DEBATES IN THE DIGITAL HUMANITIES

DEBATES IN THE DIGITAL HUMANITIES

Matthew K. Gold
EDITOR

University of Minnesota Press
Minneapolis
London

Chapter 1 was previously published as "What Is Digital Humanities and What's It Doing in English Departments?" *ADE Bulletin,* no. 150 (2010): 55–61. Chapter 2 was previously published as "The Humanities, Done Digitally," *The Chronicle of Higher Education,* May 8, 2011. Chapter 17 was previously published as "You Work at Brown. What Do You Teach?" in *#alt-academy,* Bethany Nowviskie, ed. (New York: MediaCommons, 2011). Chapter 28 was previously published as "Humanities 2.0: Promises, Perils, Predictions," *PMLA* 123, no. 3 (May 2008): 707–17.

Published by the University of Minnesota Press
111 Third Avenue South, Suite 290
Minneapolis, MN 55401-2520
http://www.upress.umn.edu

LIBRARY OF CONGRESS CATALOGING-IN-PUBLICATION DATA
Debates in the digital humanities / [edited by] Matthew K. Gold.
ISBN 978-0-8166-7794-8 (hardback)—ISBN 978-0-8166-7795-5 (pb)
1. Humanities—Study and teaching (Higher)—Data processing. 2. Humanities —Technological innovations. 3. Digital media. I. Gold, Matthew K..
AZ182.D44 2012
001.3071—dc23

2011044236

Printed in the United States of America on acid-free paper

19 18 17 16 15 14 13 12 10 9 8 7 6 5 4 3 2

Contents

Introduction

The Digital Humanities Moment

MATTHEW K. GOLD

Recent coverage of the digital humanities (DH) in popular publications such as the *New York Times*, *Nature*, the *Boston Globe*, the *Chronicle of Higher Education*, and *Inside Higher Ed* has confirmed that the digital humanities is not just "the next big thing," as the *Chronicle* claimed in 2009, but simply "the Thing," as the same publication noted in 2011 (Pannapacker). At a time when many academic institutions are facing austerity budgets, department closings, and staffing shortages, the digital humanities experienced a banner year that saw cluster hires at multiple universities, the establishment of new digital humanities centers and initiatives across the globe, and multimillion-dollar grants distributed by federal agencies and charitable foundations. Even Google entered the fray, making a series of highly publicized grants to DH scholars (Orwant).

Clearly, this is a significant moment of growth and opportunity for the field, but it has arrived amid larger questions concerning the nature and purpose of the university system. At stake in the rise of the digital humanities is not only the viability of new research methods (such as algorithmic approaches to large humanities data sets) or new pedagogical activities (such as the incorporation of geospatial data into classroom projects) but also key elements of the larger academic ecosystem that supports such work. Whether one looks at the status of peer review, the evolving nature of authorship and collaboration, the fundamental interpretive methodologies of humanities disciplines, or the controversies over tenure and casualized academic labor that have increasingly rent the fabric of university life, it is easy to see that the academy is shifting in significant ways.

And the digital humanities, more than most fields, seems positioned to address many of those changes. The recently created international group 4Humanities, for instance, argues that the digital humanities community has a "special potential and responsibility to assist humanities advocacy" because of its expertise in "making creative use of digital technology to advance humanities research and teaching" ("Mission"). In a moment of crisis, the digital humanities contributes to the sustenance of academic life as we know it, even as (and perhaps because) it upends academic life as we know it.

We've come a long way from Father Busa's digital concordances.[1] Indeed, the rapid ascent of the digital humanities in the public imagination and the concomitant expansion of its purview have masked, and at times threatened to overshadow, decades of foundational work by scholars and technologists who engaged in "digital humanities" work before it was known by that name.[2] Though longtime practitioners, having weathered decades of suspicion from more traditional colleagues, have largely welcomed an influx of newcomers into the field—the theme of the 2011 Digital Humanities Conference was "The Big Tent," a metaphor much debated in the pages that follow—some DHers have found the sudden expansion of the community to be disconcerting. Indeed, fault lines have emerged within the DH community between those who use new digital tools to aid relatively traditional scholarly projects and those who believe that DH is most powerful as a disruptive political force that has the potential to reshape fundamental aspects of academic practice.[3]

As the digital humanities has received increasing attention and newfound cachet, its discourse has grown introspective and self-reflexive. In the aftermath of the 2011 Modern Language Association Convention, many members of the field engaged in a public debate about what it means to be a "digital humanist." The debate was sparked by University of Nebraska scholar Stephan Ramsay, whose talk at the convention was bluntly titled "Who's In and Who's Out." Having been asked by the roundtable session organizer to deliver a pithy, three-minute-long take on the digital humanities, Ramsay noted increasingly capacious definitions of the field ("[DH] has most recently tended to welcome anyone and anything exemplifying a certain wired fervor," he noted) before delivering, with the mock-serious pretension that it would settle the matter once and for all, the pronouncement that, yes, there are some basic requirements one must fulfill before calling oneself a digital humanist: "Digital Humanities is not some airy Lyceum. It is a series of concrete instantiations involving money, students, funding agencies, big schools, little schools, programs, curricula, old guards, new guards, gatekeepers, and prestige. . . . Do you have to know how to code [to be a digital humanist]? I'm a tenured professor of digital humanities and I say 'yes.' . . . Personally, I think Digital Humanities is about building things. . . . If you are not making anything, you are not . . . a digital humanist" (Ramsay, "Who's In and Who's Out"). Predictably, these comments set off an intense debate during the session itself and in the ensuing online discussions. Ramsay wrote a follow-up blog post in which he softened his stance—moving from "coding" as a membership requirement to the less specific "building"—but he still noted that the fundamental commonality that can be found among digital humanists "involves moving from reading and critiquing to building and making" (Ramsay, "On Building").

These recent, definitional conversations bear the mark of a field in the midst of growing pains as its adherents expand from a small circle of like-minded scholars to a more heterogeneous set of practitioners who sometimes ask more disruptive questions. They also signal the ways in which the applied model of digital humanities work portends significant shifts in the nature of humanities scholarship. When a DH scholar attempts to include within her tenure dossier (if, indeed, the scholar is even on a tenure track and not one of a growing set of "alt-academics"[4]) not only articles and books but also, for example, code for a collaboratively built tool that enables other scholars to add descriptive metadata to digitized manuscripts, key questions about the nature of scholarship are raised. Several essays within this volume deal with such questions, and institutions such as the Modern Language Association have compiled guides to help DH scholars begin to answer them ("The Evaluation of Digital Work").

Similar definitional debates can be found in the pages that follow. Where, for instance, does new media studies leave off and digital humanities begin? Does DH need theory? Does it have a politics? Is it accessible to all members of the profession, or do steep infrastructural requirements render entry prohibitive for practitioners working at small colleges or cash-strapped public universities? Are DHers too cliquish? Do social media platforms like Twitter trivialize DH's professional discourse? Can DH provide meaningful opportunities to scholars seeking alternatives to tenure-track faculty employment? Can it save the humanities? The university?

These questions and others have vexed the public discourse around the digital humanities for a few years now, but to date such discussions have taken place predominantly on listservs, blogs, and Twitter. Few attempts have been made to collect and curate the debates in a more deliberate fashion, with the result that some conversations, especially those on Twitter—a platform used extensively by digital humanists—are hopelessly dispersed and sometimes even impossible to reconstitute only a few months after they have taken place.

Debates in the Digital Humanities seeks to redress this gap and to assess the state of the field by articulating, shaping, and preserving some of the vigorous debates surrounding the rise of the digital humanities. It is not a comprehensive view of DH or even an all-encompassing portrait of the controversies that surround it, but it does represent an attempt to clarify key points of tension and multiple visions of a rapidly shifting landscape. The contributors who provide these visions have a range of perspectives; included among them are some of the most well-known senior figures in the field, well-established midcareer scholars, rising junior scholars, "#alt-ac" digital humanists, and graduate students. This mix of new and seasoned voices mirrors the openness of digital humanities itself and reflects its strong tradition of mentorship and collaboration.

The collection builds upon and extends the pioneering volumes that have preceded it, such as *A Companion to the Digital Humanities* (Schreibman, Siemens, and Unsworth) and *A Companion to Digital Literary Studies* (Schreibman and Siemens), as well as newer and forthcoming collections such as *The American Literary Scholar in the Digital Age* (Earhart and Jewell), *Switching Codes: Thinking*

Through Digital Technology in the Humanities and Arts (Bartscherer and Coover), *#alt-academy* (Nowviskie), *Hacking the Academy* (Cohen and Scheinfeldt), and *Teaching Digital Humanities* (Hirsch). In the spirit of those texts and in line with the open-source ethos of the digital humanities, this volume will be published as both a printed book and an expanded, open-access webtext. The University of Minnesota Press is to be much commended for its willingness to share the volume in this way, a feature that will significantly extend the reach of the book.

This collection is not a celebration of the digital humanities but an interrogation of it. Several essays in the volume level pointed critiques at DH for a variety of ills: a lack of attention to issues of race, class, gender, and sexuality; a preference for research-driven projects over pedagogical ones; an absence of political commitment; an inadequate level of diversity among its practitioners; an inability to address texts under copyright; and an institutional concentration in well-funded research universities. Alongside these critiques are intriguing explorations of digital humanities theories, methods, and practices. From attempts to delineate new theories of coding as scholarship to forward-looking visions of trends in big data, the volume sketches out some of the directions in which the field is moving.

And the field of digital humanities does move quickly; the speed of discourse in DH is often noted with surprise by newcomers, especially at conferences, when Twitter feeds buzz with links to announcements, papers, prototypes, slides, white papers, photos, data visualizations, and collaborative documents. By the typical standards of the publishing industry, this text has seen a similarly rapid pace of development, going from first solicitation of essays to published book in less than a year. To have a collection of this size come together with such speed is, to put it mildly, outside the norms of print-based academic publishing. That it did so is a tribute to the intensity of the debates, the strength of the submissions, and the responsiveness of the press. But it is also a testimonial to the collaborative process through which the book was produced, a feature seen most clearly in the peer review that it received.

The book, in fact, went through three distinct stages of peer review, each of which required separate revisions: the first and most innovative process was a semipublic peer-to-peer review, in which contributors commented on one another's work. Essays then went through an editor's review, which was followed finally by a traditional blind review administered by the press.

The semipublic peer-to-peer review was modeled on a number of recent experiments in peer review, most notably Noah Wardrip-Fruin's *Expressive Processing* (2008), Kathleen Fitzpatrick's *Planned Obsolescence* (2009), *Shakespeare Quarterly*'s "Shakespeare and New Media" issue (2010), and Trebor Scholz's *Learning through Digital Media* (2011). In all of these cases, CommentPress, a WordPress blog theme built by the Institute for the Future of the Book, was used to publish draft manuscripts on a site where comments could be added to the margin beside particular paragraphs of the text (Fitzpatrick, "CommentPress"). Most of the aforementioned examples were fully public, however, meaning that anyone with the link and an interest in a particular text could read and comment on it. For *Debates in the Digital Humanities*, we chose to go with a semipublic option, meaning that the site was password protected and accessible only to the scholars involved in its production. Draft essays were placed on the site along with a list of review assignments; each contributor was responsible for adding comments to at least one other text. The process was not blind: reviewers knew who had written the text they were reading, and their comments were published under their own names. Often, debates between contributors broke out in the margins of the text.

Whether measured quantitatively or qualitatively, the peer-to-peer review process was effective. In the space of two weeks, the thirty essays that went through the process received 568 comments—an average of nearly twenty comments per essay (the median number of comments received was eighteen). Many contributors went far beyond the single essay that had been assigned to them, commenting on as many as half of the essays in the volume. Lest skeptics assume that a nonblind review process leads inevitably to superficial praise or even to a mild suppression of negative feedback, it should be noted that several features of the peer-to-peer review worked against such possibilities. The semipublic nature of the review meant that the names of reviewers were attached to the comments they left; a failure to leave substantive comments would have reflected poorly on the reviewer's own work. The fact that review assignments were shared openly among the circle of contributors created a sense of peer pressure that made it difficult for reviewers to shirk their duties. And because the peer-to-peer review was not fully open to the public, contributors seemed comfortable providing negative criticism in a more open fashion than they might have had the platform been fully public.

The peer-to-peer review website wound up imparting a sense of community and collectivity to the project as a whole. It also gave contributors a better sense of the full volume in its prepublished state. Whereas contributors to edited collections typically gain a vision of the entire book only when it is finally printed, contributors to *Debates in the Digital Humanities* were able to see the work of their peers while revising their own essays. This led some authors not only to thank fellow contributors in their acknowledgments for feedback given during peer-to-peer review but also to cite one another's essays and peer reviews. In short, rather than serving solely as a gate-keeping mechanism, this review process built a sense of cohesion around the project itself. And it was followed and supplemented by more traditional forms of review that provided opportunities for the kind of unfiltered criticism typically associated with blind review. Ultimately, this hybrid, semiopen, multistage model of peer review incorporated the innovations of completely open models of peer-to-peer review while retaining the strengths of more traditional processes.

The resulting text reflects the range of issues facing the digital humanities at the present time. It begins with the section "Defining the Digital Humanities," a subject of perennial discussion within the DH community. Other portions of the book explore the field by moving from theory to critique to practice to teaching, ending with a look toward the future of the digital humanities. Each chapter closes with a short selection of materials reprinted from scholarly blogs and wikis, reflecting both the importance of such networked spaces to digital humanities scholars and the ways in which such "middle-state" publishing both serves as a vital channel for scholarly communication and feeds into more formal publishing projects.[5]

The printed version of *Debates in the Digital Humanities* is the first iteration of this project; it will be followed by an online, expanded, open-access webtext. We are planning a website that will offer not a static version of the book, but rather an ongoing, community-based resource that can be used to track and extend discussions of current debates. Given the speed with which the digital humanities is growing, such a dynamic resource is necessary. And in that sense, this volume is but the beginning of a new set of conversations.

NOTES

I am grateful to Douglas Armato, Stephen Brier, Kathleen Fitzpatrick, Matthew Kirschenbaum, Elizabeth Losh, Stephen Ramsay, Lisa Spiro, and an anonymous reviewer for their helpful readings of earlier drafts of this introduction.

1. Father Roberto Busa, an Italian Jesuit priest, is generally credited with having founded humanities computing in 1949 when he began collaborating with IBM on a machine that could be used to create a concordance of all words ever published by Thomas Aquinas. After thirty years of work, Busa published the *Index Thomisticus* first in print and later on CD-ROM and the web. See Hockey and Busa for more information.

2. For a history of the digital humanities before it was known by that appellation, see Susan Hockey's "The History of Humanities Computing," in *A Companion to Digital Humanities*. The entire first section of that book, "Part I: History," provides a useful overview and history of digital work in various fields. See also the essays by Matthew Kirschenbaum in the present volume.

3. See the essays by Patrik Svensson and Julia Flanders in this volume for further discussion of such tensions. For recent discussions of the ways in which DH is reconfiguring traditional scholarly careers and forms, see Nowviskie's *#alt-academy* project as well as the recent announcement of *PressForward* (Cohen, "Introducing *PressForward*").

4. See Nowviskie for a description of this term and the various kinds of work it can entail.

5. For more on the concept of middle-state academic publishing, see Cohen, "Introducing *PressForward*."

BIBLIOGRAPHY

Bartscherer, Thomas, and Roderick Coover. *Switching Codes: Thinking through Digital Technology in the Humanities and Arts*. Chicago: University of Chicago Press, 2011.

Busa, Roberto. "The Annals of Humanities Computing: The Index Thomisticus." *Computers and the Humanities* 14 (1980): 83–90.

Cohen, Daniel. "Introducing *PressForward*." *Dan Cohen*. June 2011. http://www.dancohen.org/2011/06/22/introducing-pressforward/.

Cohen, Daniel, and Tom Scheinfeldt. *Hacking the Academy*. Ann Arbor: University of Michigan Press, forthcoming.

Cohen, Patricia. "Humanities 2.0 Series." *New York Times*, November 17, 2010–March 22, 2011. http://topics.nytimes.com/top/features/books/series/humanities_20/index.html.

Earhart, Amy E., and Andrew Jewell, eds. *The American Literature Scholar in the Digital Age*. Ann Arbor: University of Michigan Press, 2010.

"The Evaluation of Digital Work." Modern Language Association. http://wiki.mla.org/index.php/Evaluation_Wiki.

Fitzpatrick, Kathleen. "CommentPress: New (Social) Structures for New (Networked) Texts." *Journal of Electronic Publishing* 10, no. 3 (Fall 2007).

———. *Planned Obsolescence: Publishing, Technology, and the Future of the Academy*. New York: New York University Press, 2009. http://mediacommons.futureofthebook.org/mcpress/plannedobsolescence/.

Guess, Andy. "Rise of the Digital NEH." *Inside Higher Ed*, April 3, 2008. http://www.insidehighered.com/news/2008/04/03/digital.

Hand, Eric. "Culturomics: Word Play." *Nature* 474 (June 2011): 436–40.

Hirsch, Brett D., ed. *Teaching Digital Humanities*. Ann Arbor: University of Michigan Press, forthcoming.

Hockey, Susan. "The History of Humanities Computing." In *A Companion to Digital Humanties*, edited by Susan Schreibman, Ray Siemens, and John Unsworth. Oxford: Blackwell, 2004.

Johnson, Carolyn Y. "In Billions of Words, Digital Allies Find Tale." *Boston Globe*, December 17, 2010. http://articles.boston.com/2010-12-17/business/29280973_1_words-researchers-german-books.

"Mission." *4Humanities: Advocating for the Humanities*. http://humanistica.ualberta.ca/mission/.

Nowviskie, Bethany, ed. *#alt-academy*. New York: MediaCommons, 2011. http://mediacommons.futureofthebook.org/alt-ac/.

Orwant, Jon. "Our Commitment to the Digital Humanities." *The Official Google Blog*. July 14, 2010. http://googleblog.blogspot.com/2010/07/our-commitment-to-digital-humanities.html.

Pannapacker, William. "The MLA and the Digital Humanities." *Chronicle of Higher Education*. December 28, 2009. http://chronicle.com/blogPost/The-MLAthe-Digital/19468/.

———. "Pannapacker at MLA: Digital Humanities Triumphant?" *Chronicle of Higher Education*. January 8, 2011. http://chronicle.com/blogs/brainstorm/pannapacker-at-mla-digital-humanities-triumphant/30915.

Ramsay, Stephen. "On Building." *Stephen Ramsay*. January 11, 2011. http://lenz.unl.edu/papers/2011/01/11/on-building.html.

———. "Who's In and Who's Out." *Stephen Ramsay*. January 8, 2011. http://lenz.unl.edu/papers/2011/01/08/whos-in-and-whos-out.html.

Rowe, Katherine, ed. "Shakespeare and New Media." Special issue, *Shakespeare Quarterly* 61, no. 3 (Fall 2010). http://mediacommons.futureofthebook.org/mcpress/ShakespeareQuarterly_NewMedia/.

Scholz, R. Trebor, ed. *Learning Through Digital Media*. http://mediacommons.futureofthebook.org/mcpress/artoflearning/.

Schreibman, Susan, and Ray Siemens, eds. *A Companion to Digital Literary Studies*. Oxford: Blackwell, 2008. http://www.digitalhumanities.org/companionDLS/.

Schreibman, Susan, Ray Siemens, and John Unsworth, eds. *A Companion to Digital Humanities*. Oxford: Blackwell, 2004. http://www.digitalhumanities.org/companion/.

Wardrip-Fruin, Noah. *Expressive Processing: An Experiment in Blog-Based Peer Review*. January 22, 2008. http://grandtextauto.org/2008/01/22/expressive-processing-an-experiment-in-blog-based-peer-review/.

PART I

DEFINING THE DIGITAL HUMANITIES

What Is Digital Humanities and What's It Doing in English Departments?

MATTHEW KIRSCHENBAUM

People who say that the last battles of the computer revolution in English departments have been fought and won don't know what they're talking about. If our current use of computers in English studies is marked by any common theme at all, it is experimentation at the most basic level. As a profession, we are just learning how to live with computers, just beginning to integrate these machines effectively into writing- and reading-intensive courses, just starting to consider the implications of the multilayered literacy associated with computers.

—Cynthia Selfe, "Computers in English Departments: The Rhetoric of Technopower"

What is (or are) the "digital humanities" (DH), also known as "humanities computing"? It's tempting to say that whoever asks the question has not gone looking very hard for an answer. "What is digital humanities?" essays like this one are already genre pieces. Willard McCarty has been contributing papers on the subject for years (a monograph, too). Under the earlier appellation, John Unsworth has advised us on "What Is Humanities Computing and What Is Not." Most recently Patrik Svensson has been publishing a series of well-documented articles on multiple aspects of the topic, including the lexical shift from humanities computing to digital humanities. Moreover, as Cynthia Selfe in an *ADE Bulletin* from 1988 reminds us, computers have been part of our disciplinary lives for well over two decades now. During this time digital humanities has accumulated a robust professional apparatus that is probably more rooted in English than any other departmental home.

The contours of this professional apparatus are easily discoverable. An organization called the Alliance of Digital Humanities Organizations hosts a well-attended annual international conference called Digital Humanities. (It grew out of an earlier annual series of conferences, hosted jointly by the Association for Computers and the Humanities and the Association for Literary and Linguistic Computing since 1989.) There is Blackwell's *Companion to Digital Humanities*. There is a book series (yes, a book series), Topics in the Digital Humanities, from the University of Illinois Press. There is a refereed journal called *Digital Humanities Quarterly*, one of several that serve the field, including a newer publication, *Digital Studies/Le champ numérique*, sponsored by the Canadian Society for Digital Humanities (Société pour l'Étude des Médias Interactifs). The University of Victoria hosts the annual Digital Humanities Summer Institute to train new scholars. Crucially, there are digital humanities centers and institutes (probably at least one hundred worldwide, some of them established for a decade or more with staffs numbering in the dozens); these are served by an organization known as centerNet. There have been digital humanities manifestos (I know of at least two) and FAQs, colloquia and symposia, and workshops and special sessions. Not to mention, of course, that a gloss or explanation of digital humanities is implicit in every mission statement, every call for papers and proposals, every strategic plan and curriculum development document, every hiring request, and so forth that invokes the term. Or the countless times the question has been visited on electronic discussion lists, blogs, Facebook walls, and Twitter feeds, contributing all the flames and exhortations, celebrations, and screeds one could wish to read.

We could also, of course, simply Google the question. Google takes us to Wikipedia, and what we find there is not bad:

> The digital humanities, also known as humanities computing, is a field of study, research, teaching, and invention concerned with the intersection of computing and the disciplines of the humanities. It is methodological by nature and interdisciplinary in scope. It involves investigation, analysis, synthesis and presentation of information in electronic form. It studies how these media affect the disciplines in which they are used, and what these disciplines have to contribute to our knowledge of computing.[1]

As a working definition this serves as well as any I've seen, which is not surprising since a glance at the page's view history tab reveals individuals closely associated with the digital humanities as contributors. At its core, then, digital humanities is more akin to a common methodological outlook than an investment in any one specific set of texts or even technologies. We could attempt to refine this outlook quantitatively, using some of the very tools and techniques digital humanities has pioneered. For example, we might use a text analysis tool named Voyeur developed by Stéfan Sinclair to mine the proceedings from the annual Digital Humanities conference and develop lists of topic frequencies or collocate key terms or visualize the papers' citation networks. We could also choose to explore the question qualitatively by examining sets of projects from self-identified digital humanities centers. At the University of Maryland, where I serve as an associate director at the Maryland Institute for Technology in the Humanities, we support work from "Shakespeare to Second Life," as we're fond of saying: the Shakespeare Quartos Archive, funded by a joint grant program administered by the United Kingdom's Joint Information Systems Committee and the National Endowment for the Humanities, makes a searchable digital facsimile of each of the thirty-two extant quarto copies of *Hamlet* available online, while Preserving Virtual Worlds, a project supported by the Library of Congress, has developed and tested standards and best practices for archiving and ensuring future access to computer games, interactive fiction, and virtual communities.

Yet digital humanities is also a social undertaking. It harbors networks of people who have been working together, sharing research, arguing, competing, and collaborating for many years. Key achievements from this community, like the Text Encoding Initiative or the Orlando Project, were mostly finished before the current wave of interest in digital humanities began. Nonetheless, the rapid and remarkable rise of digital humanities as a term can be traced to a set of surprisingly specific circumstances. Unsworth, who was the founding director of the Institute for Advanced Technology in the Humanities at the University of Virginia for a decade and is currently dean of the Graduate School of Library and Information Science at the University of Illinois, has this to relate:

> The real origin of that term [digital humanities] was in conversation with Andrew McNeillie, the original acquiring editor for the Blackwell *Companion to Digital Humanities*. We started talking with him about that book project in 2001, in April, and by the end of November we'd lined up contributors and were discussing the title, for the contract. Ray [Siemens] wanted "A Companion to Humanities Computing" as that was the term commonly used at that point; the editorial and marketing folks at Blackwell wanted "Companion to Digitized Humanities." I suggested "Companion to Digital Humanities" to shift the emphasis away from simple digitization.[2]

At about the same time that Blackwell's volume was being put together, the leadership of two scholarly organizations opened discussions about creating an umbrella entity for themselves and eventually other organizations and associations with like interests. As anyone who has ever tried to run a scholarly organization will know, economies of scale are difficult to come by with only a few hundred members, and so the thought was to consolidate and share infrastructure and services. The two organizations were the aforementioned Association for Computers and the Humanities (ACH) and the Association for Literary and Linguistic Computing (ALLC). The umbrella structure that resulted was called ADHO, or the Alliance of Digital Humanities Organizations. Here is Unsworth again from the same communication: "Conversations about merging ACH and ALLC began at Tuebingen, in a bar, in a conversation between Harold Short and me, in July 2002. A couple of months later, I had set a list called 'adhoc'—allied digital humanities organizations committee, first message dated August 16, 2002. . . . We finally got things off the dime in Sweden, at the 2004 ALLC/ACH, and after waffling some more about names (ICHIO, OHCO, and others) we voted, in April of 2005, to go with ADHO, changing 'A' from 'Allied' to 'Alliance.'"[3]

By 2005 Blackwell's *Companion to Digital Humanities* had been published, and the Alliance for Digital Humanities Organizations had been established. There's one more key event to relate, and that's the launch in 2006 of the Digital Humanities Initiative by the National Endowment for the Humanities (NEH), then under the chairmanship of Bruce Cole and with leadership provided by Brett Bobley, a charismatic and imaginative individual who doubles as the agency's CIO. In an e-mail to me, Bobley describes a January 2006 lunch with another NEH staffer at which they were brainstorming ideas for what would become the Digital Humanities Initiative:

> At the lunch, I jotted down a bunch of names, including humanities computing, ehumanities, and digital humanities. When I got back to the office, I Googled all three of them and "digital humanities" seemed to be the winner. I liked it for a few reasons: due to ADHO and their annual Digital Humanities conference, the name brought up a lot of relevant hits. I believe I'd also heard from Julia Flanders about the forthcoming *Digital Humanities Quarterly* journal. I also appreciated the fact that it seemed to cast a wider net than "humanities computing" which seemed to imply a form of computing, whereas "digital humanities" implied a form of humanism. I also thought it would be an easier sell to the humanities community to have the emphasis on "humanities."[4]

In 2008 the Digital Humanities Initiative became the Office of Digital Humanities, the designation of "office" assigning the program (and its budget line) a permanent place within the agency. That *the* major federal granting agency for scholarship in the humanities, taking its cues directly from a small but active and influential group of scholars, had devoted scarce resources to launching a number of new grant opportunities, many of them programmatically innovative in and of themselves, around an endeavor termed "digital humanities" was doubtless the tipping point for the branding of DH, at least in the United States.

These events will, I think, earn a place in histories of the profession alongside other major critical movements like the Birmingham School or Yale deconstruction. In the space of a little more than five years, digital humanities had gone from being a term of convenience used by a group of researchers who had already been working together for years to something like a movement. Individual scholars routinely now self-identify as digital humanists, or DHers. There is an unusually strong sense of community and common purpose manifested, for example, in events such as the Day of Digital Humanities, organized by a team at the University of Alberta. Its second annual iteration featured over 150 participants (up from around one hundred the first year), who blogged on a shared site about the details of their workday, posted photographs of their offices and screens, and reflected on the nature of their enterprise. Digital humanities has even been the recipient of its own *Downfall* remix, the Internet meme whereby the climactic scene from the HBO film depicting Hitler's final days in the bunker is closed captioned with, in this instance, a tirade about the pernicious influence of online scholarship.

Digital humanities was also (you may have heard) big news at the 2009 Modern Language Association (MLA) Annual Convention in Philadelphia. On December 28, midway through the convention, William Pannapacker, one of the *Chronicle of Higher Education*'s officially appointed bloggers, wrote the following for the online "Brainstorm" section: "Amid all the doom and gloom of the 2009 MLA Convention, one field seems to be alive and well: the digital humanities. More than that: Among all the contending subfields, the digital humanities seem like the first 'next big thing' in a long time." (It seems fair to say that Pannapacker, who is the author of "Graduate School in the Humanities: Just Don't Go" under the pseudonym Thomas Benton, is not a man easily impressed.) Jennifer Howard, meanwhile, a veteran *Chronicle* reporter who has covered the convention before, noted that the "vitality" of digital humanities drew "overflow crowds to too-small conference rooms." There were several dozen panels devoted to the digital humanities at the MLA convention, and one could (and did) easily navigate the three-day convention by moving among them.

Crucially, digital humanities was visible in another way at the conference: the social networking service Twitter. Twitter is the love-it-or-hate-it Web 2.0 application often maligned as the final triumph of the attention-deficit generation because it limits postings to a mere 140 characters—not 140 words, 140 characters. The reason has less to do with attention spans than Twitter's origins in the messaging protocols of mobile devices, but the format encourages brief, conversational posts (tweets) that also tend to contain a fair measure of flair and wit. Unlike Facebook, Twitter allows for asymmetrical relationships: you can "follow" someone (or they can follow you) without the relationship being reciprocated. Tweeting has rapidly become an integral part of the conference scene, with a subset of attendees on Twitter providing real-time running commentary through a common "tag" (#mla09, for example), which allows everyone who follows it to tune in to the conversation. This phenomenon has some very specific ramifications. Amanda French ran the numbers and concluded that nearly half (48 percent) of attendees at the Digital Humanities 2009 conference were tweeting the sessions. By contrast, only 3 percent of MLA convention attendees tweeted; according to French's data, out of about 7,800 attendees at the MLA convention only 256 tweeted. Of these, the vast majority were people already associated with digital humanities through their existing networks of followers. Jennifer Howard, again writing for the *Chronicle*, noted the centrality of Twitter to the DH crowd and its impact on scholarly communication, going so far as to include people's Twitter identities in her roundup of major stories from the convention. *Inside Higher Ed* also devoted coverage to Twitter at the

MLA convention, noting that Rosemary G. Feal was using it to connect with individual members of the organization—not surprisingly, many of them DHers. Feal, in fact, kept up a lively stream of tweets throughout the conference, gamely mixing it up with the sometimes irreverent back-channel conversation and, in a scene out of *Small World* had it only been written twenty years later, issued an impromptu invite for her "tweeps" to join the association's elite for nightcaps in the penthouse of one of the convention hotels.

While it's not hard to see why the academic press devoured the story, there's more going on than mere shenanigans. Twitter, along with blogs and other online outlets, has inscribed the digital humanities as a network topology, that is to say lines drawn by aggregates of affinities, formally and functionally manifest in who follows whom, who friends whom, who tweets whom, and who links to what. Digital humanities has also, I would propose, lately been galvanized by a group of younger (or not so young) graduate students, faculty members (both tenure line and contingent), and other academic professionals who now wield the label "digital humanities" instrumentally amid an increasingly monstrous institutional terrain defined by declining public support for higher education, rising tuitions, shrinking endowments, the proliferation of distance education and the for-profit university, and underlying it all the conversion of full-time, tenure-track academic labor to a part-time adjunct workforce. One example is the remarkable tale of Brian Croxall, the recent Emory PhD who went viral online for a period of several weeks during and after the MLA convention. Croxall had his paper "The Absent Presence: Today's Faculty" read at the convention in absentia while he simultaneously published it on his blog after finding himself unable to afford to travel to Philadelphia because he hadn't landed any convention interviews. As numerous observers pointed out, Croxall's paper, which was heavily blogged and tweeted and received coverage in both the *Chronicle* and *Inside Higher Ed*, was undoubtedly and by many orders of magnitude the most widely seen and read paper from the 2009 MLA convention. These events were subsequently discussed in a series of cross-postings and conversations that spilled across Twitter and the blogosphere for several weeks after the convention ended. Many seemed to feel that the connection to wider academic issues was not incidental or accidental and that digital humanities, with a culture that values collaboration, openness, nonhierarchical relations, and agility, might be an instrument for real resistance or reform.

So what is digital humanities, and what is it doing in English departments? The answer to the latter portion of the question is easier. I can think of some half a dozen reasons why English departments have historically been hospitable settings for this kind of work. First, after numeric input, text has been by far the most tractable data type for computers to manipulate. Unlike images, audio, video, and so on, there is a long tradition of text-based data processing that was within the capabilities of even some of the earliest computer systems and that has for decades fed research in fields like stylistics, linguistics, and author attribution studies, all heavily associated with English departments. Second, of course, there is the long association between computers and composition, almost as long and just as rich in its lineage. Third is the pitch-perfect convergence between the intense conversations around editorial theory and method in the 1980s and the widespread means to implement electronic archives and editions very soon after; Jerome McGann is a key figure here, with his work on the *Rossetti Archive*, which he has repeatedly described as a vehicle for applied theory, standing as paradigmatic. Fourth, and at roughly the same time, is a modest but much-promoted belle-lettristic project around hypertext and other forms of electronic literature that continues to this day and is increasingly vibrant and diverse. Fifth is the openness of English departments to cultural studies, where computers and other objects of digital material culture become the centerpiece of analysis. I'm thinking here, for example, of the reader Stuart Hall and others put together around the Sony Walkman, that hipster iPod of old. Finally, today, we see the simultaneous explosion of interest in e-reading and e-book devices like the Kindle, iPad, and Nook and the advent of large-scale text digitization projects, the most significant of course being Google Books, with scholars like Franco Moretti taking up data mining and visualization to perform "distance readings" of hundreds, thousands, or even millions of books at a time.

Digital humanities, which began as a term of consensus among a relatively small group of researchers, is now backed on a growing number of campuses by a level of funding, infrastructure, and administrative commitments that would have been unthinkable even a decade ago. Even more recently, I would argue, the network effects of blogs and Twitter at a moment when the academy itself is facing massive and often wrenching changes linked to both new technologies and the changing political and economic landscape have led to the construction of "digital humanities" as a free-floating signifier, one that increasingly serves to focus the anxiety and even outrage of individual scholars over their own lack of agency amid the turmoil in their institutions and profession. This is manifested in the intensity of debates around open-access publishing, where faculty members increasingly demand the right to retain ownership of their own scholarship—meaning their own labor—and disseminate it freely to an audience apart from or parallel with more traditional structures of academic publishing, which in turn are perceived as outgrowths of dysfunctional and outmoded practices surrounding peer review, tenure, and promotion.

Whatever else it might be, then, the digital humanities today is about a scholarship (and a pedagogy) that is publicly visible in ways to which we are generally unaccustomed, a scholarship and pedagogy that are bound up with infrastructure in ways that are deeper and more explicit than we are generally accustomed to, a scholarship and pedagogy that are collaborative and depend on networks of people and that live an active, 24-7 life online. Isn't that something you want in your English department?

NOTES

This chapter was originally written for presentation at the Association of Departments of English Summer Seminar East at the University of Maryland in June 2010 and then revised for publication in the ADE Bulletin (no. 150, 2010). It wears its disciplinary bias on its sleeve. While I would happily acknowledge that there have been other important settings in the story of the development and maturation of digital humanities, including history, linguistics, and composition and rhetoric (when these last are separate programs or departments not subsumed by English), not to mention nondepartmental venues such as libraries and academic computing centers, I remain comfortable with the idea that departments of English language and literature were predominant; the reasons why are given hereafter. (And while much has been made of the "arrival" of DH at #mla09 and #mla11, in fact humanities computing panels have been a staple of the annual MLA convention since the early 1990s, as a scan of past years' programs will confirm.) So this piece, which has already enjoyed a fair amount of online circulation and comment, can perhaps best be taken not as the canonical account of what digital humanities is (Patrik Svensson in particular has done the real spadework here) but as an artifact of a particular perspective from someone who witnessed firsthand the emergence of digital humanities from the vantage point of several large departments of English at public research universities in the United States. A more specific argument about DH—the edges of which can already be discerned here—is picked up in my contribution later in this collection.

1. Wikipedia, s.v. "Digital humanities," last modified July 31, 2011, http://en.wikipedia.org/wiki/Digital_humanities

2. Unsworth, John. E-mail message to the author. April 5, 2010.

3. Unsworth, John. E-mail message to the author. April 5, 2010.

4. Bobley, Brett. "What's in a Name: NEH and 'Digital Humanities.'" E-mail message to the author. April 12, 2010.

BIBLIOGRAPHY

French, Amanda. "Make '10' Louder; or, The Amplification of Scholarly Communication." Amandafrench.net. December 30, 2009. http://amandafrench.net/blog/2009/12/30/make-10-louder/.

Howard, Jennifer. "The MLA Convention in Translation." *Chronicle of Higher Education*. December 31, 2009. http://chronicle.com/article/The-MLA-Convention-in/63379/.

McCarty, Willard. *Humanities Computing*. New York: Palgrave Macmillan, 2005.

Pannapacker, William. "The MLA and the Digital Humanities." *Chronicle of Higher Education*. December 28, 2009. http://chronicle.com/blogAuthor/Brainstorm/3/William-Pannapacker/143/.

Selfe, Cynthia. "Computers in English Departments: The Rhetoric of Technopower." *ADE Bulletin* 90 (1988): 63–67. http://www.mla.org/adefl_bulletin_c_ade_90_63&from=adefl_bulletin_t_ade90_0.

Svensson, Patrik. "Humanities Computing as Digital Humanities." *Digital Humanities Quarterly* 3, no. 3 (2009). http://digitalhumanities.org/dhq/vol/3/3/000065/000065.html.

———. "The Landscape of Digital Humanities." *Digital Humanities Quarterly* 4, no. 1 (2010). http://digitalhumanities.org/dhq/vol/4/1/000080/000080.html.

Unsworth, John. "What Is Humanities Computing and What Is Not?" *Graduate School of Library and Information Sciences.* Illinois Informatics Institute, University of Illinois, Urbana. November 8, 2002. http://computerphilologie.uni-muenchen.de/jg02/unsworth.html.

The Humanities, Done Digitally

KATHLEEN FITZPATRICK

A few months back, I gave a lunchtime talk called "Digital Humanities: Singular or Plural?" My title was in part a weak joke driven primarily by brain exhaustion. As I sat at the computer putting together my remarks, which were intended to introduce the field, I'd initially decided to title them "What Is Digital Humanities?" But then I thought "What Is the Digital Humanities?" sounded better, and I stared at the screen for a minute trying to decide if it should be "What Are the Digital Humanities?" In my precoffee, underslept haze, I honestly couldn't tell which one was correct.

At first this was just a grammatical mix-up, but at some point it occurred to me that it was actually a useful metaphor for something that's been going on in the field of late. Digital humanities has gained prominence in the last couple of years, in part because of the visibility given the field by the use of social media, particularly Twitter, at the Modern Language Association (MLA) convention and other large scholarly meetings. But that prominence and visibility have also produced a fair bit of tension within the field—every "What Is Digital Humanities?" panel aimed at explaining the field to other scholars winds up uncovering more differences of opinion among its practitioners. Sometimes those differences develop into tense debates about the borders of the field and about who's in and who's out.

My first stab at trying to define digital humanities came in a post I wrote in July 2010 for the *Chronicle of Higher Education*'s *ProfHacker* blog. In that post, I wrote that the digital humanities could be understood as "a nexus of fields within which scholars use computing technologies to investigate the kinds of questions that are traditional to the humanities, or, as is more true of my own work, ask traditional kinds of humanities-oriented questions about computing technologies."[1]

There is, however, a specific history to the term digital humanities, detailed by my friend (and scholar of English) Matthew Kirschenbaum in a 2010 article in the *Association of Departments of English Bulletin.* In 2001 the field was known as humanities computing and had been around for some decades when Susan Schreibman, Ray Siemens, and John Unsworth, three of its key practitioners, entered into discussions with Blackwell Publishing about editing a volume prospectively titled "A Companion to Humanities Computing." Blackwell wanted a title that might appeal to a wider range of readers and so proposed "A Companion to Digitized Humanities." Unsworth countered with "Digital Humanities" to keep the field from appearing to be about mere digitization, and the name has stuck, helping to characterize a robust area of research and teaching supported by a number of prestigious conferences, well-received journals, scholarly societies, and even a dedicated office within the National Endowment for the Humanities (NEH).

Digital humanities thus grows specifically out of an attempt to make "humanities computing," which sounded as though the emphasis lay on the technology, more palatable to humanists in general. The field's background in humanities computing typically, but far from exclusively, results in projects that focus on computing methods applicable to textual materials. Some of these projects have been editorial and archival in nature, producing large-scale digital text collections for scholarly study. One such project is the William Blake Archive, which presents carefully annotated scholarly editions of both the writing and visual art of the romantic-era British poet. It is sponsored by the Library of Congress and supported by the University of North Carolina at Chapel Hill, the University of Rochester, and a division of the NEH.

Tools and technical standards to support the production of such archives have been another key source of digital humanities work, including projects like the Text Encoding Initiative or the Text-Image Linking Environment. There are projects that focus on processing those large collections through a statistical analysis of a text's linguistic features, for example, or author attribution studies or studies that rely on data mining. And there are initiatives that are designed to help digital humanities archives and projects become interoperable and to facilitate the peer review of these projects.

Digital humanities as it is currently practiced isn't just located in literary studies departments; the field is broadly humanities based and includes scholars in history, musicology, performance studies, media studies, and other fields that can benefit from bringing computing technologies to bear on traditional humanities materials.

However, when many of us hear the term digital humanities today, we take the referent to be not the specific subfield that grew out of humanities computing but rather the changes that digital technologies are producing across the many fields of humanist inquiry. Disciplines such as rhetoric and composition, for instance, have long been interested in the difference that the computer makes in contemporary writing and communication, as has digital media studies.

It's certain that there's an overlap between these fields and that which has been called digital humanities—between scholars who use digital technologies in studying traditional humanities objects and those who use the methods of the contemporary humanities in studying digital objects—but clear differences lie between them. Those differences often produce significant tension, particularly between those who suggest that digital humanities should always be about *making* (whether making archives, tools, or new digital methods) and those who argue that it must expand to include *interpreting*.

The terms of this tension should begin to sound a bit familiar: this is an updated version of the theory-practice divide that has long existed in other quarters of the humanities. There has long been a separation, for instance, between studio artists and art historians or between literary scholars and creative writers, and that separation can often lead to profound misunderstandings and miscommunications. In media studies, however, we've been reckoning with the theory-practice divide for some time. After much tension between media makers and media scholars, an increasing number of programs are bringing the two modes together in a rigorously theorized praxis, recognizing that the boundaries between the critical and the creative are arbitrary. In fact, the best scholarship is always creative, and the best production is always critically aware. The digital humanities seems another space within the academy where the divide between making and interpreting might be bridged in productive ways.

Does that mean we should throw open the floodgates and declare all forms of humanities scholarship that come into contact with the digital to be digital humanities? Should we expand the definition of the field to include, as I've heard it said several times, "every medievalist with a website"? Undoubtedly not: just as there are scholars who write about film from perspectives that don't take into account the intellectual history of film studies and thus are not considered part of the field, there are scholars who work with digital materials but who remain outside the traditions and assumptions of the digital humanities.

That fact doesn't diminish the usefulness of the debates about the borders of the digital humanities as a discipline, however. As Neil Fraistat, director of the Maryland Institute for Technology in the Humanities, pointed out in a recent talk at the University of Texas at Austin, these debates can be most productive if we understand them as a means of opening ourselves to the kinds of conversations that true interdisciplinarity can support.[2] While disciplinarity is often institutionally useful, after all—allowing for the development of centers, departments, and tenure lines—it can also be turned against its adherents, restricting their movement and disciplining, literally, the knowledge they produce.

The state of things in digital humanities today rests in that creative tension between those who've been in the field for a long time and those who are coming to it today, between disciplinarity and interdisciplinarity, between making and interpreting, between the field's history and its future. Scholarly work across the humanities, as in all academic fields, is increasingly being done digitally. The particular contribution of the digital humanities, however, lies in its exploration of the difference that the digital can make to the kinds of work that we do as well as to the ways that we communicate with one another. These new modes of scholarship and communication will best flourish if they, like the digital humanities, are allowed to remain plural.

NOTES

1. See Kathleen Fitzpatrick, "Reporting from the Digital Humanities 2010 Conference," *ProfHacker*, last modified July 13, 2010, http://chronicle.com/blogs/profhacker/reporting-from-the-digital-humanities-2010-conference/25473.

2. See Neil Fraistat, "The Question(s) of Digital Humanities," Maryland Institute for Technology in the Humanities, last modified February 7, 2011, http://mith.umd.edu/the-questions-of-digital-humanities/.

PART I][*Chapter 3*

"This Is Why We Fight": Defining the Values of the Digital Humanities

LISA SPIRO

Even as the digital humanities (DH) is being hailed as the "next big thing," members of the DH community have been debating what counts as digital humanities and what does not, who is in and who is out, and whether DH is about making or theorizing, computation or communication, practice or politics. Soon after William Pannapacker declared the arrival of digital humanities at the Modern Languages Association (MLA) conference in 2009 (Pannapacker, "The MLA and the Digital Humanities"), David Parry wrote a much-debated blog post insisting that DH should aim to "challenge and change scholarship" rather than "us[e] computers to 'tag up Milton'" (Parry). MLA 2011 unleashed another round of debates, as Pannapacker pointed to a DH in-crowd, an ironic label for a group of people who have long felt like misfits (Pannapacker, "Digital Humanities Triumphant?").

Although the debate has generated intellectual energy and compelling exchanges, it also has left me frustrated by statements that seem to devalue the work of fellow digital humanists and longing for a more coherent sense of community. Even as we debate the digital humanities, We need to participate in a frank discussion about what connects us and what values we hold in common. Given that the digital humanities community includes people with different disciplines, methodological approaches, professional roles, and theoretical inclinations, it is doubtful that we will settle on a tight definition of the digital humanities—just witness the many definitions of the term offered by participants in the Day of Digital Humanities ("How do you define Humanities Computing/Digital Humanities?"). Instead of trying to pigeonhole digital humanities by prescribing particular methods or theoretical approaches, we can instead focus on a community that comes together around values such as openness and collaboration. As Matt Kirschenbaum suggests, "the digital humanities today is about a scholarship (and a pedagogy) that is publicly visible in ways to which we are generally unaccustomed, a scholarship and pedagogy that are bound up with infrastructure in ways that are deeper and more explicit than we are generally accustomed to, a scholarship and pedagogy that are collaborative and depend on networks of people and that live an active, 24-7 life online" (Kirschenbaum, 6). How the digital humanities community operates—transparently, collaboratively, through online networks—distinguishes it. Even as we acknowledge points of difference, I propose that the digital humanities community develop a flexible statement of values that it can use to communicate its identity to itself and the general public, guide its priorities, and perhaps heal its divisions. Rather than debating who is in and who is out, the DH community needs to develop a keener sense of what it stands for and what is at stake in its work. Taking an initial step toward this goal, I will discuss the rationale for creating a core values statement by drawing on the literature about professional codes, suggest a process for engaging the community in developing a values statement, explore models for and influences on DH values, and analyze the DH literature to put forward potential values.

Why the Digital Humanities Community Needs a Statement of Values

By creating a core set of values, the digital humanities community may be able to unite to confront challenges such as the lack of open access to information and hidebound policies that limit collaboration and experimentation. As Kathleen Fitzpatrick notes of the digital humanities, "the key problems that we face again and again are social rather than technological in nature: problems of encouraging participation in collaborative and collective projects, of developing sound preservation and sustainability practices, of inciting institutional change, of promoting new ways of thinking about how academic work might be done in the coming years" (Fitzpatrick, "Reporting from the Digital Humanities 2010 Conference"). Solving such problems is not simple, but an important first step may be articulating shared values that can then be used to define goals, develop collaborations, and foster participation. Most professional organizations advance a set of values or an ethical code to make clear their aspirations, set standards of behavior, "provide the foundation of institutional mission and guide professional practice and decision making" (Miller, 5). Further, values statements can enable groups to confront change while remaining true to their overarching principles (Bell).

Yet even as they help to define a community, values statements can also confine it, reflecting a static understanding of the organization or the particular biases of a powerful clique that defines the standards. Finding consensus on the few values held in common by the community is difficult (Weissinger); indeed, dissensus plays an important role in pressing an organization to consider blind spots and alternative perspectives. Thus organizations must seek community-wide input on values statements and view them as flexible and contextual rather than fixed and eternal. As I suggest later in the section "How to Produce a Values Statement," the DH community should reflect its own spirit of collaboration and flexibility in developing a values statement, opening up the process to participation via wikis and other social media.

This essay will focus on values rather than specific ethical guidelines. Whereas values "represent closely held belief[s] and ideal[s]," ethics "are stated guidelines attempting to describe standards and inform behavior so that the behavior will meet these standards" (Miller, 8). A statement of values is typically broader than an ethical code and serves in part to inspire and to help an organization set priorities, defining what it holds most important. Professional codes such as ethical guidelines or values statements fulfill several functions, including providing guidance for professionals, shaping the public's expectations of the profession, promoting professional socialization, improving the profession's reputation, "preserv[ing] entrenched professional biases," preventing unethical actions, supporting professionals in their decision making, and adjudicating disputes (Frankel, 111–12). While a statement of values won't settle debates in the digital humanities (nor should it), it will at least frame them and provide the grounds for conversation. The digital humanities profession, loosely configured as it is, has matured to the point where it needs a values statement to help articulate its mission.

HOW TO PRODUCE A VALUES STATEMENT

Producing a values statement is difficult, since it requires you to synthesize what matters to a community even as you recognize areas of potential disagreement. (As a good humanist, I am well aware of the contingencies, ideologies, and contexts that shape values.) I believe that articulating a set of values *for* a community should be done *by* the community. The process of producing a values statement may be as important as the statement itself, since that process will embody how the community operates and what it embraces. Thus the values statement should not come down on high from a Committee that meets in private, then delivers its decrees to the community. Instead, the DH community should enact an open, participatory, iterative, networked process to develop its values statement. The statement itself should be created and disseminated on a wiki, so that one can see it change from version to version, review the discussion history, and understand the dynamic, collaborative nature of knowledge creation. The community should engage in diverse efforts to solicit input and foster conversation, such as online forums, face-to-face discussions at digital humanities conferences and unconferences, and blog posts exploring key values. To ensure that the code of values is not narrowly focused but reflects the needs of the larger community, wide input should be solicited from outsiders as well as "insiders" (Frankel). But someone needs to kick off the discussion, which is what I aim to do in this essay.

In defining core values, the community needs to consider what it is excluding as well as the cultural and ideological contexts surrounding the values it promotes. Given the diversity of the community and the ways in which culture informs values, it may be difficult to arrive at consensus on the core values (Koehler). Indeed, it is likely that creating a set of core values will stimulate further debate, since different subcommunities and even individuals will have their own views about what values are most important and whether it even makes sense to come up with a core values statement. Stated values can come into conflict with the "values in practice" of community members (Morgan, Mason, and Nahon, 8). For example, the Wikipedia community split over a debate whether to include a controversial cartoon representing the prophet Muhammad in a Wikipedia article about the publication of that cartoon by a Danish newspaper, as the value of freedom of information clashed with that of "multicultural inclusivity" (Morgan, Mason, and Nahon, 9). But if the process of developing values is handled fairly and openly, conflicts can be defused and healthy discussion can move the community forward. The process of developing a set of values for the DH community can prompt self-reflection and conversation, helping the profession to mature. These values should serve as beacons illuminating different paths rather than rigid rules constraining choices. Even as the community recognizes that values are contextual rather than fixed, the process of developing a values statement can spark a concrete discussion about what the digital humanities is trying to achieve and can produce a living document that can help guide planning and decision making.

TOWARD A SET OF DIGITAL HUMANITIES VALUES

In developing a set of values, the digital humanities community can draw from several sources that reflect its own diverse influences. The values of the digital humanities represent a convergence of several sets of values, including those of the humanities; libraries, museums, and cultural heritage organizations; and networked culture. In some ways, these values can come into conflict, which may be contributing to the ongoing debates about the digital humanities. Yet at their core, they share a common aim to advance knowledge, foster innovation, and serve the public.

The values of the humanities provide the foundation for the digital humanities. Indeed, the humanities are typically defined by their focus on aesthetics and values (American Council of Learned Societies). Among core humanistic values are inquiry, critical thinking, debate, pluralism, balancing innovation and tradition, and exploration and critique (Levine et al.). Yet contemporary humanities scholarship also recognizes that values are not universal or fixed but rather reflect particular contexts and ideologies: "At its best, contemporary humanistic thinking does not peddle ideology, but rather attempts to sensitize us to the presence of ideology in our work, and to its capacity to delude us into promoting as universal values that in fact belong to one nation, one social class, one sect" (Levine et al.). We cannot assume that the values of one culture are shared by another culture; rather, values reveal the ideologies and interests of those who hold them.

The professional values of academic humanities scholars are to some extent narrower than general humanistic values, as manifested in the insistence on solo scholarship, specialization, and scholarly authority. For example, defending the humanities against conservative attacks on academic specialization and literary theory such as Lynne Cheney's *Humanities in America*, the American Council of Learned Societies (ACLS) report *Speaking for the Humanities* insists on the importance of professionalization: "It is precisely because teachers of the humanities take their subject seriously that they become specialists, allow themselves to be professionals rather than amateurs—belle lettrists who unselfconsciously sustain traditional hierarchies, traditional social and cultural exclusions, assuming that their audience is both universal and homogeneous" (Levine et al.). Driven by a conservative political agenda, *Humanities in America* takes a limited view in insisting that humanities scholarship should focus solely on "timeless . . . truth—and beauty and excellence" (Cheney, 7). Further, it is important to defend expert knowledge and the academic profession. However, the emphasis, in *Speaking for the Humanities*, on professionalization reinforces hierarchy and reveals its own elitism in its assumption that nonprofessionals will naively uphold "traditional hierarchies." Likewise, *Speaking for the Humanities* celebrates the challenge to authority and objective knowledge represented by contemporary theory but insists on the authority of the professoriate, proclaiming that the "competence of the best scholars in the humanities today is remarkable" (Levine et al.). In a sense, these values focus more on asserting the importance of scholarly authority and professional identity than on how scholars work and what they do for society.

Such emphasis on specialization and professional authority clashes with the collaborative, crowdsourced approaches of the digital humanities—though the digital humanities, too, wrestles with questions of how to value expert knowledge. As Ed Ayers suggests, IT culture and academic culture often clash, as IT is "highly unstable . . . designed to be transparent," and has "all work performed by anonymous teams," while the academy is "the most stable institution across the world . . . opaque and labyrinth," and "centered on scholarly stars" (Ayers, "The Academic Culture and the IT Culture"). The digital humanities represents a partial blending of these two cultures. Perhaps because the digital humanities includes people representing different professional positions (faculty, librarians, technologists, museum professionals, passionate amateurs, and others) and often deliberately pursues a public role for scholarship (whether through creating freely accessible digital archives or supporting networked discussion of ideas), it often better serves values such as pluralism and innovation than do the professional values of the traditional academic humanities, which often seem to be crouched in a defensive posture.

Yet the formal values statements of professional humanities organizations do offer important principles that can guide the digital humanities, including inquiry, respect, debate, and integrity. As befits a scholarly organization, the American Historical Association's (AHA) "Statement on Standards of Professional Conduct" does not simply list particular scholarly values but rather explores and contextualizes them in an essay. The document emphasizes the importance of "critical dialogue" and demonstrating "trust and respect both of one's peers and of the public at large" (American Historical Association), embracing a public role for historical scholarship. While "practicing history with integrity does not mean being neutral or having no point of view," it does require "mutual respect and constructive criticism . . . awareness of one's own biases and a readiness to follow sound method and analysis wherever they may lead," and recognizing "the receipt of any financial support" (American Historical Association). AHA's values statement seeks a balance between critical dialogue and integrity, recognizing the importance of staking out a position yet also of honoring evidence. Likewise, the Modern Language Association's code of professional ethics emphasizes freedom of inquiry, while admitting that it can come into conflict with other values. Thus the MLA acknowledges that "this freedom carries with it the responsibilities of professional conduct," including integrity, respect for diversity, and fairness (Modern Language Association, "MLA Statement of Professional Ethics").

Since the digital humanities encompasses fields such as librarianship in addition to humanities disciplines, we should also look to models such as the American Library Association's (ALA) "Core Values of Librarianship." Adopted in 2004, this list of eleven values emphasizes the civic role that libraries play in promoting access, confidentiality/privacy, democracy, diversity, education and lifelong learning, intellectual freedom, preservation, the public good, professionalism, service, and social responsibility (American Library Association). Whereas the values statements of the academic organizations emphasize what scholars do (pursue inquiry) and how they do it (with integrity), the ALA focuses on providing service and upholding the public good through access, lifelong learning, and intellectual freedom. Bridging these two communities, the digital humanities community brings together core scholarly values such as critical dialogue and free inquiry with an ethic focused on the democratic sharing of ideas.

In a sense, the digital humanities reconfigures the humanities for the Internet age, leveraging networked technologies to exchange ideas, create communities of practice, and build knowledge. *The Digital Humanities Manifesto 2.0* deliberately sets the digital humanities in the context of traditional humanistic values, arguing that DH seeks to revitalize them in a time when culture is shifting from print to digital forms of knowledge dissemination: "Knowledge of the Humanities as constituted in the modern university has shaped lives, conveyed critical skills, provided a moral compass for human experiences, given pleasure and satisfaction, inspired acts of generosity and heroism. Digital Humanities represent an effort not to downplay or 'downsize' these traditional merits but, on the contrary, to reassert and reinterpret their value in an era when our relation to information, knowledge, and cultural heritage is radically changing, when our entire cultural legacy as a species is migrating to digital formats" (UCLA Mellon Seminar in Digital Humanities). Even as the humanities continue to make a vital contribution to society, they must be "reassert[ed] and reinterpret[ed]" in a networked age. Whereas the traditional humanities typically value originality, authority, and authorship—an ethos based in part on the scarcity of information and the perceived need for gatekeepers—the *Digital Humanities Manifesto* instead promotes remixing, openness, and the wisdom of the crowd. For the digital humanities, information is not a commodity to be controlled but a social good to be shared and reused.

Internet values themselves grow out of the humanistic mission to explore and exchange ideas. As Tim O'Reilly argues, "Just as the Copernican revolution was part of a broader social revolution that turned society away from hierarchy and received knowledge, and instead sparked a spirit of inquiry and knowledge sharing, open source is part of a communications revolution designed to maximize the free sharing of ideas expressed in code" (O'Reilly). With the development of the Internet and of open-source technologies come new ways to communicate information and ideas, build communities, and promote the growth of knowledge. The digital humanities, dubbed "Humanities 2.0" by Cathy Davidson, likewise promote openness, participation, and community (Davidson).

Indeed, Internet values, as manifested in the ethos of open source, infuse the digital humanities. As Tom Scheinfeldt argues, the digital humanities community operates much like a "social network," nimble and connected: "Digital humanities takes more than tools from the Internet. It works like the Internet. It takes its values from the Internet" (Scheinfeldt, "Stuff Digital Humanists Like"). Like the Internet, the digital humanities community is distributed rather than centralized, built on trust and the freedom to invent. Yet we might also say that, like the Internet, the digital humanities community needs protocols—values—to guide its development. As Scheinfeldt suggests, we can see these Internet values reflected in the DH community's focus on openness, iterative development, and transparency, as well as in its adoption of open-source approaches to code development and community education.

In some ways, the values of print culture (which is identified with the traditional humanities) clash with those of Internet culture. As Kathleen Fitzpatrick, citing Lawrence Lessig, explains, "the networks of electronic communication carry embedded values within the codes that structure their operation, and many of the Internet's codes, and thus its values, are substantively different from those within which scholars—or at least those in the humanities—profess to operate. We must examine our values, and the ways that our new technologies may affect them, in order to make the most productive use of those new forms" (*Planned Obsolescence*). According to Fitzpatrick, the values of print authorship are typically "individuality, originality, completeness, ownership," while the values of the Internet include "open, shared protocols and codes" (*Planned Obsolescence*). At their core, both sets of values aim to promote the exchange of ideas and the progress of knowledge, but print (at least in the tradition of academic prose) typically gives greater emphasis to authority and ownership, while digital scholarship values access, conversation, fluidity, and collaboration. Likewise, Paula Petrik contrasts the ethos of traditional humanities scholarship with the ethos of digital humanities scholarship. Whereas the traditional humanities are text based and nontechnical and value solitary, specialized work resulting in a book, the digital humanities are collaborative and technical, value design, and are built upon shared information resources ("Digital Scholarship in the University Tenure and Promotion Process").

Grounded in humanistic values but catalyzed by Internet values, the digital humanities seeks to push the humanities into new territory by promoting collaboration, openness, and experimentation. Although no professional organization in the digital humanities has, to my knowledge, crafted a values statement, we can find sources for such a statement in ongoing discussions in blogs and articles, the mission statements of DH centers, and digital humanities manifestos. Taking a witty, pragmatic look at "Stuff Digital Humanists Like," Tom Scheinfeldt points to open social networks (Twitter vs. Facebook), agile development (rapid, iterative), do-it-yourself (building, making), PHP (simplicity, accessibility), and extramural grants (innovation, collaboration) ("Stuff Digital Humanists Like"). Scheinfeldt's list captures much of what animates the digital humanities community, expressing this description in terms of core technologies and technical approaches. In Diane Zorich's study of digital humanities centers, she distills key values as expressed in their mission statements, including "the enduring value of the humanities, collaboration and cross-disciplinarity, openness, civic and social responsibility, and questioning sacred cows" (Zorich). Even as the digital humanities insist on the importance of the humanities, they also seek to transform practices (or "sacred cows") such as tenure, publication, and peer review and to promote collaboration, cross-disciplinarity, and public responsibility. *The Digital Humanities Manifesto 2.0* advances values such as openness (open access, open source), collaboration, multiplicity, participation, "scholarly innovation, disciplinary cross-fertilization, and the democratization of knowledge" (UCLA Mellon Seminar in Digital Humanities). Likewise, the Paris "Manifesto for the Digital Humanities" focuses on defining the DH community as "solidary, open, welcoming and freely accessible . . . multilingual and multidisciplinary," and favoring "the advancement of knowledge, the improvement of research quality in our disciplines, the enrichment of knowledge and of collective patrimony, in the academic sphere and beyond it" ("Manifesto for the Digital Humanities"). Running throughout these statements is an overarching sense that the digital humanities should promote traditional humanistic values such as access to knowledge and civic responsibility by embracing collaboration, cross-disciplinarity, innovation, participation, and openness.

PROPOSED VALUES

Drawing from manifestos, model statements of value, and my own analysis of the rhetoric of the digital humanities, I propose the following initial list of digital humanities values. My intent is not to speak presumptuously for the community and decide on my own what it values but rather to open up the conversation. Although I wanted to keep the list of values concise, I recognize that others should probably be added, such as sharing public knowledge, curiosity, multidisciplinarity, and balancing theory and practice. With each value, I explain what it is and why it is embraced by the digital humanities community, and I also offer a few examples of how the value manifests itself, aggregating ongoing discussions in the digital humanities. This set of values signifies what the digital humanities community aspires to achieve, not necessarily what it has fully met.

Openness

Openness operates on several levels in the digital humanities, describing a commitment to the open exchange of ideas, the development of open content and software, and transparency (Zorich, 11). The digital humanities community embraces openness because of both self-interest and ethical aspirations. In order to create digital scholarship, researchers typically need access to data, tools, and dissemination platforms. As Christine Borgman argues, "Openness matters for the digital humanities for reasons of interoperability, discovery, usability, and reusability" (Borgman), since it means that scholars are better able to find and use the data they need and create systems that work together. As participants at a 2011 MLA panel on "The Open Professoriate" argued, openness allows scholars to reach larger audiences than the few who read academic journals, meet their responsibilities to be "public servants," participate in public exchanges, and become more visible (Jaschik). Ultimately, openness promotes the larger goal of the humanities "to democratize knowledge to reach out to 'publics,' share academic discoveries, and invite an array of audiences to participate in knowledge production" (Draxler et al.).

We can see openness at work throughout the digital humanities community, such as in open-source software tools, freely accessible digital collections, and open-access journals and books. In the United States, the National Endowment for the Humanities (NEH) "strongly encourages" grant applicants to release software developed through NEH support as open source (National Endowment for the Humanities). The digital humanities community has produced a number of open-source tools, including Zotero and NINES Collex. Likewise, some digital collections important to the digital humanities, such as the Rossetti Archive, use Creative Commons licenses; even more make their content freely accessible without explicitly using such open licenses. In launching *Digital Humanities Quarterly,* the editors decided to make it open access to expand the audience and connect with fields related to the digital humanities, so that "it can offer a freely accessible view of the field to those who are curious about it, and can also provide a publication venue that is visible to readers (and potential authors) from these other domains" (Flanders, Piez, and Terras). Openness thus supports related values such as transdisciplinarity, collaboration, and the democratization of knowledge.

Digital humanists are beginning to press for open access not only to digital collections, tools, and scholarship but also to educational resources and even course evaluations. As Ethan Watrall argues, open courseware benefits the global community of learners by making knowledge widely available (and is thus "the right thing to do"), the university by making visible its curriculum and offering educational resources for current students, and faculty members by documenting their educational innovations and giving them access to the pedagogical contributions of their colleagues. As part of his commitment to openness and transparency, Mark Sample makes his course evaluations public and shares his Zotero library ("Transparency, Teaching, and Taking My Evaluations Public"). As Sample argues, the work of the humanities "is so crucial that we need to share what we learn, every step along the way" ("On Hacking and Unpacking My (Zotero) Library"). Rather than cheapening knowledge by making it free, embracing openness recognizes the importance of the humanities to society.

Collaboration

As Steven Johnson argues, a "majority of breakthrough ideas emerge in collaborative environments" as the free flow of information allows people to build on ideas and think in new ways. If reforming education and solving social problems depends on tapping our "collective creative potential," then the humanities faces a "real ethical dilemma in its persistant [sic] presumption that intellectual work is fundamentally individual," argues Alex Reid. Thus one of the key contributions that the digital humanities can make is "to encourage a new kind of communal behavior, guided by a new *ethos*"(Reid).

Indeed, the digital humanities community promotes an ethos that embraces collaboration as essential to its work and mission (even as it recognizes that some work is better done in solitude). In part, that emphasis on collaboration reflects the need for people with a range of skills to contribute to digital scholarship. As Martha Nell Smith explains, "By its very nature, humanities computing demands new models of work, specifically those that exploit the technology of collaboration, for humanities computing projects cannot be realized without project managers, text encoders, scanners, visionaries, and others with a variety of responsibilities to produce effective multimedia projects." Often collaborations in the digital humanities are interdisciplinary, linking together the humanistic and computational approaches (Siemens, Unsworth, and Schreibman). Yet collaboration isn't just about being more productive but also about transforming how the humanities work. Instead of working on a project alone, a digital humanist will typically participate as part of a team, learning from others and contributing to an ongoing dialogue. By bringing together people with diverse expertise, collaboration opens up new approaches to tackling a problem, as statistical computing is applied to the study of literature or geospatial tools are used to understand historical data.

There are many indicators of the importance of collaboration to the digital humanities community. Consider, for instance, how frequently "collaboration" is a topic at digital humanities conferences. For instance, at the Digital Humanities 2010 Conference, a number of papers, posters, and workshop sessions addressed collaboration, whether as a key component of the humanities cyberinfrastructure (e.g., "Content, Compliance, Collaboration and Complexity: Creating and Sustaining Information"), a goal for online environments (e.g., "Developing a Collaborative Online Environment for History—The Experience of British History Online"), a characteristic of the digital humanities community (e.g., "A Tale of Two Cities: Implications of the Similarities and Differences in Collaborative Approaches within the Digital Libraries and Digital Humanities Communities"), or a means of accomplishing work (e.g., "An Inter-Disciplinary Approach to Web Programming: A Collaboration Between the University Archives and the Department of Computer Science") (Alliance of Digital Humanities Organisations, *Digital Humanities 2010 Conference Abstracts*). In my own preliminary analysis of collaboration in the digital humanities community, I found that, between 2004 and 2008, 48 percent of the articles published in *Literary and Linguistic Computing*, a major DH journal, were coauthored, a much higher percentage than is typical of humanities journals (Spiro). Digital humanities centers (such as the Collaboratory for Research in Computing for Humanities) strive to support collaborations (Zorich), as do digital humanities networks such as the Humanities Arts, Sciences, and Technology Advanced Collaboratory (HASTAC), a focus sometimes reflected in their names. Many digital humanities funding programs explicitly require or encourage collaboration, including the NEH's Collaborative Research Grants, Digging into Data Challenge, JISC/NEH Transatlantic Digitization Collaboration Grants, and DFG/NEH joint grants.

But it isn't just that the digital humanities community values collaboration—rather, it values collaboration that acknowledges contributions by all involved, whether they are tenured faculty, graduate students, technologists, or librarians (Nowviskie). To guide the DH community in collaborating with respect and fairness for all, the "Collaborators' Bill of Rights" affirms the community value of recognizing all involved in a collaboration and outlines how credit should be attributed and intellectual property rights of contributors respected (Kirschenbaum et al.).

Collegiality and Connectedness

As part of its commitment to openness and collaboration, the digital humanities community promotes collegiality, welcoming contributions and offering help to those who need it. Tom Scheinfeldt calls this the "niceness" of digital humanities, which he ascribes to both its collaborative nature and its focus on method rather than theory ("Why Digital Humanities is 'Nice'"). Furthermore, as Lincoln Mullen argues, inclusion may be an effective strategy for increasing the acceptance of digital scholarship: "It's the ethos that says, I'm a coder and you're not, so let me teach you, or let me build the tools you need. It's the ethos that says texts and tools should be available for all and that publicly funded research and instruction should be publicly accessible" (Mullen). If the underlying goal is the promotion of public knowledge, why not share?

We can see this commitment to collegiality in both virtual and physical spaces that bring together digital humanists. For example, *Digital Humanities Questions and Answers*[1] aims to "create a friendly and inviting space where people can help each other with questions about languages, tools, standards, best practices, pedagogy, and all things related to scholarly activity in the digital humanities (broadly defined)" (Meloni). Between September of 2010 and April 2011, *Digital Humanities Questions and Answers* has attracted over one thousand posts, attesting to the willingness of the DH community to help. Likewise, THATCamp, an "unconference" that promotes collaboration and conversation in the digital humanities, aims to be "open, . . . informal," and "non-hierarchical and non-disciplinary and inter-professional" (French). Rather than establishing an agenda in advance, THATCamps encourage participants to write short blog posts before the unconference to describe their session ideas, then charge the participants with defining the schedule during the first session. At a typical THATCamp, it doesn't matter whether you are a senior faculty member, a graduate student, a programmer, or an early career librarian; what matters is your willingness to participate and the quality of your ideas. With the participants in charge of defining the conference, sometimes individuals can dominate the discussion, and some conversations can be less inclusive than others, but the ethic of THATCamp emphasizes collaboration, productivity, and fun (French).

Recently, this idea of inclusiveness in the digital humanities has come under critique. For example, William Pannapacker noted the split between "builders and theorizers" and "an in-group, out-group dynamic" in the digital humanities ("Digital Humanities Triumphant?"), a comment echoed by others (Sulley). But as Stéfan Sinclair suggests, the digital humanities community recognizes a variety of contributions, from authoring publications to moderating discussion lists to developing software. Many of its members devote themselves to serving the community—"advocating for the digital humanities at various levels, helping to provide support and expertise for other colleagues, mentoring junior colleagues formally and informally" (Sinclair). Still, leaders of the digital humanities community have reacted with concern to the charge of exclusiveness. Geoffrey Rockwell argues for providing more paths to entry to the community, looks to THATCamp as a model for "creating a new 'we' of community," and concludes, "May we have the grace to welcome the exuberance of passion of the next generation." Likewise, John Unsworth suggests that "to expand the community further," digital humanities will need to demonstrate how it can advance humanities research, provide support for researchers and teachers who want to use digital tools and methods, and reward their efforts ("The State of Digital Humanities, 2010"). Even if the DH community has not fully met the value of collegiality and inclusiveness, it certainly aspires to.

Diversity

The digital humanities embraces diversity, recognizing that the community is more vibrant, discussions are richer, and projects are stronger if multiple perspectives are represented. Some argue that the digital humanities community pays lip service to diversity but has not engaged with it on a deeper level. As Tanner Higgin contends, "issues of cultural politics are downplayed or, more commonly, considered a given within DH. There's a disposition that the battles of race, gender, class and ecology have already been won, their lessons have been learned, and by espousing a rhetoric of equity everything will fall into place" (Higgin). Similarly, Anne Cong-Huyen asks, "where are those individuals and communities who are visibly different to examine and create or represent disparate voices and media objects?"

Given the DH community's orientation toward building and making rather than theorizing, its focus has not really been on cultural politics, although Alan Liu and others have been pressing it to engage with cultural criticism (Liu). Based on my admittedly anecdotal observations at DH gatherings, the community may not have achieved the same degree of diversity in race and ethnicity as it has in professional roles, nationalities, age, disciplines, and gender. However, the community works toward diversity as a goal. In recognition of the need for the digital humanities to be diverse, THATCamp SoCal created a position statement, "Towards an Open Digital Humanities": "Digital humanities must take active strides to include all the areas of study that comprise the humanities and must strive to include participants of diverse age, generation, skill, race, ethnicity, sexuality, ability, nationality, culture, discipline, areas of interest. Without open participation and broad outreach, the digital humanities movement limits its capacity for critical engagement" (Rivera Monclova). The community's desire to achieve diversity and inclusiveness is reflected in the theme of the 2011 Digital Humanities conference, "Big Tent Digital Humanities" (Alliance of Digital Humanities Organizations, "General CFP"). The call for papers for the conference includes "digital humanities and diversity" as a suggested topic, reflecting both the importance given to the topic and the sense that it merits deeper discussion.

Experimentation

The language of experimentation runs throughout the digital humanities, demonstrating its support of risk taking, entrepreneurship, and innovation. By leveraging information technology to explore data, digital humanities casts intellectual problems as experiments: What is the effect of modeling the data in a particular way? What happens when we visualize data or use text mining tools to discover patterns in it? (Svensson, "The Landscape of Digital Humanities"). As Willard McCarty suggests, "ours is an experimental practice, using equipment and instantiating definite methods." As in the sciences, digital humanities projects often use data, tools, and methods to examine particular questions, but the work supports interpretation and exploration. The word "experiment" turns up in Burrows's *Computation into Criticism: A Study of Jane Austen's Novels and an Experiment in Method,* which explores the use of textual analysis software to study Austen's language. Likewise, Ayers and Thomas initially included the word "experiment"—*Two American Communities on the Eve of the Civil War: An Experiment in Form and Analysis* (Ayers and Thomas)—in the title of their article for *The American Historical Review,* which tests how historians can "create or present new forms of scholarship and narrative" (Thomas, 415). However, reviewers rejected the article's use of hypertext, since it "frustrated readers' expectations for a scholarly article laid out in a certain way" (Ayers, "The Academic Culture and the IT Culture"). When Ayers and Thomas's article was finally published in the journal, it adopted a "much-simplified form" and took a new title that deemphasized its experimental approach: "The Differences Slavery Made: A Close Analysis of Two American Communities" (Ayers, "The Academic Culture and the IT Culture"). Perhaps a traditional academic journal wasn't ready for "an experiment in form and analysis" (although the language of experimentation still permeates the article).

Not all experiments succeed as originally imagined, but the digital humanities community recognizes the value of failure in the pursuit of innovation. "[T]o encourage innovations in the digital humanities," the National Endowment for the Humanities offers "Digital Humanities Start-Up Grants," which "are modeled, in part, on the 'high risk/high reward' paradigm often used by funding agencies in the sciences" (National Endowment for the Humanities). Failure is accepted as a useful result in the digital humanities, since it indicates that the experiment was likely high risk and means that we collectively learn from failure rather than reproducing it (assuming that the failure is documented). As John Unsworth argues, "If an electronic scholarly project can't fail and doesn't produce new ignorance, then it isn't worth a damn" ("Documenting the Reinvention of Text").

Many digital humanities organizations model themselves after laboratories, emphasizing the experimental, collaborative nature of their work. In defining the term "digital humanities center," Diane Zorich characterizes it as "an entity where new media and technologies are used for humanities-based research, teaching, and intellectual engagement and experimentation" (4). Indeed, a number of DH centers position themselves as labs, including the University of Virginia's Scholars' Lab, the HUMlab at Umeå University, and University of California Davis's Humanities Innovation Lab, reflecting the sense of a lab both as a space where experiments are carried out and as a community focused on exploration and experimentation. Likewise, the Stanford Literary Lab focuses on quantitative methods to study literature, where "[i]deally, research will take the form of a genuine 'experiment'" ("Stanford Literary Lab"). Stanford Literary Lab's recent investigation into automatically classifying texts by genre, *Quantitative Formalism: An Experiment* (Allison et al.), employs the language of experimentation throughout.

For the digital humanities community, experimentation suggests not only a method of testing ideas and creating knowledge but also its engagement in transforming traditional approaches to teaching and research. "Experiment" belongs in a constellation of terms such as curiosity, play, exploration, and do-it-yourself. Dan Cohen ran an experiment to see if he could disseminate a historical puzzle via Twitter and get an answer back from the research community (Cohen). Similarly, in launching *Digital Humanities Quarterly*, the editors characterize it as an experiment "in how academic journals are published," given its use of open standards such as XML and commitment to "the rhetoric of digital authoring" (Flanders, Piez, and Terras). Experimentation goes on in the classroom as well as in research and publishing. For instance, the *Looking for Whitman* project brought together classes at four different universities to explore the work of Walt Whitman, collaborate using social networking technologies, and contribute to an open repository of resources from places where Whitman once lived ("About Looking for Whitman"). Jim Groom characterizes *Looking for Whitman* as "an attempt to experiment with how [a group] of distributed faculty and students can share, collaborate, and converse out in the open" (Groom). "Experiment" thus suggests the aim to develop innovative, novel practices for humanities research and teaching.

Conclusion

To some extent, some digital humanities values may clash with the norms of the academy. For example, universities' intellectual property policies may be unfavorable toward producing open-source software. In addition, professors may find it difficult to find publishers for their work if they initially release it as open access (although some publishers—including the University of Minnesota Press, which is publishing this volume—are willing to adopt open licenses). Likewise, many humanities departments favor solo work in their tenure and promotion policies and may find it difficult to determine how to assign credit for collaborative work (Modern Language Association, *Report of the MLA Task Force on Evaluating Scholarship for Tenure and Promotion*). This resistance (or, in some cases, ignorance) makes it all the more important for the DH community to come together in putting forward values such as openness and collaboration. These values point to an overarching ethos that promotes innovative scholarship as a public good and believes that it should be practiced openly and collaboratively.

By developing a core values statement, the digital humanities community can craft a more coherent identity, use these values as guiding principles, and pass them on as part of DH education. What defines a profession is not only what it does but also what values it upholds and how it practices "professional responsibility" (Fuller and Keim). If groups share common values, they are typically governed more effectively and can motivate people to participate more actively (Zhu, Kraut, and Kittur). As Patrick Svensson notes, the DH community offers "rather strong support for expanding the territory and for achieving a higher degree of penetration" across the humanities community ("Humanities Computing as Digital Humanities"); one way to reach out is to articulate core values that those both inside and outside the community might understand and embrace. Of course, these values must operate in a specific context, where they may clash or get complicated. But they can help to guide decision making about priorities and serve as the basis for the DH community's goals. Should projects use proprietary code? What should DH curricula emphasize? What should determine the agenda of a DH center or professional organization? In tackling these questions, we can draw guidance from an explicit yet evolving set of community values.

NOTES

This essay elaborates ideas that I first articulated in "What Is She Doing Here? Crafting a Professional Identity as a Digital Humanist/Librarian," in *Alt-Academy: Alternative Academic Careers for Humanities Scholars*, edited by Bethany Nowviskie. Thanks to Liz Losh, Matt Gold, George Williams, and Rebecca Frost Davis for their helpful comments on this essay.

1. http://digitalhumanities.org/answers.

BIBLIOGRAPHY

"About Looking for Whitman." *Looking for Whitman.* 2011. http://lookingforwhitman.org/about/.

Alliance of Digital Humanities Organisations, Association for Literary and Linguistic Computing, Association for Computers and the Humanities, and Society for Digital Humanities–Société pour l'étude des médias interactif. *Digital Humanities 2010 Conference Abstracts.* King's College London, London, July 7–10, 2010. http://dh2010.cch.kcl.ac.uk/academic-programme/abstracts/papers/pdf/book-final.pdf.

———. "General CFP." Digital Humanities 2011, June 19–22. https://dh2011.stanford.edu/?page_id=97.

Allison, Sarah, et al. *Quantitative Formalism: An Experiment.* Stanford Literary Lab, 2011.

American Council of Learned Societies. "Frequently Asked Questions." 2011. http://www.acls.org/info/Default.aspx?id=198.

American Historical Association. "Statement on Standards of Professional Conduct." 1987. http://www.historians.org/pubs/free/ProfessionalStandards.cfm.

American Library Association. "Core Values of Librarianship." June 29, 2004. http://www.ala.org/ala/aboutala/offices/oif/statementspols/corevaluesstatement/corevalues.cfm#.

Ayers, Edward L. "The Academic Culture and the IT Culture: Their Effect on Teaching and Scholarship." *EDUCAUSE Review* 39, no.6 (2004): 48–62. http://www.educause

.edu/EDUCAUSE+Review/EDUCAUSEReviewMagazineVolume39/TheAcademicCultureandtheITCult/157939.

Ayers, E. L., and W. G. Thomas III. "Two American Communities on the Eve of Civil War: An Experiment in Form and Analysis." Preprint, submitted to the *American Historical Review,* January 11, 2002. http://www2.vcdh.virginia.edu/xml_docs/article/article_full.pdf.

Bell, Steven. "Core Values Must Come First." *ACRLog.* June 18, 2008.

Borgman, Christine L. "The Digital Future Is Now: A Call to Action for the Humanities." *Digital Humanities Quarterly* 3, no. 4 (2009). http://works.bepress.com/borgman/233/.

Cheney, Lynne. *Humanities in America: A Report to the President, Congress and the American People.* Washington, D.C.: National Endowment for the Humanities, 1988.

Cheverie, Joan F., Jennifer Boettcher, and John Buschman. "Digital Scholarship in the University Tenure and Promotion Process: A Report on the Sixth Scholarly Communication Symposium at Georgetown University Library." *Journal of Scholarly Publishing* 40, no. 3 (2009): 219–30.

Cohen, Dan. "The Spider and the Web: Results." *Dan Cohen's Digital Humanities Blog.* April 29, 2009. http://www.dancohen.org/2009/04/29/the-spider-and-the-web-results/.

Cong-Huyen, Anne. "Toward an 'Asian American' Digital Humanities." *Anne Cong-Huyen.* http://anitaconchita.wordpress.com/2011/01/10/an-asian-american-digital-humanities-or-digital-asian-american-criticism/.

Davidson, Cathy N. "Humanities 2.0: Promise, Perils, Predictions." *PMLA* 123, no. 3 (2008): 707–17. http://www.mlajournals.org/doi/abs/10.1632/pmla.2008.123.3.707.

Draxler, Bridget, et al. "Democratizing Knowledge." *HASTAC.* September 21, 2009. http://hastac.org/forums/hastac-scholars-discussions/democratizing-knowledge-digital-humanities.

Fitzpatrick, Kathleen. *Planned Obsolescence: Publishing, Technology, and the Future of the Academy.* New York: NYU Press, 2009. http://www.lib.umich.edu/events/kathleen-fitzpatrick-planned-obsolescence-publishing-technology-and-future-academy.

———. "Reporting from the Digital Humanities 2010 Conference." *ProfHacker.* July 13, 2010. http://chronicle.com/blogs/profhacker/reporting-from-the-digital-humanities-2010-conference/25473.

Flanders, Julia, Wendell Piez, and Melissa Terras. "Welcome to Digital Humanities Quarterly." *Digital Humanities Quarterly* 1, no. 1 (2007). http://digitalhumanities.org/dhq/vol/1/1/000007/000007.html.

Frankel, Mark S. "Professional Codes: Why, How, and With What Impact?" *Journal of Business Ethics* 8, no. 2 (1989): 109–15. http://philpapers.org/rec/FRAPCW.

French, Amanda. "About." *THATCamp.* December 21, 2010.

Fuller, Ursula, and Bob Keim. "Assessing Students' Practice of Professional Values." Madrid: ACM, 2008, 88–92.

Groom, Jim. "Looking for Whitman: A Grand, Aggregated Experiment." *bavatuesdays.* September 1, 2009. http://bavatuesdays.com/looking-for-whitman-a-grand-aggregated-experiment/.

Higgin, Tanner. "Cultural Politics, Critique and the Digital Humanities." *MediaCommons* 25 (May 2010). http://www.tannerhiggin.com/2010/05/cultural-politics-critique-and-the-digital-humanities/.

"How do you define Humanities Computing/Digital Humanities?" *Day of Digital Humanities.* March 8, 2011. http://tapor.ualberta.ca/taporwiki/index.php/How_do_you_define_Humanities_Computing_/_Digital_Humanities%3F.

Jaschik, Scott. "An Open, Digital Professoriat." *Inside Higher Ed.* January 10, 2011. http://www.insidehighered.com/news/2011/01/10/mla_embraces_digital_humanities_and_blogging.

Johnson, Steven. *Where Good Ideas Come From: The Natural History of Innovation.* 1st ed. Riverhead, 2010. Kindle edition.

Kirschenbaum, Matthew. "What Is Digital Humanities?" *ADE Bulletin* 150 (2010): 1–7. http://mkirschenbaum.wordpress.com/2011/01/22/what-is-digital-humanities/.

Kirschenbaum, Matthew, et al. "Collaborators' Bill of Rights." *Off The Tracks Workshop.* January 21, 2011.

Koehler, Wallace. "Professional Values and Ethics as Defined by 'The LIS Discipline.'" *Journal of Education for Library and Information Science* 44, no. 2 (2003): 99–119. http://www.jstor.org/pss/40323926.

Levine, George, et al. *Speaking for the Humanities.* American Council of Learned Societies, 1988. http://www.lib.muohio.edu/multifacet/record/mu3ugb1492819.

Liu, Alan. "Where Is Cultural Criticism in the Digital Humanities." Modern Language Association convention, Los Angeles, CA. January 7, 2011. http://liu.english.ucsb.edu/where-is-cultural-criticism-in-the-digital-humanities/.

"Manifesto for the Digital Humanities." *THATCamp Paris 2010.* June 3, 2010. http://tcp.hypotheses.org/411.

McCarty, Willard. "Modeling: A Study in Words and Meanings." In *Companion to Digital Humanities*, edited by Ray Siemens, John Unsworth, and Susan Schreibman. Oxford: Blackwell, 2004. http://www.digitalhumanities.org/companion/view?docId=blackwell/9781405103213/9781405103213.xml&doc.view=content&chunk.id=ss1-3-7&toc.depth=1&brand=default&anchor.id=0.

Meloni, Julie. "Announcing Digital Humanities Questions & Answers." *ProfHacker.* September 29, 2010. http://chronicle.com/blogs/profhacker/announcing-digital-humanities-questions-answers-dhanswers/26544.

Miller, Rebecca. "The Value of Values-Based Literature: An Exploration of Librarianship's Professional Discussion of Core Values." 2007. Master's thesis, University of North Carolina at Chapel Hill. http://dc.lib.unc.edu/cdm4/item_viewer.php?CISOROOT=/s_papers&CISOPTR=1012&CISOBOX=1&REC=6.

Modern Language Association. "MLA Statement of Professional Ethics." 2004. http://www.mla.org/repview_profethics.

———. *Report of the MLA Task Force on Evaluating Scholarship for Tenure and Promotion.* 2006. http://www.mla.org/tenure_promotion.

Morgan, Jonathan T., Robert M. Mason, and Karine Nahon. "Lifting the Veil." Proceedings of the 2011 iConference, Seattle, Washington, 2011. 8–15. http://portal.acm.org/citation.cfm?id=1940763.

Mullen, Lincoln. "Digital Humanities Is a Spectrum; or, We're All Digital Humanists Now." *Backward Glance.* April 29, 2010. http://lincolnmullen.com/2010/04/29/digital-humanities-is-a-spectrum-or-were-all-digital-humanists-now/.

Murray-John, Patrick. "Itches and Inclusion: Thoughts from Afar on THATCamp." *Remediation Roomy-nation.* January 2011. http://www.patrickgmj.net/node/197.

National Endowment for the Humanities. "Digital Humanities Start-Up Grants." August 6, 2010. http://www.neh.gov/grants/guidelines/digitalhumanitiesstartup.html.

Nowviskie, Bethany. "Monopolies of Invention." *Bethany Nowviskie.* December 30, 2009. http://nowviskie.org/2009/monopolies-of-invention/.

O'Reilly, Tim. "Open Source Paradigm Shift." *O'Reilly.* June 2004. http://tim.oreilly.com/articles/paradigmshift_0504.html.

Pannapacker, William. "Digital Humanities Triumphant?" *Chronicle Review's Brainstorm Blog.* January 8, 2011. http://chronicle.com/blogs/brainstorm/pannapacker-at-mla-digital-humanities-triumphant/30915.

———. "The MLA and the Digital Humanities." *Chronicle Review's Brainstorm Blog.* December 28, 2009. http://chronicle.com/blogPost/The-MLAthe-Digital/19468/.

Parry, David. "Be Online or Be Irrelevant." *academHack.* January 11, 2010. http://academhack.outsidethetext.com/home/2010/be-online-or-be-irrelevant/.

Reid, Alex. "The Creative Community and the Digital Humanities." *digital digs.* October 17, 2010. http://www.alex-reid.net/2010/10/the-creative-community-and-the-digital-humanities.html.

Rivera Monclova, Marta. "Towards an Open Digital Humanities." *THATCamp Southern California 2011.* January 11, 2011. http://socal2011.thatcamp.org/01/11/opendh/.

Rockwell, Geoffrey. "Inclusion in the Digital Humanities." *philosophi.ca.* June 19, 2010. http://www.philosophi.ca/pmwiki.php/Main/InclusionInTheDigitalHumanities.

Sample, Mark. "On Hacking and Unpacking My (Zotero) Library." *SAMPLE REALITY.* March 17, 2010.

———. "Transparency, Teaching, and Taking My Evaluations Public." *SAMPLE REALITY.* August 4, 2009. http://www.samplereality.com/2009/07/29/on-hacking-and-unpacking-my-zotero-library/.

Scheinfeldt, Tom. "Stuff Digital Humanists Like: Defining Digital Humanities by its Values." *Found History.* December 2, 2010. http://www.foundhistory.org/2010/12/02/stuff-digital-humanists-like/.

———. "Why Digital Humanities is 'Nice.'" *Found History.* May 26, 2010. http://www.foundhistory.org/2010/05/26/why-digital-humanities-is-%E2%80%9Cnice%E2%80%9D/.

Siemens, Ray, John Unsworth, and Susan Schreibman. "The Digital Humanities and Humanities Computing: An Introduction." In *Companion to Digital Humanities,* edited by Ray Siemens, John Unsworth, and Susan Schreibman. Oxford: Blackwell, 2004. http://

www.digitalhumanities.org/companion/view?docId=blackwell/9781405103213/9781405103213.xml&chunk.id=ss1-1-3

Sinclair, Stéfan. "Digital Humanities and Stardom." *Stéfan Sinclair: Scribblings & Musings of an Incorrigible Humanist.* January 9, 2011.

Smith, M. N. "Computing: What Has American Literary Study To Do with It." *American Literature* 74, no. 4 (2002): 833–57.

Spiro, Lisa. "Collaborative Authorship in the Humanities." *Digital Scholarship in the Humanities.* April 21, 2009. http://digitalscholarship.wordpress.com/2009/04/21/collaborative-authorship-in-the-humanities/.

"Stanford Literary Lab." http://litlab.stanford.edu/.

Sully, Perian. "Digital Humanities Silos and Outreach." *Musematic.* http://musematic.net/2011/01/09/dh-silos-and-outreach/.

Svensson, Patrik. "Humanities Computing as Digital Humanities." 3, no. 3 (2009). http://digitalhumanities.org/dhq/vol/3/3/000065/000065.html.

———. "The Landscape of Digital Humanities." 4, no. 1 (2010). http://digitalhumanities.org/dhq/vol/4/1/000080/000080.html.

Thomas III, William G. "Blazing Trails toward Digital History Scholarship." *Social History/Histoire Sociale* 34, no. 68 (2001): 415–26.

Thomas III, William G., and Edward L. Ayers, "An Overview: The Differences Slavery Made: A Close Analysis of Two American Communities." *American Historical Review* 108, no. 5 (December 2003). http://www.historycooperative.org/journals/ahr/108.5/thomas.html.

UCLA Mellon Seminar in Digital Humanities. *The Digital Humanities Manifesto 2.0.* 2009.

Unsworth, John. "Documenting the Reinvention of Text: The Importance of Failure." *Journal of Electronic Publishing* 3, no. 2 (1997). http://quod.lib.umich.edu/cgi/t/text/text-idx?c=jep;view=text;rgn=main;idno=3336451.0003.201.

———. "The State of Digital Humanities, 2010." June 7, 2010. http://www3.isrl.illinois.edu/~unsworth/state.of.dh.DHSI.pdf.

Watrall, Ethan. "Developing a Personal Open Courseware Strategy." *ProfHacker.* June 11, 2010. http://chronicle.com/blogPost/Developing-a-Personal-Open-/24696/.

Weissinger, Thomas. "Competing Models of Librarianship: Do Core Values Make a Difference?" *Journal of Academic Librarianship* 29, no. 1: 32–39. http://www.sciencedirect.com/science/article/pii/S0099133302004032.

Wikipedia. "BarCamp." 2011. March 15, 2011.

Zhu, H., R. Kraut, and A. Kittur. "Doing What Needs To Be Done: Effects of Goals in Self-Governed Online Production Groups." ACM Conference on Human Factors in Computing Systems, Vancouver, BC, Canada, 2011.

Zorich, Diane. *A Survey of Digital Humanities Centers in the United States.* Washington, D.C.: Council on Library and Information Resources, 2008. http://www.clir.org/pubs/reports/pub143/pub143.pdf.

Beyond the Big Tent

PATRIK SVENSSON

"Big Tent Digital Humanities" is the theme of the Digital Humanities 2011 conference at Stanford University. It is a well-chosen conference topic given the current, often fairly intense debate about the scope and direction of the digital humanities, one also exemplified by the Modern Language Association (MLA) 2011 panel on "The History and Future of the Digital Humanities" as well as a number of concurrent online discussions. This debate has a disciplinary, historical, and institutional basis and is backdropped by considerable interest in the digital humanities from universities, funding agencies, scholars, and others. Moreover, there is a basic tension between a tradition invested in technology as a tool and methodology and a range of "newcomers" starting out from other modes of engagement between the humanities and the digital (Svensson, "Landscape"). A related point of tension has to do with the scope of the digital humanities. Arguably, much of the hope and interest currently invested in the digital humanities relates to an inclusive notion of the field and a sense of the digital humanities as a way of reconfiguring the humanities (Svensson, "Envisioning"). Hence the issue of the size of the digital humanities canalizes a range of important debates and future critical choices.

This chapter explores the contemporary landscape of digital humanities starting from the discourse of "big tent" digital humanities. What is it exactly that needs to be incorporated into the tent that was not there before? Does a larger tent come with expanded responsibilities? Why do we need a tent or a bounding mechanism in the first place? Is there place for private as well as public institutions of higher education in the tent? Is a very inclusive notion of digital humanities problematic? The chapter ends with a suggestion that the community may benefit from a "no tent" approach to the digital humanities and that "trading zone" (Galison) or "meeting place" may be useful, alternative structuring devices and ideational notions.

Sizing the Digital Humanities

There can be no doubt that the digital humanities have expanded in multiple ways over the last ten years. Indeed, ten years ago, the notion of digital humanities itself was an emerging one, arising out of a relabeling process within the humanities computing community (Kirschenbaum; Svensson, "Humanities Computing"). The perceived larger size would partly seem to be a result of having a more distinct and inclusive label, although there has also obviously been a real expansion as indicated by new book series, the number of positions advertised, funding available, the growing number of digital humanities initiatives, interest from policy makers and university leadership, increased visibility, and general buzz.

The digital humanities arose from a specific epistemic tradition or set of traditions (Knorr Cetina), and with the expansion of the field comes a higher degree of heterogeneity and inclusion of other epistemic traditions (Svensson, "Humanities Computing"). This is part of what makes the digital humanities a dynamic and, to some extent, indeterminate field. It is important to note that traditional humanities computing, as well as digital humanities, frequently have had an intersectional position. In other words, digital humanities institutions tend to depend on interaction with other institutions to a larger extent than most traditional departments and disciplines. This is evident in the idea of a methodological commons (McCarty), for instance; and it is also notable that the digital humanities have often been institutionalized as centers and institutes rather than as traditional departments. Indeed, such centers may be more institutionally akin to traditional humanities centers than departments. Examples include the Centre for Computing in the Humanities (CCH) at King's College, the Institute for Advanced Technology in the Humanities (IATH) at the University of Virginia, and the Maryland Institute for Technology in the Humanities (MITH) at the University of Maryland. These centers obviously share some characteristics, such as a range of activities and strategies to do work with other parts of the humanities, as well as outside of the humanities proper. This liminal position is quite important, offering something that can be built on in order to facilitate digital humanities as a larger project. However, we also need to acknowledge that this necessitates the reassessing of traditions and possible interaction points between the humanities and the digital and allowing change not only in terms of size but also in terms of epistemic texture and institutional focus. An interesting question is whether the recent name change of the Centre for Computing in the Humanities to the Department of Digital Humanities indicates a difference in self-conception and whether it will result in a different institutional position.

Yale University: Inside or Outside the Tent?

The listed institutions all come from the humanities computing tradition. What's more, we are now seeing a range of new initiatives not anchored in this tradition as strongly, which sometimes leads to points of tension. A useful example is Yale University's relatively recent interest in digital humanities as manifested in a working group for the digital humanities started in 2009. On their website, the field is described as follows: "Digital humanities encompass an array of convergent practices that explore a world in which scholarship is not exclusively produced in print but is created and distributed through new digital technologies. This group will consider the expanding practices, vocabulary, and research methods germane to digital humanities across disciplines." This is a fairly inclusive definition, arguably compatible with a big-tent notion of the digital humanities. The discussion of Yale's interest in the digital humanities is presumably inflected by the fact that Yale is not just any newcomer but an Ivy League school and one arguably coming to the field from a different tradition (as evidenced by a close connection to media theory). In February 2010, the conference "The Past's Digital Presence" received considerable attention partly through *Humanist* editor Willard McCarty's description of it as a "watershed moment" (McCarty, *Humanist*). This gracious introduction of Yale University into the digital humanities was met with some resistance. In a subsequent *Humanist* post, University of Nebraska professor Amanda Gailey expressed some concern:

> I find that the "watershed" comment overlooks the work that many grad students have been doing at non-Ivy schools for several years now. . . . Importantly, many of us who did not attend Ivy League schools and who professionally defined ourselves as digital humanists before it became an MLA buzzword were arguably taking many more risks. . . . Frankly, I view the late arrival of the Ivies as a worrisome indicator that DH will soon be locked down by the same tired socioeconomic gatekeeping mechanisms that prevent many people with talent from succeeding at so many other academic disciplines. (Gailey)

Gailey reacts to McCarty's description of the workshop but also to the aspirations of Yale and other Ivy League schools to enter the digital humanities. There is a clear sense of pointing to the tradition of humanities computing as digital humanities here and the personal and institutional investment of digital humanists with a long-term engagement in the field. It should also be noted here that the list of readings for the Yale Digital Humanities Working Group includes pieces such as John Unsworth's 2002 paper "What Is Humanities Computing and What Is Not?" showing sensibility to the history of the field. There is probably some truth to Gailey's socioeconomic concerns (which obviously are shared by others in the community as evident in Katherine Harris's comment (Harris), although expansion would inevitably seem to lead to more heterogeneity and hence presumably a larger socioeconomic spread. Maybe a stronger interest from elite universities could even help leverage the digital humanities as a project and the humanities as Yale (as suggested by Cohen in relation to discussing the Open Content Alliance)? Also, the creation of a working group at Yale does not in itself necessarily represent an institutionally strategic move. It could be argued that the working group indicates interest from faculty, graduate students, and technology experts. Of course, such interest cannot be entirely removed from institutional politics and the overall traction of digital humanities. The fact that the working group has the web address digitalhumanities.yale.edu carries institutional meaning, and the heading "Digital Humanities at Yale" on that web page indicates a strategic position. At the same time, the breadth of the digital humanities at Yale is indicated by a subsequent conference not organized by the working group but advertised on the digital humanities website: "Yale Media Theory and History Conference" (April 22–23, 2011). Internal priorities must also be considered; perhaps scholars interested in the digital humanities at Yale need support from the wider digital humanities (DH) community in order for their initiative to take off.

An important question here concerns who is the real gatekeeper. Gailey's reluctance to acknowledge Yale as a new addition to the field appears to be due to Yale being a privileged school that had not been part of the buildup of the field. It could be argued, however, that a big-tent notion of the digital humanities must be based on an open invitation and generosity rather than past hardships. At the same time, we need to acknowledge that expanding territory and, in particular, epistemic range is not unproblematic and that boundary making is integral to disciplinary formation.

Another type of reluctance is based on the type of digital humanities that Yale is seen as representing and its associated epistemic commitments. Many of the people active in the Yale working group seem to be "traditional" scholars interested in the digital more as a digitally inflected object of inquiry. In a polemic position statement from the MLA 2011 conference, Stephen Ramsay points to "coding" or "making" as a necessary criterion to qualify for the digital humanities, and in the discussion he brings in Yale (and some other schools):

> But what if Duke or Yale were to offer a degree in Digital Humanities and they said "no" to code and "yes" to text? Or "no" to building and "yes" to theorizing? Or decided that Digital Humanities is what we used to call New Media Studies (which is the precise condition, as far as I can tell, at Dartmouth)? You might need to know how to code in order to be competitive for relevant grants with the ODH, NSF, or Mellon. Maybe that means Yale's DH ambitions will never get off the ground. Or maybe Yale is powerful enough to redefine the mission of those institutions with respect to the Humanities. Most institutions, for the record, are not. (Ramsay)

This is an intentionally provocative piece written by a single person (Ramsay), and we should be careful not to draw overly far-reaching conclusions from it. However, it is quite clear that this is an example of gatekeeping based on epistemic traditions and commitments. Funding agency structures and programs, often seen as barriers in the humanities computing tradition (cf. Terras and Smithies), are used as a gatekeeping device.

Joining Willard McCarty in approval of the Yale event was John Unsworth, another established digital humanities representative. It is notable that both McCarty and Unsworth have secure institutional positions, while scholars critiquing the Yale event were less established in the field. McCarty and Unsworth represent the core of the community, and their praise hence comes from deep inside the discipline, which may help explain some of the intensity of the discussion. Unsworth (12–13) notes that graduate students organized the conference and lists the titles of PhD projects of these graduate students. These include "The Liberal Schoolmaster" and "Literary Souvenirs: Didactic Materialism in Late Eighteenth- and Early Nineteenth-Century Fiction." Unsworth asks, "How did these students get drawn into the digital humanities?" (13). This is a very interesting question, the answer to which demonstrates that even a big tent—enacted by Unsworth—can be coupled with epistemic predispositions:

> Finally, back to that remark Willard made, about the graduate students in the Yale conference—the remark generally overlooked in the dispute about watersheds. What he said was that "quite independently of the work us older ones have done for so long, these students see the possibilities now visible and question them as befits the humanities." This is perhaps the most interesting point, and the one on which I will end. Coming up behind Christy and Harris, Gailey, Ramsay, Bogost, Kirschenbaum, McCarty, Ayers, Stallybrass, and me, is a generation of graduate students who essentially learned to do research with digital tools; they aren't necessarily aware of the history that's implicit, just barely submerged, in the exchanges we've been considering here—they actually don't care all that much about the back-story. They're interested in grabbing these tools, using these new library services, and making their own mark, and they have some interesting questions to ask. (Unsworth, 18)

The Yale graduate students are "read" as coming to the digital humanities through having "learned to do research with digital tools" and being interested in "grabbing these tools." While the conference program to some extent was tool and encoding based, the PhD titles previously listed by Unsworth would seem to indicate analytical research of more traditional type, and the question is whether these students really came to the digital humanities (if they actually came to stay) through an interest in tools and library services. Again, the point here is that this is not just a question of the size of the tent but also about how the tent is epistemologically textured.

What Types of Digital Humanities?

The place of Yale University in the digital humanities tent can be partially related to how the relationship between the humanities and the digital is conceived. In traditional digital humanities (or humanities computing), technology or tool-related methodology often serves an instrumental function (Svensson, "Humanities Computing"). I have argued elsewhere that the interrelation between the humanities and the digital can be discussed in terms of different modes of engagement: the digital or technology as tool, study object, medium, laboratory, and activist venue (Svensson, "Landscape"). If big-tent digital humanities reaches across these modes of engagement, the tool-oriented approach is only one among several possible modes of engagements.

We can see the primary role given to tools in Unsworth's discussion or in the idea of a methodological commons as a core structural component of the field. In discussing the methodological commons, McCarty writes that humanities computing has been able to transcend disciplinary and institutional boundaries through a methodological commons "for all to draw on"; and, in his thoughtful outlining of the commons, it is quite clear that we are concerned with a particular model (118). For instance, it is based on introducing data types and a set of tools to manipulate the data, and the tools in turn are derived from formal methods (136). There is considerable complexity to this issue, and tools can be both instrumental and deeply integrated into humanistic research endeavors. This said, we should be careful not to see tools as neutral artifacts. In an enlightening discussion on digital visualization tools, Johanna Drucker maintains that graphical tools such as GIS, mapping, and graphs are based on underlying assumptions, which "are cloaked in a rhetoric taken wholesale from the techniques of the empirical sciences that conceals their epistemological biases under a guise" (Drucker). While tools themselves can be epistemologically predisposed, it could be argued that placing tools and tool-related methodology at the base of digital humanities work implies a particular view of the field and, within big-tent digital humanities, possibly an exclusive stance. One central question is whether the tent can naturally be taken to include critical work construing the digital as an object of inquiry rather than as a tool.

When Unsworth notes that the young Yale scholars have "some interesting questions to ask," the epistemic perspective is not so much seen in asking or not asking analytical questions but in how one gets to the questions. If tools and related mechanisms underlie an epistemic commitment, this would be evident in the questions either being asked through the tools or arising as a result of using the tools. One pertinent question, then, is whether there is room for research in the digital humanities that does not engage with tools, or "making" in Ramsey's fairly narrow sense, and whether that work can be accepted in its own right.

It is important not to overplay these differences while being sensitive to them and to the tensions that may arise from them. In general, it is easier to be inside than outside, and it would seem quite important to be inclusive and generous when one is part of the established core of a field or discipline. Language plays a significant role here, and what seems uncontroversial from an internal perspective can be exclusionary from an outside perspective.

The DH 2011 Call for Papers: Inclusionary or Exclusionary?

Conferences are important in the formation of disciplines and fields (Klein), and the principal conference for the digital humanities is the annual conference named "Digital Humanities." This conference series is grounded in the tradition of humanities computing; it goes back to at least the early 1990s and is currently organized by the Association for Digital Humanities Organizations (ADHO). I have earlier discussed the 2009 Call for Papers for the Digital Humanities conference (Svensson, "Humanities Computing") as clearly representing a specific tradition of digital humanities rather than a more multivalent approach. As Stéfan Sinclair observes, the conference is quite competitive in terms of accepted proposals (34 percent in 2010), and there is a tendency to "push inwards toward the centre of recognized digital humanities research and practices." He argues that the conference can thus be seen to stifle growth and innovation and also points to it serving several disciplines and institutional contexts. Sinclair also notes that new conferences (such as Yale's "The Past's Digital Presence" discussed earlier) have helped to decenter the Digital Humanities conference. However, there can be no doubt that it is the main conference for the field (at least as traditionally conceived) and thus an important arena for negotiating a more inclusive notion of digital humanities.

As noted at the beginning of this chapter, the theme for the 2011 conference is "Big Tent Digital Humanities," a theme that makes it particularly relevant to look again at the Call for Papers (CFP) for the conference:

> Proposals might, for example, relate to the following aspects of digital humanities: research issues, including data mining, information design and modelling, software studies, and humanities research enabled through the digital medium; computer-based research and computer applications in literary, linguistic, cultural and historical studies, including electronic literature, public humanities, and interdisciplinary aspects of modern scholarship. Some examples might be text analysis, corpora, corpus linguistics, language processing, language learning, and endangered languages; the digital arts, architecture, music, film, theater, new media, and related areas; the creation and curation of humanities digital resources; the role of digital humanities in academic curricula.

> The range of topics covered by digital humanities can also be consulted in the journal of the associations, *Literary and Linguistic Computing* (*LLC*). (General Call for Papers, Digital Humanities 2011)

The call as a whole is definitely more inclusive than the 2009 CFP, which had a more pronounced instrumental and textual focus; but, even so, there can be no doubt that there is a particular scholarly tradition underlying the call. This may not be surprising given the history of the conference series, but the current state of the field and the theme would seem to call for a more clearly inclusive stance. Again, it is important to consider inside and outside perspectives. It may be that the call under discussion seems inclusive to the organizers of the conference, whereas it is seen as exclusionary by "outsiders" or newcomers to the field. For instance, most of the aspects listed could be said to represent tool-oriented and text-based research. Through talking about "humanities research enabled through the digital medium," the technology or medium is also given considerable agency. The long-standing humanities computing interest in cultural heritage work is evident through the focus on creation and curation of digital resources. The only aspect listed that can easily be seen as reaching outside of the tradition is the one focusing on "digital arts, architecture, music, film, theater, new media, and related areas." This is quite a significant inclusion, but it is worth noting that in contrast with the two preceding items on the list, there is no further elaboration. Rather, it could be argued that a number of internally heterogeneous "leftovers" have been subsumed under one bullet point. And while the list as a whole is presented as only suggesting examples of digital humanities areas, what is actually listed is quite important, not least to outsiders. If this is how the big tent is reflected among the suggested topic areas, it does not necessarily seem inviting, nor does it speak to those communities that do not share tool-oriented or text-based approaches to research.

In the introduction to the call, there is special focus on big-tent aspects: "With the Big Tent theme in mind, we especially invite submissions from Latin American scholars, scholars in the digital arts and music, in spatial history, and in the public humanities" ("General Call for Papers," Digital Humanities 2011). It seems that this specification is narrower than the topic area just discussed and, to an outsider, somewhat arbitrary (although the local context at Stanford would seem to be an important rationale). For instance, a new media scholar interested in the digital humanities may not feel inclined to submit a proposal, particularly because new media is not included in the big-tent specification and is instead listed together with some fairly unrelated areas without further elaboration in the list of topics.

We would expect newcomers to be prepared to make an effort and learn about the context of the conference and tradition. However, sometimes what may be clear to insiders may not be accessible to newcomers. This can be exemplified with the reference to the journal *Literary and Linguistic Computing* in the Call for Papers.

It is said that the journal can be consulted about the "range of topics covered by digital humanities." Looking at the most recent issue of the journal at the time of writing (Volume 26, Issue 1, April 2011), the articles deal with comparing treaty texts, visualization as a tool for dialect geography, authorship attribution, computer scansion of Ancient Greek Hexameter, lexical bundles, extraction of syntactic differences, and a regressive imagery dictionary. If the new media scholar interested in digital humanities imagined earlier was not stopped by the text in the Call for Papers and followed the advice to look at the journal to find out more, it is very likely that he or she would not feel included or inclined to actually register for the conference.

However, the emphasis on this particular journal is partly institutional. It was started in 1973 and has been the journal of two of the core humanities computing associations, as well as for the journal of the Association for Digital Humanities Organizations (AHDO). Furthermore, it is part of a funding mechanism for ADHO (and its organizations), as members and member organizations pay their fees through subscribing to the journal. All this means that *LLC* has a special status but not necessarily that all members of traditional digital humanities (or humanities computing) see this journal as the primary voice of the field. To an outsider, however, this arrangement may not be particularly transparent. A very simple adjustment would be to also include the *Digital Humanities Quarterly* (also supported by ADHO) as a reference in the Call for Papers. It has a considerably broader scope than *LLC* and is open access. A more radical suggestion would be to also list a few journals outside the core tradition. This would clearly indicate a big-tent sentiment and pronounced interest in other traditions.

Big Visions

I have argued elsewhere (Svensson, "Envisioning") that contemporary digital humanities can be associated with an interest in change and that the field can be used as a means to imagine the future of the humanities. This is typically more apparent in new initiatives than in traditional digital humanities. Hence one interesting question is how these "big" visions relate to a big-tent digital humanities grounded in the tradition of humanities computing.

White papers produced to make a case for the digital humanities can act as a source of material for visionary discourse. These documents are typically part of a process of lobbying for the field and establishing a digital humanities center. This is a particular type of text—typically aiming to convince university management to prioritize a certain area—but also indicative of hopes and strategies associated with the field at particular sites. I have looked at three white papers from three American universities: University of Wisconsin–Madison (UW-Madison), University of California at Los Angeles (UCLA), and Texas A&M. While the documents are site specific, so to speak, there is considerable overlap. The wish lists presented generally include space, technology, and strategic hires. Moreover, there is a common view of the digital humanities as a considerable force and "game changer" in all three documents.

The UW-Madison documents describe how the digital humanities "plugs directly into the media culture lived by our students, our peers, and our wider communities" and how the field, through its "interconnected and infrastructural dimensions," is the future of the humanities ("Enhancing Digital Humanities"). They also point out how the digital humanities currently offers a "strategic nexus through which faculty, students, and staff can analyze and direct how this future might unfold" ("Enhancing Digital Humanities"). This is an expansive vision that goes beyond affecting and changing the humanities. The UCLA white paper similarly extends beyond the humanities proper when it is argued that the field is "setting new intellectual agendas and priorities for the twenty-first century" ("The Promise of Digital Humanities"). Furthermore, emergent modes of knowledge formation and reaching new audiences for digitally inflected scholarship are emphasized. Again, we get the impression of a field that intersects with the humanities profoundly through multiple modes of engagement. The Texas A&M document presents two grand challenges for the center: "the need to investigate the relationship of computing technologies and culture, and the need to construct cyberinfrastructure for the humanities and social sciences" ("Texas Center for Digital Humanities and New Media"). The planned research—cultural records, systems, environments, and interactions in the digital age—is said to engage with one of most significant questions of our time: What does it mean to be human in the digital age? Presumably, tackling this question and the grand challenges requires a range of competencies as well as a broad engagement with the digital (and nondigital).

While we should exercise analytical caution given the genre of these documents, it seems clear that they attribute transformative power to the digital humanities and that the field and associated challenges require multivalent competencies including analytical work and engagement that may not necessarily involve digital tools, coding, or a textual focus. This would seem to suggest the importance of a broadly conceived digital humanities and the need for a larger tent than the one indicated by the Digital Humanities 2011 Call for Papers.

The Digital Humanities as a Trading Zone and Meeting Place

It may be difficult to recognize different epistemic traditions and support them within the framework of a digital humanities "tent" that may be stretched in some ways (but not others). Importantly, there is a risk that a wealth of traditions and perspectives are subsumed and conflated in a tent primarily keyed to one particular tradition. This is not merely a question of semantics and metaphorical systems but deeply concerns how we think of the future of the field. Given the foregoing discussion, the history of the field, and an inclusive view of the digital humanities,

I am suggesting an alternative model based on the digital humanities as a meeting place, innovation hub, and trading zone (see McCarty for an earlier discussion of humanities computing as a methodology-oriented trading zone). Such a notion highlights some qualities of the digital humanities—including its commitment to interdisciplinary work and deep collaboration—that could attract individuals both inside and outside the tent with an interest in the digital humanities. Arguably, such bridge building and the bringing together of epistemic traditions is not optimally done from the position of discipline or department. The liminal position of the field is thus not seen as a problem but rather as an important quality.

The notion of trading zones comes from Peter Galison and his analysis of physicists of different paradigms carrying out collaborative research despite belonging to different epistemic traditions. The concept can be used to describe "places" where interdisciplinary work occurs and where different traditions are maintained at the same time as intersectional work is carried out. We should be aware that the concept of "trading zone" is based on a trading and marketplace metaphor that construes knowledge production as trade and that comes from a scientific context.

Harry Collins, Robert Evans, and Mike Gorman point to the importance of interactional expertise (i.e., using the language of an expert community for interacting with members) for productive engagement in cross-disciplinary work. They suggest an evolution of trading zones in relation to interactional expertise, where the starting point may be a cohesive situation where different groups are encouraged to work together, while the other end of the scale represents cultures becoming more homogenous through the process of new disciplinary formation. The digital humanities can be seen as a fractioned (not homogenous) collaborative (not coerced) trading zone and a meeting place that supports deeply collaborative work, individual expression, unexpected connections, and synergetic power. The "digital," in a broad sense and in various manifestations, functions as a shared boundary object.

Arguably, the digital humanities needs to support and allow multiple modes of engagement between the humanities and the digital in order to touch at the heart of the disciplines, maximize points of interaction, tackle large research and methodology challenges, and facilitate deep integration between thinking and making. This perspective would seem to be compatible with the digital humanities as a trading zone and a meeting place. Similarly, the grand challenges identified in the white papers discussed would seem to require consorted efforts. Meeting places can make such efforts possible. Whether mostly physical or mostly digital, they can help channel dispersed resources, technologies, and intellectual energy. Furthermore, deep integration of toolmaking and interpretative perspectives requires very different kinds of competencies and work to happen in the same space. It could also be argued that there is value to unexpected meetings in creative environments in terms of expanding the digital humanities.

Digital humanities as a trading zone and meeting place also emphasizes the intermediary and facilitating function of the digital. The digital cuts across disciplines and perspectives; and, as Matt Ratto and Robert Ree observe in their study, digital media is not an industrial sector in its own right. Similarly, it could be argued that the digital humanities is not a discipline and that the intermediary role of the digital is useful to the digital humanities in multiple ways. For instance, it allows connections to all of humanities disciplines as well as to the large parts of the academy and the world outside. It is no accident that there is a growing connection between the public humanities and the digital humanities ("Digital Humanities at the University of Washington"). Also, the digital can be used as a way of canalizing interest in rethinking the humanities and the academy. This gives a strong incitement for institutions to support the digital humanities. More broadly, there is a niche to be filled in most institutions of higher education—that of intersectional meeting places. The humanities is a good place for such meeting places to emerge, and the digital humanities can thus unquestionably become a site for innovation, dialogue, and engagement with the future.

Conclusion

The digital humanities amply demonstrates that there is no one size that fits all. The heterogeneity of the field is in many ways an asset, and the current external interest and attraction presents a significant opportunity for expansion. At the same time, we need to acknowledge that there is a core community associated with the digital humanities and that the all-encompassing, inclusive digital humanities may not always seem an attractive option to it. Multitude and variation may be seen as diluting the field and taking away from a number of epistemic commitments. This is a very valid concern, and various initiatives are bound to tackle this challenge in different ways. It would seem, however, that a big-tent digital humanities should not be predominantly anchored in one tradition.

Even if the big-tent vision of the digital humanities gives the field a sense of openness and invitation, it does not necessarily remove institutional predispositions and thresholds or make the field into a blank slate. The alternative model suggested here, seeing the digital humanities as a trading zone and meeting place, places more emphasis on existing traditions and the intersectional work required to make "big" digital humanities happen. Furthermore, this model acknowledges the advantage of a liminal position and the digital as a way of connecting disciplines, perspectives, and methodologies. By seeing the field as a trading zone and meeting place, we can acknowledge disciplinary and methodological expertise, while approaching grand challenges, relating key disciplinary discourses, supporting multiple modes of engagement with the digital, and distinctly engaging with the future of the humanities.

BIBLIOGRAPHY

Cohen, Dan. "Mass Digitization of Books: Exit Microsoft, What Next?" May 29, 2008. http://www.dancohen.org/2008/05/29/mass-digitization-of-books-exit-microsoft-what-next/.

Collins, Harry, Robert Evans, and Mike Gorman. "Trading Zones and Interactional Expertise." In *Trading Zones and Interactional Expertise: Creating New Kinds of Collaboration*, edited by M. E. Gorman, 7–23. Cambridge, Mass.: MIT Press, 2010.

"Digital Humanities at the University of Washington." Simpson Center for the Humanities, University of Washington. http://depts.washington.edu/uwch/docs/digital_humanities_case_statement.pdf.

"Digital Humanities at Yale: About." Digital Humanities at Yale. http://digitalhumanities.yale.edu/.

Drucker, Johanna. "Humanities Approaches to Graphical Display." *Digital Humanities Quarterly* 5, no. 1 (2011).

"Enhancing Digital Humanities at UW-Madison: A White Paper." http://dighum.wisc.edu/FDS_White_Paper.pdf.

Galison, Peter. *Image & Logic: A Material Culture of Microphysics*. Chicago: University of Chicago Press, 1997.

Gailey, Amanda. "Yale, the Past and the Future". *Humanist*, vol. 23, post 649. 2010.

"General Call for Papers, Digital Humanities 2011." Digital Humanities 2011. https://dh2011.stanford.edu/?page_id=97.

Harris, Katherine. "Yale, the Past and the Future". *Humanist*, vol. 23, post 659. 2010.

Kirschenbaum, Matthew. "What Is Digital Humanities and What's It Doing in English Departments?" *ADE Bulletin* 150 (2010): 55–61. Reprinted in this volume.

Klein, Julie Thomson. *Crossing Boundaries: Knowledge, Disciplinarities, and Interdisciplinarities*. Charlottesville: University of Virginia Press, 1996.

Knorr Cetina, Karin. *Epistemic Cultures: How the Sciences Make Knowledge*. Cambridge, Mass.: Harvard University Press, 1999.

Livingstone, David. *Putting Science in Its Place: Geographies of Scientific Knowledge*. Chicago: Chicago University Press, 2003.

McCarty, Willard. *Humanities Computing*. New York: Palgrave, 2005.

———. "Yale, the Past and the Future." *Humanist*, vol. 23, post 647. 2010.

"The Promise of Digital Humanities: A Whitepaper. March 1, 2009–Final Version." http://www.itpb.ucla.edu/documents/2009/PromiseofDigitalHumanities.pdf.

Ramsay, Stephen. "Who's In and Who's Out." Stephen Ramsay. 2011. http://lenz.unl.edu/papers/2011/01/08/whos-in-and-whos-out.html

Ratto, Matt, and Robert Ree. "The Materialization of Information and the Digital Economy, a Report to the Knowledge Synthesis Grant on the Digital Economy." Social Sciences and Humanities Research Council, Toronto, Canada, 2010.

Sinclair, Stéfan. "Some Thoughts on the Digital Humanities Conference." Stéfan Sinclair: Scribblings and Musings by an Incorrigible Digital Humanist. February 24, 2010. http://stefansinclair.name/dh2010. Document no longer available.

Smithies, James. "Digital Humanities: The Pacific Node." James Smithies. December 5, 2010. http://jamessmithies.org/2010/12/05/digital-humanities-the-pacific-node/.

Svensson, Patrik. "Humanities Computing as Digital Humanities." *Digital Humanities Quarterly* 3, no. 3 (2009).

———. "Envisioning the Digital Humanities." Submitted to *Digital Humanities Quarterly*. Accepted for publication.

———. "The Landscape of Digital Humanities." *Digital Humanities Quarterly* 4, no. 1 2010).

Terras, Melissa. "DH2010 Plenary: Present, Not Voting: Digital Humanities in the Panopticon." Digital Humanities 2010 plenary talk manuscript, Melissa Terras' blog. 2010. http://melissaterras.blogspot.com/2010/07/dh2010-plenary-present-not-voting .html.

"Texas Center for Digital Humanities and New Media." http://www-english.tamu.edu/pers/fac/may/DHwhitepaper.pdf. Document no longer available.

Unsworth, John. "The State of Digital Humanities, 2010 (ripped from the blogosphere and twitterverse)." Talk manuscript. Digital Humanities Summer Institute, June 2010. http://www3.isrl.illinois.edu/~unsworth/state.of.dh.DHSI.pdf.

The Digital Humanities Situation

RAFAEL C. ALVARADO

Let's be honest—there is no definition of digital humanities, if by definition we mean a consistent set of theoretical concerns and research methods that might be aligned with a given discipline, whether one of the established fields or an emerging, transdisciplinary one. The category denotes no set of widely shared computational methods that contributes to the work of interpretation, no agreed upon norms or received genres for digital publication, no broad consensus on whether digital work, however defined, counts as genuine academic work. Instead of a definition, we have a genealogy, a network of family resemblances among provisional schools of thought, methodological interests, and preferred tools, a history of people who have chosen to call themselves digital humanists and who in the process of trying to define the term are creating that definition. How else to characterize the meaning of an expression that has nearly as many definitions as affiliates? It is a social category, not an ontological one.

As a social category, the term has a more or less clear set of organizational referents. Recently Matt Kirschenbaum reminded us that there is a peer-reviewed journal, a federal office, an annual conference, and an international network of academic centers associated with the term, not to mention an Oxford Companion ("What Is"). However the gap between the social and the ontological cannot avoid appearing as a kind of scandal. This is evident from the number of essays and blog posts that have emerged seeking to define the category, as well as from the playfully combative and defensive tone some remarks have taken. This anxiety of self-definition seems to indicate a new phase in the history of the field, one that may indicate the emergence of a territorial instinct in an environment of scarce resources—even as the language of the "big tent" emerges. After all, the shift from "humanities computing" to the "digital humanities" indexes a growth in the size and popularity of the community. With growth comes growing pains.

To many, the digital humanities feels like a small town that has recently been rated as a great place to raise a family. It is now inundated by developers who want to build condos for newcomers who are competing for resources and who may not understand local customs. Identity crises emerge when tacit, unspoken understandings and modes of interaction are disrupted by external contact and demographic shifts. In the quest to defend old ways and invent new ones, in-groups are defined, prophets emerge, witchcraft accusations are made, and people generally lose what communal solidarity they once had. The digital humanities community has not gone this far, but one cannot help but notice the disparity between the Woodstock feeling of THATCamp events and what appears to be the Altamont of Digital Humanities 2011.

To be sure, all digital humanists share a common bond as *humanists*, scholars devoted to the interpretation of what the art historian Erwin Panofsky called "the records left by man [sic]" (5)—works of literature, art, architecture, and other products and traces of human intellectual labor. More specifically, the sorts of humanists who have been drawn into the fold of digital humanities have had a distinct preference toward textual remains, even if we entertain pleas to consider nonverbal channels as well (usually originating from nontraditional fields, such as media studies). It remains an implicit (if discomfiting) assumption among digital humanists that, as Tim Bray puts it (in the tag line for his website, Textuality.com), "knowledge is a text based application." Consistent with this view, the typical digital humanist is a literary scholar, historian, or librarian—all traditional fields concerned with the management and interpretation of written documents. Others, such as myself, come from other backgrounds; but I believe it is no accident that the recent buzz about the discipline was spawned by talks given at the Modern Language Association (MLA) meetings.

There are also many schools of thought under the sign who do share, within themselves, a more or less coherent set of methods and concerns. There is, of course, the old guard of humanities computing, trained in the markup of textual sources using the Text Encoding Initiative's guidelines and schema and versed in the theoretical implications of this mode of representation. There is a newer community who embraces the "spatial humanities" through the use of mapping software in relation to textual (and other) sources and who has shifted our attention toward visualization and human geography—an overlooked field that should rightly have its day. Alongside these there is a long-running group of statistical critics, extending from Father Busa and IBM to Franco Moretti and Google, as well as other computational humanists who have been at it since the 1960s and who believe that counting words, applying the methods of computational linguistics, and observing patterns in large corpora will produce insights unreachable by mere reading. One could also point to the Critical Code Studies group and other schools of thought that have emerged in this space.

Taken as a whole, however, there is little connection among these groups beyond a shared interest in texts and the use of computational technologies to explore and understand them (as opposed to merely creating or distributing them). But more important, none of these groups, either in isolation or as a whole, has successfully demonstrated to the wider community of humanists that there are essential and irreplaceable gains to be had by the application of digital tools to the project of interpreting (and reinterpreting) the human record for the edification of society. To a disconcertingly large number of outsiders, the digital humanities qua humanities remains interesting but irrelevant. Anthony Grafton speaks for the majority when, in a recent *New York Times* piece (Cohen), he repeats the platitude that the digital humanities is a means and not an end. Given his stature in the field, not to mention his role as president of the American Historical Association (AHA), his recent remarks regarding his experience of a presentation on Culturomics at the AHA meetings in Boston (Grafton) may indicate a turning of the tide—but the conversion of other prominent scholars has not produced such shifts in the past.

Now, if we use the term digital humanities and cannot define it, maybe we are thinking of such definitions in the wrong way. Maybe the traditional way of defining disciplines in the academy is all wrong. Instead of saying that physics is the study of matter and energy, or history the study of what people have done in the past, maybe we should say that physics is the work of those who read Newton and Einstein, who use various branches of mathematics, and who know how to construct experiments in a certain way. Or history is the work of people who know how to navigate archives and read old tax records and diaries and other textual remains, whereas archaeologists are those who know how to manage digs and how to retrieve, classify, and interpret shards and bones.

This may sound forced for the hard sciences, but it is eminently reasonable for the humanities and social sciences. For what are the real differences between history, sociology, economics, anthropology, and archaeology? Each claims to address the structure and function of society. The answer is that each has mastered a particular domain of data—its acquisition, organization, analysis, and interpretation. Sociologists do surveys and statistics, interviews and content analysis. Cultural anthropologists do fieldwork and thick description. Economists count indicators and develop equations to relate them. Historians are very good at converting old documents and archives into stories. When an archaeologist starts to read such documents, we say she is doing "historical archaeology." Document-reading anthropologists become ethnohistorians. And so forth.

Such a definition (which philosophers will recognize as a species of pragmatism) allows us to turn our attention to the practical and situated basis of the digital humanities. In this view, digital humanists are simply humanists (or interpretive social scientists) by training who have embraced digital media and who have a more or less deep conviction that digital media can play a crucial, indeed transformative, role in the work of interpretation, broadly conceived. Beyond this all bets are off. Because the category of digital media includes essentially everything afforded to the humanist by the presence of available computing—everything from crowd sourcing and social media to natural language processing and latent semantic indexing to gaming and haptic immersion—the digital humanities is in principle associated with as many methods and tools as there are intersections between texts and technologies.

The complexity of the field is also multiplied by the modes of relationship that may characterize the intersection between computation and textuality in each case. Consider the difference between the practices of textual markup and the work associated with Critical Code Studies. The former subjects primary source texts to digital representation by means of code—XML, XSLT, and so on—whereas the latter treats code itself as text, seeking to apply principles of interpretation theory (hermeneutics, structuralism, etc.) to programming languages and, one hopes, markup languages as well. (One might include here Kirschenbaum's *Mechanisms: New Media and the Forensic Imagination*, which treats hardware itself as text.) As Stephen Ramsay has argued ("Toward"), practitioners of the former approach can be curiously uncritical of their tools and methods, checking their postmodernist perspectives at the door of the lab.

Consider also the case of databases. On the one hand, many scholars supplement their research by using data management tools to organize notes and references. On the other hand, there is an emerging school of thought, initiated by Lev Manovich, that regards the database itself as an object of criticism in its own right (Manovich). The difference between the two approaches is like night and day, although one can imagine how one may profit from the other. Still a third mode of intersection is to regard technology as an allegory of textuality. For example, Wendy Hui Kyong Chun has employed the image of the fiber optic network as a frame for the interpretation of digitally mediated social interaction and text (Chun). So not only are there as many kinds of digital humanities as there are intersections between humanities and computation technology, but that number is at least tripled, in principle, by the kind of relationship that inheres in that intersection. To a humanist, any computational technology is potentially tool, text, and metaphor.

Given this surplus of extensional meanings, there is simply no way to describe the digital humanities as anything like a discipline. Just think of the curricular requirements of such a field! Not only would it require its members to develop the deep domain knowledge of the traditional humanist—distant reading notwithstanding—it would also demand that they learn a wide range of divergent technologies (including programming languages) as well as the critical discourses to situate these technologies as texts, cultural artifacts participating in the reproduction of social and cognitive structures. Granted the occasional polymath who may master all three, the scope of such a program is simply too vast and variegated. And in fact there has been no consensus among digital humanists about the basic elements of a curriculum, a problem we share with advocates of media fluency to define a curriculum for faculty development.

So if the digital humanities is neither in fact nor in principle a discipline, then what is it? Surely, with its growing army of followers and plethora of concrete institutional manifestations, it must have some basis in a reality other than its own existence. In fact it does. The digital humanities, as both a broad collection of practices and an intense, ongoing interpretive *praxis* generative of such practices, is best thought of as having two very concrete but equally elusive dimensions. On the one hand, the digital humanities (conceived of in the plural) comprises something very much like a curriculum, an interrelated collection of subject domains and resources that, as a whole, contributes to both the construction of knowledge and the education of people. Although no one individual can master an entire curriculum, a curriculum nevertheless has a logic, a coherence, and even a center of gravity.

This leads to the second and more important dimension: that center of gravity is not a particular assemblage of technologies or methods but the ongoing, playful encounter with digital representation itself. It is the encounter that the digital humanist discovers and finds at once a revealing, satisfying, and ineffable source of fellow feeling with his colleagues. This encounter is not regarded merely as a means to an end but as an end in itself, in so much as the process of interpretation is often as rewarding as its products. I call this encounter the *situation* of digital representation, a stable but always-in-flux event space that is but a special case of the work, or praxis, of representation in general. Adult members of literate cultures for the most part have sublimated and forgotten this praxis, but it remains present to the minds of children and poets, who are always learning how to read and write.

This, I believe, is what Stephen Ramsay means by "building" ("On Building"). Or at least it is a charitable misreading (*misprision*) that retrieves the argument he makes when he suggests, essentially, that real digital humanists write code. In my rephrasing, real digital humanists are engaged in the play of representation, which profoundly involves putting things together, whether the vehicle of assembly be Lisp or Zotero. That marks a wide spectrum; but within it there is a common element of play, of productively mapping and remapping the objects and categories of scholarship onto the rapidly changing, intrinsically plastic but structurally constraining media of digital technology. Without this play—to the extent that the scholar has a standoffish, do-this-for-me attitude toward the medium—then, no, she is not a digital humanist.

Digital humanists are aware that in the current historical moment, as the older *mentalités* of print literacy continue to be displaced and reworked, the humanist has the opportunity to immerse herself in the transductive plasma of interpretation where ideas and their expressive vehicles can be mapped and remapped in a variety of forms and frameworks, a giddy play of praxis that not all generations have the good fortune of witnessing. This experience cross-cuts all the various discipline- and technology-specific instances of digital humanities work. To the extent that a common discourse is emerging to reflect on this experience across the disciplines, the digital humanities is real enough.

NOTE

This chapter originally appeared as "The Digital Humanities Situation," http://transducer.ontoligent.com/?p=717.

BIBLIOGRAPHY

Chun, Wendy Hui Kyong. *Control and Freedom: Power and Paranoia in the Age of Fiber Optics*. Cambridge, Mass.: MIT Press, 2006.

Cohen, Patricia. "Digital Keys for Unlocking the Humanities' Riches." *New York Times*, November 17, 2010. http://www.nytimes.com/2010/11/17/arts/17digital.html.

Grafton, Anthony. "Loneliness and Freedom." *Perspectives Online* 49, no. 5 (2011). http://www.historians.org/Perspectives/issues/2011/1103/1103pre1.cfm.

Kirschenbaum, Matthew G. *Mechanisms: New Media and the Forensic Imagination*. Cambridge, Mass.: MIT Press, 2008.

———. "What Is Digital Humanities?" Matthew G. Kirschenbaum. January 22, 2011. http://mkirschenbaum.wordpress.com/2011/01/22/what-is-digital-humanities/.

Manovich, Lev. "Database as Symbolic Form." *Convergence: The International Journal of Research into New Media Technologies* 5, no. 2 (1999): 80–99.

Panofsky, Erwin. *Meaning in the Visual Arts: Papers in and on Art History*. Ann Arbor: University of Michigan Press, 1955.

Ramsay, Stephen. "On Building." Stephen Ramsay. January 11, 2011. http://lenz.unl.edu/papers/2011/01/11/on-building.html.

———. "Toward an Algorithmic Criticism." *Literary and Linguistic Computing*, 18, no. 2 (2003): 167–74.

Where's the Beef? Does Digital Humanities Have to Answer Questions?

TOM SCHEINFELDT

The criticism most frequently leveled at digital humanities is what I like to call the "Where's the beef?" question—that is, what questions does digital humanities answer that can't be answered without it? What humanities arguments does digital humanities make?

Concern over the apparent lack of argument in digital humanities comes not only from outside our young discipline. Many practicing digital humanists are concerned about it as well. Rob Nelson of the University of Richmond's Digital Scholarship Lab, an accomplished digital humanist, recently ruminated, "While there have been some projects that have been developed to present arguments, they are few, and for the most part I sense that they haven't had a substantial impact among academics, at least in the field of history." A post on the *Humanist* listserv, which has covered humanities computing for over two decades, expresses one digital humanist's "dream" of "a way of interpreting with computing that would allow arguments, real arguments, to be conducted at the micro-level and their consequences made in effect instantly visible at the macro-level."[1]

These concerns are justified. Does digital humanities have to help answer questions and make arguments? Yes, of course. That's what the humanities are all about. Is it answering lots of questions currently? Probably not—hence the reason for worry.

But this suggests another, more difficult, more nuanced question: When? *When* does digital humanities have to produce new arguments? Does it have to produce new arguments now? Does it have to answer questions yet?

In 1703, the great instrument maker, mathematician, and experimenter Robert Hooke died, vacating the suggestively named position he occupied for more than forty years, curator of experiments to the Royal Society. In this role, it was Hooke's job to prepare public demonstrations of scientific phenomena for the fellows' meetings. Among Hooke's standbys in these scientific performances were animal dissections, demonstrations of the air pump (made famous by Robert Boyle but *made* by Hooke), and viewings of prepared microscope slides. Part research, part ice breaker, and part theater, one important function of these performances was to entertain the wealthier fellows of the society, many of whom were chosen for election more for their patronage than their scientific achievements.

Upon Hooke's death, the position of curator of experiments passed to Francis Hauksbee, who continued Hooke's program of public demonstrations. Many of Hauksbee's demonstrations involved the "electrical machine," essentially an evacuated glass globe that was turned on an axle and to which friction (a hand, a cloth, a piece of fur) was applied to produce a static electrical charge. Invented some years earlier, Hauksbee greatly improved the device to produce ever greater charges. Perhaps his most important improvement was the addition to the globe of a small amount of mercury, which produced a glow when the machine was fired up. In an age of candlelight and on a continent of long, dark winters, the creation of a new source of artificial light was sensational and became a popular learned entertainment not only in meetings of early scientific societies but also in aristocratic parlors across Europe. Hauksbee's machine also set off an explosion of electrical instrument making, experimentation, and descriptive work in the first half of the eighteenth century by the likes of Stephen Gray, John Desaguliers, and Pieter van Musschenbroek.

And yet not until later in the eighteenth century and early in the nineteenth century did Benjamin Franklin, Charles-Augustin de Coulomb, Alessandro Volta, and ultimately Michael Faraday provide adequate theoretical and mathematical answers to the questions of electricity raised by the electrical machine and the phenomena it produced. Only after decades of tool building, experimentation, and description were the tools sufficiently articulated and phenomena sufficiently described for theoretical arguments to be fruitfully made.[2]

There's a moral to this story. As I have argued in an earlier post, this kind of drawn-out, *longue duree*, seasonal shifting between methodological and theoretical work isn't confined to the sciences. One of the things digital humanities shares with the sciences is a heavy reliance on instruments, on tools. Sometimes new tools are built to answer preexisting questions. Sometimes, as in the case of Hauksbee's electrical machine, new questions and answers are the byproduct of the creation of new tools. Sometimes it takes a while; in the meantime, tools themselves and the whiz-bang effects they produce must be the focus of scholarly attention.

Eventually, digital humanities must make arguments. It has to answer questions. But yet? Like eighteenth-century natural philosophers confronted with a deluge of strange new tools like microscopes, air pumps, and electrical machines, maybe we need time to articulate our digital apparatus, to produce new phenomena that we can neither anticipate nor explain immediately. At the very least, we need to make room for both kinds of digital humanities, the kind that seeks to make arguments and answer questions now and the kind that builds tools and resources with questions in mind, but only in the back of its mind and only for later. We need time to experiment and even, as Bill Turkel and Kevin Kee have argued, time to play.[3]

The eighteenth-century electrical machine was a parlor trick—until it wasn't.

NOTES

This chapter originally appeared as "Where's the Beef? Does Digital Humanities Have to Answer Questions?" by Tom Scheinfeldt, *Found History*, May 12, 2010, http://www.foundhistory.org/2010/05/12/wheres-the-beef-does-digital-humanities-have-to-answer-questions/.

1. Rob Nelson, "Audiences and Arguments for Digital History," *THATCamp CHNM 2010*, April 19, 2010, http://chnm2010.thatcamp.org/04/19/audiences-and-arguments-for-digital-history/; and Willard McCarty, "Reading," *Humanist*, May 9, 2010, http://www.digitalhumanities.org/humanist/Archives/Current/Humanist.vol24.txt.

2. For more on Hooke, see J. A. Bennett, *London's Leonardo : The Life and Work of Robert Hooke* (Oxford, New York: Oxford University Press, 2003). For Hauksbee and the electrical machine, see Willem Hackmann, *Electricity from Glass: The History of the Frictional Electrical Machine, 1600–1850* (Alphen aan den Rijn, The Netherlands: Sijthoff & Noordhoff, 1978); and Terje Brundtland, "From Medicine to Natural Philosophy: Francis Hauksbee's Way to the Air-Pump," *British Journal for the History of Science* 41, no. 2 (June 1, 2008): 209–40. For eighteenth-century electricity in general, see John Heilbron, *Electricity in the 17th and 18th centuries : A Study of Early Modern Physics* (Berkeley: University of California Press, 1979) is still the standard.

3. Dan Cohen, Mills Kelly, and Tom Scheinfeldt, *Digital Campus Episode 56—Past Play*, MP3, http://digitalcampus.tv/2010/05/07/episode-56-past-play/.

Why Digital Humanities Is "Nice"

TOM SCHEINFELDT

One of the things that people often notice when they enter the field of digital humanities is how nice everybody is. This can be in stark contrast to other (unnamed) disciplines where suspicion, envy, and territoriality sometimes seem to rule. By contrast, our most commonly used bywords are "collegiality," "openness," and "collaboration." We welcome new practitioners easily, and we don't seem to get in lots of fights. We're the golden retrievers of the academy. (OK, it's not always all balloons and cotton candy, but most practitioners will agree that the tone and tenor of digital humanities is conspicuously amiable when compared to many, if not most, academic communities.)

There are several reasons for this. Certainly the fact that nearly all digital humanities is collaborative accounts for much of its congeniality—you have to get along to get anything accomplished. The fact that digital humanities is still young, small, vulnerable, and requiring of solidarity also counts for something.

But I have another theory: Digital humanities is nice because, as I have described in earlier posts, we're often more concerned with method than we are with theory. Why should a focus on method make us nice? Because methodological debates are often more easily resolved than theoretical ones. Critics approaching an issue with sharply opposed theories may argue endlessly over evidence and interpretation. Practitioners facing a methodological problem may likewise argue over which tool or method to use. Yet at some point in most methodological debates one of two things happens: either one method or another wins out empirically, or the practical needs of our projects require us simply to pick one and move on. Moreover, as Sean Takats, my colleague at the Roy Rosenzweig Center for History and New Media (CHNM), pointed out to me today, the methodological focus makes it easy for us to "call bullshit." If anyone takes an argument too far afield, the community of practitioners can always put the argument to rest by asking to see some working code, a useable standard, or some other tangible result.

In each case, the focus on method means that arguments are short, and digital humanities stays nice.

NOTE

This chapter originally appeared as "Why Digital Humanities Is 'Nice,'" by Tom Scheinfeldt, *Found History*, May 26, 2010, http://www.foundhistory.org/2010/05/26/why-digital-humanities-is-"nice"/.

An Interview with Brett Bobley

MICHAEL GAVIN AND KATHLEEN MARIE SMITH

HASTAC, or the Humanities, Arts, Science, and Technology Advanced Collaboratory, is an interdisciplinary consortium committed to exploring the collaborative potential of the digital era. In February 2009, HASTAC scholars Kathleen Marie Smith and Michael Gavin asked Brett Bobley, director of the Office of the Digital Humanities for the National Endowment for the Humanities, his thoughts about "The Future of the Digital Humanities." The following interview originally appeared on the HASTAC website as one in a series of HASTAC Scholar Discussion Forums dealing with topics of interest to the digital humanities community.

1. What are the most interesting innovations happening right now in the field of digital humanities, and is it possible to predict or anticipate what will be most important in the future?

First, let me briefly explain what we mean by "digital humanities." I use "digital humanities" as an umbrella term for a number of different activities that surround technology and humanities scholarship. Under the digital humanities rubric, I would include topics like open access to materials, intellectual property rights, tool development, digital libraries, data mining, born-digital preservation, multimedia publication, visualization, GIS, digital reconstruction, study of the impact of technology on numerous fields, technology for teaching and learning, sustainability models, media studies, and many others. It became way too exhausting to recite that entire list whenever I spoke with someone, so "digital humanities" seemed to nicely summarize the issues. (Plus, it sounded better to me than "e-humanities," which is what I used to use!)

This long list of things related to digital humanities really reinforces why my staff is so busy—it is because the impact of technology on the humanities is so profound. As Tom Scheinfeldt has written, it is a game changer (Scheinfeldt). Some people wonder if game changing is an exaggeration, but let's put it this way: technology has radically changed the way we read, the way we write, and the way we learn. Reading, writing, learning—three things that are pretty central to the humanities.

In terms of interesting innovations, I think a lot of them surround technology and how it helps you interact with humanities collections. At its heart, technology allows you to manipulate and interact with "stuff" in different ways. The stuff might be music; it might be video; it might be text; it might be images of objects. (It might even be people.) Before we look at humanities scholarship, let me throw out an analogy. Consider how, in a very short period of time, technology has changed popular music. Let's break music down to three key areas:

Access. Putting music in digital format has completely changed the access paradigm. I remember back when I was in college. I was the station manager for my campus radio station (University of Chicago, WHPK 88.5, "Cold kickin' it live!"). At the time, before the web and a few years before CDs came out, music was still remarkably regional. Whenever I was heading home to New York to visit my family, station DJs would ask me to buy records for them. Think about that for a moment—even in Chicago, one of the biggest cities in the country, there were many, many records you couldn't get your hands on. So in order to get the latest rap records coming out of New York or even a lot of imports from the UK, you had to fly to another city and bring vinyl back in your suitcase. The Internet completely and utterly changed that. Today, you can listen to a band from Australia as easily as one from your hometown.

Production and Distribution. Just a few years ago, it was nearly impossible for an unsigned band to get their music to a wide audience. Trust me, as the former head of a college radio station, most bands couldn't even make a demo tape that didn't sound horrible. But technology allows anyone with a home computer to record their music, and the web allows them to distribute it to anyone in the world.

Consumption (Listening). Digital files have enabled people to have much, much larger collections of music than they could physically store before. (Piracy helped, too, but that's another, related issue.) I carry my entire music collection on an iPod. This changes the way you listen, what you listen to, and the way you share music with others.

Now let's look at these three areas again (Access, Production, and Consumption) but in the context of humanities scholarship. What do humanists do? Well, a big part of what they do is study cultural heritage materials—books, newspapers, paintings, film, sculptures, music, ancient tablets, buildings, and so on. Pretty much everything on that list is being digitized in very large numbers. The change in access may not be quite as far along as it is for music, but it will be soon. Like with music, you'll have access to materials from all over the world. You won't have to send a book via airmail from New York to Chicago because you'll have instant access to it on your PC (or your mobile device). If you want to study materials in China, you'll be able to view them (or, for that matter, find out about them) using the web.

On the production side, we're already seeing more and more scholars producing their work for the web. It might take the form of scholarly websites, blogs, wikis, or whatever. But as with music, a scholar (even an amateur, part-time scholar) can make her work available to the entire world at very low cost of production. After all, scholars still have to eat and so be compensated for what they do best—the analysis of scholarly materials and being part of the larger scholarly conversation (so production and transmission of knowledge). Plus, keep in mind that the entire production cycle uses technology (collecting, editing, discussing with others) before the final product is created.

On the consumption side, people get their materials in all kinds of new ways. Reading has changed with the web. It has changed from a technology perspective, of course—thinking of e-readers and laptops and mobile devices (and some of the now-starting-to-get-obsolete tech products like microfiche machines). But the changes are more profound than that. The way we read is changing—bits and pieces of varied content from so many places and perspectives.

If I had to predict some interesting things for the future in the area of access, I'd sum it up in one word: scale. Big, massive, scale. That's what digitization brings—access to far, far more cultural heritage materials than you could ever access before. If you're a scholar of, say, nineteenth-century British literature, how does your work change when, for the first time, you have every book from your era at your fingertips? Far more books than you could ever read in your lifetime. How does this scale change things? How might quantitative tech-based methodologies like data mining help you to better understand a giant corpus? Help you zero in on issues? What if you are a historian and you now have access to every newspaper around the world? How might searching and mining that kind of data set radically change your results? How might well-known assumptions in various disciplines fall once confronted with hard data? Or, perhaps, how might they be altered or reenvisioned?

2. How do you see digital technology transforming work in the disciplines of the humanities? Are there disciplines in which digital technology will have less of an impact?

In my earlier answer, I spoke about how access to large collections of digitized cultural heritage materials will transform the humanities. So let's also talk a bit about digital research tools and methodologies and their impact.

More and more scholars are starting to take advantage of digital research tools. Let me note that pretty much every scholar uses a digital tool for her work: namely, a word processor. And I'm sure there must be all kinds of interesting papers about how a word processor and its ability to edit and reedit on the fly has changed scholarship. But we don't even talk about a word processor as a digital tool anymore. But that's really the point here. What might seem novel at first can become accepted even by "regular" humanities scholars over time. There are all kinds of interesting tools and methodologies. I've been seeing a lot of really interesting uses for GIS—mapping places and events, over time, in a geographical space to help gain new insight. Visualization is another technique that I think will become a great deal more common in the humanities. Scholars have always consumed materials to gain insight into why an event happened (or why the artist drew a painting that way, or why an ancient temple was constructed, etc.). Visualization may prove to be another technology that can help scholars see their materials in a new way.

There are many, many digital tools that scholars use every day to collaborate, to organize their work, and to publish it to the community. I suspect that many of these digital practices will become the norm. The tools will change (many will die out), but useful methods will stick. By the way, for a nice list of digital tools for the humanities, see Lisa Spiro's DiRT Wiki (Spiro).

Digital technology may impact some disciplines more than others. But frankly, this is hard to predict. Obviously, subdisciplines like game studies are very tech heavy. But who would have guessed that classics would be one of the most digitally savvy disciplines?

3. What roadblocks are scholars in the digital humanities encountering, and what advice do you have for graduate students and junior faculty?

The roadblock issue is much discussed. It seems like every conference I go to there is discussion of promotion and tenure issues, so this is certainly a big topic. Let me preface this by saying that I'm not a scholar myself; I'm a government grant maker and technologist. I say this because I want to make it clear that I can't speak authoritatively about how P&T (promotion and tenure) works on your campus. That said, my impression is that on some campuses, graduate students and junior faculty are strongly encouraged to steer away from digital scholarship and instead to write about "traditional" topics and publish "traditional" monographs. On the other hand, I do hear about more and more campuses where digital scholarship is highly valued and counted toward promotion.

I have a few thoughts here. First, I think it is important for people throughout the humanities community to understand that digital scholarship doesn't have to mean nontraditional. In other words, to get back to my word processor issue, have you ever heard someone say to a young philosopher, "Oh, you better not write your book about Aristotle using a *word processor*! Someone will think you're one of those crazy digital humanists and you won't get tenure!" This example seems silly, but keep in mind that it wasn't all that long ago that a word processor was newfangled technology. My point is that you can tackle "traditional" humanities topics and questions while still using the latest digital tools if you find it adds value to your work. Maybe you used data-mining techniques to see how Aristotle influenced other philosophers. That's great, but the focus of your book should be the results (the scholarship) and not necessarily the techniques you used.

One issue I'd like to see graduate programs tackle: more training in digital tools and methodologies for humanities scholarship. In the sciences, graduate students learn how to use digital tools for research and analysis. But how many graduate humanities programs include classes on using GIS, 3-D modeling, data analysis, or other methods of scholarship? I suspect the number is fairly low. I wonder if this isn't an area more graduate programs should be exploring.

4. How will digital technology in the academic system in general (for example, in the changing role of textbooks in the classroom, open-access databases, or publishing requirements for tenure) affect the way research is performed and shared?
I think research will change a great deal over the next twenty years. We have already seen this in the sciences where mining "big data" has changed the way scientists do their research (Anderson). Imagine a future where we have huge digital libraries of far more material than you ever had access to before. Now imagine automatic language translation for those documents, which greatly increases your ability to study documents from around the globe.

Let's face it: sometimes scholarship is constrained by seemingly mundane hurdles like copyright, travel costs, or language barriers. Let's take art history for a moment. If you're an art historian and you want to write a book about French painters and you get the rights to reproduce the paintings of Renoir but not Monet, which artist will you choose to focus on? You'll probably write a lot more about Renoir for strictly practical reasons. What if you're a political philosopher and you can read English, French, and Greek but not Chinese? Might there be incredible literature in Chinese that would help you understand how ideas moved through cultures and across languages? But if you can't read it, you probably won't focus on it.

5. Many of the NEH's programs involve collaboration with other institutions. What does the NEH need from administrators and researchers to make successful programs?
In the Office of Digital Humanities, we're looking for really cool projects to fund! Of course, being the government, I can't exactly make the peer review criteria "coolness factor" and expect the lawyers to be OK with that! In all seriousness, though, we're looking for innovative projects that demonstrate how technology can be brought to bear on a humanities problem and, ultimately, yield great scholarship for use by a variety of audiences, whether it be scholars, students in a formal classroom setting, or the interested public.

Administrators and researchers who are interested in applying to the Office of Digital Humanities should definitely check out the projects we have already funded. (They are all easy to find on our website; check out our Library of Funded Projects at http://www.neh.gov/ODH.) It is also important to understand how to work collaboratively. So many of today's digital projects involve teams of people from various disciplines. Each member of the team brings different strengths to the project. We often see humanities scholars teaming up with computer scientists, librarians, social scientists, and others. And the projects are richer for it. If you are developing a tool or methodology, we're very interested in broad applicability. Does this method just help your scholarship? Or can others benefit as well? Make sure you perform an environmental scan to find out what similar projects may already be under way. Also, check out Meredith Hindley's nice article on how to prepare your NEH application.

Lastly, I suggest getting out there and communicating. Use new media tools like blogs, wikis, and social networks. Go to conferences when you can. Talk to people in your field and other fields to find out what is possible and what needs to be done.

NOTE

This interview was originally published as Smith, Kathleen, and Michael Gavin. "Q&A with Brett Bobley, Director of the NEH's Office of Digital Humanities (ODH)," *HASTAC*, February 1, 2009. http://hastac.org/node/1934. Opinions expressed are those of Brett Bobley and do not necessarily reflect official positions of the National Endowment for the Humanities.

BIBLIOGRAPHY

Anderson, Chris. "The End of Theory: The Data Deluge Makes the Scientific Method Obsolete." *Wired*. Condé Nast Digital, June 23, 2008. http://www.wired.com/science/discoveries/magazine/16-07/pb_theory.

Hindley, Meredith. "How to Get a Grant from NEH: A Public Service Message." *Humanities* 29, no. 4 (July/August 2008). http://www.neh.gov/news/humanities/2008-07/GrantWriting.html.

Scheinfeldt, Tom. "Sunset for Ideology, Sunrise for Methodology." *Found History*. March 13, 2008. http://www.foundhistory.org/2008/03/13/sunset-for-ideology-sunrise-for-methodology/.

Spiro, Lisa. *Digital Research Tools (DiRT) Wiki*. https://digitalresearchtools.pbworks.com/w/page/17801672/FrontPage.

Day of DH: Defining the Digital Humanities

A Day in the Life of the Digital Humanities (*Day of DH*) is a community publication project sponsored by the University of Alberta under the direction of Geoffrey Rockwell. Each year, it brings together digital humanists from around the world to document what they do on one day, March 18. The goal of the project is to create a website that weaves together the journals of the participants into a picture that answers the question, Just what do computing humanists really do? Participants document their day through photographs and commentary in a blog-like journal. The collection of these journals with links, tags, and comments makes up the final work that is published online.

In advance of the *Day of DH*, participants are asked, How do you define humanities computing / digital humanities? The following selection of definitions was culled from 2011 answers to that question, which are posted publicly on the *Day of DH* website.[1]

> Using computational tools to do the work of the humanities.
>
> —*John Unsworth, University of Illinois, United States*

> I think of digital humanities as an umbrella term that covers a wide variety of digital work in the humanities: development of multimedia pedagogies and scholarship, designing and building tools, human computer interaction, designing and building archives, and so on. DH is interdisciplinary; by necessity it breaks down boundaries between disciplines at the local (e.g., English and history) and global (e.g., humanities and computer sciences) levels.
>
> —*Kathie Gossett, Old Dominion University, United States*

> A "community of practice" (to borrow Etienne Wenger's phrase) whereby the learning, construction, and sharing of humanities knowledge is under-

taken with the application of digital technologies in a reflexive, theoretically informed, and collaborative manner.

—Kathryn E. Piquette, Humboldt-Universität zu Berlin, Germany

A name that marks a moment of transition; the current name for humanities inquiry driven by or dependent on computers or digitally born objects of study; a temporary epithet for what will eventually be called merely Humanities.

—Mark Marino, University of Southern California, United States

I view the digital humanities as a collaborative, open, and emerging field of inquiry. A state of mind, a methodology, and theoretical approach to knowledge, it forces us to reconceive our practice. In my own work, I embrace curation as a means of reweaving and reintegrating theory and practice in history. I seek to interpret space, place, and identity in a multisensory way. I fail more often than not. But the digital humanities is like jazz in that it is about process, as well as outcome.

—Mark Tebeau, Cleveland State University, United States

I think digital humanities, like social media, is an idea that will increasingly become invisible as new methods and platforms move from being widely used to being ubiquitous. For now, digital humanities defines the overlap between humanities research and digital tools. But the humanities are the study of cultural life, and our cultural life will soon be inextricably bound up with digital media.

—Ed Finn, Stanford University, United States

A term of tactical convenience.

—Matthew Kirschenbaum, University of Maryland, United States

It is both a methodology and a community.

—Jason Farman, University of Maryland, United States

When I'm asked, I like to say that digital humanities is just one method for doing humanistic inquiry.

—Brian Croxall, Emory University, United States

The Digital Humanities is both a field with a discernable set of academic lineages, practices, and methodologies and a vague umbrella term used to describe the application of digital technology to traditional humanistic inquiry. Ultimately, what sets DH apart from many other humanities fields is its methodological commitment to building things as a way of knowing.

—*Matthew K. Gold, New York City College of Technology and CUNY Graduate Center, United States*

Digital Humanities is the integration of sophisticated, empirical techniques utilizing tools and technologies typically associated with practical sciences into the study of traditional humanities questions. It represents a more exploratory and less quantitative approach than social sciences in the use of such tools, but it also represents ambitious attempts to model nuanced human wisdom in ways that, like early flying machines, are beautiful, quite impractical and often fail.

—*Elijah Meeks, Stanford University, United States*

The use of digital tools and methods in humanities study and dissemination.

—*Geoffrey Rockwell, University of Alberta, Canada*

DH is inquiry enabled by digital methodologies or modes of research, dissemination, design, preservation, and communication that rely on algorithms, software, and/or the Internet network for processing data.

—*Tanya Clement, University of Maryland, United States*

The scholarly study and use of computers and computer culture to illuminate the human record. (BUSA Remix)

—*Ernesto Priego, University College London, United Kingdom*

Digital Humanities is a critical investigation and practice of the methods of humanities research in the digital medium.

—*Julia Flanders, Brown University, United States*

Digital humanities is a metafield, a set of coevolving new knowledge and best practices expanding from traditional humanities disciplines into born-digital research and teaching methods. Digital humanists study all objects and practices of concern to analog humanities, plus those made possible by the digital age. Digital humanists also build tools that make it possible for themselves, their students, and the world at large to engage critically with our cultural heritage.

—*Vika Zafrin, Boston University, United States*

I don't: I'm sick of trying to define it. When forced to, I'll make the referent the people instead of the ideas or methods—Digital Humanities is the thing practiced by people who self-identify as Digital Humanists. It's helpful to have a name for the field chiefly for institutional authority. Though granted I think it does involve coding/making/building/doing things with computers, things related to, you know, the humanities.

—*Amanda French, Center for History and New Media, United States*

Digital Humanities is a way to ask, redefine, and answer questions with a more intelligent set of tools.

—*Lik Hang Tsui, University of Oxford, United Kingdom*

I think it's a convenient label, but fundamentally I don't believe in it. There are people who haven't yet attempted to come to grips with how digital tools and methods can change research, teaching, and outreach in the Humanities, and those who have. The latter are Digital Humanities types. But it's all Wissenschaft.

—*Hugh Cayless, New York University, United States*

The digital humanities is what digital humanists do. What digital humanists do depends largely on academic discipline but also on level of technical expertise. Each discipline, with varying degrees of intensity, has over the years developed a set of favored methods, tools, and interests that, although shared with other disciplines, remains connected to the discipline. The task of the digital humanities, as a transcurricular practice, is to bring these practitioners into communication with each other and to cultivate a discourse that captures the shared praxis of bringing technologies of representation, computation, and communication to bear on the work of interpretation that defines the humanities.

—*Rafael Alvarado, University of Virginia, United States*

I think digital humanities is an unfortunate neologism, largely because the humanities itself is a problematic term. The biggest problem is that the tent isn't big enough! I have participated in a number of DH events and they are strikingly similar to things like Science Online.

With that said, DH is at its best when it embraces the digital not simply as a means to the traditional ends of scholarship, but when it transforms the nature of what humanists do. The digital allows for scholars, librarians, archivists, and curators to engage much more directly with each other and the public. Further, it allows them not simply to write for each other, but to build things for everyone.

—*Trevor Owens, Library of Congress, United States*

NOTE

1. For the full range of 2011 definitions see http://tapor.ualberta.ca/taporwiki/index.php/How_do_you_define_Humanities_Computing_/_Digital_Humanities%3F. The Day of DH homepage can be found at http://tapor.ualberta.ca/taporwiki/index.php/Day_of_Digital_Humanities.

PART II

THEORIZING THE DIGITAL HUMANITIES

Developing Things: Notes toward an Epistemology of Building in the Digital Humanities

STEPHEN RAMSAY AND GEOFFREY ROCKWELL

The Anxieties of Digital Work

Leave any forum on digital humanities sufficiently open, and those gathered will inevitably—and almost immediately—turn to issues surrounding credit for digital work.

It can sometimes be difficult to determine precisely what "digital work" means in the humanities, and the context in which that term is being applied can differ between scholarly but nonprofessorial positions ("alternate academic," as it is sometimes called) and the normative concerns of tenure and promotion. Yet despite this, it is clear that the object of anxiety is becoming more focused as time goes by. There might have been a time when study of "the digital" seemed generally dissonant amid more conventional studies within history, philosophy, and literature. But in more recent times, people writing conventional books and articles about "new media" seldom worry that such work won't count. People who publish in online journals undoubtedly experience more substantial resistance, but the belief that online articles don't really count seems more and more like the quaint prejudice of age than a substantive critique. Increasingly, people who publish things online that look like articles and are subjected to the usual system of peer review need not fear reprisal from a hostile review committee.

There is, however, a large group in digital humanities that experiences this anxiety about credit and what counts in a way that is far more serious and consequential. These are the people—most of whom have advanced degrees in some area of humanistic study—who have turned to building, hacking, and coding as part of their normal research activity. This is the segment of contemporary digital humanities (DH) that invented the terms "humanities computing" and later "digital humanities"—the ones for whom any other common designation (game studies, media studies, cyberculture, edutech) doesn't make as much sense. They are scholarly editors, literary critics, librarians, academic computing staff, historians, archaeologists, and classicists, but their work is all about XML, XSLT, GIS, R, CSS, and C. They build digital libraries, engage in "deep encoding" of literary texts, create 3-D models of Roman ruins, generate charts and graphs of linguistic phenomena, develop instructional applications, and even (in the most problematic case) write software to make the general task of scholarship easier for other scholars. For this group, making their work count is by no means an easy matter. A book with a bibliography is surely scholarship. Is a tool for keeping track of bibliographic data (like Zotero) scholarship? A literary critical article that is full of graphs, maps, and trees is also scholarship (if, perhaps, a little unusual). Is a software framework for generating quantitative data about literary corpora scholarship? A conference presentation about the way maps mediate a society's sense of space is unambiguously an act of scholarship. Is making a map an unambiguous act of scholarship?

There have been both passive and active attempts to address these issues by providing guidelines for the evaluation of digital work. In one of the more notable instances of active intervention, the Modern Language Association (MLA) released guidelines for such evaluation. As laudable as such efforts have been—and it should be noted that the MLA began this work over ten years ago—the guidelines themselves often beg the question by encouraging faculty members to "ask about evaluation and support" and to "negotiate and document [their] role" (Modern Language Association). For nontenure-line faculty and staff (e.g., those working in DH research groups and centers), the problem of evaluation is at least theoretically solved by a job description; if it is your job to build things in the context of the humanities, success at that task presumably resolves the question of what counts in terms of evaluation and promotion. Grant funding, too, has functioned in recent years as a form of evaluation. Grants in excess of fifty thousand dollars are quite rare in the humanities; grants exceeding twice that amount are by no means unusual in DH. Review committees (particularly those above the department level) have been more than willing to view cash awards, often with substantial indirect cost requirements, as something that most definitely counts.

But none of this resolves the core anxiety over whether the work counts as *scholarship* and whether those doing such things are still engaged in humanistic inquiry. People in DH will sometimes point to the high level of technical skill required, to the intellectual nature of the pursuit, and to the plain fact that technical projects usually entail an enormous amount of work. But even as these arguments are advanced, the detractions seem obvious. Repairing cars requires a high level of technical skill; the intellectual nature of chess is beyond dispute; mining coal is backbreaking work. No one confuses these activities with scholarship. The authors of this paper have each made strong claims for building, hacking, and coding as important—and, indeed, definitional—activities within DH. Yet we are aware that, despite enthusiasm for our ideas in some quarters, neither of us has made the case for building as a form of scholarship and a variety of humanistic inquiry. Our purpose in this chapter, therefore, is to work toward a materialist epistemology sufficient to the task of defending building as a distinct form of scholarly endeavor, both in the humanities and beyond. We do not offer particular solutions to the challenge of having work in the digital humanities count in concrete institutional terms.[1] Our hope is rather to understand our own practices more fully, with an eye toward strengthening the practical arguments our institutions commonly demand.

Thing Theory: Can DH Things Be Theories?

In December of 2008, Willard McCarty started a conversation on *Humanist* by asking whether things like the digital artifacts we build are knowledge if they aren't accompanied by some measure of discourse: "Can any such artefact ever stand for itself wholly without written commentary and explanation?" (McCarty, *Humanist*). Stan Ruecker responded that he thought "we do have categories of artifacts that both reify knowledge and communicate it" (Ruecker) and quoted Lev Manovich who, at the Digital Humanities (DH) 2007 conference, got up and said something to the effect of "a prototype is a theory. Stop apologizing for your prototypes."[2]

Manovich's statement is provocative, in part, because it answers McCarty's question by eschewing entirely the notion of an accompanying discourse. Prototypes are theories, which is to say they already contain or somehow embody that type of discourse That is most valued—namely, the theoretical. Manovich undoubtedly had in mind not the standard scientific meaning of the word "theory"—an explanation for a set of observations that can predict future observations—but something closer to the way the term is commonly used in the humanities. In the context of history or literary study, "theory" doesn't predict, but it does explain. It promises deeper understanding of something already given, like historical events or a literary work. To say that software is a theory is to say that digital works convey knowledge the way a theory does, in this more general sense.

Alan Galey and Ruecker went on to claim, in a subsequent article, that "the creation of an experimental digital prototype [should] be understood as conveying an argument about designing interfaces" (405). In this view, certain prototypes are understood to do rhetorically what a theoretical discourse does by presenting a thesis that is "contestable, defensible, and substantive" (412). They made this argument with full awareness of the institutional consequences—namely, that "digital artifacts themselves—not just their surrogate project reports—should stand as peer-reviewable forms of research, worthy of professional credit and contestable as forms of argument" (407). It is the prototype that makes the thesis, not discursive accompaniments (to borrow McCarty's formulation) like white papers, reports, and peer-reviewed papers. They illustrate their argument with specific examples, including text visualizations like Brad Paley's TextArc, offering them as graphical interpretations of a text comparable to a critical or interpretative essay.

Galey and Ruecker's vision of the explanatory power of the experimental prototype recalls the centuries-old practice of demonstration devices "deployed in public lectures to recruit audiences by using artifice to display a doctrine about nature" (Schaeffer, 157). The eighteenth-century orrery was not a scientific instrument designed for discovery but simply a tool for showing how the solar system worked—in essence, a rhetorical device that could be used in persuasive performances. Davis Baird makes the case more forcefully in *Thing Knowledge* where, as the title suggests, he traces the way scientific instruments convey knowledge within the scientific communities that have the training to interpret them. Baird goes further, however, and questions the privilege accorded to the discursive, even accusing us of ignoring the communicative power of the instrumental: "In the literary theater, lacking any arsenal of techniques to understand and advance instrumentation, textual analysis will have free play, while in the instrumental and technological theatre humanists will be relegated to the sidelines, carping at the ethical, social and—following the Heideggarian line of criticism—metaphysical problems of modern science and technology" (xvii). If Baird is right, then "building" may represent an opportunity to correct the discursive and linguistic bias of the humanities. According to this view, we should be open to communicating scholarship through artifacts, whether digital or not. It implies that print is, indeed, ill equipped to deal with entire classes of knowledge that are presumably germane to humanistic inquiry.

The problem with this explanatory approach to digital artifacts is that it doesn't apply to the most problematic—and, perhaps, the most ubiquitous—category of digital tools: namely, those tools that digital humanists develop for others to use in the ordinary course of their work as scholars. Such tools are celebrated for their transparency or, as Heidegger puts it, for the way they stand—like hammers or pencils—ready to hand. Such tools, far from being employed on the center stage in a performative context, are only noticed when they break down or refuse to work transparently. Such tools don't explain or argue but simply facilitate. Galey and Ruecker get around this in their discussion by focusing on experimental prototypes, which are not tools meant to be used. They imagine a tool like TextArc to be a visualization tool that makes an argument about interface but not an argument about the text it visualizes. They believe that TextArc's visualizations "are not really about *Hamlet* or *Alice in Wonderland* or its other sample texts; they are about TextArc's own algorithmic and aesthetic complexity" (419). While this might be true, it almost disqualifies the tool from being transparent or ready to hand. A digital artifact that transparently shows you something else might convey knowledge, but it doesn't intervene as an explanation or argument; it recedes from view before that which is represented. Where there is argument, the artifact has ceased to be a tool and has become something else. This other thing is undoubtedly worthy and necessary in many cases, but it resolves the question of whether "building is scholarship" by restricting building to the creation of things that, because they are basically discursive, already look like scholarship.

The Digital as a Theoretical Lens or Instrument

A second way to think of digital artifacts as theories would be to think of them as hermeneutical instruments through which we can interpret other phenomena. Digital artifacts like tools could then be considered as "telescopes for the mind" that show us something in a new light. We might less fancifully consider digital artifacts as "theory frameworks" for interpreting, in the same way that Jonathan Culler views Foucault's theoretical interventions.

As with prototypes, there is a history to this view. Margaret Masterson in "The Intellect's New Eye," an essay in the *Times Literary Supplement* of 1962, argued that we should go beyond using computers just to automate tedious tasks. Using the telescope as an example of a successful scientific instrument, she argued for a similar artistic and literary use of computing to "see differently." One recalls, in this connection, Steve Jobs's early presentation of the Macintosh as a "bicycle for the mind" that would (in an ad campaign some twenty years later) allow us to "Think different." Such analogies, even in their less strident formulations, reinforce the suggestion that digital artifacts like text analysis and visualization tools are theories in the very highest tradition of what it is to theorize in the humanities, because they show us the world differently.

One of us has even argued that visualization tools work like hermeneutical theories (Rockwell). A concordancing tool, for example, might be said to instantiate certain theories about the unity of a text. The concordance imagines that if you gather all the passages in the text that contain a keyword, the new text that results from this operation will be consistent with the author's intentions. Whatever other work it might perform, it is informed by this basic theoretical position. While we might regard such a position as crude in comparison to more elaborate theories of discourse, it is not hard to imagine tools that instantiate subtler theories deliberately and self-consciously (and perhaps more in keeping with present theoretical preoccupations). Further, digital instruments work a lot faster. Reading Foucault and applying his theoretical framework can take months or years of application. A web-based text analysis tool could apply its theoretical position in seconds. In fact, commercial analytical tools like Topicmarks tell you how much time you saved (as compared to having to read the primary text).[3]

We are, of course, uncomfortable thinking of theories in this highly utilitarian manner. Yet there is a tradition of philosophical pragmatism in which theories are thought of quite explicitly as tools to be used. As William James famously said, "Theories thus become instruments, not answers to enigmas, in which we can rest" (98). He wanted philosophical theories not just to explain things but to be useful and argued that the way to judge theories was to assess their usefulness or their "cash value." This instrumental view is argued historically by John Dewey in works like *Reconstruction in Philosophy:*

> Here it is enough to note that notions, theories, systems, no matter how elaborate and self-consistent they are, must be regarded as hypotheses. They are to be accepted as bases of actions which test them, not as finalities. To perceive this fact is to abolish rigid dogmas from the world. It is to recognize that conceptions, theories and systems of thought are always open to development through use. . . . They are tools. As in the case of all tools, their value resides not in themselves but in their capacity to work shown in the consequences of their use. (145)

Dewey was not a mean instrumentalist. He believed that it was necessary to reconstruct philosophy (and by extension the humanities) so that it could guide action rather than just become the solace of pedants. He wanted theories to be useful instruments for living, not the high mark of scholarship. It is by no means idly speculative to imagine that he would have recognized that computers, by virtue of their ability to automate processes, could thus instantiate theories at work. He almost certainly would not have objected to the idea of a theory packaged as an application that you can "run" on a phenomenon as an automatic instrument (provided we remained open to the idea that such theories might cease to be useful as the context changed).

If highly theorized and self-reflective visions of tools as theories fail to be sufficiently tool-like, one might say that so-called thing theories of the instrumental sort outlined here err in the opposite direction by being insufficiently open about their theoretical underpinnings. A well-tuned instrument might be used to understand something, but that doesn't mean that you, as the user, understand how the tool works. Computers, with chains of abstraction extending upward from the bare electrical principles of primitive XOR gates, are always in some sense opaque. Their theoretical assumptions have to be inferred through use or else explained through the very stand-in documentation that we are trying to avoid treating as a necessary part of the tool. For Baird, the opacity of instruments isn't a problem; it is simply part of how scientific instruments evolve in the marketplace. Early instruments might demonstrate their working (as they certainly did in the case of early computer equipment), but eventually they get boxed up and made available as easy-to-use instruments you can order—effectively installing the user at a level of abstraction far above whatever theoretical claims might lie beneath.

But the understanding of underlying theoretical claims is the sine qua non of humanistic inquiry. For tools to be theories in the way digital humanists want—in a way that makes them accessible to, for example, peer review—opacity becomes an almost insuperable problem. The only way to have any purchase on the theoretical assumptions that underlie a tool would be to use that tool. Yet it is the purpose of the tool (and this is particularly the case with digital tools) to abstract the user away from the mechanisms that would facilitate that process. In a sense, the tools most likely to fare well in that process are not tools, per se, but prototypes—perhaps especially those that are buggy, unstable, and make few concessions toward usability. One could argue that the source code provides an entry point to the theoretical assumptions of black boxes and that the open-source philosophy to which so many digital humanists subscribe provides the very transparency necessary for peer review. But it is not at all clear that all assumptions are necessarily revealed once an application is decompiled, and few people read the code of others anyway. We are back to depending on discourse.

The Digital as a Theoretical Model

Concern with the source might lead us toward formal definitions of "computation" as put forth in the context of computer science. The most minimal definition of a computer—the one that typically reigns within the rarefied fields of information theory and theory of computation—considers a computer to be any mechanism that transforms information from one state to another. Such terse conceptions aim to be widely inclusive but, like tool as prototype, often end up excluding much that we would want to acknowledge in a definition of computing as a sociological activity (whether for DH or for computer science more generally). More expansive definitions that try to allow for a wide range of activities are common. Here is a recent one from an article that begins with the question, "What is the core of computing?" (Isbell, 195):

> In our view, computing is fundamentally a modeling activity. Any modeler must establish a correspondence between one domain and another. For the computational modeler, one domain is typically a phenomenon in the world or in our imagination while the other is typically a computing machine, whether abstract or physical. The computing machine or artifact is typically manipulated through some language that provides a combination of symbolic representation of the features, objects, and states of interest as well as a visualization of transformations and interactions that can be directly compared and aligned with those in the world. The centrality of the machine makes computing models inherently executable or automatically manipulable and, in part, distinguishes computing from mathematics. Therefore, the computationalist acts as an intermediary between models, machines, and languages and prescribes objects, states, and processes. (198)

The idea of computing in the humanities as a modeling activity has been advanced before, most notably by Willard McCarty, who notes "the fundamental dependence of any computing system on an explicit, delimited conception of the world or 'model' of it" (*Humanities Computing*, 21). For McCarty, such notions help to establish a critical discourse within DH by connecting humanistic inquiry to the vast literature and philosophy of science, where "modeling has been a standard method for a very long time."

The question for those who would understand building as a scholarly activity, though, is not whether understanding the world can be rectified with the terms of humanistic inquiry; clearly, it can. If computers can be enlisted in the task of gaining this understanding, then a failure to welcome methodologies that substantially employ computational methods is surely a reactionary stance. Moreover, since one would expect the results of that methodology to appear as a "visualization of transformations and interactions," the normal output of computational methods is similarly unproblematic. We may reject the understanding of the world put forth by a humanist using computational methods and even point to the output of those methods as evidence of insufficiency or error; but, if digital humanities is about using computers to provide robust interpretations of the world (however contingent, provisional, and multiple), then it is manifestly not incommensurable with humanistic practice.

The question, rather, is whether the manipulation of features, objects, and states of interest using the language of coding or programming (however abstracted by graphical systems) constitutes theorizing. And here, the nature of the problem of building reveals itself most fully as a kind of category error. To ask whether coding is a scholarly act is like asking whether writing is a scholarly act. Writing is the technology—or better, the methodology—that lies between model and result in humanistic discourse. We have for centuries regarded writing as absolutely essential to scholarship. We esteem those who write much, penalize those who write little, and generally refer to the "literature" when evaluating the state of a discourse. But in each case, we speak metaphorically. We do not mean to propose that the act of putting words on a page is scholarship. We seek, instead, to capture metonymically the quality of the intervention that has occurred as a result of the writing. Scholars conceive the world and represent it in some altered form. That writing stands as the technical method by which this transformation is made is almost beside the point. One recalls, in this context, Marshall McLuhan's gnomic observation that the "medium is the message"—that the message of any medium or technology is the "change of scale or pace or pattern that it introduces into human affairs" (8).

Yet this analogy falters on a number of points. The act of putting words on a page (or finished works considered in isolation from readers) may not be scholarship in some restricted sense, but the separation between writing, conceiving, and transforming is hardly clear-cut. That one might come to understand a novel or an issue or a problem through the act of writing about it forms the basic pedagogy of the humanities. We assign students writing not merely to provide us with evidence that they have thought about something but rather to have that thinking occur in the first place.

In discussing this issue, then, we may borrow the phrase that inaugurated the philosophical discourse of computing. As Alan Turing proposed "What happens when a machine takes the part of [a human interlocutor] in this game?" as a replacement for "Can machines think?" (434), so may we substitute "What happens when building takes the place of writing?" as a replacement for "Is building scholarship?" The answer, too, might be similar. If the quality of the interventions that occur as a result of building are as interesting as those that are typically established through writing, then that activity is, for all intents and purposes, scholarship. The comparison strikes us as particularly strong. In reactions to the Turing test, one may easily discern a fear of machine intelligence underlying many of the counterarguments. It is neither unfair nor reductionist to suggest that fear of an automated scholarship—an automatic writing—informs many objections to the act of building and coding within the humanities. But even if that were not the case, it would still fall to the builders to present their own activities as capable of providing affordances as rich and provocative as that of writing. We believe that is a challenge that the digital humanities community (in all its many and varied forms) should accept and welcome.

NOTES

1. For those interested in the institutional evaluation of digital work, the Modern Language Association maintains a wiki of advice at http://wiki.mla.org/index.php/Evaluation_Wiki.

2. See also Galey, Ruecker, and the INKE team, "How a Prototype Argues."

3. Topicmarks, http://topicmarks.com.

BIBLIOGRAPHY

Baird, Davis. *Thing Knowledge: A Philosophy of Scientific Instruments.* Berkeley: University of California Press, 2004.

Culler, Jonathan. *Literary Theory: A Very Short Introduction.* Oxford: Oxford University Press, 2000.

Davidson, C. N. "Data Mining, Collaboration, and Institutional Infrastructure for Transforming Research and Teaching in the Human Sciences and Beyond." *CTWatch Quarterly* 3, no. 2 (2007). http://www.ctwatch.org/quarterly/articles/2007/05/data-mining-collaboration-and-institutional-infrastructure/.

Dewey, John. *Reconstruction in Philosophy*. Enlarged ed. Boston: Beacon, 1948.

Galey, Alan, Stan Ruecker, and the INKE team. "How a Prototype Argues." *Literary and Linguistic Computing* 25, no. 4 (2010): 405–24.

Heidegger, Martin. *Being and Time.* Translated by Joan Stambaugh. Albany: State University of New York Press, 1953.

Isbell, Charles L., et al. "(Re)Defining Computing Curricula by (Re)Defining Computing." *SIGCSE Bulletin* 41, no. 4 (2009): 195–207.

James, William. "What Pragmatism Means." In *Pragmatism: A Reader,* edited by Louis Menand. New York: Vintage, 1997.

Masterson, Margaret. "The Intellect's New Eye." *Times Literary Supplement,* vol. 284, April 27, 1962.

McCarty, Willard. "22.403: Writing and Pioneering." Humanist Discussion Group. http://www.digitalhumanities.org/humanist/.

———. *Humanities Computing.* New York: Palgrave, 2005.

McLuhan, Marshall. *Understanding Media: The Extensions of Man.* Boston: MIT Press, 1994.

Modern Language Association. "Guidelines for Evaluating Work with Digital Media in the Modern Languages." http://www.mla.org/guidelines_evaluation_digital.

Paley, Bradford. TextArc. http://www.textarc.org.

Rockwell, Geoffrey. "The Visual Concordance: The Design of Eye-ConTact." *Text Technology* 10, no. 1 (2001): 73–86.

Ruecker, Stan. "22.404: Thing Knowledge." Humanist Discussion Group. http://www.digitalhumanities.org/humanist/.

Schaffer, Simon. "Machine Philosophy: Demonstration Devices in Georgian Mechanics." *Osiris* 9 (1994): 157–82.

Turing, Alan. "Computing Machinery and Intelligence." *Mind: A Quarterly Review of Psychology and Philosophy* 59, no. 236 (1950): 433–60.

Humanistic Theory and Digital Scholarship

JOHANNA DRUCKER

Digital humanists have seen themselves within the longer tradition of the humanities, suggesting that the main value of their work resides in the creation, migration, or preservation of cultural materials (McGann). Using new platforms and networked environments, humanists entering the digital arena learned a great deal from the encounter. Expressed succinctly, the tasks of creating metadata, doing markup, and making classification schemes or information architectures forced humanists to make explicit many assumptions often left implicit in our work. Humanities content met digital methods and created projects in which the terms of production were, necessarily, set by technological restraints. (The forms of print media and their rhetorics, by contrast, were established by humanist scholars for whom debate, commentary, and interpretative exposition were so essential they drove the development of the book format and the paratextual apparatus.)

After several decades of digital work, the question remains whether humanists are actually doing anything different or just extending the activities that have always been their core concerns, enabled by advantages of networked digital technology (easier access to primary materials, speed of comparison, searching, etc.). Whatever the answer, the role of humanities scholars is crucial in the production and interpretation of cultural materials. It may turn out that data mining or large corpus processing and distant reading are substantially different from close reading and textual analysis and may bring new insights and techniques into the humanities (Moretti). But my second question frames a very different agenda: Have the humanities had any impact on the digital environment? Can we create graphical interfaces and digital platforms from humanistic methods?

The cultural authority of digital technology is still claimed by the fields that design the platforms and protocols on which we work. These are largely fields in which quantitative, engineering, and computational sensibilities prevail. Tools for humanities work have evolved considerably in the last decade, but during that same period a host of protocols for information visualization, data mining, geospatial representation, and other research instruments have been absorbed from disciplines whose epistemological foundations and fundamental values are at odds with, or even hostile to, the humanities. Positivistic, strictly quantitative, mechanistic, reductive and literal, these visualization and processing techniques preclude humanistic methods from their operations because of the very assumptions on which they are designed: that objects of knowledge can be understood as self-identical, self-evident, ahistorical, and autonomous.

Within a humanistic theoretical frame, all of these are precepts that have been subject to serious critical rethinking. So can we engage in the design of digital environments that embody specific theoretical principles drawn from the humanities, not merely work within platforms and protocols created by disciplines whose methodological premises are often at odds with—even hostile to—humanistic values and thought? This question is particularly pressing in light of the absorption of these visualization techniques, since they come entirely from realms outside the humanities—management, social sciences, natural sciences, business, economics, military surveillance, entertainment, gaming, and other fields in which the relativistic and comparative methods of the humanities play, at best, a small and accessory role. While it may seem like an extreme statement, I think the ideology of almost all current information visualization is anathema to humanistic thought, antipathetic to its aims and values. The persuasive and seductive rhetorical force of visualization performs such a powerful reification of information that graphics such as Google Maps are taken to be simply a presentation of "what is," as if all critical thought had been precipitously and completely jettisoned. Therefore, this is a critical moment to identify core theoretical issues in the humanities and develop digital platforms that arise from these principles.

At their base—which is to say, in the encoded protocols of operating systems, machine languages, compilers, and programming—computational environments are fundamentally resistant to qualitative approaches. We can cast an interpretative gaze on these instruments from a humanistic perspective, and we can build humanities content on their base; but we have rarely imagined creating computational protocols grounded in humanistic theory and methods. Is this even possible? Desirable? I suggest that it is essential if we are to assert the cultural authority of the humanities in a world whose fundamental medium is digital that we demonstrate that the methods and theory of the humanities have a critical purchase on the design of platforms that embody humanistic values. Humanistic methods are necessarily probabilistic rather than deterministic, performative rather than declarative. To incorporate these methods, more advanced models of simulation than the literal techniques of current visualization will need to be designed.

The humanistic tradition is not a unified monolith, and any values I suggest here, or methods, will simply reflect my own disposition and training. But I think we can fairly say that the intellectual traditions of aesthetics, hermeneutics, and interpretative practices (critical editing, textual studies, historical research) are core to the humanities. These all have their own histories, of course, and in the twentieth century humanistic assumptions were subjected to systematic critique. The insights gleaned from poststructuralism, postcolonialism, and deconstruction altered our understanding of notions of meaning, truth, authorship, identity, subjectivity, power relations, bodies, minds, nations, intelligence, nature, and almost any other ontological category of cultural thought. Computation and digital techniques have been subject to plenty of rich discussion along deconstructive and postcolonial lines. But the distinction on which I am trying to call for a next phase of digital humanities would synthesize method and theory into ways of doing as thinking. This is different from the (albeit important and insightful) directions set by digital forensics, code studies, and other analyses of digital materiality and its implications. (Kirschenbaum; Wardrip-Fruin)

The challenge is to shift humanistic study from attention to the *effects* of technology (from readings of social media, games, narrative, personae, digital texts, images, environments), to a humanistically informed theory of the *making* of technology (a humanistic computing at the level of design, modeling of information architecture, data types, interface, and protocols). To theorize humanities approaches to digital scholarship we need to consider the role of affect, notions of non–self-identicality of all expressions, the force of a constructivist approach to knowledge as knowing, observer dependent, emergent, and process-driven rather than entity-defined.

Let's backtrack a moment and review some of the ways humanistic thinking has been incorporated into digital scholarship, since some useful insights can be carried forward from this summary.

As the first phase of digital humanities reveals, the exigencies of computational method reflect its origins in the automation of calculation. Counting, sorting, searching, and finding nonambiguous instances of discrete and identifiable strings of information coded in digital form are the capacities on which digital technology performed the tasks of corpus linguistics to create Father Busa's concordance. The power of automation depended on principles that are basically *ahumanistic* principles. The creation of the concordance does not depend on interpretation even if the resulting work supports it, even if it offers a powerful instrument for extending the capacities of humanistic scholars.

The phase of digital humanities that began in the 1990s was characterized by an abundance of critical editing and repository building. Both depended on elaboration of substantial metadata and also engagement with markup languages. The scholars involved in this work certainly understood clearly the rhetorical force of argument that was embodied in the information structures they created to model content types and organize data structures. My own direct involvement with digital humanities came at the end of the 1990s, as the Perseus Project; Blake, Whitman, and Rossetti archives; the Women Writers Project; and other large-scale complex editions and repositories were already well developed. Much critical thinking was involved in the construction of these undertakings, and mature discussions of content modeling, metadata, and markup all had philosophical dimensions to them. But as one of my colleagues was fond of saying, humanists came into those conversations as relativists and left as positivists out of pragmatic recognition that certain tenets of critical theory could not be sustained in that environment. Getting the work done—putting texts into digital formats with markup that identified content—might be an interpretative exercise, but introducing ambiguity at the level of markup was untenable, not merely impractical.

Discussions about the limits of markup languages were a sign of the maturing field. Debates at the end of the 1990s focused keen attention on the ways the hierarchical structure of XML was antithetical to the formal structure of aesthetic works. The realization did not lead to new methods grounded in humanistic theory. Arguments emerged; discussion was heated, insights profound, then scholars shrugged and went back to coding. The basic conclusion was that to play in a digital sandbox one had to follow the rules of computation: disambiguation and making explicit what was so often implicit in humanities work was the price of entry. The benefits outweighed the liabilities. The capacity to aggregate all versions of Blake's prints, to assemble the many witnesses and expressions of Rossetti's double works in a single web environment in which their relations could be studied, annotated, made evident for the first time—these were remarkable leaps beyond the printed approach that had defined the horizon of possibility just a few years earlier. The combination of digital tools and networked environments pushed scholarship to a new level.

But if this is what the encounter of humanities work and digital tools was like, then what could the encounter of humanities "tools" bring to digital contexts?

The question has more in it than a simple shift of emphasis. The tools in scare quotes stands for precepts, theoretical approaches, basic ways of thinking that are fundamentally different in the two realms. Humanities approaches would proceed from a number of very specific principles. The first of these is that interpretation is performative, not mechanistic—in other words, no text is self-identical; each instance or reading constructs a text; discourses create their objects; texts (in the broad sense of linguistic, visual, acoustic, filmic works) are not static objects but encoded provocations for reading. These are familiar arguments within the digital and broader humanities community, and finding ways of showing these principles informed our work at SpecLab, particularly in the realization of the Ivanhoe platform. The project of showing interpretation, modeling it, making a composition space in which ambiguity and contradiction can coexist, where the non–self-identicality of objects can be made as evident as their codependent relation to the social fields of production from which they spring (a relation premised on the constructedness of their identity, rather than the relation of an "object" to a "context") remains undone. Perhaps it is undoable, since the very instantiation of an interpretative act would reify it in ways that create at least the illusion (or delusion) of fixity. That built-in paradox does not obviate the need to experiment with humanistic precepts in the design of digital environments, however; and that takes me to the current situation.

As we turn our attention from that first phase of textual studies and critical editing, we see the phenomena I noted appear on the horizon: data mining with all its attendant visualization techniques, engagement with geospatial tools, and the use of timelines and other graphic conventions from fields rooted in empirical investigation, management, and social sciences where predictable outcomes and repeatable results are at the desired outcomes even if they are not absolute tenets of belief. The graphical tools that are used for statistical display depend, in the first instance, on quantitative data, information that can be parameterized so that it lends itself to display. Virtually no humanistic data lends itself to such parameterization (e.g., what year should a publication be dated to in the long history of its production and reception?), and it is in fact precisely in the impossibility of creating metrics appropriate to humanistic artifacts that the qualitative character of *capta*, that which is taken as interpretation rather than *data*, comes sharply into relief.

But if the premises on which quantitative information might be abstracted from texts or corpora raise one set of issues, the use of graphical techniques from social and natural sciences raise others. Graphs and charts reify statistical information. They give it a look of certainty. Only a naive viewer, unskilled and untrained in matters of statistics or critical thought, would accept an information visualization at face value. But most humanists share with their social and natural science colleagues a willingness to accept the use of standard metrics and conventions without question in the production of these graphs (e.g., using the same sized unit for all hours of the day seems bizarre for a humanist charting the narrative of *Mrs. Dalloway* or film critic analyzing *Memento*). Even the supposedly simple act of counting entities in any study, for instance, raises a host of questions, while creating a chart on which to graph the information immediately throws the untrained humanist into a world where the difference between a bar chart and a continuous graph should be understood in professional terms. Amateur chart making provides a rash of examples of ways not to do things with numbers, but we are still only in the baby pool of information visualization, and already the waters are perilous to navigate. Statisticians are concerned with probabilities, not certainties. They do not count things; they model conditions and possible outcomes. Data mining in the humanities has largely depended on counting, sorting, ordering techniques—in essence, some automated calculations. Statistical modeling has factored less, at least to date, in the analytic tool kit of critical digital work with texts. Stylometrics, attribution studies, natural language processing, and other higher level analyses have long made use of these sophisticated modeling techniques, but graphing ambiguous and partial knowledge is still in its early stages. Archaeologists who work in reconstruction, trying to extrapolate various models of possible form from fragmentary remains, have created spectral palimpsestic methods of portraying uncertainty in their digital imagery. Some conventions from art history and architectural study include an inventory of techniques for indicating distinctions between known and projected or imagined evidence.

Probability is not the same as ambiguity or multivalent possibility within the field of humanistic inquiry. The task of calculating norms, medians, means, and averages will never be the same as the task of engaging with anomalies and taking their details as the basis of an argument. Statistics and pataphysics will never meet on the playing fields of shared understanding. They play different games, not just the same game with different rules. However, the dialogue among probabilistic methods, modeling, and visualization holds much promise for humanistic work ahead as the shift from counting and sorting to predicting and presenting uncertainty advances in the digital humanities.

But once we depart from the realms of probability into the world of empirical or positivist representation, the friendly atmosphere evaporates. The theoretical underpinnings of humanistic interpretation are fundamentally at odds with the empirical approaches on which certain conventions of temporal and spatial modeling are based. All maps are constructions, and the history of cartography, like the histories of other graphical forms of knowledge, is filled with productive debates about the ideological and rhetorical force of mapping techniques. Humanists are certainly well aware of these complexities, but the tendency to wave them aside as mere nuance in the rush to adopt Google Maps or a standard projection, even knowing full well that any presentation of an oblate spheroid (the earth) onto a flat surface (map or screen), is fraught. But more is at stake for a humanist than the technical problems of projection. Both space and time are constructs, not givens. As constructs they come into being in a codependent relation with their discursive or experiential production. If I am anxious, spatial and temporal dimensions are distinctly different than when I am not. When the world was bounded by the Mediterranean it was a different world than the one seen from space. These are not different versions of the same thing. The entire theoretical weight of constructivist approaches to knowledge stands against such a reductive pronouncement.

But the social, cultural, experiential, psychological, and phenomenological aspects of spatial and temporal modeling have had very little play in the history of graphical expressions. No space is a given, and no standard metric adequately serves the analysis and presentation of temporal experience. When we expand this discussion to include the spatial and temporal richness of cultural artifacts, the vision of a complex worldview begins to beg for digital means of exposure.

Start with a simple example to make the case. What kind of map should be used to show the locations in which cuneiform tablets were produced in the ancient near east? The configuration of linguistic boundaries and social groupings within the Mesopotamian region would offer one version of that geography. A simple outline of landmasses and landforms would offer another. A map with modern nation-states outlined for easy reference to current events and contemporary place names would offer another. None are commensurate with each other. None present the experience of geography within which the tablets were produced. How do we understand the geographically specific references to lands or cities within those texts if they are only points on a contemporary map? Most pernicious of all, because it is so ubiquitous, is the already cited Google Maps. The reification performed by a digital photography imaging system trumps in the "this is what is" game. Put the average person in front of one of those screens, and they believe they are seeing *the* world, not a constructed version of it. Savvy as we are, the concessions made in the name of efficacy may turn out to have too heavy a price if we cannot imagine alternative spatial models for experienced and situated approaches. Once those aerial maps come into play, they set a baseline against which historical maps are referenced. Then the assumption built into the analysis is that the other images are deviations from that photographic record of Google satellite. My point is not so much that we are naive users, as we may or may not be, but that the force that photographic renderings carry when they are used as the ground on which other images are referenced makes it very difficult to dislodge the subtler conviction that these satellite images are the "real" earth.

If spatial location is problematic and needs historical and cultural relativization from the outset, then navigation and motion through and across landscapes as a construction of space introduce another level of challenge. In a striking visualization created for the digital project *Mapping the Republic of Letters*, letters between eighteenth-century correspondents move from one geographic location to another as if by airmail. The perfect lines of light, looking for all the world like a contemporary graphic of air traffic, make the connection between the point of origin and place of delivery a smooth, seamless, unitary motion. All letters move at the same speed in this simulation, and all leave and arrive as if by airmail. No matter that the shape of coastlines and borders have changed or that methods of travel involved many kinds of detours, checks, delays, and roundabout routes at varying speeds and through multiple levels of diplomatic negotiations with official or unofficial interlopers. How would the variable spatial relations of communications be modeled to show these complexities? If that were possible, then the humanistic principles of cultural and historical constructions of space would be the foundation from which the visualization would arise. As it is, humanities scholars attach their analysis to the armature of preexisting graphical conventions. The primary strategy for undoing the force of reification is to introduce parallax and difference, thus taking apart any possible claim to *the* self-evident or self-identical presentation of knowledge and replacing this with a recognition of the made-ness and constructedness that inhere in *any* representation of knowledge.

Humanistic conventions for the graphical production of spatial knowledge and interpretation would spring from the premises of situatedness and enunciation. By situatedness, I am gesturing toward the principle that humanistic expression is always observer dependent. A text is produced by a reading; it exists within the hermeneutic circle of production. Scientific knowledge is no different, of course, except that its aims are toward a consensus of repeatable results that allow us to posit with a degree of certainty what the qualities of a frog are by contrast with those of a cat. We take such distinctions to be observer independent even if the system according to which we represent, name, analyze, arrive at, and value these distinctions is subject to the same analytic principles as any other expression of human knowledge. By enunciation I am suggesting we bring the idea of spatial relations in digital humanities back into conversation with the principles elaborated in film studies, architecture, cultural geography, and visual and textual studies that took seriously the analysis of ways representational systems produce a spoken subject as well as engage a speaking subject within their "regimes," as we used to say. Situatedness and enunciation are intimately bound to each other, though the first resides more squarely in individual experience and its representation, the second in the cultural systems that speak through us and produce us as social subjects. This is not the place to go back through deconstruction and poststructuralist thought and its legacy but, rather, to sketch ways these principles could inform digital humanities work going forward.

If we embark on a project to study inscriptions in the Roman forum, for instance, should we simply take a virtual simulation, a fly-through model made on a standard 3-D software platform and place the writing on the variously appropriate surfaces? Or should the ways signage works as an articulation of space, the "species of spaces" described by Georges Perec, be merged in a mash-up of Christopher Alexander's "pattern language" with Gaston Bachelard's poetics of space and the Foucauldian analysis of spatialized regimes of disciplinary control structured into and structuring architectural and social relations? A ridiculous proposition emerges from that impossible sentence. Or does it? The principles of humanistic spatial modeling arise from a system of enunciation, as a system, in which eyelines, scale, proportion, surface texture, lighting, color, depth, openings, routes of egress, degrees of security, and other tractable elements might be given a value so that the space is constructed as an effect, rather than a basis, of experience. Without minimalizing the complexity involved in realizations and aware of the risk of cartoonish special effects, my point is that by not addressing these possibilities we cede the virtual ground to a design sensibility based in engineering and games. The risk is that the persuasive force of such representations tips the balance of belief; the Roman forum of a virtual world becomes far more satisfying and real than the fragmentary evidence and analytic complexity on which humanistic scholarship arises. But the partial nature of knowledge is another crucial tenet of humanistic belief, and rendering a seamless image of "what is" prevents the imaginative critical faculties from engaging with the all important question of "what if?" The parallax views that arise in the interstices of fragmentary evidence are what give humanistic thought its purchase on the real, even with full acknowledgment that knowing is always a process of codependencies.

To finish the examples and summarize these premises, I return to the unfinished project of modeling temporality. Temporal coordinates, like spatial ones, contain many variations across history, culture, and individual experience. The experience of temporality, like that of space, is already inflected by cultural circumstance. We feel time differently, because it is a different kind of time, than other generations. Life expectancy, control over lighting, and mechanical clocks and their presence in daily routines are all structuring features of the contemporary experience of time that are fundamentally different from those of, say, citizens of Augustan Rome, pre-conquest Mayan communities, or seventeenth-century French aristocrats. Understanding the basic experience of time is a subject of humanistic research that already differentiates it from the "time" imagined by researchers checking the frequency of urination in lab rats or number of commuters on a stretch of highway during certain hours of a commute.

Within humanistic documents, time is as frequently noted in relativistic terms as in absolute ones. As the community of "tensers" makes clear, the notions of before and after, expressions of temporal sequence in the forms of verbs and auxiliaries, are evidence of the richness of expression in relation to the tensions between ambiguity and certainty in linguistic communications. The time described in aesthetic texts has other features, with its marked discontinuities, the discrepancy between times of telling and times of the told, between flashbacks and foreshadowings, recollection and anticipation. These are all features of temporality within the horizon of humanistic inquiry and study. We know these characteristics and work with them without any difficulty, except when it comes to using graphical means of expression or analysis. Then the distinction between time and temporality evaporates in the fallback position of taking timelines as an adequate measure on which to map the complexities of historical and aesthetic experience.

The experience of temporality; the representation of that experience; the temporal dimensions of narration and mutabilities of duration, extension, telescoping contraction, and explosive expansion all need a graphical language for analysis as well as for the presentation of argument. Relations among various documents and artifacts within a corpus raise another set of tangled theoretical issues, since rates at which different members of a communication network send or receive information produce the circumstances in which they collectively imagine a sequence of events. The very notion of an "event horizon" cannot be standardized within a single frame. Each participant's sense of when an event occurred will differ, and hence the liabilities of diplomacy and delicacies of policy decisions within varying temporal assumptions.

And what of incommensurate temporalities within a single frame? If I chart my life according to segments based on places I have lived, the units of time and the relation among them has one shape, still not consistent since, as with most humans, I assign the eons of childhood a different value from the fleeting units of adult life. But what if I try to divide my life into segments according to relationships, affective connections, and emotional ties? What are the seasons of the heart, the dimensions of trauma? How long does something last? This segmentation, or impossibility of even making a segmentation, does not match the first exercise. These are incommensurate chronologies and yet within a single life, and some shared milestones connect these different versions of the lived.

The original project of temporal modeling, conceived a decade ago, engaged these issues and developed a basis on which to make a graphical authoring space that would express some of these principles. Our computational muscle was not adequate for the task. I return to the points raised earlier about engaging with probabilistic systems rather than deterministic ones that rely on discrete or fixed frames of reference or standard metrics. Flexible metrics, variable, discontinuous, and multidimensional will be necessary to realize a humanistic system for the graphical analysis of temporal relations.

Just as the attempt to place James Joyce's spatial references onto a literal street map of Dublin defeats the metaphoric and allusive use of spatial reference in *Ulysses*, flattening all the imaginative spatial experience that infuses the text with images of an urban imaginary irreducible to its material counterpart, so the task of putting pins into a Google map or charting the times of lived experience on a single unvarying linear scale is a grotesque distortion—not merely of humanistic approaches to knowledge as interpretation, but the very foundation from which they arise. The modern paradigms of logic and rationality, now thoroughly subjected to post-Cartesian critique, underpin those visualizations, those seemingly self-evident maps and charts. But the humanities are not a mere afterthought, simply studying and critiquing the effects of computational methods.

Humanistic theory provides ways of thinking differently, otherwise, specific to the problems and precepts of interpretative knowing—partial, situated, enunciative, subjective, and performative. Our challenge is to take up these theoretical principles and engage them in the production of methods, ways of doing our work on an appropriate foundation. The question is not, Does digital humanities need theory? but rather, How will digital scholarship be humanistic without it?

BIBLIOGRAPHY

Kirschenbaum, Matthew. *Mechanisms: New Media and the Forensic Imagination*. Cambridge, Mass.: MIT Press, 2008.

McGann, Jerome J. *Radiant Textuality*. New York: Palgrave Macmillan, 2001.

Moretti, Franco. "Conjectures on World Literature." *New Left Review*. January–February 2000. http://www.newleftreview.org/A2094.

The Perseus Archive. http://www.perseus.tufts.edu.

The Republic of Letters. http://shc.stanford.edu/collaborations/supported-projects/mapping-republic-letters.

The Rossetti Archive. http://www.rossettiarchive.org.

The Walt Whitman Archive. http://www.whitmanarchive.org/.

Wardrip-Fruin, Noah. *Expressive Processing*. Cambridge, Mass.: MIT Press, 2009.

The Willam Blake Archive. http://www.blakearchive.org/.

The Women Writers Project. http://www.wwp.brown.edu.

This Digital Humanities Which Is Not One

JAMIE "SKYE" BIANCO

Aggression

> Cultural Studies . . . ephemera. Irrelevant.
>
> Critical theory, I mean, let's be honest, what did it ever do politically?
>
> While historians continued to ponder the pros and cons of quantitative methods and while the profession increasingly turned to cultural studies, or took the "linguistic turn," as some have called the move toward the textual and French theory, computer scientists were hammering out a common language for shared files over the Internet.

I offer these three quotations in order to frame a set of problems; and, to be clear, the authors of these three synecdochal snippets do not share much in common beyond a particular advocacy for what is now ubiquitously termed *the* digital humanities.[1]

The first citation, taken from an informal conversation with a senior colleague who self-defines as a computational humanist within a literary specialization, marks what might be thought of as two mutated legacies reemerging in contemporary digital humanities discourse: first, a tendency to treat cultural objects as enclosed, rational systems that may be fully transcoded computationally and, second, an *old* humanist tendency to claim the irrelevance and disavow the privilege of position and deterministic stratifications, which are lived by those outside a centrifugal or privileged referent through a variety of identity-based isms marking the leverage of political, economic, and social power relations. We might think of this twofold movement as an echo of T. S. Eliot's advocacy of "a continual extinction of personality [by the artist]" such that "in this depersonalization . . . art may be said to approach the condition of [so-called objective] science" ("Tradition and the Individual Talent," 10).[2]

The second quotation, more of a digital humanities inflected echo (of the Jacques Derrida, François Cussett, and Stanley Fish circuit[3]) than a statement of invention, was spoken informally in a group discussing methodology. The conversation focused on the inadequacy of print-based critical methods in the wake of informatically and computationally informed practices.[4] I share a sense of the complex limitations of the critical enterprise; and, while I find myself often describing why I feel, as Bruno Latour phrases it, "critique [has] run out of steam," it is rather surprising to repeatedly encounter the assertion that critique (often framed in a denigrated reference to "French theory") ran on a historical rail of impotence and trivialized academic navel gazing rather than running across a historically situated duration that has since changed nontrivially.

The third quotation, taken from William G. Thomas II's "Computing and the Historical Imagination," was published in the well-known, early collection *A Companion to Digital Humanities* (edited by Susan Schreibman, Ray Siemens, and John Unsworth) that, as the origin story is told, gave *the* digital humanities, our computational Adam, *his* name. What Thomas offers in this foundational, tripartite narrative is a history of recent academic history, locating together the segregated emergence of quantitative analysis, cultural studies, and the linguistic turn with the development (by computer scientists) of the Internet. He goes on to infer a clear, if not genetic, relationship between the quantitative analysis (performed with computers) in the computational humanities and the computational work that made the Internet. Thomas includes the narrative of Vannevar Bush's vision of the memex, essentially an imagined apparatus for archiving and data mining, but he does not point to Tim Berners-Lee's vision of a web of shared knowledge, culture and semantic content, which might reassemble the collective emergence of quantitative analysis, cultural studies, "the linguistic turn," and computational networks.

Ethos and Difference

Taken together, what constellations of politics are emerging through the digital humanities? And while one might legitimately ask whether the digital humanities has any acknowledged politics, I would specify my usage of the term. By the word "politics," I am asking what power relations have emerged. And because the digital humanities operates through a web of politics, people, institutions, and technics in a network of uneven, albeit ubiquitous, relations, perhaps the question might be more accurately framed as one of ethics. Does the digital humanities need an ethology or an ethical turn? Simply put, yes.

The three anecdotal moments at the head of this essay are meant to point to unsettling substrates growing in the debates of a set of fields that, until a year or two ago, were known by many names, sub- and extra-academic and disciplinary practices. What quick, concatenating, and centrifugal forces have so quickly rendered the many under the name of one, *the* digital humanities? What's in this name, its histories, legacies, and privileged modalities that assert centrality over and against differentials? Digital and multimodal compositionists, digital and new media producers, game designers, electronic literati, visual and screen studies, and theorists of any sort (French, Italian, or cosmopolite): what sort of bastards or stepchildren have we become under this nomos? And this is a grouping merely predicated on professional difference, because at the heart of the three citations I quote at the head of this essay lies an uneasy, if not abject, relationship to difference. The title of my essay, as I hope many readers will know, refers to Luce Irigaray's famous feminist essay and book, *This Sex Which Is Not One*, wherein "one" is defined as "the universal standard and privileged form in our systems of representation, oneness expresses the requirements for unitary representations of signification and identity. Within such a system, in which the masculine standard takes itself as a universal, it would be impossible to represent the duality or plurality of the female [or any other] sex" (Irigarary, 221).

It's been a long time since I've quoted a feminist like a sledgehammer, but something about the new, posttheoretical humanities, the digital humanities, smells a bit like its self- (and other-) enlightened, progress-driven, classifying, rationalizing, and disciplining (grand)father.

I feel deep political, intellectual, and pedagogical concern regarding current dominant narratives and dialogues circulating not just through problematic historical frameworks but also around the need to establish identity in order to blueprint the future of the digital humanities. The Tunisian uprising made for the first true Twitter or Internet revolution, true only in the sense that the events were socially mediated from Tunisia, assisting the actions of a people who changed a localized political situation. At the very same moment, the Twitter stream emerging from a panel focusing on the future of the digital humanities at the Modern Language Association (MLA) predominantly voiced concerns about "who's in and who's out" of the digital humanities as well as discussions of an emergent academic star network from within the field.[5] More historically framed, the contemporary drift of noncontent and nonproject-based discussions in the digital humanities often echoes the affective techno-euphoria of the libertarian (white, masculinist, meritocratic) tech boom in the 1990s with its myopic focus on tools and technicity and whose rhetorical self-positioning is expressed as that of a deserving but neglected community finally rising up to their properly privileged social and professional prestige. Unrecognized privilege? From this position, no giant leap of logic is required to understand the allergic aversion to cultural studies and critical theory that has been circulating. It's time for a discussion of the politics and particularly the ethics of the digital humanities as a set of relationships and practices within and outside of institutional structures.

The Call

Over and again, we hear an informal refrain, "The people in digital humanities are so nice!" Tom Scheinfeldt makes this assertion point blank in his blog post "Why

Digital Humanities is 'Nice'": "Digital humanities is nice because we're often more concerned with method than we are with theory. Why should a focus on method make us nice? Because methodological debates are often more easily resolved than theoretical ones." I'm not sure I follow the logic of the conclusion here, as "easily resolved" debates could just as easily point to uneven power relations or to passive aggression as much as to niceness. And putting aside the implication that methods and theory are separable, the questionable status of self-description, the sociopsychological implications of conflict avoidance, and the values of "niceness" and its "niceties" in global-knowledge work and the digital economies through which we circulate, we must ask ourselves what sort of social narrative is this—one that smoothes out potential social differences before conflict sets in? Is this the substrate for our ethics and for a theorization of the social? Who does it include and what (self- and other-) disciplines must we practice and propagate?[6]

In fact, from my experience, when issues of social, cultural, political, and theoretical origin are raised in discussions of the digital humanities among self-identified digital humanists, several versions of the same response consistently occur, and none of them is "nice." Responses range from hostility to defensiveness to utter dismissal to an accusatory mimicry of a grossly oversimplified understanding of Big Theory, as the phrase "the linguistic turn" and the lack of reference to theory as social, cultural, or political alludes. This set of responses redounds with a trumpeted faith in technocratic and instrumental means through which the digital humanities (DH) will serve up technocratic and instrumental solutions. Boiled down blithely, the theory is in the tool, and we code tools. Clearly, this position never refers to Audre Lorde's famous essays on tools nor to "the uses of anger," but it does summon their politics ("The Master's Tools Will Never Dismantle the Master's House" and "The Uses of Anger: Women Responding to Racism," in Lorde, *Sister Outsider and Other Essays*). Let me be clear: I am a digital/multimodal compositionist, a digital media practitioner, a feminist, and a critical media theorist whose ethics lie in progressive affiliation and collaborative social justice. This is not a rant against the machine or the tool. This is a rant against the resurgence of an old humanist theme, "Man and His Tool(s)." Tools don't reflect upon their own making, use, or circulation or upon the constraints under which their constitution becomes legible, much less attractive to funding. They certainly cannot account for their circulations and relations, the discourses and epistemic constellations in which they resonate. They cannot take responsibility for the social relations they inflect or control. Nor do they explain why only 10 percent of today's computer science majors are women, a huge drop from 39 percent in 1984 (Stross), and 87 percent of Wikipedia editors—that would be the first-tier online resource for information after a Google search—are men (Wikimedia). Tools may track and compile data around these questions, visualize and configure it through interactive interfaces and porous databases, but what then? What do *we do* with the data?

Digital humanists must seriously question, maybe even interrogate, to use critical terminology, our roles in the legitimization and institutionalization of computational and digital media in the humanistic nodes of the academy and in liberal arts education and not simply defend the legitimacy (or advocate for the "obvious" supremacy) of computational practices out of a ressentiment-filled righteousness that crudely tends toward a technicist culture and jockeys for position in this climate of growing institutional clout. After all, aren't critical and analytical modes of knowledge production and reception a methodological cache and database, elaborated by technological and techno-scientific practices, and one that might lend some sense of ethical direction for reinvestment in the word "humanities"? Or are the humanities in our title simply the catchall historical referent for our objects of interest and the digital simply the instrumental application that now zeros (and ones) out all previous modes of application?

Again, let me say, this is not a rant against code or computation. I believe and teach that learning to code is an essential and fundamental practice of literacy in our culture, but one among many critical literacy practices. This is a rant against the wielding of computation and code as instrumental, socially neutral or benevolent, and theoretically and politically transparent, not to mention its role in the sequel to "DH Is So Nice," the newly authored farce "The Humanist Geeks' Revenge." In this story, code circulates as the new secret password that allows its bearers to gain entry into what has been consistently and grotesquely referred to as "the cool kids' table" occupied by digital humanists.[7] Is this field actually constructing itself through the competing narratives of privileged, middle-class, white, high-school politics in tension with privileged, middle-class, white people who work "nicely" together? Let me simply suggest that factoring recent events involving social and networked media, social and corporeal violence, bodies, collaboration, and asymmetrical power relations in Tunisia, Egypt, Yemen, Syria, and Pakistan (and these are just a few recent headlines) into the discussions of DH, sociality, ethics, theory, and practices might afford a valuable shift in current perspectives (and on the topic of navel gazing) in the digital humanities.

Where Do You Want to Go Today?

> If code and software are to become objects of research for the humanities and social sciences, including philosophy, we will need to grasp both the ontic and ontological dimensions of computer code. Broadly speaking, then, this paper suggests that we take a philosophical approach to the subject of computer code, paying attention to the wider aspects of code and software, and connecting them to the materiality of this growing digital world. With this in mind, the question of code becomes central to understanding in the digital humanities, and serves as a condition of possibility for the many computational forms that mediate out experience of contemporary culture and society. (Berry)

As Berry's conclusion points out, "we will need to grasp both the ontic and ontological dimensions of computer code," and so we must ask, how might we do this? How might we suss out the qualities and materialities of code, from the most primitive to compiled and networked deployments? And to Berry's assertion, I would add the essential follow-up question, how might we grasp the ontic and ontological dimensions of relational and affective embodiment—human and nonhuman, animate and nonanimate—in a networked, computational, and codified milieu? Recently, we've seen a winnowing of what was an experimental and heterogeneous emergence of computational and digital practices, teaching and theorization from within and across disciplines to an increasingly narrow, highly technical, and powerful set of conservative and constrained areas and modes of digital research. In "Reckoning with Standards," in *Standards and Their Stories: How Quantifying, Classifying, and Formalizing Practices Shape Everyday Life*, Martha Lampland and Susan Leigh Star write of this capacity for constraining standards to "embody ethics and values" such that "to standardize an action, process, or thing means, at some level to screen out unlimited diversity. At times, it may mean to screen out even limited diversity" (8). They go on to discuss how these standardizations can be linked to "economic assessments" (8). This overcoding and compression of protofields and specific computational practices into the field of the digital humanities is directly linked to the institutional funding that privileges canonical literary and historiographic objects and narratives. These disciplinarily legible projects garner high exposure and at times media coverage, presenting a justification for the field based on its kinship to much older modes of humanistic study than those from which we have most recently "posted" and harking back to the study of high literature or true (mapable, visualized data) histories, narratives of enlightenment wiped clean of their problematic grounds. This is a turn back to an older humanism, a retro-humanism, one that preceded work in the humanities and social sciences of the last fifty-odd years and that expanded its ethics and methods to include cultural and critical critique; political, institutional, and governmental analyses; feminism, critical race, postcolonial, queer, and affect studies; biopolitics; critical science and technology studies; experimental methodologies; social theory; and, certainly, philosophical inquiry into the ontic and ontological. New methods, tools, technics, and approaches—Moretti's "distant reading," for example—have been welcome evolutions with provocative expository and critical value, but these additions to the humanities need not mean distant ethics and a severing off of critique and cultural studies. It need not mean that any of these modes will operate as they have in earlier historical moments, either. Our material and historical circumstances change.

Fortunately, we are not required to choose between the philosophical, critical, cultural, and computational; we *are* required to integrate and to experiment. And this analysis and integration need also include the widening schism and reimposition of hierarchies growing between research and teaching institutions and analogically between research and pedagogy. The heterogeneous constituencies of the digital humanities still have such tremendous opportunities to open up research modes, methods, practices, objects, narratives, locations of expertise, learning and teaching, the academy, the "crisis" in liberal arts education, and the ethics through which we engage knowledge practices at work in a global context. This is not a moment to abdicate the political, social, cultural, and philosophical, but rather one for an open discussion of their inclusion in the ethology and methods of the digital humanities.

Creative Critique: Making Digital Research, One Experiment with Method

Rather than continue this aggressive bent, or what I think of as the negativity of critique, I would like to offer a theoretically informed experimentation with method that I am pursuing that aims at a generative constellation of critique, cultural studies, literacy, pedagogy, affect, and digital computation. Context is a difference engine, especially if the work is humanistic. Sharon Daniel, activist and tactical media artist, makes this case well:

> I refuse to stand outside the context I provide. As a context provider, I am more immigrant than ethnographer, crossing over from the objective to the subjective, from the theoretical to the anecdotal, from authority . . . to unauthorized alien. As an academic I was once reluctant to include my own story when theorizing my work. But my position is not neutral; in theory or in practice, that would be an impossible place. So I have crossed over into . . . "the anecdotal," where theorizing and storytelling, together, constitute an intervention and a refusal to accept reality as it is. By employing a polyphony of voices, including my own, in order to challenge audiences to rethink the paradoxes of social exclusion that attend the lives of those who suffer from poverty, racism, and addiction, my work fulfills the role that new media documentary practices [must play]— . . . context provision. (159)

This manifesto is an attempt at an ethical relationality that underwrites the design and implementation of Sharon's technological work (from the user interface to the database). But she also calls for an affective mode of composing, the drive to produce sensations, feelings, context, and movement. The theory, design, and implementation of her work are also aesthetic relationalities derived from what I see, along with Bruno Latour, as the necessity to construct, to *make* a felt and critical mode of thinking, an open and affective intervention that, while circuiting through tracks of lived and theoretical violence, does not enact them. The construction of context as an affective interaction and circuit is what I refer to as composing creative critical media: a performative interaction, composed affectively through the production of discursive and extradiscursive sensations in order to effect a synaesthetic rhetoric—felt, seen, and heard—that forges ethical relations out of the captured, inventoried, and composed remains or ruins of injustice, harm, violence, and devastation, out of the social and political conditions in which we find ourselves. When this affective design works, it is creative and critical, rhetorical and aesthetic, embodied and virtual, activating and meaning filled, fully social, ethical and political. But this is a later stage of the process. Let me slow down.

Let's begin again with this funny term "creative critique," and I will return to drawing out a reemerging tendency from New Criticism with which I began this essay and from which I understand some of the current intolerance in the digital humanities to cultural studies and critical theory to be predicated. If we have read our T. S. Eliot, we might take the term "creative criticism" to be an oxymoron as we understand the *function* of criticism: "If so large a part of creation is really criticism, is not a large part of what is called 'critical writing' really creative? If so, is there not creative criticism in the ordinary sense? The answer seems to be, that there is no equation I have assumed as axiomatic that a creation, a work of art, is autotelic; and that criticism, by definition, is *about* something other than itself. Hence you cannot fuse creation with criticism as you can fuse criticism with creation" ("The Function of Criticism, [1923]"). Eliot's distinction between creation and criticism is predicated on a compositional response (as opposed to, say, reception or delivery) and the unidirectional *functionality* of criticism toward a given "creation," or aesthetic object. This distinction correlates to the contemporary role of digital "tools" in relation to humanistic objects of study. Tools are also *about* something other than themselves. Eliot is, of course, responding to an ongoing debate that, as we know, tracks back to the ancients and certainly to the Aristotelian separation of the poetics from rhetoric, technē from *physis*. At this moment, though, the New Criticism is finding its legs in an instrumentalization of criticism, a scientification of the methods and analog codifications and classifications of humanistic inquiry. This separation of criticism from its objects, its one-way functionality, and the invention of New Critical vocabulary understood as a set of tools has continued to enjoy long-lived deployments, long after the turn away from New Criticism as interpretive method. Yet there are other histories in this New Critical moment, debates now absent from the dominant canon and archive of literary studies (and recoverable in this instance through my poststructural and theoretical training in genealogical historicism). In 1931, just a few years after Eliot's "The Function of Criticism," J. E. Spingarn, a modernist critic few of us are likely to remember or know, published a collection of essays titled *Creative Criticism and Other Essays* in which he responds directly and indirectly to Eliot's assertion of a distinctive *function* of criticism by shifting the register of Eliot's compositional *about*: "Aesthetics takes me still farther afield into speculations on art and beauty. And so it is with every form of Criticism. Do not deceive yourself. *All criticism tends to shift the interest from the work of art to something else*. The other critics give us history, politics, biography, erudition, metaphysics. As for me, I re-dream the poet's dream. . . . I at least strive to replace one work of art by another, and art can only find its *alter ego* in art" (7–8, emphasis added). Thus, for Spingarn, objects lead to or associate with other objects such that, rather than objectified classifications, these objects form a *network*, a constellation of aboutness or interobjective referentiality that exceeds their immediate functionality and instrumentality as they become embedded in a nested and generative process of creation. In a direct way, we might understand this critical redreaming, then, as a sort of prototheory of the remix and the mash up—and certainly of digital, multimodal, inventive, creative critique.

However, one extremely significant problem remains if we are to take this strain of academic history as the basis for a contemporary ethos of computational and digital work in the academic humanities. For Eliot and Spingarn, aesthetics and creation emerge from a legacy of beauty, genius, and the sublime, a *high* art, object-centered modernism. And upon the hierarchal politics and social histories from which this understanding of aesthetics dominates New Critical discourse, the divide between criticism and critique emerges. Aesthetics, as associated with beauty and the sublime, has been a naughty word within critique and critical theory for quite some time, specifically after Theodor Adorno's critical work on aestheticism and the culture industry at large: "I constantly attempt to expose the bourgeois philosophy of idealism, which is associated with the concept of aesthetic autonomy" ("Letters to Walter Benjamin"); and, culminating in his famous quotation, "*nach Auschwitz ein Gedicht zu schreiben*" (There can be no poetry after Auschwitz), framed within the *context* of barbarity, from *Cultural Criticism and Society*, 1951. I do not have the luxury here for a full rehearsal of the movements across New Criticism, the Frankfurt School, and poststructuralism. But as computational and digital practitioners, we can no more sit back and enjoy the privileges of *our* technological sublime any more than we can disavow the ontic, political, aesthetic, technical, cultural, and pedagogical constellations constituted through and with computation and digital networks.

Recent work by Jacques Ranciere on aesthetics and critique offers a model for a generative and contextualized approach. The idealized and functionalist aesthetics of the New Critics belong to what Ranciere calls "aesthetic modernity," which relies on a particular regime, one of three that he identifies in *The Politics of Aesthetics*: "The poetic—or representative—regime of the arts [that] breaks away from the ethical regime of images" (20–21). This "ethical regime of images" offers a provocative thought mesh for computational and digital practitioners, one that is, for me, informed by Spinozian ethical relationality and by what Nicholas Bourriaud terms "relational aesthetics" or "the possibility of a relational art (an art taking as its theoretical horizon the realm of human *interactions* and its social context, rather than the assertion of an independent and private symbolic space), [which] points to a radical upheaval of the aesthetic, cultural and political goals introduced by modern art" (14, emphasis added). This concept of relations and particularly *interactions*—given the affordances of digital media—posits an opening for rethinking the roles of critique, cultural studies, and digital and computational practice through any number of digital, creative critical *interactions*.

Toni Ross pushes Bourriaud's somewhat utopian democratic concept of relational aesthetics one step further by insisting that Ranciere's work takes Bourriaud's position farther in that it "conceives of aesthetics beyond the realm of art, as the numerous ways in which a culture or society establishes, coordinates and privileges particular kinds of sensible experience or perception. His 'distribution of the sensible' produces a system of naturalized assumptions about perception based on what is allowed to be 'visible or audible, as well as what can be said, made, or done' within a particular social constellation" (172). Thus, rather than aesthetics rationally locating the innate beauty of a thing, aesthetics works procedurally in the organization of perception as an affective and embodied process. It designs and executes that which can be experienced as synaesthetically (aurally, visibly, and tacitly) legible. To intervene or critique social or political relations means to create work that offers a critical redistribution of the sensible. Representational criticism, such as interpretative analysis, does not address work at the level of ontology, the body, the affective, and the sensible. In order to get to sensation and perception, a more materially robust mode of critique is necessary. Critical theory, understood as materialist critique, offered a political corrective to interpretive criticism by populating psychosocial and political vantage points to include the receptive positions identified (and disidentified) by feminism or critical race studies, for example. But is *receptive* critique, as we understand it to circulate through the domains of cultural studies and critical theory, sufficiently ontological and sensate or sufficiently productive? At this point, no.

Keeping this revised articulation of a critical aesthetics expressed as contextual design to produce a "[re]distribution of the sensible," I want to offer a further expression of the word "critical" as it has come to function in my methodological experiments in multimodal digital production as creative critique. In 2007, Bruno Latour published an essay in *Critical Inquiry* titled "Why Has Critique Run out of Steam? From Matters of Fact to Matters of Concern," in which he begins,

> Wars. So many wars. Wars outside and wars inside. Cultural wars, science wars, and wars against terrorists. Wars against poverty and wars against the poor. Wars against ignorance and wars out of ignorance. My question is simple: Should we be at war, too, we, the scholars, the intellectuals? Is it really our duty to add fresh ruins to fields of ruins? Is it really the task of the humanities to add deconstruction to destructions? More iconoclasm to iconoclasm? What has become of critical spirit? Has it not run out of steam?

Latour's was not the first voice to raise a concern regarding the violence or negativity of receptive, critical methodologies nor to point out that critique does not offer a supplemental practice of construction to deconstruction, an active politics. Moving toward a method of constructive reception, Eve Sedgwick published *Touching Feeling: Affect, Pedagogy, Performativity* in 2003, in which she argues for reparative reading, a mode of generative interpretive reading that was meant to correct the preponderance of paranoid reading and a hermeneutics of suspicion. And while she addresses critical violence and its forcible exposures, her rhetorical tact turns to consider the characteristics and qualities that must be embodied by the receptive, passive audience for such acts: "What is the basis for assuming that it will surprise or disturb, never mind motivate, anyone to learn that a given social manifestation is artificial, self-contradictory, imitative, phantasmatic, or even violent? . . . How television-starved would someone have to be to find it shocking that ideologies contradict themselves, that simulacra don't have originals, or that gender representations are artificial?" (141). Sedgwick's turn to affect and performance theory, particularly routed through the work of Sylvan Tompkins, redirected the tendencies of critique from an epistemological milieu to a corporealized neopsychoanalytics yet still predicated on the composition of a reading. These tendencies were not entirely dissimilar to but not at all self-identical to the movements toward compositional affectivity made by Gilles Deleuze and Félix Guattari in *A Thousand Plateaux* in 1980 and throughout much of their collaborative and individual writing. Deleuze and Guattari's work, however, did not turn back toward reception and readings, nor toward the psychoanalytic, but rather toward a radical material compositionism predicated on the ethological and the ontological, fed by Baruch Spinoza, Henri Bergson, Gilbert Simondon, and others. Retrospectively, this work has come to be known as assemblage theory. Many digital media and network theorists and tactical media critics engaged Deleuze and Guattari specifically to address issues of complex powers, forces, exposures, connectivities, interactivities and nonlinear structurations in digital media.

Assemblage theory, in turn, leads us back to Latour, whose Actor Network Theory relies on both assemblage and performance. In each of these instances, an attempt to invent a production-based theoretical method is at play, methods through which the limitations, constraints, and unintended consequences of critique, forcible exposures, and practices of reading that inevitably recall the word "unveiling" and the mid-nineteenth century Marxian industrial technologies and methods from whence they came might be modulated to retain the social and political valences and work they have enacted through the academic paradigms of critical and cultural studies while addressing contemporary technological and material conditions.

Following up on his earlier challenge to the work of critique as violent exposure, Latour has taken an additional step in a recent piece in *New Literary History* with the provocative title, "An Attempt at a 'Compositionist Manifesto'" (2010), which I quote at length to give a full sense of the problem and Latour's potential methodological solution:

> In a first meaning, compositionism could stand as an alternative to critique (I don't mean a critique of critique but a *reuse* of critique; not an even more critical critique but rather critique acquired secondhand—so to speak—and *put to a different use*). To be sure, critique did a wonderful job of debunking prejudices, enlightening nations, and prodding minds, but, as I have argued elsewhere, it "ran out of steam" because it was predicated on the discovery of a true world of realities lying behind a *veil* of appearances. This beautiful staging had the great advantage of creating a huge difference of potential between the world of delusion and the world of reality. . . . But it also had the immense drawback of *creating a massive gap between what was felt and what was real.* Ironically, given the Nietzschean fervor of so many iconoclasts, critique relies on a rear world of the beyond, that is, on a transcendence that is no less transcendent for being fully secular. With critique, you may debunk, reveal, unveil, but only as long as you *establish, through this process of creative destruction*, a privileged access to the world of reality behind the veils of appearances. Critique, in other words, has all the limits of utopia: it relies on the certainty of the world beyond this world. By contrast, for compositionism, there is no world of beyond. It is all about immanence. (474–75, emphasis added)

As a compositionist, digital media practitioner, and theorist, whose understanding of the word "composition" includes but far exceeds visions of a first-year writing classroom, I was shocked by Latour's newfound way through or beyond the impasse of (1) throw the political baby out with the bathwater by moving away from critique altogether or (2) enact a "more critical critique" *of* critique, which is a zero-sum, paralytic game, correlate to the navel-gazing, linguistic-turn accusations against theory during the cultural and theory wars of the 1980s and 1990s (and reemerging now in the digital humanities). Instead, Latour's explicit way through takes up a moment in critical praxis, "this process of creative destruction"—a clever allusion to Joseph Schumpeter, which rhetorically aligns the movement of negative critique to the movement of capital as well as is an allusion to the constellated work of Walter Benjamin, Giorgio Agamben, and Carl Schmitt on establishing, that is, constitutive violence through which "you establish a privileged access to the world of reality behind the veils of appearances" (475). And from which, as Sedgwick points out, one translates the truths of this world to the dullard or naive masses, who must be constructed as deluded and hallucinatory denizens of a totalizing Matrix.

Latour locates a creationary moment in the critical impulse but one through which, up until now, a wholesale *destruction* is the created and with it "a massive gap between what was felt and what was real." So the hypothesis from this compositionist's manifesto becomes, what might happen if this critical impulse, described as "reuse" (remix) and "secondhand" (mash up), operated not through creative destruction but creative construction, or what I have been calling composing creative critique?

And I would briefly add one final problem that requires a shift in critical practice. Critique's primary action is that of exposure, and if informatic technologies have altered one aspect of politics and culture it would be a reconfiguration of what is exposed and exposable and what remains illegibly *layered*—not veiled. The Internet and digital technologies provide a set of platforms and affordances for *exposing* human actions and older, analog, informatic archives (alphabetic documentation, legal records, etc.) superbly; for example, Wikileaks and recent events in North Africa and the Middle East resonate with political affectivity and effectivity. We live exposed. Might we begin to experiment with ways to shift or move out of the utopian ideal of unveiling the already unveiled, executed through acts of destructive creation, to take up the troubling of affective disjuncture between what is felt and what is real and to move from interrogative readings to interactive, critical "reuse" compositions through what Latour terms a "progressivism" that is predicated on immanence and upon what I would argue are nontrivially changed material conditions? Furthermore, might we also begin to recognize the massive crisis in informatic literacies, layers of computational and networked codifications, in which few are able to read and write, much the less able to do so critically or tactically? And it is at this point that the affordances, affective and creative, of digital media and computation need to enter this critical and cultural assemblage. Digital and computational work simultaneously documents, establishes, and affectively produces an iteration of real worlds (small "w"), worlds both felt and real but multimodally layered worlds. And in the creation of context, relationality, and interactivity, the lived collaboration of the "user" (and in the classroom, the "student") becomes a performance, a necessary flow and return of participatory and synaesthetic rhetorics. If the critical impulse is to become inventive, creational, and social, and with it critical and cultural studies, then the entire constellation of context, affect, and embodiment must remain viably dynamic and collaborative in digital and computational work.

Coda, for the Open

Let me finish by offering and advocating for an experimental reopening of this work. Computational and digital modes offer a huge range of potential critical and cultural affordances, and the key to this potential lies in their public and accessible capacities for phenomenological transfer as affective, lived, and located experience, embodied and culturally complex, and for creative and critical making and doing, for creative critique in a world constitutive of many worlds that continue to need more critically and culturally informed constructions and always need more relational and ethical participation and interaction. Therefore, digital and computational practitioners must move away from the practices and logic of unifying standards and instrumentality, as well as rationalizing and consolidating genres—for genres, like academic disciplines, are not immanent. They are produced through labored containment and through a logic of similitude against difference. Digital and computational modes are embedded, object oriented, networked, enacted, and relational. The digital humanities is one subset of computational and digitally mediated practices, though its current discursive regime articulates itself as an iteration of the one world, a world both felt and real. But work in computation and digital media is, in fact, a radically heterogeneous and a multimodally layered—read, not visible—set of practices, constraints, and codifications that operate below the level of user interaction. In this layered invisibility lies our critical work. So no, our ethics, methods, and theory are *not transparent* in our tools—unless you have the serious know-how to critically make them or to hack them. So let's work in and teach the serious know-how of code and critique, computation and cultural studies, collaboration and multimodal composing as so many literacies, capacities, and expressivities attuned to our moment and to the contexts and conditions in which we find ourselves. Let's take up the imperatives of a relational ethics in discussion and in practices and methods through composing creative critical media.

NOTES

Enormous thanks are owed to Jentery Sayers, Tara McPherson, and of course Matt Gold for helpful editorial suggestions and citation reminders. Any and all failings belong to me.

1. I am intentionally not citing the sources of the first and second epigraphs, as my intention in using these quotations is to point to problems, not to indict individuals.

2. The echoes of New Critical scientism and objective formalism in contemporary discourses of digital humanities as a strict computational humanities will be taken up later in this essay.

3. This refers to a *New York Times* Opinionator post authored by Stanley Fish, "French Theory in America," April 6, 2008, regarding the American (mis)appropriation of French theory, spurred by the then-imminent publication of François Cussett's book, *French Theory: How Foucault, Derrida, Deleuze, & Co. Transformed the Intellectual Life of the United States*, published in 2008.

4. I have heard a version of this position publicly articulated in at least four discussions of the politics and ethics of *The* Digital Humanities from October, 2010, through March, 2011, and have elected to use the latest as an epigraph. It is also worth quoting Patricia Cohen's *New York Times* November 16, 2010, interview with Tom Scheinfeldt on this subject in "Humanities 2.0: Digital Keys for Unlocking Humanities Riches" (a title well worth critical reflection in itself): "In Mr. Scheinfeldt's view academia has moved into 'a post-theoretical age.' This 'methodological moment,' he said, is similar to the late 19th and early 20th centuries, when scholars were preoccupied with collating and cataloging the flood of information brought about by revolutions in communication, transportation and science. The practical issues of discipline building, of assembling an annotated bibliography, of defining the research agenda and what it means to be a historian 'were the main work of a great number of scholars,' he said."

The correspondence of "this 'methodological moment'" to that of "the late 19th and early 20th centuries" also parallels the impetus to return to the early twentieth-century New Critical paradigm that I have already noted and will elaborate further. What goes entirely unacknowledged in Cohen's paraphrase of Scheinfeldt's position vis-à-vis "theory" is that this articulation of "a post-theoretical age" in itself constitutes and culminates in a formal theory of nonreflexive "practice": "collati[on], . . . catalog[ues], . . . disciplin[es], . . . assembl[ages], . . . [and] defini[tions]."

5. Admittedly, I was not in attendance, so this impression may say more about who tweets what, but conversations with several folk who were in attendance and the subsequent flood of postconference dialogue through connected Twitter threads and blogs reinforced this perception.

6. This issue was *mildly* taken to task in the weeks following the MLA. Niceness conflicted with the acknowledgment of the emergence of a "star system" and uneven inclusion in *The* Digital Humanities. Matt Kirschenbaum mentioned the conflict of niceness with the "asymmetry of networked relationships" in his blogpost "The (DH) Stars Come Out In LA (January 13, 2011): "We often seek to defuse that [asymmetry of relations] with testimonials about digital humanities' 'niceness,' or more tellingly how collectively open and available we all tend to be. . . . But while being nice is good, being nice is not, or may no longer be, enough." Of course, this begs two questions I asked earlier: Is "nice" good? Is this "niceness" not the outcome of a particular distribution of "assymetr[ical]" relations?

7. While one reader took issue with this aspect of the essay and helpfully pointed me to William Pannapacker's extremely well-known redux of Modern Language Association 2011 in the *Chronicle of Higher Education*, this phrase and its social implications were already heavily circulated through DH prior to MLA11. This and several of the other conflicts this essay discusses, including the compulsive need to posit DH against Big Theory, are evident in Pannapacker's summation of the conference: "The digital humanities have some internal tensions, such as the occasional divide between builders and theorizers, and coders and non-coders. But the field, as a whole, seems to be developing an in-group, out-group dynamic that threatens to replicate the culture of Big Theory back in the 80s and 90s, which was alienating to so many people. It's perceptible in the universe of Twitter: We read it, but we do not participate. It's the *cool-kids' table*" ("Pannapacker," my italics).

BIBLIOGRAPHY

Adorno, Theodor. "Letters to Walter Benjamin (1936)." *New Left Review* 81 (1973). http://newleftreview.org/?page=article&view=14/.

———. "Cultural Criticism and Society." In *Prisms*. Cambridge, Mass: MIT Press, 1983.

Bourriaud, Nicolas. *Relational Aesthetics.* Paris: Les Presses du Reel, 2002.

Berry, David M. "The Computational Turn: Thinking about the Digital Humanities." *Culture Machine* 12 (2011). http://www.culturemachine.net/index.php/cm/article/view/440/470/.

Cohen, Patricia. "Humanities 2.0: Digital Keys for Unlocking Humanities Riches." *New York Times*, November 16, 2010. http://www.nytimes.com/2010/11/17/arts/17digital.html/.

Cussett, François. *French Theory: How Foucault, Derrida, Deleuze, & Co. Transformed the Intellectual Life of the United States*. Minneapolis: University of Minnesota Press, 2008.

Daniel, Sharon. "Hybrid Practices." *Cinema Journal* 48, no. 2 (Winter 2009): 154–59.

Deleuze, Gilles, and Félix Guattari. *A Thousand Plateaux*. Minneapolis: University of Minnesota Press, 1980.

Eliot, T. S. *Selected Prose of T. S. Eliot*. New York: Harvest Books, 1975.

———. "Tradition and the Individual Talent (1922)." Accessed March 27, 2010. http://www.bartleby.com/200/sw4.html/.

Fish, Stanley. "French Theory in America." *New York Times*, April 6, 2008. http://opinionator.blogs.nytimes.com/2008/04/06/french-theory-in-america/.

Irigaray, Luce. *This Sex Which Is Not One*. Translated by Catherine Porter. Ithaca, N.Y.: Cornell University Press, 1985.

Kirschenbaum, Matthew G. "The (DH) Stars Come Out in LA." January 11, 2011. http://mkirschenbaum.wordpress.com/2011/01/13/the-dh-stars-come-out-in-la-2/.

Lampland, Martha, and Susan Leigh Star. "Reckoning with Standards." In *Standards and Their Stories: How Quantifying, Classifying, and Formalizing Practices Shape Everyday Life*, edited by Martha Lampland and Susan Leigh Star. Ithaca, N.Y.: Cornell University Press, 2009.

Latour, Bruno. "An Attempt at a 'Compositionist Manifesto.'" *New Literary History* 41, no. 3 (Summer 2010): 471–90.

———. "Why Has Critique Run out of Steam? From Matters of Fact to Matters of Concern." *Critical Inquiry* 30, no. 2 (2008). http://www.uchicago.edu/research/jnl-crit-inq/issues/v30/30n2.Latour.html.

Lorde, Audre. *Sister Outsider and Other Essays*. Berkeley, Calif.: Crossing, 1984.

Moretti, Franco. *Graphs Maps Trees*. New York: Verso, 2005.

Pannapacker, William. "Pannapacker at MLA: Digital Humanities Triumphant?" *The Chronicle of Higher Education*. January 8, 2011. http://chronicle.com/blogs/brainstorm/pannapacker-at-mla-digital-humanities-triumphant/30915/.

Ranciere, Jacques. *The Politics of Aesthetics*. New York: Continuum, 2004.

Ross, Toni. "Aesthetic Autonomy and Interdisciplinarity: A Response to Nicolas Bourriaud's 'Relational Aesthetics.'" *Journal of Visual Art Practice* 5, no. 3 (2006): 167–81.

Scheinfeldt, Tom. "Why Digital Humanities Is 'Nice'" in *Found History*. May 26, 2010. http://www.foundhistory.org/2010/05/26/why-digital-humanities-is-%E2%80%9Cnice%E2%80%9D/. Reprinted in this volume.

Sedgwick, Eve Kosofsky. *Touching Feeling: Affect, Pedagogy, Performativity*. Durham, N.C.: Duke University Press, 2002.

Spingarn, J. E. *Creative Criticism and Other Essays*. New York: Harcourt, Brace, 1931.

Stross, Randall. "What Has Driven Women out of Computer Science?" *New York Times*, November 15, 2008. http://www.nytimes.com/2008/11/16/business/16digi.html/.

Thomas, William G. II. "Computing and the Historical Imagination." In *A Companion to Digital Humanities*, edited by Susan Schreibman, Ray Siemens, and John Unsworth. Oxford: Blackwell, 2004. http://www.digitalhumanities.org/companion/.

Wikimedia. "File:WMFstratplanSurvey1.png." *Wikimedia Strategic Plan*. February, 2011. http://strategy.wikimedia.org/wiki/File:WMFstratplanSurvey1.pngandhttp://upload.wikimedia.org/wikipedia/foundation/c/c0/WMF_StrategicPlan2011_spreads.pdf.

A Telescope for the Mind?

WILLARD MCCARTY

As to those for whom to work hard, to begin and begin again, to attempt and be mistaken, to go back and rework everything from top to bottom, and still find reason to hesitate from one step to the next—as to those, in short, for whom to work in the midst of uncertainty and apprehension is tantamount to failure, all I can say is that clearly we are not from the same planet.

—Michel Foucault, *History of Sexuality*

The phrase in my title is Margaret Masterman's; the question mark is mine. Writing in 1962 for Freeing the Mind, a series in the *Times Literary Supplement*,[1] she used the phrase to suggest computing's potential to transform our conception of the human world just as in the seventeenth century the optical telescope set in motion a fundamental rethink of our relation to the physical one. The question mark denotes my own and others' anxious interrogation of research in the digital humanities for signs that her vision, or something like it, is being realized or that demonstrable progress has been made. This interrogation is actually nothing new; it began in the professional literature during the 1960s and then became a sporadic feature of our discourse that persists to this day. I will return to present worries shortly. First allow me to rehearse a few of its early expressions. Then, following the clues these yield, I will turn to the debate that I am not at all sure we are having but which, if we did, could translate the neurotic search for justification into questions worth asking. The debate I think we should be having is, to provoke it with a question, What is this machine of ours for? Or, to make it personal, What are *we* for?

"Analogy is an identity of relationships" (Weil, 85), not of things. Thus the computer could now be to the mind, Masterman was saying, as the telescope was to seventeenth-century observers, enlarging "the whole range of what its possessors could see and do [so] that, in the end, it was a factor in changing their whole picture of the world." ("The Intellect's New Eye," 38) She suggests that by thus extending our perceptual scope and reach, computing does not simply bring formerly unknown things into view but also forces a crisis of understanding from which a new, more adequate cosmology arises. (I will return to this crisis later.) She was not alone in thinking that the computer would make a great difference to all fields of study, but she seems to have been one of the very few who argued for qualitative rather than quantitative change—different ideas rather than simply more evidence, obtained faster and more easily in greater abundance, to support ideas we already have in ways we already understand. Masterman was a linguist and philosopher; pioneer in computational linguistics; one-time student of Ludwig Wittgenstein; playwright and novelist; founder and director of the Cambridge Language Research Unit; adventurous and imaginative experimenter with computing, for example in composing haikus and arguing for the significance of such work against sometimes ferocious opposition; and part of a community of people genuinely, intelligently excited about the possibilities, however implausible, that the computer was then opening up before hype muddied the waters.[2]

Masterman begins her contribution to Freeing the Mind by distancing herself from her predecessors' evident notion that the digital computer is "a purely menial tool": "in fact . . . a kind of intellectual spade. This, it has been shown, can indeed assist a human scholar . . . by performing for him a series of irksome repetitive tasks . . . that the scholar, unaided, just cannot get through. . . . They take too long, they are backbreaking, they are eye-wearing, they strain too far human capacity for maintaining accuracy: in fact, they are both physically and intellectually crushing" (38). She had (can we have?) quite other ideas. Nevertheless the complaint pointed to a very real problem—that is, very real drudgery that at various times the demands of maritime navigation, the bureaucratic state, warfare, and scientific research inflicted on those who were professionally adept at calculation. Thus Gottfried Wilhelm Leibniz complained about enslavement to "dull but simple tasks" in the seventeenth century, Charles Babbage in the nineteenth, and Herman Goldstine in the twentieth (Goldstine, 8–12; Pratt, 20–44). All three responded by devising computational machinery. We certainly cannot and should not deny the crippling effects of the mathematical drudgery about which they all complained. But, Masterman insisted, these spadework uses, however welcome the time and effort they liberate, "provoke no new theoretic vision" ("The Intellect's New Eye", 38). Relief of others' drudgery is a noble undertaking, but to slip from laudable service of that practical need to the notion that the computer is *for* drudgery is a profound error. It is an error that became an occupational hazard among early practitioners of humanities computing.

In 1978, literary scholar Susan Wittig paused to take stock of accomplishments in computing for her field. Quoting Masterman via an article promoting content analysis for literary study (Ellis and Favat), Wittig argued that Masterman's call for more than spadework had come to naught. Although the computer "*has* added immeasurably to the ability of literary analysis to perform better and more efficiently the same tasks that they have performed for many years" (her emphasis),

Wittig wrote, it has not "enlarged our range of vision or radically changed for us the shape of the universe of esthetic discourse" (211). The problem she identified was not the machinery; as Thomas Rommel has pointed out, the basic technical requirements for making a real difference had been met at least a decade before Wittig wrote (93). The problem she identified was the "limited conceptual framework" of the then dominant but ageing literary-critical theory, New Criticism, which along with structuralist-formalist grammar held, "first, the notion that the text is a linear entity; second, the idea that the text is a one-time, completed work, firmly confined to its graphic representation, the printed page; and third, the belief that the text is autonomously independent of any other entity, that it is meaningful in and of itself" (Wittig, 211–12). The force of these theoretical assumptions was to foreshorten the horizon of possibilities to what computers could then most easily do.

A dozen years earlier, literary scholar Louis Milic, also noting the great assistance provided to the old ways, had bemoaned the failing that Masterman indicated and that, we might say, lies behind the problem Wittig complained of: "Satisfaction with such limited objectives denotes a real shortage of imagination among us. We are still not thinking of the computer as anything but a myriad of clerks or assistants in one convenient console. Most of the results . . . could have been accomplished with the available means of half a century ago. We do not yet understand the true nature of the computer. And we have not yet begun to think in ways appropriate to the nature of this machine" (4). Fourteen years later, the situation had still not changed much. Summing up his experience and observations in research that had begun almost two decades earlier, Father Roberto Busa wrote with evident impatience (evincing the prevalence of the error) that the computer was not primarily a labor-saving device to be used to free scholars from drudgery but a means to illumine ignorance by provoking us to reconsider what we think we know (Busa, "The Annals of Humanities Computing"). Four years before that in "Why Can a Computer Do So Little?" he had surveyed the "explosion" of activities in "processing non-numerical, literary information" during the previous quarter century but noted the "rather poor performance" of computing as then conceived (1). Like Wittig and much like Jerome McGann at the beginning of the twenty-first century, Busa argued that this disappointing performance pointed to our ignorance of the focal subject—in this case, language: "what is in our mouth at every moment, the mysterious world of our words" ("Why Can a Computer Do So Little?," 3). Back to the theoretical drawing board (which was by then already filling up with very different ideas).

Masterman's vision of computing—her "telescope of the mind"—was not the only one nor the most ambitious. Best known is Herbert Simon's and Allen Newell's in 1958, phrased as a mixture of exuberant claims and startling predictions of what computers would, they said, be capable of doing within the following decade (Simon and Newell, "Heuristic Problem Solving"; cf. Simon and Newell, "Reply: Heuristic Problem Solving"). The gist of these Simon gave in a lecture in November of the previous year, preceding and following them with these confident statements as they appear in his lecture note:

> IV. As of A.D. 1957 (even 1956) the essential steps have been taken to understand and simulate human judgmental heuristic activity. [. . .] Put it bluntly (hard now to shock)—Machines think! Learn! Create!
>
> V. What are the implications of this[3]

In *Alchemy and Artificial Intelligence* (1965) the philosopher Hubert Dreyfus famously took Simon and Newell to task for their pronouncements. But whatever our view of either, it is clear that by the mid-1960s signs of trouble for early visions were beginning to surface. The next year the Automatic Language Processing Advisory Committee of the U.S. National Research Council published *Language and Machines: Computers in Translation and Linguistics* (1966), a.k.a. the "black book" on machine translation, which effectively ended the lavish funding for the project (Wilks, *Grammar, Meaning and the Machine Analysis of Language*, 3–4). At the same time, however, the committee (much like Busa) recommended that efforts be redirected to research in the new field of computational linguistics "and should not be judged by any immediate or foreseeable contribution to practical translation" (ALPAC, 34). Machine translation was, they said, a research question, not a practical goal.

The like did not happen in the humanities, despite efforts such as John B. Smith's, for example, in "Computer Criticism" (1978, the year Wittig measured current achievements against Masterman's vision). More than ten years later Rosanne Potter, in her preface to a collection of papers that included a reprint of Smith's "Computer Criticism," wrote laconically that literary computing had "not been rejected, but rather neglected" by the profession (*Literary Computing and Literary Criticism: Theoretical and Practical Essays on Theme and Rhetoric,* xvi). Two years later, in her bibliographic survey of the first twenty-four years of *Computers and the Humanities*, she identified nine essays that, she wrote, "have attempted to reflect on what we are doing and why, where we are going and whether we want to go there" ("Statistical Analysis of Literature: A Retrospective on *Computers and the Humanities,* 1966–1990," 402). All of them, she noted, "warn against the same danger, seduction away from what we want to do by what the computer can do, call for the same remedy, more theory to guide empirical studies, and end with perorations about moving from the easy (data gathering) to the more creative (building new, more complex conceptual models)" ("Statistical Analysis of Literature: A Retrospective on *Computers and the Humanities*, 1966–1990," 402–3). She concluded that this was "as much self-reflection as the field was capable" ("Statistical Analysis of Literature: A Retrospective on *Computers and the Humanities,* 1966–1990," 403). And now?

In August of that year the World Wide Web was released to the public; and, as many have noted, everything changed for computing in the humanities, though slowly at first. Also that year, Mark Olsen, presiding over the development of tools for one of the early large corpora, the *Trésor de la Langue Française*, at the American and French Research on the Treasury of the French Language project (ARTFL), shocked and even outraged many of those most closely involved with the field by arguing in an Modern Language Association (MLA) paper for what Franco Moretti has more recently called "distant reading." A special issue of *Computers and the Humanities*, centered on a revised version of that paper, was published two years later (*Computers and the Humanities* 27.5–6). In it, Olsen sounded the familiar sentence: "Computer-aided literature studies have failed to have a significant impact on the field as a whole" ("Signs, Symbols and Discourses: A New Direction for Computer-Aided Literature Studies," 309). Again, but as Yaacov Choueka said in somewhat different terms in 1988, "The tools are here, what about results?"[4]

So given the catalog of failings and disappointments that emerges from the complaints of practitioners, I ask the same question that architectural designer John Hamilton Frazer recently asked of once adventurous British computer art: "What went wrong?" (Brown et al., 50). This is not an idle question, for the digital humanities especially in regard of its strong tendency to define itself as serving client disciplines, which tend to initiate collaborations, set the agenda for the research and take academic credit for the result. As the popular metaphor of "text-mining," the focus on large infrastructural projects, and the preoccupation with standards suggest, anticipation of service to be rendered moves the field toward an industrial model, in which curiosity-motivated research is subordinated to large-scale production, better to facilitate research that happens elsewhere by other means. Big Science is cited as a precedent without anyone asking about the historically documented and prominently attested consequences for the affected sciences. But to answer this historical question properly for the disciplines most affected—those for which interpretation of cultural artefacts is the central activity—would require more than any of the surveys of the last three or more decades. I am convinced, but cannot yet demonstrate, that an adequate historical account could be written and that a genuine history of the digital humanities in its first half century would greatly help us turn pitiful laments and dull facts into the stimulating questions we should be asking now. To write such an account, however, an historian would have to locate practitioners' minority concerns within the broad cultural landscape of the time and then describe the complex pattern of confluence and divergence of numerous interrelated developments.[5] These practitioners were not working in a vacuum; it is trivial to demonstrate that they were well aware of what was going on elsewhere. Why did they react (or not) as they did?

My intention here is much more modest. I want to talk about what we can do meanwhile, reflectively, to address our own predicaments beyond simply recognizing them.

A start may be made with the manner in which we now express our worries. No doubt in response to the demands for accountability from funding agencies, we have in recent years picked up the trendy phrase "evidence of value," thus asking how we might prove that money has been well spent.[6] We have, that is, shifted from the older argument for justification based on acceptance by our mainstream peers to a new one. What can we learn from it?

Roughly speaking the phrase "evidence of value" has migrated from legal disputes over property and the like to modern debates, for example, over the worth of public health care schemes (where it has become a buzzword and branded label). The question of value the phrase raises is a very old and persistent one that begins formally with ethics in the ancient world and continues today in philosophical arguments about whether affective states, such as feeling good or being excited about something, have anything to do with the value of that thing or whether a focus on evidence proves a dangerous trap. The eminently practical question of whether effort should continue to be spent in a particular way is sensible enough. There is nothing whatever wrong with it in the context of the purest, most wicked or curiosity-motivated research, for which you might say its constant presence is a necessary (though not sufficient) condition. But what do we accept as evidence for the worth or worthlessness of the effort, and who decides?

If funding agencies ask the question of whether research is worthwhile and judge the answer, then the effort is measured in funds spent, and evidence is defined as the "impact" of the research, in turn measured by citations to published work. For example, the rapporteur's report for a recent event at Cambridge, "Evidence of Value: ICT in the Arts and Humanities," begins thus: "With large sums of public money being channelled into this area, how is the 'value' of this investment assessed, what exactly are we assessing and for whom?"[7] Argument for qualitative as much as quantitative evidence was made, but what qualitative evidence might be other than claims supported by anecdote isn't clear. We can imagine a proper social scientific study of claimants' claims—how, for example, computing has changed their whole way of thinking—but would the results, however numerically expressed, be persuasive? Is any measure of "impact" critically persuasive for the humanities? To push the matter deeper, or further, are we not being naive to think that measurement simply establishes how things are in the world? Thomas Kuhn put paid to that notion for physics quite a long time ago (1961, the year before Masterman's visionary analogy).

In other words, it begins to look like the old philosophical argument, made by the consequentialists, carries the day: a preoccupation with evidence is mistaken; what matters, they say, are the consequences. We should ask, then, not where is the evidence of value. We should ask, instead, is computing fruitful for the humanities? What kinds of computing have been especially fruitful? In areas where it has not been, what's the problem? How can we fix it?

There is, of course, the practical concern with how to continue the research that we do (I don't ask whether) in the face of demands for evidence of value that often simply cannot be supplied without perverting it. If funding is contingent on providing this evidence, then the question becomes, what can we do without funding?

If funding is cut anyhow, as it has been for the humanities in the UK, then only the possibility of compromise is removed. What kinds of work can be done under the circumstances in which we find ourselves? Here is a debate we should be having, but it is not the debate I regard as most insistent, since what we can do on our own (which is really what we're left with primarily) is a matter for individual scholars to decide and find the cleverness to implement.

What lies beyond the let's-get-on-with-it scenario (where "it" has become one's own research made procedurally modest but as intellectually adventurous as can be) is the longer term question of how to improve the social circumstances of humanistic research. The question was debated briefly on the *Humanist* listserv from late October to early December 2010.[8] Here I return to a remark I reported there from the current UK science minister, David Willetts. Justifying the protected funding for the sciences, he noted that "the scientific community has assembled very powerful evidence such as in that Royal Society report, *The Scientific Century,* about what the benefits are for scientific research. Now you can argue that it's all worthwhile in its own rights, but the fact that it clearly contributes to the performance of the economy and the well-being of citizens—that's really strong evidence, and we deployed it."[9] Arguing for economic benefits is a long reach for the humanities, but "the well-being of citizens" is not. What can the digital humanities do for the humanities as a whole that helps these disciplines improve the well-being of us all?

And so I come to the debate I think we should be having.

We who have been working in the field know that the digital humanities can provide better resources for scholarship and better access to them. We know that in the process of designing and constructing these resources our collaborators often undergo significant growth in their understanding of digital tools and methods and that this sometimes, perhaps even in a significant majority of cases, fosters insight into the originating scholarly questions. Sometimes secular metanoia is not too strong a term to describe the experience. All this has for decades been the experience of those who guided collaborating scholars or were guided as scholars themselves through a gradual questioning of the original provocation to research, seeing it change as the struggle to render it computationally tractable progressed. In a sense, there is nothing new here to anyone who has ever attempted to get to the bottom of anything complex and ended up with, as Busa said, a mystery, something tacit, something that escapes the net. So not only is evidence of value to our collaborating colleagues thick on the ground, but it is also to be expected as a normal part of scholarship. But what about the argument? By definition evidence is information that backs up an argument. In other words, no argument, no evidence, only raw, uncommitted information.

The problem we have and must debate, then, is the argument or set of arguments that will convert decades of experience into (I believe, from a quarter century of it) incontrovertible evidence of *intellectual* value. We've seen and, I hope, are by now convinced that all computing in the humanities is not *for* drudgery even as it becomes more and more difficult, through ever-multiplying layers of software powered by ever-better hardware, to see what goes on behind the friendly service our devices provide. Some computing is designed to relieve us of drudgery. But to go back to Turing's scheme for indefinitely many forms of computing, whose number is limited only by the human imagination, what is computing in and of the humanities *for*? Are we for drudgery? If not, with regards to the humanities, what are we *for*?

NOTES

1. Freeing the Mind was first published as a series of essays in the *Times Literary Supplement* from March 23 to May 4, 1962, then republished as a slim volume together with selected letters to the editor later that year. It provides an excellent snapshot of nontechnical reflection on and about computing, as was characteristic of the *Times Literary Supplement* during the 1960s and 1970s.

2. As Yorick Wilks says in his biographical tribute to her, Masterman was "ahead of her time by some twenty years . . . never able to lay adequate claim to [ideas now in the common stock of artificial intelligence and machine translation] because they were unacceptable when she published them," making efforts "to tackle fundamental problems with computers . . . that had the capacity of a modern digital wristwatch," producing and inspiring numerous publications that today seem "curiously modern" (Wilks, *Language, Cohesion and Form*, 1, 4). For her work with haiku, see Masterman and McKinnon Wood, and Masterman "Computerized Haiku"; for vitriolic opposition to it see Leavis. For an idea of the diverse company with which her work associated her, see the table of contents in Reichardt's *Cybernetics, Art and Ideas*. Art critic Jasia Reichardt was responsible for the landmark *Cybernetic Serendipity* exhibition in London, August to October, 1968 (Reichardt, *Cybernetic Serendipity*). Among the exhibitors was "mechanic philosopher" and inventor of visionary "maverick machines" Gordon Pask, who was a long-time friend and research partner of Robert McKinnon Wood, Masterman's colleague at Cambridge; for more on Pask, see Bird and Di Paolo.

3. An image of the original manuscript upon which this transcription was based may be found at http://www.mccarty.org.uk/essays/McCarty,%20Telescope.pdf.

4. At the 1988 Association for Literary and Linguistic Computing Conference in Jerusalem, Choueka assigned me to the panel "Literary and Linguistic Computing: The Tools Are Here, What about Results?" The title was his. See http.sigir.org/sigirlist/issues/1988/88-4-28.

5. My historiography owes a great deal to the late Michael S. Mahoney; see the collection of his papers and the editor Thomas Haigh's discussion in Mahoney; cf. McCarty.

6. For "evidence of value" in the digital humanities, see subsequent sections in this chapter and www.crassh.cam.ac.uk/events/196/. The AHRC ICT Methods Network, under which "evidence of value" was the subject of an expert seminar, has concluded its work. Otherwise, a search of the web will turn up thousands of examples of its use in other contexts.

7. Wilson; see also www.crassh.cam.ac.uk/events/196/, and Hughes.

8. See *Humanist* 24.427–8, 431, 436 (http://www.digitalhumanities.org/humanist/, with reference to a British Academy lecture by Martha Nussbaum), 440, 445, 448, 453, 455, 464, 469, 479, 481, 483, 485, 504, 511, 515, 527, 541. As is typical with online discussions, a particular thread remains distinct for a time then begins to unravel into related matters. This one remained coherent for quite some time.

9. "The Material World," BBC Radio 4, October 21, 2010, my transcription. For the Royal Society report, see royalsociety.org/the-scientific-century/.

BIBLIOGRAPHY

ALPAC. *Language and Machines: Computers in Translation and Linguistics.* Report by the Automatic Language Processing Advisory Committee, National Academy of Sciences. Publication 1416. Washington, D.C.: National Academy of Sciences, 1966.

Bird, Jon, and Ezequiel Di Paolo. "Gordon Pask and His Maverick Machines." In *The Mechanical Mind in History,* edited by Philip Husbands, Owen Holland, and Michael Wheeler, 185–211. Cambridge, Mass.: Bradford Books, 2008.

Brown, Paul, Charlie Gere, Nicholas Lambert, and Catherine Mason, eds. *White Heat Cold Logic: British Computer Art 1960–1980.* Cambridge, Mass.: MIT Press, 2008.

Busa, R. "The Annals of Humanities Computing: The Index Thomisticus." *Computers and the Humanities* 14 (1980): 83–90.

———. "Guest Editorial: Why Can a Computer Do So Little?" *Bulletin of the Association for Literary and Linguistic Computing* 4, no. 1 (1976): 1–3.

Dreyfus, Hubert L. *Alchemy and Artificial Intelligence.* Rand Corporation Papers, P-3244. Santa Monica, Calif.: RAND Corporation, 1965.

Ellis, Allan B., and F. André Favat. "From Computer to Criticism: An Application of Automatic Content Analysis to the Study of Literature." In *The General Inquirer: A Computer Approach to Content Analysis,* edited by Philip J. Stone, Dexter C. Dumphy, Marshall S. Smith, and Daniel M. Ogilvie. Cambridge, Mass.: MIT Press, 1966. Reprint, in *Science in Literature: New Lenses for Criticism,* edited by Edward M. Jennings, 125–37. Garden City, N.Y.: Doubleday, 1970.

Foucault, Michel. *The Use of Pleasure. The History of Sexuality 2.* Translated by Robert Hurley. London: Penguin, 1992/1984.

Goldstine, Herman H. *The Computer from Pascal to von Neumann.* Princeton, N.J.: Princeton University Press, 1972.

Hughes, Lorna, ed. *The AHRC ICT Methods Network.* London: Centre for Computing in the Humanities, King's College London, 2008.

Kuhn, Thomas S. "The Function of Measurement in Modern Physical Science." *Isis* 52, no. 2 (1961): 161–93.

Leavis, F. R. "'Literarism' versus 'Scientism': The Misconception and the Menace." *Times Literary Supplement* (April 23, 1970): 441–45. Reprint, 1972 in *Nor Shall My Sword: Discourses on Pluralism, Compassion and Social Hope,* 137–60. London: Chatto & Windus, 1972.

Mahoney, Michael S. *Histories of Computing,* edited by Thomas Haigh. Cambridge, Mass.: Harvard University Press, 2011.

Masterman, Margaret. "Computerized Haiku." In *Cybernetics, Art and Ideas,* edited by Jasia Reichardt. London: Studio Vista, 1971: 175–83.

———. "The Intellect's New Eye." *Times Literary Supplement* 284 (April 17, 1962). Reprint, in *Freeing the Mind: Articles and Letters from The Times Literary Supplement during March-June, 1962,* 38–44. London: Times, 1962.

———. *Language, Cohesion and Form.* Edited by Yorick Wilks. Cambridge, UK: Cambridge University Press, 2005.

———. "The Use of Computers to Make Semantic Toy Models of Language." *Times Literary Supplement* (August 6, 1964): 690–91.

Masterman, Margaret, and Robin McKinnon Wood. "The Poet and the Computer." *Times Literary Supplement* (June 18, 1970): 667–68.

McCarty, Willard. "Foreword." In *Language Technology for Cultural Heritage: Selected Papers from the LaTeCH Workshop Series,* edited by Caroline Sporleder, Antal van den Bosch, and Kalliopi A. Zervanou, vi–xiv. Lecture Notes in Artificial Intelligence. Berlin: Springer Verlag, 2011.

Milic, Louis. "The Next Step." *Computers and the Humanities* 1, no. 1 (1966): 3–6.

Moretti, Franco. "Conjectures on World Literature." *New Left Review* 1 (2000): 54–68.

Olsen, Mark. "Signs, Symbols and Discourses: A New Direction for Computer-Aided Literature Studies." *Computers and the Humanities* 27 (1993): 309–14.

———. "What Can and Cannot Be Done with Electronic Text in Historical and Literary Research." Paper for the Modern Language Association of America Annual Meeting, San Francisco, December 1991.

Potter, Rosanne, ed. *Literary Computing and Literary Criticism: Theoretical and Practical Essays on Theme and Rhetoric.* Philadelphia, Pa.: University of Pennsylvania Press, 1989.

———. "Statistical Analysis of Literature: A Retrospective on *Computers and the Humanities,* 1966–1990." *Computers and the Humanities* 25 (1991): 401–29.

Pratt, Vernon. *Thinking Machines: The Evolution of Artificial Intelligence.* Oxford: Basil Blackwell, 1987.

Reichardt, Jasia, ed. *Cybernetic Serendipity.* New York: Frederick A. Praeger, 1969.

———. *Cybernetics, Art and Ideas.* London: Studio Vista, 1971.

Rommel, Thomas. "Literary Studies." In *A Companion to Digital Humanities,* edited by Susan Schreibman, Ray Siemens, and John Unsworth, 88–96. Oxford: Blackwell, 2004.

Simon, Herbert A., and Allen Newell. "Heuristic Problem Solving: The Next Advance in Operations Research." *Operations Research* 6, no. 1 (1958): 1–10.

———. "Reply: Heuristic Problem Solving." *Operations Research* 6, no. 3 (1958): 449–50.

Smith, John B. "Computer Criticism." *Style* 12 (1978): 326–56. Reprint, in Potter (1989): 13–44.

Weil, Simone. *Lectures on Philosophy.* Translated by Hugh Price. Cambridge, UK: Cambridge University Press, 1978/1959.

Wilks, Yorick Alexander. "Editor's Introduction." In Margaret Masterman, *Language, Cohesion and Form.* Edited by Yorick Wilks. Cambridge, UK: Cambridge University Press, 2005: 1–17.

———. *Grammar, Meaning, and the Machine Analysis of Language.* London: Routledge & Kegan Paul, 1972.

Wilson, Lee. "Evidence of Value: ICT in the Arts and Humanities. Rapporteur's Report." http://www.ahrcict.rdg.ac.uk/news/evidence%20of%20value%20v2.pdf.

Wittig, Susan. "The Computer and the Concept of Text." *Computers and the Humanities* 11 (1978): 211–15.

Sunset for Ideology, Sunrise for Methodology?

TOM SCHEINFELDT

Sometimes friends in other disciplines ask me, "So what are the big ideas in history these days?" I then proceed to fumble around for a few minutes trying to put my finger on some new ism or competing isms to describe and define today's historical discourse. Invariably, I come up short.

Growing up in the second half of the twentieth century, we are prone to think about our world in terms of ideologies and our work in terms of theories. Late twentieth-century historical discourse was dominated by a succession of ideas and theoretical frameworks. This mirrored the broader cultural and political discourse in which our work was set. For most of the last seventy-five years of the twentieth century, socialism, fascism, existentialism, structuralism, poststructuralism, conservatism, and other ideologies vied with one another broadly in our politics and narrowly at our academic conferences.

But it wasn't always so. Late nineteenth- and early twentieth-century scholarship was dominated not by big ideas but by methodological refinement and disciplinary consolidation. Denigrated in the later twentieth century as unworthy of serious attention by scholars, the nineteenth and early twentieth century, by contrast, took activities like philology, lexicology, and especially bibliography very seriously. Serious scholarship was concerned as much with organizing knowledge as it was with framing knowledge in a theoretical or ideological construct.

Take my subdiscipline, the history of science, as an example. Whereas the last few decades of research have been dominated by a debate over the relative merits of constructivism (the idea, in Jan Golinski's succinct definition, "that scientific knowledge is a human creation, made with available material and cultural resources, rather than simply the revelation of a natural order that is pre-given and independent of human action"), the history of science was in fact founded in an outpouring of bibliography.[1] The life work of the first great American historian of science, George Sarton, was not an idea but a journal (*Isis*), a professional society (the History of

Science Society), a department (Harvard's), a primer (his *Introduction to the History of Science*), and especially a bibliography (the *Isis Cumulative Bibliography*).[2] Tellingly, the great work of his greatest pupil, Robert K. Merton, was an idea: the younger Merton's "Science, Technology and Society in Seventeenth Century England" defined history of technology as social history for a generation.[3] By the time Merton was writing in the 1930s, the cultural climate had changed and the consolidating and methodological activities of the teacher were giving way to the theoretical activities of the student.

I believe we are at a similar moment of change right now that we are entering a new phase of scholarship that will be dominated not by ideas but once again by organizing activities, in terms of both organizing knowledge and organizing ourselves and our work. My difficulty in answering the question, "What's the big idea in history right now?" stems from the fact that, as a digital historian, I traffic much less in new theories than in new methods. The new technology of the Internet has shifted the work of a rapidly growing number of scholars away from thinking big thoughts to forging new tools, methods, materials, techniques, and modes or work that will enable us to harness the still unwieldy, but obviously game-changing, information technologies now sitting on our desktops and in our pockets. These concerns touch all scholars. The Center for History and New Media's Zotero research management tool is used by more than a million people, all of them grappling with the problem of information overload. And although much of the discussion remains informal, it's no accident that Wikipedia is right now one of the hottest topics for debate among scholars.

Perhaps most telling is the excitement that now (or, really, once again) surrounds the library. The buzz among librarians these days dwarfs anything I have seen in my entire career among historians. The terms "library geek" and "sexy librarian" have gained new currency as everyone begins to recognize the potential of exciting library-centered projects like Google Books.

All these things—collaborative encyclopedism, tool building, librarianship—fit uneasily into the standards of scholarship forged in the second half of the twentieth century. Most committees for promotion and tenure, for example, must value single authorship and the big idea more highly than collaborative work and methodological or disciplinary contribution. Even historians find it hard to internalize the fact that their own norms and values have and will again change over time. But change they must. In the days of George Sarton, a thorough bibliography was an achievement worthy of great respect and an office closer to the reference desk in the library an occasion for great celebration. (Sarton's small suite in study 189 of Harvard's Widener Library was the epicenter of history of science in America for more than a quarter century.) As we tumble deeper into the Internet age, I suspect it will be again.

NOTES

This chapter originally appeared as Tom Scheinfeldt, "Sunset for Ideology, Sunrise for Methodology?," *Found History*, March 13, 2008, http://www.foundhistory.org/2008/03/13/sunset-for-ideology-sunrise-for-methodology/.

1. Jan Golinski, *Making Natural Knowledge: Constructivism and the History of Science* (Cambridge, UK: Cambridge University Press, 1998), 6.

2. George Sarton, *Introduction to the History of Science* (Washington, D.C.: Carnegie Institution of Washington, 1962); *History of Science Society, Isis Cumulative Bibliography: A Bibliography of the History of Science Formed from Isis Critical Bibliographies 1–90, 1913–65* (London: Mansell, 1971).

3. Robert K. Merton, "Science, Technology and Society in Seventeenth Century England," *Osiris* 4 (January 1, 1938): 360–632.

Has Critical Theory Run Out of Time for Data-Driven Scholarship?

GARY HALL

Certainly, something that is particularly noticeable about many instances of this turn to data-driven scholarship—especially after decades when the humanities have been heavily marked by a variety of critical theories (Marxist, psychoanalytic, postcolonialist, post-Marxist)—is just how difficult they find it to understand computing and the digital as much *more* than tools, techniques, and resources and thus how naive and lacking in meaningful critique they often are (Liu; Higgen). Of course, this (at times explicit) repudiation of criticality could be viewed as part of what makes certain aspects of the digital humanities so intriguing at the moment. From this perspective, exponents of the computational turn are precisely *not* making what I have elsewhere characterized as the antipolitical gesture of conforming to accepted (and often moralistic) conceptions of politics that have been decided in advance, including those that see it only in terms of power, ideology, race, gender, class, sexuality, ecology, affect, and so forth (Hall, *Digitize*). Refusing to "go through the motions of a critical avant-garde," to borrow the words of Bruno Latour, they are responding to what is perceived as a fundamentally new cultural situation and the challenge it represents to our traditional methods of studying culture by avoiding such conventional gestures and experimenting with the development of fresh methods and approaches for the humanities instead.[1]

In a series of posts on his *Found History* blog, Tom Scheinfeldt, managing director at the Center for History and New Media at George Mason University, positions such scholarship very much in terms of a shift from a concern with theory and ideology to a concern with methodology:

> I believe . . . we are entering a new phase of scholarship that will be dominated not by ideas, but once again by organizing activities, both in terms of organizing knowledge and organizing ourselves and our work . . . as a digital historian, I traffic much less in new theories than in new methods. The new technology of

> the Internet has shifted the work of a rapidly growing number of scholars away from thinking big thoughts to forging new tools, methods, materials, techniques, and modes or work which will enable us to harness the still unwieldy, but obviously game-changing, information technologies now sitting on our desktops and in our pockets. (Scheinfeldt, "Sunset")

In this respect there may well be a degree of "relief in having escaped the culture wars of the 1980s"—for those in the United States especially—as a result of this move "into the space of methodological work" (Higgen) and what Scheinfeldt reportedly dubs "the post-theoretical age" (cited in Cohen, "Digital Keys"). The problem is, though, without such reflexive critical thinking and theories many of those whose work forms part of this computational turn find it difficult to articulate exactly what the point of what they are doing is, as Scheinfeldt readily acknowledges ("Where's the Beef?").

Witness one of the projects I mentioned earlier: the attempt by Dan Cohen and Fred Gibbs to text mine all the books published in English in the Victorian age (or at least those digitized by Google).[2] Among other things, this allows Cohen and Gibbs to show that use of the word "revolution" in book titles of the period spiked around "the French Revolution and the revolutions of 1848" (Cohen, "Searching"). But what argument is it that they are trying to make with this? How exactly is the number of times a word does or does not occur significant? What is it we are able to learn as a result of this use of computational power on their part that we didn't know already and couldn't have discovered without it (Scheinfeldt, "Where's the Beef")?

Elsewhere, in an explicit response to Cohen and Gibbs's project, Scheinfeldt suggests that the problem of theory, or the lack of it, may actually be a matter of scale and timing:

> It expects something of the scale of humanities scholarship which I'm not sure is true anymore: that a single scholar—nay, every scholar—working alone will, over the course of his or her lifetime . . . make a fundamental theoretical advance to the field.
>
> Increasingly, this expectation is something peculiar to the humanities. . . . it required the work of a generation of mathematicians and observational astronomers, gainfully employed, to enable the eventual "discovery" of Neptune . . . Since the scientific revolution, most theoretical advances play out over generations, not single careers. We don't expect all of our physics graduate students to make fundamental theoretical breakthroughs or claims about the nature of quantum mechanics, for example. There is just too much lab work to be done and data to analyzed for each person to be pointed at the end point. That work is valued for the incremental contribution to the generational research agenda that it is. (Scheinfeldt, "Response")

Yet notice how theory is again being marginalized in favour of an emphasis on STEM subjects and the adoption of expectations and approaches associated with mathematicians and astronomers in particular.

This is not to deny the importance of experimenting with the new kinds of knowledge, tools, methods, materials, and modes of working and thinking that digital media technologies create and make possible, including those drawn from computer science, in order to bring new forms of Foucauldian *dispositifs*, or what Bernard Stiegler calls *hypomnemata* (i.e., mnemonics, what Plato referred to as *pharmaka*, both poisons and cures), or what I am trying to think in terms of media gifts into play.[3] And I would potentially include in this process of experimentation techniques and methodologies drawn from computer science and other related fields such as information visualization, data mining, and so forth. Yes, of course, it is quite possible that as Daniel W. Stowell, director of the Papers of Abraham Lincoln project at the Illinois Historic Preservation Society puts it, in the future "people will use this data in ways we can't even imagine yet," both singularly and collaboratively (cited in Cohen, "Digital Keys"). Still, there is something intriguing about the way in which many defenders of the turn toward computational tools and methods in the humanities evoke a sense of time in relation to theory.

Take the argument—one I have heard put forward at a number of different events now—that critical and self-reflexive theoretical questions about the use of digital tools and data-led methodologies should be deferred for the time being, lest they have the effect of strangling at birth what could turn out to be a very different form of humanities research before it has had a chance to properly develop and take shape. Viewed in isolation, it can be difficult, if not impossible, to decide whether this particular form of "limitless" postponement (Deleuze, 5) is serving as an alibi for a naive and rather superficial form of scholarship (Meeks) or whether it is indeed acting as a responsible, political or ethical opening to the (heterogeneity and incalculability of the) future, including the future of the humanities. After all, the suggestion is that now is *not the right time* to be making any such decision or judgment, since we cannot *yet* know how humanists will *eventually* come to use these tools and data and thus what data-driven scholarship may or may not turn out to be capable of critically, politically, theoretically.

This argument would be more convincing as a responsible political or ethical call to leave the question of the use of digital tools and data-led methodologies in the humanities open if it were the only sense in which time was evoked in relation to theory in this context. Significantly, it is not. As we have seen, advocates for the computational turn do so in a number of other and often competing senses, too. These include the following:

1. That the time *of* theory is over, in the sense a particular historical period or moment has now ended (e.g., that of the culture wars of the 1980s)

2. That the time *for* theory is over, in the sense it is now the time for methodology
3. That the time to return to theory, or for theory to (re-)emerge in some new, unpredictable form that represents a fundamental breakthrough or advance, although possibly on its way, has not arrived yet and cannot necessarily be expected to do so for some time given that "most theoretical advances play out over generations" (Scheinfeldt, "Response")

All of this gives a very different inflection to the view of theoretical critique as being at best inappropriate and at worst harmful to data-driven scholarship. Even a brief glance at the history of theory's reception in the English-speaking world is sometimes enough to reveal that those who announce its time has not yet come, or is already over, that theory is in decline or even dead and that we now live in a posttheoretical world, are more often than not endeavoring to keep it at a temporal distance. Positioning their own work as being either pre- or posttheory in this way in effect gives them permission to continue with their preferred techniques and methodologies for studying culture relatively uncontested (rather than having to ask rigorous, critical and self-reflexive questions about their practices and their justifications for them). Placed in this wider context, far from helping to keep the question concerning the use of digital tools and data-led methodologies in the humanities open (or having anything particularly interesting to say about theory), the rejection of critical-theoretical ideas as untimely can be seen as both moralizing and conservative.

In saying this I am reiterating an argument initially made by Wendy Brown in the sphere of political theory. Yet can a similar case not be made with regard to the computational turn in the humanities to the effect that the "rebuff of critical theory as untimely provides the core matter for the affirmative case for it"?[4] Theory is vital from this point of view, not for conforming to accepted conceptions of political critique that see it primarily in terms of power, ideology, race, gender, class, sexuality, ecology, affect, and so forth or for sustaining conventional methods of studying culture that may no longer be appropriate to the networked nature of twenty-first century postindustrial society. Theory is vital "to contest the very sense of time invoked to declare critique untimely" (Brown, 4).

NOTES

This chapter originally appeared as "On the Limits of Openness V: There Are No Digital Humanities," *Media Gifts*, January 12, 2011. http://www.garyhall.info/journal/2011/1/27/on-the-limits-of-openness-vi-has-critical-theory-run-out-of.html.

1. This is one explanation as to why many exponents of the computational turn appear to display such little awareness of the research of "critical media scholars (like Matthew Fuller, Wendy Chun, McKenzie Wark, and many others) and hacker activists of the

past decade; research that has shown again and again how these very formalisms [i.e. 'the "quantitative" formalisms of databases and programming'] are 'qualitative,' i.e. designed by human groups and shaped by cultural, economical and political interests through and through" (Cramer). Liu encapsulates the situation as follows: "In the digital humanities, cultural criticism—in both its interpretive and advocacy modes—has been noticeably absent by comparison with the mainstream humanities or, even more strikingly, with 'new media studies' (populated as the latter is by net critics, tactical media critics, hacktivists, and so on). We digital humanists develop tools, data, metadata, and archives critically; and we have also developed critical positions on the nature of such resources (e.g., disputing whether computational methods are best used for truth-finding or, as Lisa Samuels and Jerome McGann put it, 'deformation'). But rarely do we extend the issues involved into the register of society, economics, politics, or culture in the vintage manner, for instance, of the Computer Professionals for Social Responsibility (CPSR). How the digital humanities advance, channel, or resist the great postindustrial, neoliberal, corporatist, and globalist flows of information-cum-capital, for instance, is a question rarely heard in the digital humanities associations, conferences, journals, and projects with which I am familiar. Not even the clichéd forms of such issues—e.g., 'the digital divide,' 'privacy,' 'copyright,' and so on—get much play."

2. See http://victorianbooks.org.

3. See http://garyhall.info.

4. Lest this aspect of my analysis appear somewhat unfair, I should stress that the ongoing discussion over how the digital humanities are to be defined and understood does feature a number of critics of the turn toward techniques and methodologies derived from computer science who have made a case for the continuing importance of the traditional, theoretically informed humanities. See, in their different ways, not just Higgen and Liu as referenced above but also Drucker and Fitzpatrick. For an analysis that draws attention to some of the elements of misrecognition that are in turn to be found in such a traditional, theoretically informed humanism, see my "On the Limits of Openness: Cultural Analytics and the Computational Turn in the Digital Humanities" (unpublished manuscript), especially the conclusion, and also Hall, "The Digital Humanities Beyond Computing: A Postscript."

BIBLIOGRAPHY

Brown, Wendy. *Edgework: Critical Essays on Knowledge and Politics*. Princeton and Oxford: Princeton University Press, 2005.

Cohen, Dan. "Searching for the Victorians." *Dan Cohen*. October 4, 2010. http://www.dancohen.org/2010/10/04/searching-for-the-victorians/.

Cohen, Patricia. "Digital Keys for Unlocking the Humanities' Riches." *New York Times*, November 16, 2010. http://www.nytimes.com/2010/11/17/arts/17digital.html

Cramer, Florian. "Re: Digital Humanities Manifesto." *Nettime*. January 22, 2009. http://www.mail-archive.com/nettime-l@kein.org/msg01331.html.

Deleuze, Gilles. "Postscript on Societies of Control." *October* 59 (Winter 1992): 3–7.

Drucker, Johanna. "Humanistic Approaches to the Graphical Expression of Interpretation." *MIT World*. May 20, 2010. http://mitworld.mit.edu/video/796.

Fitzpatrick, Kathleen. "Reporting from the Digital Humanities 2010 Conference." *Chronicle of Higher Education*, July 13, 2010. http://chronicle.com/blogPost/Reporting-from-the-Digital/25473/.

Hall, Gary. "The Digital Humanities Beyond Computing: A Postscript." *Culture Machine* 12 (2011). http://www.culturemachine.net/index.php/cm/article/view/441/459.

———. *Digitize This Book! The Politics of New Media, or Why We Need Open Access Now*. Minneapolis and London: University of Minnesota Press, 2008.

Higgen, Tanner. "Cultural Politics, Critique, and the Digital Humanities." *Gaming the System*. May 25, 2010. .http://www.tannerhiggin.com/2010/05/cultural-politics-critique-and-the-digital-humanities/.

Latour, Bruno. "Why Has Critique Run Out of Steam?" *Critical Inquiry* 30, no. 2 (2004). http://criticalinquiry.uchicago.edu/issues/v30/30n2.Latour.html.

Liu, Alan. "Where is Cultural Criticism in the Digital Humanities." Paper presented at the panel on "The History and Future of the Digital Humanities," Modern Language Association convention, Los Angeles, January 7, 2011. http://liu.english.ucsb.edu/where-is-cultural-criticism-in-the-digital-humanities.

Meeks, Elijah. "The Digital Humanities as Imagined Community." *Digital Humanities Specialist*. September 14, 2010. https://dhs.stanford.edu/the-digital-humanities-as/the-digital-humanities-as-imagined-community/.

Scheinfeldt, Tom. "Searching for the Victorians." Response to Dan Cohen. *Dan Cohen*. October 5, 2010. http://www.dancohen.org/2010/10/04/searching-for-the-victorians/.

———. "Sunset for Ideology, Sunrise for Methodology?" *Found History*. March 13, 2008. http://www.foundhistory.org/2008/03/13/sunset-for-ideology-sunrise-for-methodology/. Reprinted in this volume.

———. "Where's the Beef? Does Digital Humanities Have to Answer Questions?" *Found History*. March 13, 2010. http://www.foundhistory.org/2010/05/12/wheres-the-beef-does-digital-humanities-have-to-answer-questions/.

There Are No Digital Humanities

GARY HALL

Building on the work of Jean-François Lyotard and Gilles Deleuze in *The Postmodern Condition* and "Postscript on Societies of Control," respectively, let us pursue a little further the hypothesis that the externalization of knowledge onto computers, databases, and more recently mobile media environments, networked servers, and the cloud is involved in the constitution of a different form of society and human subject. To what extent do such developments cast the so-called computational turn in the humanities in a rather different light to the celebratory data fetishism that has come to dominate this rapidly emerging field? Is the direct, practical use of techniques and methodologies drawn from computer science and various fields related to it here, too, helping to produce a major alteration in the status and nature of knowledge and indeed the human subject? I'm thinking not just of the use of tools such as Anthologize, Delicious, Juxta, Mendeley, Pliny, Prezi, and Zotero to structure and disseminate scholarship and learning in the humanities. I also have in mind the generation of dynamic maps of large humanities data sets and employment of algorithmic techniques to search for and identify patterns in literary, cultural, and filmic texts as well as the way in which the interactive nature of much digital technology is enabling user data regarding people's creative activities with this media to be captured, mined, and analyzed by humanities scholars.

To be sure, in what seems to be almost the reverse of the situation Lyotard describes in *The Postmodern Condition*,[1] many of those in the humanities—and this includes some of the field's most radical thinkers—*do* now appear to be looking increasingly to science (*and* technology *and* mathematics), if not necessarily computer science specifically, to provide their research with a degree of legitimacy. Witness Franco "Bifo" Berardi's appeal to "the history of modern chemistry on the one hand, and the most recent cognitive theories on the other" (121) for confirmation of the compositionist philosophical hypothesis in his book *The Soul at Work*: "There is no object, no existent, and no person: only aggregates, temporary atomic compositions, figures that the human eye perceives as stable but that are indeed mutational, transient, frayed and indefinable" (120). It is this hypothesis, derived from Democritus, that Bifo sees as underpinning the methods of both the schizoanalysis of Deleuze and Guattari and the Italian Autonomist Theory on which his own compositionist philosophy is based. Can this turn toward the sciences (if there has indeed been such a turn, a question that is worthy of further examination) be regarded as a response on the part of the humanities to the perceived lack of credibility, if not obsolescence, of *their* metanarratives of legitimation: the life of the spirit and the Enlightenment but also Marxism, psychoanalysis, and so forth? Indeed, are the sciences today to be regarded as answering many humanities questions more convincingly than the humanities themselves?

While ideas of this kind are perhaps a little bit too neat and symmetrical to be entirely convincing, this "scientific turn" in the humanities *has* been attributed by some to a crisis of confidence. It is a crisis brought about, if not by the lack of credibility of the humanities' metanarratives of legitimation exactly then at least in part by the "imperious attitude" of the sciences. This attitude has led the latter to colonize the humanists' space in the form of biomedicine, neuroscience, theories of cognition, and so on (Kagan, 227).[2] Is the turn toward computing just the latest manifestation of and response to this crisis of confidence in the humanities? Can we go even further and ask, is it evidence that certain parts of the humanities are attempting to increase *their* connection to society[3] and to the instrumentality and functionality of society especially? Can it be merely a coincidence that such a turn toward computing is gaining momentum at a time when the UK government is emphasizing the importance of the STEMs (Science, Technology, Engineering and Mathematics) and withdrawing support and funding for the humanities? Or is one of the reasons all this is happening now due to the fact that the humanities, like the sciences themselves, are under pressure from government, business, management, industry, and increasingly the media to prove they provide value for money in instrumental, functional, performative terms? Is the interest in computing a strategic decision on the part of some of those in the humanities? As Dan Cohen and Fred Gibbs's project to text mine "the 1,681,161 books that were published in English in the UK in the long nineteenth century" shows, one can get funding from the likes of Google (Cohen, "Searching"). In fact, in the summer of 2010 "Google awarded $1 million to professors doing digital humanities research" (Cohen, "Digital Keys"; see also Orwant).

To what extent, then, is the take up of practical techniques and approaches from computing science providing some areas of the humanities with a means of defending (and refreshing) themselves in an era of global economic crisis and severe cuts to higher education, through the transformation of their knowledge and learning into quantities of information—deliverables? Can we even position the computational turn as an event created to justify such a move on the part of certain elements within the humanities (Frabetti)? And does this mean that, if we don't simply want to go along with the current movement *away* from what remains resistant to a general culture of measurement and calculation and *toward* a concern to legitimate power and control by optimizing the system's efficiency, we would be better off using a different term than "digital humanities"? After all, the idea of a computational turn implies that the humanities, thanks to the development of a new generation of powerful computers and digital tools, have somehow *become* digital, or are in the process of *becoming* digital, or are at least coming to terms with the digital and computing (Frabetti). Yet one of the things I am attempting to show by drawing on the thought of Lyotard, Deleuze, and others is that the digital is not something that can now be *added to* the humanities—for the simple reason that the (supposedly predigital) humanities can be seen to have *already had* an understanding of and engagement with computing and the digital.

NOTES

This chapter originally appeared as "On the Limits of Openness V: There Are No Digital Humanities," *Media Gifts*, January 12, 2011. http://www.garyhall.info/journal/2011/1/12/on-the-limits-of-openness-v-there-are-no-digital-humanities.html.

1. In *The Postmodern Condition*, Jean-François Lyotard showed how science, lacking the resources to legitimate itself as true, had since its beginnings with Plato relied for its legitimacy on precisely the kind of knowledge it did not even consider to be knowledge: nonscientific narrative knowledge. Specifically, science legitimated itself by producing a discourse called philosophy. It was philosophy's role to generate a discourse of legitimation for science. Lyotard proceeded to define as modern any science that legitimated itself in this way by means of a metadiscourse that explicitly appealed to a grand narrative of some sort: the life of the spirit, the Enlightenment, progress, modernity, the emancipation of humanity, the realization of the Idea.

2. Interestingly, for Kagan, "The scientists' intrusions into the philosophers' territory, which robbed the latter of part of their mission, forced them to find another assignment and many selected analyses of the coherence of the scientists' semantic texts" (Kagan, 228).

3. As Kirschenbaum writes, "Whatever else it might be then, the digital humanities today is about a scholarship (and a pedagogy) that is publicly visible in ways to which we are generally unaccustomed, a scholarship and pedagogy that are bound up with infrastructure in ways that are deeper and more explicit than we are generally accustomed to, a scholarship and pedagogy that are collaborative and depend on networks of people and that live an active 24/7 life online. Isn't that something you want in your English department?"

BIBLIOGRAPHY

Berardi, Franco "Bifo". *The Soul at Work: From Alienation to Autonomy.* Los Angeles: Semiotext(e), 2009.

Cohen, Dan. "Searching for the Victorians." *Dan Cohen*. October 4, 2010. http://www.dancohen.org/2010/10/04/searching-for-the-victorians/.

Cohen, Patricia. "Digital Keys for Unlocking the Humanities' Riches." *New York Times,* November 16, 2010. http://www.nytimes.com/2010/11/17/arts/17digital.html.

Deleuze, Gilles. "Postscript on Societies of Control." *October* 59 (Winter 1992): 3–7.

Frabetti, Federica. "Digital Again? The Humanities Between the Computational Turn and Originary Technicity." Lecture, Open Media Lecture Series, Coventry School of Art and Design. November 9, 2010. http://coventryuniversity.podbean.com/2010/11/09/open-software-and-digital-humanities-federica-frabetti/.

Orwant, Jon. "Our Commitment to the Digital Humanities." *The Official Google Blog,* July 14, 2010. http://googleblog.blogspot.com/2010/07/our-commitment-to-digital-humanities.html.

Kagan, Jerome. *The Three Cultures: Natural Sciences, Social Sciences, and the Humanities in the 21st Century*. Cambridge, UK: Cambridge University Press, 2009.

Kirschenbaum, Matthew. "What Is Digital Humanities and What's It Doing in English Departments?" *ADE Bulletin* 150 (2010). http://mkirschenbaum.files.wordpress.com/2011/01/kirschenbaum_ade150.pdf. Reprinted in this volume.

Latour, Bruno. "Why Has Critique Run Out of Steam? From Matters of Fact to Matters of Concern" *Critical Inquiry* 30, no. 2 (2004).

Lyotard, Jean-François. *The Postmodern Condition: A Report on Knowledge*. Manchester: Manchester University Press, 1986.

PART III

CRITIQUING THE DIGITAL HUMANITIES

Why Are the Digital Humanities So White? or Thinking the Histories of Race and Computation

TARA MCPHERSON

In mid-October 2008, the American Studies Association (ASA) hosted its annual conference in Albuquerque, New Mexico. According to its website, the ASA "is the nation's oldest and largest association devoted to the interdisciplinary study of American culture and history." Over the past two decades, the ASA conference has emerged as a leading venue for vibrant discussions about race, ethnicity, transnationalism, gender, and sexuality. While the ASA represents scholars with a diverse array of methodological approaches from a variety of disciplines, the society is a welcome home to academics whose work is interpretative and theoretical. During the meeting, I attended a variety of panels engaging such issues and approaches and came away feeling energized and refreshed, my intellectual imagination stoked by the many ways in which race and ethnicity were wielded as central terms of analysis throughout the long weekend.

The following week, I was off to Baltimore where I attended "Tools for Data-Driven Scholarship," a workshop funded by the National Science Foundation (NSF), the National Endowment for the Humanities, and the Institute of Museum and Library Services. This invitation-only event was cohosted by George Mason University's Center for History and New Media (CHNM) and the Maryland Institute for Technology in the Humanities (MITH), two pioneering centers of what we have recently begun to call the "digital humanities." This workshop built upon several years' conversation (particularly following the 2003 NSF Atkins Report on cyberinfrastructure) about the need for a digital infrastructure for humanities computing. The goal of the workshop was defined in the e-mail invite as a report "that discusses the needs of tools developers and users; sets forth objectives for addressing those needs; proposes infrastructure for accomplishing these objectives; and makes suggestions for a possible RFP." This meeting was also lively, full of thoughtful discussions about the possibilities for (and obstacles in the way of) a robust infrastructure for scholars engaged in computation and the humanities. The conversation certainly fired up my technological imagination and subsequently led to useful discussions with my collaborators in technological design.[1]

As I flew home following this second event, I found myself reflecting on how far my thoughts had ranged in the course a mere week: from diaspora to database, from oppression to ontology, from visual studies to visualizations. And, once again, I found myself wondering why it seemed so hard to hold together my long-standing academic interests in race, gender, and certain modes of theoretical inquiry with my more recent (if decade-old) immersion in the world of digital production and design.

While the workshop I participated in at ASA was titled "American Studies at the Digital Crossroads" and drew a nice crowd, the conference as a whole included remarkably little discussion of digital technologies (although there were some analyses of digital texts such as websites and video games.)[2] It is largely accurate, if also a generalization, to say that many in the membership of the ASA treat computation within the humanities with some level of suspicion, perceiving it to be complicit with the corporatization of higher education or as primarily technological rather than scholarly.[3] (Indeed, this attitude is shared by a large number of "traditional" humanities scholars across any number of fields or professional societies who do not work with digital media.) In a hallway chat following our workshop, one scholar framed his dis-ease as a question: "Why are the digital humanities, well, so white?" And while my memory is far from perfect, I think it is safe to say that the Baltimore workshop included no discussion of many topics much in evidence at ASA, topics including immigration, race, and neoliberalism. To be fair, this was a workshop focused on the notion of tools and infrastructure, so one might not expect such discussions. Nonetheless, this essay will argue that we desperately need to close the gap between these two modes of inquiry. Further, I will argue that the difficulties we encounter in knitting together our discussions of race (or other modes of difference) with our technological productions within the digital humanities (or in our studies of code) are actually an *effect* of the very designs of our technological systems, designs that emerged in post–World War II computational culture. These origins of the digital continue to haunt our scholarly engagements with computers, underwriting the ease with which we partition off considerations of race in our work in the digital humanities and digital media studies.

U.S. Operating Systems at Midcentury: The Intertwining of Race and UNIX

Let us turn to two fragments cut from history, during the 1960s.

FRAGMENT ONE

In the early 1960s, computer scientists at MIT were working on Project MAC, an early set of experiments in Compatible Timesharing Systems for computing. By 1965, MULTICS (Multiplexed Information and Computing Service), a mainframe timesharing operating system, was in use, with joint development by MIT, GE, and Bell Labs, a subsidiary of AT&T. The project was funded by ARPA (Advanced Research Projects Agency) of the Defense Department for two million dollars a year for eight years. MULTICS introduced early ideas about modularity in hardware structure and software architecture.

In 1969, Bell Labs stopped working on MULTICS, and that summer one of their engineers, Ken Thompson, developed the beginning of UNIX. While there are clearly influences of MULTICS on UNIX, the later system also moves away from the earlier one, pushing for increased modularity and for a simpler design able to run on cheaper computers.

In simplest terms, UNIX is an early operating system for digital computers, one that has spawned many offshoots and clones. These include MAC OS X as well as LINUX, indicating the reach of UNIX over the past forty years. The system also influenced non-UNIX operating systems like Windows NT and remains in use by many corporate IT divisions. UNIX was originally written in assembly language, but after Thompson's colleague Dennis Ritchie developed the C programming language in 1972, Thompson rewrote UNIX in that language. Basic text-formatting and editing features were added (i.e., early word processors). In 1974, Ritchie and Thompson published their work in the journal of the *Association for Computing Machinery*, and UNIX began to pick up a good deal of steam.[4]

UNIX can also be thought of as more than an operating system, as it also includes a number of utilities such as command line editors, APIs, code libraries, and so on. Furthermore, UNIX is widely understood to embody particular philosophies and cultures of computation, "operating systems" of a larger order that we will return to.

FRAGMENT TWO

Of course, for scholars of culture, of gender, and of race like the members of the ASA, dates like 1965 and 1968 have other resonances. For many of us, 1965 might not recall MULTICS but instead the assassination of Malcolm X, the founding of the United Farm Workers, the burning of Watts, or the passage of the Voting Rights Act. The mid-1960s also saw the origins of the American Indian Movement (AIM) and the launch of the National Organization for Women (NOW). The late 1960s mark the 1968 citywide walkouts of Latino youth in Los Angeles, the assassinations of Martin Luther King Jr. and Robert F. Kennedy, the Chicago Democratic Convention, the Stonewall Riots, and the founding of the Black Panthers and the Young Lords. Beyond the geographies of the United States, we might also remember the Prague Spring of 1968, Tommie Smith and John Carlos at the Mexico Summer Olympics, the Tlatelolco Massacre, the execution of Che Guevara, the Chinese Cultural Revolution, the Six-Day War, or May '68 in Paris. On the African continent, thirty-two countries gained independence from colonial rulers. In the United

States, broad cultural shifts emerged across the decade, as identity politics took root and countercultural forces challenged traditional values. Resistance to the Vietnam War mounted as the decade wore on. Abroad, movements against colonialism and oppression were notably strong.

The history just glossed as "Fragment One" is well known to code junkies and computer geeks. Numerous websites archive oral histories, programming manuals, and technical specifications for MULTICS, UNIX, and various mainframe and other hardware systems. Key players in that history, including Ken Thompson, Donald Ritchie, and Doug McIlroy, have a kind of geek-chic celebrity status, and differing versions of the histories of software and hardware development are hotly debated, including nitty-gritty details of what really counts as "a UNIX." In media studies, emerging work in "code studies" often resurrects and takes up these histories.[5]

Within American, cultural, and ethnic studies, the temporal touchstones of struggles over racial justice, antiwar activism, and legal history are also widely recognized and analyzed. Not surprisingly, these two fragments typically stand apart in parallel tracks, attracting the interest and attention of very different audiences located in the deeply siloed departments that categorize our universities.

But why?

In short, I suggest that these two moments are deeply interdependent. In fact, they coconstitute one another, comprising not independent slices of history but instead related and useful lenses into the shifting epistemological registers driving U.S. and global culture in the 1960s and after.

This history of intertwining and mutual dependence is hard to sketch. As one delves into the intricacies of UNIX (or of XML), race in America recedes far from our line of vision and inquiry. Likewise, detailed examinations into the shifting registers of race and racial visibility post-1950 do not easily lend themselves to observations about the emergence of object-oriented programming or the affordances of databases. Very few audiences who care about one lens have much patience or tolerance for the other.

Early forays into new media theory in the late 1990s and much concurrent work in the computational humanities rarely helped this problem. Theorists of new media often retreated into forms of analysis that Marsha Kinder has critiqued as "cyberstructuralist," intent on parsing media specificity and on theorizing the forms of new media while disavowing twenty-plus years of critical race theory, feminism, and other modes of overtly politicized inquiry. Much of the work in the digital humanities also proceeded as if technologies from XML to databases were neutral tools.[6] Many who had worked hard to instill race as a central mode of analysis in film, literary, and media studies throughout the late twentieth century were disheartened and outraged (if not that surprised) to find both new media theory and emerging digital tools seem indifferent to those hard-won gains.

Early analyses of race and the digital often took two forms: first, a critique of representations *in* new media or the building of digital archives about race, modes that largely were deployed at the surface of our screens, or, second, debates about access to media—that is, the digital divide. Such work rarely tied race to the analyses of form, phenomenology, or computation that were so compelling in the work of Lev Manovich, Mark Hansen, or Jay Bolter and Richard Grusin. Important works emerged from both "camps," but the camps rarely intersected. A few events attempted to force a collision between these areas, but the going was tough. For instance, at the two Race and Digital Space Conferences colleagues and I organized in 2000 and 2002, the vast majority of participants and speakers were engaged in work in the two modes mentioned earlier. The cyberstructuralists were not in attendance.

But what if this very incompatability is itself part and parcel of the organization of knowledge production that operating systems like UNIX helped to disseminate around the world? Might we ask whether there is not something *particular to the very forms* of electronic culture that seems to encourage just such a movement, a movement that partitions race off from the specificity of media forms? Put differently, might we argue that the very structures of digital computation develop at least in part to cordon off race and to contain it? Further, might we come to understand that our own critical methodologies are the heirs to this epistemological shift?

From early writings by Sherry Turkle and George Landow to more recent work by Alex Galloway and others, new media scholars have noted the parallels between the ways of knowing modeled in computer culture and the greatest hits of structuralism and poststructuralism. Critical race theorists and postcolonial scholars like Chela Sandoval and Gayatri Spivak have illustrated the structuring (if unacknowledged) role that race plays in the work of poststructuralists like Roland Barthes and Michel Foucault. We might bring these two arguments together, triangulating race, electronic culture, and poststructuralism, and, further, argue that race, particularly in the United States, is central to this undertaking, fundamentally shaping how we see and know as well as the technologies that underwrite or cement both vision and knowledge. Certain modes of racial visibility and knowing coincide or dovetail with specific ways of organizing data: if digital computing underwrites today's information economy and is the central technology of post–World War II America, these technologized ways of seeing and knowing took shape in a world also struggling with shifting knowledges about and representations of race. If, as Michael Omi and Howard Winant argue, racial formations serve as fundamental organizing principles of social relations in the United States, on both the macro and micro levels (55), how might we understand the infusion of racial organizing principles into the technological organization of knowledge after World War II?

Omi and Winant and other scholars have tracked the emergence of a "race-blind" rhetoric at midcentury, a discourse that moves from overt to more covert modes of racism and racial representation (e.g., from the era of Jim Crow to liberal colorblindness). Drawing from those 3-D postcards that bring two or more images together even while suppressing their connections, I have earlier termed the racial paradigms of the postwar era "lenticular logics." The ridged coating on 3-D postcards is actually a lenticular lens, a structural device that makes simultaneously viewing the various images contained on one card nearly impossible. The viewer can rotate the card to see any single image, but the lens itself makes seeing the images *together* very difficult, even as it conjoins them at a structural level (i.e., within the same card). In the post–civil rights United States, the lenticular is a way of organizing the world. It structures representations but also epistemologies. It also serves to secure our understandings of race in very narrow registers, fixating on sameness or difference while forestalling connection and interrelation. As I have argued elsewhere, we might think of the lenticular as a covert mode of the pretense of separate but equal, remixed for midcentury America (McPherson, 250).

A lenticular logic is a covert racial logic, a logic for the post–civil rights era. We might contrast the lenticular postcard to that wildly popular artifact of the industrial era, the stereoscope card. The stereoscope melds two different images into an imagined whole, privileging the whole; the lenticular image partitions and divides, privileging fragmentation. A lenticular logic is a logic of the fragment or the chunk, a way of seeing the world as discrete modules or nodes, a mode that suppresses relation and context. As such, the lenticular also manages and controls complexity.

And what in the world does this have to do with those engineers laboring away at Bell Labs, the heroes of the first fragment of history this essay began with? What's race got to do with that? The popularity of lenticular lenses, particularly in the form of postcards, coincides historically not just with the rise of an articulated movement for civil rights but also with the growth of electronic culture and the birth of digital computing (with both—digital computing and the civil rights movement—born in quite real ways of World War II). We might understand UNIX as the way in which the emerging logics of the lenticular and of the covert racism of color blindness get ported into our computational systems, both in terms of the specific functions of UNIX as an operating system and in the broader philosophy it embraces.

SITUATING UNIX

In moving toward UNIX from MULTICS, programmers conceptualized UNIX as a kind of tool kit of "synergistic parts" that allowed "flexibility in depth" (Raymond, 9). Programmers could "choose among multiple shells. . . . [and] programs normally provide[d] many behavior options" (6). One of the design philosophies driving UNIX is the notion that a program should do one thing and do it well (not unlike our deep disciplinary drive in many parts of the university); this privileging of the discrete, the local, and the specific emerges again and again in discussions of UNIX's origins and design philosophies.

Books for programmers that explain the UNIX philosophy revolve around a common set of rules. While slight variations on this rule set exist across programming books and online sites, Eric Raymond sets out the first nine rules as follows:

1. Rule of Modularity: Write simple parts connected by clean interfaces.
2. Rule of Clarity: Clarity is better than cleverness.
3. Rule of Composition: Design programs to be connected to other programs.
4. Rule of Separation: Separate policy from mechanism; separate interfaces from engines.
5. Rule of Simplicity: Design for simplicity; add complexity only where you must.
6. Rule of Parsimony: Write a big program only when it is clear by demonstration that nothing else will do.
7. Rule of Transparency: Design for visibility to make inspection and debugging easier.
8. Rule of Robustness: Robustness is the child of transparency and simplicity.
9. Rule of Representation: Fold knowledge into data so program logic can be stupid and robust. (13)

Other rules include the Rules of Least Surprise, Silence, Repair, Economy, Generation, Optimization, Diversity, and Extensibility.[7]

These rules implicitly translate into computational terms the chunked logics of the lenticular. For instance, Brian Kernighan wrote in a 1976 handbook on software programming that "controlling complexity is the essence of computer programming" (quoted in Raymond, 14). Complexity in UNIX is controlled in part by the Rule of Modularity, which insists that code be constructed of discrete and interchangeable parts that can be plugged together via clean interfaces. In *Design Rules, Vol. 1: The Power of Modularity*, Carliss Baldwin and Kim Clark argue that computers from 1940 to 1960 had "complex, interdependent designs," and they label this era the "premodular" phase of computing (149). While individuals within the industry, including John von Neumann, were beginning to imagine benefits to modularity in computing, Baldwin and Clark note that von Neumann's ground-breaking designs for computers in that period "fell short of true modularity" because "in no sense was the detailed design of one component going to be hidden from the others: all pieces of the system would be produced 'in full view' of the others" (157). Thus one might say that these early visions of digital computers were neither modular nor lenticular. Baldwin and Clark track the increasing modularity of hardware design from the early 1950s forward and also observe that UNIX was the first operating system to embrace modularity and adhere "to the principles of information hiding" in its design (324).

There are clearly practical advantages of such structures for coding, but they also underscore a worldview in which a troublesome part might be discarded without disrupting the whole. Tools are meant to be "encapsulated" to avoid "a tendency to involve programs with each others' internals" (Raymond, 15). Modules "don't promiscuously share global data," and problems can stay "local" (84–85). In writing about the Rule of Composition, Eric Raymond advises programmers to "make [programs] independent." He writes, "It should be easy to replace one end with a completely different implementation without disturbing the other" (15). Detachment is valued because it allows a cleaving from "the particular . . . conditions under which a design problem was posed. Abstract. Simplify. Generalize" (95). While "generalization" in UNIX has specific meanings, we might also see at work here the basic contours of a lenticular approach to the world, an approach that separates object from context, cause from effect.

In a 1976 article, "Software Tools," Bell Lab programmers Kernighan and P. J. Plauger urged programmers "to view specific jobs as special cases of general, frequently performed operations, so they can make and use general-purpose tools to solve them. We also hope to show how to design programs to look like tools and to interconnect conveniently" (1). While the language here is one of generality (as in "general purpose" tools), in fact, the tool library that is being envisioned is a series of very discrete and specific tools or programs that can operate independently of one another. They continue, "Ideally, a program should not know where its input comes from nor where its output goes. The UNIX time-sharing system provides a particularly elegant way to handle input and output redirection" (2). Programs can profitably be described as filters, even though they do quite complicated transformations on their input. One should be able to say

program-1 . . . | sort | program-2 . . .

and have the output of program-1 sorted before being passed to program-2. This has the major advantage that neither program-1 nor program-2 need know how to sort, but can concentrate on its main task (4).

In effect, the tools chunk computational programs into isolated bits where the programs' operations are meant to be "invisible to the user" and to the other programs in a sequence: "the point is that this operation is invisible to the user (or should be). . . . Instead he sees simply a program with one input and one output. Unsorted data go in one end; somewhat later, sorted data come out the other. It must be *convenient* to use a tool, not just possible" (5). Kernighan and Plauger saw the "filter concept" as a useful way to get programmers to think in discrete bits and to simplify their code, reducing the potential complexity of programs. They note that "when a job is viewed as a series of filters, the implementation simplifies, for it is broken down into a sequence of relatively independent pieces, each small and easily tested. This is a form of high-level modularization" (5). In their own way, these filters function as a kind of lenticular frame or lens, allowing only certain portions of complex data sets to be visible at a particular time to both the user and the machine.

The technical feature that allowed UNIX to achieve much of its modularity was the development by Ken Thompson (based on a suggestion by Doug McIlroy) of the pipe—that is, a vertical bar that replaced the symbol for greater than (>) in the operating system's code. As described by Doug Ritchie and Ken Thompson in a paper for the Association of Computing Machinery in 1974 (reprinted by Bell Labs in 1978), "A *read* using a pipe file descriptor waits until another process writes using the file descriptor for the same pipe. At this point, data are passed between the images of the two processes. Neither process need know that a pipe, rather than an ordinary file, is involved" (480). In this way, the ability to construct a pipeline from a series of small programs evolved, while the "hiding of internals" was also supported. The contents of a module were not central to the functioning of the pipeline; rather, the input or output (a text stream) was key. Brian Kernighan noted "that while input/output direction predates pipes, the development of pipes led to the concept of tools—software programs that would be in a 'tool box,' available when you need them" and interchangeable.[8] Pipes reduced complexity and were also linear. In "Software Tools," Kernighan and Plauger extend their discussion of pipes, noting that "a pipe provides a hidden buffering between the output of one program and the input of another program so information may pass between them without ever entering the file system" (2). They also signal the importance of pipes for issues of data security:

> And consider the sequence
>
> decrypt key <file | prog | encrypt key > newfile
>
> Here a decryption program decodes an encrypted file, passing the decoded characters to a program having no special security features. The ouput of the program is re-encrypted at the other end. If a true pipe mechanism is used, no clear-text version of the data will ever appear in a file. To simulate this sequence with temporary files risks breaching security. (3)

While the affordances of filters, pipes, and hidden data are often talked about as a matter of simple standardization and efficiency (as when Kernighan and Plauger argue that "our emphasis here has been on getting jobs done with an efficient use of people" [6]), they also clearly work in the service of new regimes of security, not an insignificant detail in the context of the cold war era. Programming manuals and UNIX guides again and again stress clarity and simplicity (don't write fancy code; say what you mean as clearly and directly as you can), but the structures of operating systems like UNIX function by hiding internal operations, skewing "clarity" in very particular directions. These manuals privilege a programmer's equivalent of common sense in the Gramscian sense. For Antonio Gramsci, common sense is a historically situated process, the way in which a particular group responds to "certain problems posed by reality which are quite specific" at a particular time (324). As programmers constituted themselves as a particular class of workers in the 1970s, they were necessarily lodged in their moment, deploying common sense and notions about simplicity to justify their innovations in code. Importantly, and as we will see, this moment is overdetermined by the ways in which the United States is widely coming to process race and other forms of difference in more covert registers, as noted earlier, even if the programmers themselves do not explicitly understand their work to be tied to such racial paradigms.[9]

Another rule of UNIX is the Rule of Diversity, which insists on a mistrust of the "one true way." Thus UNIX, in the words of one account, "embraces multiple languages, open extensible systems and customization hooks everywhere," reading much like a description of the tenets of neoliberal multiculturalism (Raymond, 24). Certain words emerge again and again throughout the ample literature on UNIX: modularity, compactness, simplicity, orthogonality. UNIX is meant to allow multitasking, portability, time sharing, and compartmentalizing. It is not much of a stretch to layer these traits over the core tenets of post-Fordism, a mode of production that begins to remake industrial-era notions of standardization in the 1960s: time-space compression, transformability, customization, a public/private blur, and so on. UNIX's intense modularity and information-hiding capacity were reinforced by its design—that is, in the ways in which it segregated the kernel from the shell. The kernel loads into the computer's memory at start-up and is "the heart" of UNIX (managing "hardware memory, job execution, and time sharing"), although it remains hidden from the user (Baldwin and Clark, 332). The shells (or programs that interpret commands) are intermediaries between the user and the computer's inner workings. They hide the details of the operating system from the user behind "the shell," extending modularity from a rule for programming in UNIX to the very design of UNIX itself.[10]

Modularity in the Social Field

This push toward modularity and the covert in digital computation also reflects other changes in the organization of social life in the United States by the 1960s. For instance, if the first half of the twentieth century laid bare its racial logics, from "Whites Only" signage to the brutalities of lynching, the second half increasingly hides its racial "kernel," burying it below a shell of neoliberal pluralism. These covert racial logics take hold at the tail end of the civil rights movement at least partially to cut off and contain the more radical logics implicit in the urban uprisings that shook Detroit, Watts, Chicago, and Newark. In fact, the urban center of Detroit was more segregated by the 1980s than in previous decades, reflecting a different inflection of the programmer's vision of the "easy removal" or containment of a troubling part. Whole areas of the city might be rendered orthogonal and disposable (also think post-Katrina New Orleans), and the urban black poor were increasingly isolated in "deteriorating city centers" (Sugrue, 198). Historian Thomas Sugrue traces the increasing unemployment rates for black men in Detroit, rates that rose dramatically from the 1950s to the 1980s, and maps a "deproletarianization" that "shaped a pattern of poverty in the postwar city that was surprisingly new" (262). Across several registers, the emerging neoliberal state begins to adopt the Rule of Modularity. For instance, we might draw an example from across the Atlantic. In her careful analysis of the effects of May 1968 and its afterlives, Kristin Ross argues that the French government contained the radical force of the uprisings by quickly moving to separate the students' rebellion from the concerns of labor, deploying a strategy of separation and containment in which both sides (students and labor) would ultimately lose (69).

Modularity in software design was meant to decrease "global complexity" and cleanly separate one "neighbor" from another (Raymond, 85). These strategies also played out in ongoing reorganizations of the political field throughout the 1960s and 1970s in both the Right and the Left. The widespread divestiture in the infrastructure of inner cities can be seen as one more insidious effect of the logic of modularity in the postwar era. But we might also understand the emergence of identity politics in the 1960s as a kind of social and political embrace of modularity and encapsulation, a mode of partitioning that turned away from the broader forms of alliance-based and globally inflected political practice that characterized both labor politics and antiracist organizing in the 1930s and 1940s.[11] While identity politics produced concrete gains in the world, particularly in terms of civil rights, we are also now coming to understand the degree to which these movements curtailed and short-circuited more radical forms of political praxis, reducing struggle to fairly discrete parameters.

Let me be clear. By drawing analogies between shifting racial and political formations and the emerging structures of digital computing in the late 1960s, I am not arguing that the programmers creating UNIX at Bell Labs and in Berkeley were *consciously* encoding new modes of racism and racial understanding into digital systems. (Indeed, many of these programmers were themselves left-leaning hippies, and the overlaps between the counterculture and early computing culture run deep, as Fred Turner has illustrated.) I also recognize that their innovations made possible the word processor I am using to write this article, a powerful tool that shapes cognition and scholarship in precise ways. Nor am I arguing for some exact correspondence between the ways in which encapsulation or modularity work in computation and how they function in the emerging regimes of neoliberalism, governmentality, and post-Fordism. Rather, I am highlighting the ways in which the organization of information and capital in the 1960s powerfully responds—across many registers—to the struggles for racial justice and democracy that so categorized the United States at the time. Many of these shifts were enacted in the name of liberalism, aimed at distancing the overt racism of the past even as they contained and cordoned off progressive radicalism. The emergence of covert racism and its rhetoric of color blindness are not so much intentional as systemic. Computation is a primary delivery method of these new systems, and it seems at best naive to imagine that cultural and computational operating systems don't mutually infect one another.

Thus we see modularity take hold not only in computation but also in the increasingly niched and regimented production of knowledge in the university after World War II. For instance, Christopher Newfield comments on the rise of New

Criticism in literature departments in the cold war era, noting its relentless formalism, a "logical corollary" to "depoliticization" (145) that "replaced agency with technique" (155). He attributes this particular tendency in literary criticism at least in part to the triumph of a managerial impulse, a turn that we might also align (even if Newfield doesn't) with the workings of modular code (itself studied as an exemplary approach to dynamic modeling systems for business management in the work of Baldwin and Clark cited earlier.)[12] He observes as well that this managerial obsession within literary criticism exhibits a surprising continuity across the 1960s and beyond. Gerald Graff has also examined the "patterned isolation" that emerges in the university after World War II, at the moment when New Criticism's methods take hold in a manner that deprivileges context and focuses on "explication for explication's sake." Graff then analyzes the routinization of literary criticism in the period, a mechanistic exercise with input and output streams of its own (227). He recognizes that university departments (his example is English) begin to operate by a field-based and modular strategy of "coverage," in which subfields proliferate and exist in their own separate chunks of knowledge, rarely contaminated by one another's "internals" (250). (He also comments that this modular strategy includes the token hiring of scholars of color who are then cordoned off within the department.) Graff locates the beginning of this patterned isolation in the run-up to the period that also brought us digital computing; he writes that it continues to play out today in disciplinary structures that have become increasingly narrow and specialized. Patterned isolation begins with the bureaucratic standardization of the university from 1890 through 1930 (61–62), but this "cut out and separate" mentality reaches a new crescendo after World War II as the organizational structure of the university pushes from simply bureaucratic and Taylorist to managerial, a shift noted as well by Christopher Newfield. Many now lament the overspecialization of the university; in effect, this tendency is a result of the additive logic of the lenticular or of the pipeline, where "content areas" or "fields" are tacked together without any sense of intersection, context, or relation. Today, we risk adding the digital humanities to our proliferating disciplinary menus without any meaningful and substantial engagement with fields such as gender studies or critical race theory.

It is interesting to note that much of the early work performed in UNIX environments was focused on document processing and communication tools and that UNIX is a computational system that very much privileges text (it centers on the text-based command line instead of on the graphical user interface, and its inputs and outputs are simple text lines). Many of the methodologies of the humanities from the cold war through the 1980s also privilege text while devaluing context and operate in their own chunked systems, suggesting telling parallels between the operating systems and privileged objects of the humanities and of the computers being developed on several university campuses in the same period.

Lev Manovich has, of course, noted the modularity of the digital era and also backtracked to early twentieth-century examples of modularity from the factory line to the creative productions of avant garde artists. In a posting to the Nettime listserv in 2005, he frames modularity as a uniquely twentieth-century phenomenon, from Henry Ford's assembly lines to the 1932 furniture designs of Belgian designer Louis Herman De Kornick. In his account, the twentieth century is characterized by an accelerating process of industrial modularization, but I think it is useful to examine the digital computer's privileged role in the process, particularly given that competing modes of computation were still quite viable until the 1960s, modes that might have pushed more toward the continuous flows of analog computing rather than the discrete tics of the digital computer. Is the modularity of the 1920s really the same as the modularity modeled in UNIX? Do these differences matter, and what might we miss if we assume a smooth and teleological triumph of modularity? How has computation pushed modularity in new directions, directions in dialogue with other cultural shifts and ruptures? Why does modularity emerge in our systems with such a vengeance across the 1960s?

I have here suggested that our technological formations are deeply bound up with our racial formations and that each undergo profound changes at midcentury. I am not so much arguing that one mode is causally related to the other but, rather, that they both represent a move toward modular knowledges, knowledges increasingly prevalent in the second half of the twentieth century. These knowledges support and enable the shift from the overt standardized bureaucracies of the 1920s and 1930s to the more dynamically modular and covert managerial systems that are increasingly prevalent as the century wears on. These latter modes of knowledge production and organization are powerful racial and technological operating systems that coincide with (and reinforce) (post)structuralist approaches to the world within the academy. Both the computer and the lenticular lens mediate images and objects, changing their relationship but frequently suppressing that process of relation, much like the divided departments of the contemporary university. The fragmentary knowledges encouraged by many forms and experiences of the digital neatly parallel the logics that underwrite the covert racism endemic to our times, operating in potential feedback loops, supporting each other. If scholars of race have highlighted how certain tendencies within poststructuralist theory simultaneously respond to and marginalize race, this maneuver is at least partially possible because of a parallel and increasing dispersion of electronic forms across culture, forms that simultaneously enact and shape these new modes of thinking.

While the examples here have focused on UNIX, it is important to recognize that the core principles of modularity that it helped bring into practice continue to impact a wide range of digital computation, especially the C programming language, itself developed for UNIX by Ritchie, based on Thompson's earlier B language. While UNIX and C devotees will bemoan the nonorthogonality and leakiness of Windows or rant about the complexity of C++, the basic argument offered earlier—that UNIX helped inaugurate modular and lenticular systems broadly across computation and culture—holds true for the black boxes of contemporary coding and numerous other instances of our digital praxis.

Today, we might see contemporary turns in computing—neural nets, clouds, semantics, and so on—as parallel to recent turns in humanities scholarship to privilege networks over nodes (particularly in new media studies and in digital culture theory) and to focus on globalization and its flows (in American studies and other disciplines). While this may simply mean we have learned our midcentury lessons and are smarter now, we might also continue to examine with rigor and detail the degree to which dominant forms of computation—what David Golumbia has aptly called "the cultural logic of computation" in his recent update of Frankfurt School pessimism for the twenty-first century—continue to respond to shifting racial and cultural formations. Might these emerging modes of computation be read as symptoms and drivers of our postracial moment, refracting in some way national anxieties (or hopes) about a decreasingly white America? We should also remain alert to how contemporary technoracial formations infect privileged ways of knowing in the academy. While both the tales of C. P. Snow circa 1959 and the Sokal science wars of the 1990s sustain the myth that science and the humanities operate in distinct realms of knowing, powerful operating systems have surged beneath the surface of what and how we know in the academy for well over half a decade. It would be foolish of us to believe that these operating systems—in this paper best categorized by UNIX and its many close siblings—do not at least partially overdetermine the very critiques we imagine that we are performing today.

Moving Beyond Our Boxes

So if we are always already complicit with the machine, what are we to do?

First, we must better understand the machines and networks that continue to powerfully shape our lives in ways that we are often ill equipped to deal with as media and humanities scholars. This necessarily involves more than simply studying our screens and the images that dance across them, moving beyond the study of representations and the rhetorics of visuality. We might read representations seeking symptoms of information capital's fault lines and successes, but we cannot read the logics of these systems and networks solely at the level of our screens. Capital is now fully organized under the sign of modularity. It operates via the algorithm and the database, via simulation and processing. Our screens are cover stories, disguising deeply divided forms of both machine and human labor. We focus exclusively on them increasingly to our peril.

Scholars in the digital humanities and in the emerging field of code studies are taking up the challenge of understanding how computational systems (especially but not only software) developed and operate. However, we must demand that these fields not replay the formalist and structuralist tendencies of new media theory circa 1998. This formalist turn displayed a stubborn technological determinism and often privileged the machine over the social. To end run such determinism, the digital humanities and code studies must also take up the questions of culture and meaning that animate so many scholars of race in fields like the *new* American studies. Likewise, scholars of race must analyze, use, and produce digital forms and not smugly assume that to engage the digital directly is to be complicit with the forces of capitalism. The lack of intellectual generosity across our fields and departments only reinforces the divide-and-conquer mentality that the most dangerous aspects of modularity underwrite. We must develop common languages that link the study of code and culture. We must historicize and politicize code studies. And, because digital media were born as much of the civil rights era as of the cold war era (and of course these eras are one and the same), our investigations must incorporate race from the outset, understanding and theorizing its function as a ghost in the digital machine. This does not mean that we should simply add race to our analysis in a modular way, neatly tacking it on or building digital archives of racial material, but that we must understand and theorize the deep imbrications of race and digital technology even when our objects of analysis (say UNIX or search engines) seem not to be about race at all. This will not be easy. In the writing of this essay, the logic of modularity continually threatened to take hold, leading me into detailed explorations of pipe structures in UNIX or departmental structures in the university, taking me far from the contours of race at midcentury. It is hard work to hold race and computation together in a systemic manner, but it is work that we must continue to undertake.

We also need to take seriously the possibility that questions of representation and of narrative and textual analysis may, in effect, divert us from studying the reorganization of capital—a reorganization dependent on the triumph of the very particular patterns of informationalization evident in code. If the study of representation may in fact be part and parcel of the very logic of modularity that such code inaugurates, a kind of distraction, it is equally plausible to argue that our very intense focus on visuality in the past twenty years of scholarship is just a different manifestation of the same distraction. There is tendency in film and media studies to treat the computer and its screens as (in Jonathan Beller's terms) a "legacy" technology to cinema. In its drive to stage continuities, such an argument tends to minimize or completely miss the fundamental material differences between cinematic visuality and the production of the visual by digital technologies. For most of the twentieth century, cinema was a profoundly visual (if also aural) form, with images etched into celluloid; the digital does not depend on vision in any analogous way.

To push my polemic to its furthest dimensions, I would argue that to study image, narrative, and visuality will never be enough if we do not engage as well the nonvisual dimensions of code and their organization of the world. Yet to trouble my own polemic, we might also understand the workings of code to have already internalized the visual to the extent that, in the heart of the labs from which UNIX emerged, the cultural processing of the visual via the register of race was already at work in the machine.

In extending our critical methodologies, we must have at least a passing familiarity with code languages, operating systems, algorithmic thinking, and systems design. We need database literacies, algorithmic literacies, computational literacies, interface literacies. We need new hybrid practitioners: artist-theorists, programming humanists, activist-scholars; theoretical archivists, critical race coders. We need new forms of graduate and undergraduate education that hone both critical and digital literacies. We have to shake ourselves out of our small, field-based boxes so that we might take seriously the possibility that our own knowledge practices are normalized, modular, and black boxed in much the same way as the code we study in our work. That is, our very scholarly practices tend to undervalue broad contexts, meaningful relation, and promiscuous border crossing. While many of us identify as interdisciplinary, very few of us extend that border crossing very far (theorists tune out the technical; the technologists are impatient of the abstract; scholars of race mock the computational, seeing it as corrupt). The intense narrowing of our academic specialties over the past fifty years can actually be seen as an effect of or as complicit with the logics of modularity and the relational database. Just as the relational database works by normalizing data—that is, by stripping it of meaningful, idiosyncratic context, creating a system of interchangeable equivalencies—our own scholarly practices tend to exist in relatively hermetically sealed boxes or nodes. Critical theory and poststructuralism have been powerful operating systems that have served us well; they were as hard to learn as the complex structures of C++, and we have dutifully learned them. They are also software systems in desperate need of updating and patching. They are lovely, and they are not enough. They cannot be all we do, but that is not to say that they are not of any value.

In universities that simply shut down "old school" departments—like at my university, German and geography; in the UK, Middlesex's philosophy program; in Arizona, perhaps all of ethnic studies; in Albany, anything they can—scholars must engage the vernacular digital forms that make us nervous, *authoring* in them in order to better understand them and to recreate in technological spaces the possibility of doing the work that moves us. We need new practices and new modes of collaboration; we need to be literate in emerging scientific and technological methodologies but also in theories of race, globalization, and gender. We'll gain that literacy at least partially through an intellectual generosity or curiosity toward colleagues whose practices are not our own. We need to privilege systemic modes of thinking that can understand relation and honor complexity, even while valuing precision and specificity. We need nimbler ways of linking the network and the node and digital form and content, and we need to understand that categories like race profoundly shape both form *and* content. In short, we need a good deal more exchange between the ASA and the digital humanities so that we might develop some shared languages and goals. We must take seriously the question, why are the digital humanities so white? but also ask why American studies is not more digital.

We must remember that computers are themselves encoders of culture. If, in the 1960s and 1970s, UNIX hardwired an emerging system of covert racism into our mainframes and our minds, then computation responds to culture as much as it controls it. Code and race are deeply intertwined, even as the structures of code labor to disavow these very connections.[13] Politically committed academics with humanities skill sets must engage technology and its production not simply as an object of our scorn, critique, or fascination but as a productive and generative space that is always emergent and never fully determined.

NOTES

1. For the past decade, I have had the privilege to work with a team of collaborators on a variety of digital projects, including the online journal *Vectors* and a new authoring platform Scalar. In Los Angeles, this team includes Steve Anderson, Craig Dietrich, and Erik Loyer (and, until recently, Raegan Kelly), among others, and it is impossible to overstate how thoroughly I have been reconfigured by the opportunity to interact with such smart and congenial people. Conversations over the years (including at the Baltimore summit) with the broader DH community have deeply shaped our approach to developing computational systems for the humanities.

This essay is a revised version of a piece originally written for *Race after the Internet,* edited by Peter Chow-White and Lisa Nakamura, forthcoming from Routledge. Feedback from Neil Fraistat, Matt Gold, David Golumbia, and Steve Ramsay helped sharpen the piece for this volume.

2. This panel was organized by Glenn Hendler and Bruce Burgett, both of whom have worked quite tirelessly to engage the ASA community in conversations about the digital humanities. In addition to the three of us, Randy Bass, Sharon Daniel, Deborah Kimmey, and Curtis Marez were also on the panel. Tim Powell had been on the original program but was unable to attend.

3. These tensions between traditional humanities scholars and computational humanists are, of course, not new. For examples of these dynamics within early waves of humanities computing, see Thomas, "Computing and the Historical Imagination," and Craig, "Stylistic Analysis and Authorship Studies." As these authors note from within the realms of authorship studies and historical studies, these tensions often played out over the differences between quantitative and qualitative analysis and via debates on the status and validity of various modes of interpretation. Two readers (Golumbia and Ramsay) of this piece during the volume's semiopen peer review process expressed discomfort with the use of the term "traditional" to describe humanities scholars who don't consider themselves DHers. I share that discomfort, particularly since the word "traditional" seems to imply conservative, not a term many would associate with the ASA today, at least in a

political sense. Instead, I mean the term simply to signal scholars in the humanities whose methodologies are not primarily dependent on digital analysis, platforms, or tools.

4. UNIX develops with some rapidity at least in part because the parent company of Bell Labs, AT&T, was unable to enter the computer business due to a 1958 consent decree. Eric Raymond notes that "Bell Labs was required to license its nontelephone technology to anyone who asked" (33). Thus a kind of counterculture chic developed around UNIX. Raymond provides a narrative version of this history, including the eventual UNIX wars, in his *The Art of UNIX Programming*. His account, while thorough, tends to romanticize the collaborative culture around UNIX. For a more objective analysis of the imbrications of the counterculture and early computing cultures, see Fred Turner's *From Counterculture to Cyberculture*. See also Tom Streeter for a consideration of liberal individualism and computing cultures.

5. Critical code studies (and software studies more generally) take up the study of computational systems in a variety of ways. For an overview of software studies, see Fuller. For emerging work in critical code studies, see the proceedings of the 2010 conference on Critical Code Studies, archived at http://vectorsjournal.org/thoughtmesh/critcode.

6. Some scholars have questioned the neutral status of digital structures such as code and databases. John Unsworth has situated UNIX as a Western cultural formation, arguing that "UNIX is deeply indebted to culturally determined notions such as private property, class membership, and hierarchies of power and effectivity. Most of these ideas are older than the modern Western culture that produced UNIX, but the constellation of cultural elements gathered together in UNIX's basic operating principles seems particularly Western and capitalist—not surprisingly, given that its creators were human extensions of one of the largest accumulations of capital in the Western world" (142). See also David Golumbia's observations on the limits of the database and of semantic computing for humanities analysis, as well as work on culturally contextual databases and ontologies undertaken by Kimberly Christen and Ramesh Srinivasan. Golumbia has further argued that object-oriented programming privileges categorization and hierarchies in a manner that has "much more to do with engineering presumptions and ideologies than with computational efficiency" (209). His work is a must read for anyone caught up in utopian readings of digital culture's empowering and participatory aspects.

7. In comments on a draft of this essay, Steve Ramsay suggested that Mike Gancarz's *The Unix Philosophy* categorizes UNIX via a related but different rule set. His rule set (4–5) is as follows:

1. Small is beautiful.
2. Make each program do one thing well.
3. Build a prototype as soon as possible.
4. Choose portability over efficiency.
5. Store data in flat text files.
6. Use software leverage to your advantage.
7. Use shell scripts to increase leverage and portability.

8. Avoid captive user interfaces.
9. Make every program a filter.

Both Raymond and Gancarz privilege many of the same elements, including modularity, portability, and a certain notion of simplicity. See, for example, Gancarz's discussion of code modules and pipes (116).

8. This quote from Kernighan is from "The Creation of the UNIX Operating System" on the Bell Labs website. See http://www.bell-labs.com/history/unix/philosophy.html.

9. For Gramsci, "common sense" is a multilayered phenomenon that can serve both dominant groups and oppressed ones. For oppressed groups, common sense may allow a method of speaking back to power and of rejiggering what counts as sensible. Kara Keeling profitably explores this possibility in her work on the black femme. Computer programmers in the 1970s are interestingly situated. They are on the one hand a subculture (often overlapping with the counterculture), but they are also part of an increasingly managerial class that will help society transition to regimes of neoliberalism and governmentality. Their dreams of libraries of code may be democratic in impulse, but they also increasingly support postindustrial forms of labor.

10. Other aspects of UNIX also encode "chunking," including the concept of the file. For a discussion of files in UNIX, see *You Are Not a Gadget* by Jaron Lanier. This account of UNIX, among other things, also argues that code and culture exist in complex feedback loops.

11. See, for instance, Patricia Sullivan's *Days of Hope* for an account of the coalition politics of the South in the 1930s and 1940s that briefly brought together antiracist activists, labor organizers, and members of the Communist Party. Such a broad alliance became increasingly difficult to sustain after the Red Scare. I would argue that a broad cultural turn to modularity and encapsulation was both a response to these earlier political alliances and a way to short circuit their viability in the 1960s. My *Reconstructing Dixie* examines the ways in which a lenticular logic infects both identity politics and the politics of difference, making productive alliance and relationality hard to achieve in either paradigm.

12. To be fair, Newfield also explores a more radical impulse in literary study in the period, evident in the likes of (surprisingly) both Harold Bloom and Raymond Williams. This impulse valued literature precisely in its ability to offer an "unmanaged exploration of experience" (152).

13. There is no smoking gun that can unequivocally prove a one-to-one equation between shifting parameters of racial representation and racism and the emergence of UNIX as a very particular development in the history of computing, one that was neither necessary nor inevitable. Such proof is not my goal here. Rather, this essay asks why the midcentury turn to modularity was so deeply compelling and so widely dispersed, from urban planning to operating systems; I argue that in the United States this reorganization cannot be understood without taking into account the ways in which the nation responded to the civil rights movement. Of course, race is not the only axis of difference

driving cultural change at this moment; how we understand the politics of gender and sexuality are also changing and are important to consider in relation to this essay's broad argument. In fact, we might understand the emergence of identity politics throughout the 1960s and 1970s as part of this very logic of modularity. But I would maintain that two broad things are true. First, society is reorganizing due to pressures within the political field (i.e., due to social movements), and that race is a particularly important vector in this reorganization. Second, all technological change is deeply situated within cultural forces, and, thus, the development of UNIX needs to be read in relation to these changes even if the relationship is not one of strict linear causality. It has been interesting to note that, when presenting this work in various venues, scholars of race typically get the argument, while others are sometimes more resistant. I would suggest that perhaps this very resistance might itself be an after effect of the triumph of modularity in the contemporary academy.

BIBLIOGRAPHY

"The Creation of the UNIX Operating System." Bell Labs. http://www.bell-labs.com/history/unix/philosophy.html.

Baldwin, Carliss, and Kim Clark. *Design Rules, Vol. 1: The Power of Modularity*. Cambridge, Mass.: MIT Press, 2000.

Beller, Jonathan. "Re: Periodizing Cinematic Production." Post on IDC Listserv. September 2, 2009. https://lists.thing.net/pipermail/idc/2009-September/003851.html.

Bolter, Jay, and Richard Grusin. *Remediations: Understanding New Media*. Cambridge, Mass.: MIT Press, 2000.

Craig, Hugh. "Stylistic Analysis and Authorship Studies." In *A Companion to Digital Humanities*, edited by Susan Schreibman, Ray Siemens, and John Unsworth. Oxford: Blackwell, 2004. http://www.digitalhumanities.org/companion/.

Fuller, Matthew. *Software Studies: A Lexicon*. Cambrigde, Mass.: MIT Press, 2008.

Galloway, Alex. *Protocol: How Control Exists after Decentralization*. Cambridge, Mass.: MIT Press, 2006.

Gancarz, Mike. *The Unix Philosophy*. Newton, Mass.: Digital, 1995.

Graff, Gerald. *Professing Literature: An Institutional History*. Chicago: University of Chicago Press, 1989.

Gramsci, Antonio. *Selections from the Prison Notebooks*. Translated and edited by Q. Hoare and G. Nowell Smith. London: Lawrence and Wishart, 1971.

Golumbia, David. *The Cultural Logic of Computation*. Cambridge, Mass.: Harvard University Press, 2009.

Hansen, Mark B. N. *Embodying Technesis: Technology Beyond Writing*. Ann Arbor: University of Michigan Press, 2000.

Keeling, Kara. *The Witch's Flight: The Cinematic, the Black Femme, and the Image of Common Sense*. Durham, N.C.: Duke University Press, 2007.

Kernighan, Brian, and P. J. Plauger. *Software Tools*. Reading, Mass.: Addison-Wesley, 1976.

———. "Software Tools." *ACM SIGSOFT Software Engineering Notes* 1, no. 1 (May 1976): 15–20.

Kernighan, Brian, and Rob Pike. *The Unix Programming Environment*. Englewood Cliffs, N.J.: Prentice-Hall, 1984.

Kernighan, Brian, and D. M. Ritchie. *The C Programming Language*. Englewood Cliffs, N.J.: Prentice-Hall, 1978. Reprint, 1988.

Kinder, Marsha. "Narrative Equivocations between Movies and Games." In *The New Media Book*, edited by Dan Harries. London: BFI, 2002: 119–32.

Landow, George. *Hypertext: The Convergence of Contemporary Critical Theory and Technology*. Baltimore, Md.: Johns Hopkins University Press, 1991.

Lanier, Jaron. *You Are Not A Gadget: A Manifesto*. New York: Knopf, 2010.

Lewis, Martin W., and Kären Wigen. "A Maritime Response to the Crisis in Area Studies." *Geographical Review* 89, no. 2 (April 1999): 162.

Manovich, Lev. *The Language of New Media*. Cambridge, Mass.: MIT Press, 2002.

———. "We Have Never Been Modular." Post to Nettime Listserv. November, 28, 2005. http://www.nettime.org/Lists-Archives/nettime-l-0511/msg00106.html.

McPherson, Tara. *Reconstructing Dixie: Race, Place and Nostalgia in the Imagined South*. Durham, N.C.: Duke University Press, 2003.

Newfield, Christopher. *Ivy and Industry: Business and the Making of the American University, 1880–1980*. Durham, N.C.: Duke University Press, 2004.

Omi, Michael, and Howard Winant. *Racial Formation in the United States: From the 1960s to the 1980s*. New York: Routledge, 1986/1989.

Raymond, Eric. *The Art of UNIX Programming*. Reading, Mass.: Addison-Wesley. 2004.

Ritchie, D. M., and K. Thompson. "The UNIX Time-Sharing System." *Bell System Technical Journal* 57, no. 6, part 2 (July–August 1978).

Ritchie, Dennis. "The Evolution of the Unix Time-Sharing System." *AT&T Bell Laboratories Technical Journal* 63, no. 6, part 2 (October 1984): 1577–93. http://cm.bell-labs.com/cm/cs/who/dmr/hist.html.

Ross, Kristin. *May '68 and Its Afterlives*. Chicago: University of Chicago Press, 2004.

Rowe, John Carlos. "Areas of Concern: Area Studies and the New American Studies." In *Transatlantic American Studies*, edited by Winfried Fluck, Donald Pease, and John Carlos Rowe. Lebanon, N.H.: University Presses of New England, forthcoming.

Salus, Peter H. *A Quarter-Century of Unix*. Reading, Mass.: Addison-Wesley. 1994.

Sandoval, Chela. *Methodology of the Oppressed*. Minneapolis: University of Minnesota Press, 2000.

Spivak, Gayatri. *In Other Worlds: Essays in Cultural Politics*. New York: Routledge, 1987.

Streeter, Thomas. "The Romantic Self and the Politics of Internet Commercialization." *Cultural Studies* 17, no. 5 (September 2003): 648–68.

Sugrue, Thomas J. *The Origins of the Urban Crisis: Race and Inequality in Post-War Detroit*. Princeton, N.J.: Princeton University Press, 1998.

Sullivan, Patricia. *Days of Hope: Race and Democracy in the New Deal Era*. Chapel Hill: University of North Carolina Press, 1996.

Thomas, William G. II. "Computing and the Historical Imagination." In *A Companion to Digital Humanities*, edited by Susan Schreibman, Ray Siemens, and John Unsworth. Oxford: Blackwell, 2004. http://www.digitalhumanities.org/companion/.

Turkle, Sherry. *Life on the Screen: Identity in the Age of the Internet*. New York: Simon and Schuster, 1997.

Turner, Fred. *From Counterculture to Cyberculture: Stewart Brand, the Whole Earth Network, and the Rise of Digital Utopianism*. Chicago: University of Chicago Press, 2006.

Unsworth, John. "Living Inside the (Operating) System: Community in Virtual Reality." In *Computer Networking and Scholarly Communication in the 21st Century*, edited by Teresa Harrison, and Timothy Stephen, 137–50. Albany, N.Y.: SUNY Press, 1996.

Hacktivism and the Humanities: Programming Protest in the Era of the Digital University

ELIZABETH LOSH

On June 16, 2009, Professor Cathy Davidson of Duke University posted an entry on the blog for the Humanities, Arts, Science, and Technology Advanced Collaboratory (HASTAC) called "Drinking the HASTAC Kool-Aid," which focused on soliciting applications for a new program coordinator for the organization. In her recruitment effort, she describes HASTAC as a "voluntary network" of scholars whose work reaches beyond academia to expand what the digital humanities could and should be. In doing so, Davidson defines HASTAC's sphere of influence in moral and ethical terms:

> It's not only "digital humanities" in the traditional sense (although the impressive and creative work happening in digital humanities is certainly one part of HASTAC) but it is "humanities" in the even more traditional sense of concern for the deep issues of humanity and society (including the role of science and technology and the state of our planet) that structure everything else in our world, issues of equity and ethics and humanity, issues of what it means to be human (on a deep level informed by science as well as morality), issues of learning and history and introspection, issues of culture, multiculturalism, community, communication, and interaction.

Although Davidson argues that this form of humanities is doubly "traditional," she also seems to be describing a kind of "hybrid humanities" of the kind praised by Patrik Svennson as "visionary" by virtue of "being situated at the periphery and fighting established structures" ("A Visionary Scope").

Davidson concludes her posting with a very different kind of call to action from her initial help-wanted message, one that speaks directly to hackers who might want to topple the theocratic Iranian regime that had just crushed prodemocracy protests contesting recent election results and had shut down the microblogging and text messaging services that had been disseminating information from political dissenters. Davidson alerts her audience that Western digital rights advocates had "received an SOS from pro-democracy activists in Tehran asking us all to use basic hacking tools to flood the propaganda sites of the ruling regime with junk traffic in order to bring them down and thereby open Twitter channels again." Accordingly she reposts the following orders for electronic civil disobedience from *Boing Boing*, the popular "directory of wonderful things": "NOTE to HACKERS—attack www.farhang.gov.ir—pls try to hack all iran gov wesites [sic]. very difficult for us,? Tweets one activist. The impact of these distributed denial of service (DDOS) attacks isn?t clear. But official online outlets like leader.ir, ahmadinejad.ir, and iribnews.ir are currently inaccessible" (Jardin). What is the connection between Davidson's eloquent defense of a broader notion of the digital humanities and her reposting of a rushed message that is peppered with misspellings, abbreviations, fragments, and ungrammatical infelicities of style? Davidson appears to be again positioning the digital humanities as a site of political activism, one that can run the gamut from the institutionally conventional to the radicalized and marginalized, recognizable as being in the tradition of campus protests about subjects such as civil rights or antimilitarism that have defined how political commitment and dissent are staged in the built environment of the university while also being part of a new vanguard of networked digital culture in which protests in the temporary autonomous zones of computational media are rhizomatic, sporadic, and even ironic in the rhetorical stances that they adopt.

Davidson's use of the trope of "drinking the Kool-Aid" seems to allude to critiques of blind obedience or collective hallucination commonly deployed by critics of cyberutopianism and its associated narratives of technoprogress and Internet liberation theology. Specifically Davidson writes that her program coordinator doesn't "have to drink the HASTAC Kool-Aid" but does "have to be willing to work really hard to support the HASTAC mission and to respect those who believe in it." In doing so, Davidson emphasizes a work ethic very much like the one described in Pekka Himanen's *The Hacker Ethic,* which mixes devotion to the spirit of informationalism with a set of highly intensive labor practices that link individuals to collectives.

By urging her readership to participate in distributed denial of service attacks aimed at the government of Iran, Davidson also links HASTAC with another frame of cultural reference, that of hacktivism, or the writing of code to promote or subvert particular political ideologies. In addition to protesting human rights violations, in the recent past hacktivists have used their programming skills as a form of civil disobedience to promote free and open software, privacy, free speech, freedom of movement, governmental transparency, information ethics, political self-determination, environmental protection, and a range of other online and offline causes. Tim Jordan argues that the "rise of hacktivism has not superceded or destroyed previous hacker politics, but has reconfigured it within a broader political landscape" that goes beyond "informational politics" (Jordan, 121). However, because hacking tends to be a kind of virtuoso performance by seasoned programmers, the ability to wield tools that expose vulnerabilities in security, privacy, or accurate data representation is often seen as the sole purview of an elite group of highly computer-literate cognoscenti very different from the print-cultured college professors and graduate students who might be expected to read Davidson's blog.

In thinking about the relationship between hacktivism and the humanities, this essay attempts to describe a range of related protest movements during a time in which there is a significant cohort of professors calling for hacking the academy that includes department chairs, heads of national centers, and those in the leadership of professional associations who are demanding fundamental changes in fair use, peer review, and tenure guidelines. There are also others who are going even further and rejecting their allegiances to traditional forms of university governance and risking tenure and even arrest by engaging in direct confrontation on a range of political issues through electronic civil disobedience. To understand these phenomena that bring either politics into academia or academia into politics, I argue that it is helpful to examine current theories both of hacking and of hacktivism, or the nonviolent use of digital tools in pursuit of political ends, and to consider how dissent by students and faculty and protest by an old guard of political organizers and a new cadre of programmers in the general public may be related. In the context of the digital humanities, hacktivism theory offers a way to broaden and deepen our understanding of the use of digital tools and of the politics of that tool use and to question the uncritical instrumentalism that so many digital humanities projects propound.

Digital Dissent

Some might argue that Davidson's appeal for hackers to bring down Iranian government sites shows a profoundly naive understanding of how human rights discourses function in the era of the Internet. In practical terms, such denial of service attacks on state-run online media may only intensify suspicions that outside agitators are interfering with the internal politics of a country with a long history of unwelcome U.S. intervention and covert warfare. Furthermore, such attacks on the state's propaganda infrastructure do little to protect the lives of human rights activists who document state violence against women, police brutality, summary execution, unauthorized detention, or other brutal forms of state control. Such activists bear witness when they post online video or publicize abuses on blogs and microblogging sites through channels independent of the information mechanisms of the authoritarian state, providing evidence with persuasive power rather than just disruption of an online user's experience (Gregory). Older broadcast or telephonic technologies may also provide useful models for a more effective form of hacktivism that respects existing culture and facilitates practical change. For example, consider how media activist Tad Hirsch designed Dialup Radio to provide political dissidents in Africa a channel for broadcasting information about corrupt or repressive regimes by using mobile phone technology, open-source code, and secure networks that preserve the anonymity of participants and support low-tech solutions (Frid-Jimenez). Other critics of Davidson might observe that the time of digital humanists might be better invested in creating a good information visualization that shows the statistical features of the election irregularities that drove many into the street, which might have more persuasive power than a vandalized government website, although it lacks the glamour of radical chic.

Certainly, not all who use software for political dissent agree that hacktivism and scholarly research are natural partners. New York University's Alexander Galloway, who directs the Radical Software Group, appears wary of uncritically accepting any ideology that affirms that distributed networks are inherently liberatory. In *The Exploit: A Theory of Networks*, Galloway and Eugene Thacker describe the Internet as both highly centralized and highly dispersed in structure and a platform for both corporate and subversive activity. In their account of network relations, the broadcast and surveillance mechanisms of hidden power brokers and the cracking of hackers who undermine authority covertly and idiosyncratically might not be so different, after all. Although Galloway's team is probably capable of infiltrating and disrupting some seemingly secure networks, he also implies that simply hacking those networks does little to foster meaningful intellectual exploration. Instead he aspires to create a new framework for critical theory to help others with "thinking topologically" (Galloway, 13) about forms of networked organization very different from hierarchical pyramids. For Galloway and Thacker, the fundamental constraints of protocol politics are of much more interest than the romantic myths of lone antiheroes. Ironically, they argue that hacktivism actually operates within the context of a "new symmetry" that places electronic civil disobedience in a static geometrical relationship with "cyberwar," which is also similar to other forms of "netwar" that do little to foster the kind of serious systematic critique that is the subject of their book (Galloway, 66). Indeed, while DDOS attacks were used recently to protest the international pursuit of WikiLeaks founder Julian Assange, such attacks have also been part of the defense mechanisms of more conventional forms of nation-state militarism complete with geographical borders and definitions of citizenship constituted by ideologies of self-determination and shared ethnicity from Estonia to East Timor.[1]

Galloway, however, makes a significant exception for academic hacktivists like himself, as he explains the aims of the Radical Software Group and subversive projects like Carnivore, which mocks an FBI surveillance system of the same name that was designed to monitor e-mail and other forms of electronic communication on a massive scale: "You might call RSG a hacker rip-off group. For example, Carnivore is nothing but a new spin on the packet sniffer, a tool that hackers and sys admins have been using for years. But the flip side is that most hackers are quite unschooled when it comes to politics and cultural theory. (Of course I'm referring to traditional hackers, not hacktivists like Critical Art Ensemble or The Yes Men.) So one of the goals of RSG is to bring a more political and theoretical awareness to hacker practice" (Quaranta). The Carnivore project website explains that "Galloway's artwork is independent of the federal digital-surveillance program, yet it functions in much the same way," although "he takes his data from volunteers," and "his program generates art" not "incriminating evidence," because rather than "sifting the flow of data—which might include personal, potentially sensitive material like Web-page contents and chat-session exchanges—in a quest for clues," the software "converts the electronic information into vibrant images and sounds" (Radical Software Group).

In response to the Iranian postelection situation, some digital humanities projects took a fundamentally different approach from either the anonymous cyberattacks promoted by Davidson or the kind of artistic translation, conversion, and reappropriation at work in Galloway's projects that subverts signification and coherence. HyperCities, a digital humanities initiative that describes itself as "a digital research and educational platform for exploring, learning about, and interacting with the layered histories of city and global spaces," supported the efforts of UCLA Iranian-American graduate student Xarene Eskandar to create a collection of geotagged social media artifacts that document the election protests in Iran with markers on electronic maps, online videos, links to microblog postings, and explanations of the significance of a range of digital ephemera by Eskandar, who wrote,

> Working against Iranian state media censorship, I wanted to keep track of the protests across the country and especially the capital, Tehran, to show they are not isolated events. My goal is to raise awareness of the magnitude of discontent, as well as keep a record of it due to the temporal nature of Twitter. State media either denied there were any protests, or they circulated false news that the unrest was only in northern Tehran, a well-to-do part of the city (and sympathetic to Western culture), and a few times they even claimed the opposition to be pro-government while broadcasting the protests with no audio. They also claimed all other provinces were calm, while in fact the protests were not limited to class, age or province and were wide-spread. (Presner)

In other words, in the terms of modern information theory, Eskandar describes her goals as facilitating signal rather than noise to spread information about the location and recurrence of protest activities rather than jam the systems of their oppressors.

More recently, the HyperCities group in the UCLA Digital Humanities Collaborative created HyperCities Egypt. Subtitled "Voices from Cairo through Social Media," it includes a Google map of Egypt's capital that reorients the viewer as the program pinpoints a new tweet every four seconds that includes hashtags associated with the street protests that toppled the Mubarak government, such as #Jan25 or #egypt. "Because it gathers tweets from those who have enabled Twitter's 'add location' function, the program also maps the precise location in Cairo from which they were sent," a news release explains. "And the Twitter users' avatars—often photos of the protesters themselves—accompany the poignant messages, providing a moving immediacy to the experience" (Sullivan). Thus multiple systems of authentication function simultaneously in the HyperCities spectacle of transparency; on-screen text is tied both to images of the urban landscape that can be zoomed in on from a satellite view and to photographs of the faces of those who bear witness.

HyperCities director Todd Presner maintains that this retasking of a digital humanities mapping tool designed to teach about urban history in sites such as ancient Rome or Weimar Berlin is completely consistent with the project's mission, because "HyperCities Egypt gives users a sense of living—and reliving—history" (Presner). The software also maps contemporary protests to share information about rapidly unfolding events organized by smart mobs with potential future participants. Presner, Eskandar, and others in HyperCities see this kind of dissemination of real-time data as continuing the scholarly work of building digital archives.

However, this form of digital humanities also borrows from contemporary activist practices that use digital mapping technologies in grassroots organizing and the human rights work of NGOs. One might argue that HyperCities Egypt and the HyperCities Tehran collections are actually much more like the mapping initiatives jointly sponsored by Google Earth and the U.S. Holocaust Memorial Museum, Crisis in Darfur and World is Witness, which use aerial digital photography and online crowd sourcing in African nations like Sudan, Rwanda, and the Democratic Republic of Congo, as well as in Bosnia-Herzegovina and Chechnya, to track both evidence of past crimes against humanity and present genocides potentially unfolding.

Thus these uses of testimony and evidence put the digital humanities in dialogue with movements for decriminalization and political abolitionism and open up new forms of electronic publication for scholars who see themselves as potential agents of change. For example, Sharon Daniel's Public Secrets and Blood Sugar websites, which use digital audio recordings of prisoners and drug addicts, were created with programming resources from the online journal *Vectors* and thus partially funded by the National Endowment for the Humanities (NEH). Yet many NEH digital humanities competitions specifically forbid endorsing any particular political point of view and would seem to promote a form of technocratic neutrality very different from the work of the most interesting practitioners in the field.

Electronic Civil Disobedience

Outright electronic civil disobedience could be described as the most militant form of political resistance in the digital humanities and one that has become more visible in panels and professional associations in recent years. Many scholars date theories of electronic civil disobedience in the academy to the early work of Critical Art Ensemble (CAE) on the subject. In their 1996 book, *Electronic Civil Disobedience and Other Unpopular Ideas,* which actually predates the group's own access to the sophisticated computer networks that they imagined capable of toppling the powerful, this collective of artist-activists that coalesced in 1987 declares that although conventional civil disobedience was "still effective as originally conceived (particularly at local levels), its efficacy fades with each passing decade" as a result of "the increasing ability of power to evade the provocations" of those who remain nostalgic for the victories of the sixties as powerful influences cease to be either "visible or stable" (*Electronic Civil Disobedience,* 9).

Although CAE founder Steve Kurtz eventually earned tenure at SUNY Buffalo, he and other members of Critical Art Ensemble remain suspicious of the arbitrary nature of the legitimating power of cultural, political, and economic institutions and suggest in their more recent work that self-interested experts—including those in university positions—often have little incentive to pursue the truth. "Amateurs have the ability to see through dominant paradigms, are freer to recombine elements of paradigms thought long dead, and can apply everyday life experience to their deliberations. Most important, however, amateurs are not invested in institutional systems of knowledge production and policy construction, and hence do not have irresistible forces guiding the outcome of their process" (*Digital Resistance,* 9). Because of this very enthusiasm for DIY science and amateur rather than professional knowledge making, Kurtz found himself the subject of a criminal bioterrorism investigation after his wife Hope died of congenital heart failure in 2004, merely because law enforcement officers who came to the scene found the presence of biotechnology equipment in the couple's home laboratory to be suspicious. Given the rapid rise of genetically modified foods and other forms of radically new biological engineering, CAE had wanted to focus attention on what they saw as "the misuse of biotechnology by private corporations operating outside the realm of democratic, public debate" with a tactical response that they called Fuzzy Biological Sabotage, or FBS, "a type of sophisticated, prank that uses harmless biological agents, including plants, insects, reptiles and even microorganisms, to operate in the gray, in-between spaces as yet unregulated by institutional regimes" (Sholette).

Gray areas of law involving technological practices that have not yet become fully regulated were also of interest to former Critical Art Ensemble member Ricardo Dominguez, who founded the Electronic Disturbance Theater (EDT) in 1998 with Carmin Karasic, Brett Stalbaum, and Stefan Wray.[2] In 2001, Dominguez traveled to Germany and visited activists who had been inspired by EDT and CAE's work on electronic civil disobedience. The first virtual sit-in was held to protest Lufthansa Airline's involvement in state-sanctioned deportations. According to Dominguez, thirteen thousand people participated in campaigns organized by *Kein Mensch ist illegal* (No Human Is Illegal) and Libertad during Lufthansa's annual shareholders' meeting. The organization and orchestration of this event occurred with the full public disclosure that had been considered also to be essential in previous Italian netstrikes against the World Trade Organization.[3] As Dominguez explains, it was important that "nothing was hidden . . . because ECD is about bringing together real bodies and digital bodies in a transparent manner which is the same tradition as Civil Disobedience—that people are willing to break a law (like blocking the street) to uphold a higher law" ("A Transparent and Civil Act").

Electronic Disturbance Theater put many earlier principles of the Critical Art Ensemble into digital practice with their series of virtual sit-ins to provide a "reconfiguration of street theater" that "facilitates direct access between macro-networks and non-digital networks" (Electronic Disturbance Theater). They organized a series of protests on the virtual real estate of official websites, first against Mexican President Ernesto Zedillo's official website and later against President Bill Clinton's White House site, the Pentagon, the School of the Americas, the Mexican Stock Exchange, and the Frankfurt Stock Exchange (Denning). For example, in the first pro-Zapatista demonstration held online by EDT, visitors might see images of masked rebels and the FloodNet branding with a message suggesting, "Use the applet below to send your own message to the error log of the institution/symbol of Mexican Neo-Liberalism of your choice" (Electronic Disturbance Theater). No actual damage to the computer infrastructure of the sites or to their security mechanisms was caused by these actions. As one website explaining Floodnet describes, the intent was merely "to disrupt access to the targeted website by flooding the host server with requests for that website" ("Brief Description of the Tactical Floodnet").

As an academic, Dominguez earned praise for his impressive output and for his innovative work in conceptual art and technological development for DIY activism, as he led the b.a.n.g. lab at the prestigious California Institute for Telecommunications and Information Technology.[4] Confident in the protections of academic freedom, Dominguez held a well-publicized virtual sit-in to stop "Nanotech and Biotech War Profiteers" from March 19 to March 20, 2008, in which he used computer servers owned by his employer, University of California (UC), San Diego, and targeted those of the Office of the President for the entire UC system. Despite his use of public resources for controversial activities, he was promoted without incident and received tenure on March 30, 2009.

University ownership of servers used for hacktivism would not become an issue for Dominguez until after a virtual sit-in on March 4, 2010, which was held to protest budget cuts and tuition hikes that were crippling access to higher education. While faculty and students marched on the state capitol building in Sacramento, some four hundred EDT supporters helped occupy the ucop.edu domain. A reporter from the *Los Angeles Times* later described the basic script for the mass action:

> "Transparency," hundreds of protesters wrote, over and over again, in the search box of the home page.
>
> The jammed website responded with an error message: "File not found."
>
> The protesters' message: Transparency doesn't exist in the UC system. (Marosi)

At the same time the b.a.n.g. lab hosted a parody website at markyudof.com, which lampooned the unpopular UC president by posting a fake resignation letter. Because of the timeline of accusations, some claim that it was actually the development of the controversial Transborder Immigrant Tool, or TBT, rather than the March 4 virtual sit-in that caused Dominguez to face the serious possibility of disciplinary consequences that included a threatened loss of tenure for expropriating public resources and criminal prosecution for violating existing computer law. After all, Fox News was running stories explaining hacktivism to their viewership, and members of the b.a.n.g. lab were receiving harassing phone calls and death threats soon after the news media reported that Dominguez's group was helping illegal immigrants by recycling cheap mobile phones and equipping them with new software to guide them in making the risky trip across the border to water caches left by humanitarian groups or to border patrol stations where they could receive first aid. This retasking of an existing technology turned the old phones into lifesaving GPS devices with easy-to-read digital compasses. According to Dominguez, the global migrant underclass unable to afford so-called smart phones would no longer be "outside of this emerging grid of hyper-geo-mapping-power" ("Transborder Immigrant Tool"), and the harsh reality of the border landscape could be digitally augmented to promote a different form of politics.[5]

The use of computing resources in more conventional digital humanities projects may seem less obviously open to debate, but Dominguez's case should function both as a cautionary tale and as an aspirational story to those operating in the mainstream of an emerging field. In other words, projects involving text encoding, electronic archiving, or GIS mapping generally use university computer resources as well, and controversies about ownership, access, and control may have consequences for digital humanities projects at least at the level of local institutional politics. Although the battles over who uses a given computer server and under what circumstances may seem less contested for a database of Jane Austen novels than a database of covert water caches in the desert, academics involved in all kinds of digital humanities projects must grapple with potentially combative IT situations in which funding can dry up or be diverted without much advance warning. Furthermore, digital humanists often also struggle for recognition of the value of their digital scholarship, which can make tussling over computer resources even more frustrating and exhausting. Ironically, Dominguez had relatively little trouble getting his digital work to count for his tenure file, and he certainly did not labor in obscurity unlike many digital humanists who foreground the authors of the past or principles of collective authorship or crowd sourcing that may cost them dearly when they must be reviewed by their print monograph–oriented peers.

Unfortunately for Dominguez, he is still unable to gain access to his FBI file or to see the reports written by the detectives who visited his office, but he was able to see documents from an official university audit that was conducted to address concerns that individuals with the b.a.n.g. lab may have misused university resources.

It is interesting to note that this document strongly asserts the value of academic freedom while also suggesting that some hacktivist practices could violate the faculty code of conduct that functions as part of the social contract of the university.

> The University of California APM-010 states that the University is committed to the principles of academic freedom, which protect freedom of inquiry and research, freedom of teaching, and freedom of expression and publication. While exercising this freedom, faculty must also abide by the Faculty Code of Conduct located in Section E of AMP-015, which addresses interaction with the community and defines two types of unacceptable conduct: 1) intentional misrepresentation of personal views as a statement of position of the University or any of its agencies; and, 2) commission of a criminal act which has led to conviction in a court of law and which clearly demonstrated unfitness to continue as a member of the faculty. ("Use of Resources")

Although Dominguez was eventually cleared of culpability and both types of "unacceptable conduct" were eventually ruled out as possibilities, these categories point to how certain online activities create slippage in delineating the difference between "personal views" and professional expertise and also raise questions about what constitutes a "criminal act" when computer algorithms perform their unit operations automatically and highly efficient digital distribution systems produce cascading effects not possible to execute from a single computer.

Of course, the figure of the protesting professor is a familiar one on college campuses, and many sympathetic faculty members rallied to Dominguez's side as he grappled with the mounting costs of legal assistance from multiple lawyers as he was faced with defending himself in a complex case involving many legal and procedural issues within the jurisdiction of federal, state, local, and campus authorities and specific technologies that had never before been litigated or regulated (*Prof. Ricardo Dominguez*). In addition to fundraising efforts, letters of support were soon posted on websites and Facebook pages and disseminated via listservs and e-mail. One letter from the "Faculty Coalition" emphasized appeals to authority, the litmus tests of peer review, and the stature of Dominguez as a "defining figure in the migration of performance art from physical space to virtual space"; it also pointed out the irony that Dominguez was being persecuted for precisely what he received tenure for (UCSD Coalition Letter). In contrast, the letter of support from the Visual Arts Department emphasized academic freedom rather than peer review and Dominguez's obligations to those outside the university rather than those within it.

> It is the unique mission of a public university to make higher education available to all, and not just the wealthy and privileged. As faculty in one the most respected public education systems in the world we thus feel a unique responsibility. It is essential to understand that the "public" is not monolithic, but is

> composed of diverse and often conflicting constituencies. It is our mandate as educators to explore these points of tension and reconciliation in our research and our teaching. Clearly we are living through a period of profound technological change. It is in the nature of such moments that these changes also transform our understanding of culture and politics, introducing new concepts of public identity and space, and new modes of political action and cultural expression. This is precisely the task that Professor Dominguez has taken on in his research. If UCSD is to retain its international reputation for excellence it's essential that the principles of academic and artistic freedom be defended against the growing pressures exerted by incipient privatization and political extremism. (Visual Arts Letter of Support for Ricardo Dominguez)

The ideal of the public intellectual could be said to be at the core of many arguments for bringing more hacktivists into the digital humanities. Hacktivism brings university scholarship into the headlines and makes it possible to articulate arguments about the relevance of the digital humanities that go beyond cultural heritage claims that rarely get much public attention. Despite the dismay of university administrators, who are often hesitant to recognize computer programming as a form of campus free speech, faculty and students continue to deploy code to further activist agendas. Yet media reports about hacktivist conduct by faculty, graduate students, and undergraduates rarely place these computer-coded expressions of protest in the context of other kinds of campus activism or critical engagement (Losh, *Virtualpolitik*, 199–238). Whether a scholarly researcher is generating electronic boarding passes to protest homeland security policies or using data-mining techniques to identify self-interested Wikipedia edits by corporations and politicians, the attention goes to the programmer's identity as a hacker, rather than as a member of the academy, even though such conduct may be both socially useful and morally justified and thus fully in keeping with the university's mission to serve the public.[6]

Critical Information Studies

The digital ephemera created by Dominguez's hacktivism have also become objects of study in the humanities. However, as scholars work collectively to interpret varied practices that include the "political coding" and "performative hacking" that bring together the efforts of hacker-programmers and artist-activists from the postmodern left (Samuelson), it may be more accurate to describe this research as "hybrid humanities" rather than "digital humanities," because those doing it often are studying art practices, conducting field work, or emulating code rather than merely explicating textual artifacts in a narrow interpretation of the tradition of humanities scholarship. Some literary scholars who are drawn to Dominguez's work have approached it as a hypertext in which "a multi-layered networked narrative" links to evidence of the discursive practices of different communities "within a narrative and performative framework" that includes hacking, activism, and net art (Deseriis). Others have focused on close reading the text of the actual computer code generated by Electronic Disturbance Theater or the b.a.n.g. lab, much as one might read a poem with close attention to its rhetorical address, allusions, and tropes, while also acknowledging the importance of "reframing" code and thus preserving the "context of its circulation and creation" (Marino). However, as one of the creators of the code for the Transborder Immigrant Tool, Brett Stalbaum, observed at a recent Critical Code Studies Conference, basic code "fluency" may be more important than more sophisticated forms of scholarly interpretation, particularly when university administrators and investigators from law enforcement lack the basic "ability to even look at source code" with comprehension and thus routinely mischaracterize the purpose and function of what he called a "public safety tool" (Stalbaum).

According to a story in the *Chronicle of Higher Education* about a new cohort of "digitally incorrect" professors who seem determined to flout their hacktivist principles, such misunderstandings may be increasingly more likely to occur now that the university must grapple with assimilating "the first generation of new-media artists who migrated to academe," a group that includes not only Dominguez but also "Mark Tribe, now at Brown University, and the social-activist pranksters the Yes Men, Andy Bichlbaum (real name: Jacques Servin), at Parsons the New School for Design, and Mike Bonanno (real name: Igor Vamos), at Rensselaer Polytechnic Institute" (Goldstein). Many of these new-media political dissenters use the tools of tactical media as it is imagined most broadly by theorists like Geert Lovink to include not only computer code but also other kinds of small-scale media appropriation, such as "pirated radio waves, video art, animations, hoaxes, wi-fi networks, musical jam sessions, Xerox cultures, performances, grassroots robotics, cinema screenings, street graffiti" (Lovink, 189). Although specific niche areas like "intellectual property hacktivism" may seem limited in effect (Irr), practitioners often earn considerable public interest and support from computer users fed up with digital-rights management and entertained by witty satire.

Because pursuit of the media spotlight is an essential part of hacktivism and tactical media activism, conflicts can break out among seemingly like-minded academics, particularly when authenticity might be valued over irony. For example, Kembrew McLeod irritated many colleagues when he dressed up as a robot and accosted former president Bill Clinton at a televised public event about the seemingly trivial matter of the former president's criticism of hip hop artist Sista Souljah fifteen years earlier. McLeod, a tenured professor at the University of Iowa and creator of the documentary *Copyright Criminals,* had first achieved fame for trying to trademark the phrase "freedom of expression" as "an ironic comment that demonstrates how our culture has become commodified and privately owned" and has since declared, despite rising to a recognized position of tenured stability in his chosen profession, "I still solemnly swear to put the 'ass' back in associate professor (just as I put the 'ass' in assistant professor for six years)" ("My Trademark of Freedom of Expression").

Although McLeod subsequently defended his heckling of Clinton in an unapologetic column in the *Washington Post* called "I, Roboprofessor," which reaffirmed his enthusiasm for performance rather than regulatory compliance, self-described friends of McLeod still posted disapproving blog entries about being unwilling to overlook the hypocrisy of McLeod criticizing Clinton for his media opportunism by taking part in a spectacle of media opportunism of his own.

One of McLeod's friends and critics, Siva Vaidhyanathan, has argued that Critical Information Studies (CIS) could serve as the common field uniting this new vanguard of academics who are neither cyberutopian cheerleaders for computer technologies nor dour reactionaries eager to crush subversive digital practices and who strive to influence actual policy through their teaching and research: "CIS interrogates the structures, functions, habits, norms, and practices that guide global flows of information and cultural elements. Instead of being concerned merely with one's right to speak (or sing or publish), CIS asks questions about access, costs, and chilling effects on, within, and among audiences, citizens, emerging cultural creators, indigenous cultural groups, teachers, and students. Central to these issues is the idea of 'semiotic democracy,' or the ability of citizens to employ the signs and symbols ubiquitous in their environments in manners that they determine" ("Afterword: Critical Information Studies"). Vaidhyanathan envisions a big-tent form of digital humanities that "necessarily stretches to a wide array of scholarly subjects, employs multiple complementary methodologies, and influences conversations far beyond the gates of the university" by engaging economists, sociologists, linguists, anthropologists, ethnomusicologists, communication scholars, lawyers, computer scientists, philosophers, and librarians in a common endeavor ("Afterword: Critical Information Studies"). For Vaidhyanathan, the digital humanities is not merely about curating and managing particular digital collections; it is also about thinking about systemic and structural problems and opportunities related to the political and legal status of digital files and data infrastructures. He is particularly enthusiastic about the advocacy roles assumed by contemporary digital librarians and their collaborators and points to the political work of the American Library Association against the onerous Digital Millennium Copyright Act as a model for other professional academic associations.

Although Vaidhyanathan and others promulgate CIS as an interdisciplinary field of study that could serve as the logical successor to the areas of academic inquiry in cultural studies that arose from the protests of the 1960s and 1970s, which is now "needed to make sense of important phenomena such as copyright policy, electronic voting, encryption, the state of libraries, the preservation of ancient cultural traditions, and markets for cultural production" ("Afterword: Critical Information Studies"), advocacy for these issues in the university setting does not necessarily achieve the kind of visibility that was associated with previous movements that assembled crowds of individuals for face-to-face interactions in physical public space to achieve an end to the Vietnam War, milestones on civil rights issues, affirmative action, or divestment in South Africa. Despite the fact that the Iraq War and the Iranian elections have also been important to hacktivist activities promoted by the academy, the networked publics of these communities of interest are often not a visible presence in the university. Even though Vaidhyanathan notes in the section "Code Switching: Activism and Hacktivism" in his Critical Information Studies Manifesto that CIS contributors often "translate their more rarified scholarly work via blogs and other open Websites" or "announce the publication of drafts of their work and invite feedback through their Weblogs," the existence of these remote and dispersed public audiences usually does little to persuade either university administrators or policy makers to pursue fundamental or unpopular political changes.

Hacking the Academy

The assumption that a rising new-media professorate of the kind described by the *Chronicle of Higher Education* would eventually replace more conservative faculty members has not necessarily proved true any more than the so-called digital generation has taken over policy making in other traditional institutions. After all, what Diane Harley has called the "tournament culture" of publish-or-perish academia can only offer diminishing resources to newcomers, and practicing digital humanists continue to be underrepresented in tenure-track positions. Moreover, scholars such as Mimi Ito, who observe the computer practices of present-day digital youth, note that online behavior oriented toward conformity, popularity, and gossip continues to be far more common than activism and hacking, so hacktivism is likely to continue to be a minority movement within the culture at large for a very long time.

Nonetheless, there are calls for change in the university and for forming larger coalitions between marginalized social actors and political interests; some of these calls are even coming from within the ivory tower itself. Two notable recent collections, *Learning Through Digital Media: Experiments in Technology and Pedagogy* and *Hacking the Academy,* emphasize the role of everyday practices rather than abstract principles in moving the digital humanities forward to take a more significant role in the university and in society at large. Both collections were composed and edited using social media and online publishing tools: *Learning Through Digital Media* used open-source CommentPress software as a platform for peer review, and *Hacking the Academy* was aggregated largely from blog entries from nearly two hundred interested academics who responded to the challenge to create "a book crowdsourced in a week" (Scheinfeldt and Cohen).

As editors Tom Scheinfeldt and Dan Cohen explained in their call for submissions at the start of the one-week collective authoring frenzy, "in keeping with the spirit of hacking, the book will itself be an exercise in reimagining the edited volume," so that any "blog post, video response, or other media created for the volume and tweeted (or tagged) with the hashtag #hackacad will be aggregated at hackingtheacademy.org" (Scheinfeldt and Cohen). Of course, many might argue that it is significant that *Hacking the Academy* only pays homage to the spirit of hacking rather than its practice because its project is located within the academy and operates principally through sanctioned reform and because it ultimately retains the gatekeeper model that is antithetical to hacking because only a fraction of the posts submitted for the book will appear in the printed text. In contrast, many affiliated with *Learning Through Digital Media* are known for drawing on their prehistories as activists and artists and for pointing to a politics not framed by academic structures. Nonetheless, comparing these two books in similar terms in this volume can be fruitful for locating central themes in recent conversations about praxis in the digital humanities.

For example, both books profess to be deeply concerned with changing power relations in the university. Although the table of contents of *Learning Through Digital Media* reads like a how-to manual that is organized according to one's interest in particular tools, editor Trebor Scholz, who is well known in tactical media and hacktivist circles, is adamant that instrumentalist tool literacy approaches do little to effect or respond to cultural change. "Learning with digital media isn't solely about using this or that software package or cloud computing service. The altered roles of the teacher and the student substantially change teaching itself. Learning with digital media isn't about giving our well-worn teaching practices a hip appearance; it is, more fundamentally, about exploring radically new approaches to instruction. The future of learning will not be determined by tools but by the re-organization of power relationships and institutional protocols" (Scholz). Scholz argues in *Learning Through Digital Media* that such learning is characterized by an enthusiasm for cocreation and a synergy with informal peer-to-peer teaching that can "prepare learners for democratic citizenship, . . . community development," and critical engagement with the world. His collection champions teaching with digital media–ripping software like Handbrake to subvert anticopying restrictions and a pedagogy oriented around net art computer programs like Freedom and Anti-Social that mock Web 2.0 multitasking.

Hacking the Academy opens with a series of provocative questions that suggest that professors and other senior experts might be outsourced entirely: "Can an algorithm edit a journal? Can a library exist without books? Can students build and manage their own learning management platforms? Can a conference be held without a program? Can Twitter replace a scholarly society?" (Scheinfeldt and Cohen).

> As recently as the mid-2000s, questions like these would have been unthinkable. But today serious scholars are asking whether the institutions of the academy as they have existed for decades, even centuries, aren't becoming obsolete. Every aspect of scholarly infrastructure is being questioned, and even more importantly, being hacked. Sympathetic scholars of traditionally disparate disciplines are cancelling their association memberships and building their own networks on Facebook and Twitter. Journals are being compiled automatically

> from self-published blog posts. Newly minted Ph.D.'s are foregoing the tenure track for alternative academic careers that blur the lines between research, teaching, and service. Graduate students are looking beyond the categories of the traditional C.V. and building expansive professional identities and popular followings through social media. Educational technologists are "punking" established technology vendors by rolling their own open source infrastructure. (Scheinfeldt and Cohen)

Sections in *Hacking the Academy* are headed with titles such as "Scholarly Societies and Conferences," "Academic Employment, Tenure, and Scholarly Identity," and "Departments and Disciplines," which suggest that these institutional interests are ready for the radical reforms that authors recommend.

In arguing for what seems to be the digital overthrow of the university, these *Hacking the Academy* scholars champion personal visibility, public profiling, web-based organizing strategies, and literacy in code in ways that can be read as completely consistent with hacktivism (Van Veen); but I might note that the omission of an explicit discussion about digital rights and broader forms of public engagement that involve computational media is still disappointing. In sketching out the domain of its brave, new, often professor-less world, *Hacking the Academy* is careful to include a section called "Criticisms of This Book," which contains a blog entry that I wrote during the one-week authoring frenzy that asks, "Will 'Hacking the Academy' Be Understood as 'Backing the Academy'?" In it, I call for "a joint defense of work done outside of the academy in the name of fair use, free culture, open access, open source, collective intelligence, network neutrality, user privacy, and digital inclusion" and a coordinated attack on the distance learning models that libertarian fellow travelers might be pushing to privatize public institutions with online instruction (Losh).

> Instead of talking about "hacking," I have argued that we should be talking about "hacktivism" and curricular, scholarly, and societal changes that focus on digital rights and responsibilities more generally . . . There is no doubt that movements for civil rights, women's rights, gay rights, the rights of ethnic minorities from both immigrant and indigenous populations, and the rights of the disabled have transformed not only the academy but also the larger society as a whole. What would it mean to have campus protests, walkouts, and strikes to champion digital rights and how could it change the mission of the university itself? If the antiwar movement moved universities and governments toward transparency, what could a movement specifically concerned with information transparency do?

In other words, in my opinion, those interested in "hacking the academy" express too little interest in "hacking the world," and experiments in open peer review and creative commons publishing in the academy are too often oriented around the self-interest of academics needing tenure rather than the shared interests of world citizens defending the dignity or survival of others.

At the 2011 annual convention of the Modern Language Association, noted humanities scholar Alan Liu made a similar plea for more political engagement within the digital humanities and specifically for taking hacktivism and tactical media activism more seriously in the field.

> In the digital humanities, cultural criticism—in both its interpretive and advocacy modes—has been noticeably absent by comparison with the mainstream humanities or, even more strikingly, with "new media studies" (populated as the latter is by net critics, tactical media critics, hacktivists, and so on). We digital humanists develop tools, data, metadata, and archives critically; and we have also developed critical positions on the nature of such resources . . . But rarely do we extend the issues involved into the register of society, economics, politics, or culture in the vintage manner, for instance, of the Computer Professionals for Social Responsibility (CPSR). How the digital humanities advance, channel, or resist the great postindustrial, neoliberal, corporatist, and globalist flows of information-cum-capital, for instance, is a question rarely heard in the digital humanities associations, conferences, journals, and projects with which I am familiar. Not even the clichéd forms of such issues—e.g., "the digital divide," "privacy," "copyright," and so on—get much play.

Liu argues that these predictable catalogs of digital humanities products (tools, data, metadata, and archives), modes of institutional membership (associations, conferences, journals, and projects), and stock issues (the digital divide, privacy, and copyright) add up to little critical thinking about neoliberalism at best and collaboration with the enemy at worst.

In contrast, there are those who argue that the digital humanities is reaching too far and is risking the stability of academic culture itself. Ironically, this often happens as a direct result of creative misreadings that take the wishful thinking of digital humanities manifestos and provocations far too literally. For example, Ashley Dawson, coauthor of *Dangerous Professors: Academic Freedom and the National Security Campus,* takes the recent Digital Humanities Manifesto entirely at its word when the coauthors proclaim that the digital humanities has "a utopian core shaped by its genealogical descent from the counterculture?cyberculture intertwinglings of the 60s and 70s" that affirms "the value of the open, the infinite, the expansive, the university/museum/archive/library without walls" along with a radical "democratization of culture and scholarship" ("A Digital Humanities Manifesto")

After reading this utopian rhetoric, Dawson worries that academic freedom itself might be at risk because of pressure from a well-intentioned but ultimately naive digital humanities in favor of massive deinstitutionalization, deskilling, and globalization of the academy that could have disastrously counterintuitive results for the left.

> The links between the movement for a radical democratic, anti-capitalist networked commons and initiatives in the Digital Humanities such as open access publishing are laid out quite clearly . . . Notice, however, that the claims of Digital Humanities extend beyond simply making scholarly research more widely available, as valuable as such initiates are—particularly in terms of redressing the widening knowledge gap between the global North and South. In addition, the digital revolution is represented in the manifesto as transforming the character of research itself, shaking down established disciplinary walls and promoting novel forms of collaborative inquiry.

It is worth noting that Dawson shares with Liu an anxiety that, like transnational corporations, "universities have sought to profit from the intellectual property produced in research labs, libraries, and classrooms" and "to monetize knowledge" (Dawson) even in the formerly unprofitable humanities with new digital humanities initiatives that can capitalize on the economic extraction model of contemporary global capitalism.

Challenges to the Digital Humanities

Alan Liu and Cathy Davidson are certainly closer to the center of the digital humanities as it is currently defined, and Ricardo Dominguez and Kembrew McLeod are definitely located farther away on its ideological peripheries, but they all argue for the formation of new modes of institutional critique and a rethinking of the profession, particularly—in Liu's case—as impersonal and dehumanized distance learning becomes a very real possibility in transforming public education for the worse.

However, the popular base of the digital humanities might still have a vested interest in disciplining faculty who devote themselves not only to hacking but also to pirating and pranking. This is particularly true for more entrenched digital humanists who see themselves as part of a tight-knit community devoted to a what Patrik Svensson has called a "tradition of humanities computing" and its associated "epistemic commitment" to understanding "information technology as a tool and written texts as a primary object of study" in a field devoted to linguistic analysis rather than social change ("Humanities Computing"). These humanities computing specialists who represent, for Svensson, the establishment in the digital humanities tend to focus on the practical rather than ideological aspects of information technology and to seek the coherence and legibility in a given corpus, not its disruptive potential. Furthermore, because humanities computing specialists are people who have often fought for computing resources for decades, frequently without the star status and influence that high-profile hacktivists and tactical media activists might enjoy as tenured faculty members, they may also express resentment over the privileges accorded to newer academic stars.

Looking at all these case studies and surveying recent work at the intersections of hacktivism and the digital humanities by Davidson, Galloway, Presner, Dominguez, McLeod, Vaidhyanathan, and Liu, we are left with an important question: is hacktivism relevant to the digital humanities? I suppose it depends on the form of the digital humanities in question.

Certainly, the history of the digital humanities, as described by Tara McPherson, tells of founding fathers who turned to humanities computing not because they were in love with the aquarianism of Ted Nelson but because they were in full retreat from new forms of scholarship rooted in questioning ideologies of race, gender, and class as the academy underwent a fundamental transformation in the post-free-speech seventies. For McPherson, this original digital humanities, defined by white male conservatism, was about seeking enclaves, not networks, and deploying strategies, not tactics. However, both McPherson and Patrik Svensson have argued that the digital humanities has become profoundly polymorphic in the present day. As Svensson explains, "The territory of the digital humanities is currently under negotiation. While there is no doubt that the field is expanding, it is not entirely clear what is included and how the landscape can be understood or structured. These ongoing negotiations occur on multiple levels, from an individual graduate student and local institutions to national funding agencies and international institutional networking. They are consequently situated institutionally, physically, politically and epistemically" ("The Landscape"). In practice, the question might ultimately turn out to be, "Does hacktivism want digital humanists?" rather than, "Does the digital humanities want hacktivists?" In other words, what incentives do hacktivists have to join the ranks of the digital humanities and take part in their frequently arcane and soporific journals and conferences? Elsewhere, I have argued that game studies might turn out not to be at home in the digital humanities either ("Playing Against Type"), given the fact that research in computer games often values participant observation rather than disinterested analysis and adopts the stance of the playful life-hacker rather than the dutiful enforcer of standards. For scholars coming from the world of game studies, digital life and real life intermingle, the exploit functions as a site of intervention, and breaking systems is just part of the fun. If the digital humanities foregrounds neutral disembodied approaches and taxonomies of abstracted data, the most interesting work in game studies often takes the opposite approach by embracing either feminist perspectives that emphasize embodied interactions or methods derived from object-oriented ontology that foreground material assemblages and constraints. Recently Douglas Eyman and others associated with the techrhet listserv have also announced that they would rather be affiliated with digital rhetoric than with the digital humanities and have cast aspersions on the pursuit of funding by recent digital humanities converts, when a large community has existed around the journals *Computers and Composition* and *Kairos* and the conference Computers and Writing that dates back to the early 1980s.

Of course, when digital rhetorician and game studies scholar Ian Bogost maintains that more academics need to venture into what Quentin Meillassoux calls "the great outdoors," Bogost isn't merely talking about engagement with conventional politics in the sense of issue politics with a large "P."

> The "broader concerns" that public intellectualism ought to concern itself with are so much larger than politics. Ontology, not ethics, must offer us first principles . . . "The public" is a big place. It's not just a place for states and voters and ballot propositions. It's also a place for legwarmers and silicone breast implants and hot vinegar pickled green beans. (Bogost, "We Think in Public")

For Bogost, the stakes of being a public intellectual are less about being identified as a prominent liberal or conservative professor of record in the media and more about engaging with issues of everyday concern in material culture. He argues that public intellectuals should be interested in interpreting the concrete details of daily life in meaningful ways rather than merely spouting abstractions.

In answering Bogost's objection that public intellectuals tend to stay inside the ivory tower, it's worth noting that many hacktivists not only address the issues of a deliberative public culture defined by the two-party system and English common law but also create works about the quotidian materiality of technology and human culture and the contingent character of consumer comforts in the developed world. For example, hacktivists affiliated with CAE and EDT have created art projects designed to draw attention to the chemical composition and physical properties of genetically modified food and of nanotechnology that creates "beer bottles that are less likely to break, coating in glass that makes it easier to clean, improved water filtration systems, pants that liquid rolls right off of and stronger tennis rackets" (Bennett). Moreover, issues of interest to hacktivists rarely fall neatly along the party lines of the supposed political correctness that Bogost describes. For example, laws for network neutrality, liberalization of copyright laws, and increased passenger privacy have all been thwarted by prominent liberal legislators as well as conservative ones.

During the recent Day of Digital Humanities, Bogost contended that the digital humanities needed to make a similar commitment to "getting real" and to overcoming the legacy of idealism that it inherited ("Getting Real"). To support his argument, he cited the response of fellow academic blogger Alex Reid to evangelize for a fundamentally different kind of digital humanities that could engage with matters relevant to the specific and the everyday:

> For centuries (if not always), the humanities have dealt with objects: books, historical artifacts, works of art, performances, films, etc. . . . We have largely dealt with these objects in two ways. 1) We have addressed our human response,

> our ability to represent these objects to ourselves. 2) We have spoken of "culture" and "materiality" but in a vague, abstract way. As such, when we speak of the digital we have focused on the digital as a mode of representation and we have consider[ed] "digital culture" in broad and abstract terms. A realist ontology allows us to investigate objects in new ways. It makes the laptop, the mobile phone, the AR network, the procedurality of the video game all sites for humanistic investigation in new ways. (Reid)

Bogost remarks that only "age, ignorance, truculence, or idiocy" can explain why "the humanities have tried desperately to pretend that the material world is the same as ever" ("Getting Real").

Perhaps it is not heretical to say that the digital humanities is actually more about bit rot and obsolete file formats than it is about spreadsheets with clean data and perfect, high-definition information visualizations that capture every detail with total fidelity. Because being responsible for digital humanities projects forces scholars to care about mundane matters like maintaining servers and replacing routers and even getting the right kind of heating and cooling systems, this peculiar breed of academic must also come to understand the instability and materiality of the archive rather than its permanence and abstraction. Even the digital files that are migrated into the cloud exist somewhere in time and space. Adopting basic principles of redundancy and distribution in contemporary archival practices should not be mistaken for delivering on a promise of immortality and omnipresence. Futuristic technologies like satellites and data barges still involve all the legal complexities of property and territory in specific geopolitical domains. As more digital humanities projects, such as the recent Digging into Data challenge from the NEH, require international collaboration, the geopolitical, logistical, and material complications of the digital humanities are likely to become of even greater concern. Of course, narratives of progress are much more likely to attract funding than narratives of failure, but the digital humanities has important failure stories to tell that are instructive for the academy as a whole, because universities are increasingly dependent on global networks and computer technologies.

In the end, both the hacktivist and the more mainstream digital humanist must be sensitive to the vulnerability and imperfection of digital knowledge systems to pursue their avocations on a day-to-day basis. In considering the need for supporting a truly hacktivist digital humanities, perhaps we can imagine the forms of activism that they both could undertake and the publics who might respond to their collaborations. As Bruno Latour has argued, the mundane and the institutional can be part of the same assemblage, and everyday politics with a small "p" frequently intersects with epic politics with a capital "P." In thinking about the relationship between forms of symbolic representation that humanists care about and forms of political representation that activists care about, perhaps we need to break some systems to understand how they are made.

NOTES

1. See recent stories about how the United States and Israel have used cyberattacks against the Iranian government such as "Inside The United States' Secret Sabotage of Iran" from National Public Radio, http://www.npr.org/2011/05/09/135854490/inside-the-united-states-secret-sabotage-of-iran.

2. The current group, which describes itself as Electronic Disturbance Theater 2.0, includes Dominguez, Stalbaum, Micha Cárdenas, Elle Mehrmand, and Amy Sara Carroll. Cárdenas and Mehrmand are currently my colleagues in the Culture, Art, and Technology Program at the University of California San Diego's Sixth College.

3. As a performance artist, Dominguez has also deployed radical transparency as a mode of aesthetic hyperbole. While in New York he participated in Josh Harris's famed no-privacy Y2K communal utopian/dystopian happening, "Quiet: We Live in Public." He reminisces about the experience in "We Live In Public and Warhol Highjack," http://bang.calit2.net/2009/08/we-live-in-public-and-warhol-highjack/.

4. The acronym stands for "Bits. Atoms. Neurons. Genes." The group is also known for its critical stance on the nanotechnology research funded by the same institute and housed in the same building.

5. For more on the border as a site for tactical media activism with digital technologies, see Rita Raley, *Tactical Media*.

6. For defenses of the ethics of hacktivism, see Mark Manion and Abby Goodrum, "Terrorism or Civil Disobedience: Toward a Hacktivist Ethic," and Goodrum, "The Ethics of Hacktivism."

BIBLIOGRAPHY

Bennett, Darrin. "Art Explores the Science of the Very Small." Voice of San Diego. December 3, 2009. http://www.voiceofsandiego.org/news/article_97561ac3-b3ed-58a3-88e3-d0c4b0b511a1.html

Bogost, Ian. "Getting Real." *Ian Bogost: Videogame Theory, Criticism, Design.* March 9, 2011. http://www.bogost.com/blog/getting_real.shtml.

———. "We Think in Public." *Ian Bogost: Videogame Theory, Criticism, Design.* October 10, 2010. http://www.bogost.com/writing/we_think_in_public_1.shtml.

"Brief Description of the Tactical FloodNet." Thing.net. http://www.thing.net/~rdom/zapsTactical/workings.htm.

"Cae Defense Fund." Critical Art Ensemble. http://www.caedefensefund.org/overview.html.

Consalvo, Mia. *Cheating: Gaining Advantage in Videogames.* Cambridge, Mass.: MIT Press, 2007.

"Critical Art Ensemble Timeline." *TDR: The Drama Review* 44, no. 4 (2000): 132–35.

Critical Art Ensemble. *Digital Resistance: Explorations in Tactical Media.* New York: Autonomedia, 2001.

———. *Electronic Civil Disobedience and Other Unpopular Ideas.* Brooklyn, N.Y.: Autonomedia, 1996.

Davidson, Cathy N. "Drinking the HASTAC Kool-Aid." *HASTAC.* June 16, 2009. http://www.hastac.org/blogs/cathy-davidson/drinking-hastac-kool-aid.

Dawson, Ashley. "Academic Freedom and the Digital Revolution." *AAUP Journal of Academic Freedom* 1 (2010).

Della Porta, Donatella, and Mario Diani. *Social Movements: An Introduction.* Malden, Mass.: Wiley-Blackwell, 2006.

Denning, Dorothy. "Activism, Hacktivism, and Cyberterrorism." http://www.iwar.org.uk/cyberterror/resources/denning.htm.

Deseriis, Marco. "No End in Sight: Networked Art as a Participatory Form of Storytelling." *Networked: A (networked_book) About (networked_art).* http://deseriis.networkedbook.org/no-end-in-sight-networked-art-as-a-participatory-form-of-storytelling/.

"The Digital Humanities Manifesto 2.0." April 3, 2011. http://manifesto.humanities.ucla.edu/2009/05/29/the-digital-humanities-manifesto-20/.

Dominguez, Ricardo. "A Transparent and Civil Act of Disobedience." The Thing. June 12, 2005. http://post.thing.net/node/304.

———. "UCSD Hacktivism 'Affective – Not Effective!'—Fox News." b.a.n.g. May 11, 2010. http://bang.calit2.net/2010/05/ucsd-hacktivism-fox-news-eeek/.

———. "Use of Resources Investigation–Transborder Immigrant Tool AMAS Audit Project 2010–75." E-mail message to author. July 21, 2010.

———. "We Live In Public and Warhol Highjack." b.a.n.g. 31 August 2009. http://bang.calit2.net/2009/08/we-live-in-public-and-warhol-highjack/.

———. "Why I Made a Formal Statement to the UCSD Police." b.a.n.g. 23 July 2010. http://bang.calit2.net/2010/07/why-i-made-a-formal-statement-to-the-ucsd-police-4/.

"The Electronic Disturbance Theater." March 28, 2011. http://archives.openflows.org/hacktivism/hacktivism00945.html.

"Electronic Disturbance Theater—Mark Tribe—Brown University Wiki." https://wiki.brown.edu/confluence/display/MarkTribe/Electronic+Disturbance+Theater.

Eyman, Douglas. "Are You a Digital Humanist?" Computers and Writing. University of Michigan, May 21, 2011.

Frid-Jimenez, Amber. "Tad Hirsch on Activist Infrastructure." *Zones of Emergency.* March 25, 2008. http://www.zonesofemergency.net/2008/03/25/tad-hirsch-on-activist-infrastructure/.

Galloway, Alexander R., and Eugene Thacker. *The Exploit: A Theory of Networks.* Minneapolis: University of Minnesota Press, 2007.

Goldstein, Evan R. "Digitally Incorrect." *Chronicle of Higher Education,* October 3, 2010. http://chronicle.com/article/Digitally Incorrect/124649/.

Goodrum, Abby. "The Ethics of Hacktivism." *Journal of Information Ethics* 9 (2000): 51–59.

Gregory, Sam. "Cameras Everywhere: Ubiquitous Video Documentation of Human Rights, New Forms of Video Advocacy, and Considerations of Safety, Security, Dignity and

Consent." *Journal of Human Rights Practice* 2, no. 2 (2010): 191–207. September 19, 2010.

Harley, Diane, and University of California, Berkeley. *Assessing the Future Landscape of Scholarly Communication an Exploration of Faculty Values and Needs in Seven Disciplines.* Berkeley, Calif.?: Center for Studies in Higher Education, 2010.

Himanen, Pekka. *The Hacker Ethic.* New York: Random House, 2001.

Irr, Caren. "On ®TMark, or, The Limits of Intellectual Property Hacktivism." *Electronic Book Review.* April 2, 2011.

Itō, Mizuko. *Hanging Out, Messing Around, and Geeking Out: Kids Living and Learning with New Media.* Cambridge, Mass.: MIT Press, 2010.

Jardin, Xeni. "Iran: Activists Launch Hack Attacks on Tehran Regime." *Boing Boing.* June 15, 2009. http://boingboing.net/2009/06/15/iran-activists-launc.html.

Jordan, Tim. *Activism! Direct Action, Hacktivism and the Future of Society.* London: Reaktion Books, 2002.

Latour, Bruno. "Letter to Paul Drake in Support of Professor Ricardo Dominguez." Facebook. http://es-es.facebook.com/topic.php?uid=338590116750&topic=14328.

Liu, Alan. "Where Is Cultural Criticism in the Digital Humanities?" *Alan Liu.* 2011. http://liu.english.ucsb.edu/where-is-cultural-criticism-in-the-digital-humanities/.

Losh, Elizabeth. "Playing Against Type: Game Studies and the Digital Humanities." The Digital and the Human(ities), Texas Institute for Literary and Textual Studies 2010–2011. University of Texas, Austin, 2011.

———. *Virtualpolitik: An Electronic History of Government Media-making in a Time of War, Scandal, Disaster, Miscommunication, and Mistakes.* Cambridge, Mass.: MIT Press, 2009.

———. "Will 'Hacking the Academy' Be Understood as 'Backing the Academy'?" *Virtualpolitik.* May 23, 2010. http://virtualpolitik.blogspot.com/2010/05/will-hacking-academy-be-understood-as.html.

Lovink, Geert. *Zero Comments: Blogging and Critical Internet Culture.* New York: Routledge, 2008.

Manion, Mark, and Abby Goodrum. "Terrorism or Civil Disobedience: Toward a Hacktivist Ethic." In *Internet Security: Hacking, Counterhacking, and Society,* edited by Kenneth Einar Himma, 61–72. Sudbury, Mass.: Jones & Bartlett Learning, 2007.

"Mapping Initiatives." United States Holocaust Museum. http://www.ushmm.org/maps/.

Marino, Mark. "Reading the Transborder Immigrant Tool," HASTAC. January 18, 2011. http://www.hastac.org/blogs/markcmarino/reading-transborder-immigrant-tool-mla-11-cross-post.

Marosi, Richard. "UC San Diego Professor Who Studies Disobedience Gains Followers—and Investigators." *Los Angeles Times,* May 7, 2010. http://articles.latimes.com/2010/may/07/local/la-me-ucsd-professor-20100507-53.

McLeod, Kembrew. "I, Roboprofessor–" *Washington Post,* December 19, 2007. http://www.washingtonpost.com/wp-dyn/content/article/2007/12/19/AR2007121901000.html.

———. "My Trademark of Freedom of Expression." Kembrew.com. http://kembrew.com/prank/my-trademark-of-freedom-of-expression/.

McPherson, Tara. "Introduction: Media Studies and the Digital Humanities." *Cinema Journal* 48, no. 2 (2008): 119–23. http://muse.jhu.edu/journals/cj/summary/v048/48.2.mcpherson.html

Presner, Todd. "New Featured Collection: Election Protests in Iran + New Interview with Creator." HyperCities. December 8, 2009. http://hypercities.com/blog/2009/12/08/new-featured-collection-election-protests-in-iran/.

"Prof. Ricardo Dominguez Discusses Struggle to Retain Academic Freedom and Tenure." The Internet Archive. April 6, 2010. http://www.archive.org/details/Prof.RicardoDominguezDiscussesStruggleToRetainAcademicFreedomAndTenure.

Quaranta, Domenico. "Looking for a Counter-Protocol: Interview with Alexander Galloway." *Domenico Quaranta.* 2005. http://domenicoquaranta.com/2009/09/looking-for-a-counter-protocol-interview-with-alexander-galloway/.

"Radical Software Group (RSG): CARNIVORE." First Pulse Projects. http://www.firstpulseprojects.net/rsg.html.

Raley, Rita. *Tactical Media.* Minneapolis: University of Minnesota Press, 2009.

Reid, Alex. "Digital Humanities: Two Venn Diagrams." *Digital Digs.* March 9, 2011. http://www.alex-reid.net/2011/03/digital-humanities-two-venn-diagrams.html.

"Robot Heckles Bill Clinton on Behalf of Sister Souljah During Iowa Stop." *Iowa Independent.* December 11, 2007. http://iowaindependent.com/1619/robot-heckles-bill-clinton-on-behalf-of-sister-souljah-during-iowa-stop.

Samuelson, Alexandra. "Hacktivism and the Future of Political Participation." Alexandrasamuel.com. 2004. http://alexandrasamuel.com/dissertation/pdfs/index.html.

Scheinfeldt, Tom, and Dan Cohen. "Hacking the Academy: What This Is, and How to Contribute." *Hacking the Academy.* http://hackingtheacademy.org/what-this-is-and-how-to-contribute/.

Scholz, Trebor. *Learning Through Digital Media.* New York: Institute for Distributed Creativity, 2011.

Schueller, Malini Johar, and Ashley Dawson. *Dangerous Professors: Academic Freedom and the National Security Campus.* Ann Arbor: University of Michigan Press, 2009.

Shepard, David. "HyperCities Egypt: Voices from Cairo through Social Media." HyperCities. February 8, 2011. http://hypercities.com/blog/2011/02/08/new-project-hypercities-egypt/.

Sholette, Gregory. "Disciplining the Avant-Garde: The United States Versus the Critical Art Ensemble." *Circa* 112 (2005): 50–59. http://www.jstor.org/pss/25564316.

Shuster, Mike. "Inside The United States' Secret Sabotage Of Iran." *National Public Radio*. May 9, 2011. http://www.npr.org/2011/05/09/135854490/inside-the-united-states-secret-sabotage-of-iran

Stallbaum, Brett. "Briefing on Transborder Immigrant Tool Source Code and Persecution of Professor Ricardo Dominguez." ThoughtMesh. April 2, 2011. http://thoughtmesh.net/publish/376.php.

———. "Ricardo Dominguez/Transborder Immigrant Tool Academic Freedom Timeline November 2009 Through May 5th 2010." WalkingTools. http://www.walkingtools.net/DominguezTBT-timeline.pdf.

Sullivan, Meg. "New UCLA Project Streams Twitter Updates from Egypt Unrest on Digital Map of Cairo." *UCLA Newsroom*, February 7, 2011. http://newsroom.ucla.edu/portal/ucla/ucla-unveils-digitial-archive-191921.aspx.

Svensson, Patrik. "Humanities Computing as Digital Humanities." *Digital Humanities Quarterly* 3, no. 3 (2009). http://www.digitalhumanities.org/dhq/vol/3/3/000065/000065.html.

———. "The Landscape of Digital Humanities." *Digital Humanities Quarterly* 4, no. 1 (2010). http://digitalhumanities.org/dhq/vol/4/1/000080/000080.html.

———. "A Visionary Scope of the Digital Humanities." *HUMLab Blog*. February 23, 2011. http://blog.humlab.umu.se/?p=2894.

"Transborder Immigrant Tool." The Thing. April 3, 2011. http://post.thing.net/node/1642.

"UCSD Coalition Letter to V. C. Paul Drake Re: Ricardo Dominguez | UC-AFT." University Council—American Federation of Teachers. http://ucaft.org/content/ucsd-coalition-letter-vc-paul-drake-re-ricardo-dominguez.

Vaidhyanathan, Siva. "Afterword: Critical Information Studies." *Cultural Studies* 20, no. 2–3 (2006): 292–315.

———. "Kembrew's 'Bill Clinton Moment.'" *Sivacracy*. December 23, 2007. *Sivacracy*. http://www.sivacracy.net/2007/12/robot_sivacracy_friend_kembrew_1.html.

———. "Robot, Sivacracy Friend Kembrew McLeod Heckles President Clinton." *Sivacracy*. http://www.sivacracy.net/2007/12/robot_sivacracy_friend_kembrew.html.

Visual Arts Letter of Support for Richardo Dominguez. May 18, 2010. http://va-grad.ucsd.edu/~drupal/node/1492.

Van Veen, Tobias C. "Hackers, Hacktivists, and Script Kiddies." http://www.quadrantcrossing.org/papers/02Capital-Hackers_%20Lit.Review-tV.pdf.

Wray, Stefan. "On Electronic Civil Disobedience." New York, N.Y., 1998. http://www.thing.net/~rdom/ecd/oecd.html.

Unseen and Unremarked On: Don DeLillo and the Failure of the Digital Humanities

MARK L. SAMPLE

This professorship deals with events that almost took place, events that definitely took place but remained unseen and unremarked on . . . and events that probably took place but were definitely not chronicled. Potential events are often more important than real events.

—Morehouse Professor of Latent History, in *Great Jones Street*

Like Don DeLillo's professor of latent history, presented only half-mockingly in *Great Jones Street*, DeLillo's third novel—and perhaps his most Pynchonesque, a meditation upon language, celebrity, and paranoia—let us consider the unchronicled and potential events of DeLillo's own publishing history, the events that remain unseen and unremarked on. Unseen and unremarked on by literary scholars and humanists in general but, more to the point, unseen and unremarked on by the digital humanities.

That is, what have the digital humanities failed to notice about Don DeLillo?

Or, to broaden the question and absolve the humanities of any wrongdoing, in what ways has the digital age left behind scholars of DeLillo's work?

Or, to be more inclusive and hastening to interest even those uninterested in DeLillo's consistently prescient observations of the postmodern era, which editors in the past have assured me I must do in order to publish on DeLillo's lesser known short stories, many of which encapsulate in a few pages what DeLillo works out in hundreds in his novels, a feat academic publishers assume no other scholar would want to read about unless connected somehow to one of DeLillo's big ideas arrayed in his important novels—ideas such as terrorism and simulation—as I say, to interest even those uninterested in such minutia, let's rephrase the question this way (and adapt a passive voice as an extra measure, so as to avoid offending anyone): how have scholars of contemporary American literature been left behind by the rise of digital tools and the methodologies afforded by those tools that have otherwise been a boon to literary scholars working on earlier eras of American literature?

Or, as I said, what have the digital humanities failed to notice about Don DeLillo?

I should clarify this question, though, lest it seem too specific. DeLillo is merely a convenient stand-in. We might just as easily substitute for his name any other towering figure of late twentieth- and early twenty-first-century American literature: Toni Morrison, Philip Roth, Dan Brown. The results will be the same. Unless one is willing to infringe on copyright, break a publisher's DRM, or wait approximately four generations when these authors' works will likely fall into the public domain, barring some as of yet unknown though predictable act of ~~corporate America~~ Congress, the kind of groundbreaking work being done on seventeenth-, eighteenth-, nineteenth-, and even twentieth-century literature simply will not happen for DeLillo and his contemporaries.[1] Digital editions, online archives, text mining, data visualizations—these are the bread and butter of scholars working on pre-twentieth-century literature within the digital humanities. As Andrew Jewell and Amy Earhart explain in their introduction to a recent collection called *The American Literature Scholar in the Digital Age*, "utilizing digitization and computational power makes possible new ways of seeing, collecting, editing, visualizing, and analyzing works of literature. These new methods are at the core of professional academic life, altering not only what we can read through unprecedented access to textual information but also how we articulate our scholarly response to materials" (Earhart and Jewell, 2). This is all true, but like most truths it is not true for all. It is not true for scholars of DeLillo's work, which stands apart from the dominant methodological and analytical advances of the digital humanities.

Although it's risky to generalize about the digital humanities, it is safe to say that the work of the digital humanities is ultimately premised upon a simple, practical fact: it requires a digital object, either a born-digital object or an analog object that has been somehow scanned, photographed, mapped, or modeled in a digital environment. In the context of literary studies, this usually means a large corpora of digitized texts, such as the complete works of Shakespeare, the multiple versions of Whitman's *Leaves of Grass*, or every single book published in England during the nineteenth century.

None of this is available in any substantive, legal way for DeLillo's work, nor will it be. There is no debate about that. It is indisputable.[2]

But what if I were wrong?

What if there was a world in which the digital humanities could lend its considerable institutional and collaborative weight to the study of DeLillo's fiction?

Let us imagine, then, several alternate histories of DeLillo's work. First, an official publication history, the seamless kind that every scholarly monograph on DeLillo reproduces, though my version will already begin to tug at loose threads. Then a second history, one we might think of as DeLillo's latent history, those events that remain "unseen and unremarked on," revealed only by archival research of largely textual and certainly nondigital documents. And finally, let us take this notion of latent history to its logical conclusion, going beyond recovering what has been unseen and unremarked on to imagining the "potential events" of DeLillo's history, which would be "more important than real events," redefining DeLillo studies, not to mention our entire understanding of contemporary American literature.

Timeline I: Excerpt from DeLillo's Official Publication History

(This is not a Timeline. This is an Argument.)

1960

Don DeLillo, a young copywriter at the legendary Ogilvy and Mather Advertising Agency, publishes his first short story, "The River Jordan," in *Epoch*, a literary journal out of Cornell University. "The River Jordan" has never been republished. There is no electronic version of *Epoch*.

1968

DeLillo publishes "Baghdad Towers West," also in *Epoch*. By 1968, *Epoch* has published four out of five of DeLillo's earliest short stories. "Baghdad Towers West" has never been republished. There is no electronic version of *Epoch*.

1970

DeLillo publishes "The Uniforms," a rewriting of Godard's 1967 film *Weekend* (VHS available from Amazon.com for $94.95 new). "The Uniforms" appears in the *Carolina Quarterly*, digital copies of which exist for volumes 55 and on. "The Uniforms" was published in volume 22.

1972

Sports Illustrated publishes "Total Loss Weekend," DeLillo's story of a man whose wagers on dozens of college and pro sporting events on a single October weekend conclude with "misery, paranoia, bitterness, defeat" (100). Though no DeLillo scholar has ever recognized this curious fact, "Total Loss Weekend" is DeLillo's second appearance in *Sports Illustrated*. His first appearance was earlier the same year, when the first eight chapters of *End Zone* (1972) were published under the awkward title "Pop, Pop, Hit Those People." This was the April 17, 1972, issue, with a victorious Jack Nicklaus on the cover and the story itself interspersed with advertisements for Spalding golf balls, La Corona filter tips, and Puerto Rican rum. I can describe these ads because the full text and facsimiles of original pages of both "Total

Loss Weekend" and "Pop, Pop, Hit Those People" are available online in the *Sports Illustrated Vault*. These two texts are the only pieces of DeLillo's short fiction to be available digitally until "Midnight in Dostoevsky" appears on the *New Yorker* website thirty-seven years later.

These two stories were not, of course, available digitally that whole time; they went online only when Time Warner opened the *Sports Illustrated Vault* in 2008. Reading straight from the Web 2.0 playbook with nonsensical phrases that have been attached to new digital initiatives throughout the ages, Jeff Price, the president of *Sports Illustrated Digital* describes the *Sports Illustrated Vault*: "By combining SI archives with cutting-edge technology, web tools and sport functionality search capability [sic] we have created a destination that will grow through the active participation of site visitors and through search engine discovery" ("Sports Illustrated Vault Debuts").

1973

"The Uniforms" is reprinted in *Cutting Edges: Young American Fiction for the '70s*. "The Uniforms" is the only stand-alone story of DeLillo's ever to be republished. *Cutting Edges* is available in 198 libraries worldwide, none of them near you. In an appendix to *Cutting Edges*, DeLillo notes that he wrote "The Uniforms" as "a challenge to writers of radical intent" (533), who ought to experiment with the form of the novel. DeLillo explains,

> Fiction is trying to move outward into space, science, history and technology. It's even changing its typographical contours. Writers want their stories to be touched, petted, and, in some cases, sexually assaulted. In a cellar in Ludwigshafen, a ninety-four-year-old printer has been working for two decades on different mediums of type—malleable, multidimensional, pigmented. Type as paint. Dark colors for somber words. Books the size of refrigerators. ("Appendix to 'The Uniforms,'" 532)

It is entirely fitting that DeLillo imagines the future of the book in terms of the largest of kitchen appliances, the massive, humming refrigerator. Fitting, because as much as DeLillo has been an astute observer of the media age, meditating time and time again upon the meaning of technology in modern American lives, he himself has been personally resistant to digital technology, choosing to write on the same manual Olympia typewriter for the past forty years. No lightweight Kindles or sleek iPads figure in DeLillo's premonitions of the future of the book.

(DeLillo's most recent seven novels are available as downloadable Kindle e-books. DeLillo's eight novels prior to *White Noise* are not, despite Amazon founder Jeff Bezos's stated goal of making "any book, ever printed, in any language available in less than 60 seconds" [Jones]).

(n.b. Publish: From the Classical Latin *public re*, meaning to make public property, to place at the disposal of the community, to make public, to make generally known, to exhibit publicly [Oxford English Dictionary, 3rd Edition, September 2007]).

1985

White Noise, DeLilllo's breakthrough novel, is published. This is the first DeLillo novel to later become available digitally. The Kindle version of *White Noise* begins with this combination warning/plea:

> The scanning, uploading and distribution of this book via the Internet or via any other means without the permission of the publisher is illegal and punishable by law. Please purchase only authorized electronic editions, and do not participate in or encourage electronic piracy of copyrighted materials. Your support of the author's rights is appreciated.

1991

DeLillo publishes *Mao II*, widely seen as an extended meditation on the Rushdie Affair and the role of the writer in the age of terrorism.

2004

The Harry Ransom Humanities Research Center (HRC) at the University of Texas at Austin acquires the Don DeLillo Papers, 125 boxes of DeLillo's manuscripts, notebooks, research clippings, and correspondence. The acquisition costs the HRC five hundred thousand dollars. Though the archive is open to the public, there are no plans to digitize any of the material in the collection, according to Richard Workman, an associate librarian at the Harry Ransom Center (Workman).

Timeline II: Excerpts from DeLillo's Latent History

(Unseen and unremarked on)

1962

DeLillo's short story "Buy Me Some Peanuts and Crackerjacks" is rejected from *Esquire*, in part because, as one editor noted, "The weltschmertz is not Chekovian, but Chayevskian" (Hills, 1). The story is never printed and no extant copy exists.

1966

A story called "The Meridians of Sleep" is rejected from the *New Yorker*. In the letter to DeLillo's agent, the magazine's legendary fiction editor Roger Angell kindly hopes that "Mr. DeLillo won't be too disappointed by this rejection, for he has a good deal to be optimistic about. I think he may have a considerable future as a writer" (Angell, 1).

Also in 1966, the *Kenyon Review* accepts the short story "Cinema" for publication, though the journal recommends that DeLillo consider changing the title to "Coming Sun. Mon. Tues." The *Kenyon Review* also suggests removing the "page 3 reference to Dachau" (Macauley, 1). DeLillo replaces "Dachau" with "Vietnam or Mississippi" in the final version.

1969

Jack Hicks, the editor of the *Carolina Quarterly*, appreciates the "Godard touches and murmurs" of "The Uniforms" and accepts it for publication at five dollars per page (1969, "Letter to Don DeLillo," 1).

1971

Jack Hicks contacts DeLillo about an anthology called *Routines* (published in 1973 as *Cutting Edges*), which will include "The Uniforms." Hicks asks DeLillo for material for the appendix of the anthology, which should include a "frame of reference" for the story, as well as some thoughts about "what fiction should/will do in the 1970s" (1971, "Letter to Don DeLillo," 1).

It is in this "frame of reference" for "The Uniforms" that DeLillo imagines that "in a cellar in Ludwigshafen, a ninety-four-year-old printer has been working for two decades on different mediums of type—malleable, multidimensional, pigmented" ("Appendix to 'The Uniforms,'" 532). Explaining why he turned a Godard film into a short story, DeLillo argues that "thousands of short stories and novels have been made into movies. I simply tried to reverse the process. Until elastic type is perfected, I submit this mode of work as a legitimate challenge to writers of radical intent" (533). Twice in DeLillo's 325-word "frame of reference," he evokes the notion of malleability, elasticity. Throughout his career, DeLillo will consistently seek elasticity in the source material for his fiction. He will not, however, embrace "elastic type" of the kind that digital technology makes readily possible.

1972

End Zone, with its first eight chapters appearing simultaneously in *Sports Illustrated* (see "Timeline I: Excerpt from Delillo's Official Publication History"), is published.

Other titles DeLillo had considered for this novel about football, nuclear war, and trauma include *Modes of Disaster Technology* and *The Self-Erasing Word* (DeLillo, "The Self-Erasing Word").

1985

White Noise, DeLilllo's breakthrough novel, is published. DeLillo's original title for the novel was *Panasonic*, a name the Matsushita corporation refused to give the rights to (Salamon, K1). DeLillo's list of alternative titles contained two columns of forty-four other possibilities, some of which were typed, others handwritten, and a few crossed out: Book of the Dead, The American Book of the Dead, Life-Savers, Blacksmith, Germantown, The Dead Motel, Dylar, Point Omega, Flying Saucers, Nyodene, Maladyne, The Blacksmith Book, The Art of Dying, The Power of Night, A Guide to Dying, Reno Amusements, Particle Smashing, Falling Bodies, White Noise, Donald Duck, Ultrasonic, Mein Kamp, Sirens, Doomsday, The Doomsday Book, Dying Words, Atlantic & Pacific, Escape, Simuvac, Superstition, Deathless, Eternity, Darkness, Necropolis, All Souls, Megabyte, Penny Dreadful, Psychic Data, Panasonic, Ultrasound, Matshushita, Panasonic Way, Air Waves, Secaucus (DeLillo, Notebook).

1991

DeLillo publishes *Mao II*, widely seen as an extended meditation on the Rushdie Affair and the role of the writer in the age of terrorism. But the novel is just as easily a reflection on the role of the writer in the age of digital reproduction.

In DeLillo's handwritten notes for *Mao II*, he writes "Reclusive Writer: In the world of glut + bloat, the withheld work of art becomes the only meaningful object" (DeLillo, Notes in Notebook). Significantly, in the novel, DeLillo attributes this sentiment not to Bill Gray, the reclusive novelist at the heart of *Mao II* but to Scott, Gray's personal assistant and eventual archivist. "The withheld work of art is the only eloquence left," Scott tells Gray (67). And Scott will indeed withhold all Gray's writings, hoarding them. Once Bill Gray leaves the country, becoming entangled with a terrorist organization, Scott sets to organizing Gray's papers. "He could arrange the reader mail geographically or maybe book by book," Scott muses, "although there was a great deal of mail that referred to both books or neither book" (143). Later Scott goes about "restructuring the mail by country. Once that was done he would put each country in chronological order so he might easily locate a letter sent from Belgium, say, in 1972. There was no practical reason why he'd ever want to find such a letter or any other piece of reader mail in particular. The point is that he would have it all in place" (184). With his point "that he would have it all in place," Scott's actions lampoon the idea of an archive. What goes in and in what order and why is arbitrary. In *Mao II*, the archive is organized according to whimsical principles that reveal little about its contents. Order trumps the ordered.

Meanwhile in Greece, Bill Gray is questioned at every turn by an intermediary for the terrorists about the possibility of writing with a word processor. "I find the machine helps me organize my thoughts," the terrorist intermediary tells Bill, continuing, it "gives me a text susceptible to revision. I would think for a man who clearly reworks and refines as much as you do, a word processor would be a major blessing" (137–38). Later on the man persists with this praise of word processing, telling Bill that "it's completely liberating. You don't deal with heavy settled artifacts. You transform freely, fling words back and forth" (164).

Here the macro and the micro, the archive and the manuscript, both risk revision; liberation; and, DeLillo seems to suggest, their very mooring onto meaning. It is the return of the death of the author, replaced by what Barthes calls a "modern scriptor" who is "born simultaneously with the text," neither "preceding" nor "exceeding" it (145). Perhaps this is the danger of the digital for DeLillo but also its lure? Perhaps this is why Bill Gray must literally die toward the end of *Mao II*, because he refuses to die symbolically?

1997

"The reason I use a manual typewriter," DeLillo writes in a letter to David Foster Wallace in 1997, "concerns the sculptural quality I find in words on paper, the architecture of the letters individually and in combination, a sensation advanced (for me) by the mechanical nature of the process—finger striking key, hammer striking page. Electronic intervention would dull the sensuous gratification I get from this process—a gratification I try to soak my prose in" ("Letter to David Foster Wallace," 1).

2003

The author, a doctoral student at the University of Pennsylvania, attends a DeLillo reading at the Philadelphia Free Library. As DeLillo signs a copy of *Cosmopolis*, the author thrusts a sealed letter into DeLillo's hands that begins, "Please forgive this clumsy introduction—a sealed letter thrust into the hands of an unsuspecting novelist might very well appear as a scene in one of your novels" (Sample, 1) The letter goes on to explain that the author is writing his dissertation on DeLillo's early fiction and "would welcome the opportunity to talk or correspond with you about your fiction." Grimacing and looking more than a little perturbed, DeLillo brusquely tells the author that "everything I have to say about my books is in my books."

A week later a letter arrives from New York, addressed to the author, typed on manual Olympia typewriter by Don DeLillo, in which DeLillo repeats, more kindly this time, that he prefers not to revisit his novels: "I'm not a student of my own fiction and I don't necessarily want to know everything that's happening there, or everything that may be swimming the space between the reader and the book" ("Letter to Mark Sample," 1).

2004

If Don DeLillo's most ambitious novels never reached the size of refrigerators—though *Underworld* (1997) comes close—then at least the manuscripts for those books approached the largest of kitchen appliances in weight, heft, and density. Beginning with *The Names* (1982), DeLillo used a separate page for every draft paragraph, no matter how small the paragraph. He held on to those pages, even for early drafts, and they piled, piled up high: "I want those pages nearby," DeLillo told the *Paris Review* in 1993, "because there's always a chance I'll have to refer to something that's scrawled at the bottom of a sheet of paper somewhere. Discarded pages mark the physical dimensions of a writer's labor—you know, how many shots it took to get a certain paragraph right" (Begley, 281).

Records, archives, the "physical dimensions" of the page, and the evidence of a "writer's labor." DeLillo's work is shot through with these themes. This is one reason Bill Gray abhors the "lightweight, malleable" form of word-processed text (161)—it leaves no trace. It is abstracted from the knowable world, unlike his typewriter where the long, meandering hours and days of his physical presence become intertwined with the machine, measured by the accumulation of hair: "hair that drifts into the typewriter, each strand collecting dust along its lengths and fuzzing up among the hammers and interacting parts, hair that sticks to the felt mat the way a winding fiber leeches on to soap so he has to gouge it out with a thumbnail, all his cells, scales and granules, all his faded pigment, the endless must of all this galling hair that's batched and wadded in the works" (199).

Going on in the *Paris Review* interview, DeLillo speaks of the sheer physical presence of earlier drafts of work, of their "awesome accumulation, the gross tonnage, of first draft pages. The first draft of *Libra* sits in ten manuscript boxes. I like knowing it's in the house. I feel connected to it. It's the complete book, the full experience containable on paper" (Begley, 281).

As of 2004, those boxes and many more, and all the dust and detritus and sloughed-off cells among them, were no longer in DeLillo's house. DeLillo's papers, all of them, 125 boxes of material containing thousands of pages of DeLillo's personal and professional correspondence, handwritten notes, research materials, drafts, and proofs were acquired for five hundred thousand dollars by the Harry Ransom Humanities Research Center at the University of Texas at Austin.

It is an old-fashioned archive. It is not digital and cannot be conquered by digital means. It is purely physical, like the "gross tonnage" of his drafts. Though the archive is open to the public, it will resist "electronic intervention." As Richard Workman, an associate librarian at the Harry Ransom Center writes, "because most of our collections are under copyright, and because placement on the web is a form of publication, we have special problems in this regard. We can't do it without the creator's permission, and not many living writers or their heirs are ready to take the step of publishing their entire archives. In DeLillo's case, in particular, I doubt he would agree to any such project" (Workman).

DeLillo's papers were "eerily immaculate," as D. T. Max puts it in a *New Yorker* article about the Harry Ransom Center, even before the library received them (66). They are meticulously ordered, especially the latter boxes, and there is no echo of Bill Gray's fictional archives, repeatedly rearranged according to some new arbitrary scheme. Still, there are surprises in the archive—rejection letters, legal wrangling over brand names, honorary degrees turned down, discussions of royalties, surprising changes in early drafts of novels, and letters from critics and fans including, wedged between a letter to Thomas Pynchon and a letter to the organizer of a book club reading *White Noise*, the very letter this author had thrust into DeLillo's hands a year earlier as well as DeLillo's reply to that letter.

Except by those who explore the archive and share their understanding of it, these surprises in the archive will remain unseen and unremarked on. Latent.

Timeline III: Excerpts from a Potential History

(Potential events are often more important than real events.)

1991

Researchers at MIT develop MaoMOO, a multiple-user, text-based virtual world inspired by *Mao II*. Funded in part by DARPA, the Department of Defense's Advanced Research Projects Agency, MaoMOO lets users explore the cell in Beirut in which terrorists are holding an unnamed writer hostage.

1995

For the tenth anniversary of *White Noise*, its publisher Viking teams with the Voyager Company to create the *White Noise Omnibus* CD-ROM, an interactive multimedia experience. The CD-ROM contains the full text of *White Noise* as well as draft texts (scanned from DeLillo's original typescript manuscript), interviews with scholar Frank Lentricchia, and GIF images of the barn that inspired DeLillo's idea of the most photographed barn in America. Available for MS-DOS, Windows 95, and Mac, the CD-ROM is a critical success. However, the disintegration of the CD-ROM market and implosion of Voyager in 1997 means the CD-ROM never finds a popular audience. Rare and playable only with twenty-year-old technology, the *White Noise Omnibus* CD-ROM is now considered to be a collector's item.

1996

Curt Gardner launches Don DeLillo's America, a website dedicated to tracking DeLillo's writing and his interviews, as well as keeping current on the scholarly work being done on DeLillo. The site serves as a virtual meeting place for fans and critics alike, and in 1997 Scribner allows the site to host an unformatted TXT file containing *Underworld*, DeLillo's eleventh novel, in its entirety. The plan backfires, however, when it is discovered that Gopher servers in Lithuania are distributing a corrupt version of the text file, which contains embedded within it an executable macro virus that, when opened in Microsoft Word 95, deletes the host computer's "My Documents" folder.

1999

An English professor skilled in computational analysis uses word frequency counts to compare the text of the *White Noise Omnibus* CD-ROM with a scanned and OCR'd version of the raucous but out-of-print novel *Amazons* by Cleo Birdwell, long suspected to be the work of DeLillo. The professor's computer proves with a +/– 10 percent error rate that DeLillo is the author of *Amazons*, primarily based on the recurrence of the name "Murray Jay Siskind" in both novels. The English professor publishes his findings in the journal *Social Text*, concluding that "now that the author has been found, the text is explained."

2002

Scholars using the TextArc visualization tool to data-mine the *Underworld* TXT file demonstrate a startling correlation between the words "waste," "desert," and "nuclear" in *Underworld*.

2005

Using the latest tools in GIS and 3-D climatological modeling, researchers prove that the "airborne toxic event" depicted in *White Noise* would have had a significantly different viscosity, velocity, and impact zone than what DeLillo describes. The researchers suggest that the entire Gladney family should have died before reaching safety.

2009

With funding from the National Endowment for the Arts (NEA), the National Endowment for the Humanities (NEH), and the National Science Foundation (NSF), a team of humanist and computer scientists at a nationally renowned digital humanities lab recreate the vast research complex at the center of DeLillo's *Ratner's Star* (1976) as an immersive 3-D virtual environment using the Unreal game engine. Players can interact with nonplayable characters (NPCs), gather treasure, and attempt to decode the same radio signal from outer space that appears in *Ratner's Star*. Just as the novel itself is unreadable, *Ratner's Star: The Legend of Endor's Code* is unplayable.

2013

As part of the marketing campaign for David Cronenberg's cinematic adaptation of DeLillo's *Cosmopolis* (2003), the film studio teams with 42 Entertainment and the Harry Ransom Center to launch an ARG (alternate reality game) in which the Don DeLillo Papers play a key role. Core mechanics of the ARG include clues planted within the archive itself, such as letters from Murray Jay Siskind and other fictional characters, USB flash drives containing conversations between DeLillo and Cronenberg, keys to safety deposit boxes, and maps to other locations where further clues can be found.

DeLillo on the Outside of the Digital Humanities

"What does it all mean, signify, or demonstrate?" DeLillo wondered in 1971 in his "frame of reference" for "The Uniforms" ("Appendix to 'The Uniforms,'" 533). We might ask the same of these three timelines. What do they mean, signify, or demonstrate?

When I suggest that the digital humanities have failed scholars of Don DeLillo or other contemporary fiction, I am being unfair. The digital humanities are not responsible, nor are digital humanists. As my timeline of potential events suggests, if there were readily available digital versions of DeLillo's work, there would be no end to the computations that clever humanists could perform on them. Many of these projects might have failed or been misguided and overreaching, yet I do not doubt that the judicious use of visualizations, graphs, charts, maps, concordances, and other structures of meaning would reveal even greater depth to DeLillo's work than we already know to be there.

But the fact remains that the most promising, rewarded, or recognized work in the digital humanities has centered upon texts and artifacts in the public domain. The typical approaches to the digital humanities function quite well for medievalists, Renaissance scholars, Victorianists, nineteenth-century Americanists, or even modernists. Nearly everything scholars in these fields study is in the public domain and has been subjected to numerous and competing forms of digitization. But what if you study a living novelist, whose works are most decidedly copyrighted? What if you research a living novelist, whose life's work resides not on hard drives but in boxes and boxes of notes, drafts, and manuscripts?

The failure of the digital humanities to which I refer in my chapter title is not the failure to be able to do with DeLillo what we can do with Whitman or Blake. The failure is simply that nobody is talking about this disconnect. If the digital humanities are to be the future of the humanities, then we should be talking about what it means that a significant group of contemporary writers and thinkers are not a part of this future, at least not yet.[3]

Yet—again, as I have parodied in the timeline of potential events—perhaps there are advantages to being left alone, to being forced outside the constantly advancing, sprawling digital humanities machine. Of the three timelines I present, I much prefer the second, the exploration of DeLillo's latent history, rooted in dust and documents, deterioration and decay.

DeLillo has often said—and thematized in his novels—some version of his response to a question Anthony DeCurtis asked in a 1988 interview about being marginal, or marginalized: "I think I have an idea of what it's like to be an outsider in this society," DeLillo told DeCurtis (DeCurtis, 288). In an undated letter to Jonathan Franzen, DeLillo revisits this idea, telling the younger novelist that "a writer ought to function as an outsider . . . he ought to be skeptical about the values of society and ready to write in opposition to them" ("Letter to Jonathan Franzen," 1).

Perhaps it's fitting, then, that DeLillo's work will remain outside the culture of the digital humanities. Perhaps there's some value in a text or a collection of texts, a vast collection of texts, millions of words' worth of texts, that cannot be accommodated by the latest trends in literary scholarship. A corpora that cannot be assimilated and reduced to a database or a graph, a body of texts accessible only through physical engagement.

I doubt anyone in this collection believes that it's an either/or choice, that the digital humanities is an all-or-nothing affair. Archival research can exist—and does exist—alongside digital editions, visualizations, modeling, and so on. What DeLillo teaches us, though, is that we ought to be skeptical. Just as DeLillo suggests that novelists should "be ready to write in opposition" to the values of society, scholars, too, should be ready to study in opposition to the dominant values of contemporary scholarship. We may be surrounded by the digital in our reading, writing, teaching, and scholarship, but we must not be circumscribed by it.[4] We must, I think, strive to remain cognizant of the latent and the potential realities of the digital humanities. The potential is easy to see. The latent, by its very nature, is hidden. It is our mission to uncover it.

NOTES

1. DRM: digital rights management, any number of copy protection schemes used by publishers or distributors to ensure that e-books are not shared, loaned, or otherwise endowed with any resemblance to a physical book. My estimate of four generations of copyright protection is based on current U.S. law, under which DeLillo's first five novels (*Americana* through *Players*) are copyrighted until ninety-five years after their publication date, while every novel published after 1977 (*Running Dog* through *Point Omega*) is copyrighted seventy years beyond the death of the author—the literal death of the author,

not some Barthesian poststructuralist disappearance of the author that begins as soon as the words, a "tissue of quotations," are written (Barthes, 146).

2. This point is disputable. The dispute, however, is pointless. The HATHI Trust Digital Library and Google Books have both scanned some of DeLillo's novels, a fact that would appear to contradict my argument that DeLillo has been left behind by the digital humanities. But the limited range and depth of the functionality offered by either HATHI or Google only highlight their failure. HATHI has scanned exactly one DeLillo novel, *White Noise*; that novel is full-text searchable, but the results show only page numbers of the search terms. Google Book Search at least goes a step further, showing three-line "snippets" for ten of DeLillo's fifteen novels. What Google offers is a glorified index of individual novels, useful for teaching and finding quick references but a shadow of the massive text-mining and data-visualization operations upon which humanities computing has been built.

3. John Unsworth has identified T. S. Eliot's "The Waste Land" (1922) as both a literal and metaphorical demarcation between public domain texts that can be freely studied using the tools of the digital humanities and copyrighted texts that are far more difficult to subject to nonconsumptive research—that is, research that relies on computational analysis of a text rather than the reading of a text (see Unsworth). DeLillo's work, as does the work of every writer published in the United States since 1923, clearly dwells in a digital waste land, a kind of forbidden territory tantalizingly out of reach for digital humanists.

4. See, for example, the work of Lincoln Mullen and Alex Reid, who have both suggested that all humanists are digital humanists now.

BIBLIOGRAPHY

Angell, Roger. "Letter to Don DeLillo." February 18, 1966. Box 104, Folder 4. Don DeLillo Papers.

Barthes, Roland. "The Death of the Author." In *Image-Music-Text*, translated by Stephen Heath, 142–48. New York: Hill and Wang, 1977.

Begley, Adam. "The Art of Fiction CXXXV." *Paris Review* 35, no. 128 (1993): 274–306.

DeCurtis, Anthony. "'An Outsider in This Society': An Interview with Don DeLillo." *SAQ* 89, no. 2 (1990): 281–304.

DeLillo, Don. "Appendix to 'The Uniforms.'" In *Cutting Edges: Young American Fiction for the '70s*, edited by Jack Hicks, 532–33. New York: Holt, 1973.

———. *Great Jones Street*. New York: Penguin, 1994.

———. "Letter to David Foster Wallace." February 5, 1997. Box 101, Folder 10. Don DeLillo Papers.

———. "Letter to Jonathan Franzen." Undated. Box 109, Folder 3. Don DeLillo Papers.

———. "Letter to Mark Sample." April 27, 2003. Box 109, Folder 3. Don DeLillo Papers.

———. *Mao II*. New York: Penguin, 1992.

———. Notebook. Undated. Box 81, Folder 1. Don DeLillo Papers.

———. Notes in Notebook. Undated. Box 38, Folder 1. Don DeLillo Papers.
———. "Total Loss Weekend." *Sports Illustrated,* November 27, 1972, 98–120. http://sportsillustrated.cnn.com/vault/article/magazine/MAG1086811/index.htm.
———. "The Self-Erasing Word." Undated. Box 20, Folder 1. Don DeLillo Papers.
Don DeLillo Papers. Harry Ransom Humanities Research Center, University of Texas at Austin.
Earhart, Amy, and Andrew Jewell. *The American Literature Scholar in the Digital Age.* Ann Arbor: University of Michigan Press and University of Michigan Library, 2011.
Hicks, Jack. "Letter to Don DeLillo." October 1, 1969. Box 104, Folder 4. Don DeLillo Papers.
———. "Letter to Don DeLillo." December 31, 1971. Box 104, Folder 4. Don DeLillo Papers.
Hills, Rust. "Letter to Don DeLillo." April 23, 1962. Box 104, Folder 4. Don DeLillo Papers.
Jones, Philip. "Simon & Schuster Makes Kindle Push." TheBookSeller.com. February 6, 2008. http://www.thebookseller.com/news/simon-schuster-makes-kindle-push.html.
Macauley, Robie. "Letter to Don DeLillo." March 19, 1966. Box 104, Folder 4. Don DeLillo Papers.
Max, D. T. "Final Destination." *New Yorker*, June 11, 2007, 54–71.
Mullen, Lincoln. "Digital Humanities Is a Spectrum; or, We're All Digital Humanists Now." *Backward Glance.* April 29, 2010.
Reid, Alex. "Digital Humanities: Two Venn Diagrams." *Digital Digs.* March 9, 2011. http://www.alex-reid.net/2011/03/digital-humanities-two-venn-diagrams.html.
Salamon, Jeff. "Underword; Excavating the Writing Process of Don DeLillo, America's Most Paranoid Novelist." *Austin American-Stateman,* February 6, 2005, K1.
Sample, Mark. "Letter to Don DeLillo." April 24, 2003. Personal Correspondence.
"Sports Illustrated VAULT Debuts." Sports Collectors Daily. March 23, 2008. http://www.sportscollectorsdaily.com/sports-illustrated-vault-debuts/.
Unsworth, John. "Datta-Mine-ing." Digital Humanities Symposium. Texas Institute for Literary and Textual Studies, University of Texas at Austin. May 27, 2011. http://www3.isrl.illinois.edu/~unsworth/tilts3.2011.JMU.pdf.
Workman, Richard. "RE: Question About Don DeLillo Papers." Message to Mark Sample. March 29, 2011.

Disability, Universal Design, and the Digital Humanities

GEORGE H. WILLIAMS

Over the last several decades, scholars have developed standards for how best to create, organize, present, and preserve digital information so that future generations of teachers, students, scholars, and librarians may still use it. What has remained neglected for the most part, however, are the needs of people with disabilities. As a result, many of the otherwise most valuable digital resources are useless for people who are—for example—deaf or hard of hearing, as well as for people who are blind, have low vision, or have difficulty distinguishing particular colors. While professionals working in educational technology and commercial web design have made significant progress in meeting the needs of such users, the humanities scholars creating digital projects all too often fail to take these needs into account. This situation would be much improved if more projects embraced the concept of universal design, the idea that we should always keep the largest possible audience in mind as we make design decisions, ensuring that our final product serves the needs of those with disabilities as well as those without.

It is imperative that digital humanities work take into account the important insights of disability studies in the humanities, an interdisciplinary field that considers disability "not so much a property of bodies as a product of cultural rules about what bodies should be or do," in the words of Rosemarie Garland-Thomson, a prominent figure in the field (6). Digital knowledge tools that assume everyone approaches information with the same abilities and using the same methods risk excluding a large percentage of people. In fact, such tools actually do the work of disabling people by preventing them from using digital resources altogether. We must broaden our understanding of the ways in which people use digital resources. For example, visually impaired people take advantage of digital technologies for "accessibility," technologies that (with their oral/aural and tactile interfaces) are fascinatingly different than the standard screen-keyboard-mouse combination, forcing us to rethink our embodied relationship to data. Learning to create scholarly digital archives that take into account these human differences is a necessary task no one has yet undertaken.

In what follows I consider the somewhat arbitrary concept of disability and assistive technology, argue why the digital humanities community should adopt a universal design approach, explain what a universal design approach would look like, and then offer a few specific suggestions for collaborative projects that should be undertaken by digital humanists.

Questioning Disability

I first became interested in these issues as a graduate student working with Garland-Thomson when she was a faculty fellow at the Maryland Institute for Technology in the Humanities (MITH) in the fall of 2001. During this experience, I was forced to reevaluate my assumptions about using computers and designing web pages. Garland-Thomson worked with the staff at MITH to create an online academic resource site for disability studies, and we decided to design the website with maximum accessibility. To do so, we needed to think about the needs of people who are blind, have low vision, or have difficulty navigating because of the clutter that often accumulates on web pages. (We had no plans to include audio, so addressing the needs of people who are deaf or hard of hearing was not in our plan.) At the same time, we aimed for a visual design that would appeal to sighted users. We kept the layout simple and added certain features specifically for certain kinds of users. For example, because tech-savvy blind people often have their computer read websites out loud using what is known as screen-reading software, many find it tedious to listen to the identical detailed navigation menu on every page within a given site. To solve this problem, we inserted a tiny image—a transparent GIF exactly one pixel square, to be exact—at the beginning of each page with an alt attribute that read, "Skip to main content." This image would be invisible to sighted users, but those listening to the page with screen-reading software—which reads aloud the alt attributes of images embedded in an HTML page—could use that GIF as their cue to jump past what they did not need to hear in order to get to the information that they did want to hear. We also made sure that every image tag had an alt attribute where necessary, although in general we kept images to a minimum. For advice on accessibility issues, we worked with a blind person who used screen-reading software to listen to the web, rather than reading it off of a visual display as a sighted person would do. She demonstrated this software for me, and I was surprised by how quickly the words were spoken by the synthesized voice that came from her laptop's speakers. In fact, I could not understand anything at all that she was doing. To accommodate me, she adjusted the settings to slow down significantly the synthesized speech, at which point I could understand the words but still found myself unable to orient myself on a given page or within a given website. This scenario caused me to reevaluate my understanding of what it means to be disabled, as she clearly was using abilities that I did not—and still do not—have: I had not trained myself to be able to process auditory information as efficiently as she could.

Walter Ong famously wrote, "Technologies are artificial, but . . . artificiality is natural to humans" (81). Ong's concern is with writing as a fundamentally artificial process that has been so "internalized" by humans that it appears to be as natural to us as talking. Ong's observation is part of a larger cultural critique that highlights the socially constructed nature of the ways we perceive technology and its role in our lives. To those of us who are more or less comfortable with the existing dominant model of using computers, anything different, like a fast screen reader, seems alien, and the potential shortcomings of our familiar model of some combination of keyboard, mouse, and visual display remain invisible to us. We classify some software and hardware tools as "assistive technology"—sometimes the term "adaptive technology" is used instead—because they have been designed specifically to assist those people with "special needs." We might consider, however, that there is no "natural" way to interact with the 1's and 0's that make up the data we are interested in creating, transmitting, receiving, and using; there is only the model we have chosen to think of as natural. All technology is assistive, in the end.

Finally, we would do well to be aware of the range of "assistive"-technology software applications and hardware devices that do not work in the same ways as the devices used by nondisabled people. In addition to being compatible with desktop computers, laptops, smart phones, and tablet devices, the materials we create should also work well with such tools as refreshable braille displays, digital talking book devices, screen reader applications, and screen magnification software.

Universal Design Defined

The term "universal design" was invented by architect Ronald Mace, founder of North Carolina State University's (NCSU) Center for Universal Design. According to the NCSU College of Design, the term "describe[s] the concept of designing all products and the built environment to be aesthetic and usable to the greatest extent possible by everyone, regardless of their age, ability, or status in life" ("Ronald L. Mace"). Wendy Chisolm and Matt May write that to embrace universal design principles is to "approach every problem . . . with the ultimate goal of providing the greatest benefit to the greatest number of people possible" (2). Mace argues for the importance of distinguishing between universal design principles and accessibility principles. To embrace accessibility is to focus design efforts on people who are disabled, ensuring that all barriers have been removed. To embrace universal design, by contrast, is to focus "not specifically on people with disabilities, but all people" (Mace). Something created to assist a person with a disability—to make their environment more accessible in some way—might not be affordable or aesthetically pleasing even if it is usable and helpful. Something created using universal design principles, on the other hand, is designed "for a very broad definition of user that encourages attractive, marketable products that are more usable by everyone" (Mace). Devoting efforts to accessibility might improve the built environment for disabled people, but devoting efforts to universal design improves the built environment for all people. Mace cites the example of the automatic garage door opener as a consumer product created with universal design principles: it is affordable; it appeals to and is useful to people both with and without disabilities. Another frequently cited example of universal design is the sidewalk curb cut; initially created to allow people in wheelchairs to cross the street more easily, curb cuts became recognized as useful also to other people such as someone making a delivery with a dolly, a traveler pulling luggage on wheels, a parent pushing a child in a stroller, or a person walking beside their bicycle. Whether in a physical or a digital environment, designers are always making choices about accessibility. However, not all designers are aware of how their choices affect accessibility. Universal design is design that involves conscious decisions about accessibility for all, and it is a philosophy that should be adopted more widely by digital humanities scholars.

Why Universal Design?

Before I recommend how to adopt universal design principles, I need to explain the several reasons why we should do so. First, ensuring that digital resources created with federal funding are accessible is the law in many countries. In the United States, for example, the Federal Rehabilitation Act of 1973 was amended in 1998 with what is now referred to as Section 508 to require that all federal agencies "developing, procuring, maintaining, or using electronic and information technology" ensure that disabled people "have access to and use of information and data that is comparable to the access to and use of the information and data" by people who are not disabled (U.S. General Services Administration, "Section 508 of the Rehabilitation Act, as Amended by the Workforce Investment Act of 1998."). American government agencies that fund digital humanities projects do not currently require proof of accessibility, but there is no reason to assume that this will always be the case. In addition to the United States, the list of nations with laws or policies requiring web accessibility includes Australia, Canada, Germany, Israel, India, Italy, Ireland, Japan, Korea, Portugal, and Spain (Chisolm and May, 14–15). At some point in the future, project directors seeking government funding could be turned down if they are unable to demonstrate in their grant proposals that the results of their work will be accessible. Rather than wait until such time at which the laws begin to be enforced, we should start now to follow the existing guidelines for accessibility and to develop our own guidelines and tools for authoring and evaluating accessible resources. Not all digital humanities projects are created with government funding, of course, but enough of them are that this is a significant issue. Furthermore, instructors who wish to use digital humanities resources in their courses will need to ensure that those resources are accessible if they teach at an institution that receives any sort of government funding. Otherwise, they make themselves and their institution vulnerable to legal action.

Second, universal design is efficient. In order to adhere to the "alternative means of access" subsection of Section 508, American web designers used to create alternative, accessible versions of their content to parallel the original content. However, coding everything twice—first for nondisabled people and then again for disabled people—is time consuming and expensive. Fortunately, web standards have developed enough that this duplication of effort is no longer necessary. Instead, it is now possible to create just one version of a resource and to make design choices that ensure the resource suits the needs of all users, disabled and nondisabled alike. The ability to separate structure from presentation is particularly useful in this regard.

Third, applying universal design principles to digital resources will make those resources more likely to be compatible with multiple devices. To create an online resource that only works with a desktop or laptop computer is to exclude people who would prefer to access the resource with a smart phone, a tablet, or some other mobile device. The Web Accessibility Initiative of the World Wide Web Consortium points out that there is "significant overlap between making a website accessible for a mobile device and for people with disabilities" (Henry, "Web Content Accessibility"). Compatibility with mobile devices is important because an increasing number of people are using such devices to access the web. In the United States, for example, young adults between the ages of eighteen and thirty-three make up the largest segment of the population of web users at 35 percent (Zickuhr, 4), and 65 percent of those between the ages of eighteen and twenty-nine use a mobile device to go online (Smith, 5). Furthermore, those more likely to use a mobile device for online access include African Americans, Hispanics, and individuals from lower-income households (Smith, 10). If the digital humanities is to create resources accessible by a diverse array of people, then compatibility with mobile devices is a necessity.

Fourth and finally, it is the right thing to do. We recognize the importance of open access for scholarly materials, but "open access means more than simply making stuff available," as Jeremy Boggs, humanities design architect at the University of Virginia's Scholars' Lab, has said. We would never use a proprietary format for preserving and sharing our work, in part because to do so would be to exclude those people who cannot afford or do not have access to the necessary software to use that format. However, few of us think twice about whether or not the format we have chosen and the design choices we have made exclude disabled people. It might be tempting to assume that few, if any, disabled people are interested in or need to make use of our work, but by creating barriers to access we are ensuring that such people will never have the opportunity to participate in the digital humanities. According to a report from the Pew Research Center's Internet and American Life Project, 81 percent of all adults report using the Internet, but only 54 percent of disabled adults do (Fox, "Americans," 3). Of course, disabled adults are also more likely to be older, to have lower incomes, and to have less education than nondisabled adults, and all of these demographic factors are correlated with lower levels of Internet use (Fox, "What People"). However, inaccessible design choices remain a significant barrier to information for disabled people, and removing those barriers to information can only contribute to higher levels of education and perhaps higher levels of income as well. If our goals include the ability to share our work with as wide and diverse an audience as possible, then we should embrace universal design principles.

Designing for Accessibility

It is beyond the scope of this chapter to reiterate the specific guidelines for designing accessible web resources, especially when so many useful guidelines already exist. Digital humanists interested in learning more about these guidelines would do well to start with the Web Accessibility Initiative website hosted by the World Wide Web Consortium, where they will find a wide variety of specific recommendations as well as references to additional resources. Many helpful tutorials may be found on other sites, of course, but the Web Accessibility Initiative guidelines specifically and the World Wide Web Consortium guidelines more generally are widely considered to be web standards followed by those who create and maintain web-based resources. There are, however, specific projects that the digital humanities community should undertake in order to improve greatly the accessibility of the resources we create as well as the ease with which we make those resources accessible.

Specific Project Ideas

ACCESSIBILITY TOOLS FOR CONTENT MANAGEMENT SYSTEMS

Accessibility would be much easier for most content creators to achieve if a suite of free and open-source accessibility tools were developed for popular content management systems (CMS).[1] A list of the most commonly used CMSes for digital humanities projects would include—but not be limited to—WordPress, Drupal, Omeka, MediaWiki, and Joomla. Each of these has a number of appealing features: they are relatively easy to install, often available as one-click-installation options through commercial web-hosting services; they are free and open-source projects; and their appearance and functions may be customized through the use of such add-ons as themes, plug-ins, modules, and extensions. A valuable project would be for the digital humanities community to develop a collection of add-ons that would integrate easily with these CMSes and improve the accessibility of the websites they deliver. Making available a ready-made set of accessibility tools for developers to add to their sites would allow individual projects to avoid the work of developing and evaluating their own accessibility features independently of one another. These tools could not only provide end users with a more accessible interface but also provide content creators with built-in accessibility evaluation functions, facilitating good design choices from the ground up rather than after a site has already been completed.

FORMAT TRANSLATION TOOLS

In July of 2010, the Center for History and New Media at George Mason University hosted a workshop involving twelve digital humanists who were tasked with creating a useful digital humanities tool in one week. The result was Anthologize, "a free, open-source plugin that transforms WordPress 3.0 into a platform for publishing electronic texts" ("About," Anthologize). Anthologize imports texts from RSS feeds and then translates them into one of a handful of alternate formats: ePub, PDF, TEI (plus HTML), or RTF. Blind people who use the web are in need of a digital humanities project that either extends Anthologize or creates a similar tool so that RSS feeds may be converted easily and automatically into XML formats that work with digital talking book devices or with braille output devices.

A digital talking book is an XML document created to be compatible with any of a number of devices that will read the document aloud. The format includes metadata that facilitates navigation between different sections of the document, and it may include recordings of a person reading the document aloud, or it may be designed to be read aloud as synthesized speech by a device ("ANSI/NISO Z39.86"). Since 1996, the DAISY Consortium has been working to establish and promote an open standard for digital talking books ("About Us"). One of their most powerful products is the DAISY Pipeline, "a cross-platform, open source framework for DTB-related document transformations" ("DAISY Pipeline"). A well-structured document in a format like TEI or HTML is ideally suited to be automatically translated into the DAISY format through a software process that makes use of the DAISY Pipeline. A CMS add-on like Anthologize that accomplishes this task efficiently, automatically, and easily would be an extremely powerful tool in the hands of content creators, allowing them to easily make their texts available as digital talking books, providing access to information for the many people who make use of digital talking books as their primary method of reading.

People literate in braille often prefer to read by that method rather than by listening to texts. Reading content through braille provides a deeper understanding of that content for many, yet producing well-formatted braille files is accomplished through one of two expensive methods.[2] First, professionals who are certified braille translators may be hired to create well-formatted braille. Second, a number of commercial braille translation software applications may be used; the most reliable applications cost several hundred dollars and are cost prohibitive to low-income users and nonspecialized content creators. A CMS add-on like Anthologize could be such a translator if it incorporated Liblouis, a widely used open-source braille translation engine. Such an add-on would allow braille readers to access online texts through such devices as refreshable braille displays or braille embossers. Clearly, creating a free and easy-to-use online braille translator would make a tremendous difference in the lives of individuals who need braille translations of online content and in the ability of content creators to reach braille-literate audiences.

TOOLS FOR CROWDSOURCED CAPTIONS, SUBTITLES, AND TRANSCRIPTS

Online information presented in audio or video format is not accessible to deaf and hard-of-hearing end users without captions. These individuals benefit from online captioning as well as from written transcriptions presented as separate and independent documents. Creating captions and transcriptions makes such information subject to search and computer analysis in ways not currently possible with audio and video alone. Additionally, individuals without disabilities often find transcriptions easier to follow. The time and expense of captioning or transcribing is a significant obstacle to making accessible an online project featuring several hours of video or audio. Currently, a number of desktop software applications provide an interface designed to facilitate captioning videos or transcribing audio. However, none of them that I have found are free, and because they are not online tools none of them allow projects to take advantage of one of the web's most powerful and relatively new practices: crowdsourcing.

"Crowdsourcing" is a term coined by Jeff Howe in 2006 to describe online projects that make use of free or extremely inexpensive labor provided by "enthusiasts" around the world who are interested in donating their time to a project that interests them. Several digital humanities projects have experimented with taking this approach to transcribing digital images of documents, with mixed results: nonexpert transcribers sometimes make a significant number of mistakes when transcribing material written in an unfamiliar hand (Cohen). However, a digital file in which the audio has been clearly recorded stands to result in a more accurate transcription, even by nonexpert transcribers. The Center for History and New Media is currently developing a promising online tool named Scripto, which "will allow users to contribute transcriptions to online documentary projects" ("About," Scripto). Transcriptions of images of documents greatly enhance accessibility for people who are blind because screen readers will be able to read aloud the transcriptions while image-only documents are inaccessible. People who are deaf or hard of hearing, however, are in need of a digital humanities project that presents a user-friendly interface like Scripto for hearing people to caption videos or transcribe audio. Universal Subtitles, created by the Participatory Culture Foundation, is an admirable example of such an interface ("Frequently Asked Questions"). However, captions created with this interface are stored on the Universal Subtitles server, rather than in a project's content management system. An extremely valuable digital humanities accessibility project would be one that facilitates crowdsourced transcriptions and captions but that works with a variety of different content management systems, saving the resulting text in the relevant database field of the CMS or in a shared, open repository.

Conclusion: Reciprocal Benefits

People with disabilities will benefit significantly if the digital humanities community pursues projects such as these and begins to take seriously the need to adopt universal design principles. However, by working to meet the needs of disabled people—and by working with disabled people through usability testing—the digital humanities community will also benefit significantly as it rethinks its assumptions about how digital devices could and should work with and for people. Graham Pullin, a senior lecturer in the University of Dundee School of Computing, has observed that the prevailing assumption in product design is that new developments in the mainstream slowly "trickle-down" to "specialist products for people with disabilities" (xiii). However, as Pullin points out, sometimes the effect works the other way, "when the issues around disability catalyze new design thinking and influence a broader design culture in return" (xiii). What I am arguing is that infusing the digital humanities with universal design principles will result in just this kind of reciprocal relationship.

Matthew Kirschenbaum has described "the current state of new media studies" as one "in which the graphical user interface is often uncritically accepted as the ground zero of the user's experience" (34). In arguing that computer storage deserves more critical attention from scholars than it has traditionally received, Kirschenbaum adopts Nick Montfort's term "screen essentialism" to describe the fallacy of assuming that all computer interaction occurs through the interface of the screen. Montfort points out that screen essentialism obscures the diversity of computing interfaces that have existed prior to the appearance of the modern electronic screen; in particular, as he describes, early computing programs relied on paper interfaces. Montfort's point is historical, but screen essentialism also obscures the diversity of contemporary interfaces used by people with disabilities and, increasingly, by all people.

Blind computer users, for example, have no use for a screen, and they most often use an interface that is either tactile, in the form of refreshable braille devices, or audible, in the form of screen-reading software or digital books. We might also reconsider our "essentialist" thinking about the keyboard and the mouse and not just because of the technologies that we perceive to be specific to disabled people. Speech recognition technologies, while far from perfect, are already accurate enough to allow writers—if that is still the correct term—to compose documents without the need for typing. And the growth of touch screens, primarily but not exclusively available on mobile devices, bring the possibility of a mouse-less future ever closer. Both of these technologies are extremely useful for people who are disabled, but they are used for the most part by people who are not. To continue to create projects designed primarily for the screen-keyboard-mouse environment would be foolish: if a resource doesn't work on a device that lacks one of those components, then that resource is already worthless to a significant number of computer users, disabled and nondisabled alike. As we observe contemporary computing devices proliferate and diversify, we need to plan for a future in which our current digital resources continue to be not only useful but usable.

NOTES

1. I am grateful to Jennifer Guiliano for this suggestion.

2. My understanding of braille and braille technologies would not have been possible without advice and input from Tina Herzberg.

BIBLIOGRAPHY

"About." Anthologize. Center for History and New Media, 2010. http://anthologize.org/.

"About." Scripto. Center for History and New Media, 2010. http://scripto.org/.

"About Us." DAISY Consortium. 2011. http://www.daisy.org/.

Abou-Zahra, Shadi, ed. "Evaluating Web Sites for Accessibility: Overview." Web Accessibility Initiative. World Wide Web Consortium, 2011. http://www.w3.org/WAI/.

———, ed. "How People with Disabilities Use the Web: Overview." Web Accessibility Initiative. World Wide Web Consortium, 2011. http://www.w3.org/WAI/.

"ANSI/NISO Z39.86–Specifications for the Digital Talking Book." NISO. National Information Standards Organization, April 12, 2005. http://www.niso.org/.

Boggs, Jeremy. Instant message to author. February 21, 2011.

Chisholm, Wendy, and Matthew May. *Universal Design for Web Applications.* Sebastopol, Calif.: O'Reilly Media, 2009.

Cohen, Patricia. "Scholars Recruit Public for Project." *New York Times,* December 27, 2010. http://www.nytimes.com/.

"DAISY Pipeline: DTB-related Document Transformations." *DAISY Pipeline.* DAISY Consortium, 2011. http://www.daisy.org/.

Fox, Susannah. "Americans Living with Disability and Their Technology Profile." Pew Research Center's Internet & American Life Project. January 21, 2011. http://www.pewinternet.org/.

———. "What People Living with Disability Can Teach Us." Pew Research Center's Internet & American Life Project. January 26, 2011. http://www.pewinternet.org/.

"Frequently Asked Questions." *Universal Subtitles.* Participatory Culture Foundation, 2010. http://www.universalsubtitles.org/.

Garland-Thomson, Rosemarie. *Extraordinary Bodies: Figuring Physical Disability in American Culture and Literature.* New York: Columbia University Press, 1997.

Henry, Shawn Lawton, ed. "Web Content Accessibility Guidelines (WCAG) Overview." *Web Accessibility Initiative*. World Wide Web Consortium, 2011. http://www.w3.org/WAI/.

Henry, Shawn Lawton, and Liam McGee, eds. "Accessibility." *Web Design and Applications*. World Wide Web Consortium, 2010. http://www.w3.org/standards/Webdesign/.

Howe, Jeff. "The Rise of Crowdsourcing." *Wired.com,* Condé Nast Digital, June 2006. http://www.wired.com/.

Kirschenbaum, Matthew G. *Mechanisms: New Media and the Forensic Imagination*. Cambridge, Mass.: MIT Press, 2008.

"Liblouis–A Braille Translation and Back-Translation Library." Google Code. Google, 2010. http://code.google.com/.

Mace, Ron. "A Perspective on Universal Design," edited by Jan Reagan. Center for Universal Design. North Carolina State University, 2008. http://www.design.ncsu.edu/cud/.

Montfort, Nick. "Continuous Paper: MLA." *Nick Montfort*. January 1, 2005. http://nickm.com/.

Ong, Walter J. *Orality and Literacy: The Technologizing of the Word*. London: Routledge, 1982.

Pullin, Graham. *Design Meets Disability*. Cambridge, Mass.: MIT Press, 2009.

NSCU College of Design. "Ronald L. Mace." North Carolina State University, 2011. http://design.ncsu.edu/alumni-friends/alumni-profiles/ronald-mace.

Smith, Aaron. "Mobile Access 2010." *Pew Research Center's Internet & American Life Project*. July 7, 2010. http://www.pewinternet.org/.

Thorp, Justin, and Shawn Lawton Henry, eds. "Web Content Accessibility and Mobile Web: Making a Web Site Accessible Both for People with Disabilities and for Mobile Devices." *Web Accessibility Initiative*. World Wide Web Consortium, 2008. http://www.w3.org/WAI/mobile/.

U.S. Department of Commerce. *Exploring the Digital Nation: Home Broadband Internet Adoption in the United States*. Economics & Statistics Administration, and National Telecommunications and Information Administration, November 2010. http://www.ntia.doc.gov/.

U.S. Department of Justice. "Americans with Disabilities Act of 1990, as Amended with ADA Amendments Act of 2008." ADA Home Page. July 15, 2009. http://www.ada.gov/.

U.S. General Services Administration. "How do I Evaluate My Software Applications or Website for Accessibility?" Section508.gov. http://www.section508.gov/.

———. "Section 508 of the Rehabilitation Act, as Amended by the Workforce Investment Act of 1998." *Section508.gov*. January 2010. http://www.section508.gov/.

———. "Technology Tools." *Section508.gov*. http://www.section508.gov/.

Web Accessibility Initiative. World Wide Web Consortium, 2011. http://www.w3.org/WAI/.

Zickuhr, Kathryn. "Generations 2010." *Pew Research Center's Internet & American Life Project*. December 16, 2010. http://www.pewinternet.org/.

The Digital Humanities and Its Users

CHARLIE EDWARDS

In her poignant and piercing intervention, "Eternal September of the Digital Humanities," Bethany Nowviskie reflects on how "our daily voicing of the practice of digital humanities (and not just on special days—every day) helps to shape and delimit and advance it." She continues, "That voicing operates wholeheartedly to welcome people and fresh ideas in, if sometimes to press uncomfortably (one intends, salutarily) against the inevitable changes they will bring." Recently, though, the voices of digital humanities (DH) have been discordant, talking of pioneers and parvenus, makers and tweeters, workers and lurkers. Others—notoriously—have figured themselves as the out-group to DH's in-group, the dull ground against which the "stars" of DH shine (Pannapacker). Here, though, we will focus on what I hope may be a more unifying image: the user. I will try to frame DH not as a field defined by its borders, and the skills required to breach those borders, but instead—in an analogy that should appeal to the community's tool builders—as a system with users. This can help us to make some important moves. It allows us to shift the debate from charged hermeneutics ("Are DHers inclusive?") to practical heuristics ("Which features of DH as a system enhance or undermine access and participation?"). It compels us to acknowledge that DH, as a system, has serious usability issues that affect both new and experienced users. And it suggests how these problems, contingent as they are on the system's current design, might be addressed.

Usability has typically been defined and evaluated in terms of a system's ease of learning, ease of use, efficiency, and user satisfaction.[1] How, though, can this be relevant to an academic field? If DH is a system, any academic discipline is a system. Should entry to a discipline, use of its theories and methods, be "easy"? William Pannapacker finds DH inaccessible: "It's perceptible in the universe of Twitter: We read it, but we do not participate. It's the cool-kids' table." But are the barriers to entry that "outsiders" perceive really usability issues, or simply points on DH's inevitable learning curve? As one DHer tweets in response, acerbically, "Wonder if DH seems exclusivist to some because the gateway to full participation can include real, definable skills."[2] Surely the painstaking acquisition of specialist knowledge is an essential aspect of professionalization in any field. Yet surely also a field that marks its difference as the "digital" owes some explanation not just of what can be accomplished digitally but also of how those digital moves are to be made. Humanists are summoned by DHers to "build" (Ramsay "On Building"), enjoined by others to "be online or be irrelevant" (Parry), implicitly deprecated in the title of Patricia Cohen's *New York Times* coverage, "Humanities 2.0." But, as we will find, the gateways to participation, even the paths to the gateways, are obscure.

There are other ways, however, in which the concept of usability can be seen as problematic, both in itself and in its application here. As a business practice, usability and user experience (UX) design claims success in directing the user to a specific end: adoption of a site, retention on the site to view ads, seamless completion of commercial transactions. What implications might this have for DH? Pannapacker likens the atmospherics of DH to the "alienating" culture of Big Theory in the 1980s and 1990s, so I invoke one of the biggest theorists of the period perhaps inadvisedly. But Derrida has reminded us, "Metaphor is never innocent. It orients research and fixes results" (17). And this particular metaphor could involve some risk. Does it (as does, arguably, the entire project of usability) subscribe to a naive determinism that draws a straight line between wireframe design and desired outcome? Does it rest on an undertheorized, instrumental conception of technology that seeks only to achieve a smooth, seductive fit of tool to hand? After all, the usability.gov home page ventriloquizes the user: "Please don't make me think!" This summons in turn a nightmare vision: the user as consumer, passive and unreflective. This figure, with the crass n00b,[3] haunts texts such as "Eternal September" and the comments thereon. By corollary, does viewing DH as a system render DH as "applied" (versus "pure") humanities, submitting to the service orientation that Nowviskie in her post explicitly resists? Does it, in other words, offer up DH as a prosthesis for the humanities to wield?

To me, these questions are not mere artifacts of the metaphor but deeply relevant as DH moves forward. Pannapacker's post claims to mark the moment of the field's transformation from "the next big thing" to simply "The Thing"; his headline posits DH as "triumphant." While common sense argues skepticism here, nonetheless DH does seem to have reached a pivot point in its development. "Eternal September" references the moment in 1993 when Usenet, a discussion system favored by early adopters, was inundated by naive users introduced by the mainstream service provider AOL. But we are also given a glimpse of the user experience: "about thirty days in, newbies had either acclimatized to Usenet or they had dropped away." Until recently even DH's tool builders have paid scant attention to usability, as Matthew Kirschenbaum notes in his discussion of the topic, "So the Colors Cover the Wires." Now, though, DH does seem to be changing in response to its new users, as we will see. But in offering alternatives for users beyond compliance and abandonment, how will the role of those users be conceived? What forms of participation will be enabled? It is not the user as such but the user as consumer that renders the builder as service provider, proffering DH as tool to hand. Yet DH's direction in this regard is far from clear.

Traditionally, the most common methods of usability assessment are formal testing—in which selected representative users are observed interacting with the system to perform specified tasks, sometimes in a lab environment—and heuristic evaluation, where an expert reviews the system's interface against a set of best practices. This essay, I freely admit, does neither. Instead, it traces a history of the user in DH, before turning to examine DH as system. More recent thinking on usability shifts the emphasis from system to user and her lived experience of the system in its context of use (McCarthy and Wright, 5).[4] So as the essay explores the online landscape—the "user interface," as it were—of the digital humanities in its current design, it focuses on reading traces of users' situated experiences in blog posts, in comment threads, and on Twitter, then lays out this user's informal analysis of the results. I will propose that DH and its possible futures are likely to be shaped, delimited, or advanced by how DHers choose to design and build their conceptions of the user, and the extent to which *all* users can participate in that process.

DH and Its Users; or, Missing Masses?

A UX designer typically begins by asking two basic questions: who is to use the system, and for what ends? It need hardly be said that regarding DH these are contested points; for evidence, we can simply look at Pannapacker's blog post, the multiple definitions of DH generated every year by the University of Alberta's international Day of Digital Humanities event, and indeed this collection itself. But the responses to these questions have also changed over time. As Patrik Svensson describes in "Humanities Computing as Digital Humanities," the field in its initial expression (humanities computing) had very different "epistemic commitments" from those articulated under the rubric of "digital humanities," and the renaming is far from unproblematic. Indeed DH can be seen, perhaps, as a legacy application that at its core was not designed for widespread use and that struggles to integrate more recent modules that have this as their goal.

The origin story of DH tells of a stand-alone tool developed initially for a single user, Roberto Busa—his *Index Thomisticus*, a concordance of the works of St. Thomas Aquinas (Hockey). Looking at DH tools literally rather than metaphorically, they have often been designed by researchers for researchers (often themselves). As even prominent tool builders acknowledge, the uptake for many DH tools has remained small, the users almost coextensive with the makers, even where the goal of the development team has been to reach a broader audience. Multiple explanations for this have been offered from within the field. The lack of enthusiasm among "traditional" humanists for computer-assisted textual analysis, for example, is often explained by a humanistic tendency to associate computation with empiricism, positivism, and other such suspect enterprises (Mueller; Ramsay, "In Praise of

Pattern"). John Bradley, however, points to the system design, suggesting "computing humanists" and their "colleagues down the hall" have different mental models of the role of computing in literary study. The latter are, even now, operating under the "conduit model" in which the computer is simply a text delivery mechanism. Computing humanists, meanwhile, have built tools based on their own models, models that do not reflect how "traditional" literary scholars actually do their work. Whatever the cause, the effect seems clear. Martin Mueller conducted a distant reading of the titles of monographs and articles in scholarly journals, his aim being to measure mainstream interest in what he terms "literary informatics." He concludes that it remains a niche activity, of interest only to those who participate in it. It has had, he says—and he is deeply involved in such work—"virtually no impact on major disciplinary trends" (305).

Widening the lens to DH more generally, Oya Rieger's newer research supports Mueller's conclusions. In her study of faculty at Cornell's Society for the Humanities, Rieger asked about their familiarity with the digital humanities. The results: only four of forty-five participants were actually engaged in what they regarded as DH work; four more had an understanding of it; nineteen had heard the phrase but couldn't explain its meaning; and the rest were entirely unfamiliar with the term. She found, moreover, that the scholarly practices of the participants were unaltered, aside from the adoption of generic tools such as search engines—technology as conduit, to use Bradley's term. Meanwhile, "many tools and techniques that are being associated with sophisticated digital practices, such as data mining or visualization, remain accessible and relevant to only a handful of scholars." Of course, it is entirely possible that with recent coverage of DH in venues such as the *Chronicle of Higher Education* and the *New York Times*[5]—and the propulsive rhetoric of that coverage—the figures Rieger quotes may now have changed. But based on the history of the field one might have real skepticism about DH's potential to attract, let alone retain, the deluge of new users that "Eternal September" images. On this view, in fact, Eternal September may be moot.

Recently, however, some DHers have adopted a more inclusive mode of tool building, as Tom Scheinfeldt describes. "At CHNM," he writes, "we judge our tools by one key metric above all others: use. Successful tools are tools that are used . . . any open source software project's goal should be use by as many of its potential users as possible" ("Lessons from One Week | One Tool"). This, he explains, brings many benefits to the project:

> A large and enthusiastic user base is key to a successful open source software project's continued success. If people use a product, they will invest in that product. They will provide valuable user testing. They will support the project in its efforts to secure financial support. They will help market the product, creating a virtuous circle. Sustainability, even for free software, is grounded in a committed customer base.

CHNM's tools, such as Zotero, Omeka, and the newly announced Scripto, reflect this orientation: they are polished and professional, with attractive interfaces and a robust user documentation and support infrastructure.

This approach is very different from that of earlier DH projects, which focused on the system's raw functionality rather than the user's experience. But it is a persuasive one, not least to funding agencies. Instead of, or in addition to, developing bespoke tools designed to serve a small group of researchers at single institutions via discrete projects, DHers may increasingly develop products aimed at large numbers of users across institutions and outside the academy. And with the attention to usability and outreach that Scheinfeldt describes, such initiatives may very well attract new users not just to the tools themselves but also to DH in general. But this trajectory raises two critical questions regarding the newcomers: First, can DH accommodate them, and if so, how? And second, how do they relate to the field? We will turn to the first issue shortly. As to the second, we should acknowledge that even as funding for DH efforts is being justified by recourse to usage, it is far from clear how DH's new users will map onto the field. Do they even have a place within it?

Rieger's study of faculty in the humanities begins by commenting on the "richness and diversity" of existing discussions of DH but notes that "what seem to be missing are accounts from a wide range of scholars who are not characterized as 'doing digital humanities'"; this lack, indeed, is the driver for her work. Not coincidentally, however, accounts *of* them are also missing. Thanks to its name, those in the field struggle to name those conceived as outside it: are they "traditional," or "analog," humanists? And if we examine the emergent folksonomy of DH, it is difficult to find a term that those others might identify with. Here, for instance, is how Matthew Jockers of Stanford Literary Lab parses the field: "Group 'A' is composed of researchers who study digital objects; Group 'B' is composed of researchers who utilize digital tools to study objects (digital or otherwise)." Group B accommodates use, it is true, but Jockers's emphasis is on research; it does not explicitly account for other modes, such as work that focuses on pedagogy. We should note that his post is occasioned by an encounter with the other, a colleague who "asked in all earnestness, 'what do I need to do to break into this field of Digital Humanities?'" This is a reminder that the metaphor of the lab, ubiquitous in DH, has its own associations: experimentation and collaboration are there, to be sure, but it also conjures a bright pristine working environment sealed to all but the eminently qualified. To generalize, most humanists are not in the habit of breaking into laboratories.

It is understandable, perhaps, but surely not inevitable that "traditional" humanists are defined by exclusion. In fact, as Svensson notes, it is rather strange: "if the methodology and tools are central to the enterprise it seems counter-intuitive to disassociate yourself from many of the potential users (and co-creators) of the tools" (49). The effect is that these users become visible only if we trace the outlines of the negative space created by DH's self-definitions. For instance, the provocation Steve Ramsay issued at the 2011 Modern Language Association (MLA) Convention,

"Who's In and Who's Out," promotes the "builder" or "maker" as paradigmatic DHer. But even though he insists he is "willing to entertain highly expansive definitions of what it means to build something," it is doubtful that Ramsay intends the term to accommodate end users, and the humanities as such only appear as a target of "methodologization."

In these examples "traditional" humanists appear, if at all, in peripheral vision, like Bradley's "colleague down the hall." Where are their points of entry? How can they have agency, value? They are shadows. In a comment on Steve Ramsay's "On Building," Alan Liu teases out the almost buried metaphor: in the world of construction, "there is a whole ecology of positions and roles necessary for building—including also the client, urban planners, politicians, architectural critics, professors of engineering, etc." He worries that we risk "builder essentialism" in promoting the work of the coder over the "multiplicity of builder roles" necessarily involved. "It takes," he says, "a village or, as Bruno Latour puts it, an actor-network." Latour's famous essay "Where Are the Missing Masses? The Sociology of a Few Mundane Artifacts" accuses his fellow sociologists of discriminating between humans and nonhumans, the missing masses: "I do not hold this bias (this one at least) and see only actors—some human, some nonhuman, some skilled, some unskilled—that exchange their properties." These actors are bound together in a network, or, more accurately, the network is produced in their interactions. Is it fanciful to suggest that DHers risk reversing that bias? That in its focus on delimiting the field based on qualifications, DH can be seen as privileging not just the coder over less technical contributors but also that which is built over those who will use it? Are users, and especially newbie users, the missing masses of DH?

Two of DH's most recent and most successful projects, in fact, are specifically aimed at engaging the unskilled. Transcribe Bentham, based at University College London, has trained amateurs of all stripes to serve as paleographers transcribing the papers of philosopher Jeremy Bentham. And DHAnswers, the Q&A forum recently developed by the Association for Computers and the Humanities and *ProfHacker*, enables its members to pose questions to the DH community on topics ranging from "What is DH?" to "Lightweight data management/storage/transformation for use with web services." The importance of end users here is obvious—they are essential to the functioning of both projects. Viewed as an actor-network, however, we can see that DHAnswers should not only be regarded as a service provided by expert practitioners for those in need of help. It is also a place of exchange in which those asking the questions act as strong levers inducing the community to document its knowledge.

Both of these projects provide defined pathways for end-user contributions. But what Scheinfeldt describes in "Lessons from One Week | One Tool"—the open source software development model—goes further. He shows not only how the user *qua* user actually supports the project but also how the user community generates a special type of user, the volunteer developer who is key to the project's success:

"They find and fix bugs. They provide end user support. They write documentation. They add new features and functionality. They provide vision and critical assessment." At least in theory, then, open source development offers a paradigm for DH as a whole that can incorporate the full range of its users, regardless of technical skill set. Such a model imagines each user as full member of the community, whether as end user or developer-user, where the end user is on a continuum with the developer-user, and that continuum acts as an optional pathway to more technical forms of engagement. At its best, this represents more than the hand-waving "fuzziness" about "community and comity, collaboration and cooperation" that Ramsay deplores in "Who's In and Who's Out," but rather the lived experience of people working in the field. We can see this when Patrick Murray-John describes a "mini-collaboration" on Twitter in which he (a programmer) and Mark Sample (a confessed nonprogrammer) debugged and tested a widget he had built, concluding that this is how he thinks DH will "work and develop": "collaborations—on whatever scale—between humanists at different positions on the 'I am a coder'–'I ain't a coder' spectrum." And scholar-builder Stéfan Sinclair tweets,[6] "I would add to @ sramsay's post that there can be a fine (and oftentimes porous) line between using and building." By contrast, one could suggest that part of the shock that the recent unanticipated release of Google's text analysis tool, the Ngram Viewer, administered to the DH community was its abrupt demotion of skilled makers in the text analysis domain to read-only end users of the tool's limited affordances. They became, in other words, consumers. The multivalent user must be actively enabled and can be intentionally or unintentionally disabled by the system design.

Google may have brought text analysis to the masses but does not engage with them in this work. The site does not invite users to "contact us" or provide feedback, let alone participate in its making. Interfaces can be seen as performing a protective, even prophylactic, function; on this view, limiting the user's options minimizes the load the system must bear. But the user is not merely mass to be supported, as Transcribe Bentham and DHAnswers demonstrate. If DHers feel the system's new users as an inertial drag, it may be because the design itself is exerting resistance.

DH as User Experience

Until recently, however, DH as a system has grown by accretion rather than design. Much as they build tools, standards, and methods from scratch, DHers also adopt and adapt things that come to hand—Twitter is one example—and incorporate them into their workflow. The design of DH is to some extent "found" design. But these acts of finding and appropriating nonetheless should be regarded as design choices that have consequences, some beneficial for all users, others less so. In his "Stuff Digital Humanists Like," Tom Scheinfeldt makes what he acknowledges is a strong claim: that the stuff digital humanists like (Twitter, PHP, and so on) "work better" than their alternatives. In what follows I will borrow Scheinfeldt's method, examining three key features of DH and attempting to evaluate how they "work" for their users at a tactical level. But we will also test another of his arguments—one that, like this essay, proposes an analogy. "Digital humanities takes more than tools from the Internet," he writes ("Stuff Digital Humanists Like"). "It works like the Internet. It takes its values from the Internet." These values are built into the very architecture of the web, which, he explains, emphasizes the nodes rather than the network as sources of innovation, assuming "that the network should be dumb and the terminals should be smart." And just as the Internet functions by trusting those nodes to distribute the information sent to them, so does DH: "we allow all comers, we assume that their contributions will be positive, and we expect that they will share their work for the benefit of the community at large" (ibid.).

We will see, though, that the vision Scheinfeldt describes is as yet incompletely realized in DH's system design. Rather it is unevenly distributed, and the user finds herself falling into the gaps between that vision and her everyday experience of the field. This is not because DHers do not subscribe to the values that Scheinfeldt articulates. On the contrary, many in the community are working hard to improve DH's outreach and infrastructure. But Lisa Spiro's essay in this collection has as its premise the observation that DH has not, to date, cohered as a community around a set of shared values. And the implementation of values in system design is neither commonplace nor a straightforward transaction. Even researchers whose work specifically focuses on values in technology design have noted that, while design for usability is by now thoroughly mainstream, "we are still at the shaky beginnings of thinking systematically about the practice of designing with values in mind" (Flanagan, Howe, and Nissenbaum, 323). As our exploration of the DH user experience will show, the current design presents real challenges for both new and established users and in practice strains against the values DHers endorse.

GOOGLING THE DIGITAL HUMANITIES

Let's begin with an experiment. Asked recently to address the question "What Is Digital Humanities and What's It Doing in English Departments?" Matt Kirschenbaum told his audience, "It's tempting to say that whoever asks the question has not gone looking very hard for an answer." (In a comment on the associated blog post he is blunter still, writing of "intellectual laziness.") He characterizes DH as having a "robust professional apparatus" that is "easily discoverable" and demonstrates this by Googling the term and consulting its entry in Wikipedia. If we follow his example we can certainly get a sense of the field: Google lists first (at time of writing) the Wikipedia entry for digital humanities, then the Association of Digital Humanities Organizations (ADHO) site, *Digital Humanities Quarterly*, the Digital Humanities 2011 conference (titled "Big Tent Digital Humanities"), two entries for the National Endowment for the Humanities's Office of Digital Humanities, and so on. But think of the participant in Rieger's study who commented, "When I hear 'digital humanities,' I think about funding. Only those with connections to established centers are able to do it." There would be little in Google's result set to make him think otherwise. Almost all the sites listed in the first pages are associated with major initiatives and premier institutions. This also means that smaller projects—especially those addressing topics that are underrepresented in the field—continue to be hidden from view.

The presence of any "big tent" to unite DH's disparate parts is also far from apparent. Currently, at least, there is no site that explains, advocates, and showcases work of the DH community, in its full range, to all its potential audiences (general public, faculty, students, curators, librarians, administrators, funders, and so on), that invites users in and helps them navigate the field. And surveying the sites that users might reach from the Wikipedia page, Google's search results, and the ADHO's list of resources, very few set their work explicitly in the context of the digital humanities, articulate their mission in terms that are accessible to a broader audience, or link to other sites in the community.[7] Institutional, not shared, identity is to the fore; as Neil Fraistat, director of the Maryland Institute for Technology in the Humanities (MITH), acknowledges in his contribution to this collection, the major DH institutions "rarely collaborate with other centers, with whom they compete for funding and prestige." It is not surprising, then, that it's hard to detect a feeling of community in the search results and that they reflect instead DH's fragmentation. But from a user's perspective, the lack of connective tissue between even key components of DH means that Google is actually essential to navigate the field—the problem being that to Google something one already needs to know that it exists.

In his discussion of "Inclusion in the Digital Humanities," Geoffrey Rockwell has argued for both maintaining DH as a commons (we will return to this concept in a moment) and creating "well-articulated onramps"—professional training, graduate programs, and so on—that will allow people to access it. But signposts to the commons, to the on-ramps, are also needed to make them discoverable by the very people who need them most. Surely, though, Google or Wikipedia should not function as the home page for the digital humanities, its core navigation. This is not to propose an AOL for DH, a blandly corporate interface layer. Rather that the DH community, not the algorithm of a proprietary tool, should decide how its work is presented and made accessible and navigable for its users. If experienced users protest that newbies are finding only the most noticeable parts of DH and mistaking them for the whole, it's important to remember that they—we—confront a complex and fractured field largely without a guide.

TWEETING THE DIGITAL HUMANITIES

DHers have adopted Twitter to such a degree that it is in danger of defining the field by synecdoche in the broader imaginary. They have found Twitter's core functionality profoundly compelling, in spite of its usability issues. (Notoriously, it appears first in Google Instant's suggested answers to the query "how to use.") Kirschenbaum, for instance, tweets,[8] "Q: Has Twitter done more as DH cyberinfrastructure than any dedicated effort to date?" DHers use it for information sharing, discussion, and community building, though its effectiveness and appropriateness for each has been questioned. Bethany Nowviskie's post "Uninvited Guests" and the associated comments explore the tension between openness and privacy in tweeting at academic conferences, and she acknowledges sympathetically that new users are likely to feel "a little inept and lost." In the aftermath of the 2011 MLA Convention, Mark Sample worried about the "Twitter Hegemony" that rendered nonparticipants as silent, and Perian Sully pointed to the lack of communication between users of Twitter and other existing online communities such as museum listservs, advising DHers to "stop using Twitter as the vehicle for outreach." These are significant problems. But if indeed Twitter—like Google—is a critical component of DH's cyberinfrastructure, three additional weaknesses stand out.

First, just as Google promotes well-connected sites, so DH's chosen network privileges those who are, or are reciprocally linked to, well-connected users. Twitter's asymmetric follow model does provide extraordinary access to DH's "stars," along with a weaker version of the seductive telepresence familiar from earlier modes such as instant messaging. But as Kirschenbaum has discussed ("The [DH] Stars Come Out in LA"), the lack of mutuality in Twitter relationships can simply replicate or "reify" the offline hierarchies of DH. In practice, this means that *the net here is not neutral* but biased in favor of those with more and better connections. Their messages are the most likely to be distributed, their voices the most likely to be amplified. User-defined modes exist that slice across this bias: the use of hashtags, for instance, through which the voices of all users tweeting on a particular topic can be heard, regardless of status, and many Twitter users generously adopt a principal of reciprocal following. But the bias is there, and disproportionately and daily inhibits the reach of new users and those at the margins of the DH network who have limited access to its more powerful nodes.

This problem impacts existing users, too, perhaps especially the stars themselves. One commenter on Kirschenbaum's "The (DH) Stars Come Out in LA," Jordan Grant, a self-described DH newcomer, observes, "I 'follow' and listen to DH stars because they serve as essential hubs for new information and ideas—from job announcements to emerging research to this very blog post. *Without the stars, I don't know how well the DH community would function*" (emphasis added). That is quite a load to bear. We could suggest, in fact, that part of the wearying "always 'on'" nature of the role that Nowviskie describes in "Eternal September" stems from that responsibility—to act as hub, catching and rebroadcasting messages that are important to the community. Established users, for instance, form the crowd that sources *DHNow*, the online journal of the digital humanities, which is powered by their tweets.[9] And as we have seen, users with weaker connections rely on them to communicate their messages effectively. It is not only Twitter as network but stars as nodes that are critical components of the DH infrastructure—they are cybernetically welded into it.

Another issue affects all users who actively attempt to follow the field: while Twitter is very good at disseminating information, it is notoriously bad at making it persistent. Here, for instance, are a couple of tweets from Kathleen Fitzpatrick[10]: "Some weeks back somebody wrote a great post about returning to blogging from Twitter as a means of creating a more permanent archive . . . but now I can't track that post down. (Irony? Perhaps.) Anyhow, if you remember that post, would you let me know? Thanks!" David Berry has likened Twitter to the stock ticker, noting the impact of the ticker on its users when it was introduced in the late nineteenth century. Users were reported to have entered a trance-like state, marked by "attention, vigilance and constant observation." Coping with a real-time feed of the kind of information that flows across the DH network, however—information that users actually may want to retain—is very demanding. And users absent themselves at a cost, as Fitzpatrick notes[11]: "Funny how far out of the loop I now feel if I spend a day offline." For information capture, Twitter is a mode better suited to the *flâneur* than the DH *bricoleur*. In "So the Colors Cover the Wires," Kirschenbaum recalls the "baroque array of spoofs, tricks, workarounds, fixes, and kludges" that characterized web development in the mid-1990s (with the uneven results that spawned the usability industry). But nostalgia for that moment may be premature: every day, hundreds of individual acts of writing to storage take place, using our own "baroque array" of practices—favoriting, bookmarking, RSSing, archiving, harvesting, extracting—all subject to the whims of Twitter's infrastructure and changing business practices. This is part of the invisible work of keeping up with DH, tedious but necessary, inefficient and seemingly inevitable, since it is built into the current system design.[12]

WRITING THE DIGITAL HUMANITIES: CENTERS AND NODES

The centerless, distributed nature of the Internet that Scheinfeldt references gives it its flexibility and extensibility, its resilience and failover capabilities. And it is an important feature of DH, for the same reasons. In his post "On the Death of the Digital Humanities Center," Mark Sample fears for the future of the DH center, and we know that his fears are justified. Only recently, Transcribe Bentham, an exemplary project, announced that it had exhausted the funding that supports its public outreach and collaboration efforts.[13] Sample advises us, "Act as if there's no such thing as a digital humanities center." We should instead form our own networks and alliances outside established institutional structures: "To survive and thrive, digital humanists must be agile, mobile, insurgent. Decentralized and nonhierarchical. Centers, no. Camps, yes." But a commenter, Kathy, raises a critical issue: "Ok, Mark, this is great advice. But, how will those camps and discrete collaborative relationships have any wider impact? Everyone will re-invent the wheel every time?" The problems that Kathy describes, however, already beset DH. Whether DH centers proliferate or etiolate, DH has no center, and this, to my view, is its biggest usability problem.

DH's weak front end complicates the user's ability to discover and navigate the system as a whole, as we have seen. The field's reliance on Twitter as a backbone for scholarly communication renders key information only fragmentarily and fleetingly readable, requiring individual users' persistence to make it persistent. But the centerless model, to be effective, relies on a seamless interoperability that simply does not exist in DH. Like the other issues we have explored, this has very practical implications. As Kim Knight reports in her MLA 2011 talk for a panel on "The Institution(alization) of Digital Humanities," the diffusion of what she calls DH's "ecology" means that "one must actively traverse the terrain of the ecology, looking for connections, all of the time." She is "100% certain," she says, that there is work going on in her area of specialization of which she is totally unaware. In fact, DH is an enormously complex, multifunction, distributed system that is largely undocumented. There are of course many rich resources available—the Digital Research Tools (DiRT) wiki, for example, or the supporting information provided by the Text Encoding Initiative, to give just two examples. (We will see more.) But without some kind of shared knowledge base, such resources are very hard to find. And users need to be able to find information before they can read it.[14] Under these circumstances, if new users ask the same questions again and again, if we reinvent the wheel (and we do), who can blame us? No wonder the dread of Eternal September: a forum such as DHAnswers is the place where people go when they fail to find an answer to their questions in the user documentation; it is not usually the first port of call.

Where we *can* point to DH projects, information about how they were made is typically not available; this is true even of open-source work. Jeremy Boggs, a DH scholar-builder, writes in his post "Participating in the Bazaar: Sharing Code in the Digital Humanities," "I would argue that, right now, the digital humanities is getting really good at shopping/browsing at the bazaar, but not actually sharing. We seem to have no problem using open source tools and applications, but very rarely are we actually giving back, or making the development and sharing of open source code a central part of our work." Sample proposes that DH centers can and do act as a "Digital Humanities Commons," for "knowledge and resources we can all share and build upon." But Kathy counters, "It's not happening yet, the sharing." When users do attempt to share information, many of them, especially those outside of the major centers, have nowhere to put it. Users—including users at the margins—consistently create things of value for the DH community. Here are just a few small examples from recent months: a Google document collating knowledge on transcribing documents generated at MITH's Application Programming Interface (API) workshop in February 2011, another from THATCamp Texas 2011 with a rich collection of links and thoughts related to DH pedagogy, Sheila Brennan's list of suggestions on "Navigating DH for Cultural Heritage Professionals," and CUNY's *Digital Humanities Resource Guide*. Useful artifacts, all of which appeared on Twitter, then disappeared from view. In other words, DH's users are actively building plug-ins but have nowhere to plug them in. The design of the system, its lack of a writeable core, militates against one of the most prized virtues of system building: reuse. And once again this problem disproportionately affects the newest and least connected users. To be clear, I'm not advocating here a command and control model—quite the reverse. But for DH to be truly usable, the center needs to be smart enough to enable the nodes to be smarter.

Shaping the Digital Humanities

Learning about the digital humanities, navigating the field, communicating across it, contributing to it—all these things are difficult in DH, as we have seen. The problems users face are not mere annoyances, though, as they may appear to some expert users; in each case they work to inhibit access and undermine community. There is danger, however, in proposing design as a solution here, even beyond the determinism this would imply. In naming DH an "ecology" Knight captures the anxiety that accompanies this moment in DH's evolution. The messiness of DH, like any ecology is, she writes, its "condition of existence." What impact might a designed intervention have? This tension exists in regard to usability, too. For Jakob Nielsen, one of the movement's leading protagonists, usability is a website's "condition for survival" ("Usability 101"). But it has also been associated with a dogmatic excess of design. Clay Shirky, for instance, has argued that Nielsen's demands for standardization are too prescriptive and would be a homogenizing force that stifles the web's natural modes of growth and innovation: "The Internet's ability to be adapted slowly, imperfectly, and in many conflicting directions all at once is precisely what makes it so powerful." There is much creativity in the act of kludging. Outside institutionally endorsed DH centers, indeed, DH could be viewed end to end as a grand kludge, with users improvising tools, techniques, funding, project teams, and career paths to advance their larger visions. What might be lost in systematizing DH's ecosystem?

On the other hand, can we assume that DH will maintain homeostasis in a way that balances the needs of all its users? So far, it has not. Nielsen states that a usability test with only five users will discover 85 percent of the design problems in a system; many more than five users experience DH as exclusive. At THATCamp SoCal 2011, held just after the MLA Convention ended, participants created a position statement that reads, in full,

> We recognize that a wide diversity of people is necessary to make digital humanities function. As such, digital humanities must take active strides to include all the areas of study that comprise the humanities and must strive to include participants of diverse age, generation, skill, race, ethnicity, sexuality, ability, nationality, culture, discipline, areas of interest. Without open participation and

> broad outreach, the digital humanities movement limits its capacity for critical engagement.

To these users, DH is already homogenized. While in Knight's view, the primary threat to DH's ecology is "the process of discipline formation," DH is not as undisciplined as it seems. Not only does it have the "professional apparatus" that Kirschenbaum describes, but its "daily voicing" has inevitably settled into habitual practices. Perhaps the bigger threat is that DH's disciplinary formations might solidify around unrecognized inequities.

If we were to propose a design for DH, then, where might we look for a model? Several analogies have been offered in the course of this piece: DH has appeared as Usenet, as Twitter, as the Internet itself. I will suggest one more. In "Lessons from One Week | One Tool," Scheinfeldt shares his prescriptions for a successful open-source development community: "open communication channels, . . . access to the project's development road map" so developers know where their work is most needed, and "technical entry points" where they can "hone their chops on small bits of functionality before digging into the core code base." Most of all, they need "a sense of community, a sense of shared purpose, and a sense that their volunteer contributions are valued." All of this, he tells us, must be "planned, managed, and built into the software architecture" (ibid.). A visit to Omeka.org or WordPress.org shows such a community in action—a community that, as we discussed earlier, includes the full range of users, from novices to experienced programmers. These sites speak to all users, showcase what is possible using the software, provide forums and rich user documentation; they not only invite the user to "get involved" but guide her to specific ways she can contribute according to her skill set. Importantly, as the WordPress site tells us, "Everything you see here, from the documentation to the code itself, was created by and for the community."[15]

It might seem uncontroversial, anodyne even, to propose the open-source software development model as a paradigm for DH. But much as it is employed and invoked within the field, key enabling features are not yet embodied in the system's design, as we have seen. If there were a DH road map, for example, where would it be? Who would have created it? Who would know about it, and how? There are lessons here for DH. For one thing, in very practical terms, we might suggest that a shared knowledge base on the example of WordPress's documentation wiki, the Codex—a DH Codex, if you like—could alleviate much of the difficulty of the current user experience: making information findable, lifting the communication burden from DH's "stars," and providing the ability for anyone to contribute, so that the field would truly reflect the range of its participants' concerns. Such a space, a true DH Commons, could have larger implications, however. It could reify not institutional structures but radical interdisciplinariness, supporting both weak forms of collaboration, such as linking and commenting, and strong collaboration through shared development of resources. It could offer a loose and simple framework that would only minimally constrain creative messiness, enabling not top-down direction but communal self-organization. It could grow and flex to accommodate a generous definition of the field; if a user, any user, felt that DH elided, say, accessibility issues, she could create a page and begin the process of sharing her knowledge, simultaneously opening the possibility (not, of course, the certainty) of drawing together a worldwide community of practice around that knowledge; to Kim Knight's point, maybe the terrain *could* be mapped after all, its contours and lacunae made visible. The DH community could debate its values there, collectively define best practices for implementing them, and collaboratively develop a road map for DH's future initiatives. It could enact the metaphor of DH as "meeting place" that Svensson advocates in his contribution to this collection.

Naive? Perhaps. We should not overestimate the inclusiveness of the open source model, of course; declaring a system open does not make it so, and even the Ur-collaboration, Wikipedia, has struggled with diversity issues, as its self-study has revealed.[16] And yet DH does seem to be navigating an outward turn. Last year saw the launch of DHAnswers and Lisa Spiro's initiative to "Open Up Digital Humanities Education." Recently, Project Bamboo, the multiyear, multi-institution effort aimed at creating shared cyberinfrastructure, released the proof-of-concept text analysis tool, Woodchipper. The associated website invites users to participate in alpha testing and links to a wiki where users can provide feedback. And the Scholars' Lab, under the direction of Bethany Nowviskie, has created Spatial Humanities, "a place to ask questions, discover research, learn from tutorials, and explore innovative projects" that use spatial technologies and that allows users to contribute to a knowledge base. If to date, DH as a system has tended to evolve, significant elements of it are now being proactively and quite literally designed. When implemented on a large scale and with large financial investments, however, such infrastructure can become the equivalent of a definitive edition in textual scholarship: unsupplantable for a generation. But our small, local, and particular decisions also shape DH, as Nowviskie reminds us; inescapably, we are all designing DH.

Here, then, are a few questions, questions that are equally applicable locally and institutionally, literally and metaphorically, as we shape our communities and practices as well as our tools: Which users will be included in designing and building DH? How participatory and reflexive will that process be? How will the design balance efficiency, ease of use, and user agency? There are arguments to be made against implementations that privilege a frictionless usability over summoning the user to thought, that emulate the app rather than the open web. So, will the colors cover the wires? Will those users who wish to engage more deeply be permitted to trace the wires to their source, even to the core? Or will the interface enforce a clean line between who's in and who's out, makers and users, producers and consumers? How will the concept of the user be inscribed, or circumscribed, in DH's emergent design?

Of course, as Latour reminds us, "circumscription only defines how a setup itself has built-in plugs and interfaces; as the name indicates, this tracing of circles, walls, and entry points inside the text or the machine does not prove that readers and users will obey" (237). Fortunately, a system cannot legislate behavior or desire. McCarthy and Wright note that users "appropriate the physical and conceptual space created by producers for their own interests and needs; they are not just passive consumers" (11). Users will navigate their own paths through the interface of DH, paths of innovation and resistance. Another possibility, of course, is that they will not use the system at all. Notwithstanding the claims of usability consultants, adoption is stubbornly unpredictable. Laura Mitchell, a commenter on Perian Sully's post, draws a telling parallel with gender studies, her own area of expertise: "Despite at least 40 years of exacting scholarship, gender remains a sub-field, a fundamental aspect of human social existence that scholars can choose to ignore if they want to. And DH??" The analogy DH's critics like to make is with Big Theory, and this is the implication: that one day we will look back on DH as just another wave that broke over the academy, eroded its formations perhaps in some small places, and then receded, leaving a few tranquil rock pools behind. Mitchell's concern is that the skills newcomers need to acquire form a real barrier to entering DH and thus will limit its reach. The open-source model, however, suggests that our field's current focus on qualification, on boundary setting, is unnecessary and that the choice between emptying the term "digital humanities" of meaning on the one hand and defending it as specialist redoubt on the other is a false one. Instead it offers another vision: that by working, individually and collectively, to adopt and actively enable a flexible and extensible conception of the user, we can include all comers as diverse actors in the network of DH.

NOTES

1. See for example the description provided by the U.S. Government at usability.gov (under "Basics").

2. Doug Reside, Twitter, January 9, 2011, 9:20 a.m., http://twitter.com/#!/dougreside/status/24108348106346496.

3. See http://en.wikipedia.org/wiki/Leet#n00b.

4. Many thanks to Patrik Svensson for suggesting this point and for his provocative comments on an earlier draft, which were immensely helpful in shaping the essay for publication. I am also deeply grateful to Matthew Gold for his kind and generous advice, encouragement, and patience throughout the editorial process.

5. See Pannapacker and Cohen, respectively.

6. Stéfan Sinclair, Twitter, January 11, 2011. 8:46 p.m., http://twitter.com/#!/sgsinclair/status/25005558222295040.

7. Melissa Terras has raised the issue and importance of DH's digital identity in her acclaimed plenary address to the Digital Humanities 2010 conference.

8. Matthew G. Kirschenbaum, Twitter, July 3, 2010, 12:00 p.m., http://twitter.com/#!/mkirschenbaum/status/17659459594.

9. At time of writing *DHNow* was being redesigned and in a state of transition (see PressForward.org).

10. Kathleen Fitzpatrick, Twitter, March 1, 2011, 8:06 a.m., http://twitter.com/#!/kfitz/statuses/42571484153135104, and March 1, 2011, 8:07 a.m., http://twitter.com/#!/kfitz/statuses/42571609311154177.

11. Kathleen Fitzpatrick, Twitter, February 26, 2011, 11:29 a.m., http://twitter.com/#!/kfitz/statuses/41535448685740032.

12. To date *DHNow* has mitigated this problem to some degree, but since, like Google, it promotes links according to their connectedness, those transmitted from the margins of the field (and the conversations that take place in less easily linkable venues, such as the *Humanist* e-mail listserv) have been much less frequently represented there.

13. See http://chronicle.com/blogs/wiredcampus/facing-budget-woes-prominent-crowd sourcing-project-will-scale-back/30322.

14. Note that the United Kingdom and region is served by arts-humanities.net, but this is only lightly used by DHers from the United States (http://www.arts-humanities .net/).

15. See WordPress.org's About page, http://wordpress.org/about/.

16. See Gardner. Note, however, that a key focus of the response is to "improve the newbie experience."

BIBLIOGRAPHY

Berry, David M. "The Ontology of Twitter." *Stunlaw: A Critical Review of Politics, Arts and Technology*. February 13, 2011, http://stunlaw.blogspot.com/2011/02/ontology-of-twitter.html.

Bradley, John. "What You (Fore)see Is What You Get: Thinking About Usage Paradigms for Computer Assisted Text Analysis." *TEXT Technology* 14, no. 2 (2005): 1-19, http://texttechnology.mcmaster.ca/pdf/vol14_2/bradley14-2.pdf.

Brennan, Sheila A. "Navigating DH for Cultural Heritage Professionals." *Lot 49*. January 10, 2011, http://www.lotfortynine.org/2011/01/navigating-dh-for-cultural-heritage-professionals/.

Boggs, Jeremy. "Participating in the Bazaar: Sharing Code in the Digital Humanities." *Clioweb*. June 10, 2010, http://clioweb.org/2010/06/10/participating-in-the-bazaar-sharing-code-in-the-digital-humanities/.

Cohen, Patricia. "Humanities 2.0: Digital Keys for Unlocking the Humanities' Riches." *New York Times*, November 17, 2010, http://www.nytimes.com/2010/11/17/arts/17digital.html.

CUNY Digital Humanities Resource Guide. CUNY Digital Humanities Initiative, http://commons.gc.cuny.edu/wiki/index.php/The_CUNY_Digital_Humanities_Resource_Guide.

Derrida, Jacques. *Writing and Difference*. Chicago: University of Chicago Press, 1978.

DiRT Digital Research Tools Wiki. Rice University, https://digitalresearchtools.pbworks.com/w/page/17801672/FrontPage.

Flanagan, Mary, Daniel C. Howe, and Helen Nissenbaum. "Embodying Values in Technology: Theory and Practice." In *Information Technology and Moral Philosophy*, edited by Jeroen van den Hoven and John Weckert, 322–53. Cambridge, UK: Cambridge University Press, 2008.

Fraistat, Neil. "The Function of Digital Humanities Centers at the Present Time." In *Debates in the Digital Humanities*, edited by Matthew K. Gold. Minneapolis: University of Minnesota Press, 2012.

Gardner, Sue. "March 2011 Update." *Wikimedia Strategic Planning Wiki*, http://strategy.wikimedia.org/wiki/March_2011_Update.

Hockey, Susan. "The History of Humanities Computing." In *A Companion to Digital Humanities*, edited by Susan Schreibman, Ray Siemens, and John Unsworth. Oxford: Blackwell, 2004, http://www.digitalhumanities.org/companion/.

"How do you define Humanities Computing/Digital Humanities?" *TaporWiki*. University of Alberta, http://tapor.ualberta.ca/taporwiki/index.php/How_do_you_define_Humanities_Computing_/_Digital_Humanities%3F. Reprinted in this volume.

Jockers, Matthew L. "Digital Humanities: Methodology and Questions." *Matthew L. Jockers*. April 23, 2010, https://www.stanford.edu/~mjockers/cgi-bin/drupal/node/43.

Kirschenbaum, Matthew G. "The (DH) Stars Come Out in LA." *Matthew G. Kirschenbaum*. January 13, 2011, http://mkirschenbaum.wordpress.com/2011/01/13/the-dh-stars-come-out-in-la-2/.

———. "'So the Colors Cover the Wires': Interface, Aesthetics, and Usability." In *A Companion to Digital Humanities*, edited by Susan Schreibman, Ray Siemens, and John Unsworth. Oxford: Blackwell, 2004, http://www.digitalhumanities.org/companion/.

———. "What Is Digital Humanities?" *Matthew G. Kirschenbaum*. January 22, 2011, http://mkirschenbaum.wordpress.com/2011/01/22/what-is-digital-humanities/.

———. "What Is Digital Humanities and What's It Doing in English Departments?" Text of article to appear in *ADE Bulletin*, no. 150 (2010). http://mkirschenbaum.files.wordpress.com/2011/03/ade-final.pdf. Reprinted in this volume.

Knight, Kim. "MLA 2011 Paper for 'The Institution(alization) of Digital Humanities.'" *Kim Knight*. January 14, 2011, http://kimknight.com/?p=801.

Latour, Bruno. "Where Are the Missing Masses? The Sociology of a Few Mundane Artifacts." In *Shaping Technology/Building Society*, edited by Weibe Bijker and John Law, 225–259. Cambridge, Mass.: MIT Press, 1992.

Lindemann, Marilee. "MLA 2011: The Great Untweeted." *Roxie's World*. January 16, 2011, http://roxies-world.blogspot.com/2011/01/mla-2011-great-untweeted.html.

McCarthy, John, and Peter Wright. *Technology as Experience*. Cambridge, Mass.: MIT Press, 2004.

Mueller, Martin. "Digital Shakespeare, or Towards a Literary Informatics." *Shakespeare* 4, no. 3 (December 2008): 300–17.

Murray-John, Patrick. "Why I Love Twitter Number N+1: Mini-Collaboration." *Remediation Roomy-nation*, http://www.patrickgmj.net/node/179.

Nielsen, Jakob. "Usability 101: Introduction to Usability." *Jakob Nielsen's Alertbox*. August 25, 2003, http://www.useit.com/alertbox/20030825.html.

———. "Why You Only Need to Test with 5 Users." *Jakob Nielsen's Alertbox*. March 19, 2000, http://www.useit.com/alertbox/20000319.html.

"Notes from Pedagogy Sessions." *THATCamp Texas*, http://texas2011.thatcamp.org/04/19/notes-from-pedagogy-sessions/.

Nowviskie, Bethany. "Eternal September of the Digital Humanities." *Bethany Nowviskie*. October 15, 2010, http://nowviskie.org/2010/eternal-september-of-the-digital-humanities/. Reprinted in this volume.

———. "Uninvited Guests: Regarding Twitter at Invitation-Only Academic Events." *Bethany Nowviskie*. April 25, 2010, http://nowviskie.org/2010/uninvited-guests/.

Pannapacker, William. "Pannapacker at MLA: Digital Humanities Triumphant?" *Chronicle of Higher Education*, January 8, 2011, http://chronicle.com/blogs/brainstorm/pannapacker-at-mla-digital-humanities-triumphant/30915. Reprinted in this volume.

Parry, David. "Be Online or Be Irrelevant." *AcademHack*. January 11, 2010, http://academhack.outsidethetext.com/home/2010/be-online-or-be-irrelevant/.

PhDeviate et al. "Towards an Open Digital Humanities." *THATCamp SoCal 2011*. January 11, 2011, http://socal2011.thatcamp.org/01/11/opendh/.

Ramsay, Stephen. "In Praise of Pattern." *TEXT Technology* 14, no. 2 (2005): 177–90, http://texttechnology.mcmaster.ca/pdf/vol14_2/ramsay14-2.pdf.

———. "On Building." *Stephen Ramsay*. January 11, 2011, http://lenz.unl.edu/papers/2011/01/11/on-building.html.

———. "Who's In and Who's Out." *Stephen Ramsay*. January 8, 2011, http://lenz.unl.edu/papers/2011/01/08/whos-in-and-whos-out.html.

Rieger, Oya Y. "Framing Digital Humanities: The Role of New Media in Humanities Scholarship." *First Monday* 15, no. 10, October 4, 2010, http://firstmonday.org/htbin/cgiwrap/bin/ojs/index.php/fm/article/view/3198/2628.

Rockwell, Geoffrey. "Inclusion in the Digital Humanities." *Philosophi.ca*, http://www.philosophi.ca/pmwiki.php/Main/InclusionInTheDigitalHumanities.

Sample, Mark. "Academics and Social Media: #mla11, Free WiFi, and the Question of Inclusion." *ProfHacker*. January 14, 2011, http://chronicle.com/blogs/profhacker/academics-and-social-media-mla11-free-wifi-and-the-question-of-inclusion/29945.

———. "On the Death of the Digital Humanities Center." *Sample Reality*. March 26, 2010, http://www.samplereality.com/2010/03/26/on-the-death-of-the-digital-humanities-center/.

Scheinfeldt, Tom. "Lessons from One Week | One Tool–Part 2, Use." *Found History*. August 2, 2010, http://www.foundhistory.org/2010/08/02/lessons-from-one-week-one-tool-part-2-use.

———. "Stuff Digital Humanists Like: Defining Digital Humanities by its Values." *Found History*. December 2, 2010, http://www.foundhistory.org/2010/12/02/stuff-digital-humanists-like/.

Shirky, Clay. "Open Letter to Jakob Nielsen." *Clay Shirky*, http://www.shirky.com/writings/nielsen.html.

Spatial Humanities. Scholars' Lab, University of Virginia, http://spatial.scholarslab.org/.

Spiro, Lisa. "Opening Up Digital Humanities Education." *Digital Scholarship in the Humanities*. September 8, 2010, http://digitalscholarship.wordpress.com/2010/09/08/opening-up-digital-humanities-education/.

Sully, Perian. "Digital Humanities Silos and Outreach." *Musematic*. January 9, 2011, http://musematic.net/2011/01/09/dh-silos-and-outreach.

Svensson, Patrik. "Humanities Computing as Digital Humanities." *Digital Humanities Quarterly* 3, no. 3 (Summer 2009), http://digitalhumanities.org/dhq/vol/3/3/000065/000065.html.

Terras, Melissa. "DH2010 Plenary: Present, Not Voting: Digital Humanities in the Panopticon." *Melissa Terras*. July 10, 2010, http://melissaterras.blogspot.com/2010/07/dh2010-plenary-present-not-voting.html.

"Transcribing Handwritten Documents." Maryland Institute for Technologies in the Humanities, http://bit.ly/DHapiTRANSCRIBE.

Woodchipper. Maryland Institute for Technologies in the Humanities, http://mith.umd.edu/corporacamp/tool.php.

Digital Humanities Triumphant?

WILLIAM PANNAPACKER

Last year when I blogged about the Modern Language Association (MLA), I said that the digital humanities seems like the "next big thing," and quite naturally, the digital humanists were indignant because they've been doing their thing for more than twenty years (and maybe even longer than that).

At a standing-room only session I attended yesterday, "The History and Future of the Digital Humanities," one panelist noted that there has been some defensiveness about the field, partly because it has included so many alt-academics who felt disrespected by the traditional academy: "Harrumph . . . Playing with electronic toys is not scholarship. Where are your peer-reviewed articles?" I know from experience that there are plenty of people in the profession who know little about this established field and even regard it with disdain as something disturbingly outré and dangerous to the mission of the humanities. During the discussion at that session, Matthew Kirschenbaum, author of *Mechanisms: New Media and the Forensic Imagination*, which won the MLA's First Book Award last year, observed that "if you don't know what the digital humanities is, you haven't looked very hard."

I mean, come on, just start with the Wikipedia entry: http://en.wikipedia.org/wiki/Digital_humanities. The digital humanities are not some flashy new theory that might go out of fashion. At this point, the digital humanities are "the thing." There's no "next" about it. And it won't be long until the digital humanities are, quite simply, "the humanities."

Consider the quantity, quality, and comprehensiveness of the digital humanities panels at this year's MLA convention.[1]

The digital humanities have some internal tensions, such as the occasional divide between builders and theorizers and coders and noncoders. But the field, as a whole, seems to be developing an in-group, out-group dynamic that threatens to replicate the culture of Big Theory back in the 80s and 90s, which was alienating to so many people. It's perceptible in the universe of Twitter: we read it, but we do not participate. It's the cool kids' table.

So the digital humanities seem more exclusive, more cliquish, than they did even one year ago. There are identifiable stars who know they are stars, and some of the senior figures in the field, like Alan Liu, seem like gods among us. And maybe most important of all: there's money, most obviously represented by Brett Bobley from the NEH's Office of Digital Humanities—looking just a little like Jeff Goldblum in *Jurassic Park*.

If this keeps up, I might start wearing ironic T-shirts under my black sport coat.

There's justice in this turn of events: well-earned success for a community that has long regarded itself as facing uncomprehending resistance. At the same time, the tendency to become like Big Theory may change the attractive ethics of the field, described by one panelist "as community, collaboration, and goodwill." The grassroots days seem to be ending.

As this process develops, how will it affect the majority of the profession, those who teach at community colleges, for-profit schools, and teaching-intensive institutions? The growing tendency of the digital humanities to become an elite community—always pursuing the cutting edge—may leave most of us behind, struggling to catch up with limited support; and humanities education, in general, will be unchanged by the innovation and excitement promised by the digital humanities at this year's MLA convention.

NOTES

This chapter originally appeared as "Pannapacker at MLA: Digital Humanities Triumphant?" (http://chronicle.com/blogs/brainstorm/pannapacker-at-mla-digital-humanities-triumphant/30915).

1. http://www.hastac.org/blogs/marksample/digital-humanities-sessions-2011-mla.

What Do Girls Dig?

BETHANY NOWVISKIE

"Has data-mining in the humanities emerged as a gentleman's sport? Two and a half conversations about gender, language, and the 'Digging into Data Challenge.'" A two-day conference has been announced, associated with an international funding program, rightly (I think) hailed as transformative for the humanities.

> Amazing line-up of speakers for Digging into Data Challenge conference. Free to attend, but you must register! http://bit.ly/gbnHoF
>
> **brettbobley**
> April 6, 2011 at 16:54

I was excited. I clicked the link. I scrolled down. I did a double take, which means I scrolled up and then down again. Next, I scrolled very slowly, counting.

I almost didn't tweet this, but then I did:

> 2 of 33 speakers at the (very cool!) Digging into Data event are women. Casting no aspersions on NEH here! but I wonder: what do girls dig?
>
> **nowviskie**
> April 6, 2011 at 18:00

Instant feedback:

> @nowviskie I was wondering the very same thing.
>
> **kfitz**
> April 6, 2011 at 18:02

> “ @nowviskie Cast aspersions. If they can't find girl geeks IN THE HUMANITIES...
>
> **reporat**
> April 6, 2011 at 18:03

> “ @kfitz @RepoRat I'm so used to being the only woman in the room, that I only notice it in a conference program when it's over the top.
>
> **nowviskie**
> April 6, 2011 at 18:05

> “ @nowviskie @reporat Sad but true.
>
> **kfitz**
> April 6, 2011 at 18:06

> “ @nowviskie @brettbobley @kfitz But: two of these speakers are not like the others, two of these ppl are not the same. IMWTK why so many ARE!
>
> **mlaconvention**
> April 6, 2011 at 18:06

There were some other comments, and retweets, too. I was starting to feel a little sheepish about sparking a negative and public discussion of an issue uncomfortable for many, and about which I often feel ambivalent—but I knew that the group would shortly hear from the Office of Digital Humanities at the National Endowment for the Humanities (NEH), one of several funders of the program. These guys are always plugged in and ever responsive.

> “ @mlaconvention @nowviskie @kfitz We noticed too. The speakers are the project PIs. Welcome suggestions to encourage women to apply.
>
> **brettbobley**
> April 6, 2011 at 18:26

If you “welcome suggestions” on Twitter, you will get them. More with the instant feedback:

> “ @brettbobley @nowviskie @kfitz Ask them by name.
>
> **mlaconvention**
> April 6, 2011 at 18:29

> @brettbobley This is hard for me to comment on because data mining isn't really my personal brand of DH. But has that itself been gendered?
>
> **nowviskie** 
> April 6, 2011 at 18:33

> +1. "Voluntary" is a euphemism for privilege. RT @mlaconvention: @brettbobley @nowviskie @kfitz Ask them by name.
>
> **ncecire** 
> April 6, 2011 at 18:31

> @brettbobley @nowviskie @kfitz ask them by name, wk w them to prep proposal, assign mentor team
>
> **mlaconvention** 
> April 6, 2011 at 18:30

> @mlaconvention those are good ideas -- thank you. I will talk to my colleagues about it right away.
>
> **brettbobley** 
> April 6, 2011 at 18:45

> @brettbobley If you're serious about it, the answer I'm aware of is "don't wait for them to come to you; GO FIND THEM."
>
> **reporat** 
> April 6, 2011 at 18:36

> @RepoRat that's good advice, thank you. I will talk to my colleagues about that tomorrow.
>
> **brettbobley** 
> April 6, 2011 at 18:47

> @brettbobley great! A strong netwk of women are reason i got my current gig.
>
> **mlaconvention** 
> April 6, 2011 at 18:52

Those were the serious suggestions, taken seriously. (Another NEH staffer picked up the thread on my Facebook page and gave a very sensitive and cogent response, including an appeal for names of particular researchers and communities of practice to reach out to.)

Meanwhile, things on Twitter *seemed* to get silly. But maybe these questions about the *rhetoric* of data mining actually get at another side of a serious issue. At the very least, they gesture at a subtler, but equally worthwhile brand of digital humanities outreach: attention to our language.

So . . . what do girls dig?

> “@nowviskie Lace and frippery and such.
>
> **miriamkp**
> April 6, 2011 at 18:18

> “@miriamkp Boys & unicorns & SPARKLES. Actually, I don't want to make a big deal of it, but given that women are well-represented in DH...[+]
>
> **nowviskie**
> April 6, 2011 at 18:21

> “@miriamkp It does make me wonder if there's something in the overall rhetoric around data mining worth taking a look at. [-]
>
> **nowviskie**
> April 6, 2011 at 18:22

> “@nowviskie Actually, that's a good point. I hear "data mining" and think, whoa, that's some serious business. Maybe not for me.
>
> **miriamkp**
> April 6, 2011 at 18:22

> “@miriamkp Well, there's the whole "digging in" trope, too. Can't decide: just not my personal brand of scholarship, or rhetorical turn-off?
>
> **nowviskie**
> April 6, 2011 at 18:27

> “@nowviskie It's subtle, but yeah. Like, "YAR, data! I shall DIG you!"
>
> **miriamkp**
> April 6, 2011 at 18:39

On Facebook—where a colleague pointed out what he called a similar “boys on the podium” gender imbalance in a “future of academic libraries” symposium ("the future is manly!")—the discussion generated a steady, ridiculous, and slightly dangerous stream of jokes. A manly future for libraries in beer and electric guitars. Flowered gloves and gardening trowels as more appropriate for ladylike digging into data. A duty to lie back and think of England as our data furrows are ploughed.

That last one was mine. And since I started this whole mess, and in a rather flippant way, you may think I'm *just full* of snark.

In fact, I believe NEH and other "Digging into Data" supporters do a consistently brilliant job of identifying sensitive and qualified peer reviewers and funding worthy projects. NEH's digital humanities programs, in particular, always strike me as broadly representative of the actual makeup of the field.

I'm sure that gender imbalance in this area has little to do with the *Digging into Data* grant-making process and more with broader issues, going all the way back (yes, that chestnut) to Science, Technology, Engineering, and Mathematics (STEM) education for girls in the public schools. But mostly, I suspect, all this is about the number of female academics both qualified and inclined to do data-mining work, and who find themselves both at a stage of their careers and possessed of adequate collaborative networks to support their applications for such grants.

Although it wasn't exactly what I was going for, I respect my pals' advocacy, highlighted earlier, for funders' launching of an aggressive campaign to identify and mentor more women applicants for programs like "Digging into Data." And clearly there's institutional work to be done on the level of our schools, colleges, and universities. Personally, however, I feel less strongly about both of those things than I do about the need for the entire digital humanities (DH) community to be as thoughtful as possible about the way we describe this kind of work—about the language we use.

I've heard three kinds of responses from female colleagues and students about the "Digging into Data" Challenge. One (the rarest) is simple enthusiasm; though it's interesting that presumably few women applied and none of their projects were compelling enough to fund. Another is trepidation: Is this too hardcore? Involving too much math or statistical analysis I never learned? Do I understand the scholarly possibilities and have the support network I'd need? In other words: this is a challenge. Am I *competitive?* (in every sense of that word).

The third kind of response (which includes my own) has more to do with framing and rhetoric. I suspect I haven't gotten super-interested in this kind of work because I've heard few descriptions of it that really speak to my own interpretive/hermeneutic/experiential/design-oriented approach to DH. (Though the one that looks at quilts as a source for visual and stylistic analysis is very cool.) And I have a hunch that it's not just me—that the disconnect from certain brands of digital methods felt by many researchers of my ilk (note that ilk is not gender) has more to do with the language being used for methodological and research-findings descriptions, and the intellectual orientation of the people doing the describing, than with the nature of, say, data mining itself.

It's easy to make a joke about imperialist and gendered undertones in the "digging in" rhetoric, but to some degree the advertising campaign for this program set the tone, for a broad and new community, of DH's engagement with data mining. So that's what I was after, when I raised the issue with an offhand comment or two online.

Improved outreach to particular underrepresented groups is never a bad idea, but I'd prefer to see NEH and its funding partners (and individual DH centers and the Alliance of Digital Humanities Organizations and our publications, etc.) start by becoming more thoughtful about the language we all use to describe and to signal data mining to a very broad community of researchers. After all, digital humanities nerds, *we* are still the minority in most of our departments, are we not?

A little attention to audience and rhetoric can go a long way toward making applications and results of digital methods seem comprehensible, inspiring, and potentially transformative. Even to scholars who didn't think digging and delving was their (dainty, fine-china) cup of tea.

And there's always this option—an idea, I assume, free for the taking:

> “@nowviskie @miriamkp Boys & Unicorns & SPARKLES should be a new blog for women in DH :)
>
> **afamiglietti**
> April 6, 2011 at 18:23

NOTE

This chapter was originally published on April 7, 2011, at http://nowviskie.org/2011/what-do-girls-dig/ and http://storify.com/nowviskie/, first as an experiment in using the online Storify system, then in beta release. Storify allows users to annotate and weave together narrative strands from social media. All quotations are from publicly accessible posts to Twitter, a microblogging service through which much real-time conversation on the digital humanities takes place.

The Turtlenecked Hairshirt

IAN BOGOST

In a reflection on all the recent hubbub about the sordid state of the humanities and the recently proposed possibility of a cure in the form of the digital humanities, Cathy Davidson offers the following lament:

> When I think of what the humanities offer . . . it is astonishing to me (and tragic) that we are not central. We are very, very good at blaming others for our marginalization. I truly believe that most universities would be entirely grateful for a visionary humanities program that addressed the critical needs of literacies for the twenty-first century. That would not have to be all we need to do, but why we aren't making that our mission, staking that as our invaluable inestimable value in a radically changing world, is beyond my comprehension.[1]

The only possible answer is that it's us.

The problem is not the humanities as a discipline. (Who can blame a discipline?) The problem is its members. We are insufferable. We do not want change. We do not want centrality. We do not want to speak to nor interact with the world. We mistake the tiny pastures of private ideals with the megalopolis of real lives. We spin from our mouths retrograde dreams of the second coming of the nineteenth century while simultaneously dismissing out of our sphincters the far more earnest ambitions of the public at large—religion, economy, family, craft, science.

Humanists work hard but at all the wrong things, the commonest of which is the fetid fester of a hypothetical socialist dream world, one that has become far more disconnected with labor and material than the neoliberalism it claims to replace.

Humanism does not deserve to carry the standard for humans, for frankly it despises them.

We don't make reform our mission because we secretly hate the idea of partaking of and in the greater world, even as we purport to give it voice, to speak of its ills through critical esoterics no public ear could ever grasp. Instead we colonize that world—all in the name of liberation, of course—in order to return its spoils to our fetid den of Lacanian self-denial. We masticate on culture for the pleasure of praising our own steaming shit.

We are not central because we have chosen to be marginal, for to be central would be to violate the necessity of marginality. We practice the monastic worship of a secular God we divined in order to kill again, mistaking ourselves for the madmen of our fantasies. We are masochists in hedonists' clothing. We are tweed demolitionists.

If there is one reason things "digital" might release humanism from its turtlenecked hairshirt it is precisely because computing has revealed a world full of things: hairdressers, recipes, pornographers, typefaces, Bible studies, scandals, magnetic disks, rugby players, dereferenced pointers, cardboard void fill, pro-lifers, snowstorms. The digital world is replete. It resists any efforts to be colonized by the postcolonialists. We cannot escape it by holing up in Berkeley waiting for the taurus of time to roll around to 1968. It will find us and it will videotape our kittens.

It's not the digital that marks the future of the humanities—it's what things digital point to: a great outdoors.[2] A real world. A world of humans, things, and ideas. A world of the commonplace. A world that prepares jello salads. A world that litigates, that chews gum, that mixes cement. A world that rusts, that photosynthesizes, that ebbs. The philosophy of tomorrow should not be digital democracy but a democracy of objects.[3]

If we want the humanities to become central, it is not the humanities that must change but its members. We must want to be of the world, rather than hidden from it. We must be brutal. We must invoke wrath instead of liberation. We must cull. We must burn away the dead wood to let new growth flourish. If we don't, we will suffocate under the noxious rot of our own decay.

NOTES

This chapter originally appeared as "The Turtlenecked Hairshirt: Fetid and Fragrant Futures for the Humanities" (http://www.bogost.com/blog/the_turtlenecked_hairshirt.shtml).

1. http://www.hastac.org/blogs/cathy-davidson/future-humanities.

2. Quentin Meillassoux, *After Finitude: An Essay on the Necessity of Contingency*, trans. Ray Brassier (London: Continuum, 2010), 7, 29, 50.

3. Levi Bryant, *The Democracy of Objects* (Ann Arbor, Mich.: Open Humanities, 2011).

Eternal September of the Digital Humanities

BETHANY NOWVISKIE

Here's where I am. It's nearly Halloween, and kids have settled into school routines. I have little ones in my own house and big ones in the Scholars' Lab[1]—the youngest of whom are newly, this year, exactly half my age. Other[2] kids[3] are dead,[4] and it's still bothering me a good deal. Mornings in Virginia feel cold now, and acorns are everywhere underfoot. We're tracking leaves inside.

It's a melancholy way to begin a post, but it situates us.

It's October 2010 in *the social scene* of the digital humanities, and (yes, I'm feeling wry) our gathering swallows Twitter in the skies.

I tweet[5] a lot. It's a mixture—the writing *and* the reading—of shallow, smart, and sweet. I answer lots of e-mail, too—lots of messages from strangers asking questions. We're doing a good job, my team, and people are asking how. I stuck my neck out on a thing or two, and people are asking why, or for more. This fall, I worked with friends to launch a website that I'm proud of[6]—which is for strangers asking questions. I've stopped answering to[7] the phone.

There's a bit of a joke around the Scholars' Lab, about the degree to which the boss lady is not *service oriented*. It's funny (as they say) because it's true. But it's only true insofar as I let it be, and most local colleagues realize that I put on this persona consciously, as a useful corrective or (at least) a countering provocation to that strong and puzzling tendency I have noted as a scholar come to work in libraries: the degree to which the most beautiful quality of librarianship—that it is a service vocation—becomes the thing that makes the faculty, on the whole, value us so little. Service as servile. The staffer, the alternative academic,[8] the librarian, the nontenure-track digital humanist as intellectual partner? Not so long as we indulge our innate helpfulness too much. And not so long as we are hesitant to assert our own, personal research agendas—the very things that, to some of us once expected to join the professoriate, felt too self-indulgent to be borne.

I've written[9] about[10] these things.[11] Others have, too.[12] And—even though service under any banner is undervalued in the academy, and a full-fledged digital humanities center administratively embedded among library services is a rarity—near and far, DH stays nice.[13] (Just think, how many other academic disciplines or interdisciplines work so hard to manifest as "a community of practice that is solidary, open, welcoming and freely accessible"—a "collective experience," a "common good?")[14]

Here's the irony. And it's how we'll move from a dwindling Virginia October to the eternal September of the digital humanities.

If, on the local scene, I strive to give a habitation and a name to the administrator (yes,[15] even[16] that[17]) as driven intellectual partner, for outreach and service to the DH crowd, I'm your girl. The kinds of things I volunteer to organize and do (hosting training institutes,[18] grad fellowships,[19] and friendly unconferences;[20] helping raise the big tent;[21] and providing signposts[22] or lacing bootstraps[23] for bootstrapping[24]), together with my role as vice president and outreach chair for the Association for Computers and the Humanities,[25] put me in a position to observe and appreciate the depth of generosity in digital humanities (DH). A truly remarkable and frankly heartwarming percentage of the DH community gives unstintingly[26] of its precious time[27] in these ways,[28] solely for the purpose of easing the path[29] for others. And it's not all organized initiatives. To a degree I have not noted before, the DH community has become conscious that we operate in a panopticon,[30] where our daily voicing[31] of the practice of digital humanities (and not just on special days—every day[32]) helps to shape and delimit and advance it. That voicing operates wholeheartedly to welcome people and fresh ideas in, if sometimes to press uncomfortably (one intends, salutarily) against the inevitable changes they will bring. Some of us take this unending, quotidian responsibility too seriously.

I hear, and hear about, our back-channel conversations.

"Eternal September" is a notion that comes from Usenet[33] culture—the early peer-to-peer newsgroups and alt discussions[34] that were, for many of us, an introduction to networked discourse and digital identity. Because Usenet activity centered in colleges and universities, a large influx of new students each September had disruptive effects[35] on its established, internal standards of conduct, or netiquette.[36] About thirty days in, newbies had either acclimatized to Usenet or they had dropped away, and the regular roiling of September could be left behind for another eleven months. As the mid-1990s approached, Internet access became more common and less metered by the academic calendar. Once AOL began offering Usenet to its subscribers, September was eternal.

The Wikipedia article for "Eternal September"[37] reads, "See also: Elitism."

I mention this because I am not unaware of the awkwardness of my position. I have worked in humanities computing for fourteen years. I direct a department dedicated to digital scholarship. I'm a steering or program committee member or executive councilor or associate director of several DH groups and an officer of (arguably) its primary professional society. My dissertation and almost all of my publications and public presentations have been in the area of digital research, scholarship, and pedagogy. (Still, I still have a hard time thinking of myself as a DH insider, or as part of the establishment. This comes, I'm sure, of a profound respect for the two living generations of computing humanists under whom I trained—and because I matured in the field before Twitter[38] and THATCamp[39] made everybody instant pals.)

That said, I am positioned to hear the private rumblings of many of the people most inclined—indeed, perhaps *most known* for their inclination to be generous to colleagues in the digital humanities, old and new, and that over the course of years and sometimes decades. I also hear from some I'd consider new to this field, but experienced in ways that make them sensitive to the tides of online collectives. What I most hear is a tension between goodwill and exhaustion—outreach and retreat. I'm sympathetic to the weariness of these people, treading water, always "on." I feel it, too. But it's their voicing of frustration and possible disengagement that alarms me.

DH is not in Usenet's eternal September, precisely. That is, truly rude or tone deaf or plainly infelicitous tweets, comments, and postings are few enough that they're of little import, even when they grate. I also remain hopeful that we'll soon figure out, among so many bright and sensitive readers, the right balance of promotion for our programs (large or small) with *genuine* expressions of enthusiasm for our work—the rhetoric of always-on.[40] And for the most part, niceness itself is catching (which may be part of the problem[41]). Fatigue will come in waves, to different segments of the networked community at different moments. So it goes. But the "Eternal September" of the digital humanities runs deeper than simple overwork, and most threatens to exhaust us all when our newer colleagues, who are most visible online, make two assumptions: they think that all this is new;[42] and they think that the current scene[43] is all there is.

Most of us are newer and more insular than we realize.

What does it mean[44] to practice as digital humanists? Some cold mornings, I don't care. We are here to help each other figure it out along the way—by enacting community, building systems of all sorts, doing work that matters in quarters predictable and unexpected. We are *devoted* now like nothing I've seen before. But have you begun to sense how many good people are feeling deeply tired this autumn?

Some of you are hiding it. Some of us should take a breath.

NOTES

Published October 15, 2010, at http://nowviskie.org/2010/eternal-september-of-the-digital-humanities/. Hyperlinks in the original post have been converted to note numbers, with URLs in endnotes.

1. http://lib.virginia.edu/scholarslab.
2. http://en.wikipedia.org/wiki/Morgan_Dana_Harrington.
3. http://en.wikipedia.org/wiki/Murder_of_Yeardley_Love.
4. http://en.wikipedia.org/wiki/Suicide_of_Tyler_Clementi.
5. http://twitter.com/nowviskie.
6. http://digitalhumanities.org/answers.
7. http://twitter.com/foundhistory/status/23933400866.
8. http://nowviskie.org/2010/alt-ac/.

9. http://nowviskie.org/2009/monopolies-of-invention/.

10. http://nowviskie.org/2010/on-compensation/.

11. http://nowviskie.org/2010/fight-club-soap/.

12. http://lenz.unl.edu/papers/2010/10/08/care-of-the-soul.html.

13. http://www.foundhistory.org/2010/05/26/why-digital-humanities-is-%e2%80%9cnice%e2%80%9d/.

14. http://tcp.hypotheses.org/411.

15. http://twitter.com/nowviskie/status/26286764524.

16. http://twitter.com/nowviskie/status/26286775422.

17. http://twitter.com/nowviskie/status/26288196899.

18. http://spatial.scholarslab.org/.

19. http://lib.virginia.edu/scholarslab/about/fellowship.html.

20. http://virginia2010.thatcamp.org/.

21. https://dh2011.stanford.edu/.

22. http://twitter.com/briancroxall/status/5899059507.

23. http://digitalhumanities.org/answers/topic/new-to-the-life-of-digital-humanities-best-ways-to-start-getting-my-feet-wet.

24. http://digitalhumanities.org/answers/topic/what-is-digital-humanities.

25. http://ach.org/.

26. http://digitalhumanities.org/.

27. http://tbe.kantl.be/TBE/.

28. http://commons.gc.cuny.edu/wiki/index.php/The_CUNY_Digital_Humanities_Resource_Guide.

29. http://dhsi.org.

30. http://melissaterras.blogspot.com/2010/07/dh2010-plenary-present-not-voting.html.

31. http://tapor.ualberta.ca/taporwiki/index.php/Day_in_the_Life_of_the_Digital_Humanities.

32. http://digitalhumanitiesnow.org.

33. http://en.wikipedia.org/wiki/Usenet.

34. http://en.wikipedia.org/wiki/Alt.*_hierarchy.

35. http://nowviskie.org/2010/uninvited-guests/.

36. http://en.wikipedia.org/wiki/Netiquette.

37. http://en.wikipedia.org/wiki/Eternal_September.

38. http://search.twitter.com/search?q=%23digitalhumanities.

39. http://thatcamp.org.

40. http://twitter.com/#!/nowviskie/status/27368640861.

41. http://twitter.com/#!/samplereality/status/26558892458.

42. http://parezcoydigo.wordpress.com/2010/10/14/how-far-have-we-come-in-the-digital-humanities/.

43. http://twitter.com/dancohen/digitalhumanities.

44. http://digitalhumanities.org/answers/topic/doing-dh-v-theorizing-dh#post-437.

PART IV

PRACTICING THE DIGITAL HUMANITIES

Canons, Close Reading, and the Evolution of Method

MATTHEW WILKENS

I have a point from which to start: canons exist, and we should do something about them. The digital humanities offer a potential solution to this problem, but only if we are willing to reconsider our priorities for digital work in ways that emphasize quantitative methods and the large corpora on which they depend.

I wouldn't have thought the first proposition, concerning canons and the need to work around them, was a dicey claim until I was scolded recently by a senior colleague who told me that I was thirty years out of date for making it. The idea being that we'd had this fight a generation ago, and the canon had lost. But I was right and he, I'm sorry to say, was wrong. Ask any grad student reading for her comps or English professor who might confess to having skipped Hamlet. As I say, canons exist. Not, perhaps, in the Arnoldian-Bloomian sense of *the* canon, a single list of great books, and in any case certainly not the *same* list of dead white male authors that once defined the field. But in the more pluralist sense of books one really needs to have read to take part in the discipline? And of books many of us teach in common to our own students? Certainly. These are canons. They exist.

So why, a few decades after the question of canonicity as such was in any way current, do we still have these things? If we all agree that canons are bad, why haven't we done away with them? Why do we merely tinker around the edges, adding a Morrison here and subtracting a Dryden there? What are we going to do about this problem? And more to the immediate point, what does any of this have to do with digital humanities and with debates internal to digital work?

The Problem of Abundance

The answer to the question "Why do we still have canons?" is as simple to articulate as it is apparently difficult to solve. We don't read any faster than we ever did, even as the quantity of text produced grows larger by the year. If we need to read books in order to extract information from them and if we need to have read things in common in order to talk about them, we're going to spend most of our time dealing with a relatively small set of texts. The composition of that set will change over time, but it will never get any bigger. This is a canon.[1]

To put things in perspective, consider the scale of literary production over the last few decades as shown in Figure 14.1. Two things stand out: First, there are a lot of new books being published every year, and the number has grown rapidly over the last decade. Even excluding electronic editions and print-on-demand titles (as these figures do), we're seeing fifty thousand or more new works of long-form fiction annually in the United States alone (and at least as many again in the rest of the world at a time when national divisions are growing less relevant to cultural production). The overall U.S. market for books isn't growing beyond the larger economy (publishing revenues as a share of GDP have been constant, at about 0.2 percent, for decades [see Greco et al.]), but it's now being split among far more titles. This is likely the result of decreasing publishing costs in everything from acquisitions to distribution and marketing. The surge in quantity of published texts is surely a good thing insofar as it represents—in raw terms, at least—greater access to the market for a wider range of authors and a more diverse choice of books for readers. But it also means that each of us reads only a truly minuscule fraction of contemporary fiction (on the order of 0.1 percent, often much less). We could call this situation the problem of abundance. It is plainly getting worse with time.

We should notice, too—this is the second observation concerning Figure 14.1—that although the number of titles published annually was much lower prior to 2000,

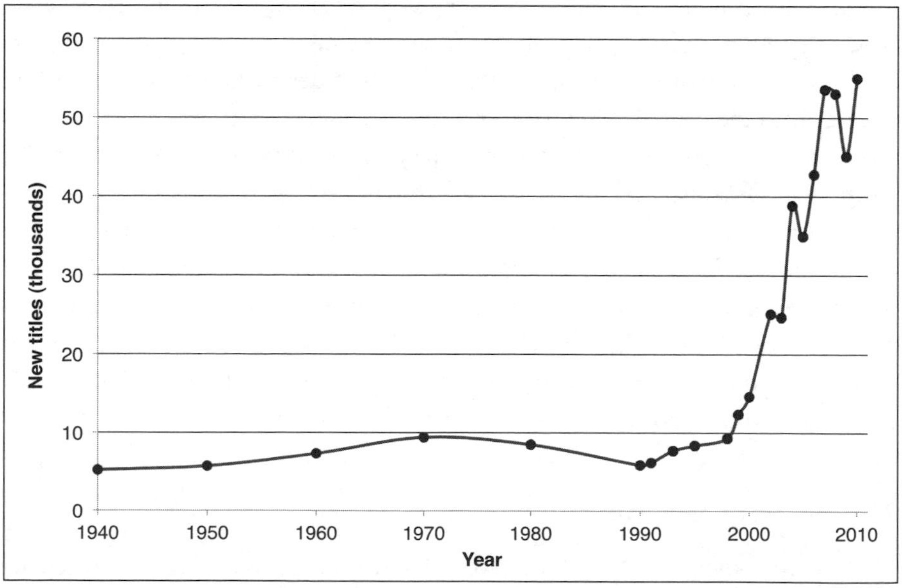

Figure 14.1. Number of new fiction titles published annually in the United States between 1940 and 2010. Sources: Greco et al. (1940–1991); R. R. Bowker (1993–2010). Title output for 1991 and earlier adjusted (upward, by a factor of three) to account for Bowker's subsequent changes in methodology.

it wasn't low in any absolute sense. There have been thousands of new novels published every year for decades. Looking further back, British publishers were bringing out more than a novel a week, on average, as early as the late eighteenth century (Moretti, 7, citing several studies); and American publishers managed the same feat by the mid-nineteenth century (Wright). So although the scale of the inadequacy of our reading is greater now than it was even a decade ago, the fact that we haven't been able to keep up with contemporary literary production is nothing new. We've had a version of the problem of abundance for centuries, whether we've cared to acknowledge it or not.

Another way of putting the issue would be to say that we need to decide what to ignore. And the answer with which we've contented ourselves for generations is, "Pretty much everything ever written." Even when we read diligently, we don't read very much. What little we do read is deeply nonrepresentative of the full field of literary and cultural production, as critics of our existing canons have rightly observed for decades. In the contemporary case, we read largely those few books that are actively promoted by the major publishing houses and in any case almost exclusively books that have been vetted through commercial publication. When we try to do better, to be more inclusive or representative in both form and content, we do so both with a deep set of ingrained cultural biases that are largely invisible to us and (because we've read so little) in ignorance of their alternatives. This is to say that we don't really have any firm sense of how we would even try to set about fixing our canons, because we have no idea how they're currently skewed. We're doing little better, frankly, than we were with the dead white male bunch fifty or a hundred years ago, and we're just as smug in our false sense of intellectual scope. The problem, moreover, is getting worse as the store of unread books grows with each passing week.

So canons—even in their current, mildly multiculturalist form—are an enormous problem, one that follows from our single working method as literary scholars—that is, from the need to perform always and only close reading as a means of cultural analysis. It's probably clear where I'm going with this, at least to some of those who work in digital literary studies. We need to do less close reading and more of anything and everything else that might help us extract information from and about texts as indicators of larger cultural issues. That includes bibliometrics and book historical work, data mining and quantitative text analysis, economic study of the book trade and of other cultural industries, geospatial analysis, and so on. Franco Moretti's work is an obvious model here, as is that of people like Michael Witmore on early modern drama and Nicholas Dames on social structures in nineteenth-century fiction.

Example: Text Extraction and Mapping

One example of what I have in mind is shown in Figure 14.2, which presents a map of the locations mentioned in a corpus of thirty-seven American literary texts published in 1851. There are some squarely canonical works included in this collection, including *Moby Dick* and *House of the Seven Gables*, but the large majority are obscure novels by the likes of T. S. Arthur and Sylvanus Cobb. I certainly haven't read many of them, nor am I likely to spend months doing so. The texts are drawn from the Wright American Fiction Collection[2] and represent about a third of the total American literary works published that year.[3] The Wright collection is based on Lyle Wright's *American Fiction, 1851–1875: A Contribution Toward a Bibliography*, which attempts to identify and list every work of long-form fiction by an American author published in the United States between the relevant dates. Place names were extracted using a tool called Geodict, which looks for strings of text that match a large database of named locations.[4] A bit of cleanup on the extracted places was necessary, mostly because many personal names and common adjectives are also the names of cities somewhere in the world. I erred on the conservative side, excluding any such named places found and requiring a leading preposition for cities and regions. If anything, some valid places have likely been excluded. But the results are fascinating.

Two points of particular interest concerning the figure in this map: First, there are more international locations than one might have expected. True, many of them are in Britain and western Europe, but these are American novels, not British or other reprints, so even that fact might surprise us. And there are also multiple mentions of locations in South America, Africa, India, China, Russia, Australia, the Middle East, and so on. The imaginative landscape of American fiction in the mid-nineteenth century appears to be pretty diversely outward looking in a way that hasn't yet received much attention. Indeed, one of the defining features of our standard model of the period is that its fiction is strongly introspective at

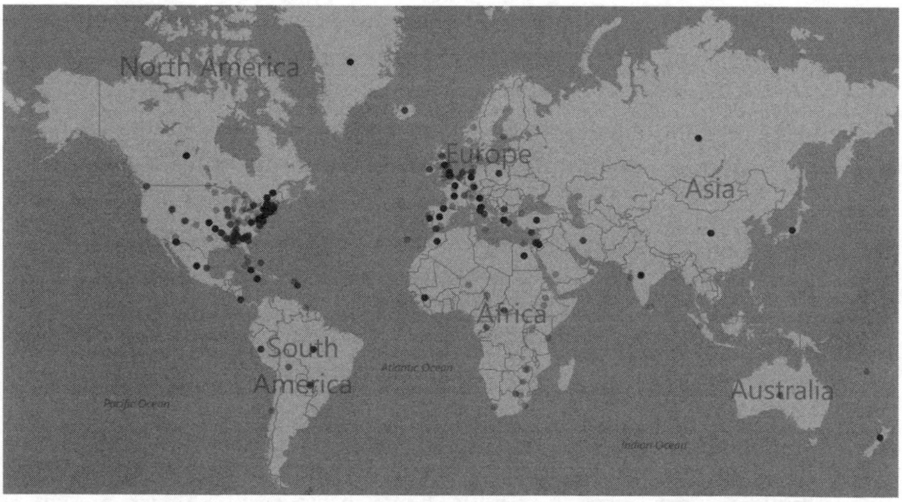

Figure 14.2. Places named in thirty-seven U.S. novels published in 1851.

both the personal and national levels, concerned largely with American identity and belonging.

Second, there's the distinct cluster of named places in the American South. At some level, this probably shouldn't be surprising, since we're talking about books that appeared just a decade before the Civil War, and the South was certainly on people's minds. But it doesn't fit very well with the stories we currently tell about Romanticism and the American Renaissance, which are centered firmly in New England during the early 1850s and dominate our understanding of the period. Perhaps we need to at least consider the possibility that American regionalism took hold significantly earlier than we usually claim.

How do these results compare with other years represented in the Wright corpus? Consider Figures 14.3 and 14.4. The maps for these years—1852 and 1874, respectively—are a bit noisier than 1851 because they've undergone less intensive data curation, but the patterns of location distribution are broadly similar to those observed earlier.[5] Two features stand out, however, in a comparison of locations appearing before and after the Civil War:

1. The density of named locations in the American west is noticeably greater in 1874 than in 1852.
2. The emergence of a second, distinct cluster of locations in the south-central United States, vaguely discernible in the earlier maps, is more pronounced in the 1874 map.

Both of these developments offer potential evidence for a revised understanding of American regionalism, particularly insofar as the dates at which the west and south-central regions become part of the imaginative landscape of American fiction significantly precede the presence of meaningful publishing activity in either area. We will want to know more about both the social history of westward expansion and the specific uses to which these locations are put in the period's literature before drawing any strong conclusions concerning their relevance, but it's clear that information of this kind can make up an important part of any new story about the course of American fiction in the nineteenth century.

There's also something to be said, however, about the striking overall similarity of all three maps. The Civil War is *the* periodizing event of American literary history. The books in question (more than a hundred from each period 1851–53 and 1873–75) were written roughly a generation apart and a decade before and after the war. If ever we should expect significant literary change in response to rapid social transformation, the Wright corpus is a strong candidate in which to observe it. So the question is, do we see a meaningful shift in a relevant aspect of literary production before and after the Civil War evinced in the data? To which the answer is, it depends on what we mean by meaningful. Our working image of important shifts in literary and cultural production is one derived from our experience with a

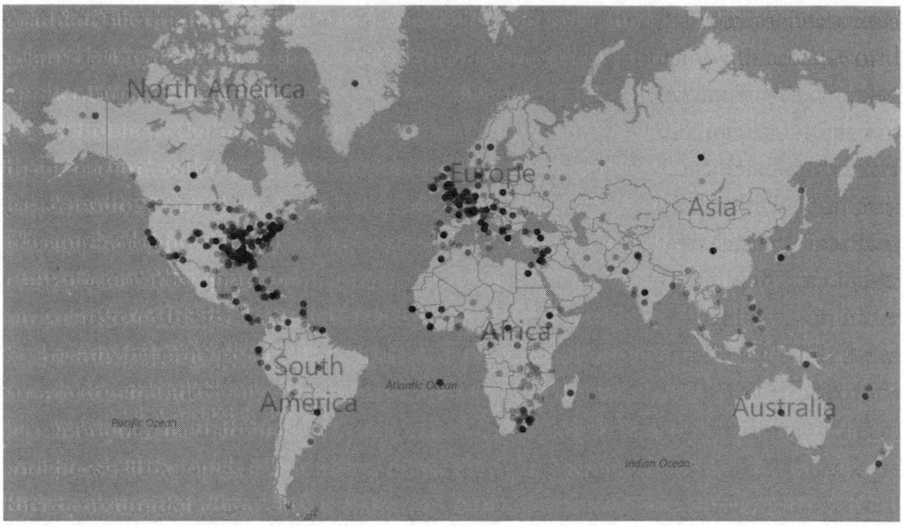

Figure 14.3. Places named in forty-five U.S. novels published in 1852.

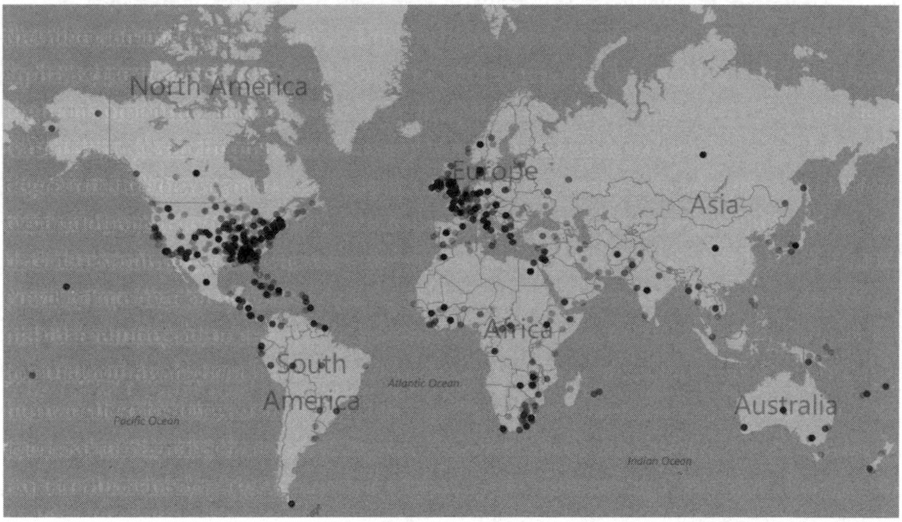

Figure 14.4. Places named in thirty-eight U.S. novels published in 1874.

handful of purportedly significant or representative works. We have, by working of necessity with very few texts and constructing highly detailed accounts of their particular differences, perhaps allowed ourselves to see period differences (and other classificatory distinctions) as more far reaching than they really are. This isn't to say that differences between periods, genres, nations, genders, and so on don't exist but only that they may consist in small but important variations on larger underlying continuities.

A scheme of literary classification based on small changes in overall literary production certainly isn't a repudiation of, for instance, periodization as such, but it does have serious implications concerning our work with the larger corpora that have long been outside our methodological grasp. As we begin to ask questions concerning the patterns and differences between and among hundreds or thousands of books, we will almost certainly encounter many more instances of data that resemble the maps presented here, in which we observe small variations in features that are broadly shared across corpora. One available interpretation of this fact—an interpretation based on our established model of event-based change—will be that no significant underlying change has occurred. Perhaps we will go so far as to say that literary history is best understood as an essentially unbroken chain of (at most) gradual evolutionary steps. Perhaps. But we should also be aware that we currently have very little concept of what major variations in the form or content of large bodies of literature might look like. It's certainly possible for small absolute variations of a given metric to be culturally (or physically, for that matter) significant in other contexts. Think, for instance, of the difference between a close national election and a comfortably one-sided vote. If our response to variations of, say, *only* 10 or 20 percent is that they fall far short of our idea of transformational, it may be our concept of transformation that needs to change.

One further methodological note: The techniques involved here can be readily extended with little additional time or labor to new texts as they become available. This is important because it allows us to test our hypothesis against new material and in different configurations and eras, something that would be difficult or impossible to do by hand. There's no guarantee, of course, that we'll be able to explain what we find or that it will fit neatly with what we've seen so far, but that's a feature, not a bug. It's good to have more material for evaluation and analysis. The relative speed of these methods is also an advantage insofar as it allows us to look for potentially interesting features without committing months or years to extracting them via close reading. We may very well still need to read some of the texts closely, but text-mining methods allow us to direct our scarce attention to those materials in which we already have reason to believe we will find relevant information. Though we're not used to framing our work in terms of rapid hypothesis testing and feature extraction, the process isn't radically different from what we already do on a much smaller scale. Speed and scalability are major benefits of this strand of computational work.

Consequences and Conclusions

I think the maps presented earlier offer interesting preliminary results, ones that demonstrate the first steps in a type of analysis that remains literary and cultural but that doesn't depend on close reading alone nor suffer the material limits such reading imposes. I think we should do more of this—not necessarily more geolocation extraction in mid-nineteenth-century American fiction (though what I've shown obviously doesn't exhaust that project) but certainly more algorithmic and quantitative analysis of piles of text much too large to tackle "directly." ("Directly" gets scare quotes because it's a deeply misleading synonym for close reading in this context.)

If we do that—shift more of our critical capacity to such projects—there will be a couple of important consequences. For one thing, we'll almost certainly become worse close readers. Our time is finite; the less of it we devote to an activity, the less we'll develop our skill in that area. Exactly how much our reading suffers and how much we should care are matters of reasonable debate; they depend on both the extent of the shift and the shape of the skill-experience curve for close reading. My sense is that we'll come out all right and that it's a trade—a few more numbers in return for a bit less text—well worth making. We gain a lot by having available to us the kinds of evidence text mining (for example) provides, enough that the outcome will almost certainly be a net positive for the field. But I'm willing to admit that the proof will be in the practice and that the practice is, while promising, as yet pretty limited. The important point, though, is that the decay of close reading as such is a negative in itself only if we mistakenly equate literary and cultural analysis with their current working method.

Second—and here's the heart of the debate for those of us already engaged in digital projects of one sort or another—we'll need to see a related reallocation of resources within DH itself. Over the last couple of decades, many of our most visible projects have been organized around canonical texts, authors, and cultural artifacts. They have been motivated by a desire to understand those (quite limited) objects more robustly and completely, on a model plainly derived from conventional humanities scholarship. That wasn't a mistake, nor are those projects without significant value. They've contributed to our understanding of, for example, Rossetti and Whitman, Stowe and Dickinson, Shakespeare and Spenser. And they've helped legitimate digital work in the eyes of suspicious colleagues by showing how far we can extend our traditional scholarship with new technologies. They've provided scholars around the world—including those outside the centers of university power—with improved access to rare materials and improved pedagogy by the same means. But we shouldn't ignore the fact that they've also often been large, expensive undertakings built on the assumption that we already know which authors and texts are the ones to which we should devote our scarce resources. And to the extent that they've succeeded, they've also reinforced the canonicity of their subjects by increasing the amount of critical attention paid to them.

What's required for computational and quantitative work—the kind of work that undermines rather than reinforces canons—is more material, less elaborately developed. The Wright collection, on which the maps are based, is a partial example of the kind of resource that's best suited to this next development in digital humanities research. It includes (or will include) every known American literary text published in the United States between 1851 and 1875 and makes them available in machine-readable form with basic metadata. Google Books and the Hathi Trust aim for the same thing on a much larger scale, currently covering a large portion of the extant public domain and offering the hope of computational access to most of the books (in and out of copyright) held in major research libraries. None of these projects are cheap. But on a per-volume basis, they're very affordable, largely because they avoid extensive human intervention (via detailed markup, for example) in the preparation of the texts. And of course the Google and Hathi corpora were produced with remarkably limited direct costs to the academic departments that will use them, particularly in light of their magnitude. The texts they include are deeply impoverished compared to those curated in author- and subject-specific archival projects. But they're more than adequate for many of our analytical purposes, which, again, need not turn solely on close textual hermeneutics.

It will still cost a good deal to make use of these what we might call "bare" repositories. The time, money, and attention they demand will have to come from somewhere. My point, though, is that if (as seems likely) we can't pull those resources from entirely new pools outside the discipline—that is to say, if we can't just expand the discipline so as to do everything we already do, plus a great many new things—then we should be willing to make sacrifices not only in traditional or analog humanities but also in the types of first-wave digital projects that made the name and reputation of DH. This will hurt, but it will also result in categorically better, more broadly based, more inclusive, and finally more useful humanities scholarship. It will do so by giving us our first real chance to break the grip of small, arbitrarily assembled canons on our thinking about large-scale cultural production. It's an opportunity not to be missed and a chance to put our money—real and figurative—where our mouths have been for two generations. We've complained about canons for a long time. Now that we might do without them, are we willing to try? And to accept the trade-offs involved? I think we should be.

NOTES

1. How many canons are there? The answer depends on how many people need to have read a given set of materials in order to constitute a field of study. This was once more or less everyone, but then the field was also very small when that was true. My best guess is that the number is at least a hundred or more at the very lowest end—and a couple orders of magnitude more than that at the high end—which would give us a few dozen subfields in English, give or take. That strikes me as roughly accurate.

2. Wright American Fiction Project, http://www.letrs.indiana.edu/web/w/wright2.

3. Why only a third? Those are all the texts available in high-quality machine-readable format with good metadata (via the MONK Project, http://monkproject.org) at the moment.

4. Peter Warden, Geodict, http://datasciencetoolkit.org.

5. Data are also available for 1853, 1873, and 1875, each showing substantially similar features. The intervening years—1854 through 1872—have as yet too few digitized volumes for reliable use. The cluster of locations in southern Africa is a known identification error.

BIBLIOGRAPHY

Elson, David K., Nicholas Dames, and Kathleen R. McKeown. "Extracting Social Networks From Literary Fiction." In *Proceedings of the 48th Annual Meeting of the Association for Computational Linguistics,* 138–47. Uppsala, Sweden, 2010.

Greco, Albert, Clara Rodrguez, and Robert Wharton. *The Culture and Commerce of Publishing in the 21st Century*. Stanford, Calif.: Stanford University Press, 2007.

Hope, Jonathan, and Michael Witmore. "The Hundredth Psalm to the Tune of 'Green Sleeves': Digital Approaches to Shakespeare's Language of Genre." *Shakespeare Quarterly* 61, no. 3 (2010): 357–90.

Moretti, Franco. *Maps, Graphs, Trees: Abstract Models for a Literary History*. New York: Verso, 2005.

R. R. Bowker. "New Book Titles & Editions, 2002–2009." April 14, 2010, http://www.bowker.com/index.php/book-industry-statistics.

———. "U.S. Book Production, 1993–2004." April 14, 2010, http://www.bowker.com/bookwire/decadebookproduction.html.

Wright, Lyle H. *American Fiction 1851–1875: A Contribution Toward a Bibliography*. Rev. ed. San Marino, Calif.: Huntington Library Press, 1965.

Electronic Errata: Digital Publishing, Open Review, and the Futures of Correction

PAUL FYFE

It is hardly possible to write a history of information separately from a history of the corruption of the press.

—Walter Benjamin, *Charles Baudelaire: A Lyric Poet in the Era of High Capitalism*

In writing about mid-nineteenth century newspapers, Walter Benjamin notes the prevalence of the réclame, a paid publisher's advertisement printed instead as an editorial notice and hidden within the miscellany of the page. For Benjamin, this "corruption of the press" was so widespread as to necessarily inform any "history of information" (28). But Benjamin's insight can also apply by corrupting the very word "corrupt" to mean something like "error." As bibliographers and textual critics well know, it is hardly possible to write the history of information without attention to errors, accidents, variants, and changes—the dynamics of corruption and correction that pattern the history of published print. As this essay will argue, it is also hardly possible to write the future history of information—an enterprise in which the essays in this volume are very much involved—separately from those same dynamics as they manifest, in new ways as well as old, in online and digital publishing. But we have yet to do so.

As Steven Berlin Johnson argues, "[t]he history of knowledge conventionally focuses on breakthrough ideas and conceptual leaps. But the blind spots on the map, the dark continents of error and prejudice, carry their own mystery as well. . . . These questions, too, deserve their own discipline—the sociology of error" (*Ghost Map*, 15). This essay undertakes such questions for the current moment in electronic publishing by looking to the history of printing errors and the labor of correction. That history offers valuable perspectives on the proliferating effects of "accidentals" and error within the automation, syndication, and algorithmic relations of the web. It further informs how scholarly publishing's digital futures might (or might not) deal with the issue, including open review, crowdsourced or distributed corrections, automated redundancy systems in libraries, and intelligent computing agents. The history of error also opens some theoretical perspectives (sometimes noted as lacking in digital humanities discussions), suggesting that, even if we do not dedicate technology or labor to these issues, the digital humanities needs to reckon conceptually with what, in a different context, John Unsworth called "the importance of failure." Scholarly publishing will inevitably change, but before its print-based model totters into the grave we need clearer commitments about the error proofing it has traditionally undertaken as well as the consequences of reinventing or abandoning such functions altogether as we move to new formats.[1]

Certainly, the discussions about the digital transformation of publishing, especially (though not exclusively) the publishing of critical work and scholarly resources, have mapped an array of important issues whose problems and opportunities need to be resolved, including peer review, credentialing, collaboration, intellectual property, multimodal textuality, encoding standards, access, and sustainability.[2] But largely absent from these discussions, or playing only a minor role, is the fate or future of copyediting, fact checking, the often thankless tasks of verification and correction that usually happen behind the publishing scenes. This omission is at once entirely consistent with the historical instability of copyediting (as I will suggest) and uniquely problematic from a contemporary perspective. While "Jhon Milton" is an easy enough error to catch (nonetheless his e-book *Areopagitica* is currently for sale on Amazon [Trettien]), the typographical, factual, and citation errors that characterize any publishing endeavor, online or in print, will not be resolved by casual or professional use in the ways commentators have envisioned.[3] Electronic errata have potentially cascading effects that we would do well to consider in imagining futures for digital publishing and networked scholarly communication.[4] So, also, do new regimes of correction have limitations and theoretical compromises that we should not ignore.

Before situating this argument historically, I want to make two major caveats about the present moment. Discussions of online publishing and digital projects have in fact deeply considered the problems of "error" in terms of preservation and their own technical obsolescence, including everything from hardware to browser interoperability to the degradation of links or "link rot." Second, there has been abundant attention to the errors of digitization, OCR, and metadata cataloguing, exemplified in Geoffrey Nunberg's ongoing critique of the Google Books initiative and projects like MIT's "culturomics" initiative that depend on the integrity of Google's data. Furthermore, any programmer worth her silicon knows the simple equation of "garbage in, garbage out" (GIGO), which underwrites the integrity of data and code. My argument is not that we are ignoring error but rather that we have not sufficiently considered error correction as a structural feature and theoretical premise within the transition to digital publishing.

This is not a conservative argument seeking a return to the good old ways. In fact, ignoring the particulars or correction ironically threatens to replicate a conservative notion of textuality that digital publishing was supposed to displace. Nor is this just scholarly nitpicking. If publishing errors seem mundane or even trivial compared to the greater transformations in digital scholarship, they have the potential for aggregate effects on the network and discourse we are producing. It may be that we decide that such errata do not warrant much technical concern or that they should fall down the scale of scholarly values as recalibrated by digital or open publishing. But these positions need to be articulated; we need clearer plans for the obsolescence of academic correction. Even if this essay floats a balloon that is quickly shot down, it will have drawn the necessary fire to a target that has hitherto flown beneath the radar. We begin with a trip backward, a historical detour that is also a shortcut to the present.

The Disappearance of the Reading Boy

I will hazard a generalization that getting copyedited is a consistently unsettling experience in academic life—at least in a professional life which has been governed by a regime of writing and peer review. On the otherwise mostly pleasant trajectory of, say, submitting a finished article, having it acknowledged or accepted, making further substantive revisions, and then sending it off for publication, the copyedited proofs one receives can come as a bit of a shock. Such was my reaction on receiving copyedits on an accepted article: I thought I was *done*, having scrupulously checked the text each time before submission and having survived peer review and its recommendations. But starkly indicated on the returned manuscript pages were anonymous testimonies to surprising grammatical inconsistencies, the occasional sloppiness of citation, lurking typos, and the flat-out misquoting of sources, several of them arcane. Why hadn't I seen them? Why had no one pointed them out before? And who was behind all this, doing the work on the page and in the library to check all this text and references?

There is no copyeditor listed on the masthead of the journal issue in which that article was published.[5] Perhaps it was the editor or assistant editor. More likely it was an (unlisted and unsalaried) editorial assistant—and probably a graduate student employed by the publisher for preprint quality control that is distinctly separate from the editorial functions of peer review. During my time as a graduate student, I actually had such a job, working to check facts, confirm citations, and copyedit quoted materials for a peer-reviewed journal—specifically, for *Postmodern Culture (PMC),* the first peer-reviewed academic journal to publish entirely online and for free. As forward thinking as *PMC* was in relation to emergent trends in digital publishing and open access, it preserved the very traditional protocols of peer review and correction as well as the distinction between them. Indeed, they had to be kept intact for *PMC* to leverage its more revolutionary proposal of open digital publishing.

With all due respect, this was a boring and tedious job. The workflow requires a different kind of attention than reading the articles or reviewing their arguments. Instead, the assistant confirms the page number, bibliographical citation, and textual accuracy of every piece of quoted, referenced, or footnoted material in a given manuscript. The assistant scurries all over the stacks in the library, hoarding armloads of books to check a mere fragment in any one of them. The assistant becomes the scourge of the interlibrary loan department, winging out endless requests for copies of materials the library does not have. From today's vantage point, the assistant seems like the motor arm in a Rube Goldberg reinvention of a database, scrambling the physical world for the items that a digitized network would so easily trace. Databases and electronic versions of sources might resolve some of these logistical difficulties, but they invite other obstacles, including access policies, the integrity of digitized materials, and coverage. Then and now, the editorial assistant has to undertake a serious amount of mundane labor. I am very grateful someone did that for me, whoever you are.

Such an assistant or fact-checking process is not necessarily a part of every scholarly publishing venture. But the assistant embodies a particular attitude toward correction whose institutional evolution is worth considering. Though the messy details of book history may seem remote from the digital transformation of publishing, they set the conceptual terms and labor conditions that have reached a crucial moment of redefinition. The anonymity and transient labor of the journal fact-checker or copyeditor is itself a historical legacy of the publishing business at large. Proofreading has a history as long as writing itself, but, in print publishing, the figure of a specialized in-house proofreader only emerges in the seventeenth century in continental Europe, subsequently adopted in the mid-eighteenth century by English printers. This was the "corrector": typically only employed by larger publishing houses, correctors were "not as a rule trained printers, but were men of education specially employed, sometimes on a part-time basis" (Gaskell, 172). Then, as now, the corrector occupied an ambiguous middle ground between editorial and production, between the managerial and technical realms. In Philip Gaskell's hierarchy of labor of the English book trade to 1800, the corrector falls right on the threshold between business owners, printing masters, and overseers (all with fixed wages) and the journeymen, apprentices, and juvenile runners who worked for them (all paid piecemeal) (171–74). Though expected to be well educated and to exert editorial influence on the copy, they were not in the salaried echelon of a house's editorial or commercial management. Though paid piecemeal, working with in-process sheets and collaborating with the compositors and printers assembling them, they were not allied to the working press. The corrector overlapped with each domain and properly belonged to neither.

Even when a press did not employ correctors, such as in smaller houses, their very absence suggests the professional ambiguities and shifting responsibilities of the corrector's role. In these cases, "correction was normally carried out by the master or a senior journeyman; less commonly the corrector was the author or the author's representative" (Gaskell, 111). In other words, correction could happen on either side of the masters/men or publisher/author divides. Sometimes, publishing firm partners and senior editors got involved in the process, as when houses undertook significantly complicated or expensive work (Gaskell, 113). On the other end of the spectrum, correction was already taking place during the very setting of type: "it had been the compositor's duty to correct or normalize the spelling, punctuation, and capitalization (known nowadays as the 'accidentals') of the manuscript" and ensure the integrity of the "substantives" (Gaskell, 110, 111). As the compositor slotted lead type into his stick, he was silently doing the typographical and editorial work that the corrector would come to check. A corrector was required because the compositor had incentives to overlook his own mistakes, since doing so would be charged to his time.

In underwriting the added value of error-free print, the corrector's allegiance was to the management, but his typical work partner hailed from the opposite side of the labor hierarchy. This was the "reading boy" or "copyholder" who would read aloud from the manuscript copy while the corrector checked the printed proofs. He would then return the proofs (in various states: the all-important first proof, revise proofs, press proofs) to the compositor, marked up in the standardized graphical codes of copyediting which "remain essentially unchanged today" (Gaskell, 113). What has definitively changed is the corrector's workflow: checking a printed proof while listening to the reading boy, then switching roles as physical fatigue warranted. The reading was a professional performance with its own auditory conventions; a reader pronounced grammatical marks and used sing-song inflections for variations in type: capitalization, emphasis, conjunctive and possessive apostrophes, and so on.[6] It also announced a publisher's relation to source text that would profoundly change by 1900, as manuscripts increasingly came into the house having already been edited for errors, or otherwise declaring themselves as proofed copytext to begin with—with no small thanks to the increasing popularity of typescript. The jobs of compositors and correctors changed: they were no longer silently normalizing the "accidental" errors of the text but instead obliged to preserve accidentals and substantive errors in the proofs just as they appeared in manuscript. Attending that change was a shift from aural to ocular correction, or the visual collation of a work in different stages of production. As a consequence, "the reading-boy disappeared in English printing houses around 1900" (Gaskell, 353).

A century later, his partner the corrector has not fared much better, particularly since the advent of new media, which, as I will argue later, shifts correction even further from aural to ocular into synthetic or automated realms. But correctors, reading boys, editorial assistants, and copyeditors are losing their places for more conspicuous reasons. Though this is not exclusively an economic issue, the financial impact of new media upon old media, as well as coinciding economic downturns, have made the considerable costs of correction seem like an unnecessary burden. Having always occupied a tenuous middle ground between management and production, editorial positions of various kinds have been subject to significant cuts.[7] From a different perspective, emerging enthusiasm about unfiltered publishing online has privileged speed, accessibility, and distribution over the comparatively tedious labor of editorial nitpicking. In effect, the corrector's function has been dismissed or elsewhere absorbed by publishers and independent content producers across the continuum of scholarly publishing. But the consequences for its seeming disappearance or reinvention are significant.

Revaluing Review and Correction

As with the death of the author, the disappearance of the corrector raises the specter of what might be called, after Foucault, the corrector function: a relation of value between a printed text and its typographical, factual, and stylistic integrity. The historical quirks and ambiguous status of the corrector underscore how such a function is constantly being negotiated through the economic, social, and technological conditions of the present, or within the discourse of publishing. According to a variety of observers, that discourse is experiencing a paradigmatic shift with the advent of digital publishing in various commercial, civilian, and scholarly forms. So, too, are its structuring relations and values in flux—very much including correction and the notion of a published or finished text. Looking at the genealogy of the corrector, we can still find its functions in the present (such as with copyeditors, graduate editorial assistants, etc.), but what are its futures? Will the prepublication function of correction continue to make sense? Or how will it evolve?

For scholarly publishers and university presses, digital publishing has heralded a major transformation in their businesses. But attention to correction, in either its traditional or its future incarnations, seems notably absent from some of the more conspicuous forums in which university presses have worried or speculated about their futures.[8] While the industry is quick to celebrate its role in "improving work through peer review/editing," the particular values or necessities of correction go relatively unmentioned (Brown et al., 36). Peter Dougherty suggests in his "Checklist for Scholarly Publishers" in transitioning to the digital future that "[e]ditorially, our work is cut out for us"; however, attention to the editorial integrity of copy remains implicit at best. A recent Association of American University Presses report on *Sustaining Scholarly Publishing* suggests several new aspects of correction including "[q]uality assurance and filtration, presentational enhancement, metadata crafting and maintenance, . . . [and] establishing authoritative versions," but they remain abstractions in the background of the report's abiding concern for business models (4). Taken together, these forecasts skew toward the managerial and technical domains, toward modified business models and digital production strategies. Obviously, scholarly publishers have some serious and pressing concerns, but the declining attention to correction starts with publishers themselves.

From a different perspective, the inattention to correction seems symptomatic of changing attitudes about its necessity. In an important blog post titled "The Social Contract of Scholarly Publishing," Dan Cohen recounts a conversation with his mentor and collaborator Roy Rosenzweig about a book manuscript they had recently finished. In an unguarded moment, Cohen asks, "So, what now?" Isn't the book for all intents and purposes finished? Couldn't it be published online immediately? "Isn't it 95% done? What's the last five percent for?" Rosenzweig's response sketches out what Cohen calls "the magic of the last stage of scholarly production between the final draft and the published book." It amounts to the mystification of the scholarly fetish. As Rosenzweig replies, "What happens now is the creation of the *social contract* between the authors and the readers. We agree to spend considerable time ridding the manuscript of minor errors, and the press spends additional time on other corrections and layout, and readers respond to these signals—a lack of typos, nicely formatted footnotes, a bibliography, specialized fonts, and a high-quality physical presentation—by agreeing to give the book a serious read." With a quick jerk, Rosenzweig pulls the curtain of this social contract, exposing the hoary, wizard-like scholar as a fabrication in smoke. The "magic" of scholarly prestige is produced by the business of publishing. By contrast, click an "Update" button in WordPress and poof! It's gone—and with it, all the social, disciplinary, or institutional credibility of our faith in the 5 percent. Cohen wants to change this equation, as do a host of scholars imagining (and actively realizing) the possibilities of near-instantaneous, inexpensive, networked scholarly communication on the web. In a follow-up post titled "Open Access Publishing and Scholarly Values," Cohen completes the arc of the argument: the social contracts of peer-reviewed print scholarship are rapidly expiring, and digitally open-access scholarship is driving the reformulation of scholarly values at large. Forget the 5 percent. The "added value" of the traditional scholarly publishing model no longer adds up.

In these posts, Cohen does not address what futures might be afforded to the corrector function. Perhaps there are none. It is certainly possible to think about copyediting and fact checking as tactical elements in the cost-recovery model of closed or for-profit publishing. In other words, such correctness is not scholarly integrity ipso facto but as much a by-product of the historical development of publishing as the material features of the book, notions of authorship, and peer review. Corrected and copyedited texts are saleable and signify in a reputational economy because they have been processed in ways that users are unlikely to replicate or undertake themselves. Correction is the "added value" of publication, part of an increasingly outmoded business plan or a contractual relic of scholarly values that ought to be renegotiated. In an e-mail, Cohen suggests that "we could regain the lost opportunity cost of other scholarly endeavors" by simply forgiving minor errors, as is commonly practiced on the open web, since the "true quality" of such work will remain intact.

Cohen and Tom Scheinfeldt have experimented with dispensing the 5 percent altogether—and then some. With *Hacking the Academy*, they crowdsourced a book in one week, inviting contributions from anyone in a range of forms and media. Cohen and Scheinfeldt collected many of them for an open-access volume published by University of Michigan's digitalculturebooks series. Scheinfeldt reports that he and Cohen are responsible for all the copyediting, which is still laborious but out of necessity less than is usually undertaken for academic volumes. As Scheinfeldt speculates, this situation will likely become the norm: in addition to more speed, "less nitpicking overall, more work thrown back on the editor/author, and more responsibility on the reader to read texts critically for factual and other errors." If, by 1900, texts declared themselves correct on arrival at a publisher, we may soon see correction become a postpublication process, if it happens at all. The first shift eliminated the reading boy and changed the dominant mode of correction from aural to ocular. The current shift may eliminate the editorial nitpicker entirely, displacing correction onto the reader or to autocorrecting functions of networks.

Scheinfeldt is sanguine about the economics of this situation, including its uncompensated outsourcing of work, but he is also optimistic about its potentials. Why belabor the 5 percent when a new model of publishing repays it twice over with intellectual and social dividends? Shana Kimball—editor of the *Journal of Electronic Publishing* as well as head of publishing services, outreach and strategic development at the University of Michigan's Scholarly Publishing Office—thoughtfully asks, "[m]ight scholars decide that speed, agility, and network effects of open, web-based forms of scholarly communication trump perfection and error-correction in some cases? Perhaps the quality, say, of self-published scholarly blogs would be good enough for certain purposes, when it's not worth the time and expense (and these functions are quite expensive) of careful editorial nit-picking." In this scenario, other functions of correction or "value" might emerge: not governed by commercial publishers or closed peer-review practices but opened to the collective input and dynamic adjustments of the web.

Kathleen Fitzpatrick's *Planned Obsolescence: Publishing, Technology, and the Future of the Academy* is perhaps the most comprehensive and eloquent assessment of this situation—as well as an interesting performance of its own argument online. Fitzpatrick's target is peer review: the conventional system of prepublication peer evaluation that functions variously—according to whom one asks in what discipline—to sort through the mass of works in progress, to improve or add intellectual value to scholarship, to control quality and prevent errors, and to serve as a gatekeeper and credentialing mechanism for academia. In tangling with these aspects of digital publication, *Planned Obsolescence* does not explicitly engage the functions of correction that, as we have seen, are often kept distinct from editorial direction and the peer-review process. Like scholarly publishers themselves, Fitzpatrick's attention is drawn elsewhere—again, justifiably so but in ways that are also suggestive of how debates about digital publishing and peer review are largely taking place on different terrain.

These debates have instead concentrated on new forms of review including in-process open review, peer-to-peer review, postpublication review, no review at all, or automated/synthetic review as an effect of usage and search engine ranking algorithms. *Planned Obsolescence* was itself subject to both traditional peer review through New York University (NYU) Press and open review on the web, as the draft was published online with CommentPress, allowing for open user comments by page and paragraph. To Fitzpatrick's great credit, she posted both of her official reader's reports (by Lisa Spiro, with permission) along with exposing her prepublication manuscript to public scrutiny and commentary. Examining these documents and their assembled commentary reveals a genuine intellectual generosity in each mode, and Fitzpatrick acknowledges the contributions of each in improving the manuscript. So, too, does each mode offer the occasional correction or copyeditorial note on typos and style, but only sporadically. Fitzpatrick reports that the open review did offer a fair bit of such suggestions but that commenters primarily engaged with the argument—which is exactly what she wanted ("Re: open review"). The revised manuscript was itself sent out for professional copyediting by NYU Press.

This method of open review is seeing more trials elsewhere. The journal *Shakespeare Quarterly* (*SQ*) has undertaken several rounds of preprint open review on the web. The comments during its initial experiment, like those for *Planned Obsolescence*, favor an engagement with the argument rather than pointing out errors. The "FAQ" for the second trial advises potential reviewers that "the most useful feedback is that which an author can use to strengthen an argument," though short comments are fine. According to associate editor Sarah Werner, *SQ* is neither expecting nor relying on open review to provide stylistic, citational, and factual correction. It happens in places but is still conducted after the review trial is over: "each article is fact-checked by either the Managing Editor or the Production Editor, and the article is copy-edited by the Managing Editor and the Editor." Werner suggests that "both of those are things that even the best, most careful writers have a hard time doing for their own work." Furthermore, "fact-checking provides reassurance that the argument the author is making is reliable and gives the necessary tools for other scholars to do their own assessment with the sources." Just as *PMC* kept its familiar editorial foundations upon which to innovate, *SQ* remains a fairly traditional academic journal, committed to the added intellectual values of editorial work. Werner worries that "the biggest danger of scholarship moving toward online and open forms is that editing might get thrown out with the bathwater." The question is, can (or will) nontraditional digital and open publishing absorb the corrector functions still currently in place?

The writer Seth Godin has quipped that "finding people to fix your typos is easy" as "most people have been brainwashed into believing that their job is to copyedit the world, not to design it." But such a presumption about the ubiquity of online correction trivializes its labor and intellectual functions. In an e-mail, Fitzpatrick writes "that this kind of editorial work still remains important" but expresses hope that "a fair bit of it might usefully be crowdsourced" ("Re: open review"). Cohen agrees that "some of it could be crowdsourced, but there is something to having one or two people really work hard on polishing a text" ("Re: open review"). It is hard work, and not everyone is volunteering for it. Fitzpatrick is extremely aware of the sustainability challenges of crowdsourced labor and indeed has done much to focus discussions of open review and digital publishing on this important concern. Stevan Harnad, a pioneer of open review in the sciences, explains the strains upon its sustainability this way: "The expert population in any given speciality [sic] is a scarce resource, already overharvested by classical peer review, so one wonders who would have the time or inclination to add journeyman commentary services to this load on their own initiative, particularly once it is no longer a rare novelty, and the entire raw, unpoliced literature is routinely appearing in this form first." Not least for this reason, Harnad concludes that "open peer commentary [is] an extremely powerful and important *supplement* to peer review, but certainly no *substitute* for it" (original emphasis). While Harnad does not specifically engage questions of correction either, his argument can make sense of correction's labor by analogy: open correction might supplement, but not substitute, for its disciplined undertaking. Indeed, the particular aspects of correction's labor may make it more difficult to sustain or crowdsource than peer review. While a commenter might be compelled to offer their time and expertise "to strengthen an argument" ("FAQ"), are they likely to undertake the tedious nonreading aspects of factual accuracy and citation checking?[9] Or, as Silvia Hunter points out, to have the professional background to protect authors from legal issues like copyright infringement or libel? Are you, dear reader, checking the accuracy of all my quotes and references as you go? Or, conversely, are you prepared to relinquish them to the voluntary or automated curation of the open web or to their own scholarly obsolescence?

New Schemes for Correction

Various scenarios are already in play for the implementation, reinvention, or dismissal of the duties of formal scholarly publishing as it migrates to digital and online forms. For example, the platform for Open Journal Systems (OJS) comes with built-in roles for a wide range of editorial functions for users to customize. Its workflow replicates the traditional structures of peer-reviewed scholarly publishing, distinguishing between editorial guidance, peer review, and copyediting by the sequential transactions of electronic documents (Willinsky et al.). In Gerry Coulter's report on "Launching (and Sustaining) a Scholarly Journal on the Internet: *The International*

Journal of Baudrillard Studies," he explains how a thematically focused, online academic journal with low financial overhead can function. Coulter claims that "someone has to be responsible, during the final proofreading of articles," to adhere to standards of spelling, citation, and encoding. He and the assistant editor, Mary Ellen Donnan, copyedit "each paper before and after the HTML process . . . to ensure consistency and quality."[10] The distinction Coulter maintains between peer review and proofreading is suggestive of another useful distinction between professional gatekeeping and bibliographic control. Especially with a widely distributed, polyglot international journal published using standard web encoding, Coulter wants bibliographic consistency not simply as a matter of quality or value or credibility but also as a function of access and scholarly interoperability. In other words, correction may have a unique scholarly value that emerges from the conditions of open, international, online publishing.

Other systems of correction are more decentralized, distributed across a broad user base of experts and amateurs alike. The classic example is, of course, Wikipedia, whose dynamic textuality and versioning invite a different understanding of correction as curation.[11] Theoretically, no centralized authority dictates the standards of bibliographic control, which are instead continually negotiated by a community of users along with standards of accuracy, coverage, consistency, and so on.[12] The 2007 ITHAKA report suggests an analogous future for university publishing in which "continuous publishing ([or] 'dynamic content') will enable scholars to continually update or correct 'published' works" (Brown et al., 14). Such distributed and dynamic correction might not even have to take self-conscious or scholarly forms. It can also be outsourced, as with the example of reCAPTCHA, wherein users recommend accurate transcriptions of ambiguous snippets of texts that their sources—the *New York Times* and Google Books—cannot effectively deal with ("What Is reCAPTCHA?"). The corrector function of reCAPTCHA is practically clandestine, integrated into unrelated user processes (such as log-in events). In this case, bibliographic control only depends on any particular user's assessment of what standard characters a string of OCRed text might index. These projects run on the web's "cognitive surplus," in Clay Shirky's phrase. But depending on that surplus to stimulate the editing of academic work might presume a larger crowd than can reasonably be sourced.

Responding to this challenge, other distributed systems encourage users to participate in editing source texts through social media and gaming elements. For example, the National Library of Finland's "Digitalkoot" or "Digital Volunteers" project enlists users to recommend transcriptions for otherwise ambiguous OCRed text from the library's newspaper archive ("Digitalkoot"). Once registered on the site, users can choose to play several typing games in the style of lightweight anytime games like the hugely popular mobile app *Angry Birds*. Some projects balance the expected interest of users in the source material with other kinds of incentives. In the Transcribe Bentham project, users join a community to transcribe images of manuscripts that are then reviewed by editors and will be aggregated into *The Collected Works of Jeremy Bentham* in print. The "Benthamometer" registers the project's progress as a whole while individual users accumulate "points" in competition with one another. The online Bite-Size Edits Project, spawned by the blog *Book Oven*, also uses a points scheme to entice its users to recommend improvements to snippets of creative writing. Users can cash in their accumulated points for selected books. *Dickens Journalism Online* is conducting a closed trial of distributed proofreading among academics, appealing to their interest in the material to generate a high-quality online resource. Project Gutenberg's distributed proofreaders project was based on a similar concept of engaged volunteerism (Hart).

Other models look past user interactions to experiment with automating the labor of correction. In reviewing current approaches to digital preservation, Fitzpatrick considers the LOCKSS model (Lots of Copies Keeps Stuff Safe) pioneered by Stanford University Libraries. In this model, digital materials from participating libraries in various forms, editions, versions, and formats are aggregated across "an open source, peer-to-peer, decentralized digital preservation infrastructure" ("What is the LOCKSS program?"). Fitzpatrick explains that, "as the project's name suggests, the redundancy of its distributed files creates a safety net for the material" (*Planned Obsolescence,* 40). But while LOCKSS is a distributed system, it also exerts its own central bibliographic control: a LOCKSS Box crawls for content, which it then compares to similar content on the network of other libraries' LOCKSS boxes, automatically repairing differences or damage. These automatic corrections result from peer-to-peer "opinion polls"—an automated relational system that synchronizes content based on the predominance of certain copies (Maniatis et al.). The LOCKSS system preserves the integrity of content on the level of bits and bytes and also automatically migrates content formats to stave off obsolescence. While LOCKSS primarily deals with things already published, the CLOCKSS (Controlled LOCKSS) initiative archives "*all* journal content to which publishers allow access, both presentation files and source files" (*Planned Obsolescence,* 40). CLOCKSS adds to the complex relations of postpublished versions of files some of the various states of their evolution. In each case, as Fitzpatrick suggests, "the network is self-correcting" (*Planned Obsolescence,* 40).

Correction is not the only strategy to deal with error: search and recommendation engines like Google and Reference Extract are practicing error avoidance. In other words, these engines source the opinions and usage events of a community to derive some measure of credibility in returning and ranking results. These kinds of systems have already been compared to automated peer review (O'Malley, "Googling"), though they are more complex in accumulating data about the entire network. They do not just build in recommendations but map the patterns of what data are accessed by whom and why. That information can supply normalizing functions like automatic search suggestions, spelling correction, and citation indexing that restore a measure of correction to the work of peer review.

These examples are not meant to exhaust the current or potential approaches to correction in digital publishing or even to "error" in code, rich media, or metadata. Instead, they map a spectrum of attention to correction: from reinventing the traditional labor of academic publishing in digital environments, to distributing that labor openly and widely, to delegating it to automated agents, to dismissing its relative importance within the grander scheme of what open, digital publishing can achieve. None of these positions predominates; indeed, that might suggest an unlikely consensus that correction doesn't amount to a "stop press" problem but can be resolved according to various needs. I will argue otherwise, not to claim that copyedited textual integrity is an independent scholarly value to be preserved at all costs in whatever media we operate, but rather to suggest how errata manifests and proliferates in its newer media and production contexts. Because the enterprise of digital publishing is remediating scholarly methods as well as resources, the evolving functions of correction have an important role in promoting the textual productivity and network effects of our published work.

The Function of Error

The web remains a textual medium. Its abundant multimodal data are inscribed by a simple character set with which we are typographically and numerically fluent—as are the protocols, ontologies, and schemata by which the web is constituted. The relational integrity of such data on and within the web is key, and facilitating the relation and interchange of data has been among the primary goals of the "semantic web." The challenges are formidable, including (in the definition of the P2P Foundation) "resolving or mediating potential heterogeneities" from the proliferating and "discrete categories of potential mismatches." Even beyond the problem of "semantic mediation" or resolving "what does the data mean (its semantics)," Mike Bergman suggests that we still face "crucial challenges in . . . reasoning over that data (inference and pragmatics), and whether the data is authoritative or can be trusted. These are the daunting—and largely remaining challenges—of the Semantic Web." At the risk of oversimplifying the technical specificities and complexities of this undertaking, I would suggest that these goals can be usefully related to the corrector function: resolving mismatches, clarifying semantic relations, and authorizing trust in a textual media and its relational economy of ideas. If that analogy holds, then correction has a future that is vital to the evolution of the web.

Almost everyone concerned with digital publishing acknowledges that it must mean more than finding an electronic equivalence with print. The future of scholarly publishing gets right to the heart of the semantic web. In a talk titled "The Glass Box and the Commonplace Book," Steven Johnson outlined what he considers two paths for the future of text: text in "glass boxes" (closed, nonreactive forms for looking at) and text in "commonplace books" (open, dynamic forms for interacting with). We can easily relate these metaphors to scholarly publishing, though Johnson is more broadly interested in the systemic intelligence of the web itself. He proposes a notion of "textual productivity" for how the web semantically processes and networks texts through its cascading algorithms, completely beyond the scope of any given writer or designer. Publishing in open forms facilitates these effects. Johnson argues that, "by creating fluid networks of words, by creating those digital-age commonplaces, we increase the textual productivity of the system. . . . [This] may be the single most important fact about the Web's growth over the past fifteen years."

For many scholars, this argument only underscores why scholarly publishing should open itself to the serendipitous productivity of the semantic web. But the relative inattention to correction in new publishing models may impede the very textual productivity by which the semantic web works. Because networked scholarly communication will increasingly operate through structured metadata and automated relational processes, it is imperative to consider the particular hindrances of errors within this scheme. In this sense, correction works more as "semantic debugging" for the scholarly network. Because new models of scholarly publishing are making fewer affordances for correctors, we ought to imagine the outlooks for a historical function upon which the technical promises of the future may significantly depend.

Consider again the entirely commonplace errors of misquoting or incorrectly citing sources in a research article.[13] In my copyedited manuscript, I was stunned that someone tracked through databases and far-flung print sources to confirm the referential integrity of my text, the accuracy of quoted materials. Had that not happened, those errors have the potential to proliferate through a "textual productivity" all their own.[14] Perhaps open review would have caught them, but I doubt it. Perhaps they would be discovered and altered through usage in a "continuous" or "dynamic" publishing model, but there is low traffic on the long tail of academic inquiry.[15] Furthermore, many research sources (especially those containing historical objects) are themselves relatively untrafficked or only available offline. It could be argued that these citations could be compared to electronic surrogates of their sources or similar citations or quotes published elsewhere, generating a "correct" version through redundancy—the principle underwriting LOCKSS as well as search engine page ranking. Of course, the power of redundancy works both ways, as errors or contested representations can themselves proliferate enough to take the spotlight.[16]

It may become increasingly important for citations to be proofread rigorously. In the sciences at least, open publication is earning practitioners and institutional capital through an architecture of recognition: "[t]he most important driver for this change is the availability of highly accurate bibliographic and citation databases" (Hindawi, 100). Accuracy here is key, and it depends on relations that databases formalize, which in turn depend on cataloguing, description, and citational integrity, which themselves depend on the contingencies of input. Citations are prone to error as well as to intentional manipulation. For example, Jöran Beel and Bela Gipp have researched how academic content can be optimized for search engines as well as how it can exploit their relational architecture. In the first case, they emphasize the importance of good metadata and consistency in citations, names, special characters, and so on, which can otherwise hurt rankings (Beel, Gipp, and Eilde, 184). In the second, they used a "fake book," "fake articles," "fake authors," and "nonsensical text" to successfully manipulate the information and rankings in online directories (Beel and Gipp). The automated network of citations, whether generated by academic-themed search engines, portals, and archives or else constituted by the associative functions of the open web at large, will significantly be shaped by the proliferation of data in accurate or perverse forms.

The interoperability of conventional citation styles (e.g., MLA, APA, Chicago, etc.) presents another challenge, as the included data can vary between them. Among the potential solutions is to describe the data capaciously enough to encompass the differences of styles and unique usages or to assign universal references to cited documents. But the universality of online referencing has problems all its own considering the tenuousness of electronic linkage. As Fitzpatrick argues, "[o]ur digital publications thus must employ a system of bibliographic identification that allows object identifiers to resolve dynamically into the correct URL as materials move" (*Planned Obsolescence,* 38). She notes the increasing popularity of the Handle System and digital object identifiers (DOI), which can be integrated with "resolvers" to access local pathways and resources for users in any variety of circumstances. Universal identifiers and automated resolution are the twin arms in a new system of bibliographic control. Errors or contingencies can be accommodated on the fly.

We are seeing "self-correcting networks" that improve as their data expand, including distributed or automated textual correction, networks of citation and resource access, and digital object storage systems like LOCKSS. But automation has issues. As even the casual user of word processing software knows, the auto-correct function should give us pause. Auto-correction is as liable to produce errors in "normalizing" data as it is in correcting them. This may particularly apply to cases, such as in some humanities research, where the objects or lexicons are often well outside the norm or the horizons of digital access. Of course, with the pace of digitization, that situation will change. It is possible to imagine artificial intelligence agents as the next generation of auto-complete software, able to deal with acute semantic puzzles and the remotest bits of brainy trivia. Automation would certainly answer some of the labor challenges of correction.[17] It is also possible to imagine, instead of an agent, automated correction as an emergent property of the information commons as a whole.

Or it is possible to imagine that, once displaced into automated environments, we will simply stop caring. Or so copyeditors worry. For Adam Deville, a professor and editor of an academic journal himself, the decreasing interest in and practice of correction amounts to nothing less than an "epistemological crisis" (170). Hunter worries about "the possibility of a total breakdown in scholarly communication" (7). These anxieties can be forgiven of a professional community that has seen its fortunes decline. Such academic apocalypse is unlikely: there will be minor breakdowns along the new routes of networked scholarly communication, and from these we are learning how to renegotiate the editorial and corrector functions for the digital future. In doing so, we need to consider not merely the problems of error but the editorial theory that the digital futures of publishing articulate or come to embody whether by intention, emergence, or neglect.

In *Radiant Textuality*, Jerome McGann considers the implications of social text theory for cultural objects on the web. McGann argues that texts in any media are n-dimensional, but the web exposes textual radiance in strikingly evident and often unpredictable ways. The arc of McGann's thinking can be traced back to his intervention in *A Critique of Modern Textual Criticism*, wherein he challenged a prevailing theory of copytext and the practice of editorial idealism. They had combined to produce textual editions that synthesized various sources and relied upon editorial judgments of authorial intention or best possible variants. But because the web is unbound, online editions can manifest all the witnesses and variants available to digitization. The *Rossetti Archive* was designed to test exactly this, and its editorial procedures required multiple and redundant levels of proofreading by its employees.[18] The results are, in the language of the archive, "trusted objects"—wherein "trust" describes scholarly integrity for users as well as interoperability with the tools being concurrently developed by the Networked Infrastructure for Nineteenth-Century Electronic Scholarship (NINES), including collation, annotation, and exhibition software. The archive's bibliographic control is not antithetical to radiance but instead helps to expose its textual manifestations.

The trouble with dynamic curation, textual redundancy engines like LOCKSS, and any self-correcting network is that they threaten to resuscitate an editorial idealism on the web. Furthermore, the automation of correction can displace editorial judgments into the synthetic functions of server polling or algorithms whose logic may be increasingly difficult to extract or kept private by commercial entities. Instead of a network of radiant texts, these functions may produce a "copyweb" of idealized content. From another angle, the editorial forgiveness of errors for the sake of scholarship's "true quality" also risks the problematic interventions of twentieth-century bibliography. As Philip Gaskell declared, "[l]et us carry out the author's intentions whenever we can, but not to the extent of taking pride in reproducing the manifest inadequacies of his accidentals" (359). But for the web and its semantic, structured, relational futures, the accidentals are often essential.

Simultaneously radiant and self-idealizing, dynamically new and obsolete, the web challenges us to reset our editorial thresholds within its spectrum and to grapple with the economic, logistical, and theoretical consequences of doing so. As has been argued about digital preservation, so for digital publishing our biggest challenges are not primarily technical but social (Kirschenbaum, 21). And in whatever professional networks, collaborations, open fields, or institutional arrangements we engineer to address them, correction—or at least a better appreciation of its consequences—must have a place.

NOTES

1. This is an argument about scholarly labor and attention—not necessarily an argument against error, which has its own unique functions, as Johnson suggests. Kathryn Schultz argues in her recent book *Being Wrong: Adventures in the Margin of Error* that "wrongness is a vital part of how we learn and change" (5). According to Daniel Rourke, "errors, noise and mistake" might encode some of the more exciting possibilities of the web's technical and creative evolution.

2. Kathleen Fitzpatrick's *Planned Obsolescence* offers a terrific survey of these topics and the discussions they have generated.

3. Trettien offers a fascinating tour of "zombie editions" of Milton and their assorted errors. See Esposito for a related discussion of the errors in the public domain copy of *Pride and Prejudice* preloaded on Amazon's Kindle, driving from the original print source, digital scans, OCR, and metadata.

4. What counts as an error? Rather than precisely defining or categorizing them, this essay considers errors in a differential relation with the labor of correcting them, a relation that changes with historical and production contexts.

5. That is not unusual, according to long-time academic copyeditor Sylvia Hunter: "[c]opy (or manuscript) editors are rarely mentioned on journal mastheads; we seldom make our way into authors' acknowledgement footnotes; we toil in silence, invisible" (8).

6. One might imagine the great Victor Borges's routine on "Phonetic Pronunciation."

7. Some telling perspectives from the field: As Merill Perlman, former chief of copy desks at the *New York Times*, sarcastically complains, "Who needs copy editors? They just get in the way. Without them, blog postings can go up faster; without them, readers get a writer's words unfiltered; without them, a publication can save lots of money" (Thomas). Sylvia Hunter suggests "that some scholarly journal publishers in the United States were considering, or had already begun, phasing out the crucial stages between final manuscript submission and typesetting. In other words—neatly defeating all of our own well-reasoned arguments about the value added to research by scholarly publishers—slapping a nice cover on exactly the same text that the author has already posted on her Web site" (7). Adam Deville blames electronic writing and publishing for putting increasing pressure on the decreasing resources of copyediting. My own experience as an "editor" at a new media company came to a close in the early 2000s when nearly the entire editorial department was laid off; the management and the technical staff survived.

8. I take the following as representative: an American Council of Learned Societies report *Crises and Opportunities: The Futures of Scholarly Publishing*; "University Press

Forum: Variations on a Digital Theme," in the *Journal of Scholarly Publishing* 38, no. 4 (July 2007); the ITHAKA organization's report on "University Publishing in a Digital Age" (2007); a special issue of the *Journal of Electronic Publishing* on "Reimagining the University Press" (vol. 13, no. 2, Fall 2010); and the Association of American University Presses report on *Sustaining Scholarly Publishing: New Business Models for University Presses* (March 2011).

9. I put this to an unscientific test, carelessly selecting a humanities article on Philica.com ("The instant, open-access Journal of Everything") to work on. But instead of engaging in the "transparent peer-review" the website seeks from its users, I put on the old editorial assistant hat and turned up a handful of errors: typos in citations, capitalization errors, absent words, sentence fragments, and so on. I will risk not sharing the specifics, as it seems churlish to identify an author who really is not at fault: everyone makes these mistakes and struggles to catch their own.

10. In his article "Scholar as E-Publisher," Thomas H. P. Gould concurs that long-tail niche journals will still require editorial and technical staff that are separate from open peer review functions but does not identify correction (442).

11. See Fitzpatrick, *Planned Obsolescence* (31) for a fuller discussion of the concept.

12. *Wikipedia*'s own openness looks a little different in practice. As David Golumbia has pointed out, a small core of under two hundred *Wikipedia* editors now operate just like any other editors, maintaining the standards of bibliographic control across the site.

13. For a more expansive and colorful list of the kinds of errors academic copyeditors testify to continually finding, see Adam Deville (169) and Sylvia Hunter (8–9).

14. There is a counter argument that errors in print are even more insidious: "When some of these things sit around in the scientific literature for a long time, they can do damage: they can influence what people work on, they can influence whole fields," according to David Goldstein, the director of Duke University's Center for Human Genome Variation (Mandavilli).

15. A telling quote from a discussion of open review in the sciences: "'Most papers sit in a wasteland of silence, attracting no attention whatsoever,' says Phil Davis, a communications researcher at Cornell University in Ithaca, New York, and executive editor of The Scholarly Kitchen, a blog run by the Society for Scholarly Publishing in Wheat Ridge, Colorado" (Mandavilli).

16. "Google bombs" offer an interesting example ofthe intentional manipulation of collective agreement. Even with the best of intentions (or without intention at all), the "group think" of a specialized online community can amplify errors with cascading effects, as Sunstein has argued (75).

17. In a Twitter post on March 2, 2011, Tim Carmody (@tcarmody) asks, "Can we put Watson from Jeopardy to work correcting bad OCR? (I'm looking at you, Google Books.)"

18. Including a version of aural sing-song proofreading of transcription and markup done by assistants in pairs, which ironically (though unintentionally) adapts the proofing practices that were possibly undertaken for Rossetti's own books.

BIBLIOGRAPHY

Alonso, Carlos J., Cathy N. Davidson, John M. Unsworth, and Lynne Withey. *Crises and Opportunities: The Futures of Scholarly Publishing*. New York: American Council of Learned Societies, 2003.

Association of American University Presses. *Sustaining Scholarly Publishing: New Business Models for University Presses*. New York: Association of American University Presses, 2011. http://mediacommons.futureofthebook.org/mcpress/sustaining/.

Bartlett, Rebecca A., Richard Brown, Kathleen Keane, Bruce Wilcox, Niko Pfund, and Thomas Bacher. "University Press Forum: Variations on a Digital Theme." *Journal of Scholarly Publishing* 38, no. 4 (July 2007): 211–28. http://muse.jhu.edu/journals/scp/summary/v038/38.4bartlett01.html.

Beel, Jöran, and Bela Gipp. "Academic Search Engine Spam and Google Scholar's Resilience Against it." *Journal of Electronic Publishing* 13, no. 3 (December 2010). Web http://hdl.handle.net/2027/spo.3336451.0013.305.

Beel, Jöran, Bela Gipp, and Erik Eilde. "Academic Search Engine Optimization (ASEO)." *Journal of Scholarly Publishing* 41, no. 2 (January 2010): 176–90. http://muse.jhu.edu/journals/journal_of_scholarly_publishing/v041/41.2.beel.html.

Benjamin, Walter. *Charles Baudelaire: A Lyric Poet in the Era of High Capitalism*. Translated by Harry Zohn. London; New York: Verso, 1973.

Bergman, Mike. "What Is the Structured Web?" *AI3*. July 18, 2007. http://www.mkbergman.com/390/what-is-the-structured-web/.

Brown, Laura, Rebecca Griffiths, and Matthew Rascoff. *University Publishing in a Digital Age*. New York: ITHAKA, 2007.

Cohen, Dan. "Open Access Publishing and Scholarly Values." *Dan Cohen's Digital Humanities Blog*. May 27, 2010. http://www.dancohen.org/2010/05/27/open-access-publishing-and-scholarly values/.

———. "Re: open review, digital publishing, and copyediting." E-mail to Paul Fyfe. March 9, 2011.

———. "The Social Contract of Scholarly Publishing." *Dan Cohen's Digital Humanities Blog*. March 5, 2010. http://www.dancohen.org/2010/03/05/the-social-contract-of-scholarly publishing/.

Coulter, Gerry. "Launching (and Sustaining) a Scholarly Journal on the Internet: *The International Journal of Baudrillard Studies*." *Journal of Electronic Publishing* 13, no. 1 (Winter 2010). http://hdl.handle.net/2027/spo.3336451.0013.104.

Deville, Adam. "Sinners Well Edited." *Journal of Scholarly Publishing* 39, no. 2 (January 2008): 168–73.

"Digitalkoot: Electrifying Our Cultural Heritage." Helsinki: National Library of Finland, 2011. http://www.digitalkoot.fi/.

Dougherty, Peter J. "Reimagining the University Press: A Checklist for Scholarly Publishers." *Journal of Electronic Publishing* 13, no. 2 (Fall 2010). http://hdl.handle.net/2027/spo.3336451.0013.202.

Esposito, Joseph. "The Terrible Price of Free: On E-reading Jane Austen via Google's Ebooks." *The Scholarly Kitchen.* March 14, 2011. http://scholarlykitchen.sspnet.org/2011/03/14/the-terrible-price-of-free-on-e-reading-jane-austen-via-googles-ebooks/.

""FAQ." Open Review: "Shakespeare and Performance." *Shakespeare Quarterly*. February 2011. http://mediacommons.futureofthebook.org/mcpress/shakespearequarterly performance/faq/.

Fitzpatrick, Kathleen. *Planned Obsolescence: Publishing, Technology, and the Future of the Academy*. Media Commons, 2002–present. http://mediacommons.futureofthebook .org/mcpress/plannedobsolescence/.

———. "Re: open review, digital publishing, and copyediting." E-mail to Paul Fyfe. February 16, 2011.

Gaskell, Philip. *A New Introduction to Bibliography*. New Castle, Del.: Oak Knoll, 1972.

Godin, Seth. "Who Will Say Go?" *Seth Godin's Blog*. March 1, 2011. http://sethgodin.type pad.com/seths_blog/2011/03/who-will-say-go.html.

Gould, Thomas H. P. "Scholar as E-Publisher." *Journal of Scholarly Publishing* 41, no. 4 (July2010):428–448.http://muse.jhu.edu/journals/journal_of_scholarly_publishing/v041/41.4.gould.html.

Harnad, Stevan. "The Invisible Hand of Peer Review." *Exploit Interactive* 5 (April 2000). http://www.exploit-lib.org/issue5/peer-review/.

Hart, Michael. "Gutenberg: The History and Philosophy of Project Gutenberg." *Project Gutenberg*. August 1992. http://www.gutenberg.org/wiki/Gutenberg:The_History _and_Philosophy_of_Project_Gutenberg_by_Michael_Hart.

Hindawi, Ahmed. "2020: A Publishing Odyssey." *Serials* 22, no. 2 (July 2009): 99–103. http://knol.google.com/k/2020-a-publishing-odyssey#.

Hunter, Sylvia. "Why Copy Editors Matter." *Journal of Scholarly Publishing* 36, no. 1 (October 2004): 6–14. http://muse.jhu.edu/journals/journal_of_scholarly_publishing/v036/36.1hunter.html.

Johnson, Steven Berlin. *The Ghost Map*. New York: Riverhead, 2006.

———. "The Glass Box and the Commonplace Book." stevenberlinjohnson.com. April 23, 2010. http://www.stevenberlinjohnson.com/2010/04/the-glass-box-and-the-common place-book.html.

Kimball, Shana. "Re: open review, digital publishing, and copyediting." E-mail to Paul Fyfe. February 20, 2011.

Kirschenbaum, Matthew G. *Mechanisms: New Media and the Forensic Imagination*. Cambridge, Mass.: MIT Press, 2008.

Lankes, R. David, ed. *Reference Extract*. Syracuse University, 2011. http://www.reference xtract.org/.

Mandavilli, Apoorva. "Peer Review: Trial by Twitter." *Nature* 469 (January 19, 2011): 286–87. http://www.nature.com/news/2011/110119/full/469286a.html.

Maniatis, Petros, et al. "Preserving Peer Replicas by Rate-Limited Sampled Voting." In *ACM SIGOPS Operating Systems Review,* 44–59. New York: ACM, 2003. http://cs.rochester .edu/meetings/sosp2003/papers/p140-maniatis.pdf.

McGann, Jerome J. *A Critique of Modern Textual Criticism.* 1983. Charlottesville; London: University Press of Virginia, 1992.

———. *Radiant Textuality: Literature After the World Wide Web.* New York: Palgrave, 2001.

McGuire, Hugh, Andy MacDonald, and Janina Szkut, eds. *Bite-Sized Edits.* Montreal, 2011. http://bookoven.com/projects/bitesizeedit/.

Nunberg, Geoffrey. "Counting on Google Books." *Chronicle of Higher Education.* December 16, 2010. http://chronicle.com/article/Counting-on-Google-Books/125735/.

———. "Google's Book Search: A Disaster for Scholars." *Chronicle of Higher Education.* August 31, 2009. http://chronicle.com/article/Googles-Book-Search-A/48245/.

O'Malley, Mike. "Academic Editor 2.0." *The Aporetic.* March 3, 2011. http://theaporetic.com/?p=1679.

———. "Googling Peer Review." *The Aporetic.* October 19, 2010. http://theaporetic.com/?p=446.

P2P Foundation. "Semantic Web." http://p2pfoundation.net/Semantic_Web.

Pochoda, Phil. "UP 2.0: Some Theses on the Future of Academic Publishing." *Journal of Electronic Publishing* 13, no. 1 (Winter 2010). http://hdl.handle.net/2027/spo.3336451.0013.102.

Rourke, Daniel. "Errors in Things and the 'Friendly Medium.'" Research Seminar Series in Open Media. Coventry School of Art and Design. February 15, 2011. http://machinemachine.net/text/ideas/errors-in-things-and-the-friendly medium.

Scheinfeldt, Tom. "Re: open review, digital publishing, and copyediting." E-mail to Paul Fyfe. March 8, 2011.

Schulz, Kathryn. *Being Wrong: Adventures in the Margin of Error.* New York: HarperCollins, 2010.

Shaw, John, and Michael Slater, eds. *Dickens Journalism Online (DJO).* University of Buckingham, 2006–present. http://www.buckingham.ac.uk/djo.

Shirky, Clay. *Here Comes Everybody: The Power of Organizing Without Organizations.* New York: Penguin, 2008.

Sunstein, Cass R. *Infotopia: How Many Minds Produce Knowledge.* New York: Oxford University Press, 2006.

Thomas, Ashley. "The Importance of Copy Editing, Copy Editors: Some Folks Just Don't Get It. Points to Ponder from Merrill Perlman." Temple University Editing Residency (blog). July 8, 2008. http://djnf08.wordpress.com/2008/07/08/the-importance-of-copy-editing-copy-editors-some-folks-just-dont-get-it-points-to-ponder-from-merrill-perlman/.

Transcribe Bentham. Bentham Project, University College of London. 2010–present. http://www.ucl.ac.uk/Bentham-Project/transcribe_bentham.

Trettien, Whitney. "Zombie Editions: An Archaeology of POD Areopagiticas." *diapsalmata.* December 15, 2010. http://blog.whitneyannetrettien.com/2010/12/zombie-editions-archaeology-of-pod.html.

Unsworth, John. "Documenting the Reinvention of Text: The Importance of Failure." *Journal of Electronic Publishing* 3, no. 2 (1997). http://hdl.handle.net/2027/spo.3336451.0003.201.

Werner, Sarah. "Re: open review, digital publishing, and copyediting." E-mail to Paul Fyfe. March 9, 2011.

"What Is the LOCKSS Program?" LOCKSS Program. Stanford University, 2004–present. http://lockss.stanford.edu/lockss/Home.

"What Is reCAPTCHA?" Google. Stanford, Calif., 2011. http://www.google.com/recaptcha/learnmore.

Willinsky, John, Kevin Stranack, Alec Smecher, and James MacGregor. "Open Journal Systems: A Complete Guide to Online Publishing." 2nd ed. Burnaby, B.C., Canada: Simon Fraser University Library, 2010. http://pkp.sfu.ca/ojs/docs/userguide/2.3.3/index.html.

The Function of Digital Humanities Centers at the Present Time

NEIL FRAISTAT

The emergence of the digital humanities as a coherent field was accompanied by and partially a result of the evolution of the Humanities Computing Center as an institution, as could be found in such exemplary early centers in the United States as Princeton and Rutgers' Center for Electronic Texts in the Humanities (1991), the University of Virginia's Institute of Advanced Technology in the Humanities (1993), and Brown University's Scholarly Technology Group (1994). They and other earlier centers at such places as Oxford and King's College London became important laboratories for the application of information technology to the humanities; powerful advocates for the significance of such work; crucial focal points for the theorization of the digital humanities as a field; local nodes of cyberinfrastructure; and influential models for the ever-increasing number of other digital humanities centers that have appeared on the scene, including the Maryland Institute for Technology and the Humanities (1999), the Stanford Humanities Lab (2000), and the University of Nebraska's Center for Digital Research in the Humanities (2005).

Through their own in-house research, digital humanities centers have produced important new digital resources and tools that benefit the humanities community as a whole. Equally important, digital humanities centers are key sites for bridging the daunting gap between new technology and humanities scholars, serving as the crosswalks between cyberinfrastructure and users, where scholars learn how to introduce into their research computational methods, encoding practices, and tools and where users of digital resources can be transformed into producers. Centers not only model the kind of collaborative and interdisciplinary work that will increasingly come to define humanities scholarship; they also enable graduate students and faculty to learn from each other while working on projects of common intellectual interest. The lectures, symposia, and workshops hosted by centers benefit those at other institutions without centers themselves but who are able to attend in person or virtually. Centers, in short, can be invaluable community resources.

But individual centers are also at risk of being silos, overly focused on their home institutions. They rarely collaborate with other centers, with whom they compete for funding and prestige, and when working in isolation they are unable to address the larger problems of the field. Especially on campuses where there is an existing "traditional" humanities center, digital humanities centers even run the risk of being silos on their own campuses if they don't work actively at collaboration. Tensions on campus can also exist when a center that aspires to be treated as a research unit is treated by administrators as a service unit instead, and the perceived divisions between "research" centers and "service" centers, in turn, create professional hierarchies that can inhibit the formation of potentially fruitful collaborations among centers. Centers also siphon off grant funding from schools unable to afford a digital humanities center of their own and thus can make it harder for scholars at such places to participate in the larger projects. Are they crucial to the future of the field, or deleterious to it? Or to point the question more finely, in what ways and under what circumstances might digital humanities centers be seen as more crucial to the field than deleterious? What exactly is the function of the digital humanities center at the present time?

The potential value of digital humanities centers to individual scholars and to the field as a whole is stated poignantly by Mark Sample in a blog entry "On the Death of the Digital Humanities Center." In elegiac tones, Sample mourns, at first, proleptically for centers that will have come and gone and for centers that never will be but then also for all those in the field who are laboring now without the support of a digital humanities center:

> Most of us working in the digital humanities will never have the opportunity to collaborate with a dedicated center or institute. We'll never have the chance to work with programmers who speak the language of the humanities as well as Perl, Python, or PHP. We'll never be able to turn to colleagues who routinely navigate grant applications and budget deadlines, who are paid to know about the latest digital tools and trends—but who'd know about them and share their knowledge even if they weren't paid a dime. We'll never have an institutional advocate on campus who can speak with a single voice to administrators, to students, to donors, to publishers, to communities about the value of the digital humanities.

While Sample is concerned in this post about how digital humanities can further itself as a field without being dependent on centers, he recognizes that centers provide significant benefits to those beyond a particular center's own campus, and he himself teaches at George Mason University, home to one of the most highly regarded digital humanities centers in the world.

As Sample also recognizes, "there is no single model for the digital humanities center. Some focus on pedagogy. Others on research. Some build things. Others host things. Some do it all." To these variants, we might add that some are primarily service units, some primarily research, some a mixture of both. Some centers focus explicitly on digital humanities; some engage the humanities but are organized around media studies, or code studies—disciplines that are increasingly converging with digital humanities. North American centers tend to arise from the bottom up, European and Asian centers from the top down. North American centers tend to focus exclusively on humanities and, sometimes, the interpretive social sciences. European and Asian centers are more likely to be dispersed through the disciplines, or to be organized as virtual rather than physically located centers. Such generalities, however, only get us so far.

At a 2009 meeting between directors of traditional humanities centers and directors of digital humanities centers that was sponsored by the Scholarly Communications Institute, the first question asked of the digital humanities center directors by our counterparts at humanities centers was, "What do you actually *do* at digital humanities centers? Literally, what goes on during a typical day?" We were a bit taken aback by this question, but a few of us responded with enough concrete particulars to achieve a grounded understanding between both groups. Similarly, I want first to provide a specific sense of the things a representative digital humanities center actually does before I address the general function of the digital humanities center as an institution. To that end, let's take a brief tour of the center that I direct, the Maryland Institute for Technology in the Humanities, or, as it is more commonly known, MITH. Of course, our tour will have to be simulated through words, much like such early text adventure games as *ADVENTURE* and *Zork*, which have become important objects of study at MITH.

MITH: The Center as Digital Humanities Adventure

Walk with me, then, through the front door of MITH. We'll turn right and walk past the office of Dave Lester, MITH's assistant director, who is in a meeting with our software architect Jim Smith, our R&D developer Travis Brown, and our project coordinator Seth Denbo. The group is discussing the design of Project Bamboo's Corpora Space,[1] through which humanities scholars will be able to use sophisticated digital tools across the boundaries of large, distributed content collections. This Mellon-funded project, in which MITH is working with a team of scholars and technologists at ten partner universities—including Oxford, Australian National University, Berkeley, Northwestern, Wisconsin, and Tufts—illustrates how centers provide the means for local campus research capacity to be networked internationally and to produce cyberinfrastructure for the common good.

Continuing our walk to the far end of MITH, we arrive at a small kitchenette where we can grab a cup of coffee and chat with Grant Dickie who works in a nearby cubicle. Grant developed the interface and technical infrastructure for the *Shakespeare Quartos Archive*,[2] an electronic environment for the scholarly study of all known pre-1641 quartos of Shakespeare's plays, living artifacts that tell the story of how such plays as *Hamlet*, *King Lear*, and *Midsummer Night's Dream* first circulated in print. This project was funded by the National Endowment for the Humanities (NEH) and Joint Information Systems Committee (JISC), and our project partners were the British Library, the Bodleian Library, and the Folger Shakespeare Library. As we approach Grant, we can see that he is intently working on TILE, the Text-Image Linking Environment, a new web-based, modular, collaborative image markup tool for both manual and semiautomated linking of encoded text and image of text to image annotation.[3] Funded by the NEH, TILE will be released to the digital humanities community as a set of componentized services and is a concrete example of how tools produced at digital humanities centers benefit the larger community, like such well known tools as Zotero and Omeka, which were produced by George Mason's Rosenzweig Center for History and New Media.

Taking our cups of coffee with us, we head back into the center aisle of MITH, where ten paces to our right we see a Microsoft Surface at which Alex Quinn, a MITH graduate research assistant from Computer Science and the Human Computer Interaction Lab, is working to develop interfaces to enhance museum visitors' interaction with two prize objects in the Smithsonian's Sackler and Freer Gallery of Art: a thirty-foot-long fourteenth-century Chinese scroll and a sixteenth-century Turkish manuscript, the creation of which was the subject of Nobel Laureate Orhan Pamuk's novel *My Name is Red*. The first in MITH's new research initiative on emerging interfaces for museums and libraries, this project has been funded internally by seed grants from the University of Maryland's vice president for research and dean of the libraries and is an example of how digital humanities centers are increasingly engaging in a form of "public humanities" that benefits the general public through work done with institutions of cultural memory and performing arts.

As we proceed toward MITH's seminar room at the far end of the main aisle, we pass the workstation of Frank Hildy, a current MITH faculty fellow from the Theatre Department, who is developing with us the *Theatre Finder*, a collaboratively edited, peer-reviewed, online database of historic theatre architecture from the Minoan "theatrical areas" on the island of Crete to the last theatre built before 1815. Frank is among some thirty faculty and graduate student fellows whose work has been supported by MITH over the years in projects that have ranged from well before 1776 in the *Early Americas Digital Archive* to *Soweto '76*, which explores the ways that multimedia digital archives can help foster a social justice–based agenda for marginalized communities, particularly in South Africa. When MITH faculty fellow Angel David Nieves, the project director of *Soweto '76*, moved from the University of Maryland to Hamilton College, he initiated a very successful digital humanities initiative there,[4] an example of how existing centers can, as it were, cross-pollinate the field.

Moving about five feet farther down the central aisle from Frank Hildy, we find Rachel Donahue, a MITH graduate research assistant from the University of Maryland's iSchool, who is preparing for the weekly meeting of MITH's Preserving

Virtual Worlds Group, led by Matt Kirschenbaum, one of our associate directors, and by Kari Kraus, a faculty member in the iSchool and English Department. Our group has worked with researchers at Stanford, the University of Illinois, and the Rochester Institute of Technology on a grant from the Library of Congress to help improve the capacity of libraries, museums, and archives to preserve computer games, virtual worlds, and interactive fiction. The project team, which has already published a two-hundred-page report on preservation strategies, was short-listed for the prestigious Digital Preservation Coalition Prize and has recently received a large grant from the Institute of Museum and Library Services (IMLS) to continue their work (Kirschenbaum et al.).

After walking another five feet farther down the central aisle, we stand in front of three doors. To our right is Matt's office. To our left is the office of MITH's business manager, Chris Grogan, who has been completing the paperwork for the second phase of *OAC*, or the *Open Annotation Collaboration*,[5] whose purpose is to create an interoperable web annotation environment that enables the sharing of annotations across the boundaries of annotation clients, annotation servers, and content collections. The founding partners of this Mellon-funded project include the University of Illinois and George Mason's Rosenzweig Center for History and New Media.

Directly in front of us, at the end of our tour, is MITH's seminar room, which houses the Deena Larsen Collection,[6] a rich archive of early-era personal computers and software for researchers from within or beyond the campus interested in early hypertext and electronic literature and for MITH's own in-house research in digital curation and preservation. In the seminar room, we also teach classes, hold meetings and consultations, and host on Tuesday afternoons Digital Dialogues, a talk or presentation featuring either an invited guest to the campus or a member of our local research community. Since 2005, MITH has hosted over eighty of these Digital Dialogues, featuring many of the most prominent names in the field and attended by people throughout the greater Washington, D.C., area. For those who can't attend in person, we release each Digital Dialogue as a podcast.

Retracing our steps, toward the door, we pass my office, in front of which I bid you farewell in order to join the faculty members from our dance, kinesiology, and computer science departments who are working with MITH on a project for the digital documentation and preservation of dance, in partnership with the Kennedy Center, the New York Public Library, Lincoln Center, and the Advanced Computing Center for the Arts and Design at Ohio State University.

This tableaux did not take shape overnight. MITH was made possible twelve years ago by a major Challenge Grant from NEH under the joint auspices of the University of Maryland's College of Arts and Humanities, Libraries, and Office of Information Technology. It began with a director and two graduate research assistants and over the years has grown to ten faculty and full-time personnel as well as about a dozen full- or part-time staff members supported through grant funding, graduate assistantships, federal work study, and internships—by most measures a relatively large digital humanities center.

Complementing MITH's research and intellectual mission is a host of conferences, public programs, workshops, and events, most of which are free and open to the community. In the past year alone, MITH has hosted workshops on computer forensics for born-digital materials, advanced Text Encoding Initiative (TEI) manuscript encoding, alternative digital humanities academic careers, and the building of Application Programming Interfaces (APIs). MITH is also developing certificate programs and degrees in digital humanities. In partnership with the Computer Science Department and the iSchool, it has recently initiated Digital Cultures and Creativity, an innovative curriculum and learning community for first- and second-year students that combines art, imagination, and global citizenship with new media and new technologies. We conceive of MITH as an applied think tank, a place where theory and practice meet on a daily and a broadly interdisciplinary basis. Located in McKeldin Library at the heart of the campus, MITH serves as a campus-wide hub and regional destination for those interested in the digital humanities and new media.

This extended sketch of MITH is meant to convey as concretely as possible the diverse kinds of research and the complex blend of faculty, staff, students, disciplines, partnerships, audiences, and funding streams that revolve around a major digital humanities center. As MITH helps to illustrate, digital humanities centers have a great capacity for focusing, maximizing, and networking local knowledge, local resources, and local communities of practice for benefits that extend far beyond the immediate campus community. There is a limit to what any one center can accomplish on its own, however, which is why MITH helped to launch centerNet, an international network of digital humanities centers.[7]

The Local Center and the Global Network

In the preface to *A Survey of Digital Humanities Centers in the United States*, a report published by the Council of Library and Information Resources, Amy Friedlander appreciates that many digital humanities centers have "incubated important research, fostered a generation of humanities scholars who are comfortable with the technology, devised creative modes of governance, assembled diverse portfolios of funding strategies, and built significant digital collections and suites of tools" (Zorich, vi–vii). But she warns that since most centers are "focused on their home institutions, they are at risk of becoming silos" and that such "institutional parochialism can inhibit the building of shared resources, like repositories, or of services, like long-term preservation, that represent a shared infrastructure where the impact of the shared resource is enhanced precisely because multiple parties contribute to and use it"(vii). In the main body of the report, Diane Zorich similarly claims that "the independent nature of existing centers does not effectively leverage resources community-wide; . . . large-scale, coordinated efforts to address the 'big' issues in building humanities cyberinfrastructure . . . are missing from the current landscape. Collaborations among existing centers are small and focus on individual partner interests that do not scale up to address community wide needs" (4–5).

The pull of local campus pressures can indeed work against external collaboration, and the consequent insularity of many centers leaves them ignorant about the work actively being done by the others. The competition among centers for prestige and relatively scarce funding resources exacerbates this problem, as does the difficulty of working across national boundaries, cultural divides, and language communities. These centripetal forces are powerful; and, to the extent that they are not overcome, they drastically limit the significance of the work done by individual centers.

It was precisely to address these pressing issues, to network the local with the global, and to establish individual digital humanities centers as key nodes of international cyberinfrastructure that centerNet was born at an American summit meeting of digital humanities centers and funders in April 2007 cohosted by the NEH and MITH. The American term "cyberinfrastructure," much like the European term "e-science," can be defined as the linking together of computing systems, data storage systems, tools and data repositories, visualization and virtual research environments, people, and communities of practice by software, shared standards, and high performance networks in order "to improve research productivity and enable breakthroughs not otherwise possible" (Stewart). The importance of digital humanities centers "as crucial seedbeds of innovation" and key nodes of American cyberinfrastructure was stressed in *Our Cultural Commonwealth,* a report on cyberinfrastructure for the humanities and social sciences, commissioned by the American Council of Learned Societies and released in 2006, which served as the immediate catalyst of the summit meeting.

Currently consisting of some 250 members from over 140 digital humanities centers in twenty countries, centerNet has four regional steering committees: in Asia Pacific, Europe, North America, and the UK and Ireland. Its initiatives include the following:

- Promoting regional meetings, workshops, and conferences for the purposes of intellectual exchange, solidifying community, and the professional development of staff and graduate students
- Connecting centers around the world along the lines of their methodological affinities for sharing expertise and collaborative project development
- Nurturing a new generation of hybrid scholars, working in staff positions that combine service and research components
- Developing collaboratively new curricular models
- Legitimating the field and the value of digital humanities centers, especially in countries where digital humanities is only just emerging

- Developing mechanisms for assessing digital humanities centers and peer review among centers
- Advocating on behalf of the field, both within and outside the academy
- Working with funders to shape new opportunities that foster international collaborations and lobbying on behalf of our funders
- Working with other large cyberinfrastructure projects such as DARIAH and CLARIN
- Establishing formal affiliations with like-minded organizations, including those already established with the Consortium of Humanities Centers and Institutes (CHCI),[8] CHAIN, the Digital Library Federation, and 4Humanities

The Center as Agent of Transformation

Underlying centerNet's various initiatives is a strategic vision of the place of the digital humanities center in the institutional history of the academy. Over a hundred years ago, the current disciplinary structure of the humanities assumed its present shape, and though the world has changed much since then humanities disciplines have not.[9] New programs in such areas as gender studies, race studies, and cultural studies, among others, have often been relegated to the province of the humanities centers that started to appear in significant numbers in the second half of the twentieth century, precisely in order to accommodate what the traditional humanities departments could not in the form of interdisciplinary or cross-disciplinary studies.

More recently, digital humanities centers have sprung up to accommodate the challenges to the traditional humanities posed by new media and technologies and the particular forms of knowledge and cross-disciplinarity they entail.[10] Humanities centers of both kinds have thus been historically positioned to dream the future of the university, so to speak, to take the lead in scholarly innovation and disciplinary transformation. Their ultimate function at the present time is not just to help set the agenda for the new humanities to come but to work in practical ways to help bring this transformation about. Crucial to realizing this goal is centerNet's five-year formal affiliation with the CHCI, through which both organizations have agreed to work together to build scholarly and technical capacity in the field of digital humanities by way of shared grant projects, shared training, and shared events, beginning with a joint conference at the University of Toronto in June 2011.

The digital humanities center as an institution can enable such large transformations to start close to home. As Amy Friedlander notes,

> In an environment where scholars identify with their disciplines rather than with their departments, and where significant professional affiliations or communities of interest may transcend the boundaries of scholars' colleges and universities, centers offer interdisciplinary "third places"—a term sociologist Ray Oldenburg has used to identify a social space, distinct from home and workplace. Third

> places foster important ties and are critical to community life. Familiar examples are barbershops, beauty salons, and coffee shops where, in the age of wireless, we see tables of students hunched over laptops, textbooks, and notepads. (Zorich, vi)

For Friedlander, within the kind of "third place" typified by digital humanities centers, "technology is simultaneously a driver and an opportunity, and the centers, whether virtual or physical, effectively become safe places, hospitable to innovation and experimentation, as well as anchors from which to base the intellectual analog of civil society in which third places are vital parts" (Zorich, vi). Such "safe places" are crucial not only because all the cyberinfrastructure in the world won't amount to much if scholars within the humanities disciplines aren't using it but also because they mitigate the risks posed by the kind of interdisciplinary teamwork that *A Digital Humanities Manifesto* correctly identifies as the "new model for the production and reproduction of humanistic knowledge" (para. 10).

The ultimate function of the digital humanities center at the present time, then, is to be an agent of change. As Steve Ramsay has observed in his blog posting "Centers of Attention," "We like to marvel at the technological wonders that proceed from things like servers, but in this case—I would say, in all cases—the miracle of 'computers in the humanities' is the way it forced even a highly balkanized academy into new kinds of social formations. Anyone involved with any of these big centers will tell you that they are rare sites of genuine collaboration and intellectual synergy—that they explode disciplinary boundaries and even the cherished hierarchies of academic rank." Ramsay also notes that the capacity of individual centers to produce such transformations is dependent on the degree to which its university administrators treat them as research units, valuing them "not because of the services they provide, but because of the culture they represent—a culture that has always been about the two things we value most: the advancement of knowledge and the education of students." Even the longstanding division in which a humanities faculty position is primarily equated with research while a staff position is equated with service is being altered in digital humanities centers, which are increasingly being staffed by a new kind of hybrid scholar with advanced degrees in the humanities and their own research agendas.[11]

A Digital Humanities Manifesto is right to claim that "Interdisciplinarity/transdisciplinarity/multidisciplinarity are empty words unless they imply changes in language, practice, method, and output" (para. 5). These kinds of changes are social, cultural, and even economic as much as they are technological. But they are also profoundly international in their effect and potential effectiveness and might therefore be called the "cosmopolitics" of the digital humanities, to adapt Kant's term for the "universal community" that cuts across all national borders. To the extent that digital humanities centers can work together despite the formidable forces that keep them apart, they can engage at this cosmopolitical level. If the function of digital humanities centers at the present time is indeed disciplinary innovation and transformation, work together they must.

So much for the function of digital humanities centers at the present time; what about the future? If digital humanities centers are successful in fomenting such change, would they still be necessary? Are they a "transitional model," helping to produce their own obsolescence? As more and more humanities centers incorporate and welcome the digital, will there still be a need for stand-alone digital humanities centers? Would this even be an undesirable scenario? Many of these same questions are now being asked about the digital humanities itself as a field. The jury, as they say, is still out. In a collection of essays about debates in the digital humanities, the ultimate sustainability of digital humanities centers is one debate yet to be had. But I suspect that the humanities will in one way or another always need an institutional space for technical innovation, that disciplinary transformations beget and require still other kinds of change, and that to the extent digital humanities centers are willing, able, and necessary to fulfill this need, they will be around long into the future.

NOTES

1. Project Bamboo. http://www.projectbamboo.org.
2. The Shakespeare Quartos Archive. http://mith.umd.edu/research/?project=58.
3. The Text-Image Linking Environment (TILE). http://mith.umd.edu/tile.
4. Digital Humanities Initiative, Hamilton College. http://www.dhinitiative.org/about/mission.php.
5. Open Annotation Collaboration. http://www.openannotation.org.
6. The Deena Larsen Collection. http://mith.umd.edu/larsen/dlcs.
7. centerNet. http://digitalhumanities.org/centernet.
8. Consortium of Humanities Centers and Institutes (CHCI). http://chcinetwork.org.
9. For a detailed history and critique of humanities disciplines that informs my own discussion here, see Chandler and Davidson, *Fate of Disciplines*, esp. Chandler's introduction, 729–46.
10. For an early attempt to provide a taxonomy of centers, see McCarty and Kirschenbaum, "Institutional Models." The centerNet website provides the most up-to-date list of current centers, along with descriptions of them.
11. For a detailed discussion and analysis of this phenomenon, see Clement and Reside and the following essay in this volume by Julia Flanders.

BIBLIOGRAPHY

American Council of Learned Societies, Commission on Cyberinfrastructure for the Humanities and Social Sciences. *Our Cultural Commonwealth.* New York: ACLS, 2006.

Bauer, Ralph. *Early Americas Digital Archive.* http://www.mith2.umd.edu/eada.

Chandler, James, and Arnold I. Davidson. *The Fate of the Disciplines.* Special Issue, *Critical Inquiry* 35, no. 4 (2009).

Clement, Tanya, and Doug Reside. "Off the Tracks: Laying New Lines for Digital Humanities Scholars." NEH White Paper. Forthcoming, 2011. http://mith.umd.edu/offthetracks/.

A Digital Humanities Manifesto. http://manifesto.humanities.ucla.edu/2008/12/15/digital-humanities-manifesto.

Friedlander, Amy. Preface to *A Survey of Digital Humanities Centers in the United States.* Report published by the Council of Library and Information Resources.

Kirschenbaum, Matthew, Richard Ovendon, and Gabriela Redwine. *Digital Forensics and Born-Digital Content in Cultural Heritage Collections.* Washington, D.C.: Council of Library and Information Resources, 2010.

McCarty, Willard, and Matthew G. Kirschenbaum. "Institutional Models for Humanities Computing." *Literary and Linguistic Computing* 18, no. 3 (2003): 465–89.

Nieves, Angel David. *Soweto '76, A Living Digital Archive.* http://www.soweto76archive.org.

Ramsay, Stephen. "Centers of Attention." *Stephen Ramsay.* April 27, 2010. http://lenz.unl.edu/papers/2010/04/27/centers-of-attention.html.

Sample, Mark. "On the Death of the Digital Humanities Center." *Sample Reality.* March 26, 2010. http://www.samplereality.com/2010/03/26/on-the-death-of-the-digital-humanities-center/.

Stewart, Craig. *Indiana University Cyberinfrastructure Newsletter.* March 2007. http://pti.iu.edu/ci/iu-cyberinfrastructure-news-march-2007.

Zorich, Diane. *A Survey of Digital Humanities Centers in the United States.* Washington, D.C.: Council of Library and Information Resources, 2008.

Time, Labor, and "Alternate Careers" in Digital Humanities Knowledge Work

JULIA FLANDERS

The quick transition of "#alt-ac" from Twitter hashtag to term of art has been an index of its evident utility: as a rubric for discussing a topic that has long been in need of a name, a terminology, and an agenda. The alternativeness of careers in digital humanities has in fact been a subject of long debate and much concern; many early researchers in what was then termed "humanities computing" were located in liminal and academically precarious institutional spaces such as newly created instructional technology support units and grant-funded research groups. Much energy was devoted—then as now—to discussion of how and whether this domain could become a discipline, with its own faculty positions and academic legitimation. And although those faculty positions and degree programs are starting to appear, many jobs in what is now called "digital humanities" are still para-academic, though their funding and institutional position has been consolidated somewhat. What has received less discussion, interestingly, is the word "career" itself. Its origins in horse racing ("the ground on which a race is run, a racecourse . . . a short gallop at full speed"[1]) are long past but not irrelevant: the word articulates a sense both of boundaries for a specific type of effort and of the intensity and directedness of the effort itself. In professional terms, a career has both direction and impetus; it is inescapably competitive.

The phrase "alternate careers" is thus remarkable at second glance not for suggesting that there are alternatives but for the centrality it still accords to those academic careers that are not alternate. This centrality is not just an effect of graduate study and not only perceptible within the academy; it shapes the way universities are understood as workplaces even by those who stand outside them. So, for instance, when I mentioned to the person who was fixing my truck that I worked at Brown University, without giving further detail, he assumed that I was a professor there. (If he was being deliberately flattering, the point is surely the same.) As a guess, this was not only wrong but a poor play of the odds: faculty positions make up only about 30 percent of all full-time employees at Brown, whereas 45 percent are some other kind of professional: technical, administrative, legal, executive, and managerial. Thus on the basis of pure statistics (and even allowing for my apparent level of education and socioeconomic positioning), I am much more likely to be anything but a faculty member. The professoriate, though, provides the characteristic paradigm through which we understand the nature and function of the university: an institution composed of professional faculty whose job is to teach students and to perform research.

This idealized view stands in for the real complexity of the university as an institutional ecology of work—in which every hour of faculty work is brought into being by hundreds of hours of time spent maintaining the physical and administrative space within which that work is conducted: libraries, network, payroll, buildings, and all the rest of it. But it also stands in for, and obscures, the real complexity of even the "purely academic work" that goes on within the university. The sketchy wireframe figure of the professor suggests a division of labor and a level of intellectual independence that, in the emerging age of digital scholarship, is increasingly obsolete. It also suggests a strongly defined intellectual and professional career trajectory that, as Alan Liu astutely observes in *The Laws of Cool,* may no longer be characteristic of modern knowledge work: "to be a professional-managerial-technical worker now is to stake one's authority on an even more precarious knowledge that has to be re-earned with every new technological change."[2]

To fill in these complexities is to gain a clearer understanding of how other kinds of academic jobs stand in relation to that of the tenured faculty and also to see how those relationships have been structured in the academic imaginary. These "alternative" or "para-academic" jobs within the academy have a great deal to teach us about how academic labor is quantified, about different models of work and work product, and about the ways that aptitude, skill, expertise, and productivity are weighed in assessing different kinds of work.

Situating the discussion within the domain of digital humanities puts these issues into more specific focus. It brings into view a wider range of work practices and roles: the novel job descriptions that arise out of digital humanities project work but also the novel forms of academic practice that even conventional academics find themselves undertaking when they embark on a digital project. But it also sharpens our attention to the question of what "knowledge work" really is and where its boundaries lie. The tension within the domain of digital humanities work between the practical and the theoretical, the technical and the scholarly, recapitulates a familiar dialectic within the traditional academy but does so in a way that prods us toward a new synthesis. If we understand "knowledge work" as a material practice, we may come closer to demystifying it.

In what follows I am going to set out some case studies based on my own work experience and try to unpack their significance and what they can reveal about different kinds of academic work.

Teaching Fellowship

My first job in the academy, as for so many people, was as a graduate teaching fellow. Precisely because of the self-evidence of that term as a designator of a certain kind of job, let me be deliberately obtuse and pretend that we know nothing about how such jobs work and what they entail. From my viewpoint as an early stage graduate student at Brown in 1991, the significant parameters were essentially these. My pretax income for the academic year was $12,500, and my formal work responsibilities were to prepare and teach two undergraduate writing courses of my own design. The time commitment for my teaching responsibilities was assumed to be approximately twenty hours per week. In addition, it was assumed that I would undertake my own research and make progress toward my PhD.

A few points are worth noting here: first, that the research I conducted as a student (preparing for professional advancement through field exams, writing conference papers, and participating in the intellectual life of the department by attending public lectures and university seminars) was not considered work, or at least not compensable work. In my first year, like all graduate students at Brown with financial aid, I received a fellowship that provided me with a living stipend and a tuition waiver, but even in that case my research would not have been characterized as work I was doing for the university. Students are positioned as net gainers from, rather than contributors to, the reservoir of knowledge the university contains, and the fellowship stipends they receive are characterized as "aid" rather than as compensation. And second, although the compensation for the formal "work" portion of my activities was reasonable (formally, about twenty-five dollars per hour for twenty-six weeks' work at twenty hours per week), as an annual income it was quite modest, and yet it would have seemed remarkable and inappropriate to hold any additional job. In other words, while formally compensating me for only part of my time, the university implicitly laid claim to all of it.[3] What is interesting about this point is not the question of whether that claim is legitimate but rather the effect it had on me: namely, the idea that I was accountable for all my time to the PhD program I was in, not just for my paid duties or even for a standard forty-hour work week, but potentially all the hours not devoted to sleeping and eating. Anecdotal evidence suggests that this erosion of a boundary between the professional and personal space is a familiar and very common effect of graduate study, and (even more anecdotally) I would observe that the people who typically enter a graduate program are likely to have the kind of personality that lends itself to this erosion: highly motivated with a strong sense of duty and an established habit of hard work and deferral of personal pleasure (or an ability to experience hard work *as* pleasure). In my own case, lacking any common sense about how to set practical boundaries on the work to be accomplished, I tended to feel that the research work required of me was effectively limitless: that no amount of effort could be sufficient to really complete it and that therefore no time could legitimately be spent on anything else.

Salary I: Free-Floating

My second job at Brown was as a full-time staff employee at the Women Writers Project (WWP), working as the managing editor for a series of books the WWP was publishing at the time with Oxford University Press, at an annual salary of twenty thousand dollars. Again, it may be useful to take a deliberately naive look at this job to understand how it was conceptualized. The WWP at that time was an independent unit reporting to the dean of the faculty, and its funding was derived partly from grants and partly from the university. It had originated in the English Department, and its agenda was still largely set by its faculty advisors, but its grant funding was awarded in large part because of its exploration of the use of digital technology, and the project was thus recognizable (to contemporary observers) as a hybrid: a project with a literary research agenda, using technology as a tool in furthering scholarly goals. The project was codirected by Susanne Woods (a full professor of English) and Allen Renear (a member of the staff in Computing and Information Services but holding a PhD in Philosophy). Its other professional staff included a programmer and the managing editor position that I held. Despite its traditional title, this job had an unusual profile, resulting from the experimental way in which these books were being produced: by converting the WWP's SGML files into a format that could be read by FrameMaker, which we then used to produce camera-ready copy following the press's specifications. My sole qualifications for the job were a familiarity with the content of the books and the management of the series (as a result of earlier proofreading work) and a willingness to learn anything else required by the job: page layout, FrameMaker, book production processes, the principles of textual editing, and enough about SGML to work with the project's programmer to troubleshoot the conversion mechanism.

It is worth noting that this job, like many jobs at the time in what was not yet being called "digital humanities," had no discernable career trajectory. The project's directors had other "real" jobs (as faculty, as permanent staff in the IT organization), and the project's programmer could, by gaining further experience and skills, advance to other more senior programming jobs; but the managing editor position (for a graduate student who was still in principle planning to become a faculty member at some point) did not look like part of a track of professional advancement, at least not within the academy. The job skills cohered only in the context of the work of the WWP, but even there they did not represent either a permanent niche or a developmental stage toward one. The job was in effect an emergency response to a sudden and temporary need.

Consultant

In 1994, a few years after my start at the WWP, the project was absorbed into the newly formed Scholarly Technology Group (STG) and became part of Brown's Computing and Information Services (CIS) department. My own job responsibilities by this time had changed: I was working as the WWP's textbase editor, with responsibility for overseeing and documenting the WWP's text encoding work and research on applying the newly published Text Encoding Initiative (TEI) P3 Guidelines to our textbase. However, a more dramatic change was the way in which our work was conceptualized in fiscal terms. STG was organized as a "cost center," with some funding from the university but also the ability (and the responsibility) to bring in income from outside sources such as grants and contracts. A significant part of STG's early development was the establishment of a fiscal model in which all STG projects (including the WWP) were understood as paying customers of the STG organization. For each staff member, STG set a level of overhead based on the amount of time that person could be expected to work on projects (rather than administration or other nonbillable tasks), and an overall overhead rate was determined that could be applied to all STG work as part of the billing structure. So, for example, if I was assumed to have 60 percent billable time (or approximately one thousand billable hours per year), then each hour worked not only would need to be charged at the hourly fraction of my salary and benefits but would also need to include an overhead amount to cover the 40 percent of my time that could not be billed out, plus the time that our office administrator spent handling payroll and grant administration, and so forth.

I'll have occasion to revisit this financial model later in this essay, but it is worth observing here that it provided a fascinating view into how academic work is conceptualized. From STG's point of view, this model was absolutely essential to the group's successful operation because STG was expected to cover the bulk of its own costs through grants, contracts, and other external income. As a result, any nonbillable work (such as basic administrative operations, the maintenance of our servers, keeping up with e-mail, attending meetings, participating in university bureaucracy) had to be paid for through the billable hours that were paid by projects. Each hour of project work, in other words, stood on the back of a fairly substantial apparatus that was necessary to make that hour possible. Without the e-mail, the payroll, the servers, and so forth, project work wouldn't be possible. However, for many collaborators and funding agencies, this model appeared not only counterintuitive but deeply troubling because it made our work look much more expensive than anyone else's. An hour of work from a staff member being paid forty thousand dollars per year cost far more than the fraction of salary and benefits that person actually received. However, that additional cost represented the actual cost of bringing that work to market, so to speak. The concept of overhead is of course familiar in another form (that of indirect costs), but indirect costs are not typically charged in the kinds of mutual exchanges of labor that we were often engaged in.

The result of this cost model for STG and WWP staff was also interesting. All of us became used to thinking of ourselves as consultants: people who might work on many different projects during the course of the year as called upon. One did not necessarily identify strongly with any single project, but one became adept at projecting oneself imaginatively into the space of each project, in turn, mastering its particular constraints and terminology so as to be able to act (program, design, research, encode, etc.) appropriately within the project context. This provisional identification with multiple projects gave us all a peculiar facility for seeing projects at a kind of metalevel: understanding their commonalities *as projects* and observing the types of problems and design challenges that emerged repeatedly. We gained a similar understanding of the disciplinary language and motivations that inhabited such projects: again, not as a matter of personal identification as a scholar in a certain field but rather as someone who is able to observe disciplines from a perspective slightly to one side.

Salary II

At a certain point, STG was reorganized to eliminate its reliance on outside funding and reduce its level of financial risk, and at this point the WWP was moved outside of STG and established as a separate unit, also within CIS but funded entirely on soft money. My job during this period was thus that of a typical salaried staff member, except that all the funding for myself and my WWP colleagues had to be raised either through grants or through licensing income from Women Writers Online (which by this time was starting to generate significant revenue). The result of this multiplicity of funding sources, however, was to reproduce in many ways the fiscal psychology of our time as consultants, in the sense that we remained very much aware of how our time was being spent and funded. In a year when the WWP had a grant from the National Endowment for the Humanities (NEH), part of our time would be allocated to the work for that grant (and paid from the grant ledger) while the rest would be allocated to WWP activities (and paid from license income). From time to time, when a shortfall in grant funding left us with a deficit, some staff time was "bought" by STG for specific projects.

Most recently, the WWP and STG have both been moved into the university library as part of its Center for Digital Scholarship. Although this move has not changed the WWP's fiscal arrangements, it has meant a subtle shift in how our work is construed in relation to the scholarly mission of the university. As a member of the library staff, my PhD in English no longer looks like a professional anomaly as it did in CIS, and the WWP's cultivation of a scholarly community for our publications, conference, and outreach programs is easier to harmonize with the digital dimensions of our research. Perhaps most importantly, the idea that we conduct research seems natural and in keeping with the library's larger mission.

Freelance

Running in parallel to this entire narrative is another with an entirely different developmental trajectory. Since 2000, my partner and I have had a small consulting business through which we have worked on an eclectic range of projects, ranging from simple database development to digital publication to grant writing. Like my teaching activities at the University of Illinois discussed later, this is for me a strictly evenings and weekends and vacation activity (though for my partner it is his job). Almost all our projects have some connection with digital tools, formats, or activities,[4] but it is not our purely *digital* expertise that is most important in these projects but rather our *digital humanities* expertise: in the sense that our literacy in a range of humanities disciplines and our skills in writing, strategic planning, and information design are essential in making our digital expertise useful to our clients. The success of the consultancy, in other words, arises directly out of (and has as its necessary precondition) an engagement with academic practices, standards, and subject domains. In an early interaction, one client said that what she found valuable about our intervention was that it mediated usefully between purely technical information on the one hand (which did not address her conceptual questions) and purely philosophical information on the other (which failed to address the practicalities of typesetting and work flow). We enabled her to understand how the decisions she was making about information modeling would affect both the intellectual content of the electronic publication and the realities of getting it produced.

Like all knowledge work that identifies itself as a species of "consulting," what we are doing in this role is situating ourselves as apart from—and even to a certain extent "above"—the knowledge domains of our clients. Just as critical theory came in the 1980s to occupy a position of metanarrative with respect to the traditional academic disciplines, so consultancy positions itself as a kind of metaknowledge, an expertise concerning the ways in which knowledge work is conducted. It's useful in the context of this essay to understand the value of this type of work—and indeed I have been arguing in favor of it throughout—but it is also important to put some critical pressure on the terms of its self-valuation.

The value of this kind of consulting work—for both the consultant and the client—is the self-consciousness it provides concerning the nature of the work being done and the terms on which it is conducted. A typical situation for a consultant is to be asked for help addressing what is taken to be a small practical problem. In the process of learning the context for addressing this problem, the consultant and client discover that in fact the practical problem arises from a deeper set of issues that had not been fully analyzed or understood, because the client was too close to them (or lacked the perspective) to see them. The consultancy relationship forces the client to articulate, for a stranger, premises and assumptions that may never have been stated plainly before—indeed, may never have risen to the level of visibility. For the client, self-consciousness results from having to bring all of this to articulation, and the result is often a better (because more explicit, transparent, and widely shared) set of intellectual configurations within the client's project or environment. For instance, work processes might be explicitly documented; latent disagreements might be brought to the surface and resolved; methodological inconsistencies or lacunae might be examined and rationalized.

Self-consciousness in the consultant arises partly from habitual exposure to infinite variety of beliefs, ways of doing things, and systems of value and partly from the constant projection of oneself into other people's imaginative spaces. The consultant must identify, however briefly and professionally, with the client's situation in order to provide useful advice while retaining enough distance to provide advice that goes beyond what the client would come up with on his or her own. Even as we treat self-consciousness as an *outcome* of this work, though, it may turn out to be more importantly a *precondition* of it, in the sense that people with this turn of mind (or training) will tend to approach their work in this spirit and may gravitate toward consulting roles no matter what their actual jobs.

With these points in mind, it is interesting to observe that digital humanities, as an institutional phenomenon, has evolved very substantially out of groups that were originally positioned as "service" units and staffed by people with advanced degrees in the humanities: in other words, people with substantial subject expertise who had gravitated toward a consulting role and found it congenial and intellectually inspiring. The research arising out of this domain, at its most rigorous and most characteristic, is on questions of method. Indeed, digital humanities has taken and been given responsibility for reforming the humanities disciplines, in virtue of the fact that it requires an attention precisely to method. By formalizing humanities research practices and rendering explicit the premises on which they rest, digital humanists also make possible critique and change.

My own professional preparation for working as a consultant, as this narrative has already shown, was in fact my acculturation as a para-academic: my various jobs in publishing, editing, supporting, teaching, grant writing, and studying. What interests me most about this work, though, has to do with the ways that various kinds of knowledge—technical, scholarly, practical—are valued. I suggest that there are at least two forms of valuable knowledge in play. The first is the knowledge that the client values because they are glad they don't have it (or have responsibility for it): they value it in the consultant because it represents what they think they are buying. Technical knowledge falls into this category: in my case, knowledge of XML, databases, electronic publication systems, digital project management. The second, more problematic category is the knowledge that makes the first type usable to the client—namely, the metaknowledge through which the consultant grasps the client's subject area. In my case, this includes familiarity with scholarly editing and with methods of literary scholarship; and, despite the fact that my technical knowledge would be unusable without it, this knowledge also constitutes a kind of subtle structural irritant in the consulting relationship. Precisely because of its potential value (if I were being considered as a colleague), it must be explicitly devalued here to show that I am not so considered: it creates a necessity for gestures of demarcation by which the boundaries of my role can be drawn, with technical knowledge on the inside and subject knowledge on the outside.[5]

I'd like to describe one project in particular that may be illuminating in this context, namely the work that my partnership has been doing on the Modern Language Association's (MLA) New Variorum Shakespeare (NVS) Editions, starting in 2003. Our work has been focused on developing specifications for representing these editions in TEI and XML and for accomplishing the encoding of the three most recent editions, plus associated other tasks. As already suggested, our technical expertise (in this case, familiarity with markup languages and XML publishing) had an obvious relevance and importance, but arguably more important was the ability to understand and explain the editorial significance of technical decisions and to serve as a bridge between the two strands of the project: the project's editorial work (conducted by senior humanities faculty) and the project's technical implementation (overseen by professional staff at the MLA who manage the production of the editions in print and digital form but for whom the XML is largely unfamiliar terrain).

For this project, we began by examining the intellectual specifications for the edition, which were described in the editorial guidelines: these prescribed (most significantly) the organization of readings from the textual witnesses that are collated for each edition, the organization and presentation of the commentary in which the editor summarizes the history of criticism on each line of the play, and the arrangement and representation of the play text. From this information we were able to create an information model of the edition: essentially, an understanding of what the informationally significant components of the edition are and how they are functionally related to one another. For example, each textual note (representing the set of variant readings on a given word) must contain both a reference back to the line containing the word in question and a formally organized arrangement of readings; each reading in turn contains the textual variant and a reference to the witness(es) where that variant is attested. We then formalized this information model in a TEI schema, through which these informational nodes and relationships could be expressed and constrained.[6] Finally, we wrote comprehensive documentation of the encoding practices required to produce a TEI version of an NVS edition and tested the entire system through the process of encoding three successive editions and creating working output of various types.

This development process, effecting as it did a complete translation of editorial methodology from one medium into another, also produced an interesting shift of perspective. In a classic edition project—such as the NVS notably was when it was a print-only edition—there are many kinds of knowledge in operation, including the literary and editorial knowledge that is responsible for what in FRBR (Functional Requirements for Bibliographic Records) terms would be called the "work" and its "expression,"[7] the knowledge of production systems such as copyediting and book design that is responsible for creating a high-quality "manifestation," and the knowledge of publication-related activities such as printing and bookbinding that go into producing the individual "items" that one can buy and shelve and read. In this universe the editorial knowledge that produces the work is understood to operate at the highest level: it directs and motivates the others and carries a kind of cultural authority as knowledge work in relation to their instrumentality. At the start of our work on the NVS, this relationship between types of knowledge was also in operation with respect to the digital implementation of the project: the XML encoding of the text was being treated as part of a typesetting process and was being executed in that spirit, as a way of producing a manifestation or set of items rather than as a process with implications higher up in FRBR's great chain of being. The discourse around the use of XML was substantially instrumental: it concerned the practicalities of supporting a digital interface and generating PDF output and similar issues.

Treating this work as information modeling, however, has produced a subtle shift in these relationships. Most significantly, it has repositioned the TEI/XML: no longer solely as part of a production workflow aimed at producing output but rather as the formal (and authoritative) instantiation of the knowledge that constitutes the edition, as the information model for the edition itself. Where in the print production process the editorial manuscript was taken as the most informationally rich artifact in the ecology (whose contents would be translated into an effective print carrier for those ideas), in the digital process the editorial manuscript is a precursor to that state: the XML encoding brings information structures that are *latent* or *implicit* in the manuscript into formal visibility. Once completed, the XML data carries in itself the information needed to generate all the possible manifestations of the edition: in print, in PDF, in interactive forms, in visualizations derived from the data, in Braille, and so forth. The knowledge that in this work process is positioned as "technical," in other words, actually turns out to be the metaknowledge through which the original motives of the NVS editions can be projected into a different medium with different representational properties.

Faculty

The final dimension to this complicated professional identity is in many ways the most conventional: a turn to university teaching. Since 2005 I have held an appointment as an adjunct instructor at the Graduate School of Library and Information Science at the University of Illinois at Urbana-Champaign (UIUC), teaching a course on electronic publication standards and technologies each fall through their distance learning program (known as LEEP). I am paid by the course at typical adjunct rates, and I teach (including class sessions, responding to student work and questions, and all administrative functions) during the evenings and weekends. From UIUC's point of view, the appointment is 25 percent of a full-time equivalent (FTE) (a four-course load being a full-time job), and in fact the time commitment does work out to approximately ten to twelve hours per week.[8]

Because the LEEP program enables students to complete a Master of Library Science (MLS) degree without moving their residence or leaving their jobs (in many cases LEEP students continue to work full time), many or most of the students in my class are already engaged in careers in digital publishing, librarianship, and other kinds of work for which an MLS degree is a strong credential. For them, the knowledge associated with digital technologies is both instrumental (a job skill that can immediately be applied in very practical ways) and foundational (a set of concepts and technologies that intersect with and enrich other dimensions of library and information science). For many of them, their working lives within the academy will be very much like mine, though probably less peripatetic; as librarians their work will be positioned at the intersection of three different paradigms of knowledge: subject expertise, "practical" or "technical" skills, and a kind of metaknowledge that inheres in their mastery of information science (i.e., the organization and management of knowledge *across* and *apart from* specific subject areas). Depending on the specific job and institutional location they find themselves in, any of these three domains may be construed as yielding "research" on which they might publish, present at professional conferences, and gain professional advancement.

What does my professional experience and training look like within this ecology? What from my history is taken to be relevant for these students, and how (the reader might ask) does someone who took fifteen years to complete a PhD in English Literature look like a plausible faculty member in a school of library science? Interestingly enough, what has proven most useful (and what students most remark on in their evaluations of the class) is the kind of embedded knowledge I represent: the understanding of methods, approaches, and strategies that arise out of real-world experience at a functioning digital publication project (i.e., the Women Writers Project). The course I teach covers a number of highly technical subjects (schema writing, XML, metadata), but its emphasis is strongly on how we can understand the significance and contextual utility of these technologies within a set of larger strategic concerns. Although on paper I only became a plausible hire with the completion of my PhD, the credential that really grounds the teaching I do is actually the fifteen years I spent *not* completing that degree and working instead in the variety of roles detailed earlier.

Stepping Back, Further Thoughts

These examples, for all their variety of institutional location and functional modality, are actually remarkably consonant with one another: one striking observation here may in fact be their similarity with respect to the actual work being done, coupled with the range of ways in which this same essential set of tasks can be framed and paid for. At the same time, from another perspective their differences are most salient: for the typical humanities faculty member, most of these paradigms of work are equally alien; only the first will look truly familiar (the adjunct faculty position is familiar but not to be identified with). Examining these two cases for their commonalities, we can suggest that what characterizes mainstream academic work is two qualities. The first is the unlimitedness of the responsibility: work interpenetrates life, and we do what is necessary. For instance, we attend conferences without there being a question of whether it's our "own" time or our employer's time; there is no concept of "vacation" during the academic year and very little functional conception of "business hours" except as a personal heuristic device. The second, related characteristic is the way time is conceptualized as a function of work practice. Time for academics is not regulated in detail, only in blocks. (For nine months you are paid; for three months you are free to do other things; at all times you should be working on your next book.)

Most digital humanities work, however—as performed by library staff, IT staff, and other para-academic staff who are not faculty—is conceptualized according to one of the other models: hourly, by FTE, or as an agenda of projects that granularizes and regulates the work in quantifiable ways. Increasingly, the use of project management tools to facilitate oversight and coordination of work within IT organizations has also opened up the opportunity to track time, and this has fostered an organizational culture in which detailed managerial knowledge of time spent on specific tasks and on overhead is considered virtuous and even essential. As we have seen, in an organization like the early STG, such tracking was a structural requirement for billing; but, even in organizations where the idea of "billing" time to a project is simply an enabling metaphor, the use of time management as a way of understanding work processes and achieving greater efficiency and productivity is clearly immensely appealing.

These terms of value—efficiency, productivity—are not inapplicable to traditional academic models of work, but their applicability is considered strictly voluntary, qualitative, and relative. We can gauge the importance of voluntariness here by observing the shock and disgust with which attempts to increase productivity (e.g., by increasing class size or stipulating specific levels of scholarly output) by external enforcement are greeted: academic work is considered to have the privilege of self-regulation, being in this respect more like the work of a poet than of a journalist. The importance of qualitative rather than quantitative measures of work is similarly a kind of class marker: the cases in which specific metrics are typically applied (e.g., number of students and courses taught, quantity of committee work) are those that are least felt to be characteristically *scholarly* work. Quantifying scholarly output can only be done at the crudest level (e.g., number of books or articles published), and the relative and comparative nature of these assessments quickly becomes apparent: a monumental, groundbreaking book is worth much more (but how much more?)

than a slighter intervention, and it takes a complex apparatus of review to establish, even approximately, the relative value of different scholarly productions.

For the para-academic digital humanities workforce, these different paradigms of value operate and interact in complex ways. In my own experience working in an IT organization (with time regulated by the hour or the project), the tension between quantitative and qualitative measures of productivity was a constant source of methodological self-consciousness. Within the most local organizational context (the Scholarly Technology Group, whose name sums up the conundrum), this tension was understood to be an interesting problem rather than a practical difficulty: we knew ourselves to be doing cutting-edge research at the same time as we were producing useful projects, and at a metalevel we were fascinated by the interplay of these two undertakings. However, the parent organization (the more unequivocally named Computing and Information Services department) understood our work to be much simpler to define and measure: we were supporting faculty projects, and completing those projects successfully was a desirable and quantifiable outcome.[9] As a historical matter, it is also worth noting the evolution of these practices and expectations: members of CIS from its earliest days remembered a time when the organization was much more research oriented, developing experimental software tools and providing much more improvisational and open-ended forms of support. The transformation into a modern IT organization involved the importation of work and management practices that were explicitly derived from the corporate rather than the academic world.

What are the larger effects of accounting for time and regulating it in these ways? One important effect is that time and work appear fungible and interconvertible. The calculus of time and effort by which we know the cost and value of an hour of an employee's time is also the basis for assessing how those resources could be used otherwise. On the spreadsheet that tracks the project, that unit of funding (time, product) could be spent to purchase an equivalent quantum of time or product from some other source: from a vendor, from an undergraduate, from a consultant, from an automated process running on an expensive piece of equipment. The precise quantification of time and effort permits (and motivates) a more direct comparison of work according to metrics of productivity and speed and permits a managerial consciousness to become aware of all the different ways of accomplishing the same task with available resources.

This last formulation—accomplishing the same task with available resources—reverses the narrative of academic work that is on view at liberal arts colleges and research universities, in which a thoughtful person pursues his or her original ideas and is rewarded for completing and communicating them. In this narrative, the defining and motivating force is the individual mind, with its unique profile of subject knowledge and animating research vision. The managerial consciousness turns this narrative on its head by suggesting that in fact the task and available resources are the forces that most significantly define our work and that the choice of person is almost a casual matter that could go one way or another without much effect on the outcome. We can see this reversal even more clearly in the way that—extending the idea of fungibility—this quantification of time also permits us to deal, managerially, with fractions of people. It is common in project discussions (and I find myself speaking this way quite often) to say something along the lines of "We need about a quarter of a person for a year," or "That project will take half a programmer." Witticisms about "which half?" aside, the effect of this model of work is to treat people as resources—as a kind of pool from which one can draw off a quantum of work when needed. The result of this fractionalization may be felt as a positive or negative effect: either of fragmented attention or of fascinating variety. But in either case it constitutes a displacement of autonomy concerning what to work on when and how long to take, from the staff member to the managerial consciousness—again, a reversal of the classic narrative of academic work.

It is tempting to suggest that this labor is—structurally, at least—alienated and to some extent exploited. While we can immediately distance ourselves from the melodrama of comparing a programmer who makes sixty thousand dollars a year with a food services worker making a fraction of that amount, we can fruitfully pause over the marked difference between this kind of para-academic labor and the characteristic model of labor by which the academy is recognizable. What *is* the effect of this fungibility, this depersonalization of labor on the para-academic staff? What is my life like as a worker (and a self-conscious manager) in these conditions?

One point worth making at the outset is that many of the people in the para-academic jobs like mine are (like me) people who originally planned to be academics in the traditional sense. Of my seven closest colleagues during the past four years, five have pursued (and four completed) a PhD. Our expectations of what work should be like are strongly colored by the cultural value and professional allure of research, and we expect to be valued for our individual contributions and expertise, not for our ability to contribute a seamless module to a work product. Our paradigm for professional output is authorship, even if actual authoring is something we rarely have enough time to accomplish.

One would expect the result of this mismatch of training and job paradigm to be disappointment, and in some cases it is. But in a way, my colleagues and I are anomalies: a transitional phase between an older, secure academic identity with which we strongly identify and a new, authentically para-academic identity that is still coming into being. Trained with the intellectual self-assurance of academics (but tempted away or derailed from that professional path), we do our work *as if it were scholarship*, cheerfully and ironically aware that we are also in some sense a fungible labor pool. Having been hired and acculturated in our jobs at a time (say, 1993) when those jobs were absolutely unique—and in some cases created specifically for us—we have no doubts about our own unique configurations of expertise and experience. Our work may be modeled as fungible, but we ourselves do not feel at risk. Moreover, because of our characteristic interest in metaknowledge as consultants and digital humanists, we construct a satisfying and holistic research narrative out of self-study: a quasi-anthropological scrutiny of our work environments that constitutes a form of suture.

But in 2025, what will the now-commonplace jobs (web programmer, digital project coordinator, programmer/analyst, and so forth) look like as professional identities, especially to people who may never have imagined themselves as scholars in the first place? In particular, I wonder whether the digital humanities may cease to operate as a locus of metaknowledge if (or, less optimistically, when) digital modes of scholarship are naturalized within the traditional disciplines. In that case, would these para-academic jobs lose their distinctive structural role in the ecology, their ability to foreground method? Or, from another angle, does the inevitable naturalization of these jobs as a routine career (rather than an odd alternative to a mainstream narrative) reduce the incumbents' sensitivity precisely to issues of method, discourse, and professional identity? Will a new set of credentials arise through which these jobs can be trained for and aimed at, avoiding the sense of professional anomaly that (in my experience at least) produces such a useful form of outsiderism?

Coda

Those who catch me in moments of professional frustration have heard my standard vision of a truly alternative career: becoming a goat farmer. As fond as I am of goats, what this idea really represents for me is a reminder that ultimately what we do is work and that there's useful work to be done wherever we look. Those of us who work in the academy and the para-academy are lucky to have jobs that are (for the most part) steady, physically harmless, flexible, full of cultural value, and opportunities to learn. If our jobs also give us a sense of identity, that is both a bonus and a pitfall: a source of inspiration and also an opportunity to confuse our own worth with what the job seems to confer on us. This is a risk to which the academy seems peculiarly prone: witness the fact that for most PhD candidates the idea of accepting a job other than a tenure-track faculty position is tantamount to an admission of failure. The reason why Mr. Silva assumed that I was Professor Flanders—the reason that no alternative is visible to him—is that no alternative can be articulated by the profession itself. And yet the vast preponderance of actual *work* involved in creating humanities scholarship and scholarly resources is not done by faculty. As we already noted, for every hour of scholarly research in an office or library, countless other hours are spent building and maintaining the vast research apparatus of books, databases, libraries, servers, networks, cataloguing and metadata standards, thesauri, and systems of access. If the academic mission, in its broadest sense, is worth doing, all parts of it are worth doing. Our own location within this landscape—the job we were hired to do—is in the final analysis a space of work like any other, with contours determined by our aptitudes and training.

For this reason, I think one of the most interesting effects of the digital humanities upon academic job roles is the pressure it puts on what we think of as our own proper work domains. In the archetypal digital humanities collaboration, traditional faculty explore forms of work that would ordinarily look "technical" or even menial (such as text encoding, metadata creation, or transcription); programmers contribute to editorial decisions; and students coauthor papers with senior scholars in a kind of Bakhtinian carnival of overturned professional usages. Examples of this are real and yet also imaginary, in the sense that they are not taken as actual models to be generalized but as exceptional cases that we can celebrate without imitating. Nonetheless, in my own experience these interactions have had very specific, beneficial effects on all participants that are worth generalizing if we can. For faculty, involvement in other kinds of work provides a perspective that cuts across the grain of standard academic work practices, and it gives a vivid and well-grounded understanding of how scholarly ideas are instantiated in digital research projects. For technical staff, these collaborative relationships produce a much richer intellectual context for their work and also convey a sense of the complexity of humanities data and research problems, which in turn makes for better, more thoughtful technical work. For students, the opportunity to work on real-world projects with professional collaborators gives unparalleled exposure to real intellectual problems, job demands, and professional skills across a wide range of roles, which in turn may yield a more fully realized sense of the landscape of academic work.

With these benefits in mind, there are a few things that we can do to encourage these interactions and to develop a professional academic ecology that is less typecast, that obscures less thoroughly the diversity of working roles that contribute to the production of scholarship (digital or not):

1. Make it practically possible and professionally rewarding (or, at the very least, not damaging) for graduate students to hold jobs while pursuing advanced degrees. This would involve rethinking our sense of the timing of graduate study and its completion: instead of rushing students through coursework, exams, and dissertations only to launch them into a holding pattern (potentially for several years) as postdocs, finished but still enrolled students, or visiting assistant lecturers, graduate programs would need to allow a bit more time for the completion of the degree and ensure that students graduate with some diversity of skills and work experience.
2. Devote resources to creating meaningful job and internship opportunities at digital humanities research projects, scholarly publications, conferences, and other professional activities with the goal of integrating students as collaborators into these kinds of work at the outset.
3. Encourage and reward coauthoring of research by faculty, students, and para-academic staff. This involves actions on the part of departments (to create a welcoming intellectual climate for such work) and on the part of

journals, conferences, and their peer review structures to encourage and solicit such work and to evaluate it appropriately.

NOTES

1. Oxford English Dictionary Online, s.v. "career, n," accessed September 12, 2011, http://www.oed.com/view/Entry/27911?rskey=JoMCBM&result=1&isAdvanced=false.

2. Alan Liu, *The Laws of Cool* (Chicago: University of Chicago Press, 2004), 19.

3. When I was a graduate student I was permitted to hold other on-campus jobs without any limitation on the number of hours worked, but more recently the graduate school has placed fairly strict limitations on the number of hours graduate students may work while receiving financial aid (i.e., fellowships and teaching assistantships).

4. With a few notable exceptions: one or two small bookbinding projects and a handmade rudder for a sailboat.

5. From a practical perspective this is an entirely reasonable clarification, since it makes clear where each set of responsibilities lies—it would not do for me to imagine that I am part of the editorial team, simply because I am helping write the grant.

6. It is worth noting for the curious that the resulting schema is a TEI customization, in which some modification of TEI structures and some new elements were required to accommodate the structural and practical requirements of the NVS editions.

7. In FRBR , the entity termed the "work" as a purely intellectual object that is made present in language as an "expression," then instantiated in specific publications as a "manifestation," and finally given physical form in specific, individual "items" that can be held in the hand, defaced, annotated, and thumped for emphasis. See http://www.oclc.org/research/activities/past/orprojects/frbr/default.htm.

8. From Brown's point of view, this work is a potential conflict of interest and poses some interesting questions about what it means to be exempt staff. In principle, full-time salaried work at Brown means being available to work as required by the demands of one's job description, without being paid overtime, so an evening job constitutes a potential source of competition for my time. In practice this has not been a problem as long as I keep my work hours at Brown strictly free of non-Brown work activities and complete my Brown-related work satisfactorily.

9. The management instruments arising out of this relationship were fascinating in themselves: complex spreadsheets with columns showing dated progress and taxonomies of project status with elaborate accompanying commentary explaining why each project was a special case.

Can Information Be Unfettered? Race and the New Digital Humanities Canon

AMY E. EARHART

In the 1990s, the rallying cry of proponents of the Internet was the democratization of knowledge made possible by the developing technological infrastructure. Lost or excluded texts began to be published on the net, some developed by scholars, others by fans, and still others by libraries and museums. I remember the possibilities that these materials offered for the literary scholar. I could create a website for students that linked the recovered e-text of Harriet Wilson's *Our Nig*, period images of slaves, and the variety of African American cultural and historical documents found on the then-fledgling Schomburg Research Center website. The seemingly expansive materials for use on the web were far more complete than materials found in print anthologies or other such course materials. For scholars interested in reinserting writers of color into critical discussions, the recovery efforts were a boon. We imagined that the free access to materials on the web would allow those previously cut off from intellectual capital to gain materials and knowledge that might be leveraged to change the social position of people of color. The new space of the Internet would allow those who had been silenced to have a voice. Hypertext theorist Jay David Bolter promoted the freeing power of the web-based environment as a space that encouraged "the abandonment of the ideal of high culture (literature, music, the fine arts) as a unifying force. If there is no single culture, but only a network of interest groups, then there is no single favored literature or music" (233). As the 1990s drew to a close, and the number of digitally recovered texts seemed to grow each day, Bolter's prediction seemed correct. However, a review of digitized materials production and the current treatment of race in the digital canon suggests that Bolter's hopes have not been realized.

I want to focus my discussion by examining a subset of the digital humanities, digital texts.[1] I'm interested in the digital work being produced by those associated with academia and those with strong connections to traditional humanities fields including history, literature, classics, art history, and archeology, among others. My focus includes pay-walled scholarly production, such as the excellent *Clotel* project published by Virginia's Rotunda Press, and open-access materials but excludes large-scale digital projects produced by for-profit publishers, such as Gale-Cengage, or nonscholarly produced projects, such as Google Books. I am also most interested in projects that make something. Here I would like to echo Stephen Ramsay's recent argument that "Digital Humanities is about building things." While Ramsay has come under fire for his insistence on the applied nature of digital humanities, the history of digital humanities reveals the centrality of building to the field. In fact, scholars invested in early work on race in digital humanities insisted on building editions and digital texts as an activist intervention in the closed canon. While we should continue to explore tool building, visualization, and data mining as crucial areas within digital humanities, the narrow digital canon should remind us why we cannot stop digital edition work.

While those invested in digital text production should continue to flesh out the digital canon, other areas of digital humanities, such as tool building and visualization, should also be invested in the investigation of canon on their work. For example, the Metadata Offer New Knowledge (MONK) project has harnessed materials from Documenting the American South, Early American Fiction, Early English Books Online (EEBO), Eighteenth Century Collections Online (ECCO), Nineteenth-Century Fiction, Shakespeare, and Wright American Fiction 1850–75. While the purpose of MONK is not text recovery but visual analysis, a broad understanding of the literature of this period is only as good as the data from which the analysis draws. In the case of MONK, a quick search reveals that texts by Sojourner Truth, Sui Sin Far, and Maria Christina Mena—authors of color included in most standard anthologies of American literature—are absent.[2] Add to this MONK's claim that "for users of public domain materials, MONK provides quite good coverage of 19th century American fiction," and we are reminded that a more direct analysis of the position of race in digital humanities work is necessary (Unsworth and Muller, 2). We shouldn't be surprised at the lack of certain texts used in the MONK project, as the digitized humanities corpora is scant and the project's primary goal was to develop a prototype of data-mining work rather than an inclusive data set. However, the emphasis on "good coverage" should concern digital humanists. As a field where collaborative teams are able to produce better results than that of the lone scholar, it is important to include project participants that can help speak to the importance of cultural criticism. Without careful and systematic analysis of our digital canons, we not only reproduce antiquated understandings of the canon but also reify them through our technological imprimatur.

Unlike related fields, digital humanities has historically deemphasized theoretical examination of the digital utilizing cultural studies frameworks. Those working within rhetoric, media, and communication, and particularly those working in game studies, have constructed a body of scholarly work that interrogates the theoretical implications of race construction within technology.[3] With superb work being produced by scholars such as Lisa Nakamura, Beth Kolko, and Tara McPherson, these fields have begun the difficult work of theorizing the way in which technology impacts the digital object. In digital humanities, however, we have much theoretical work to do in the selection of materials and application of digital tools to them.

To understand the current position of race and digital humanities work, we must turn to the emergence of the World Wide Web. As the web began to gain popularity in the 1990s, it was portrayed as an idealized, democratic, and free space. *Time* magazine's 1994 story "Battle for the Soul of the Internet" is indicative of the understanding of the newly popular space, uncolonized and free. The original users of the web, scientists, computer geeks, and hackers, according to the story, were battling against the corporate market intent on invading their open space. Advocates of the free web were interested in three ideas: "1) Access to computers should be unlimited and total; 2) All information should be free; 3) Mistrust authority and promote decentralization," all designed to allow "bubbles" of information to rise from the bottom, sowing "seeds of revolutionary change" ("Battle for the Soul of the Internet"). Scholars, too, began to see the net as a space that altered power structures. As Paul Delany notes,

> The Internet has thus mutated into an unforeseen and unplanned information space. Its virtues can all be attributed to its collegial political economy: in a word, its openness. Internet's most important features are its relatively small hardware investment, a weak (but not ineffective) central administration, little censorship, and an absence of specifiable "bottom-line" objectives. Its explosive growth in the last few years confirms the dynamism of a collegial cyberspace culture in which millions of users exchange information, collaborate on creative projects, and have their say on any subject they care about. (Childers and Delaney)

The revolutionary power of the net was based on the belief that the open digital environment was unpoliced and unregulated, open to all who wanted to participate. The low cost, the "small hardwave investment" that Delany points to, was also crucial, as it allowed scholars to produce their materials more cheaply, increasing the types and numbers of texts available. In his 1996 essay "Principles for Electronics Archives, Scholarly Editions, and Tutorials," Peter Shillingsburg concurs it "eventually will cost less to produce and therefore, one assumes, to purchase a compact disk than it costs to produce and purchase Hans Gabler's edition of *Ulysses*" (25). While, in hindsight, we have rejected this view as too simplistic, it was a common refrain in the early, heady days of digital recovery, and the decentralization and shifting power structures, as related by these statements, became part of the narrative and the mythology that in no small part drove the digital literary studies recovery projects that grew in the 1990s.

For scholars interested in reworking the canon, the web seemed an unfettered space that allowed the scholar direct control of what would be digitized and how it would be presented. Susan Fraiman, director of the Orlando Project, lauded the expansive digital environment, remarking that "what is new in the twenty-first century, however, is that now the guest list of history-making women is electronic—and there are always more seats at the table" (143). The belief in the web as a space in which the canon might be broken was likewise espoused by the editors of *Romantic Circles*: "One of the strengths of Web publishing is that it facilitates—even favors—the production of editions of texts and resources of so-called non-canonical authors and works. This is in part a function of the relative simplicity of HTML (and all of the simpler document-type-descriptions of SGML) and of 'workstation publishing' in general when compared to traditional commercial or academic letterpress production and distribution methods" (Fraistat, Jones, and Stahmer). The ease of publication, identified by the editors, was what allowed the broad range of small-scale recovery projects to explode around the web in this early period. The insistence on the web's ability to build new canons, of an applied approach to the digital tied to a theoretical model, is a hallmark of past and current digital humanities work.

The importance of building tools for digital work, common to and controversial in contemporary digital humanities, has deep roots in this early recovery work. The applied/theoretical model voiced by digital humanists also fits historically into the work of cultural studies scholars prior to the mainstream Internet. For example, Jean Fagan Yellin's work on Harriet Jacobs's *Incidents in the Life of a Slave Girl* took various trajectories of inquiry, but her 1987 Harvard University Press edition, the edition that brought the important volume to the center of the African American literary tradition, was an applied piece set within her larger scholarly body of work. In recovering the text and conducting the painstaking research required to do so, Yellin has followed a model familiar to those working with digital projects—application driven scholarship. This model of building, grown from the cultural studies recovery tradition, would expand as additional scholars began to explore the digital as a tool by which to recover texts by writers of color.

During the 1990s and early 2000s, in many ways the most productive age of digital recovery to date, projects fell into two distinctive scholarly groups. One group was the small-scale project in which scholars worked individually or as small collectives. These projects, including *The Charles Chesnutt Archive, Voices from the Gaps,* and *The Online Archive of Nineteenth-Century U.S. Women's Writings*, were mostly unfunded and produced outside of digital humanities centers or libraries. The second type of project was produced by e-text centers, digital humanities centers, or libraries and museums. Individual scholarly participation was less central to such work. These projects include the *Emory Women Writers Resource Project*; the various projects produced by the Virginia Center for Digital History, including the *Valley of the Shadow* and *Race and Place: An African-American Community in the Jim Crow South*; and the digital *Schomburg Library of Nineteenth-Century Black Women Writers*.

Of these two types of projects, the dominance of small-scale recovery efforts nurtured by an individual scholar who wanted to bring lost texts to scholarly and public attention is surprising. Simple HTML projects such as *The Charles Chesnutt Archive*, by Stephanie Browner; *Voices from the Gaps*, by Toni McNaron and Carol Miller; and *The Online Archive of Nineteenth-Century U.S. Women's Writings*, by Glynis Carr, were developed without the support of a digital humanities center, technological collaborators, or external funding. Some projects, such as *The Charles Chesnutt Archive*, were positioned as undergraduate teaching and learning tools, with undergraduate student partners in the recovery process.

Alan Liu's *Voice of the Shuttle* provides a good measure of the huge number of early recovery projects focused on literature and history written by and about people of color. A quick perusal of "The Minority Studies" section, however, reveals that a tremendous number of the projects have become lost. For example, of the six sites listed in "General Resources in Minority Literature," half cannot be located, suggesting that they have been removed or lost. The same trend is found with other projects listed on the site. While only 50 percent of the projects in the "General Resources in Chicano/Latino Literature" section are still online, other areas, such as Asian American literature, have a higher percentage of active projects.[4] Digital humanists are fond of talking about sustainability as a problem for current and future works, but it is clear that we already have sustained a good deal of loss within the broadly defined digital canon.

Cocurrent to the DIY projects were institutional initiatives focused on bringing lost texts to view. Much of this work occurred within e-text centers, such as Rutgers University's Center for Electronic Texts in the Humanities (CETH); fledgling digital humanities centers, such as the University of Virginia's Institute for Advanced Technology in the Humanities (IATH); and museums and libraries, including the New York Public Library. With limited exceptions, a majority of the early projects reinforced canonical bias. Catherine Decker argues that the canon crops up in these projects because of their funding and institutional affiliations: "The reasons for the canonicity of the bulk of the electronic texts available on the web are hardly elusive: most of the large textbases are located at and funded by major universities (or grants to university scholars that include a cut for the university at which the project is situated)." Martha Nell Smith extends this contention and argues that digital humanities developed as a space to which practitioners hoped to flee from the shifts in the profession that arose out of the cultural studies movement. In "The Human Touch: Software of the Highest Order, Revisiting Editing as Interpretation," Smith highlights the digital humanities' retreat into modes of analytics, objective approaches as "safe" alternatives to the messy fluidities found in literary studies. She notes, "It was as if these matters of objective and hard science provided an oasis for folks who did not want to clutter sharp, disciplined, methodical philosophy with considerations of the gender-, race-, and class-determined facts of life . . . Humanities computing seemed to offer a space free from all this messiness and a return to objective questions of representation" (4). If Smith is correct, then we not only have a selection problem in digital humanities but also have a historical structural problem that might be more difficult to reverse.

One only needs to review the current work in digital literary studies to see that we have not escaped the traditional canon by turning to new methods of publication. The proliferation of early projects I have cataloged remain but a trace in the current digital canon. A search of websites referenced by the Modern Language Association (MLA) bibliography reveals almost one thousand individual sites, yet very few of these projects are represented in MLA presentations, leaving many new to the field to assume that there are a small number of digital projects, often focused around a core group of digital humanities practitioners. The perception of limited projects and practitioners is what has driven the recent controversy of the digital humanities star system, highlighted by William Pannapacker's post-MLA 2011 blog post, "Digital Humanities Triumphant?" While I, along with many others, reject Pannapacker's representation of key digital humanities scholars as the cool kids at the high-school lunch table, the perception of the exclusionary world of digital humanities is reinforced by a perception of limited projects. Impacting the perception of digital humanities as exclusive, in both practice and product, is the granting model. Examination of funded projects reveals that the shift toward innovation has focused on technological innovation, not on innovative restructuring of the canon through recovery. The National Endowment of Humanities (NEH) awarded 141 Digital Humanities Start-Up Grants from 2007 through 2010. Of those grants, only twenty-nine were focused on diverse communities and sixteen on the preservation or recovery of diverse community texts. It is striking to examine the authors and historical figures individually cited in the list of funding: Shakespeare, Petrach, Melville, Jefferson, David Livingstone,[5] and Whitman. While there are grants to support work on indigenous populations, African and African American materials, and Asian American materials, in addition to others, the funding of named great men of history deserves scrutiny and even, perhaps, a specific funding program to encourage recovery efforts (NEH).

There may be many reasons for the lack of attention to noncanonical texts. Margaret Ezell cautions that we have not revised the way in which we understand texts and because of this elision certain texts, particularly noncanonical texts, are not being digitized. She argues that "while we increasingly have the ability to digitalize any text we please . . . editors do not please to select certain types of material and this is in part because perhaps we are not yet changing some of the basic assumptions about what an 'edition' does, or in Hunter's terms, what is 'appropriate'" ("Editing Early Modern Women's Manuscripts," 107). Additional reasons for exclusion are structural, such as the cost of production. Ken Price has discussed "the strong correlation between the 'significance' on which successful grant writing depends and the traditional canon" (281). Susan Belasco, for example, believes "that the traditional standards for tenure and promotion are, in fact, more entrenched than ever and worse—more restrictive and un-imaginative than they were for an earlier generation" (333). Or, as Martha Nell Smith has argued, the digital humanities community might be adverse to the expansion of the canon and the work that has been reinserted into the mix. All of these possible explanations deserve critical attention if the digital humanities community wants to promote a broader digital canon.

While a good many of the early small-scale digital projects have been displaced or lost from our current digital canon, a few have managed not only to survive but to thrive. *19: Interdisciplinary Studies in the Nineteenth Century* is one such project. Begun as a simple HTML journal, scholars affiliated with the project participated in a Nineteenth-Century Scholarship Online (NINES) summer workshop during which they learned to encode with the international standard of TEI/XML. Once the project was re-marked with TEI, it was brought into the NINES federated collection of nineteenth-century materials, helping expand its user base and take an important step toward long-term sustainability. It provides a positive example of how we might take the institutional structures that have developed in relation to the digital humanities canon and leverage them to support small-scale projects. *19: Interdisciplinary Studies in the Nineteenth Century* also provides a pivotal clue that might explain why certain projects are currently excluded from the digital canon and others are not. The archive demonstrates that project value is created by editorial principles, content, *and* technological infrastructure. Projects like *19* have been revitalized by alignment with an institution, whether a collective, like NINES, a digital humanities center, like the Maryland Institute for Technology in the Humanities (MITH), or a library, like the University of Nebraska. The case of *19* suggests that standards and institution have become a core part of project success and sustainability, crucial to the canonization of digital work. Ken Price alludes to the new canon criteria when he argues that "people ready to embrace high quality work wherever it is found hold in highest regard digital work that features a rigorous editorial process and adheres to international standards (for example, TEI/XML)" (275). If institutional affiliation and technological standards are necessary components to the success of a project, then digital humanists must investigate how we might provide both to DIY scholars. Groups like NINES, which provide workshops and outreach, have modeled potential ways by which to generate such parameters. Additional efforts must follow.

If, indeed, we are beginning to construct a digital canon that weighs content and technological choices equally, then it is crucial for digital humanists to theorize the technological with the same rigor as we theorize the content. Alan Liu has more broadly seen the problem as an absence of cultural criticism, noting that "rarely do we extend the issues involved into the register of society, economics, politics, or culture" into our digital work. If we do not theorize our technological approaches with a mind toward cultural constructions, we will continue to exclude certain materials from digitization. One possible model is found in the partnership of Timothy Powell and the Ojibwe elders, who have created the *Gibagadinamaagoom* archive.

Powell has written extensively on the crucial impact of technological application to indigenous cultural materials and argues that current work needs to be revamped so that "digital technology can more accurately and artistically represent the indigenous origins and spiritual story lines of expressive culture on these [the Americas] continents" (Powell and Aitken, 253). Part of Powell's response to cultural inclusion was to construct a partnership that shifted ownership of cultural materials from that of the scholar to the Ojibwe elders, in effect creating a mechanism by which the tribe might control their own cultural materials.

My digital project, *The Nineteenth-Century Digital Concord Archive*, is similarly invested in exploring how to appropriately apply technological standards to shifting constructions of race represented in textual materials. Our current challenge is how we represent varying representations of blackness found in the census in a database. How do we represent, technologically, the identification of the same person as West Indian, Mulatto, or black? Amanda Gailey's recent article, "A Case of Heavy Editing: The Example of Race and Children's Literature in the Gilded Age," reveals the depth of theoretical inquiry that Gailey has invested in applying TEI appropriately to complex texts that bear markers of postbellum racial construction, particularly in the decision to utilize TEI to facilitate searching. Gailey notes that "we will use the <orig> and <reg> combination instead of the <sic> and <cor> combination (meaning *sic* and "correction"), as the former pair makes no claim about the rightness or wrongness of the readings, only how standardized their spellings are" (136). The TEI tag selection is in keeping with current cultural criticism regarding race and language, which rejects the superiority of standard English. The choice of <orig> and <reg> reveals that Gailey refuses to value one language usage over the other, as would be implied through the choice of the <sic> and <cor> tags. These examples provide a helpful way to imagine the next steps involved in digital humanities work and the treatment of race. While we need to continue to consider how to invigorate a robust digital recovery, we also have a good bit of theoretical work to do in the selection, editing, and technological manipulation of our materials.

One of the powerful things about the early period of digital literary studies is the DIY approach that many scholars embraced, the sheer joy and freedom of bringing important texts to the larger scholarly community. As we move from simple HTML sites to TEI and visualization projects, as we move from individual or small collective projects to larger team projects, from nonbudgeted projects to large, externally funded projects, we see fewer scholars working with digital textual recovery. This should concern digital humanists, and we should accordingly begin to strategize how we might reverse this trend. Small steps are under way. We need to examine the canon that we, as digital humanists, are constructing, a canon that skews toward traditional texts and excludes crucial work by women, people of color, and the GLBTQ community. We need to reinvigorate the spirit of previous scholars who believed that textual recovery was crucial to their work, who saw the digital as a way to enact changes in the canon. If, as Jerome McGann suggests, "the entirety of our cultural inheritance will be transformed and reedited in digital forms" (72), then we must ensure that our representation of culture does not exclude work by people of color.

NOTES

1. I use the term "digital text" to include digital edition and digital text. I see these as two distinctive types of textual production. I define a digital edition as a project that emphasizes textual variants using traditional bibliographical methods. A digital text is one version of a text that has been brought digital.

2. For example, all of these authors are included in *The Bedford Anthology of American Literature* and *The Heath Anthology of American Literature.*

3. I recognize that there is an ongoing discussion of how to view the distinction between media studies and digital humanities. My point is that the larger body of digital humanities work has been less concerned with cultural issues than the work produced by those who self-identify as media, rhetoric, communication, and film studies scholars.

4. I utilized a general Google search to locate the projects. If they were not found through this search, I located the institution or scholar associated with the materials to see if materials had been moved elsewhere.

5. David Livingstone is a Victorian explorer of Africa. The grant was awarded to create an online scholarly edition of his Nwangwe field diary.

BIBLIOGRAPHY

"Battle for the Soul of the Internet." *Time,* July 25, 1994. http://www.time.com/time/magazine/article/0,9171,981132,00.html.

Belasco, Susan. "The Responsibility Is Ours: The Failure of Infrastructure and the Limits of Scholarship." *Legacy: A Journal of American Women Writers* 26, no. 2 (2009): 329–36.

Bobley, Brett. "New from ODH: Summary Findings of NEH Digital Humanities Start-Up Grants (2007–2010)." National Endowment for the Humanities, Office of Digital Humanities, September 7, 2010. http://www.neh.gov/ODH/ODHUpdate/tabid/108/EntryId/144/New-from-ODH-Summary-Findings-of-NEH-Digital-Humanities-Start-Up-Grants-2007-2010.aspx.

Bolter, J. D. *Writing Space: The Computer, Hypertext, and the History of Writing.* Boston: Houghton Mifflin, 1991.

Childers, Peter, and Paul Delany. "Introduction: Two Versions of Cyberspace." *Works and Days* 23, no. 4 (1994): 61–78. http://www.sfu.ca/delany/wkndays.htm.

Decker, Catherine. "Crossing Old Barriers: The WorldWideWeb, Academia, and the Romantic Novel." *Romanticism on the Net* 10 (1998). http://www.erudit.org/revue/ron/1998/v/n10/005794ar.html.

Ezell, Margaret J. M. "Editing Early Modern Women's Manuscripts: Theory, Electronic Editions, and the Accidental Copy-Text." *Literature Compass* 7, no. 2 (2010): 102–9. http://onlinelibrary.wiley.com/doi/10.1111/j.1741-4113.2009.00682.x/full.

———. "The Myth of Judith Shakespeare: Creating the Canon of Women's Literature." *New Literary History* 21, no. 3 (1990): 579–92.

———. *Writing Women's Literary History*. Baltimore: Johns Hopkins University Press, 1993.

Fraiman, Susan. "In Search of Our Mother's Gardens–With Help from a New Digital Resource for Literary Scholars." *Modern Philology* 106, no. 1 (2008): 142–48.

Fraistat, Neil, Steven E. Jones, and Carl Stahmer. "The Canon, the Web, and the Digitization of Romanticism." *Romanticism on the Net* 10 (1998). http://www.erudit.org/revue/ron/1998/v/n10/005801ar.html

Gailey, Amanda. "A Case for Heavy Editing: The Example of Race and Children's Literature in the Gilded Age." In *The American Literature Scholar in the Digital Age,* edited by Amy E. Earhart and Andrew Jewell, 125–44. Ann Arbor: University of Michigan Press, 2010.

Kirschenbaum, Matthew. "What Is Digital Humanities and What's It Doing in English Departments?" *ADE Bulletin* 150 (2010): 55–61. http://mkirschenbaum.files.wordpress.com/2011/01/kirschenbaum_ade150.pdf. Reprinted in this volume.

Liu, Alan. "Where Is Cultural Criticism in the Digital Humanities." *Alan Liu*. January 2011. http://liu.english.ucsb.edu/where-is-cultural-criticism-in-the-digital-humanities/.

McGann, Jerome. "Culture and Technology: The Way We Live Now, What Is To Be Done?" *New Literary History* 36, no. 1 (2005): 71–82. http://muse.jhu.edu/journals/new_literary_history/v036/36.1mcgann.html.

National Endowment for the Humanities. "Digital Humanities Start-up Grants." August 6, 2010. http://www.neh.gov/grants/guidelines/digitalhumanitiesstartup.html.

Omeka. Roy Rosenzweig Center for History and New Media. George Mason University. http://omeka.org/

Powell, Timothy B., and Larry P. Aitken. "Encoding Culture: Building a Digital Archive Based on Traditional Ojibwe Teachings." In *The American Literature Scholar in the Digital Age,* edited by Amy E. Earhart and Andrew Jewell, 250–74. Ann Arbor: University of Michigan Press, 2010.

Price, Ken. "Digital Scholarship, Economics, and the American Literary Canon." *Literature Compass* 6, no. 2 (2009): 274–90. http://onlinelibrary.wiley.com/doi/10.1111/j.1741-4113.2009.00622.x/full.

Ramsay, Stephen. "Who's in and Who's Out." Stephen Ramsay Blog. January 8, 2011. http://lenz.unl.edu/papers/2011/01/08/whos-in-and-whos-out.html.

Shillingsburg, Peter L. "Principles for Electronic Archives, Scholarly Editions, and Tutorials." In *The Literary Text in the Digital Age*, edited by Richard J. Finneran, 23–35. Ann Arbor: University of Michigan Press, 1996.

Smith, Martha Nell. "The Human Touch: Software of the Highest Order: Revisiting Editing as Interpretation." *Textual Cultures* 2, no. 1 (2007): 1–15.

Spencer, Amy. *DIY: The Rise of Lo-FI Culture*. London: Marion Boyars, 2005.

Unsworth, John, and Martin Muller. *The MONK Project Final Report*. 2009. http://www.monkproject.org/MONKProjectFinalReport.pdf.

The Social Contract of Scholarly Publishing

DANIEL J. COHEN

When Roy Rosenzweig and I finished writing a full draft of our book *Digital History*, we sat down at a table and looked at the stack of printouts.

"So, what now?" I said to Roy naively. "Couldn't we just publish what we have on the web with the click of a button? What value does the gap between this stack and the finished product have? Isn't it 95 percent done? What's the last five percent for?"

We stared at the stack some more.

Roy finally broke the silence, explaining the magic of the last stage of scholarly production between the final draft and the published book: "What happens now is the creation of the *social contract* between the authors and the readers. We agree to spend considerable time ridding the manuscript of minor errors, and the press spends additional time on other corrections and layout, and readers respond to these signals—a lack of typos, nicely formatted footnotes, a bibliography, specialized fonts, and a high-quality physical presentation—by agreeing to give the book a serious read."

I have frequently replayed that conversation in my mind, wondering about the constitution of this social contract in scholarly publishing, which is deeply related to questions of academic value and reward.

For the ease of conversation, let's call the two sides of the social contract of scholarly publishing the *supply side* and the *demand side*. The supply side is the creation of scholarly works, including writing, peer review, editing, and the form of publication. The demand side is much more elusive—the mental state of the audience that leads them to "buy" what the supply side has produced. In order for the social contract to work, for engaged reading to happen, and for credit to be given to the author (or editor of a scholarly collection), both sides need to be aligned properly.

The social contract of the book is profoundly entrenched and powerful—almost mythological—especially in the humanities. As John Updike put it in his diatribe against the digital[1] (and most humanities scholars and tenure committees would still agree), "The printed, bound and paid-for book was—still is, for the moment—more exacting, more demanding, of its producer and consumer both. It is the site of an encounter, in silence, of two minds, one following in the other's steps but invited to imagine, to argue, to concur on a level of reflection beyond that of personal encounter, with all its merely social conventions, its merciful padding of blather and mutual forgiveness."

As academic projects have experimented with the web over the past two decades, we have seen intense thinking about the supply side. Robust academic work has been reenvisioned in many ways: as topical portals, interactive maps, deep textual databases, new kinds of presses, primary source collections, and even software. Most of these projects strive to reproduce the magic of the traditional social contract of the book, even as they experiment with form.

The demand side, however, has languished. Far fewer efforts have been made to influence the mental state of the scholarly audience. The unspoken assumption is that the reader is more or less unchangeable in this respect, only able to respond to and validate works that have the traditional marks of the social contract: having survived a strong filtering process, near-perfect copyediting, the imprimatur of a press.

We need to work much more on the demand side if we want to move the social contract forward into the digital age. Despite Updike's ode to the book, there *are* social conventions surrounding print that are worth challenging. Much of the reputational analysis that occurs in the professional humanities relies on cues beyond the scholarly content itself. The act of scanning a CV is fraught with these conventions.

Can we change the views of humanities scholars so that they may accept, as some legal scholars already do, the great blog post as being as influential as the great law review article? Can we get humanities faculty, as many tenured economists already do, to publish more in open access journals? Can we accomplish the humanities equivalent of FiveThirtyEight.com, which provides as good, if not better, in-depth political analysis than most newspapers, earning the grudging respect of journalists and political theorists? Can we get our colleagues to recognize outstanding academic work wherever and however it is published?

I believe that to do so, we may have to think less like humanities scholars and more like social scientists. Behavioral economists know that although the perception of value can come from the intrinsic worth of the good itself (e.g., the quality of a wine, already rather subjective), it is often influenced by many other factors, such as price and packaging (the wine bottle, how the wine is presented for tasting). These elements trigger a reaction based on stereotypes—if it's expensive and looks well wrapped, it must be valuable. The book and article have an abundance of these value triggers from generations of use, but we are just beginning to understand equivalent value triggers online—thus the critical importance of web design and why the logo of a trusted institution or a university press can still matter greatly, even if it appears on a website rather than a book.

Social psychologists have also thought deeply about the potent grip of these idols of our tribe. They are aware of how cultural norms establish and propagate themselves and tell us how the imposition of limits creates hierarchies of recognition. Thinking in their way, along with the way the web works, one potential solution on the demand side might come not from the scarcity of production, as it did in a print world, but from the scarcity of attention. That is, value will be perceived in any community-accepted process that narrows the seemingly limitless texts to read or websites to view. *Curation* becomes more important than publication once publication ceases to be limited.

NOTES

This chapter originally appeared as "The Social Contract of Scholarly Publishing" (http://www.dancohen.org/2010/03/05/the-social-contract-of-scholarly-publishing/).

1. http://www.nytimes.com/2006/06/25/books/review/25updike.html.

Introducing Digital Humanities Now

DANIEL J. COHEN

Do the digital humanities need journals? Although I'm very supportive of the new journals that have launched in the last year and although I plan to write for them from time to time, there's something discordant about a nascent field—one so steeped in new technology and new methods of scholarly communication—adopting a format that is struggling in the face of digital media.

I often say to nondigital humanists that every Friday at five I know all of the most important books, articles, projects, and news of the week—without the benefit of a journal, a newsletter, or indeed any kind of formal publication by a scholarly society. I pick up this knowledge by osmosis from the people I follow online.

I subscribe to the blogs of everyone working centrally or tangentially to digital humanities. As I have argued[1] from the start[2] and against the skeptics and traditionalists who think blogs can only be narcissistic, half-baked diaries, these outlets are just publishing platforms by another name, and in my area there are an incredible number of substantive ones.

More recently, social media such as Twitter has provided a surprisingly good set of pointers toward worthy materials I should be reading or exploring. (And as happened with blogs five years ago, the critics are now dismissing Twitter as unscholarly, missing the filtering function it somehow generates among so many unfiltered tweets.) I follow as many digital humanists as I can on Twitter and created a comprehensive list of people in digital humanities.[3] (You can follow me @dancohen.)

For a while I've been trying to figure out a way to show this distilled "Friday at five" view of digital humanities to those new to the field or those who don't have time to read many blogs or tweets. This week I saw a tweet from Tom Scheinfeldt[4] (who in turn saw a tweet from James Neal[5]) about a new service called Twittertim.es,[6] which creates a real-time publication consisting of articles highlighted by people you follow on Twitter. I had a thought: what if I combined the activities of several hundred digital humanities scholars with Twittertim.es?

Digital Humanities Now (*DHN*)[7] is a new web publication that is the experimental result of this thought. It aggregates thousands of tweets and the hundreds of articles and projects those tweets point to and boils everything down to the most-discussed items, with commentary from Twitter. A slightly longer discussion of how the publication was created can be found on the *DHN* "About" page.[8]

Does the process behind *DHN* work? From the early returns, the algorithms have done fairly well, putting on the front page articles on grading in a digital age and bringing high-speed networking to liberal arts colleges, Google's law archive search, and (appropriately enough) a talk on how to deal with streams of content given limited attention. Perhaps *Digital Humanities Now* will show a need for the light touch of a discerning editor. This could certainly be added on top of the raw feed of all interest items[9] (about fifty a day, out of which only two or three make it into *DHN*), but I like the automated simplicity of *DHN* 1.0.

Despite what I'm sure will be some early hiccups, my gut is that some version of this idea could serve as a rather decent new form of publication that focuses the attention of those in a particular field on important new developments and scholarly products. I'm not holding my breath that someday scholars will put an appearance in *DHN* on their CVs. But as I recently told an audience of executive directors of scholarly societies at an American Council of Learned Societies meeting, if you don't do something like this, someone else will.

I suppose *DHN* is a prod to them and others to think about new forms of scholarly validation and attention beyond the journal. Ultimately, journals will need the digital humanities more than we need them.

NOTES

This chapter originally appeared as "Introducing Digital Humanities Now" (http://www.dancohen.org/2009/11/18/introducing-digital-humanities-now/).

1. http://www.dancohen.org/2008/12/05/leave-the-blogging-to-us/.
2. http://www.dancohen.org/2005/12/16/creating-a-blog-from-scratch-part-1-what-is-a-blog-anyway/.
3. http://twitter.com/dancohen/digitalhumanities/members.
4. http://www.foundhistory.org/, http://twitter.com/#!/foundhistory.
5. https://twitter.com/#!/james3neal.
6. http://tweetedtimes.com/.
7. http://digitalhumanitiesnow.org/.
8. http://digitalhumanitiesnow.org/about/.
9. http://feeds.feedburner.com/DigitalHumanitiesNow.

Text: A Massively Addressable Object

MICHAEL WITMORE

At the Working Group for Digital Inquiry at Wisconsin, we've just begun our first experiment with a new order of magnitude of texts. Jonathan Hope and I started working with thirty-six items about six years ago when we began to study Shakespeare's First Folio plays (Witmore and Hope). Last year, we expanded to three-hundred and twenty items with the help of Martin Mueller at Northwestern, exploring the field of early modern drama. Now that the University of Wisconsin has negotiated a license with the University of Michigan to begin working with the files from the Text Creation Partnership (TCP), which contains over twenty-seven thousand items from early modern print, we can up the number again. By January, we will have begun our first one-thousand item experiment, spanning items printed in Britain and North America from 1530 through 1809. Robin Valenza and I, along with our colleagues in computer sciences and the library, will begin working up the data in the spring. Stay tuned for results.

New experiments provide opportunities for thought that precede the results. What does it mean to collect, tag, and store an array of texts at this level of generality? What does it mean to be an "item" or "computational object" within this collection? What is such a collection? In this post, I want to think further about the nature of the text objects and populations of texts we are working with.

What is the distinguishing feature of the digitized text—that ideal object of analysis considered in all its hypothetical relations with other ideal objects? The question itself goes against the grain of recent materialist criticism, which focuses on the physical existence of books and practices involved in making and circulating them. Unlike someone buying an early modern book in the bookstalls around St. Paul's four hundred years ago, we encounter our TCP texts as computational objects. That doesn't mean that they are immaterial, however. Human labor has transformed them from microfilm facsimiles of real pages into diplomatic quality digital transcripts, marked up in TEI so that different formatting features can be distinguished. That labor is as real as any other.

What distinguishes this text object from others? I would argue that a text is a text because it is *massively addressable at different levels of scale*. Addressable here means that one can query a position within the text at a certain level of abstraction. In an earlier post, for example, I argued that a text might be thought of as a vector through a metatable of all possible words (Witmore). Why is it possible to think of a text in this fashion? Because a text can be queried at the level of single words and then related to other texts at the same level of abstraction: the table of all possible words could be defined as the aggregate of points of address at a given level of abstraction (the word, as in Google's new Ngram corpus). Now, we are discussing ideal objects here; addressability implies different levels of abstraction (character, word, phrase, line, etc.), which are stipulative or nominal: such levels are not material properties of texts or Pythagorean ideals; they are, rather, conventions.

Here's the twist. We have physical manifestations of ideal objects (the ideal *1 Henry VI*, for example), but these manifestations are only provisional realizations of that ideal. (I am using the word manifestation in the sense advanced in the Online Computer Library Center's Functional Requirements for Bibliographic Records [FRBR] hierarchy.[1]) The book or physical instance, then, is *one of many levels of address*. Backing out into a larger population, we might take a genre of works to be the relevant level of address. Or we could talk about individual lines of print, all the nouns in every line, every third character in every third line. All this variation implies massive flexibility in levels of address. And more provocatively, when we create a digitized population of texts, our modes of address become more and more abstract: all concrete nouns in all the items in the collection, for example, or every item identified as a "History" by Heminges and Condell in the First Folio. Every level is a provisional unity: stable for the purposes of address but also stable because it is the object of address. Books are such provisional unities. So are all the proper names in the phone book.

The ontological status of the individual text is the same as that of the population of texts: both are massively addressable, and when they are stored electronically we are able to act on this flexibility in more immediate ways through iterative searches and comparisons. At first glance, this might seem like a Galilean insight, similar to his discipline-collapsing claim that the laws that apply to heavens (astronomy) are identical with the ones that apply to the sublunar realm (physics). But it is not.

Physical texts were *already* massively addressable before they were ever digitized, and this variation in address was and is registered at the level of the page, chapter, the binding of quires, and the like. When we encounter an index or marginal note in a printed text—for example, a marginal inscription linking a given passage of a text to some other in a different text—we are seeing an act of address. Indeed, the very existence of such notes and indexes implies just this flexibility of address.

What makes a text a text—its susceptibility to varying levels of address—is a feature of book culture and the flexibility of the textual imagination. We address ourselves to this level, in this work, and think about its relation to some other.

"Oh, this passage in *Hamlet* points to a verse in the Geneva bible," we say. To have this thought is to dispose relevant elements in the data set in much the same way a spreadsheet aggregates a text in ways that allow for layered access. A reader is a maker of such a momentary *dispositif* or device, and reading might be described as the continual redisposition of levels of address in this manner. We need a phenomenology of these acts, one that would allow us to link quantitative work on a culture's "built environment" of words to the kinesthetic and imaginative dimensions of life at a given moment.

A physical text or manifestation is a provisional unity. There exists a potentially infinite array of such unities, some of which are already lost to us in history: what was a relevant level of address for a thirteenth-century monk reading a manuscript? Other provisional unities can be operationalized now, as we are doing in our experiment at Wisconsin, gathering one thousand texts and then counting them in different ways. Grammar, as we understand it now, affords us a level of abstraction at which texts can be stabilized: we lemmatize texts algorithmically before modernizing them, and this lemmatization implies provisional unities in the form of grammatical objects of address.

One hundred years from now, the available computational objects may be related to one another in new ways. I can only imagine what these are: every fourth word in every fourth document, assuming one could stabilize something like "word length" in any real sense. (The idea of a word is itself an artifact of manuscript culture, one that could be perpetuated in print through the affordances of moveable type.) What makes such thought experiments possible is, once again, the addressability of texts as such. Like a phone book, they aggregate elements and make these elements available in multiple ways. You could even think of such an aggregation as the substance of another aggregation, for example, "all the phone numbers belonging to people whose last name begins with A." But unlike a phonebook, the digitized text can be reconfigured almost instantly into various layers of arbitrarily defined abstraction (characters, words, lines, works, genres). The mode of storage or virtualization is precisely what allows the object to be addressed in multiple ways.

Textuality *is* massive addressability. This condition of texts is realized in various manifestations, supported by different historical practices of reading and printing. The material affordances of a given medium put constraints on such practices: the practice of "discontinuous reading" described by Peter Stallybrass, for example, develops alongside the fingerable discrete leaves of a codex. But addressability as such: *this* is a condition rather than a technology, action, or event. And its limits cannot be exhausted at a given moment. We cannot, in a Borgesian mood, query all the possible data sets that will appear in the fullness of time. And we cannot import future query types into the present. But we can and do approximate such future searches when we automate our modes of address in unsupervised multivariate statistical analysis—for example, factor analysis or Principle Component Analysis (PCA). We want all the phonebooks. And we can simulate some of them now.

NOTES

This chapter originally appeared as "Text: A Massively Addressable Object" (http://winedarksea.org/?p=926).

1. http://www.oclc.org/research/publications/library/2003/lavoie_frbr.pdf.

BIBLIOGRAPHY

Hope, Jonathan, and Michael Witmore. "The Hundredth Psalm to the Tune of 'Green Sleeves': Digital Approaches to Shakespeare's Language of Genre." *Shakespeare Quarterly* 61, no. 3 (2010): 357–90.

Witmore, Michael. "Texts as Objects II: Object Oriented Philosophy. And Criticism?" *Wine Dark Sea*. September 17, 2009. http://winedarksea.org/?p=381.

The Ancestral Text

MICHAEL WITMORE

In this post I want to understand the consequences of "massive addressability" (Witmore) for "philosophies of access"—philosophies that assert that all beings exist only as correlates of our own consciousness. The term "philosophy of access" is used by members of the speculative realist school: it seems to have been coined largely as a means of rejecting everything the term names. Members of this school dismiss the idea that speculative analysis of the nature of beings can be replaced by an apparently more basic inquiry into how we access the world, an access obtained through either language or consciousness. The major turn to "access" occurs with Kant, but the move is continued in an explicitly linguistic register by Heidegger, Wittgenstein, Derrida, and a range of poststructuralists.

One reason for jettisoning the priority of access, according to Ray Brassier, is that it violates "the basic materialist requirement that being, though perfectly intelligible, remain irreducible to thought" ("The Enigma of Realism"). As will become clear, I am sympathetic to this materialist requirement and more broadly to the speculative realist project of dethroning language as our *one and only* mode of access to the world. (There are plenty of ways of appreciating the power and complexity of language without making it the wellspring of Being, as some interpreters of Heidegger have insisted.) Our quantitative work with texts adds an unexpected twist to these debates: as objects of massive and variable address, texts are "handled" in precisely the ways usually reserved for nonlinguistic entities. When taken as objects of quantitative description, texts possess qualities that—at some point in the future—could be said to have existed in the present, *regardless* of our knowledge of them. There is thus a temporal asymmetry surrounding quantitative statements about texts: if one accepts the initial choices about what gets counted, such statements can be "true" now even if they can only be produced and recognized later. Does this asymmetry, then, mean that language itself, "though perfectly intelligible, remain[s] irreducible to thought" (Brassier)? Do iterative methods allow us to satisfy Brassier's materialist requirement in the realm of language itself?

Let us begin with the question of addressability and access. The research described on this blog involves the creation of digitized corpora of texts and the mathematical description of elements within that corpus. These descriptions obtain at varying degrees of abstractions (nouns describing sensible objects, past verb forms with an auxiliary, etc.). If we say that we know something quantitatively about a given corpus, then we are saying that we know it on the basis of a set of relations among elements that we have provisionally decided to treat as countable unities. Our work is willfully abstract in the sense that, at crucial moments of the analysis, we foreground relations as such, relations that will then be reunited with experience. When I say that objects of the following kind—"Shakespearean texts identified as comedies in the First Folio"—contain more of a certain type of thing (first- and second-person singular pronouns) than objects of a different kind (Shakespeare's tragedies, histories), I am making a claim about a relation between groups and what they contain. These groupings and the types of things that we use to sort them are provisional unities: the circle we draw around a subset of texts in a population could be drawn another way if we had chosen to count other things. And so, we must recognize several reasons why claims about these relations might always be revised.

Every decision about what to count offers a caricature of the corpus and the modes of access this corpus allows. A caricature is essentially a narrowing of address: it allows us to make contact with an object in some of the ways Graham Harman has described in his work on vicarious causation. One can argue, for example, that the unity "Shakespeare's Folio comedies" is really a subset of a larger grouping or that the group can itself be subdivided into smaller groups. Similarly, one might say that the individual plays in a given group aren't really discrete entities and so cannot be accurately counted in or out of that group. There are certain words that *Hamlet* may or may not contain, for example, because print variants and multiple sources have made *Hamlet* a leaky unity. (Accommodating such leaky unities is one of the major challenges of digital text curation.) Finally, I could argue that addressing these texts on the level of grammar—counting first- and second-person singular pronouns—is just one of many modes of address. Perhaps we will discover that these pronouns are fundamentally linked to semantic patterns that we haven't yet decided to study but should. All of these alternatives demonstrate the provisional nature of any decision to count and categorize things: such decisions are interpretive, which is why iterative criticism is not going to put humanities professors out of business. But such counting decisions are not—and this point is crucial—simply another metaphoric reduction of the world. Principal component analysis (PCA), cluster analysis, and the other techniques we use are clearly *inhuman* in the number of comparisons they are able to make. The detour through mathematics is a detour *away* from consciousness, even if that detour produces findings that ultimately converge with consciousness (i.e., groupings produced by human reading).

Once the counting decisions are made, our claims to know something *in a statistical sense* about texts boils down to a claim that a particular set of relations pertains among entities in the corpus. Indeed, considered mathematically, the things we call texts, genres, or styles simply *are* such sets of relations—the mathematical reduction being one of many possible caricatures. But counting is a very interesting caricature: it yields what is there now—a real set of relations—but is nevertheless impossible to contemplate at present. Once claims about texts become mathematical descriptions of relations, such statements possess what the philosopher Quentin Meillassoux calls ancestrality, a quality he associates primarily with statements about the *natural* world. Criticizing the ascendance of what he calls the Kantian dogma of correlationism—the assumption that everything that can be said "to be" exists only as correlate of consciousness—Meillassoux argues that the idealist or critical turn in Continental philosophy has impoverished our ability to think about anything that exceeds the correlation between mind and world. This "Great Outdoors," he goes on to suggest, is a preserve that an explicitly speculative philosophy must now rediscover, one that Meillassoux believes becomes available to us through mathematics. So, for example, Meillassoux would agree with the statement, "the earth existed 4.5 billion years ago," precisely because it can be formulated mathematically using measured decay rates of carbon isotopes. The statement itself may be ideal, but the reality it points to is not. What places the Great Outdoors out of doors, then, is its indifference to our existence or presence as an observer. Indeed, for Meillassoux, it is *only* those things that are "mathematically conceivable" that exceed the post-Kantian idealist correlation. For Meillassoux, "all those aspects of the object that can be formulated in mathematical terms can be meaningfully conceived as properties of the object in itself." Clearly such a statement is a goad for those who place mind or natural language at the center of philosophy. But the statement is also a philosophical rallying cry: be curious about objects or entities that do not reference human correlates! I find this maxim appealing in the wake of the "language is everything" strain of contemporary theory, which is itself a caricature of the work of Wittgenstein, Derrida, and others. Such exaggerations have been damaging to those of us working in the humanities, not least because they suggest that our colleagues in the sciences do *nothing but* work with words. By making language everything—and, not accidentally, making literary studies the gatekeeper of all disciplines—this line of thought amounts to a new kind of species narcissism. Meillassoux and others are finding ways to not talk about language all the time, which seems like a good thing to me.

But would Meillassoux, Harman, and other speculative realists consider texts to be part of the Great Outdoors? Wouldn't they have to? After all, statements about groupings in the corpus can be true now even when there is no human being to recognize that truth as a correlate of thought. Precisely *because* texts are susceptible to address and analysis on a potentially infinite variety of levels we can be confident that a future scholar will find a way of counting things that turns up a new but as yet unrecognized grouping. Human reading turned up such a thing when scholars in the late nineteenth century "discovered" the genre of Shakespeare's late romances. (Jonathan Hope and I have, moreover, redescribed these groupings statistically [Witmore and Hope].) Like our future mathematical sleuth might do a century from now, nineteenth-century scholars were arguing that romance was already a *real* feature of the Shakespearean corpus, albeit one that no one had yet recognized. They had, in effect, picked out a new object by emphasizing a new set of relations among elements in a collection of words. Couldn't we expect another genre to emerge from this sort of analysis—a genre X, let's say—given sufficient time and resources? Would we accept such a genre if derived through iterative means?

I can imagine a day, one hundred years from now, when we have different dictionaries that address the text on levels we have not thought to explore at present. What if someone creates a dictionary that allows me to use differences in a word's linguistic origin (Latinate, Anglo-Saxon, etc.) to relate the contents of one text to another? What if a statistical procedure is developed that allows us to "see" groupings we *could* recognize today but simply have not developed the mathematics to expose? When you pair the condition of massive addressability with (1) the possibility of new tokenizations (new elements or strata of address) or (2) the possibility that all token counts past and future can be subjected to new mathematical procedures, you arrive at a situation in which something that is arguably true now about a collection of texts can only be known in the future.

And if something can be true about an object now without itself being a correlate of human consciousness, isn't that something part of the *natural world,* the one that is supposed to be excluded from the charmed circle of the correlation? Does this make texts more like objects in nature, or objects in nature more like texts? Either way, the Great Outdoors has become larger.

NOTE

This chapter originally appeared as "The Ancesteral Text" (http://winedarksea.org/?p=979).

BIBLIOGRAPHY

Brassier, Ray. "The Enigma of Realism: On Quentin Meillassoux's After Finitude." In *Collapse: Philosophical Research and Development*. Vol. 2. 2007.

Meillassoux, Quentin. *After Finitude: An Essay on the Necessity of Contingency*. New York: Continuum, 2008.

Witmore, Michael. "Text: A Massively Addressable Object." In *Wine Dark Sea*. December 31, 2010. http://winedarksea.org/?p=926.

Witmore, Michael, and Jonathan Hope. "Shakespeare by the Numbers: On the Linguistic Texture of the Late Plays." In *Early Modern Tragicomedy*, edited by Subha Mukherji and Raphael Lyne, 133–53. Woodbridge, Suffolk, UK: D. S. Brewer, 2007.

PART V

TEACHING THE DIGITAL HUMANITIES

Digital Humanities and the "Ugly Stepchildren" of American Higher Education

LUKE WALTZER

For the past three decades, the humanities in American public higher education have suffered recurrent crises. In moments of general fiscal austerity, class sizes in the humanities have risen, departments and programs have been threatened or eliminated, and searches for open faculty positions have been abandoned. Even in times of stable budgets, tenure-track positions have remained elusive, and resources available to those scholars doing work in the humanities have been scarce. This context has been so persistent that it has taken on an air of permanence.

The general implications for instruction and pedagogical innovation in the humanities from this "new normal" are well documented: contact time with students has declined, and the ratio of classes being taught by contingent faculty has increased. General education curricula have, for the most part, not kept pace with changes in institutional structure that have led to more adjuncts teaching larger classes with strained institutional support. Most university curricula have not adjusted to the material realities of the college experience, where the vast majority of students lead lives that are exponentially more digital and networked than they were when those curricula were designed. General education requirements have not been sufficiently reoriented to the changing demands of the job market, which require, at the very least, that students be able to navigate increasingly complicated information systems. Most universities have failed to relay to students why studying the humanities is important or relevant in this context, and so it is little wonder that ever-increasing percentages of students are landing in nonhumanities majors, choosing instead courses of study that promise to certify them for a specific place in the economy, which may or may not in fact exist (Menand, 50–54).

These conditions are encouraging too many college students to see knowledge as something they purchase in the form of a degree, as opposed to something flexible and broadly applicable that they gain through deep, engaging experience. This new normal has done much to undermine the place of the humanities in college instruction. In this context, pedagogy, curriculum development, and the scholarship of teaching and learning remain what Steve Brier has called "the ugly stepchildren of the university." Those particular paths of inquiry continue to be undervalued by institutions and less energetically pursued by academics than the discipline-based research with which the majority of humanists began their careers.

In contrast to these troubling realities, the digital humanities appear to be on the ascendance. The job market for academic humanists in the past three years has been the weakest in over a generation, yet jobs in the digital humanities are becoming more plentiful. In 2010 through 2011, there were cluster hires of digital humanities faculty at a number of research universities, including the University of Iowa, Georgia State University, the University of Maryland, and the University of Wisconsin, among others. There has also been an increase in what Bethany Nowviskie has called "#alt-ac" positions doing the digital humanities—"alternative academic careers"—including postdocs, jobs in libraries, and administrative and staff positions at newly founded or expanding digital humanities centers ("#alt-ac"). New conferences and camps seem to emerge monthly, and they're always well attended despite eroding travel support from colleges and universities. The Alliance of Digital Humanities Organizations, formed in 2005, brings together previously disparate international organizations, supports five influential journals, and organizes a massive annual conference in the field. At each of the past two Modern Language Association meetings—perhaps the most influential general meeting in the humanities—various reports lauded "the arrival of the digital humanities" (Pannapaker; Howard; and "News: Tweetup at the MLA"). Although the extent to which that arrival is complete has been debated, there can be little argument that the field is a more significant presence in the academy than it was ten, or even five, years ago. With the increase in the number of humanists who blog and use Twitter, the digital humanities conversation is always happening.

Contributing to this sense of arrival, beyond the jobs and intensifying discourse, was the creation of an Office of the Digital Humanities (ODH) at the National Endowment for the Humanities (NEH) in 2008. The ODH funded 145 projects from 2008 through spring of 2011; and, while its annual operating budget of around 4.5 million dollars pales in comparison to endowments managed by many universities and the investments in university-based research and development made by science and industry over the past half century, the initiative has been extremely influential in shaping the progression of the digital humanities in American colleges, universities, libraries, and museums (National Endowment for the Humanities 2011). Other funding sources over the past half decade—such as the MacArthur Foundation's HASTAC Digital Media and Learning Grants (forty-four multiyear awards ranging in funding from forty-five thousand dollars to more than five million dollars), Google's 2010 Digital Humanities Research Awards (twelve one- to two-year grants totaling almost one million dollars), and the Andrew Mellon Foundation's Grants to universities (totaling more than one hundred and twenty million dollars in 2009) and libraries and museums (more than thirty-six million dollars in 2009, with significant amounts earmarked for various digitization projects)—have also mapped a sense of opportunity onto the digital humanities landscape (Digital Media and Learning Recent Grants; Orwant; The Andrew Mellon Foundation). Even though "humanities computing" has been around in some capacity for over half a century, we seem, in the past few years, to have reached a tipping point that has made the digital humanities more permanent and influential within the academic landscape (Kirschenbaum, "Digital Humanities As/Is a Tactical Term").

The discordance between a roiled university system where the very role of the humanities is being challenged and an obviously invigorated subfield begs pause and deeper consideration. This task is made easier by the fact that much work in the digital humanities over the past two years has been keenly self-aware. This very volume itself is intended to highlight some key debates in an effort to clarify the field. Yet few scholars or practitioners have directly addressed the glaring tension between a subfield that booms while its parent struggles to maintain footing.

Though work in the digital humanities has done much to reorient academic thinking to new information and communication realities, it has not yet done enough to show how the values and lessons at the core of the field might reshape the role of the humanities in the university of the future. What's troubling is that it could. More so than just about any other subfield, the digital humanities possess the capability to invigorate humanities instruction in higher education and to reassert how the humanities can help us understand and shape the world around us. Every college student engages some form of humanistic inquiry in order to fulfill general education requirements. Even beyond general education, regardless of discipline, the very idea of a "curriculum" requires that faculty and administrators delve into the questions of, what must our students learn in their time on campus, and how? Debating how knowledge is and should be made necessitates a certain amount of humanistic inquiry, and to be most relevant such processes must be acclimated to the technological and communicative revolution within which we are living. There are multiple paths, then, for work in the digital humanities to influence the future of higher education in vibrant ways. Even Stanley Fish has found in the digital humanities a rejoinder to those administrators "who still think of the humanities as the province of precious insights that offer little to those who are charged with the task of making sense of the world" (Fish).

Digital humanists are certainly aware of this potential. As Matthew Kirschenbaum has noted, "'What is digital humanities?' essays . . . are already genre pieces" ("What Is the Digital Humanities and What's It Doing in English Departments?"). There are several lines of argument within this genre, yet the common streak that runs through most is the belief that the digital humanities, whatever its boundaries, does and must continue to generate ideas that can transform what it means to do the humanities (Ramsay; Svensson 2011; Pressner and Schnapp et al.). Much in the past five years has already brought this to pass: ideas originating from self-identified digital humanists have pushed academic book publishing to embrace open access and offered new models for peer review; have fostered the development of new, accessible tools that are applicable to the range of work that humanists and nonhumanists do inside and outside of the academy; have issued a sustained challenge to the ways that academic conferences are organized and performed; and have asserted the value and importance of academic professionals who don't happen to be on the tenure track. Interventions into each of these areas of academic life relentlessly assert the values of openness, community, collaboration, democracy, and getting stuff done.

These values are professed and expressed in online conversations and in conferences by colleagues communicating across institutions, and those discussions and efforts to build community are undoubtedly good things. But interventions from the digital humanities into the various roles that the humanities play *within* individual colleges and universities have been far less forceful and assertive, and it's here where the upward trajectory of the field comes into starkest tension with the tenuous place of the humanities in American higher education. Even though many digital humanists think and speak of themselves and their work as rising in opposition to the traditional structures of the academy, much current work in the digital humanities also values research and scholarship far more than teaching, learning, and curriculum development. In this sense, the digital humanities are hard to distinguish significantly from other academic disciplines.

The "ugly stepchildren" of the university need protection, attention, and reinvigoration as higher education undergoes wrenching changes. Of course, it shouldn't be up to any single subfield to save the parent field or the university. Humanities computing and the digital humanities have never really taken on the university as a subject. As has been written elsewhere, the digital humanities is not new but rather is the latest stage of inquiry at the intersection of digits and the humanities that stretches back to the 1940s. This history reads much like the development of a traditional research subfield, one that values esoteric knowledge and has been mostly propelled by literature scholars who used computers to index text and examine large data sets. The field has gone through periods of professionalization, standardization, collaboration with industry, and incursions by other subdisciplines, such as when historians explored cliometrics in the 1970s (Schreibman, Siemens, and Unsworth; Hockey; and Thomas).

The advent of the World Wide Web has been the single most influential development in the field in the past two decades. Earlier uses of the web in the humanities were oriented toward making scholarship and methodologies more widely accessible and to exploring the implications of embedding various media within texts. Current uses of the web within the digital humanities are extending these projects but are also more fully embracing the connective possibilities of the Internet. Those possibilities existed in the excitement over listservs dating back to the 1980s but have become ever more multimodal, vibrant, and open in the past five to seven years.

The very sociality of the digital humanities is the central component of its current phase, and that—when combined with the influx of funding opportunities—has drawn scores of newcomers and, in turn, sparked recent efforts to define the field and set some boundaries. For much of its history, humanities computing was the realm of seasoned specialists whose search for deeper understanding of a particular field brought them to digital tools: the Austen scholar who wondered what meaning might be unveiled by crunching the words in her texts and by extension how such understandings might alter criticism or linguistic analysis, or the Civil War historian who sought to tell the story of two communities during the war by presenting various primary sources chronologically in close proximity to one another and inviting the visitor to perform some research—in the process creating a new model for how archives and libraries might approach the web (Burrows; Ayers). In the past few years, however, work and prestige in the digital humanities, because of the combination of networks and opportunity, has spread both vertically and horizontally. Graduate students and junior scholars are more confidently embracing what digital tools can mean for their work and are more likely than their predecessors to imagine a career path that revolves around their identities as digital humanists. The digital humanities is no longer a field one arrives at through one's research; it has become a destination in and of itself, a jumping-off point for the building of a scholarly identity.

This is a moment of empowerment for many doing work in the field, and it features movement from the periphery of American higher education toward the center. When power relationships change, politics often come into play. The history of the field has never been explicitly political, and its relationship with other attempts to transform the role of the humanities in the university system, such as the residential college movement or the recurrent debates over general education, has been incidental. Yet there have been a few noteworthy exceptions, and they suggest how the intersection of humanistic inquiry and technological innovation can be harnessed to newly empower individuals or groups.

In the 1980s and 1990s, the City University of New York's American Social History Project and George Mason's Center for History and New Media (now the Roy Rosenzweig Center for History and New Media) were founded by social historians who were deeply interested in how technology might popularize the study of history from the bottom up. Randy Bass's work at Georgetown, with the Crossroads and Visible Knowledge Projects and the Center for New Designs in Learning and Scholarship, has explored how technology and the networks it enables can open up pedagogical processes to inquiry, intervention, and reinvention. These projects were eminently political not just because they emerged out of work in labor and social history but also because each asserted that technology is not merely a tool for doing work along the lines that humanities academics have always pursued. They sought first and foremost to explore how technology might transform the operation of the humanities within the academy by opening up new possibilities and contexts for teaching and learning.[1] They were exceptional because they both produced great scholarship and focused on pedagogy and curriculum development. The most celebrated work in the digital humanities over the past decade has not often shared those priorities but instead has revolved around the research, tool, and network building that have always defined the field.

This is not to say that the current stage of work in the digital humanities is completely without politics. The celebration of openness, sharing, and collaboration that prevails within the field is itself an attempt to be the type of change digital humanists want to see in a more progressive university. The recognition of those of us, like me, who have ended up on the #alt-ac path as central to the humanities is one of the sharper critiques that digital humanists have leveled at higher education.[2] These are people whose work is often support oriented and who spend their time building curricula; organizing faculty development initiatives; and planting, congealing, and connecting communities of practice. Yet when looking at the #alt-ac landscape closely, it's difficult to see how the demands of that career path differ significantly from those of a tenure-track route. To qualify for an #alt-ac position, one must show ability as a scholar by presenting at conferences, keeping up with scholarship in multiple fields, and promoting one's work. To progress along an #alt-ac path, one must produce scholarship or other types of work on a similar scale and timeline as a faculty member, even though only the rare #alt-ac position allows space and autonomy in the daily workflow for scholarship of any type. These are overwhelmingly nontenure-track positions, and many are short term.

The very presence and growing prominence of #alt-ac work is evidence that cracks have opened in the academy that are being filled by talented people, many of whom would prefer to be on the tenure track. If folks in the digital humanities had their way, those positions would not be space fillers but rather secure jobs that come with allowances for some of the generative autonomy that faculty enjoy ("Alternative Academic Careers"). Yet there is little indication that the labor structure of the academy will adjust to accommodate the inglorious work that so many #alt-ac academics are actually doing. And beyond proclamations that these positions are necessary and valuable, a range of conditions limit the ability of those working in the digital humanities to make a very forceful case that the university's labor structure should evolve.

One of those conditions is the dependence of the digital humanities upon grants. While the increase in funding available to digital humanities projects is welcome and has led to many innovative projects, an overdependence on grants can shape a field in a particular way. Grants in the humanities last a short period of time, which make them unlikely to fund the long-term positions that are needed to mount any kind of sustained challenge to current employment practices in the humanities. They are competitive, which can lead to skewed reporting on process and results, and reward polish, which often favors the experienced over the novice. They are external, which can force the orientation of the organizations that compete for them outward rather than toward the structure of the local institution and creates the pressure to always be producing. Tom Scheinfeldt, the managing director of the Roy Rosenzweig Center for History and New Media, has noted the challenges of winning and balancing enough grants to maintain stability in staffing (Scheinfeldt). Each of these components might potentially diminish the ability of groups doing digital humanities work to transform colleges and universities and assert their values locally. And each also nudges the field toward research and tool building, pursuits that produce more demonstrably tangible results than innovations focused on hard-to-measure areas like curriculum and pedagogy.

There is ample evidence that the grant procedures in the digital humanities are fair, welcoming to newcomers, and supportive of projects at a variety of stages. The NEH's ODH especially is well known for its openness, availability, and support during grant application processes and after grants are awarded and for building community between the projects it funds. But the "Common Questions" section of the NEH's website notes that the "NEH does not fund projects that deal solely with pedagogical theory or that are intended to improve writing, speaking, or thinking skills apart from a focus on specific humanities content." A generous reading of this guidance to visitors would acknowledge that pedagogical theory designed around specific humanities content is often more strongly constructed. And a preceding statement does note that one of the goals of the grants is to "strengthen teaching and learning in schools and colleges." But in a less generous reading, this statement implies that pedagogy and curricula are secondary factors in the humanities. This is reflected among the many pioneering projects supported by the NEH. Though many will likely produce resources that are valuable in the classroom, there are currently very few that have focused specifically on the undergraduate student as humanities doer (National Endowment for the Humanities, "Videos of 2010 DH Start-Up Grant Lightning Round Presentations").

The belief that work and prestige in the digital humanities has focused more on tools and scholarship than on pedagogy and curricula is present beyond the consideration of funding. Katherine Harris has argued that "teaching is invisible labor" repeatedly on her blog, on Twitter, and at conferences, noting that in the digital humanities this is just as true as it is elsewhere. Her comments are imbued with the insider/outsider tension that many academics feel and talk about when it comes to the digital humanities. 4/4 teaching loads and full administrative plates hamper the ability of many scholars to keep up with the conversation and to contribute to new work in the digital humanities. Harris argues that faculty members who focus on taking the core principles of the digital humanities into their assignment design should be seen as just as central to the field as the toolmakers, and just as worthy of prestige.

Other critics have said that beyond undervaluing questions of pedagogy and curricula, work in the digital humanities has failed to articulate a social and political role within and beyond the university. In the wake of widespread confusion about which papers got accepted to the Digital Humanities 2011 Conference—a conference devoted to "Big Tent Digital Humanities"—Alex Reid sensed that the field was rejecting large questions about the impact of technology on the contemporary human condition and reverting to a focus on software writing, indexing, and data mining. "Perhaps humanists, digital and otherwise, would prefer to cede questions of literacy, pedagogy, and contemporary media to other non-humanistic or quasi-humanistic fields," he concluded (Reid).

Alan Liu has argued that digital humanists should do more to engage and transform the traditional social and political role of the humanities both inside and beyond the university. He traces the vectors through which work in the digital humanities has pushed practices in the humanities in new directions: from "writing to authoring/collaborating," from "reading to social computing," from "interpreting to data-mining," from "critical judgment to information credibility," from "peer reviewing to commenting," and from "teaching to co-developing" ("Digital Humanities and Academic Change"). But he also details the structures within and around which the digital humanities have developed, arguing that it has created only the conditions for "evolutionary change" instead of "revolutionary change" (ibid).

The field has not produced enough of the "cultural criticism" that gives research in the humanities meaning and impact beyond the esoteric. Liu and several other scholars launched the advocacy site *4Humanities* in November 2010, and it promises to provide proponents of the humanities with "a stockpile of digital tools, collaboration methods, royalty-free designs and images, best practices, new-media expertise, and customizable newsfeeds of issues and events relevant to the state of the humanities in any local or national context" (Liu, "Digital Humanities and Academic Change"). At current reading—admittedly early in the life of *4Humanities*—the site is an irregularly updated group blog and index of digital humanities projects whose posts assert the value of the humanities and link to similar media. The stridency and grandiosity of the *4Humanities* mission statement is important and necessary, but there does not seem to be a detailed plan at this stage for realizing the group's goals.

Such plans are crucial, necessary, and incredibly difficult to implement. Too few digital humanities projects take the extra steps to argue for their generalizable value or even to create the conditions for broad adoption. There are many explanations for this, not least of all the question of digital humanists' responsibility for service, which Liu addresses in his work and Bethany Nowviskie has also written about (Nowviskie, "Eternal September of the Digital Humanities"). The majority of the resources invested in digital humanities projects go toward producing tools, often with some funding left over for marketing. There tends to be less effort given to the grinding and frustrating process of supporting a tool after it has been produced. Such steps are necessary for building a user base, fixing bugs, and creating the conditions for additional community development.[3]

Take, for instance, the impressive *Hypercities* project, "a collaborative research and educational platform for traveling back in time to explore the historical layers of city spaces in an interactive, hypermedia environment" (*Hypercities*). *Hypercities* is funded by the MacArthur Foundation and is developed at the UCLA Center for the Digital Humanities. The site allows visitors to drill down into geolocated historical maps and to build multimedia collections on top. This is a fantastic resource for humanities instruction at various levels, and yet there are obstacles that limit its impact. At the time this essay is being written, more than two years after *Hypercities* was launched, the documentation for the project is spotty, FAQs and forum pages are under construction, and the only content on a page labeled "Getting Started" is an eight-minute video that offers an overview of the platform but no explanation of how one can actually begin working on it. The site lists a handful of classes that are using *Hypercities* as of spring 2011, but each of those was taught by a researcher who was personally involved in building the site.

It is not clear to what extent *Hypercities* is being used for teaching and learning beyond the orbit of the Center for Digital Humanities at UCLA. *Hypercities* may very well have plans for making more robust documentation and support for their young platform. But there is a feeling that projects like this, which embrace "perpetual beta" and focus more on delivering whiz-bang components than doing the less glamorous—and less recognized—work of outreach, community development, and support, especially around questions of pedagogy and curriculum development. Yet those questions are perhaps just as important to securing and extending the reach of innovations as the innovations themselves. It is in those moments of engagement with those who aren't already part of the conversation where the values embedded in the individual digital humanities project become most generalized, accessible, and influential.

Pedagogy and curricula remain the best avenues to assert, protect, and energize the role of the humanities in higher education, particularly via the general education programs that, unfortunately, so few full-time faculty members get excited about teaching. These curricula are often expected to fulfill multiple goals, including introducing students to the college experience, providing remediation where needed, giving students broad exposure to the humanities, and building broad information literacy. But in many cases, large general education courses are foisted upon adjuncts who are unsupported and who often don't know how their courses fit in with other parts of the curriculum. Yet it remains here where a college's values are most evident and here where ideas from the digital humanities can have the most transformative impact.

Several colleges are realizing that their curricula need to adapt to the challenges emerging from rapidly changing modes of information exchange and communication. The 2011 *Horizon Report* identified digital media literacy as "a key skill in every discipline and profession" and noted that while some colleges and universities are starting to integrate these skills into curricula, the progress is slow and uncoordinated (Johnson, Smith, Willis, Levine, and Haywood). A few programs and centers have emerged that attempt to do this via specific student projects, including Maryland's Digital Cultures and Creativity Program, the University of California's Digital Media and Learning Center, University of Virginia's Digital Media Lab, and University of North Carolina's Media Resources Center.

The University of Mary Washington (UMW) has built an online publishing platform—UMW Blogs—that has for five years pushed the school's curriculum to embrace the opportunities of networked teaching and learning and the exploration of processes of digital identity formation. The platform emerged in large part due to the inspiration of faculty member Gardner Campbell's time on campus and the fervent experimentation of instructional technologist Jim Groom and his comrades at the Division of Teaching and Learning Technologies. It has benefited from partnerships with several committed faculty members. Led by Jeffrey McClurken, a group of faculty and staff at UMW is now seeking to systematize what they have learned via work on UMW Blogs in the form of a Digital Knowledge Initiative (DKI). This would create a Digital Knowledge Center to support students who are looking to adapt new technologies into their learning and to help faculty members who are seeking to integrate digital work into their courses.[4] A broader goal would be to foster and institutionalize a college-wide conversation about teaching and learning with digital tools and to develop curricula and support practices that would best equip students to critically produce, consume, and assess information during their college years and beyond.

New York City College of Technology's current project—"A Living Laboratory: Redesigning General Education for a 21st Century College of Technology"—offers an exciting reconceptualization of the traditional general education curriculum. This project has four connected goals: "a redesign of the college's general education curriculum to enrich connections between the courses taken by students throughout their four years at the college; the creation of a state-of-the-art digital platform for teaching and learning; the integration of comprehensive outcomes assessment into the curriculum; and the establishment of a restricted endowment to support the new Center for the Study of the Brooklyn Waterfront" (Brooklyn Eagle). The imprint of the digital humanities is visible in this project, especially in its multi- and interdisciplinarity, its reliance on open digital tools, and its emphasis on creating new models of collaboration between students, faculty members, administrators, and the community around the college. Matthew K. Gold—the editor of this volume—is the primary investigator on the 3.1-million-dollar Department of Education grant, and Gold not only has been an active participant in the digital humanities community but also has been instrumental in extending that conversation throughout the twenty-three-campus City University of New York (CUNY) system. He is the director of the CUNY Academic Commons and a cofounder of the CUNY Digital Humanities Initiative and was also the project director of "Looking for Whitman: The Poetry of Place in the Life and Work of Walt Whitman." The last project was the beneficiary of two Digital Humanities Start-Up Grants from the NEH's ODH, and "A Living Laboratory" builds directly on both the structure and "place-based pedagogy" explored in the Whitman experiment in a way that promises to transform what it means to teach and learn at City Tech (*Looking for Whitman*).[5]

The initiatives at both UMW and City Tech have emerged in deep dialogue with developments in the digital humanities. Importantly, those dialogues have been led by individuals who also possess a deep sense of and long-standing commitment to the particular missions and needs of each individual institution. Each project has the potential to fundamentally alter the curriculum of the college and could also shift (for at least the medium term, if not longer) the labor structure that supports instruction in the humanities on each campus. It is not coincidental that both UWM and CUNY have long traditions of support for experiential and radical pedagogy.[6] Such commitments are preconditions for work in the digital humanities to have a truly transformative impact on a college's humanities instruction.

Ultimately, of course, it shouldn't be up to the digital humanities or any one field to "fix" the problems in American higher education. Those problems are reflective of much broader social and political conditions. Yet the digital humanities can—and, indeed, is uniquely positioned to—invigorate arguments about why the humanities matters, how it relates to our progress as a society, and why universities must protect and promote it vigorously in the face of increased pressure to quantify its relevance. Participants in the digital humanities and the funding agencies that support their work can learn from initiatives like those at UMW and City Tech that tool production, iteration, conferences, and a few cluster hires here and there will not dramatically alter the landscape of higher education. But more bridges that connect the digital humanities to the myriad spaces the humanities occupy within the structure of the academy just might. To really make a lasting impact on higher education, digital humanists must give more systematic, consistent, resilient, multilayered attention to the invisible, ugly stepchildren of the university.

NOTES

1. I was a participant in the Crossroads Project in 1995 through 1996 as an undergraduate in the Program in American Culture at the University of Michigan and worked for and learned much from Steve Brier and Joshua Brown at the American Social History Project from 1999 through 2003.

2. Since completing a PhD in American History, I have become an educational technologist. I now administer a large open-source publishing platform at Baruch College out

of the Bernard L. Schwartz Communication Institute, where I also help design and run faculty development initiatives and edit a weblog, Cac.ophony.org, that explores issues in communication across the curriculum.

3. Writing and updating documentation is something I've struggled with immensely since launching Blogs@Baruch in Fall 2008. This problem seems recognized within the community, as the Roy Rosenzweig Center for History and New Media recently formed a "Documentation Working Group" in an attempt to bolster outreach and communication in support of its open-source archive tool, Omeka (Brennan).

4. Thanks to Jeffrey W. McClurken and Jim Groom for sharing and discussing this Quality Enhancement Proposal as it was under consideration by the university. Ultimately, another proposal was selected. The DKI is not dead, however, and the proposal's findings will deeply inform curriculum and cocurricular development at the college.

5. Two other NEH-funded faculty development projects—"Water and Work: The History and Ecology of Downtown Brooklyn" and "Along the Shore: Changing and Preserving the Landmarks of Brooklyn's Industrial Waterfront"—also served as prototypes for the grant.

6. See Steve Brier's essay, "Where's the Pedagogy? The Role of Teaching and Learning in the Digital Humanities," in this volume for more on CUNY's tradition of innovative pedagogy.

BIBLIOGRAPHY

Andrew Mellon Foundation. "The Andrew W. Mellon Foundation: President's Report, 2009." http://www.mellon.org/news_publications/annual-reports-essays/presidents-reports/2009.

Ayers, Edward L., ed. *The Valley of the Shadow: Two Communities in the American Civil War*. Virginia Center for Digital History, University of Virginia. 2001. http://valley.lib.virginia.edu/.

Brennan, Sheila. "Help Us Make Omeka Better." *Omeka*. April 28, 2011. http://omeka.org/blog/2011/04/28/help-us-make-omeka-better/.

Brooklyn Eagle. "City Tech Will Use Downtown as 'Lab,' Thanks to $3M Grant." *Brooklyn Daily Eagle*, December 10, 2010. http://www.brooklyneagle.com/categories/category.php?category_id=31&id=40086

Brier, Steve. Comment on "On EdTech and the Digital Humanities," by Luke Waltzer. *Bloviate*. October 21, 2010. http://lukewaltzer.com/on-edtech-and-the-digital-humanities/.

Burrows, J. F. *Computation into Criticism?: A Study of Jane Austen's Novels and an Experiment in Method*. Oxfordshire: Oxford University Press, 1987.

"Digital Media and Learning: Recent Grants." MacFound.org. http://www.macfound.org/site/c.lkLXJ8MQKrH/b.947073/k.4CD8/Domestic_Grantmaking__Education__Recent_Grants.htm.

Fish, Stanley. "The Triumph of the Humanities." NYTimes.com, June 22, 2011. http://opinionator.blogs.nytimes.com/2011/06/13/the-triumph-of-the-humanities/.

Harris, Katherine. "Failure? DHC 2011 Kerfuffle." *Triproftri*. March 2, 2011. http://triproftri.wordpress.com/2011/03/02/failure-dhc-2011-kerfuffle/.

———. "In/Out, DH, Pedagogy, or Where It All Started (MLA 2011)." *Triproftri*. March 1, 2011. http://triproftri.wordpress.com/2011/03/01/inout-dh-pedagogy-or-where-it-all-started/.

Hockey, Susan. "The History of Humanities Computing." In *Companion to Digital Humanities (Blackwell Companions to Literature and Culture)*, edited by Ray Siemens, John Unsworth, and Susan Schreibman. Oxford: Blackwell, 2004. http://www.digitalhumanities.org/companion/view?docId=blackwell/9781405103213/9781405103213.xml&chunk.id=ss1-2-1.

Howard, Jennifer. "The MLA Convention in Translation." *Chronicle of Higher Education*. December 31, 2009. http://chronicle.com/article/The-MLA-Convention-in/63379/.

Hypercities. http://hypercities.com/.

Johnson, Larry, Rachel Smith, Holly Willis, Alan Levine, and Keene Haywood. *2011 Horizon Report*. Austin, Tex.: New Media Consortium, 2011.

Kirschenbaum, Matthew. "Digital Humanities As/Is a Tactical Term." In *Debates in the Digital Humanities,* edited by Matthew K. Gold. Minneapolis: University of Minnesota Press, 2012.

———. "What Is Digital Humanities and What's It Doing in English Departments?" *ADE Bulletin*. 150 (2010): 55–61. http://mkirschenbaum.wordpress.com/2011/01/22/what-is-digital-humanities/. Reprinted in this volume.

Liu, Alan. "Digital Humanities and Academic Change." *English Language Notes* 47(2009): 17–35.

———. "Where Is the Cultural Criticism in the Digital Humanities." *Alan Liu*. http://liu.english.ucsb.edu/where-is-cultural-criticism-in-the-digital-humanities/.

"Looking for Whitman." http://lookingforwhitman.org.

Menand, Louis. *The Marketplace of Ideas: Reform and Resistance in the American University*. New York: W. W. Norton, 2010.

National Endowment for the Humanities. "Appropriations Request for Fiscal Year 2012." February 2011. http://www.nea.gov/about/Budget/NEA-FY12-Appropriations-Request.pdf.

———. "Common Questions," http://www.neh.gov/grants/commonquestions.html.

———. "Videos of 2010 DH Start-Up Grant Lightning Round Presentations." Office of Digital Humanities. http://www.neh.gov/ODH/ODHHome/tabid/36/EntryId/155/Videos-of-2010-DH-Start-Up-Grant-Lightning-Round-Presentations.aspx.

"News: Tweetup at the MLA." *Inside Higher Education*. January 4, 2010. http://www.insidehighered.com/news/2010/01/04/tweeps.

Nowviskie, Bethany, ed. "Alternative Academic Careers." *#alt-academy*. 2011. http://mediacommons.futureofthebook.org/alt-ac/cluster/alternative-academic-careers-humanities-scholars.

———. "#alt-ac: alternate academic careers for humanities scholars." *Bethany Nowviskie*. January 3, 2010. http://nowviskie.org/2010/alt-ac/.

———. "Eternal September of the Digital Humanities." *Bethany Nowviskie*. October 15, 2010. http://nowviskie.org/2010/eternal-september-of-the-digital-humanities/.

Nussbaum, Martha C. *Cultivating Humanity: A Classical Defense of Reform in Liberal Education*. Cambridge, Mass.: Harvard University Press, 1998.

Orwant, John. "Our Commitment to the Digital Humanities." *The Official Google Blog*. July 14, 2010. http://googleblog.blogspot.com/2010/07/our-commitment-to-digital-humanities.html.

Pannapaker, William. "The MLA and the Digital Humanities." *Chronicle of Higher Education*. December 28, 2009. http://chronicle.com/blogPost/The-MLAthe-Digital/19468/.

Pressner, Todd, and Jeffrey Schnapp et al. "The Digital Humanities Manifesto 2.0." May 29, 2009. http://manifesto.humanities.ucla.edu/2009/05/29/the-digital-humanities-manifesto-20/.

Ramsay, Stephen. "Who's In and Who's Out," *Stephen Ramsay*. January 8, 2011. http://lenz.unl.edu/papers/2011/01/08/whos-in-and-whos-out.html.

"Recent Grants." MacFound Digital Media and Learning. http://www.macfound.org/site/c.lkLXJ8MQKrH/b.947073/k.4CD8/Domestic_Grantmaking__Education__Recent_Grants.htm.

Reid, Alex. "Digital Digs: The Digital Humanities Divide." *Digital Digs*. February 17, 2011. http://www.alex-reid.net/2011/02/the-digital-humanities-divide.html.

Scheinfeldt, Tom. "Introduction: 'Tenure is broken. Please give me tenure'." *#alt-academy*. June 23, 2011. http://mediacommons.futureofthebook.org/alt-ac/pieces/toward-third-way-rethinking-academic-employment.

Schreibman, Susan, Ray Siemens, and John Unsworth. "The Digital Humanities and Humanities Computing: An Introduction." In *Companion to Digital Humanities (Blackwell Companions to Literature and Culture)*, edited by Ray Siemens, John Unsworth, and Susan Schreibman. Oxford: Blackwell, 2004. http://www.digitalhumanities.org/companion/view?docId=blackwell/9781405103213/9781405103213.xml&chunk.id=ss1-1-3.

Sinclair, Stéfan. "Digital Humanities and Stardom." *Stéfan Sinclair*. January 9, 2011. http://stefansinclair.name/dh-stardom.

Svensson, Patrik. "Humanities Computing as Digital Humanities." *Digital Humanities Quarterly* 3, no. 3 (Summer 2009). http://digitalhumanities.org/dhq/vol/3/3/000065/000065.html.

———. "The Landscape of Digital Humanities." *Digital Humanities Quarterly* 4, no. 1 (Summer 2010). http://digitalhumanities.org/dhq/vol/4/1/000080/000080.html.

———. "A Visionary Scope of the Digital Humanities." *The Humlab Blog*. February 23, 2011. http://blog.humlab.umu.se/?p=2894.

Thomas, William G. II, "Computing and the Historical Imagination." In *Companion to Digital Humanities (Blackwell Companions to Literature and Culture)*, edited by Ray Siemens, John Unsworth, and Susan Schreibman. Oxford: Blackwell, 2004. http://digital

humanities.org/companion/view?docId=blackwell/9781405103213/9781405103213.xml&chunk.id=ss1-2-5.

United States National Science Foundation. "FY 2010 Performance and Financial Highlights." February 15, 2011. http://www.nsf.gov/pubs/2011/nsf11002/nsf11002.pdf.

Graduate Education and the Ethics of the Digital Humanities

ALEXANDER REID

Among the many challenges and opportunities that are emerging from the rapid expansion of, and growing interest in, the digital humanities is the question of how to prepare graduate students for academic careers in the humanities (to say nothing of potential nonacademic or para-academic professional opportunities that might arise in the context of digital humanities). According to a Modern Language Association (MLA) study of 2007 through 2008 doctoral recipients in English and foreign languages, the median time from a Bachelor's degree to a PhD is ten to eleven years (2). As such, graduate students entering doctoral programs in 2011 will likely not be receiving their degrees until the end of the decade. Assuming even the most fortunate of degree paths, they will likely not be coming up for tenure until 2025. Given the volatility of digital culture and the digital humanities, it is difficult to know how to prepare entering graduate students for that job market or their careers beyond. To what extent do we imagine that all humanities doctoral students should have fluency with digital scholarly and pedagogical methods? Today, the typical literary studies graduate student might be expected to have a baseline fluency in a range of critical, theoretical methods as well as the ability to teach at least one literary survey course. In the future, will there be—and should there be—some digital component to this shared baseline knowledge? Will all humanities doctoral students need to have fluency with digital scholarly and pedagogical methods? And for those graduate students who specialize in the digital humanities, how will that field be defined? Is it a distinct field or a series of methodologies attached to existing disciplines (e.g., one might be a Victorianist who uses digital humanities research methods)? These questions become even more complicated as one intersects digital humanities with other fields of study. As a rhetorician who studies digital rhetoric, I know that the requirements for digital work in my field are different from those in literary studies or comparative literature and that those differences only proliferate as one includes other humanistic disciplines. Digital humanities clearly means different things depending on one's disciplinary perspective, and yet, to some degree, there is also an emerging entity that is digital humanities itself that confronts traditional humanities disciplines and demands attention.

To a large extent, the answers to these questions depend on how one defines the digital humanities, and that definition is currently in flux. The history of the term, as explained by Matthew Kirschenbaum, begins in 2002 with John Unsworth in the field previously known as humanities computing (2). Kirschenbaum recounts Unsworth's participation in the decision that led to the title of Blackwell's *Companion to the Digital Humanities* (published in 2004) as well as to the creation of the Alliance for the Digital Humanities Organizations in 2005 and finally the National Endowment for the Humanities' (NEH) creation of a Digital Humanities Initiative in 2006. Each of these namings essentially equated digital humanities with the prior field of humanities computing. While humanities computing has a long history, dating back to the earliest days of computers, there are other humanities research practices involving the study of computers and related technologies with well-established practices. Research in computers and composition dates to the beginning of the 1980s, with the first issue of the journal *Computers and Composition* appearing in 1983. New media studies emerges, along with the "new" media itself, from the field of media studies, which itself has been active since at least the middle of the last century. Certainly new media studies as the study of Internet culture develops in the 1990s along with that technology. In a similar vein, the cultural study of technology dates back to the earliest days of cultural studies and Raymond Williams's investigation of television. As with new media studies, the study of digital culture emerges alongside the increasing prevalence of digital technologies. One might also point to video game studies as a particular specialized field of digital research emerging in the 1990s, though clearly with a longer history in the study of games.

When humanities computing was known as such, it existed in relative comfort alongside these other modes of investigation. Indeed, on local levels, there were likely common points of interest between, for example, someone in humanities computing and someone in computers and composition regarding department expenditures on technology or university computing policies. However, there was little crossover between humanities computing and these other fields in terms of scholarship or pedagogy. That is, the issues that might arise in scholarly work or in a course on humanities computing are quite different from those that one would typically find in any of these other fields. As I view it, there is a significant shift in emphasis that separates humanities computing from these other fields. Humanities computing is primarily focused on the digital and or computational study of the humanities, while these other areas, though each unique in its own right, share a common focus in the humanities' study of digital technology and culture. That is not to say that scholars in humanities computing are *not* interested in studying digital technologies from a humanities perspective; nor do I mean to suggest that scholars in these other fields are *not* interested in establishing computational methods or building digital tools for conducting their research. It would seem that each of these areas has its own mix of technical facility and critical methods. The cultural study of technology is largely undertaken using traditional methods of scholarship. In computers and composition, my own field, it is not uncommon for specialists to have skills in digital media production and less commonly programming and to employ these in the study of digital technologies. In humanities computing, technical ability is a necessity; and, while there is certainly an awareness of a critical engagement with technology, most of the scholarship undertaken is directed as traditional humanistic areas of study—for example, Jerome McGann's archive project, "The Complete Writings and Pictures of Dante Gabriel Rossetti." Such a project clearly requires a critical engagement with technology. However, the project is not itself a scholarly study of digital technology; it is research into Rossetti's works. In reviewing the content, or even the titles, of journal articles and conference presentations in the fields of humanities computing, computers and composition, new media studies, the cultural study of technology, games studies, and so on, there is a clear difference in emphasis between humanities computing and the others, where humanities computing is primarily interested in computing as a research method and these other fields primarily focus on computing as an object of study. This observation is not meant as a critique of any field but simply as a recognition that a scholar who identified with humanities computing would not likely be mistaken for being in one of these others.

Scholars in these research areas have coexisted with little conflict, but the creation of the term "digital humanities," and the NEH's subsequent adoption of that term to organize its funding of technology-related humanities research, brought them into a new relationship with one another, creating an umbrella term with which they must contend. I have seen this in my own professional experience, though there are many scholars who could tell similar stories. I first taught in a computer lab in 1992 and have been teaching using a variety of technologies since. I was the editor of an online literary magazine in 1996. My dissertation, completed in 1997, included a study of the role of technology in composition. Since then, my scholarship and teaching has operated in the areas of computers and composition, new media studies, and the cultural study of technology. In short, I have been engaged in the humanistic study of technology for nearly twenty years, but I have never once thought of myself as being in the field of humanities computing. On the other hand, how could I not think of myself as a digital humanist? That said, I do not mean to put too much emphasis on the particular genesis of the term "digital humanities." Given the global, information revolution over the past two decades, it is not surprising that significant changes have taken place in the humanities use and study of digital technology.

While such differences can be viewed as another rehearsal of familiar territorial battles among academics, there are larger issues at stake. Growing concerns over the general defunding of the humanities have led some to look to the digital humanities as a means to revitalize the humanities as a whole. In November 2010, a group of digital humanities scholars, led by Alan Liu, Geoffrey Rockwell, and Melissa Terras, formed a group called 4Humanities with a primary mission of using the digital humanities to advocate for the humanities. As the 4Humanities mission statement observes, the digital humanities "catch the eye of administrators and funding agencies who otherwise dismiss the humanities as yesterday's news. They connect across disciplines with science and engineering fields. They have the potential to use new technologies to help the humanities communicate with, and adapt to, contemporary society" ("Mission"). However, one might wonder if this growing interest from administrators, funding agencies, and others is in humanities computing, now renamed, or in the larger umbrella of digital humanities. In part the answer to this question might be framed in terms of the *Horizon Report*, an annual document produced collaboratively by EDUCAUSE and the New Media Consortium, which identifies technologies "on the horizon" for adoption in higher education. The 2011 report observes, "Digital media literacy continues its rise in importance as a key skill in every discipline and profession" and identifies this as the number one critical challenge facing higher education in terms of technology (Johnson et al., 3). In a similar vein, HASTAC, the Humanities, Arts, Sciences and Technology Advanced Collaboratory, asks in its mission statement, "What would our research, technology design, and thinking look like if we took seriously the momentous opportunities and challenges for learning posed by our digital era? What happens when we stop privileging traditional ways of organizing knowledge (by fields, disciplines, and majors or minors) and turn attention instead to alternative modes of creating, innovating, and critiquing that better address the interconnected, interactive global nature of knowledge today, both in the classroom and beyond?" Such questions, along with the concerns regarding new media literacy, would certainly seem to fall within the purview of the humanities and thus would seem to be central questions of a digital humanities for the future, and yet these would not be the kinds of research questions that have traditionally defined humanities computing. They would, however, be precisely the kinds of questions asked by computers and composition, new media studies, the cultural studies of technology, and even games studies as they enter into concerns of serious or educational gaming.

In short, we find ourselves at a difficult crossroads in the digital humanities. If we define digital humanities in its narrowest sense as the use of computational means to study traditional humanistic content, then it is likely fair to say that it can and will remain a kind of methodological specialization, akin to being a Marxist or feminist critic. Humanities computing appears poised to grow in numbers of scholars, and it is likely that all humanities graduate students will be expected to have some knowledge of the field, just as they are expected to know something of Marx or feminism today. Nevertheless, it is difficult to imagine a near future where every humanities department feels it is necessary to have a humanities computing specialist. However, if we expand our notion of digital humanities, then a very different picture emerges. The humanities at large faces an uncertain future. Digital technologies are raising increasingly pressing questions for humanists and higher education. If we think of the humanities educational mission as one that is founded on literacy, not just in the sense of a basic reading and writing literacy, but in the sense of a broader cultural literacy, then the growing need to teach digital literacy impacts all humanities faculty. As relatively uncommon as an insistence on humanities computing in job ads for literary scholars is today (growing but still uncommon), it is quite typical for faculty teaching rhetoric and composition to be expected to use technology for teaching and be able to teach digital or "multimodal" composition. When one adds searches for humanities computing faculty to searches for digital culture, new media studies, game studies, technical/professional writing, and digitally proficient rhetoric and composition faculty, then one begins to see a faster expanding demand for digital humanities, broadly conceived. And those numbers would just be within English studies. From this view, it is not unreasonable to expect that all incoming humanities graduate students will require a yet undefined digital literacy just as they acquire a shared humanistic (print?) literacy today.

Furthermore, just as digital media are transforming every aspect of the way we communicate, they will inevitably shift the way humanities scholars conduct their research. This shift in humanities research practices will not be determined by new technologies any more than the development of typewriters, industrial printing, and other late industrial technologies "determined" the shape of twentieth-century humanities scholarship. However, just as one might recognize that twentieth-century scholarship relied upon, and emerged in connection with, the communication technologies of the period, one might equally recognize that the scholarly practices of this century will develop in relation to emerging digital technologies. As such, today's graduate students will not only face a professional career where they will need to help students develop a digital literacy; they will also be employing an as-yet-undeveloped, specialized digital literacy of their own as teachers and scholars. As a result, while undefined and perhaps always in flux with the ongoing churn of digital innovation, graduate students in the humanities face multiple, related but also dissimilar, challenges. They will require a critical understanding and technical facility with a broadly conceived digital literacy that would be roughly analogous to contemporary humanities faculty understanding and facility with print literacy. They will require some level of technical facility with digital production and programming, though the particulars of that will certainly vary among fields and disciplines. Finally, as teachers they will require a technical facility and critical, *pedagogical* understanding of the use of emerging technologies in the classroom.

Legacy Research

When we look at our legacy scholarly and teaching practices, it is possible to historicize them in several ways. One might look back to the classical Greek philosophical dialogue or identify any number of other historical starting points for various humanities disciplines. No doubt, the contemporary humanities share rhetorical and scholarly practices that extend deep into history. At the same time, disciplines have specific rhetorical and scholarly practices that identify them as disciplinary. That is, for example, a journal article in literary studies has specific discursive features that make it not simply an "essay" or an "argument." These features, I would argue, are largely the product of the late industrial period. That is, the general shape and scope of published research reflects access to information; the speed of communication; and the difficulties of composing, editing, and publishing scholarship. Before the second industrial revolution in the United States, scholarly practices were quite different. Indeed the entire project of higher education was revolutionized during the late nineteenth century. Specifically, for language and literary study, the first MLA convention, and subsequently the first issue of MLA's flagship publication *PMLA*, came about in the 1880s. Professional organizations and related journals in history and philosophy date from the same period. Not coincidentally, as many scholars have noted (see Berlin, Connors, Graff, Russell, and Scholes, for example), this professionalization of humanities scholarship occurs during a time of rapid expansion for higher education. As James Berlin notes, in 1870 in the United States, 5,553 faculty taught at 563 institutions; by 1900, there were 23,868 faculty-held positions at 977 institutions (22–23). This increase mirrored the demand for a new educated class of the American workforce during the second industrial revolution. Undoubtedly industrialization not only provided technological means for travel, communication, and publication but also ushered in a new era of professionalism and approaches to management that was reflected in both the administration of universities and the organization of disciplines.

Industrialization not only prodded the growth of higher education; it directly supported the development of scholarly practices in the humanities. While the earliest MLA conventions were likely facilitated by rail travel, contemporary national conferences were built on air travel, a national highway system, and the general process of urbanization that led to conference centers and such: MLA is just one of many national conferences in many industries. Similarly *PMLA* becomes one of many periodicals in an age of industrial printing, and scholarly monographs fit into a larger publishing industry. An investigation of the various assemblages[1] or networks that have participated in the formation of humanities discourses could extend interminably. However, I think it is fair to say that the typical length of a journal article (around seven thousand words) or conference presentation (twenty minutes) is not a reflection of some tangible, epistemological structure in humanities research: under different technological constraints, these would likely be different. The economic limits that constrain the number of articles in a journal or how often a journal publishes no longer apply to digital publication. The traditional rationale for national conferences as the best if not only way for scholars to meet and communicate no longer applies. Similarly, many limits on the length of monographs and the number of monographs a press might publish shift in the movement to digital production and distribution.

Of course, such this shift from industrial to digital assemblages accounts for more than the length or frequency of publication. These assemblages play a central role in the establishment of pedagogical and scholarly practices and consequently on the professional, ethical relations we have established with one another. For instance, unlike a laboratory, which requires a team of people to operate, the default mode for humanities academic labor has been for a professor to work independently. Of course, independence is a relative term. All scholars draw upon other scholars in a variety of ways. However, typically, humanities scholars work alone while searching databases, archives, and library shelves; reading monographs, essays, and articles; and composing their scholarship. It is unusual for humanities scholarship to appear with more than two authors, let alone the long lists of authors that will accompany work in the sciences, for example. While late industrial technologies did not determine these practices, they became part of the assemblage of scholarly production. And just as it would be difficult for a single person to produce scientific scholarship without collaborators, it is challenging to collaborate in the humanities. Given that the assemblage operates effectively with a single author, one essentially has to invent new roles for additional participants. While there are certainly examples of notable, long-standing collaborations in the humanities, they are the exceptions to the rule.

As the humanities shift into a digital assemblage, however, these practices are changing, and this is already apparent in digital humanities fields, where research indicates a growing amount of collaboration (Meyer et al.). As with the sciences, digital humanities projects can require a broad range of expertise and a significant amount of labor, more than one person could expect to undertake. As Alan Liu notes, "It requires a full team of researchers with diverse skills in programming, database design, visualization, text analysis and encoding, statistics, discourse analysis, website design, ethics (including complex 'human subjects' research rules), and so on, to pursue ambitious digital projects at a grant-competitive level premised on making a difference in today's world" (27). In other words, there is a growing body of digital humanities work that requires collaboration. More broadly, however, the development of networked communication has facilitated collaboration for humanities scholars undertaking more traditional scholarship as well. I could publish this chapter on my blog as soon as it is finished and alert my colleagues via Twitter, Facebook, e-mail listservs, and so on. I would likely receive more, and more immediate, feedback from my colleagues that way then I will ever receive from publishing this chapter in a printed book. In fact, I wouldn't even need to wait until I was finished. I could publish this part today and the rest later. However, I could go beyond a publish, feedback, and conversation model to engage in more substantive collaboration of a scholarly work. That is, while the traditional scholarly model asks authors to respond to the requests and feedback of reviewers and editors, the author remains the sole person to make meaningful changes to the text (aside from editorial corrections). This practice is extended to the web when, for example, one authors a blog and invites comments. Though blog comments are public, where editorial and reviewer comments often are not, the blogger retains sole control of the texts he or she posts. However, social media obviously also allows for both real-time and asynchronous collaboration, resulting in a composition with multiple authors.

In short, from a technological perspective, it would be fairly easy to collaborate with a number of scholarly colleagues. From every other perspective, though, it could be quite difficult. Put simply, while we have all been carefully and extensively trained to research and write articles and monographs, we have little or no preparation for working as a networked community. In our defense, for most contemporary academics, such networks did not exist when they were in graduate school. Our scholarly discourses and practices were built in a century when information was relatively scarce and communication was comparatively difficult. Today, the conditions are so different that it is only the weight of institutional inertia that keeps us grinding forward, even as academic publishers fail, journal subscriptions dwindle, and humanities funding disappears. Though humanists are skilled at recognizing the historical contexts of the objects they study, they have largely overlooked the historically contingent nature of their own scholarly practices. As unlikely as a near future (i.e., the next fifteen to twenty years) without journal articles might be, it is equally unlikely that scholarly practices will move forward without being significantly transformed by emerging technologies. Currently, we have little understanding about what practices will develop in the next decade, even though we face the task of preparing graduate students for that decade today.

In this context, one encounters a *third* digital humanities. It is not simply the digital/computational study of the humanities or the humanistic study of the digital; it is the way in which the humanities as a whole shifts from a print paradigm to a digital one. It is in this sense that all the humanities becomes subsumed within the digital, and it is at this level that the concern for a digital education in graduate programs affects everyone in the humanities.

Teaching and Digital Literacy

Because humanities graduate students tend to come directly from humanities undergraduate majors and most of those majors provide little education regarding digital technologies, the typical student enters his or her graduate education as a novice in regards to the digital. Certainly there are exceptions to this rule. Students who developed an undergraduate interest in the digital could certainly have found an education in it. However, an education in the digital humanities or more generally in digital technology is hardly a common feature of an undergraduate career in the humanities, though in humanistic fields that verge into the social sciences or the arts, such as communications, fine arts, or media study, one is at least more likely to find departments where traditional humanities courses intermingle with courses in digital production or the study of digital media. Undoubtedly, for graduate students who are interested in specializing in humanities computing, specific programs at specific institutions will continue to develop. As is the case with most humanistic fields, certain institutions offer better training in this particular area of specialization than others. It will be interesting to see how graduate programs across the country decide to address the need for digital humanities specialists (in the narrowest sense of the term) in their own departments and hence the need to offer digital humanities courses to their own graduate students. Perhaps digital humanities specialists will function similarly to computers and writing specialists in rhetoric and composition. There are certain institutions that are notably strong in the field of computers and composition, but it is also the case that virtually any doctoral program in rhetoric and composition would include at least one professor who could provide graduate students with curriculum in technology. To give a counterexample, it would not be the case that the typical doctoral program in literary studies would offer courses in digital humanities, though some certainly do. Perhaps it is the case that humanistic disciplines that are focused, at least on the undergraduate level, in teaching production of some kind—for example, writers (rhetoric), journalists (communication), artists (fine arts)—are also more likely to offer graduate curriculum that prepares students in these areas and, not surprisingly, to hire faculty with discipline-specific digital knowledge and skill. Returning to my example of the field of rhetoric and composition, given that many openings now explicitly look for candidates with some digital expertise, it would seem unwise to enter a rhetoric and composition graduate program in 2011 without some plan to develop that expertise. Notably, this is a shift that has occurred in the last decade. As quickly as technological specializations in rhetoric and composition have grown, the general expectation of digital literacy for all writing faculty has expanded even faster. It is possible that the demand for digital humanities specialists in other disciplines will grow just as quickly. However, the real question for digital humanities is not how many specialists of different stripes will be sought on the job market but how quickly expectations for digital literacy among all humanists will rise. As such, the more pressing question for graduate education is not how graduate students who are interested in the digital humanities will gain that education but rather how graduate students as a whole will be educated to meet the humanities' digital future.

At my institution, the State University of New York at Buffalo (UB), we are neither particularly ahead nor particularly behind in terms of the digital humanities. We have a modestly funded "initiative" that supports digital humanities research done by faculty and graduate students. In our English department of approximately fifty faculty and one hundred and eighty master's and doctoral students, around 10 percent have received funding from our digital humanities initiative. Mostly that represents some curiosity or tangential interest in digital practices rather than any sustained digital humanistic inquiry, but UB remains at the stage of piquing nascent faculty interest in the digital. On different fronts, however, there are more pressing demands. The never-ending search for more revenue has led UB to expand its summer course offerings, and the primary way the English department has responded to this call is by developing online composition courses, which are taught by our graduate teaching assistants. This has required a substantial push in professional development to prepare TAs for this new digital task. Where two years ago only a handful of our sixty-five TAs would have had experience in teaching online, by the end of the 2011 summer, nearly half of our TAs will have done so. Teaching an online composition course requires relatively modest technical skills. Essentially, one needs to be able to make fairly full use of a course management system. However, the pedagogical demands for online teaching are quite challenging. Typically, face-to-face composition courses are taught through class discussion, small group work, and short lectures. None of these activities translates simply to an online environment. As such, teaching online requires the development of a new digitally mediated literacy through which the instructor can communicate with students and foster discussion and interaction in the class. In addition, our composition program has instituted a requirement whereby every composition course includes at least one formal "digital composition" assignment. While the requirement remains vague, the graduate TAs and adjunct instructors have developed a variety of assignments that require students to produce slidecasts, web pages, or video. The TAs have needed to develop a facility with some consumer-level digital production tools, ranging from slideware and image editors to audio and video editing, as well as knowledge of various social media platforms they might employ (blogs, wikis, etc.). Again, while the technical learning curves of such tools are not especially steep, there remain more challenging goals, such as developing a rhetorical skill with the technology (i.e., it's one thing to make a slideshow, but making an interesting one is a different challenge) and then figuring out how to teach these lessons to their students. Thus, even though most of our doctoral students are pursuing dissertation projects that are not in the digital humanities, the other demands of the department have begun to require them to develop a digital literacy.

The interesting result is that the graduate students encounter humanistic, rhetorical, and ethical questions regarding digital technologies as teachers first rather than as students or scholars. They wonder how to create and sustain online discussion forums or motivate their students to write longer blog posts. They struggle with creating and evaluating digital composition assignments. They ask questions about copyright and make decisions about public and closed online spaces and open source versus proprietary applications. Unfortunately they do so with only the cursory support of a few professional development workshops and with little or no experience doing digital work in their own coursework. While generations of novice teachers have largely had to discover for themselves their own teaching styles, at least they could draw on their experiences with faculty as a model for their own pedagogies. While all faculty discover that some essay assignments work better than others, at least they all knew what an essay was. For graduate teaching assistants facing the demands of teaching digital literacy through digital media, there is a very different challenge. Of course, it may still be possible for humanities graduate students to avoid using digital technologies in their teaching and not address the challenges of helping their students communicate in digital media. It is certainly possible for graduate students to write dissertations with a minimal use of digital technologies (e.g., word processors, library databases). However, it is now certainly a *choice* they must make.

Similarly, graduate faculty must also make a choice or, more accurately, a wager. If we believe that the demands and expectations for teaching and using digital technology in the next decade will not increase appreciably, then we are likely free to continue organizing our departments and curricula as we currently do. We can continue to hire according to existing models of what our departments should look like, models that have not changed much in the last twenty or thirty years. If, however, we find reason in the arguments put forth by groups like HASTAC, 4Humanities, or EDUCAUSE, then we have reason to believe that there will be a growing expectation that humanists will be able to address the educational and intellectual challenges of our digital culture. And if we believe that, then we face the difficult tasks of hiring faculty, reworking curriculum, and perhaps even developing professionally ourselves to meet those challenges.

Aside from hiring, which is almost always a contentious matter, the greatest difficulty for both graduate students and faculty will be discovering ways to infuse digital media into their teaching and scholarship. While developing a real facility with programming and design may remain a specialization, learning to use mainstream social media and digital production tools on a basic how-to level is not hard. Though we tend to speak of steep learning curves for faculty facing technology, the widespread participation in social media from YouTube to Wikipedia should be evidence in itself that learning the basics is not the challenge. Put differently, it's easy to set up a blog, and one can learn how to post in a few minutes. Maintaining a blog over an extended period of time is an entirely different matter. One not only faces rhetorical and compositional challenges in determining appropriate subject matter and developing a regular blogging practice but also must address the changing technological contexts in which the blog operates. Contemporary bloggers employ a variety of media, intersect with Twitter, Facebook, and other social media, and drive their content to a variety of devices in a way that bloggers five years ago would not have. In a similar vein, one could learn the basics for using a half-dozen of the most popular digital tools in a few days, but keeping up with the continual churn of new devices, applications, and practices would demand ongoing attention. The short duration of the specific kinds of expertise one might receive in technological training (e.g., learning how to use a particular application) is a phenomenon that is unusual in the humanities. Humanities faculty and students expect their education to have some real durability. That is, if one reads a novel in a course, one expects that the reading of that novel and much of the scholarly conversation surrounding it will be durable knowledge, probably for the rest of one's career. In contrast, lessons in Dreamweaver are durable for maybe one or two versions. Perhaps the surrounding discussion of principles of web design and HTML lasts a little longer, but as it turns out, they, too, are quickly supplanted by a different, social media version of the web.

However, durability is only part of the problem. The real difficulty lies in creating opportunities for the technologies to be put to work. Developing facility with digital media must be tied fairly closely to pedagogical or research objectives. Otherwise, any training one receives will lie fallow and potentially become outmoded before one returns to it. In teaching, this is a little easier than it is with scholarship. At the University at Buffalo, the need to offer online courses and the institution of a digital composition requirement for our first-year writing courses created both a need for graduate students to develop some digital literacy and an opportunity for them to put that literacy to work in their teaching. Of course such practices are not without their resistances. If one viewed an existing course, like a first-year composition course, as complete already, then adding digital components would understandably be viewed as extra work. Instead, successfully infusing digital media into any curriculum requires rethinking the entire work of a course, not its goals necessarily but its *work*. That is, for example, a literary survey course would have the same fundamental goals as always in introducing students to the primary features of literature from a given historical moment, and clearly the primary activity of that course would remain the students reading those works. However, the conversations among the students and faculty, the major assignments students undertake, the research they do, the larger communities with whom they might interact, and ultimately, as a result, the activities within the classroom might all be transformed. Why undertake such changes? Hopefully not to meet some top-down bureaucratic pressure or to pursue some trend but rather because such infusion might be the best and most likely way for the humanities to investigate how their traditional objects and methods of study shift from the print cultures in which they were born into the emerging digital culture where they must learn to thrive. Certainly this is the approach we have taken with our composition program, where traditional activities like journal writing, in-class workshop groups, and class discussion are now mixed with blogging, web-based peer review, and online forums. In terms of graduate education, the hope is that following several semesters of infusing digital technology because it is required programmatically that TAs will gain enough expertise and confidence to explore the use of technology in other, noncomposition courses. It is important to note again, though, that composition is a somewhat unique example in the humanities. Like general education courses in the arts, which might ask students to engage in digital photography or graphic design, composition courses have always focused on production. On the other hand, those humanities disciplines that have always focused on interpretation, like literary studies, have aligned themselves quite differently in relation to technology. In those fields, the tradition has not been to introduce students to new technological methods, as it has been with composition or the arts, which have been putting undergraduates in front of computers for thirty years. Perhaps for this reason, the broad introduction of digital work across these fields has come more quickly and seamlessly (though certainly not without challenges) than in other areas of the humanities.

Digital Spaces and the Ethics of Scholarship

Unfortunately, making an analogous transition toward digital scholarly practices in other humanities disciplines is more difficult. While some graduate students may relish the opportunity to break new ground, and really all dissertation writers have in their mind at least some pressure to make an "original" contribution, it is unfair to ask graduate students to bear the burden of inventing new digital scholarly practices. For graduate students who would specialize in digital humanities, computers and writing, new media studies, and another existing areas, there are already established paradigms to work from. That is, one knows not only generally what a computers and writing dissertation looks like but also the kind of work that one does to produce one. The questions for graduate students and assistant professors in these fields instead tend to whether or not other humanists and departments will recognize and value their research. My interest in this chapter, however, has been with the larger question of how the humanities as a whole will rise to the general shift of digital media. In my view, this shift is analogous to the late nineteenth-century shift that brought us the journal article and later the monograph, as well as the national professional conference. This shift is also analogous to the one we face with our teaching. However, in the case of teaching, we face expectations to teach students digital literacy as a primary goal of humanities curriculum, in addition to using digital media as a means to achieve other goals. In scholarship, while we might face external economic pressures to publish digitally, for the most part we are answerable only to ourselves in determining how we will use digital media as researchers.

Conversations about the impact of digital technologies on humanities research practices have focused on two areas: the creation and use of digital tools for analyzing humanities texts and publishing born-digital scholarship. I would not be surprised if there came a time in this century when digital research tools and born-digital scholarly composition were as common as close reading and essay writing are today, but that time may not come for several decades. In the shorter term, it is the larger ecology of social media that is relevant. Just as digital pedagogy explores the use of social media to expand conversations beyond the classroom and connect students with larger communities, humanities scholars need to explore the possibility of establishing networked communities and employing social media to connect with a larger audience. As with teaching, learning the basic how-tos is relatively simple; the challenge is adapting one's scholarly practices to incorporate social media. Certainly some humanists, particularly digital humanists, have been blogging, tweeting, uploading videos, and sharing links, among other activities, for several years; and, even though this is a small fraction of humanist scholars, overall it is evident that social media, in comparison to traditional scholarly practices, offer means to practice and share scholarship that make it easier to communicate and collaborate with one's colleagues, while also sharing one's work with a larger audience. When one thinks of this "larger audience," one might think of the general public, and to some extent that is the case. However, most academics may continue to write for more specialized, professional audiences than a general public and for them, social media will also enable access to a larger audience in their own fields and across the humanities.

However, incorporating a social media practice into humanities scholarship is not easy. There are several obstacles. One can find celebrations, critiques, attacks, and defenses of the academic use of social media across the Internet. It's not my intention to rehearse those arguments here. Instead, as I suggested earlier, as academics we simply have a wager to make. Either we believe that the humanities can survive as an essentially print-based intellectual practice or we believe the humanities will need to adapt to contemporary communication and information technologies. If one believes the former, then I suppose one has little concern for the issues I have raised here. If, however, one believes the latter, then the question is not whether academics, and graduate students in particular, need to adapt to digital media, but how.

The challenges, in the end, are ethical, and by this I mean that the challenges stem from the values we place on particular activities and the specific relations we establish among ourselves. While digital media will not, in any straightforward, deterministic way, alter the underlying goals of humanities research (e.g., literary scholars will continue to study literature for largely the same reasons as they do today), they will alter our everyday practices. That is, quite simply, the technologies and applications we will use to conduct research, communicate with one another, collaborate (potentially) on projects, compose our scholarship, review and edit our work, and publish our findings will change. Alongside these technological changes, we will need to rethink how we value emerging scholarly practices, new forms of professional service, and the professional development they will require. In terms of graduate school, then, the objective must be to introduce students to new practices and encourage the students' development of these practices. In suggesting this, I do not mean putting graduate students in situations where they must argue that blogging, for example, should "count" as a scholarly activity along the continuum of other scholarly publishing. If such arguments are to be made, the task should not fall upon our most vulnerable members. Instead, the value of a digital social media practice should be reflected in the better articles, essay collections, and monographs that scholars produce through its practice. In time, such publishing genres will probably transform, but that transformation, while likely to be informed by the larger ecology of digital practices, should not be confused for that ecology.

When one looks at the operation of social media in humanities graduate programs, if one sees anything, one typically sees individual course blogs and wikis, the blogs and tweets of individual faculty and students, and perhaps department-level representation in Facebook. These presences represent a kind of remediation of the traditional and ongoing organization of curriculum and scholarship. A course blog or wiki typically has a one-semester duration; and, even if it persists from one iteration of a course to the next, its primary audience remains those in the course. Individual faculty and students in social media likely have audiences that stretch beyond departments; but generally those presences, to the extent that they are scholarly, remain vertical within one's specialization and are not likely to gain the attention of one's department colleagues. Projects such as the CUNY Academic Commons; the Humanities, Arts, Science, and Technology Advanced Collaboratory (HASTAC); and MediaCommons each serve as a platform for academic collaboration across institutions and across disciplines. Graduate students and faculty might participate in these communities as a way of reaching beyond local departments. However this still leaves open the question of how a department-level community will work. Where projects on both the small, individual scale (like a blog) and on a large scale (like HASTAC) operate on the basis of shared academic interests, departments are imagined as microcosms of the disparate interests of a discipline or, as in the case of many English departments, multiple disciplines. Department structures such as bylaws, committees, and curriculum serve to manage those disparate interests if not combine them in some felicitous way for students. As I have been discussing, the digital humanities can and does enter humanities departments as a specialization, as one of many interests (i.e., one can hire a digital humanities specialist). However, digital media and technologies also impact the humanities across specializations, altering the relations among faculty and students. To give a single example: fifteen years ago it would have been largely impractical on a technological basis for the conversations and work undertaken in one graduate course to be taken up in relation to the conversations and work undertaken in another course being offered in the same term. Today, from a technological perspective, it would be easy for a department community to conduct academic conversations in a public forum. Perhaps it would be risky. Perhaps it would not be pedagogically effective, though in making that claim we would have to be certain we still knew what the aims of graduate education ought to be. However, these are ultimately ethical concerns, concerns regarding what we *should* do. They are not concerns regarding what we *can* do.

What might a department-level public forum of this type be like? Undoubtedly, the first fear would be that the kinds of departmental political in-fighting seen on faculty listservs and in department meetings would be made public in some embarrassing way. Exposure, as always, is a prime inhibitor for faculty in social media. To what extent would a department administrator find it necessary to moderate online conversation? Would faculty and students ultimately be able to differentiate between an intellectually productive discussion of differences and some all-out war of words?

And would the shift into a public space help to bring about such a discourse where previous forums did not? One thing is certain: a civil discourse about scholarly and intellectual issues across specializations and philosophical-political positions in the humanities would need to be invented. If the digital humanities could usher in such a discourse, then it would truly be a boon.

Some intermediary gestures would include a nonpublic, department-level content management system (e.g., Drupal). Clearly not all conversations need to be fully public anyway. This would allow graduate students to develop some facility with a social media presence and to explore some of the potential collaborations networks make possible while mitigating some of the fears of exposure. Another possibility would be a public space that was focused on a particular area of specialization, for example, rhetoric and composition. A blog of this kind would not be limited to a particular course but would be composed by students and faculty across a program in this area and addressed publicly to others in the field. There are many examples of successful academic group blogs in various fields that might be employed as models. A community site of this kind would provide a way for graduate students to develop a professional-digital identity, collaborate with their departmental colleagues, and establish connections with others in the field. Ideally, such sites, if initiated at multiple institutions, would ultimately aggregate into a larger conversation that graduate students could take with them as the moved into other academic positions. This arrangement would be of mutual benefit and would draw links between local community conversations and the larger initiatives we see with HASTAC, MediaCommons, and CUNY's Academic Commons. One of the big challenges recent graduates face when moving into new academic positions, often at smaller schools, is the loss of their academic community. Sites of this type would mitigate that feeling. In turn, current graduate students could certainly benefit from the experiences of a program's recent graduates.

Though I have written here about specific social media technologies, in the end, the reformation of graduate education in the face of digital humanities is not a matter of using blogs or wikis or creating Twitter or YouTube accounts. The challenge is not to figure out how to use an iPad in a classroom or a video camera or GPS data for one's research. It is not about learning to use specific technologies or programming languages. Or rather, it is about all these things and a hundred others yet to come. Fundamentally the challenge lies in recognizing our humanities disciplines as they have been shaped by twentieth-century technologies and realizing that they must be shaped anew. In doing so, we need to examine the ways in which our ethics have developed in the context of past technological networks so that we may engage directly in establishing new ethical practices that meet the challenges and take advantage of the opportunities that digital media present us. Graduate education is one of many sites where this work must be done as we meet our commitment to prepare those entering our field to work in a digital future that is admittedly difficult to foresee. In my view, this is the central task of the digital humanities, broadly conceived.

NOTE

1. The concept of assemblage is developed in the work of Gilles Deleuze and Félix Guattari and then later in Manuel DeLanda. As DeLanda explains, assemblage theory "was meant to apply to a wide variety of wholes constructed from heterogeneous parts. Entities ranging from atoms and molecules to biological organisms, species and ecosystems may be usefully treated as assemblages and therefore as entities that are products of historical processes. This implies, of course, that one uses the term 'historical' to include cosmological and evolutionary history, not only human history. Assemblage theory may also be applied to social entities, but the very fact that it cuts across the nature-culture divide is evidence of its realist credentials" (3). Assemblage theory provides a method for investigating the "heterogeneous parts" involved in the development of disciplinary paradigms. In the case of humanities, scholarly assemblages cannot be solely cultural or discursive but intersect a variety of objects, including, most notably, the communications technologies of the early twentieth century.

BIBLIOGRAPHY

"About HASTAC." *HASTAC: Humanities, Arts, Science, and Technology Advanced Collaboratory.* http://hastac.org/about.

Berlin, James. *Rhetorics, Poetics, and Culture.* West Lafeyette, Ind.: Parlor, 2003.

Connors, Robert. *Composition-Rhetoric: Backgrounds, Theory, and Pedagogy*. Pittsburgh, Penn.: University of Pittsburgh Press, 1997.

Delanda, Manuel. *A New Philosophy of Society: Assemblage Theory and Social Complexity*. London, UK: Continuum, 2006.

Deleuze, Gilles, and Félix Guattari. *A Thousand Plateaus: Capitalism and Schizophrenia.* Translated by Brian Massumi. Minneapolis: University of Minnesota Press, 1987.

Graff, Gerald. *Professing Literature: An Institutional History.* Chicago: University of Chicago Press, 1987.

Johnson, Larry, et al. *The 2011 Horizon Report.* Austin, Tex.: New Media Consortium, 2011. http://www.nmc.org/publications/2011-horizon-report.

Kirschenbaum, Matthew. "What Is Digital Humanities and What's It Doing in English Departments?" *ADE Bulletin* 150 (2010): 1–7. Reprinted in this volume.

Liu, Alan. "Digital Humanities and Academic Change." *English Language Notes* 47, no. 1 (2009): 17–35.

Meyer, Eric T., Kathryn Eccles, Michael Thelwall, and Christine Madsen. *Final Report to JISC on the Usage and Impact Study of JISC-funded Phase 1 Digitisation Projects and the Toolkit for the Impact of Digitised Scholarly Resources (TIDSR).* Oxford: Oxford

Internet Institute, 2009. http://microsites.oii.ox.ac.uk/tidsr/system/files/TIDSR_Final Report_20July2009.pdf.

"Mission." *4Humanities*. http://humanistica.ualberta.ca/mission/.

MLA Office of Research. *Report on the Survey of Earned Doctorates, 2007–08*. New York: MLA, 2010.

Russell, David. *Writing in the Academic Disciplines, Second Edition: A Curricular History*. Carbondale: Southern Illinois University Press, 2002.

Scholes, Robert. *The Rise and Fall of English Studies: Reconstructing English as a Discipline*. New Haven, Conn.: Yale University Press, 1998.

Should Liberal Arts Campuses Do Digital Humanities? Process and Products in the Small College World

BRYAN ALEXANDER AND REBECCA FROST DAVIS

This is a boom time for the digital humanities. As this chapter is being written, projects proliferate while dialogue around the movement grows, as marked by online discussion, conference presence, articles, and books. Academic instantiations of digital humanities are building, even in a recession, from individual courses to faculty positions to academic programs to digital humanities centers. The movement's influence has been felt outside the walls of academia, as 2010 saw Google funding digital humanities projects around the Google Books collection and Patricia Cohen publishing her Humanities 2.0 series of articles in the *New York Times* about digital methodologies in the humanities (Parry). At a time when the academic humanities seems otherwise threatened and contracting, the digital humanities remains a viable growth area, even a potential source of salvation for threatened disciplines.[1]

Like many intellectual or social movements, the digital humanities (DH) advance not uniformly but unevenly, moving from certain academic positions to specific niches. So far, the enterprise has largely been the creature of doctoral and research universities (formerly Research-I under the Carnegie Classifications; "Carnegie") and several state campuses, at least on the high-profile production end. Community colleges, most large state and regional universities, small schools, and many private campuses have been comparatively underinvolved (Unsworth, "The State of Digital Humanities").

In this chapter, we examine the liberal arts sector, small colleges and universities focused on traditional-age undergraduate education, ones that have apparently played little role in the digital humanities movement.[2] Our argument starts from the sector's relative silence, as we identify a series of reasonable objections to the engagement of liberal arts colleges in the digital humanities. After we summarize (and, in some case, ventriloquize) these objections, we identify responses. This is not a symmetrical sequence, with each dour "no" met by a cheerful "yes," as some arguments are met by cases of ongoing practice that don't map precisely onto the criticism. Other charges are answered only on a small scale, which doesn't necessarily speak to the entire sector. We chose this uncomfortable call-and-response framing in order to take criticism seriously, while letting us fully delineate the liberal arts sector's achievements. The mismatch between critique and liberal arts practice uncovered by this framing is revealing. Ultimately, those achievements have come to constitute a different mode for the digital humanities, a separate path worth identifying, understanding, and encouraging, one based on emphasizing a distributed, socially engaged *process* over a focus on publicly shared *products*.

A point about perspective: the authors are a program officer and researcher for the National Institute for Technology in Liberal Education (NITLE). We are also humanists (classical studies and English, respectively), former small liberal arts college teaching faculty, and digital practitioners. Our stance is therefore an unusual one, combining current interinstitutional work with a history of on-campus immersion. We are invested in the topic but do not hold a current campus practitioner's standpoint. We hope to combine understanding of the small campus experience with a view of national trends cross the sector. Finally, we wish to elicit discussion.

Obstacles

Should liberal arts campuses engage with the digital humanities movement? There are several serious arguments for disengagement, including problems of logistics, infrastructure, and campus identity.

One institutional objection stems from the size and concomitant resource base that characterizes most small liberal arts colleges. Because of their small scale, such colleges and universities may lack the proper infrastructure to support digital humanities work. For many digital humanists, *the* key piece of college infrastructure is the digital humanities center. In her *Survey of Digital Humanities Centers in the United States*, Diane Zorich defines the center as "an entity where new media and technologies are used for humanities-based research, teaching, and intellectual engagement and experimentation. The goals of the center are to further humanities scholarship, create new forms of knowledge, and explore technology's impact on humanities-based disciplines" (4). Functionally, such centers provide locations for interdisciplinary, interdepartmental collaboration; centralized computing support and expertise for a variety of projects; and help in securing funding. They are resource centers, information clearing houses, interpersonal networking nodes, and advocates for the field. These centers are comparatively new in the university landscape; the centers in Zorich's survey have a median founding date of 1999 (9). Zorich also finds a typical trajectory for the development of most centers in which an initial stimulus, "a grant, a strategic discussion, or an entrepreneurial individual," starts a development that moves in an unstructured fashion "from project (singular activity) to program (long-term activity) to center (multiple activities)" (9–10). In all of these cases, it seems that a critical mass of digital research projects and other activities must be reached to justify a center and its staff.

Unfortunately, digital humanities centers are relatively rare in the small college world, as they are generally predicated on a campus being large and resourced well enough to allocate significant funds to what may be perceived as a niche effort. Small colleges typically lack the numbers to develop the critical mass that has led to the creation of centers at large institutions. Moreover, digital humanities centers are relatively new arrivals on liberal arts campuses, which makes them potentially less appealing than already established paradepartmental entities, such as teaching and learning or writing centers, which are fairly common at small colleges. As members of the *Digital Campus* podcast noted, life as an isolated digital humanist is a challenge, especially without the place to meet, support for getting grants, and technical staff that a center provides (Cohen, French, Kelly, and Scheinfeldt). How can digital humanists assemble the combination of skills and technology infrastructure needed to conduct digital humanities work such as coding, media production and aggregation, and the creation and development of information architecture, not to mention conducting the essential work within a humanities subject? Furthermore, the digital humanities center integrates professional populations along with personal skill sets: faculty members, librarians, and technologists. Without an anchoring department, individual digital humanists at small colleges often lack the social capital to create or participate in already existing cross-sector teams.

Small colleges may not have accumulated the critical mass to create a digital humanities center due to a third obstacle to the digital humanities in the liberal arts world, namely that sector's pedagogical focus. Not only is a digital humanities center inappropriately resource demanding, but such centers do not usually focus on undergraduate teaching, the central task of a liberal arts campus. While many digital humanities centers do support some teaching, their ultimate goal is to "train the next generation of digital humanities researchers, scholars, and professionals" (Zorich, 20). Those receiving such training are more likely to be graduate students or interested faculty seeking professional development. Both cases are outside the mainstream of liberal education practice—teaching undergraduates.

While defining liberal education is nontrivial—in fact, it's a classic conversation generator—it is not controversial to recognize one generally inoffensive description: schooling focused on undergraduate education. As Jo Ellen Parker describes it, "The defining characteristics of liberal education in this logic are not disciplines but practices—practices like group study, undergraduate research, faculty mentoring, student presentations, and other forms of active learning." To the extent that liberal arts campuses follow this suite of practices, they are working in a way very different from a large university producing digital content for general consumption. Liberal arts campuses devote the balance of their energies to the classroom rather than the outside world of content consumers, the residential student body in discussion-based clusters rather than the res publica, small groups of physically colocated students rather than fellow advanced scholars distributed around the world. Their tradition, reward structure, student expectation, and alumni perspective all turn on this richly rewarding student–professor interaction rather than more public, outward-facing types of sharing and publication. Therefore, on-campus critics could construe work in the classic digital humanities as marginal or off mission—perhaps dangerously so, during the Great Recession era of funding crisis.

If the pedagogical nature of liberal education presents a problem for practicing digital humanities, then the unclear identity of digital humanities offers yet another difficulty. It is famously difficult for observers and participants to agree on a definition of digital humanities; and, as Matthew Kirschenbaum has observed, essays defining the term are already genre pieces (55). Consider the definitional range Kirschenbaum explores from the perspective of literature departments: digital humanities are based on technologies, or analytical methods, or the emergence of certain research-supporting social structures demarcated by funding or social movement dynamics or network topology.[3] Other sources offer a similar diversity. The digital humanities are about scholars, or about projects, or tools, or about technology itself. They are the entire humanities in transformation, or a narrow strand therein. The digital world invades the humanities, forcing us to think through new categories and reinvent our world, or cyberculture nestles firmly within our established critical theory tradition ("How Do You Define"). Whatever digital humanities is, it is emergent, dynamic, inclusive, evolving, and very fresh. It is an ongoing, Poundian "make it new!"

We can suggest many reasons for this definitional uncertainty. Although the digital humanities have a history of practice under various names—for example, humanities computing—the current name, digital humanities, remains relatively new within the academy. Kirschenbaum traces its origin to the publication of Blackwell's *Companion to Digital Humanities* in 2004 (Schreibman, Siemens, and Unsworth), the creation of the Alliance for Digital Humanities Organizations in 2005, and the launch of the Digital Humanities Initiative (now the Office of Digital Humanities) at the National Endowment for the Humanities (NEH) in 2006. Beyond the scholastic history, digital technologies change rapidly, as do the practices around them, driving digital humanities into a state of perpetual reinvention (websites, then Web 2.0, then apps, then games, then . . .). Additionally, the most recent recession has perhaps crimped academic progress generally, constricting budgets for people and materials, slowing the output of recognizable digital humanities work. Interdisciplinarity presents its usual challenges: difficulty in winning champions and resources in a discipline-structured environment. Similarly, the cross-population nature of digital humanities work, which requires faculty members, librarians, and technologists, makes it hard to garner interest in digital humanities projects. The combination of newness, technology change, and inclusion of multiple sectors and disciplines make (re)defining the digital humanities both problematic and necessary.

These definitional debates are, of course, fraught with practical implications, impacting careers and campuses. For example, the classic production-versus-theory argument (opposing hands-on work to reflective criticism, an argument about resources and ethos), a familiar one to the institutionalization of film and media studies, recurs here. To do digital humanities is to create digital humanities projects, argued Stephen Ramsay during a high-profile MLA 2011 discussion: "I think Digital Humanities is about building things . . . if you aren't building, you are not engaged in the 'methodologization' of the humanities, which, to me, is the hallmark of the discipline that was already decades old when I came to it" ("Who's In and Who's Out"). Such a focus might describe the field's developmental arc: "There's always been a profound—and profoundly exciting and enabling—commonality to everyone who finds their way to digital humanities. And that commonality, I think, involves moving from reading and critiquing to building and making" (Ramsay, "On Building"). Ramsay sees the process of creation as radically different from that of study (viz. critical media studies). Production summons up a distinct set of competencies, resources, and challenges, all in an especially emergent way that the observer or critic has no immediate access to.

The implications of Ramsay's definition exacerbate the small college production problem outlined earlier. By extension, small liberal arts colleges cannot pursue digital humanities projects due to their lack of centers and incompatibility of mission, and their inability to produce further disables them from truly engaging with the field on both individual and institutional levels. Put another way, the definitional problem makes it more difficult to argue for resource allocation to efforts stakeholders cannot readily apprehend.

The combination of small institutional size, lack of supporting infrastructure, pedagogical focus, and uncertain definition yields still another challenge for the digital humanities at small liberal arts colleges. These campuses lack visibility in the digital humanities world, as it is constituted through social networks, projects, and conferences. The relative lack of visibility for small liberal arts colleges in this world is clear from a survey of Twitter activity (see Dan Cohen's Twitter list, "Digital Humanists") or from a glance at Project Bamboo, a multi-institutional planning project aimed at discussing shared approaches to the digital humanities. The latter's planning and discussion were dominated by research universities, from planning through workshops (2008–2010) to the 2010 project group's composition (Millon, Project Bamboo).

Or consider participation in the Digital Humanities Conference, the annual international conference for digital scholarship in the humanities, sponsored by the Alliance of Digital Humanities Organizations (ADHO). At the 2010 conference, of the one hundred and forty institutions of various types listed on the program, only two were North American small liberal arts colleges. Granted, the conference took place in London; but, even at Digital Humanities 2009 in Maryland, five presenters and two posters from a total of three hundred and sixty participants were scholars at small liberal arts colleges.

George Mason scholar Tom Scheinfeldt has argued that, in addition to Twitter and conferences, the federal grant-making process plays an important role in sustaining the digital humanities community by keeping it in conversation and collaboration ("Stuff Digital Humanists Like"). But if digital humanists at small liberal arts colleges cannot create projects, then they will also miss out on this part of the community. The numbers for the NEH Digital Humanities Start-Up Grant program bear this out. According to the *Summary Findings of NEH Digital Humanities Start-Up Grants (2007–2010)*, of the 1,110 grant applications, less than 50 came from liberal arts colleges, while over 400 came from doctoral research institutions (Office of Digital Humanities, 18). The same report includes potential evidence of the effects of these perception issues. One principal investigator on a start-up grant who had so far failed to secure additional funding refers to "hesitation on the part of granting agencies to fund projects that rely on undergraduate work" (Office of Digital Humanities, 31). If small liberal arts colleges and universities participate in production or even study, that work lacks presence in the overall movement. That lack of impact can rebound on a small campus, creating a negative incentive for increased contribution.

Hand in hand with poor visibility comes the isolation of digital humanists working at small liberal arts colleges. Isolation impacts individuals, their work, and their projects in general. Such digital humanists lack physically proximate colleagues with whom they can collaborate or discuss their work. This disconnection reduces their opportunities for learning about standards, resources, and ongoing projects from peers. One result is that their work may not be interoperable with other projects or may even reduplicate efforts (Davis and Dombrowski). At a number of large research institutions, digital humanities centers play a key isolation reduction role by providing technology; expertise; information about tools, standards, and ongoing projects; as well as introductions to prominent figures in the digital humanities community who can serve as guides and mentors.

The Twitter network, the blogosphere, and other online community venues and shared resources may alleviate these problems to a certain extent, but digital humanists at small campuses are still disconnected from in-person meetings and collaborations. They can also feel isolated by the particular political and academic structures of their own institutions. Perhaps the liberal arts campus's residential ethos and emphasis on face-to-face teaching acculturates humanists on those campuses to prefer collocated conversations more strongly than do their colleagues in other sectors. While the impact of isolation is magnified for the scholar working at an institution without a digital humanities center, such organizations are hardly a panacea. As Diane Zorich explains, "The silo-like nature of centers also results in overlapping agendas and activities, particularly in areas of training, digitization of collections, and metadata development" (42). This shared challenge of isolation offers one reason why the plight of the small college digital humanist should matter to the larger world of digital humanities.

Patterns of Engagement

What responses can be offered to these critiques? One answer is simple assent to each charge. A lack of institutional support, lines not opened, courses not approved, funds unallocated: there are many avenues for disengagement either at the policy level or in practical terms. A second type of response, however, evokes actual liberal arts digital humanities practices, making these available for analysis. The first category of response requires little adumbration here, partly because discussion of it involves proving an absence, or establishing a negative. The second category, current practice, is more interesting, especially as many projects address the objections outlined earlier.

To begin, we *are* seeing the creation of some digital humanities centers—at the University of Richmond, Hamilton College, and Occidental College—though with a particular liberal arts inflection. The Digital Scholarship Lab at the University of Richmond enjoys, perhaps, the highest level of institutional support, since noted digital humanist Ed Ayers is the president of the university. The lab's mission statement makes clear its production focus: "The Digital Scholarship Lab develops innovative digital humanities projects that contribute to research and teaching at and beyond the University of Richmond. It seeks to reach a wide audience by developing projects that integrate thoughtful interpretation in the humanities and social sciences with innovations in new media" ("About the Digital Scholarship Lab"). In addition to continuing projects like the History Engine started by Ayers at the University of Virginia, the lab also supports new projects including two that have received Digital Humanities Start-Up Grants from the National Endowment for the Humanities: "Landscapes of the American Past: Visualizing Emancipation" and "Visualizing the Past: Tools and Techniques for Understanding Historical Processes." This lab, with its focus on production of tools and projects, seems most like the digital humanities center familiar from large research institutions, although at least two of its projects—the History Engine and "Americans in Paris"—provide opportunities for undergraduate contributions integrated into courses ("History Engine," Jones).

By contrast, both Hamilton and Occidental Colleges have a more explicit pedagogical focus integrated into the overall mission of their centers. Each also secured grant funding from the Liberal Arts College Program of the Andrew W. Mellon Foundation in 2010 ("Mellon Awards $800K for Digital Humanities Initiative"; "Occidental Awarded $700,000 Mellon Grant for Digital Scholarship"). With its funding, the Digital Humanities Initiative (DHi) at Hamilton College has hired a programmer and is supporting faculty projects, which take the form of digital multimedia collections. One significant requirement is that all projects must have a curricular element. DHi both builds on preexisting digital projects and pulls together faculty from all over campus. At the same time, this initiative illustrates the challenges of definition and visibility for the digital humanities on small liberal arts campuses. When one of the authors of this chapter visited there, she was struck by the repeated comment, "I didn't know I was doing digital humanities." Recognizing that other small liberal arts colleges do not have the resources to establish a center, Hamilton College is currently piloting some infrastructure to support these collections and wants to create a shared infrastructure in the cloud that can be used by other colleges (Simons, Nieves, and Hamlin). Essentially, Hamilton could act as a digital humanities center for other small liberal arts colleges.

The pedagogical focus becomes even clearer in our third example of a liberal arts digital humanities center. At Occidental College, the Center for Digital Learning and Research (CDLR) is part of a larger vision to transform the college for the twenty-first century. Like other centers, the CDLR centralizes expertise and becomes a nexus for collaboration on campus. Its staff consists of existing positions from both the library and information technology with the addition of its director and grant-funded postdocs ("Center for Digital Learning and Research"). A summer institute for faculty and ongoing support of faculty projects aim to transform teaching and learning. As part of this plan, the digital humanities provide an avenue for envisioning a new kind of education in which "faculty and students use digital resources to pose new questions, discover and create knowledge in distributed and collaborative ways, work with scholars and information globally without physically leaving campus, and simultaneously gather and share data in the field" (Chamberlain). The mission of this center, then, explicitly focuses on undergraduate education rather than on the production of digital humanities projects. Instead, digital methodologies are seen as a means to achieving that classroom-based end. While such centers share with centers at research institutions the functions of offering a location for interdisciplinary collaboration, thereby centralizing expertise and attracting funding, they have a distinct mission that focuses on undergraduate education, akin to the focus of teaching and learning centers and in keeping with the identity of small liberal arts colleges.

Despite these examples, most liberal arts campuses do not currently maintain a digital humanities center, nor do they plan on doing so in the near future. The first challenge we identified is thus only partially addressed by current practice. If the center model is not a normative one, can these small colleges and universities develop other institutional anchors to support the multidisciplinary, collaborative work of digital humanities? We have observed other structures emerging that fulfill the various functions of the center by unbundling them, including community building and on-campus advocacy and developing computing expertise and support for finding funding.

To combat the sense of isolation and lack of visibility on campus, one programmatic function focuses on creating a sense of community. Both Wheaton

College's Digital Scholarship Working Group and the Tri-Co Digital Humanities Consortium—which includes Bryn Mawr, Haverford, and Swarthmore Colleges (Hamlin; "Tri-Co Digital Humanities")—represent the coming together of groups of faculty who share an interest in digital humanities. Inspired by their faculty, students at Haverford and Bryn Mawr also created an undergraduate digital humanities group that hosted "Re:Humanities," an undergraduate digital humanities conference that pulled in students from other institutions like Hamilton College. These communities have helped advocate for the value of digital humanities work and raise its profile in the campus community.

Part of advocacy for the digital humanities on campus includes integrating it with an institution's mission and culture. For example, both Hamilton and Occidental Colleges have a pedagogical focus for their digital humanities centers in keeping with their institution's academic mission. From a different angle, the Humanities Program at the University of Puget Sound includes digital work in what is ostensibly a nondigital program, the Humanities Teaching Collective, directed by Professor Kent Hooper. Viewing the digital as a necessary part of humanities today, Hooper has integrated a collaboratively taught course on digital humanities within the humanities sequence at the University Puget Sound. When the associate dean was asked about what sort of structure they had to support the digital humanities, she replied, "Kent *is* our structure" (DeMarais). Such linkage of digital humanities with one person on campus may pose a danger. That person may be dismissed as an early adopter or the effort may run the risk of losing impetus if that person leaves (Moore). Nevertheless, Hooper has been able to integrate the digital humanities into Puget Sound's humanities program with the support of the administration, library, and information technology.

We find a similar integration of digital humanities into existing campus curricular programs at Wheaton College in Norton, Massachusetts. While large institutions need centers to operate outside curricular structures (i.e., outside departments) to promote interdisciplinary collaboration, at small colleges the tradition of interdisciplinary work is linked to the values of liberal education. The Association of American Colleges and Universities (AAC&U) includes interdisciplinary, integrative learning among its list of essential learning outcomes for liberal education. At Wheaton College, students have to take connected courses that link not just across disciplines but also across divisions as required by the integrative learning program, Connections. Out of that context arose the Lexomics Project, which combines computer science, statistics, and Old English texts (LeBlanc, Armstrong, and Gousie, "Lexomics"). Lexomics received an NEH Digital Humanities Start-Up Grant in 2008, and students contributed to the project which uses text mining to study Old English texts and determine authorship based on stylistic characteristics. The project secured additional funding in the form of an NEH Preservation and Access Grant in 2011 ("Four Professors Win NEH Grants"). Since such interdisciplinary approaches are typical of the digital humanities, the Connections program that made this possible provided the perfect environment. Both the University of Puget Sound and Wheaton College demonstrate that one successful strategy for promoting digital humanities is to find those existing structures and programs on campus that might fit with the digital humanities and to leverage them.

A third center function we see unbundled on the small college campus is computing expertise and support. Rather than creating a separate center, many colleges take advantage of the existing structures that already centralize computing and information support on campus. At the University of Puget Sound, the Library, Media, and Information Services Committee plays an active role in supporting their humanities program. At Willamette University, Michael Spalti, Associate University Librarian for Systems, essentially has played the role of a digital humanities center director: he was project director for an NEH Digital Humanities Start-Up Grant ("Bridging the Gap: Connecting Authors to Museum and Archival Collections"); he was the driving force behind Willamette's involvement in Project Bamboo; he organized and found funding for faculty workshops; and he has been a planner and the Willamette contact for digital humanities collaboration within NITLE. Similarly, at Lewis and Clark College, the library is supporting a new NEH Digital Humanities Start-Up Grant project, "Intellectual Property and International Collaboration in the Digital Humanities: The Moroccan Jewish Community Archives" (Kosansky). At Occidental College, the Center for Digital Learning and Research (CDLR) is connected to a developing Academic Commons in the library. It also pulls together staff from the library and IT. At Wheaton College, support for participation in the Text Encoding Initiative (TEI) comes from Library and Information Services, with materials coming from the college archives.

It's notable that most of these collaborative support examples occur where the information technology and library organizations are merged, or where a close working relationship exists between the two. Hamilton College's HILLgroup (Hamilton Information and Learning Liaisons) and Information Commons represent almost a decade of collaboration among faculty, librarians, and technologists. Wheaton and Occidental also have merged organizations. And at the University of Puget Sound, inclusion of digital work within the Humanities Teaching Collective models collaboration among faculty, librarians, and technologists typical of digital humanities projects. Essentially, these colleges have already centralized services in a way that can support digital humanities projects without having to create a separate structure to centralize expertise. Further, in these cases, small campus size, rather than being an obstacle to digital humanities work, may become an enabling virtue because it obviates the need for a separate center to house such work.

If these unbundled approaches do represent a separate mode of supporting digital humanities, their ability to secure grant funding represents an additional measure of their success. Besides the aforementioned grants for Wheaton, Willamette, and Lewis and Clark Colleges, faculty at Wheaton College have secured two Digital Humanities Start-Up Grants from the National Endowment for the Humanities

(Leblanc; Tomasek, "Digital History Project"); and the Tri-Co Digital Humanities Consortium will benefit from a million-dollar grant awarded to Bryn Mawr College ("Andrew W. Mellon Foundation"). While this funding level does not reach that of major digital humanities centers, it does demonstrate that major funding entities see the unbundled model as a viable alternative to digital humanities centers.

The presence of unbundled digital humanities center functions at small liberal arts colleges suggests that centers may, in fact, *not* be required to enable effective digital humanities work. It may well be that the functions described are waypoints on the journey to building up the critical mass needed for a digital humanities center. Then again, they may represent an alternate method of supporting digital humanities at small liberal arts colleges, one that will never lead to a center. Centers arose at large research institutions to help centralize efforts of community building, computing expertise, and advocacy spread across a large campus; the small size of liberal arts colleges mitigates the need for a separate structure to perform this centralizing function. In that case, assessing the viability of the digital humanities at small liberal arts colleges by the presence or lack of a digital humanities center is applying the wrong criterion to the question.

As we have seen, existing campus structures and intracampus collaborations can approximate the function of digital humanities centers for centralizing expertise and promoting interdisciplinary work on campus, but they do not necessarily help with the challenges of isolation and lack of visibility in the broader digital humanities community. For those challenges, digital humanists at small colleges have turned to interinstitutional collaboration. Many of the liberal arts colleges that have successful digital humanities activities have benefitted from relationships with research institutions. Kathryn Tomasek at Wheaton College has described how her proximity to Brown University has allowed her and her colleagues to learn TEI and hear speakers from the digital humanities world ("Brown Groupies?"). Likewise, Occidental College leveraged speakers from the University of Southern California and the University of California, Los Angeles, for their grant-funded summer institute on digital scholarship. Essentially, these small colleges take advantage of the networking and professional development opportunities of digital humanities centers at large institutions, especially when enabled by physical proximity. Regional THATCamps offer another nearby networking and professional development opportunity to connect digital humanists at a variety of institutions. One of the authors of this chapter helped plan THATCamp Liberal Arts Colleges, a THATCamp focused on institutional type rather than region that seeks specifically to counter the isolation of digital humanists at small colleges while raising their visibility within the larger community ("THATCamp: The Humanities"; "THATCamp Liberal Arts").

Small colleges may also join collaborative, interinstitutional digital humanities projects supported by large research institutions. Swarthmore faculty and students collaborate with faculty, librarians, and technologists at the University of Pennsylvania on the Early Novels Database (END), which seeks to provide rich bibliographic information for a collection of early fiction (Buurma, Levine, and Li). The project won a NITLE Community Contribution Award for Digital Humanities and the Undergraduate in October 2010 ("Digital Humanities and the Undergraduate"). Since small colleges commonly do not have infrastructure or expertise to support large-scale digital projects, opportunities like these provide effective means to integrate their faculty, staff, and students into the digital humanities world.

Although many of these collaborations are organized around specific projects, we are also seeing large-scale multi-institutional projects aimed at building resources and pooling expertise. These are constructed to match the needs of both small liberal arts colleges and large research institutions. For example, the TAPAS project, or TEI Archiving, Preservation, and Access Service, aggregates expertise and labor of technology staff at small liberal arts colleges to help publish and archive high-quality scholarly data marked up according to TEI standards ("A New Part of Your Digital Humanities Toolkit"). Such data markup offers a relatively accessible way to engage students in digital humanities work, as shown by the Wheaton College Digital History Project, in which students transcribe and markup materials from the Wheaton College archive (Tomasek et al.). Since small colleges often lack resources such as server space, technical expertise, and advanced XML publication tools, publication and archiving of this work becomes a challenge. The TAPAS project started as Publishing TEI Documents for Small Colleges, a project funded by an Institute of Museum and Library Services (IMLS) planning grant to Wheaton College in collaboration with Dickinson and Mount Holyoke Colleges. In the course of the planning grant, participants realized that the service was also needed by large institutions, and Brown University is now partnering with the project to be the base of the service.

This kind of collaboration recognizes common needs at small and large institutions while integrating small colleges as equal partners in a productive process. It goes a long way toward raising the profile of small colleges in the digital humanities community and demonstrating their capacity to make meaningful contributions even at the level of producing tools. In addition, such multi-institutional collaborations have the added benefit of combating the tendency to form silos that Zorich identified for digital humanities centers. Due to their small size, liberal arts colleges have no illusions about their ability to go it alone. Their needs may prove a useful indicator of needs within the digital humanities community as a whole, needs that would benefit from the approach of large-scale shared infrastructure. Liberal arts colleges can thus help chart a more widely distributed version of the digital humanities in the future.

A related response to our opening objections involves the strategic use of resources. Perhaps liberal arts campuses are engaging digital humanities through a narrow selection of technologies and areas. We have just noted a good deal of work on text markup technologies, such as TEI; we have not discovered a parallel body of work in, for example, semantic text analysis, or the creation of large-scale digital audio archives, or the development of open source tools (e.g., Zotero). Liberal arts campuses are smaller than most others and have recently suffered from the general recession. It is therefore appropriate for them to advance on several well-chosen axes, rather than across a general front. If this model is correct, then we should expect to see visible signs of liberal arts digital humanities engagement (conference presentations, published articles, Web 2.0 discussions) only in certain areas.

So far we have concentrated on ways in which small liberal arts colleges have strategically approximated the functions of large digital humanities centers by establishing their own centers, finding preexisting structures with analogous functions, and forming strategic partnerships with each other and larger institutions. Now we turn to an aspect of digital humanities linked to the particular identity of small liberal arts colleges—that is, their focus on undergraduate education. Liberal arts campuses focus digital humanities work specifically in the classroom experience, combining digital humanities research with teaching. Rather than emphasizing professionally mediated content and tool creation (cf. Ramsay, earlier), this approach turns faculty energies away from the production model, defining a very different form of digital humanities.

In a recent *Digital Humanities Quarterly* article, Chris Blackwell and Thomas Martin point to the prevalence of undergraduate research in the sciences, especially student-faculty collaborative research, but note the relative dearth of such examples in the humanities where the independent student thesis is the norm. This lack of collaboration is particularly troubling to small liberal arts colleges because such collaborative research, with close interaction between students and faculty, is a hallmark of their educational model (Lopatto). Mark Schantz points to more barriers to undergraduate research in the humanities: limited expertise, the independent researcher model that is typical of the humanities, and challenges of scalability in finding faculty time and attention to support undergraduate research ("Undergraduate Research," 26). The independent thesis model, however, is one existing structure that has allowed some undergraduates to pursue digital humanities research, turning a problem to an advantage. For example, Jen Rajchel produced the first online senior thesis in the English Department at Bryn Mawr College: "Mooring Gaps: Marianne Moore's Bryn Mawr Poetry" (Davis, Rajchel). While the idea of the individual thesis is a traditional practice at Bryn Mawr, Rajchel departed from the norm in constructing her thesis online. In this way, she was able to innovate within an existing program rather than completely break from tradition. Such measured progress may help make the digital humanities more palatable on the liberal arts campus.

Collaborative undergraduate research in the humanities, however, represents a departure from the norm for small liberal arts colleges. Blackwell and Martin argue persuasively that the digital humanities, along with some changes in practice, can open up collaborative research options for classical studies undergraduates both in and out of the classroom. Many of the examples mentioned previously, such as the

Wheaton College Digital History Project, the Early Novels Database (END), or the Lexomics Project, demonstrate those research options existing in other humanities disciplines, including history and English.

The Homer Multitext Project, described by Blackwell and Martin, presents an excellent example of student-faculty collaborative research in digital humanities (Dué and Ebbott). Although the project is based at the Center for Hellenic Studies of Harvard University, undergraduates at the College of the Holy Cross, Furman University, and the University of Houston collaborate on it. Recently, one of the authors of this chapter interviewed Mary Ebbot, coeditor of the Homer Multitext Project and associate professor of classics at the College of the Holy Cross about how she has integrated this project into undergraduate courses. In a Fall 2008 advanced Greek course on Homer, Professor Ebbot had her students take responsibility for one section of Homer; transcribe, translate, and provide commentary on the scholia, or marginal annotations; and map the text to the digital images of the manuscript. These high-resolution images allowed the students better views of the manuscript than were available to the handful of traditional classicists who had access to the physical manuscripts in the past. Now, not only have the images been made available online, but they are even available as an iPad app (Smith, "'Touch' the Venutus A"). In 2010, Holy Cross students did similar work as part of a summer research program. That fall, Ebbot's colleague, Neel Smith, organized a group of students, including first years, to volunteer to spend their Friday afternoons doing the same work (Smith, "New Content, New Contributors"). These students have developed a research community with which they share insights about how to decipher the writing on Byzantine manuscripts. Part of the intellectual excitement experienced by students stems from the opportunity to generate original work on primary material, rather than rehashing old arguments or synthesizing secondary literature ("Ebbot").

The Homer Multitext Project approaches the lab model familiar from the sciences. Amy Earhart suggests that the practices of the science lab offer a potential model for collaboration in the digital humanities, with students working under supervision by faculty and older students until they are ready for independent research (31–33). Collaborative work on a common project within the lab helps professionalize students in their discipline of classics. The collaborative model also helps with issues of scalability: students contribute to faculty projects, rather than taking away from faculty research time; and they support each other, rather than relying solely on faculty members for support and supervision. Overall, while the independent researcher model may represent an easier transition for integrating digital methodologies into undergraduate research in the humanities, the collaborative model will be more productive in the end, more in line with practice in the digital humanities, more in keeping with the world of webs and networks, and therefore a better option for the future of liberal education.

We should also consider the Homer Multitext Project as an example of applied learning, another of the key learning outcomes for liberal education identified by

AAC&U. In terms of pedagogical theory, this is problem-based learning, a pedagogical approach in which groups of students attack a problem with a real-world application. In "Bringing Our Brains to the Humanities: Increasing the Value of Our Classes while Supporting Our Futures," Sheila Cavanaugh argues that typical humanities classrooms do not take into account recent pedagogical theory; she suggests problem-based learning as one potentially fruitful and corrective approach. The applied-learning opportunities of digital humanities projects make them especially ripe for this approach. By giving students a limited amount of information—say, a section of the Homer manuscript—and some guidance, faculty can limit the scope and scaffold the learning process. Under this model of learning, students should learn both the process of inquiry and the actual content answer to the problem. After such scaffolded learning experiences, students will be ready for more independent research of the Homer manuscripts. This process-over-product focus distinguishes the digital humanities as practiced at small liberal arts colleges from the production focus in much of the digital humanities community.

For liberal arts colleges, applied learning has further benefits when it moves into the local community. Consider SmartChoices, a project led by Jack Dougherty, associate professor of educational studies at Trinity College in Hartford, Connecticut. Winner of NITLE's Community Contribution Award in 2010, SmartChoices is "a Web-based map and data sorting application that empowers parents to navigate and compare the growing number of public school options in metropolitan Hartford" (Dougherty). It was developed at Trinity by a team of students, faculty, and academic computing staff in collaboration with two nonprofit urban school reform organizations. Students on the project engaged in several high-impact practices valued in liberal education—including applied learning, service learning, and undergraduate research—and also developed their knowledge as citizens (Kuh). This kind of public engagement makes a powerful argument for the value of liberal education and digital humanities. Our undergraduates can play an important role translating our digital humanities work to the general public. Not all of these students will become digital humanists, but they will take a digital humanities perspective with them wherever they go, after having had an impact on their local communities.

The focus on the undergraduate curriculum at small liberal arts colleges offers the digital humanities a path for expansion beyond research centers at large universities to other types of institutions and beyond. While teaching is obviously important for most faculty members (allowing for variance by campus type), the discussion of pedagogy in the digital humanities has largely focused on teaching the field of digital humanities or preparing future digital humanists. By contrast, small liberal arts colleges focus on how the digital humanities effectively fulfill the learning outcomes of undergraduate liberal education. Thus they answer objections to their engagement with the digital humanities with their own brand of digital humanities, one predicated upon integration within undergraduate teaching and shared with all institutions that teach undergraduates.

Forking the Digital Humanities Code

Our descriptions of the ways liberal education addresses obstacles to digital humanities engagement have been uneven and partial so far. The examples we cite overcome some problems in an indirect or oblique way. Taken together, perhaps we are witnessing a fork in the digital humanities development path, to borrow a term from software development. Liberal arts campuses have taken the digital humanities source code and built a different application with it than their research university peers are currently constructing. Their focus is often on teaching and learning, not open content production. Institutional shapes differ from the now-classic digital humanities center. This looks like a specifically liberal arts route across the digital humanities landscape. Perhaps these small colleges and universities will decide, as an aggregate, not to follow that path any longer, either disengaging en masse or generating small-scale versions of research university models. But if those scenarios do not occur and the current record persists, liberal arts colleges and universities may break new ground with their focus on undergraduate education and their occasionally unbundled/uncentered support model.

If that is correct, then two implications arise. First, as liberal arts digital humanities work grows, those campuses will be sending undergraduates into digital humanities graduate studies programs. The research-I university will have a different type of humanist to train, one with a new and distinct background. These fresh graduate students may well present a deeper interest in teaching and learning implications than their peers, for example. They may also have a face-to-face understanding of digital humanities work. They may consider the humanities in terms of networks rather than centers, as a diffuse web rather than unified field.

Second, if liberal arts campuses continue this work and share some proportion of it with the world via the open web, then that work will connect with small campuses beyond the United States and that nation's unique liberal education experience. The system of American-style liberal arts colleges abroad, for example, could adopt the liberal arts path rather than the research university version. That group's very active library collaboration, the AMICAL consortium, could play a role in this by sharing practices. And as American-style liberal education flourishes in hitherto unfamiliar markets like China, this liberal arts brand of the digital humanities may follow. More broadly, a global education system eager to boost training during a worldwide recession may well find much utility in the liberal arts digital humanities model, grounded as it is in teaching and learning. A humanities-oriented cyberinfrastructure would support such international, interinstitutional collaboration if it developed shared workspaces, collaborative workflows, and other linked work tools (Unsworth, "Our Cultural Commonwealth").

We wish to conclude by expanding our discussions beyond institutional constraints. The liberal arts digital humanities method can impact the public understanding of the digital humanities, or the humanities in general. First, the liberal arts emphasis on involving undergraduates, local communities, and multiple campuses might contribute to a sense of humanities belonging to everyone, not just trained professionals. Standing at the intersection between the general public and academia, undergraduates are particularly well positioned to bridge the gap, performing public outreach for academic digital humanities work. They may also fill the same needs as the public in crowdsourcing projects, while avoiding concerns about minimum expertise. In the liberal arts tradition, helping students become active citizens engaged in civic life is a longstanding good, supported by nondigital programs like service learning (Schneider). Perhaps this sector's digital humanities approach keys into that outcome, developing a capacity for new forms of citizenship in a networked world. It may specifically help bridge the widening gap between academic humanities and broader American culture. Further, the liberal arts emphasis on lifelong learning could nudge some graduates to play a digital humanities advocacy role for decades to come.

Second, the rise of intercampus projects not affiliated with a single institution could reinforce the perception that digital humanities involves fluid, collaborative efforts. In an era when the humanities in general are under terrific budgetary pressures, such hacking of public awareness could prove influential. The liberal arts digital humanities fork may appear as a form of humanism oriented toward the commonweal. Understood in those terms, it could play a role in arguing for the humanities as a public good in policy and budgeting discussions.

This returns our "fork" back to the very nature of liberal education once again. One aspect of the liberal arts ethos is community engagement. As Jo Ellen Parker notes, "this approach [to understanding liberal education] tends to value the development of skills specifically believed to be central to effective citizenship—literacy, numeracy, sometimes public speaking, scientific and statistical literacy, familiarity with social and political science, and critical thinking. It tends to value curricular engagement with current social and political issues alongside the extracurricular development of ethical reflection and socially responsible character traits in students, seeing student life as an educational sphere in its own right in which leadership, rhetorical, and community-building skills can be practiced." This pedagogical goal of boosting students' civic engagement is a very different academic process than that of publishing digital humanities projects to the web or other venues. The latter is a kind of *product*, a scholarly "output" shared with the world. In contrast the set of liberal arts digital humanities practices we've outlined makes more sense in terms of *process*. The skills of collaboration across disciplines and institutions, working with primary sources and archives, strategically selecting technologies under financial constraints, and working within networks and connecting with local communities: these practices start from microcommunities then ultimately rise to an ethical level of civic engagement. To focus on a triumphantly finished digital product masks the networked processes within which it grew and grows further. In engaging the digital humanities movement in their own way, liberal arts campuses have reconnected with their deepest traditions and with the world.

NOTES

1. Luke Waltzer explores this tension within this volume in his chapter, "Digital Humanities and the 'Ugly-Stepchildren' of American Higher Education."

2. For an explication of various definitions of liberal arts colleges, see Parker, "What's So 'Liberal' About Higher Ed?" For a recent examination of the sector, see Ferrall, *Liberal Arts at the Brink.*

3. Thanks to Mark Sample for this reference.

BIBLIOGRAPHY

"ADHO | Alliance of Digital Humanities Organizations." Alliance of Digital Humanities Organizations. 2011. http://digitalhumanities.org/.

AMICAL. "Home." AMICAL Consortium. http://www.amicalnet.org/.

"Andrew W. Mellon Foundation Gives $1 Million Grant to Bryn Mawr College." Sage Nonprofit Solutions. April 27, 2011. http://www.saleslogix.com/NA/Nonprofit/Newsroom/IndustryDetails?id=c5973c9e-242d-4932-8515-6d4d8115080d.

Association of American Colleges and Universities (AAC&U). "Essential Learning Outcomes." *Liberal Education and America's Promise (LEAP).* http://www.aacu.org/leap/vision.cfm.

Blackwell, Christopher, and Thomas R. Martin. "Technology, Collaboration, and Undergraduate Research." *Digital Humanities Quarterly* 3, no. 1 (2009). http://www.digitalhumanities.org/dhq/vol/3/1/000024/000024.html.

Buurma, Rachel Sagner, Anna Tione Levine, and Richard Li. "The Early Novels Database: A Case Study." *Academic Commons: Digital Humanities and the Undergrad.* (April, 2011). http://www.academiccommons.org/commons/essay/early-novels-database.

Carnegie Foundation for the Advancement of Teaching. "The Carnegie Classification of Institutions of Higher Education." 2010. http://classifications.carnegiefoundationorg/.

Cavanagh, Sheila. "Bringing Our Brains to the Humanities: Increasing the Value of Our Classes while Supporting Our Futures." *Pedagogy* 10, no. 1 (2010): 131–42.

Chamberlain, Daniel. Personal communication with authors. October 28, 2010.

Cohen, Dan. "digitalhumanities" Twitter List. http://twitter.com/#!/dancohen/digitalhumanities/members.

Cohen, Dan, Amanda French, Mills Kelly, and Tom Scheifeldt. "Stimulus Plan." *Digital Campus.* September 27, 2010. http://digitalcampus.tv.

Cohen, Patricia. "Digital Humanities Boots Up on Some Campuses." *New York Times,* March 21, 2011. http://www.nytimes.com/2011/03/22/books/digital-humanities-boots-up-on-some-campuses.html.

———. "For Bentham and Others, Scholars Enlist Public to Transcribe Papers." *New York Times,* December 27, 2010. http://www.nytimes.com/2010/12/28/books/28transcribe.html.

———. "Humanities Scholars Embrace Digital Technology." *New York Times,* November 16, 2010. http://www.nytimes.com/2010/11/17/arts/17digital.html.

———. "In 500 Billion Words, a New Window on Culture." *New York Times,* December 16, 2010. http://www.nytimes.com/2010/12/17/books/17words.html.

———. "Victorian Literature, Statistically Analyzed With New Process." *New York Times,* December 3, 2010. http://www.nytimes.com/2010/12/04/books/04victorian.html.

Davis, Rebecca Frost. "Learning from an Undergraduate Digital Humanities Project." *Techne.* December 1, 2010. http://blogs.nitle.org/2010/12/01/learning-from-an-undergraduate-digital-humanities-project/.

Davis, Rebecca Frost, and Quinn Dombrowski. *Divided and Conquered: How Multivarious Isolation Is Suppressing Digital Humanities Scholarship.* National Institute for Technology in Liberal Education, 2011. http://www.nitle.org/live/files/36-divided-and-conquered.

DeMarais, Alyce. Personal interview with Rebecca Frost Davis. July 23, 2010.

"Digital Humanities and the Undergraduate: Campus Projects Recognized." National Institute for Technology in Liberal Education. October 12, 2010. http://www.nitle.org/live/news/134-digital-humanities-and-the-undergraduate-campus.

Digital Scholarship Lab. "About the Digital Scholarship Lab." University of Richmond, 2010. http://dsl.richmond.edu/about/.

"Digital Scholarship Lab." University of Richmond, 2011. http://dsl.richmond.edu/.

Dougherty, Jack. "SmartChoices: A Geospatial Tool for Community Outreach and Educational Research." *Academic Commons. Charting the New Knowledge Terrain.* (September, 2010). http://www.academiccommons.org/commons/essay/smartchoices-geospatial-tool.

Dué, Casey, and Mary Ebbott, eds. *The Homer Multitext Project.* Washington, D.C.: Center for Hellenic Studies of Harvard University, 2010. http://www.homermultitext.org/.

Earhart, Amy. "Challenging Gaps: Redesigning Collaboration in the Digital Humanities." In *The American Literature Scholar in the Digital Age,* edited by Amy Earhart and Andrew Jewell, 27–43. Ann Arbor: University of Michigan Press, 2010.

Ebbott, Mary. Personal interview with Rebecca Frost Davis. March 1, 2011.

Ferrall, Victor E., Jr. *Liberal Arts at the Brink.* Cambridge, Mass.: Harvard University Press, 2011.

Hamlin, Scott. "Digital Humanities on the Rise at Small Liberal Arts Colleges." *Insert_Clever_Name_Here/.* July 9, 2010. http://scottphamlin.wordpress.com/2010/07/09/digital-humanities-on-the-rise-at-small-liberal-arts-colleges/.

"History Engine." The University of Richmond. 2009. http://historyengine.richmond.edu/.

"How Do You Define Humanities Computing/Digital Humanities?" Taporwiki. 2011. http://tapor.ualberta.ca/taporwiki/index.php/How_do_you_define_Humanities_Computing_/_Digital_Humanities%3F.

Jones, Suzanne. "Americans in Paris." University of Richmond. Fall, 2010. http://tocqueville.richmond.edu/AmericansInParis.html.

Kirschenbaum, Matthew G. "What Is Digital Humanities and What's It Doing in English Departments?" *ADE Bulletin* 150 (2010). http://mkirschenbaum.files.wordpress.com/2011/03/ade-final.pdf. Reprinted in this volume.

Kosansky, Oren. "Intellectual Property and International Collaboration in the Digital Humanities: The Moroccan Jewish Community Archives." Library of Funded Projects. Washington, D.C.: National Endowment for the Humanities, Office of Digital Humanities, July 1, 2010. http://www.neh.gov/ODH/Default.aspx?tabid=111&id=193.

Kuh, George. Excerpt from *High-Impact Educational Practices: What They Are, Who Has Access to Them, and Why They Matter*. Washington, D.C.: Association of American Colleges and Universities, 2008. http://www.aacu.org/leap/hip.cfm.

LeBlanc, Mark. "Pattern Recognition Through Computational Stylistics: Old English and Beyond." *Library of Funded Projects*. Washington, D.C.: National Endowment for the Humanities, Office of Digital Humanities, February 1, 2008. http://www.neh.gov/ODH/Default.aspx?tabid=111&id=46.

LeBlanc, Mark D., Tom Armstrong, and Michael B. Gousie. "Connecting Across Campus." In *Proceedings of the 41st ACM Technical Symposium on Computer Science Education*, 52–56. New York: ACM, 2010.

"Lexomics." Wheaton College. June 30, 2010. http://wheatoncollege.edu/lexomics/.

Lopatto, David. "Undergraduate Research as a Catalyst for Liberal Learning." *Peer Review* 22, no. 1 (2006): 22–26.

"Mellon Awards $800K for Digital Humanities Initiative." Hamilton College, News, Sports, Events. September 23, 2010. http://www.hamilton.edu/news/story/mellon-foundation-awards-800k-for-digital-humanities-initiative.

Millon, Emma. "Projcct Bamboo: Building Shared Infrastructure for Humanities Research." *Maryland Institute for Technology in the Humanities Blog*. July 1, 2011. http://mith.umd.edu/project-bamboo-building-shared-infrastructure-for-humanities-research/.

Moore, Geoffrey. *Crossing the Chasm*. New York: HarperBusiness, 1991.

"A New Part of Your Digital Humanities Toolkit." *TAPAS Project*. http://tapasproject.org/.

"Occidental Awarded $700,000 Mellon Grant for Digital Scholarship." Occidental College. April 16, 2010. http://www.oxy.edu/x9846.xml.

Occidental College. "Center for Digital Learning & Research." *Scholarship Technology*. 2011. http://www.oxy.edu/cdlr.xml.

Office of Digital Humanities, National Endowment for the Humanities. *Summary Findings of NEH Digital Humanities Start-Up Grants (2007–2010)*. 2010. http://www.neh.gov/ODH/ODHUpdate/tabid/108/EntryId/144/New-from-ODH-Summary-Findings-of-NEH-Digital-Humanities-Start-Up-Grants-2007-2010.aspx.

Parker, Jo Ellen. "What's So 'Liberal' About Higher Ed?" *Academic Commons* (September, 2006). http://www.academiccommons.org/commons/essay/parker-whats-so-liberal-about-higher-ed.

Parry, Marc. "Google Awards First Grants for New Digital Humanities Research Program." *Wired Campus.* July 14, 2010. http://chronicle.com/blogPost/Google-Awards-First-Grants-for/25506/%20%20.

"Project Bamboo." Project Bamboo. 2011. http://www.projectbamboo.org/.

Rajchel, Jen. "Mooring Gaps: Marianne Moore's Bryn Mawr Poetry." Bryn Mawr College, 2010. http://mooreandpoetry.blogs.brynmawr.edu/.

Ramsay, Stephen. "On Building." Stephen Ramsay. January 11, 2011. http://lenz.unl.edu/papers/2011/01/11/on-building.html.

———. "Who's In and Who's Out." Modern Language Association Convention. January 7, 2011. http://lenz.unl.edu/papers/2011/01/08/whos-in-and-whos-out.html.

"Re:Humanities–An undergraduate symposium on digital media." Haverford College. 2010. http://news.haverford.edu/blogs/rehumanities/.

Schantz, Mark. "Undergraduate Research in the Humanities: Challenges and Prospects." *Council on Undergraduate Research Quarterly* 29, no. 2 (2008): 26.

Scheinfeldt, Tom. "Stuff Digital Humanists Like: Defining Digital Humanities by its Values." *Found History.* December 2, 2010. http://www.foundhistory.org/2010/12/02/stuff-digital-humanists-like/.

Schneider, Carol Geary. "Practicing Liberal Education: Formative Themes in the Reinvention of Liberal Learning." Association of American Colleges and Universities, 2003. http://www.aacu.org/publications/practicing_liberal_education.cfm.

Schreibman, Susan, Ray Siemens, and John Unsworth, eds. *Companion to Digital Humanities (Blackwell Companions to Literature and Culture).* Oxford: Blackwell, 2004. http://www.digitalhumanities.org/companion/.

Simons, Janet, Angel David Nieves, and Scott Hamlin. "Infrastructure and Support for Digital Scholarship in the Clouds." Online Presentation, Digital Scholarship Seminars. December 10, 2010. http://www.nitle.org/live/events/103-digital-scholarship.

Smith, Neel. "New Content, New Contributors." *The Homer Multitext Project Blog.* February 28, 2011. http://homermultitext.blogspot.com/2011/02/new-content-new-contributors.html.

———. "'Touch' the Venetus A." *The Homer Multitext Project Blog.* March 10, 2011. http://homermultitext.blogspot.com/2011/03/touch-venetus.html.

Spalti, Michael. "Bridging the Gap: Connecting Authors to Museum and Archival Collections." *Library of Funded Projects. National Endowment for the Humanities, Office of Digital Humanities,* July 1, 2008. http://www.neh.gov/ODH/Default.aspx?tabid=111&id=82.

"Text Encoding Initiative (TEI)." Text Encoding Initiative. Accessed, March 23, 2011. http://www.tei-c.org/index.xml.

"THATCamp: The Humanities and Technology Camp." http://thatcamp.org/.

"THATCamp Liberal Arts Colleges 2011." The Humanities And Technology Camp." 2011. http://lac2011.thatcamp.org/

Tomasek, Kathryn. "Brown Groupies?" *Doing History Digitally.* April 25, 2010. http://kathryntomasek.wordpress.com/2010/04/25/brown-groupies/.

———. "Digital History Project Receives Start-Up Grant from NEH Office of Digital Humanities." Digital History Project, Wheaton College. April 1, 2011. http://wheatoncollege.edu/digital-history-project/2011/04/01/digital-history-project-receives-startup-grant-neh-office-digital-humanities/.

Tomasek, Kathryn, et al. "Encoding Text, Revealing Meaning: Implications of the Text Encoding Initiative (TEI) for Small Liberal Arts Colleges." *International Journal of Technology, Knowledge and Society* 1, no. 3 (2006): 157–64.

"Tri-Co Digital Humanities." Bryn Mawr College. 2011. http://www.brynmawr.edu/tdh/.

Unsworth, John. "Our Cultural Commonwealth: The Report of the American Council of Learned Societies Commission on Cyberinfrastructure for the Humanities and Social Sciences." *American Council of Learned Societies*, 2006. http://acls.org/uploadedFiles/Publications/Programs/Our_Cultural_Commonwealth.pdf.

———. "The State of Digital Humanities." Plenary address for the 2010 Digital Humanities Summer Institute, June 2010. http://www3.isrl.illinois.edu/~unsworth/state.of.dh.digital humanitiesSI.pdf.

Waltzer, Luke. "Digital Humanities and the 'Ugly-Stepchildren' of American Higher Education." *Debates in the Digital Humanities*, edited by Matthew K. Gold. Minneapolis: University of Minnesota Press, 2012.

Wheaton College. "Connections." The Wheaton Curriculum. September 8, 2010. http://wheatoncollege.edu/academics/the-wheaton-curriculum/connections/.

Wheaton College. "Four Professors Win NEH Grants." News & Events. May 9, 2011. http://wheatoncollege.edu/news/2011/05/09/professors-win-neh-grants/.

Zorich, Diane. *A Survey of Digital Humanities Centers in the United States.* Washington, D.C.: Council on Library and Information Resources, 2008. http://www.clir.org/pubs/reports/pub143/contents.html.

PART V][*Chapter 22*

Where's the Pedagogy? The Role of Teaching and Learning in the Digital Humanities

STEPHEN BRIER

The digital humanities (DH) has experienced impressive growth over the past three or four years, sweeping across a number of academic fields and, in the process, helping to reshape and reframe discussion and debate about the nature of scholarly research, peer review and publication, and academic promotion and tenure. "Digital humanities" already generates more than four-hundred thousand unique results in a Google search. The print and online pages of the *Chronicle of Higher Education*, that reliable bellwether of all trends academic, document the impact that the digital humanities has had in and on universities and colleges, both here and abroad. *Chronicle*, which appears forty-five times a year, has published no fewer than ninety-five articles on DH over the past three years alone, many of which are part of the new and popular *ProfHacker* blog that *Chronicle* recently launched to make the publication more relevant to the up-and-coming academic generation. Younger scholars, especially those currently pursuing or having recently received doctoral degrees in fields in the humanities, interpretive social sciences, and the arts, seem particularly taken with the possibilities of using digital innovations and techniques to reimagine their disciplines and the very nature of their future academic work and life.[1] The National Endowment for the Humanities (NEH), a mainstay of financial support for the humanities since its creation in 1965, was well ahead of this particular academic curve, launching its Digital Humanities Initiative in 2006; two years later it evolved into the Office of Digital Humanities.

But this recent rush toward the technological new has tended to focus too narrowly, in my judgment, on the academic research and publication aspects of the digital humanities, in the process reinforcing disciplinary "silos" and traditional academic issues while also minimizing and often obscuring the larger implications of DH for how we teach in universities and colleges and how we prepare the next generation of graduate students for careers inside and outside of the academy. Pedagogy is not totally ignored by DH's growing cadre of practitioners; rather, teaching and learning are something of an afterthought for many DHers. Matthew Kirschenbaum, the associate director of the Maryland Institute for Technology in the Humanities, in a recent essay on the rise of the digital humanities, emphasizes the research aspects of DH, noting its growing impact on academic scholarship, publishing, peer review, and tenure and promotion in English departments. Kirschenbaum hardly mentions DH's role in teaching and learning until the article's final paragraph, when the word "pedagogy" makes a sudden appearance several times (61). DHers seem far more engaged by the intellectual possibilities of using (to take but one example) digital technologies to mine vast and newly available databases of information on a range of subjects and issues. A good illustration of this focus on digital research can be seen in the various academic research projects spawned by Google's controversial library books scanning project and the heavy publicized Google digital humanities grant competition that encouraged humanities faculty members to use the huge database generated by the company.[2]

This emphasis on digital research can also be seen in many recent DH academic publications. For example, one of the key DH academic journals, *Digital Humanities Quarterly* (*DHQ*), based at Brown University, has published nine online issues since its debut in spring 2007. Its pages feature scholarly work from across the globe representing a mix of humanities disciplines and focusing on a range of interesting DH-related topics. While *DHQ*'s mission statement indicates a desire to "provide a forum for theorists, researchers and teachers to share their work," its actual definition of DH reveals a narrower emphasis on academic research: "Digital humanities is a diverse and still emerging field that encompasses the practice of humanities research in and through information technology, and the exploration of how the humanities may evolve through their engagement with technology, media, and computational methods."[3] A search of the titles of the ninety plus articles *DHQ* has published over its first three years confirms this emphasis on research over teaching: only two article titles include references to teaching or pedagogy while nineteen titles include the word "research." Full-text searches of the contents of the ninety articles published to date in *DHQ* reveal a less marked disparity between research and teaching and pedagogy: while the word "research" garners eighty-one hits in total (nine of every ten articles that *DHQ* has published), "teaching" and "learning" each total at least forty hits (and twenty-six when paired), while "pedagogy" appears a mere nine times (averaging about one of every ten articles). This quick and somewhat unnuanced survey of *DHQ* suggests that, while research is the dominant focus of much of what scholars choose to publish in the journal, there is some interest in and focus on (albeit a limited one) the broader implications of DH work for teaching and learning.[4]

Brett Bobley, director of the NEH's Office of Digital Humanities, recently offered a broad definition of the digital humanities in a January 2011 radio interview, noting that "digital humanities is really applying digital technology to doing traditional study and also trying to determine how do you use technology best in a classroom setting. So it's really about both the research and the education."[5] Yet the cover of the Office of Digital Humanities' September 2010 "Summary Findings of NEH Digital Humanities Start-Up Grants (2007–2010)"—which features a Wordle word cloud drawn from the text of the abstracts of all of the office's funded start-up grants—does not include the words "teaching," "learning," "classroom," or "pedagogy." The word "research," on the other hand, is among the ten most frequently used words in all the abstracts, along with "project," "director," "digital," and "humanities." Again, this does not mean that none of the NEH-supported digital humanities start-up projects funded over the past three years was concerned or engaged with questions of teaching and learning. Several focused, at least in part, on the application of the digital humanities to classroom teaching or graduate education. Rather, the absence of key words like pedagogy and teaching in the abstracts suggests that these approaches are not yet primary in terms of digital humanists' own conceptions of their work, at least among those who apply to the NEH's Office of Digital Humanities for funding support.[6]

Instead of belaboring this point about the primacy of the research focus in the current DH world, this essay will look instead at DH through the lens of the scholarship of teaching and learning,[7] exploring in particular the pedagogical implications of digital technologies for the ways we educate the current generation of college students. Building on my own and my City University of New York (CUNY) colleagues' diverse efforts and experiences in incorporating digital technologies into a variety of CUNY educational programs and initiatives at both the undergraduate and graduate levels, this essay will offer an alternative vision of the digital humanities that is engaged in the project of improving the quality of classroom teaching practices and learning outcomes.

The City University of New York is a good place to focus such a discussion about the scholarship of teaching and learning and the impact of digital technologies in general and the digital humanities in specific. From its origins in the mid-nineteenth century, CUNY's stated purpose was to educate "the children of the whole people,"[8] as expressed by the first president of the Free Academy (later the City College) on the occasion of its opening in 1849. Over the course of the next 160 years, CUNY (which was only consolidated in its current incarnation in 1961) became the nation's largest urban public university system, this year enrolling more than 260,000 matriculating students and an equal number of continuing and professional education students on twenty-three different campuses across the city's five boroughs. CUNY's extraordinary growth over the past half century required that its faculty and administrators be willing to undertake (or at least minimally tolerate) a series of radical experiments in pedagogy and open access that have put CUNY at the forefront of national efforts to effect educational change and transformation, including (but not limited to) pioneering efforts in the digital humanities and the educational uses of digital technologies. CUNY's long-standing focus on innovative pedagogy inflects the institution's orientation and that of its faculty and doctoral students toward digital technology. It's not that CUNY faculty and doctoral students are disinterested in the kinds of research questions that digital humanities work has chosen to focus on; rather, our interest in digital humanities is significantly shaped by our institution's deep and abiding commitment to educate successive waves of the city's working-class students. Let me illustrate CUNY's special focus on innovative pedagogy by reviewing a series of major digital projects and initiatives undertaken by CUNY faculty members and doctoral students over the past two decades.

The Writing Across the Curriculum (WAC) Initiative

CUNY threw open its doors to thousands of new working-class students when it launched its open admissions experiment in 1969. Open admissions allowed all high school graduates from any New York City public school to gain entry to CUNY's senior and community colleges on the basis of having received a high school diploma. This approach put tremendous pressure on the system to provide remedial instruction in math and especially in writing, given the New York City public schools' acknowledged failures in these years (Traub, 43–80). Mina Shaughnessy, who began teaching basic writing at City College in 1967 on the eve of the open admissions era (which lasted three decades in all), emerged as an internationally recognized expert on teaching writing to underprepared working-class students entering CUNY. Those students received remedial writing (and mathematics) instruction through the City College of New York's (and later CUNY's) Search for Education, Elevation, and Knowledge (SEEK) program. Shaughnessy, through her emphasis on writing as an academic discipline, inspired several generations of CUNY teachers of writing who carried on and significantly broadened her work in the decades following her death in 1978.[9]

Responding to increasing pressure to improve CUNY's flagging academic reputation emanating from the administration of Mayor Rudolph Giuliani and from New York City opinion makers including the *New York Post,* CUNY's Board of Trustees voted to end the university's open admissions "experiment" in 1999. With the demise of open admissions, the CUNY administration launched the Writing Across the Curriculum (WAC) initiative in the same year. WAC represented a continuation of CUNY's commitment to teach writing skills as a critical component of educating CUNY's working-class student body. The WAC program was built on the deployment of dozens of doctoral-level writing fellows at various CUNY senior and community college campuses. Many WAC fellows were composition/rhetoric doctoral students studying in the CUNY Graduate Center's English PhD Program; they articulated a special academic interest in and commitment to theorizing and improving the teaching of writing skills and practices. The WAC program grew dramatically over the next decade, with as many as 150 writing fellows employed each year, embracing the use of a variety of teaching methodologies to improve writing across all courses and academic programs at CUNY community and senior colleges, as well as at the CUNY Law School and the CUNY School of Professional Studies.[10]

Almost from the outset of the WAC program, writing fellows helped push the integration of digital technologies into WAC pedagogy. At Baruch College, for example, home to CUNY's business school, the WAC program launched Blogs@ Baruch in 2008, an online publishing and academic networking platform, built in WordPress and BuddyPress, which is used for course weblogs, student journals and publications, curriculum development, administrative communication, and faculty development. Twenty-seven writing fellows and three full-time staff collaborate with hundreds of Baruch faculty members, supporting nearly four-hundred course sections with an enrollment of more than fourteen thousand Baruch students annually. The use of writing fellows and social media and other digital technologies to enhance teaching and learning has grown in the past several years on many CUNY campuses (though nowhere quite as dramatically as at Baruch).[11]

The American Social History Project/Center for Media and Learning/ New Media Lab

The American Social History Project (ASHP), which I cofounded at CUNY in 1981 with the late social historian Herbert Gutman, was a pioneer in the development of digital history, an early exemplar of digital humanities work. Among the project's most important accomplishments was its Who Built America? (WBA) multimedia U.S. history curriculum, which included textbooks, videotapes, and teacher and student guides that were widely used to transform the teaching of American history in college and high school history classrooms in New York City and across the country. The WBA multimedia curriculum also included perhaps the nation's first digital publication in U.S. history, the CD-ROM *Who Built America? From the Centennial Celebration of 1876 to the Great War of 1914*, conceived and written by the late Roy Rosenzweig, Steve Brier, and Joshua Brown and published by the Voyager Company in 1993.[12]

A hallmark of the WBA multimedia curriculum and of ASHP's digital humanities work in general has been the project's quarter-century-long commitment to using digital media to enhance the quality of teaching and learning of history at the high school and undergraduate levels. Working closely and collaboratively with humanities teachers across the country in a series of grant-supported projects over the past two decades, the ASHP staff helped pioneer a set of active learning strategies to improve history teaching, emphasizing, for example, the uses of primary source documents and visual source materials available online as a way to encourage students' deeper immersion in historical thinking and history making.

In 1999, ASHP expanded its digital reach beyond history by creating the New Media Lab (NML) at the CUNY Graduate Center, which provides an interdisciplinary laboratory environment for doctoral faculty and students to work collaboratively to integrate digital media into their academic scholarship, regardless of academic discipline. The NML has hosted the development and production of a number of digital humanities projects by CUNY faculty and doctoral students, including (to name but two) the Phylo Project (which mapped the intellectual, institutional, and personal interconnections in the academic field of philosophy) and the Virtual Poetry Project, a web-based multimedia exploration of Latin American poets and poetry.[13]

The Interactive Technology and Pedagogy Doctoral Certificate Program

The Interactive Technology and Pedagogy Certificate Program (ITP) at the CUNY Graduate Center, which I conceived and have coordinated since its founding in 2002, is an interdisciplinary program that provides doctoral students from a range of academic disciplines with opportunities to reflect on the broader theory behind and pedagogical implications of digital technology usage in the academy. The program features theoretical and conceptual discussions about the cultural, economic, legal, political, and personal impact of technological transformation across time; hands-on engagement with a range of digital technology tools, including blogs and wikis; as well as ongoing conversations about how these digital tools can best be used to enhance academic research and the quality of teaching and learning. Since so many Graduate Center doctoral students are employed at various CUNY campuses as instructors, with sole responsibility for teaching large introductory survey courses to undergraduates in their academic disciplines, the uses of digital technology to improve pedagogy is of particular interest to our doctoral students. A number of ITP certificate holders have been able to use their skills in digital technology and pedagogy to find both traditional academic positions in universities and colleges around the country and internationally as well as nontraditional digital humanities and digital pedagogy positions and postdocs. These ITP graduates, along with New Media Lab participants and American Social History Project staff, are committed to using cutting-edge digital research techniques, innovative presentational forms, and open and active pedagogical approaches to teaching and learning to improve the quality of their current and future academic work.[14]

The Instructional Technology Fellows Program at the Macaulay Honors College

The founding of CUNY's Macaulay Honors College (MHC) in 2001 included a commitment to hire and deploy a corps of Instructional Technology Fellows (ITFs), advanced doctoral students at CUNY's Graduate Center drawn from diverse academic disciplines. The twenty-five ITFs currently employed by MHC are assigned to eight different CUNY campus honors programs and at the central MHC facility. Like the CUNY writing fellows, ITFs work closely with MHC faculty and undergraduates to help them use digital tools—including blogs, wikis, discussion forums, and podcasts—"to support collaboration, integrative learning, community building, and student-centered pedagogies."[15] The ITFs are among CUNY's most advanced digital scholars and teachers, with broad knowledge about the uses of digital technology and digital pedagogy. And like the ITP certificate holders, the MHC ITFs have a solid record in securing full-time academic positions at colleges and universities once they finish their two or three years at Macaulay and complete their PhDs. MHC Associate Dean Joseph Ugoretz has suggested that the success of Macaulay's ITFs in the academic job market is the result of at least as much of their experiences as digital pedagogues as their skill as digital scholars.[16]

"Looking for Whitman"

A good example of a recent CUNY digital humanities project that combines digital research and digital pedagogy is "Looking for Whitman: The Poetry of Place in the Life and Work of Walt Whitman," conceived and headed by Matthew K. Gold at New York City College of Technology, CUNY (NYCCT). The semester-long project was designed to bring together undergraduates enrolled in four different courses at four geographically dispersed college campuses (NYCCT and New York University [NYU] in New York City, University of Mary Washington in Virginia, and Rutgers–Camden in New Jersey) to collaborate on an exploration of Whitman's poetry in relationship to specific places in which Whitman lived and labored. The participating students and faculty members regularly shared ideas, research, and feedback about Whitman's life and writing on the project's WordPress site. The four-month effort ended in April 2010 with a face-to-face "generative" conference held at Rutgers–Camden, which not only included reports on what had been accomplished by the students on each of the four campuses during the previous fall semester but also featured continued creation of scholarly content and student presentations about Whitman's life and poetry, all captured on digital video and displayed on the project's website. "Looking for Whitman" is a model for how digital scholarship and digital pedagogy can be combined to enhance undergraduate teaching as well as how social networking tools can help bridge very real geographical, economic, and cultural gaps among and between universities and colleges.[17]

The CUNY Academic Commons

The development in 2009 of the CUNY Academic Commons (AC) was a critical step taken by CUNY faculty members and administrators, led by George Otte and Matthew K. Gold, to create a unified platform for scholarly communication across CUNY that could pull together individual academics working with or interested in digital technologies and pedagogies under a single, broad, digital umbrella. The Academic Commons was conceived as an accessible, collaborative public arena on the Internet (http://www.commons.gc.cuny.edu), built in WordPress and BuddyPress, which is, in the words of one of the ACs operating documents, "dedicated to the free expression of our users in a collaborative [shared] environment. We are a community that seeks to use the Academic Commons as a means of fulfilling our highest aspirations for integrating technology into our teaching, learning, and collaborating."[18]

The AC's emphasis is on building academic community in all its diverse permutations and forms. In the eighteen months since its launch, the AC has garnered nearly two thousand CUNY members (only CUNY faculty members, staff, and doctoral students are eligible to join) who use the AC's group sites, blogs, and wikis to find and inform one another, to teach doctoral courses, and to collaborate on digital and other types of academic projects and groups (including, it should be noted, CUNYPie, a group of CUNY academics/fanatics in search of the best pizza served in New York City's five boroughs). The AC has already generated extensive notice in the academic press (including feature articles in the *Chronicle of Higher Education*, *Educause Review*, and other online academic publications) as well as inquiries from numerous universities and colleges looking to emulate CUNY's efforts by creating their own academic commons.

The existence of AC proved especially helpful last year when a group of faculty and doctoral students from across the CUNY system, under the aegis of the CUNY Digital Studies Group, which I founded and cochair, decided to organize a major conference, "The Digital University: Power Relations, Publishing, Authority and Community in the 21st Century Academy." The conference, supported by the Graduate Center's Center for the Humanities, was an effort to broaden notions of the digital humanities beyond academic scholarship and publication to include digital approaches to teaching, learning, and pedagogy. The all-day event, held at the CUNY Graduate Center in April 2010, drew more than 140 scholars and teachers from around the world, was the subject of a vigorous and sustained Twitter stream (#du10), and featured a series of smaller workshops and a keynote address by Siva Vaidhyanathan, which engaged critical issues related to academic scholarship, academic publication, peer review, and digital pedagogy.[19]

Digital Humanities Initiative

The success of "The Digital University" conference and its focus on the transformational possibilities of the digital humanities in the university led a group of CUNY faculty and doctoral students to launch the Digital Humanities Initiative (DHI) at CUNY. The DHI, cochaired by Matthew K. Gold and Charlie Edwards (a doctoral student in English and in the ITP certificate program), has in less than a year attracted more than one hundred DHers to its ranks from across the CUNY system. The group, in the words of its mission statement, is "aimed at building connections and community among those at CUNY who are applying digital technologies to scholarship and pedagogy in the humanities."[20] It is important to note the equal weight given in the mission statement to scholarship and pedagogy. Working under the aegis of the Digital Studies Group, the DHI has sponsored a series of talks and lectures on a range of DH-related research topics, including presentations by Tom Scheinfeldt of GMU's Center for History and New Media; Kathleen Fitzpatrick of Pomona College's Media Studies Program; David Hoover of NYU's English Department; and Patrik Svensson, director of HUMlab at Umeå University, Sweden. Consonant with its commitment to focus its work particularly on questions of pedagogy, the DHI has also offered several roundtable presentations on the relationship of DH to teaching and learning, including sharing of ideas and approaches to using off-the-shelf open source tools, including WordPress plug-ins to create paperless and networked classrooms. And at one of its first sessions in fall 2010, the DHI heard CUNY educational technologists Mikhail Gershovich, Joe Ugoretz, and Luke Waltzer discuss technology and pedagogy in the context of their teaching work at Baruch College and at the Macaulay Honors College.

Looking Ahead

I have provided this somewhat breathless survey of diverse projects and educational reform efforts at CUNY because they share a common focus on bridging the gap between digital scholarship and digital pedagogy. Each was designed to encourage CUNY faculty and doctoral students to engage in an extended conversation about the best strategies for improving classroom teaching and, increasingly over the past two decades, centering those conversations and strategies on the uses of digital technologies to enhance the prospects for improving teaching and learning. CUNY's growing focus over the past two decades on the scholarship of teaching and learning has by no means been limited to the digital humanities, narrowly defined. If we are willing to broaden our definition of digital humanities beyond academic research and related issues of academic publication, peer review, and tenure and promotion to encompass critical questions about ways to improve teaching and learning, then CUNY's various digital pedagogy projects and strategies offer an alternative pathway to broaden the impact of the digital humanities movement and make it more relevant to the ongoing and increasingly beleaguered educational mission of contemporary colleges and universities.

NOTES

1. The *Chronicle of Higher Education* is online at http://chronicle.com/section/Home/5; the *Chronicle*'s *ProfHacker* blog is at http://chronicle.com/blogs/profhacker/. The National Institute for Technology in Liberal Education recently (Summer 2010) defined the digital humanities as encompassing the humanities, interpretive social sciences, and the arts, an approach that echoes some funders' definition (cf. Mellon Foundation) and other national digital humanities projects (cf. Project Bamboo). See http://blogs.nitle.org/2010/08/31/nitle-launches-digital-humanities-initiative/.

2. Other scholars have pointed to DH's general exclusion of issues of pedagogy, including Katherine Harris at California State University, Long Beach, who has been particularly vocal about this issue. See her blog for comments on DH and pedagogy: http://triproftri.wordpress.com/. Professor Harris and I helped carry the pedagogy banner at several of the workshops at Project Bamboo, an ongoing international organizing effort, funded by the Mellon Foundation and headed up by the University of California Berkeley and the University of Chicago, to build a set of collaborative digital humanities tools to enhance academic scholarship. See http://googleblog.blogspot.com/2010/07/our-commitment-to-digital-humanities.html, accessed March 19, 2011, for Google's statement announcing the first recipients of its digital humanities research grants.

3. Quotations from the "About *DHQ*" section of *DHQ*'s website: http://digitalhumanities.org/DHQ/about/about.html.

4. Searches were conducted from the *DHQ*'s home page: http://digitalhumanities.org/DHQ/.

5. The *Kojo Nnamdi Show*, January 11, 2011, WAMU 88.5 FM, American University Radio podcast and transcript: http://thekojonnamdishow.org/shows/2011-01-11/history-meets-high-tech-digital-humanities/transcript.

6. The Office of Digital Humanities (ODH) report can be found at http://www.neh.gov/whoweare/cio/odhfiles/Summary.Report.ODH.SUG.pdf.

7. The simplest definition of the scholarship of teaching and learning has been offered by the eponymous Carnegie Academy at Illinois State University: "systematic reflection on teaching and learning made public." See http://www.sotl.ilstu.edu/.

8. Association of the Bar of the City of New York, Report of the Commission on the Future of CUNY: Part I Remediation and Access: To Educate the "Children of the Whole People," 1999. http://www2.nycbar.org/Publications/reports/show_html_new.php?rid=47.

9. Background information on Shaughnessy can be found on Wikipedia (http://en.wikipedia.org/wiki/Mina_P._Shaughnessy) and in Jane Maher's biography, *Mina P. Shaughnessy: Her Life and Work*.

10. CUNY's dean of undergraduate education produced a history of CUNY's Writing Across the Curriculum Program, "Writing Across the Curriculum at CUNY: A Ten-Year Review," which can be found at http://www.cuny.edu/about/administration/offices/ue/wac/WAC10YearReportJune2010.pdf.

11. Information about Blogs@Baruch provided by Mikhail Gershovich, telephone interview with the author, March 26, 2011. Gershovich is the director of the Bernard Schwartz Communications Institute (BSCI), Baruch College (CUNY). BSCI oversees the WAC program at the college. The integration of digital media at Baruch and its impact on the college's freshman seminars can be seen by reading the multiple blog posts and viewing the student-produced videos at http://blsciblogs.baruch.cuny.edu/fro/. The Schwartz Institute and its pioneering work in CUNY's WAC program were featured in Fara Warner's online article, "Improving Communication Is Everyone's Responsibility," http://www.changemag

.org/Archives/Back%20Issues/November-December%202008/full-improving-communication.html.

12. Information about the WBA multimedia curriculum can be found at http://ashp.cuny.edu/who-america/. Developing the first WBA CD-ROM in 1991 and 1992 might well qualify Rosenzweig, Brown, and Brier for special status as "premature digital humanists." For those unfamiliar with the historical reference, this phrase echoes the U.S. Communist Party's labeling of those who fought (and in many cases died) to defend the Spanish Republic in 1936 as "premature antifascists."

13. ASHP received research center status in CUNY in 1992 with the founding of the Center for Media and Learning (CML). ASHP and CML have been led by Josh Brown since 1998. Information about ASHP, CML, and the New Media Lab can be found at http://ashp.cuny.edu/and http://nml.cuny.edu/. The Phylo Project can be viewed at http://phylo.info. The Visual Poetry Project can be viewed at http://nml.cuny.edu/poetryproject/vpp/index.php/vpp/index.

14. Information about the Interactive Technology and Pedagogy Certificate Program can be found at http://web.gc.cuny.edu/itp/.

15. Quote is from the description of the Macaulay Honors College's uses of instructional technology on the school's website: http://macaulay.cuny.edu/academics/technology.php.

16. Joseph Ugoretz, e-mail message to the author, March 27, 2011.

17. The *Looking for Whitman* WordPress site can be found at http://lookingforwhitman.org.

18. CUNY Academic Commons Terms of Service, http://commons.gc.cuny.edu/about/tos/.

19. The conference's website (http://digitaluniversity.gc.cuny.edu/) offers the most complete sense of what we hoped to accomplish and what actually transpired.

20. DHI's mission statement can be found at http://commons.gc.cuny.edu/groups/digital-humanities-initiative/.

BIBLIOGRAPHY

Digital Humanities Quarterly. Alliance of Digital Humanities Organizations. http://digitalhumanities.org/dhq/.

"History Meets High-Tech: Digital Humanities." *Kojo Nnamdi Show*. WAMU 88.5 FM, American University Radio. January 11, 2011. http://thekojonnamdishow.org/shows/2011-01-11/history-meets-high-tech-digital-humanities.

Kirschenbaum, Matthew. "What Is Digital Humanities and What's It Doing in English Departments?" *ADE Bulletin*. 150 (2010): 55–61. Reprinted in this volume.

Maher, Jane. *Mina P. Shaughnessy: Her Life and Work.* Urbana, Ill.: National Council of Teachers of English, 1997.

Office of the Digital Humanities, National Endowment for the Humanities. "Summary Findings of NEH Digital Humanities Start-Up Grants (2007–2010)." September 2010. http://www.neh.gov/whoweare/cio/odhfiles/Summary.Report.ODH.SUG.pdf.

"Our Commitment to Digital Humanities." *Official Google Blog.* http://googleblog.blogspot.com/2010/07/our-commitment-to-digital-humanities.html.

Traub, James. *City on a Hill: Testing the American Dream at City College.* Reading, Mass.: Addison Wesley, 1994.

University Dean for Undergraduate Education. "Writing Across the Curriculum at CUNY: A Ten-Year Review." City University of New York, Office of Academic Affairs, 2010. http://www.cuny.edu/about/administration/offices/ue/wac/WAC10YearReportJune2010.pdf.

Warner, Fara. "Improving Communication Is Everyone's Responsibility." *Change: The Magazine of Higher Learning. Taylor and Francis Group* (November/December 2008): 26–33.http://www.changemag.org/Archives/Back%20Issues/November-December%202008/full-improving-communication.html.

Visualizing Millions of Words

MILLS KELLY

One of the very first posts I wrote for this blog was about visualizing information and some of the new online tools that had cropped up to make it a little easier to think about the relationships between data—words, people, and so on (Kelly). Interesting as they were, those tools were all very limited in their scope and application, especially when compared to Google's newly rolled out Ngram viewer.[1] This new tool, brought to you by the good people at GoogleLabs, lets users compare the relationships between words or short phrases, across 5.2 million books (and apparently journals) in Google's database of scanned works.

The data produced with this tool are not without criticism (Parry).[2] I will leave it to the literary scholars and the linguists to hash out the thornier issues here. My own concern is how using a tool such as this one can help students of the past make sense of the past in new or different ways. Among the many things I've learned from my students over the years is that they can be pretty persistent in their belief that words have been used in much the same way over time, that they have meant the same things (generally) over time, and that words or phrases that are common today were probably common in the past—assuming those words existed. They (my students) know that such assumptions are problematic for all the obvious reasons, but that doesn't stop them from holding to these assumptions anyway.

I just spent an hour or so playing with the Ngram tool, putting in various words or phrases, and I can already imagine a simple assignment for students in a historical methods course. I would begin such an assignment by asking them to play with word pairs such as war/peace. By using Ngram, they would see that peace (red) overtook war (blue) in 1743 as a word that appeared in books in English (at least in books Google has scanned to date).

Intriguing as this "finding" is, the lesson that I would then focus on with my students is that what they are looking at in such a graph is nothing more or less than the frequency with which a word is used in a book (and only books) published over the centuries. While such frequencies do reflect something, it is not clear from one graph just what that something is. So instead of an answer, a graph like this one is a doorway that leads to a room filled with questions, each of which must be answered by the historian before he or she knows something worth knowing.

After introducing my students to that room full of questions, I would then show them a slightly more sophisticated (emphasis on slightly) use of this tool. My current research is on the history of human trafficking. The term "human trafficking" (green) is a very recent formulation in books written in English. More common in prior decades were the terms "white slave trade" (blue) and "traffic in women and children" (red). This offers students a way to see the waxing and waning of these formulations over the past century.

But this also demonstrates a nice lesson in paying attention to what one is looking at. Google's database of available books runs through 2008. The graph I describe ends in 2000. If I expand the lower axis to 2008, the lines look quite different. My hope would be to use tricks like this to demonstrate to my students how essential it is that they think critically about the data being represented to them in any graphical form.

While I doubt that I'll ever assign Edward Tufte's work to my undergraduates, I do think that an exercise such as this one with the Ngram viewer will make it possible to introduce the work of Tufte and others in a way that will be more accessible to undergraduates. If they've already played with tools like the Ngram viewer, then the more theoretical and technical discussions will make a lot more sense and will seem a lot more relevant. I think they will also be more likely to see the value in what Stephen Ramsay calls the "hermeneutics of screwing around."[3]

NOTES

This chapter originally appeared as "Visualizing Millions of Words" (http://edwired.org/2010/12/17/visualizing-millions-of-words/).

1. http://ngrams.googlelabs.com/.
2. http://chronicle.com/article/Scholars-Elicit-a-Cultural/125731/.
3. http://library.brown.edu/cds/pages/705.

BIBLIOGRAPHY

Kelly, Mills. "Visualizing Information." *Edwired*. October 25, 2005. http://edwired.org/2005/10/25/visualizing-information/.

Parry, Mark. "Scholars Elicit a 'Cultural Genome' From 5.2 Million Google-Digitized Books." *Chronicle of Higher Education*, December 26, 2010. http://chronicle.com/article/Scholars-Elicit-a-Cultural/125731/.

Ramsay, Stephen. "The Hermeneutics of Screwing Around." Playing With History Conference. THEN/HiER. Niagra-on-the-Lake, Canada. April 17, 2010. http://www.playingwithhistory.com/wp-content/uploads/2010/04/hermeneutics.pdf.

What's Wrong with Writing Essays

MARK L. SAMPLE

As a professor invested in critical thinking—that is, in *difficult thinking*—I have become increasingly disillusioned with the traditional student paper. Just as the only thing a standardized test measures is how well a student can take a standardized test, the only thing an essay measures is how well a student can conform to the rigid thesis/defense model that, in the hands of novice scholars, eliminates complexity, ambiguity, and most traces of critical thinking.

I don't believe that my mission as a professor is to turn my students into miniature versions of myself or of any other professor. Yet that is the chief function that the traditional student essay serves. And even if I *did* want to churn out copycat professors, the essay fails exceedingly well at this. Somehow the student essay has come to stand in for all the research, dialogue, revision, and work that professional scholars engage in.

It doesn't.

The student essay is a twitch in a void, a compressed outpouring of energy (if we're lucky) that means nothing to no one. Randy Bass, a longtime collaborator of mine at Georgetown University, has said that nowhere but school would we ask somebody to write something that nobody will ever read.

This is the primary reason I've integrated more and more *public* writing into my classes. I strive to instill in my students the sense that what they think and what they say and what they write matters—to me; to them; to their classmates; and, through open access blogs and wikis, to the world.

In addition to making student writing public, I've also begun taking the words out of writing. Why must writing, especially writing that captures critical thinking, be composed of words? Why not images? Why not sound? Why not objects? The word *text*, after all, derives from the Latin *textus*, meaning "that which is woven," strands of different material intertwined together. Let the warp be words and the weft be something else entirely.

With this in mind, I am moving away from asking students to write, toward asking them instead to *weave*—to build, to fabricate, to design. I don't want my students to become miniature scholars. I want them to be aspiring Rauschenbergs, assembling mixed media combines, all the while through their engagement with seemingly incongruous materials developing a critical thinking practice about the process and the product. I call this type of critical thinking *creative analysis*.

In my video game studies class, I asked students to design an abstract visualization of a Nintendo Entertainment System (NES) video game, a kind of model that would capture some of the game's complexity and reveal underlying patterns to the way actions, space, and time unfold in the game. One student "mapped" *Sid Meier's Pirates!* (1991) onto a piece of driftwood. This "captain's log," covered with screenshots and overlayed with axes measuring time and action, evokes the static nature of the game more than words ever can. Like Meier's *Civilization*, much of *Pirates!* is given over to configurations, selecting from menus and other nondiegetic actions. Pitched battles on the high seas, what would seem to be the highlight of any game about pirates, are rare; and, though a flat photograph (see Notes) of the log doesn't do justice to the actual object in all its physicality, you can see some of that absence of action here, where the top of the log is full of blank wood.

The wood says what words cannot.

NOTES

This chapter originally appeared as "What's Wrong with Writing Essays" (http://www.samplereality.com/2009/03/12/whats-wrong-with-writing-essays/). A photograph of the "captain's log" may be found there.

Looking for Whitman: A Grand, Aggregated Experiment

MATTHEW K. GOLD AND JIM GROOM

Unscrew the locks from the doors!
Unscrew the doors themselves from their jambs!

—Walt Whitman, *Leaves of Grass*

In the spring of 2009, students from four universities converged on a single website in a collaborative effort to research and explore the poetry of Walt Whitman. Conceived of as a multicampus experiment in digital pedagogy seeking to break through the institutional barriers that, even in the age of the Internet, so often divide one university classroom from another, "Looking for Whitman: The Poetry of Place in the Life and Work of Walt Whitman" was sponsored by two Start-Up Grants from the National Endowment for the Humanities (NEH) Office of Digital Humanities.[1] The project brought together five courses on Walt Whitman, each running concurrently at a college located in a place where Whitman himself had lived and worked, in an attempt to see how a group of distributed faculty and students could share, collaborate, research, and converse out in the open through a rich infrastructure of social media.

While each course ran on a face-to-face basis at its respective university, a large majority of the work took place online. The project served as an opportunity to illustrate how loosely networked learning spaces could be used to reimagine the possibilities for connection among students and faculty working on related projects at a disparate range of institutions. As a case study for linked courses across universities, it framed the importance of an open and porous learning ecosystem that used network effects to aggregate and amplify student work, building a larger, focused conversation around the relationship of particular literary texts to particular geographical spaces.

The colleges chosen for participation in the project—New York City College of Technology (CUNY), New York University (NYU), University of Mary Washington, and Rutgers University-Camden—represented a wide range of institutional profiles:

an open-admissions public college of technology, a private research-intensive university, a public liberal arts college, and a public research university, each with very different types of students. Beyond that, the courses explicitly and intentionally engaged various levels of the curriculum and learners with very different types of backgrounds and knowledge bases. The class at University of Mary Washington consisted of senior English majors who were taking the course as a capstone experience. There were two classes at Rutgers; one contained a mix of undergraduate English majors and master's-level students, while the other was open to students in master's and doctoral degree programs who were taking a methods course that served as an introduction to graduate English studies. At City Tech, meanwhile, undergraduate students with little training in literature were taking a course on Whitman as part of their general education requirements. The project gained an international angle when NYU faculty member Karen Karbiener received a Fulbright Fellowship to Serbia and decided to make her American Studies class at the University of Novi Sad part of the project.

Mixing all of these students together in a single online space—especially one that placed a great deal of emphasis on social interaction—might seem at best a bad idea and at worst a dangerous one. What could graduate students studying literature and preparing for comprehensive exams learn from undergraduate students taking gen-ed courses at an urban school of technology? Would students flame one another on a course site that emphasized social media? Would undergrads be intimidated by graduate students who were doing research in their fields of specialization? How would these students connect to one another across individual institutional cultures and socioeconomic differences? And above all, how would they collectively engage Whitman's work and connect his texts to the places in which they had been written?

A look around the *Looking for Whitman* website and its diverse array of assignments and projects will demonstrate the meaningful connections created through this pedagogical experiment. From videos that remixed Whitman's work to detailed annotations and explications of his poems to a collaboratively built museum devoted to Whitman-related material artifacts, student projects demonstrated the power of networked academic study. Of course, that work did not take place without complications; we're just beginning to sort through the evaluation data associated with the project, and we're especially looking forward to tabulating student responses to the extensive survey we circulated at the close of the semester.

Still, it's not too early to say that the radical potential of projects like *Looking for Whitman*—and perhaps of digital humanities pedagogy more generally—lies in their ability to connect learners in ways that hack around the artificial boundaries of selectivity and elitism that educational institutions have long erected around themselves. And if one result of that hacking is the creation of more open, more diverse, more egalitarian learning environments that engage a broader spectrum of students and institutions in the hope that they, like Whitman himself, might stitch together common fabrics from diverse threads, the digital humanities might find that it has a social mission that complements its technological one.

NOTES

Parts of this chapter originally appeared as "Looking for Whitman: A Grand, Aggregated Experiment" (http://bavatuesdays.com/looking-for-whitman-a-grand-aggregated-experiment/) and "Hacking Together Egalitarian Educational Communities; Some Notes on the Looking for Whitman Project" (http://mkgold.net/blog/2010/05/28/hacking-together-egalitarian-educational-communities-some-notes-on-the-looking-for-whitman-project/).

1. *Looking for Whitman*. http://lookingforwhitman.org.

The Public Course Blog: The Required Reading We Write Ourselves for the Course That Never Ends

TREVOR OWENS

Ninety-two blog posts,
one hundred and ninety-five comments,
twenty projects.

This is the digital footprint of my digital history seminar, the first course I ever taught. In designing it, I did what came naturally to me: I bought the domain name Dighist.org and set up a public course blog. This blog served as a common place for us to think aloud and work together publicly; it also played a valuable role in the face-to-face class, and it will continue to serve a valuable role in the future. The blog was not simply a supplement to the course; rather, it played a cognitive role in the distributed structure of the class, moving it from knowledge consumption to knowledge production. It allowed us to disseminate the thinking that happened in our class beyond those who registered to take the course at American University. In what follows, I will suggest the potential value that can come from new students in new iterations of the course "inhabiting" the same course blog in the future.

The Course Blog as a Spider's Web

In *Supersizing the Mind Embodiment, Action, and Cognitive Extension*, philosopher Andy Clark adapts the idea of niche construction from evolutionary biology to an idea of cognitive niche construction, which he applies to the way people use tools. In evolutionary biology, niche construction refers to the "varying degrees, organisms chose their own habitats, mates, and resources and construct important components of their local environments such as nest, holes, burrows, paths, webs, dams, and chemical environments" (131). In each of these cases, animals' behavior has altered their environment, and those alterations then become the basis for further adaptation. One of the primary examples of this kind of interaction is the spider's web. Specifically, "the existence of the web modifies the sources of natural selection within the spider's selective niche, allowing subsequent selection for web-based forms of camouflage and communication" (61).

During our course, the blog served a similar role to a spider's web. The structure of the blog changed what it meant to do "class" in the classroom. As we interacted with the blog, as it provided a structure for us to share our thoughts and ideas and displayed those thoughts and ideas to anyone on the web, it pushed us to think differently about our course time. Our writing counted, our writing mattered, in a way that is different from many courses, especially at the undergraduate level. Students were not just writing papers for me to evaluate; they were composing public writing for an audience that included both their classmates and anyone from the broader digital history community. They were writing about exciting new projects that their academic community might not have even been aware of. On several occasions I would tell one of the students who had reviewed a particular software application that the creator of that software had read and posted a tweet with a link to the student's review. After making clear that students could blog under their real names and take credit and responsibility for their thoughts and ideas or blog under pseudonyms, nearly everyone opted to use their names and receive credit for their ideas on the web. We were writing for an audience, and that changed how we all approached writing about history and the production of history.

Like a Beaver Dam, the Blog We Built Together Will House the Next Generation

The spider's web is interesting as an example of how an organism's use of tools changes the cycles of feedback in their evolution. The example of a beaver's dam adds another layer of complexity. As Clark points out, dams are created and inhabited by a collective group of individual beavers. Further, beaver dams extended through time, outliving the lives of the individual beavers who occupy them. Future beavers adapt to the niche that the beavers before them had created and the altered physical landscape that that dam has produced. What matters for Clark in this case is that "niche-construction activity leads to new feedback cycles" (62). I intend the course blog site, Dighist.org, to persist into the future like a beaver's dam. The thinking and work of my students, as manifest in the structure of the content they have produced, will play an active role in the thinking and work of future students who occupy the space.

The Technological Husk of the Course Will Be Reinhabited

According to American University, my course is over. End of semester. Students received their grades. But the grades are the least interesting part of what makes a course a course. Not only am I keeping the content up, I intend to use this same WordPress instance for future iterations of the course. Whoever joins future digital history courses I teach is going to register for this blog and start posting. I will move the current syllabus to an archived syllabus page and post the future student projects right above the existing set. The next set of students will understand that they are not starting a class from scratch; they will build on the work of course alumni just as future students will later build off of their work.

When I started this course, I told students that the course blog would be the required reading that we write ourselves. Next time, I will add that the course blog is the required reading we are writing for ourselves and for future inhabitants of the course. Some of the particularly interesting reviews of software applications are going to become course content in future iterations of the syllabus. Some of the particularly interesting student web projects are going to become examples I will use in class. Some of the particularly interesting student papers will become course readings. Students from this first session of the course are welcome to continue posting and commenting on the blog.

All too often, we think about instructional technology as something that supplements the features of face-to-face instruction. If we want to think this way, then that is in fact what these technologies are going to do. BlackBoard is happy to put a closed course blog inside of its learning management system. Their blogs adapt the features of the technology of a blog for a closed system. That isn't really blogging. Blogging involves certain technical requirements, posting bits of text on the web and generally allowing others to comment on those posts. Beyond this, however, blogging is a cultural phenomena. As a genre of public writing, it has an emergent set of norms and rules that we should learn by doing. In short, blogging is actually a set of skills that is worth cultivating. When we start to think of the technology of blogging in this light, it becomes something that, instead of supplementing instruction, disrupts and transforms education.

NOTES

This chapter originally appeared as "Digital History: The Course That Never Ends" (http://www.trevorowens.org/ . . . /digital-history-the-course-that-never-ends/).

BIBLIOGRAPHY

Clark, Andy. *Supersizing the Mind: Embodiment, Action, and Cognitive Extension*. Oxford: Oxford University Press, 2008.

PART VI

ENVISIONING THE FUTURE OF THE DIGITAL HUMANITIES

Digital Humanities As/Is a Tactical Term

MATTHEW KIRSCHENBAUM

2011, tools, quarterly, victoria, now, jobs, projects, startup grant, companion, blog

—Top ten Google Instant appendages to a search on "digital humanities" as of April 28, 2011, 10:35 AM EDT

This Strange Confluence

Digital humanities is a tactical term.

In a previous essay, "What Is Digital Humanities and What's It Doing in English Departments?" I suggested that for those seeking to define digital humanities, the then-current Wikipedia definition (and top Google hit) served about as well as any and could save a lot of headache and, second, that the term "digital humanities" itself has a specific, recoverable history, originating with circumstances (which I documented) having primarily to do with marketing and uptake, and, third, that the term is now being "wielded instrumentally" by those seeking to effect change "amid the increasingly monstrous institutional terrain" of the contemporary academy. All these arguments suggest that the term is indeed tactical, by which I mean that attempts to arrive at models, mappings, and definitions—with concomitant implications for who's in and who's out, what is and what isn't, and appropriate ratios of "hack" to "yack"—are often self-defeating, not only because they are sometimes divisive, but also because they risk effacing the material history of the term as it has evolved within individual institutions over roughly the last decade.

To assert that digital humanities is a "tactical" coinage is not simply to indulge in neopragmatic relativism. Rather, it is to insist on the reality of circumstances in which it is unabashedly deployed to get things done—"things" that might include getting a faculty line or funding a staff position, establishing a curriculum, revamping a lab, or launching a center. At a moment when the academy in general and the humanities in particular are the objects of massive and wrenching changes, digital humanities emerges as a rare vector for jujitsu, simultaneously serving to position the humanities at the very forefront of certain value-laden agendas—entrepreneurship, openness and public engagement, future-oriented thinking, collaboration, interdisciplinarity, big data, industry tie-ins, and distance or distributed education—while at the same time allowing for various forms of intrainstitutional mobility as new courses are approved, new colleagues are hired, new resources are allotted, and old resources are reallocated.

None of this, I should make clear at the outset, is to suggest any cynicism with regard to the intellectual integrity of the many projects and initiatives that proceed under the banner of the digital humanities: on the contrary, the availability of a billion-word corpus from the HathiTrust or digital images of a medieval manuscript captured in multispectral bands is just as "real" as the institutional considerations I've mentioned, and the desire to do work with these remarkable materials is genuine. How could it not be? As "The Digital Humanities Manifesto 2.0" also insists,

> The phrase [digital humanities] has use-value to the degree that it can serve as an umbrella under which to group both people and projects seeking to reshape and reinvigorate contemporary arts and humanities practices, and expand their boundaries. It has use value to the degree one underscores its semantic edges: the edge where digital remains contaminated by dirty fingers, which is to say by notions of tactility and making that bridge the (non-)gap between the physical and the virtual; the edge where humanities suggests a multiplication of the human or humanity itself as a value that can (re)shape the very development and use of digital tools.

At the same time, however, I believe that those who insist that "digital" humanities is but a transitory term that will soon fall away in favor of just the humanities once again, or perhaps humanities 2.0, are mistaken. Once a course is on the books as "Introduction to Digital Humanities," it is there for the long haul. Once a center is named, names are hard to change—who wants to have to redo the letterhead and the stenciling on the wall?

The institutional structures we create thus tend to have long half-lives. An academic infrastructure that includes a journal named *Digital Humanities Quarterly*, a governing body named the Alliance of Digital Humanities Organizations, a federal agency with an Office of Digital Humanities, and a major annual educational effort named the Digital Humanities Summer Institute (to take just a few examples) are not easily shifted. Behind these labels lie some very deep investments—of reputation, process, and labor, as well as actual capital. The paperwork, branding, and identity construction are only part of what makes digital humanities tactical, however; the other distinctive component at our current moment is the role of the network, in particular social media, and Twitter most particularly of all. While it may seem odd or tendentious to rapidly whittle down to the range of digital tools and platforms to one particular technology (and privately held corporate entity), the fact is that Twitter more than any other technology or platform is—at the very moment when digital humanities is achieving its institutional apotheosis—the backchannel and professional grapevine for hundreds of people who self-identify as digital humanists. They use it daily to share information, establish contacts, ask and answer questions, bullshit, banter, rant, vent, kid, and carry on. The significance, however, is not just in people using Twitter to tweet at like-minded others but also in the algorithmic and ecological ways that the network effects of the online digital humanities "community" are reified and refracted through a range of different aggregators, reputation generators, metrical indicators, and status markers to present a visible and reified topology for the digital humanities as a whole. The obvious fact that not every digital humanist is actually on Twitter is thus beside the point for purposes of this argument. Rather, the deployment of the specific character string as a hashtag exposes it to algorithmic eyes that formally map and define what the digital humanities are or is at any given moment.

On the one hand, then, digital humanities is a term possessed of enough currency and escape velocity to penetrate layers of administrative strata to get funds allocated, initiatives under way, and plans set in motion. On the other hand, it is a populist term, self-identified and self-perpetuating through the algorithmic structures of contemporary social media. In what follows I will explore an example of each and then offer some concluding comments about the implications of this strange confluence.

And the Name

Timing, as they say, is everything. In the fall of 1999, my first semester away from the University of Virginia where I had spent the last seven years on my PhD (I had just left for a tenure-track job at the University of Kentucky), the Institute for Advanced Technology in the Humanities convened a seminar titled "Is Humanities Computing an Academic Discipline?" The noncredit seminar was directed by Bethany Nowviskie (then a graduate student) and John Unsworth and consisted of a series of weekly conversations, punctuated by visits from distinguished scholars who were invited to give public presentations on the topic.[1] Deliberately eclectic and interdisciplinary in range, the speakers included Espen Aarseth, Susan Hockey, Willard McCarty, Stuart Moulthrop, Geoffrey Rockwell, and several others. Text analysis and text encoding, hypertext fiction, and computational linguistics were all represented as potentially constitutive of humanities computing as an academic discipline. There was at least one overt motivation to the proceedings: "Participants in this fall's seminar," read a press release, "will discuss the nature of humanities computing (Is it, in fact, a field of scholarly inquiry?) and whether the University should offer a degree program in it."[2]

Unsurprisingly as these things go, the conclusion reached by the seminar was that a degree program *should* be offered, and two academic years later in 2001–2, a second seminar, this time with funding from the National Endowment for the

Humanities, was convened.[3] Titled "Digital Humanities Curriculum Seminar," it was codirected by Unsworth and Johanna Drucker (who had also arrived at the university just as I was departing). Not only does the lack of an interrogative in the title furnish an up-front answer to the question posed by the earlier seminar, the lexical shift to digital humanities already seems a fait accompli. The agenda was also conspicuously more focused, with some two dozen faculty and graduate students participating as well as (again) a set of visiting speakers and consultants (myself among them). The key deliverable was a finished syllabus for a newly designed two-semester course in "Knowledge Representation," which would form the backbone of the graduate curriculum. Also by 2001, as indicated by a May 25 address to the Congress of Social Sciences and Humanities, Université Laval, Québec, Unsworth had in hand a draft proposal for a master's degree in digital humanities to be housed within the newly established program in media studies at Virginia.[4]

For a variety of reasons, this ambitious and prescient proposal for a master's in digital humanities at one of the flagship American institutions for work in the field was never realized. The proposal eventually died somewhere in the University of Virginia's administrative ether (how and why it is not my story to tell). But a closer analysis of some of the key documents from this period of institutional self-reflection, 1999 through 2002, helps illuminate what I mean by the "tactical" nature of digital humanities.

A number of items and records associated with both Virginia seminars remain publicly available on the web, and these are instructive (as well as often all too familiar in terms of the kind of questions and "debates"—to echo the present volume's title—engaged). This much is clear: by the end of the first semester, the instinct of the group was for keeping "humanities computing" at arm's length. Indeed, reading the December 10, 1999, minutes, we find a direct rewrite of the governing question of the seminar: "Should we have an M.A. in Digital Media?" the document (whose electronic file is titled "conclusions.html") begins by asking.[5] "Digital" thus replaces "computing," and "media" has muscled in on "humanities." Looking further back in the online archive to the first meeting for which there are recorded minutes (September 24, 1999), we find, immediately after mention of the assigned readings for that week—they are Espen Aarseth's "Humanistic Informatics and its Relation to the Humanities" and Willard McCarty's "What Is Humanities Computing"—the following notation: "Opposing models: humanities computing as theoretical discipline and as a practice based on collegial service."[6] Theory and "discipline" are thus opposed to "service" from the outset. Other oppositions follow: "philology" (McCarty) and "hypermedia" (Aarseth), humanities computing as discipline (McCarty) versus media studies (Aarseth). The institutional landscape is thus defined as one of media studies versus humanities computing, with McCarty (especially) laboring mightily to recapitulate the latter as a scholarly (and theoretical) undertaking, as distinct from service-oriented academic computing.

By the time we get to December 1999, however, only a few months later, the question seems to have been decided, at least within the seminar. Concerns over legitimization, status, and intrainstitutional relationships predominate. "Clear statement of central research questions will go a long way toward legitimizing a Digital Media program and separating it from the 'collegial service' model pervasive in Humanities Computing" (http://www.iath.virginia.edu/hcs/conclusions.html), the minutes of the concluding session record. While still, to some extent, using "humanities computing" and "digital media" interchangeably, at this point the record of the discussion also introduces a third term, "knowledge representation." Originating in the work of John Sowa (who would be an invited guest in the follow-on seminar), it is presented as the constitutive element of a humanities computing (or digital media) research agenda: "The general consensus of the seminar is that this problem should be articulated in terms of 'knowledge representation'—that we are now confronted with new ways of understanding, creating, and teaching information. The structures of and modes of representing that information should be an object of study" (http://www.iath.virginia.edu/hcs/conclusions.html).

A tactically aware reading of the foregoing would note that tension had clearly centered on the gerund "computing" and its service connotations (and we might note that a verb functioning as a noun occupies a service posture even as a part of speech). "Media," as a proper noun, enters the deliberations of the group already backed by the disciplinary machinery of "media studies" (also the name of the then new program at Virginia in which the curriculum would eventually be housed) and thus seems to offer a safer landing place. In addition, there is the implicit shift in emphasis from computing as numeric calculation to media and the representational spaces they inhabit—a move also compatible with the introduction of "knowledge representation" into the terms under discussion.[7]

How we then get from "digital media" to "digital humanities" is an open question. There is no discussion of the lexical shift in the materials available online for the 2001–2 seminar, which is simply titled, ex cathedra, "Digital Humanities Curriculum Seminar." The key substitution—"humanities" for "media"—seems straightforward enough, on the one hand serving to topically define the scope of the endeavor while also producing a novel construction to rescue it from the flats of the generic phrase "digital media." And it preserves, by chiasmus, one half of the former appellation, though "humanities" is now simply a noun modified by an adjective. In retrospect, then, the real work of the first seminar concerned the move from humanities computing to digital media, with the subsequent displacement of "media" by "humanities" most likely an ancillary maneuver and in any case not something that the conveners of the second seminar saw fit to comment on overtly at the time.

At this point, some chronological housekeeping is in order. Readers will recall that in my earlier essay on "What Is Digital Humanities?" I traced the putative origin of the term back to the decision to use it as the title for the Blackwell's Companion volume, as recounted in an e-mail to me from John Unsworth, who describes a November 2001 editorial meeting with the publisher's marketing representative. It is clear, however, that the term was already in circulation among the curriculum group at Virginia and that this was the backdrop for Unsworth's advocacy of it in other contexts. A third key component was the founding of the Alliance of Digital Humanities Organizations shortly thereafter, where Unsworth again played a central role with digital humanities emerging as the term of choice for this new governance body—also detailed in my earlier essay. The editors' introduction to the Blackwell volume, meanwhile, offers some oblique commentary on the matter: titled "The Digital Humanities and Humanities Computing," it seems to grant the two terms equal billing, but in fact digital humanities emerges as the wider ranging locution, with humanities computing solidified but circumscribed as its "interdisciplinary core" (Schreibman, Siemens, Unsworth, xxiv). Nonetheless, digital humanities, which would surely have been a novel construction for many readers when the volume first came into their hands in 2004, is never explicitly glossed, merely presented as the de facto name of what the editors declare in their opening sentence to be a "field" (xxiii). Patrik Svensson has done some useful quantitative work that helps fill in the rest of this picture, tracking, for example, the appearance of "humanities computing" as opposed to "digital humanities" on the influential Humanist listserv. He notes only a few scattered instances of the latter term prior to 2001, all of them casual nominal constructions such as "digital humanities object" or "environment"; afterwards, "digital humanities" rapidly gains traction until 2006–7 when the usage ratio roughly balances.

There is one more feature of the aborted Virginia master's proposal to which I will briefly call attention. This concerns the question of whether the degree should be a stand-alone offering or whether it should exist as a "track" within an existing departmental master's program. The December 1999 minutes put the question this way: "There was some discussion about staying 'above' or 'below' the SCHEV approval threshold. One option would be to start with a program within an existing department and work [to] attract students and faculty. When the program is a working success, then we could move to create a separate department. However, the seminar group seemed decided that the need for new faculty, facilities, and research agendas precludes starting small. Now seems to be the time to campaign aggressively for a large-scale Digital Media program." SCHEV is the State Council of Higher Education for Virginia, and what's at stake here is the nature of the approval process that would be required for the new master's. To establish the degree as an independent program would eventually require the blessing of this statewide body; to establish it within the contours of an existing departmental program would sidestep that necessity. It is clear that there was a mood of confidence in the seminar, a feeling that the moment was right for a big push, one with consequences not only for the degree as such but also at the level of personnel and facilities like classrooms and labs. Crucially, such a move would be advanced under the banner of digital media (or, as it later turned out, digital humanities) and *not* humanities computing. While the minutes can only record so much, it would seem incontrovertible that there was a calculus of sorts that the newer two terms would prove more efficacious, less fraught (avoiding, for example, any hint of competition with computer science), more compatible with the institution's sense of itself and collective purpose ("digital media" doubtless seemed like a good fit for a school that had just invested heavily in media studies), and generally broader in its appeal and potential for rapid uptake. These are tactical considerations. While the degree program never materialized (it certainly never made it to SCHEV), the discussions generated by the process have proven influential. And the name stuck.

And Virtual Alike

Digital humanities is a mobile and tactical signifier, whether from the standpoint of universities, publishers, scholarly organizations, funders, the press, or its actual practitioners. But in a Web 2.0 world of tweets, streams, and feeds, it is also more than a signifier, mobile or otherwise. Signifiers become keywords and tags, and these are the means by which distributed communities self-organize across the social and semantic contours of the contemporary Internet. First Google and now Twitter (these two services especially, I think) have, in essence, reified the digital humanities as a network topology, that is to say lines drawn by aggregates of elective affinities that are formally and tangibly manifest in who follows who, who friends who, who retweets who, and who links to what. Digital humanities (and its universal truncation DH), in other words, are *identifiers* routinely operationalized through various network services.

Twitter is not, of course, the first social and scholarly communications environment to serve the digital humanities. The aforementioned Humanist listserv, launched in 1987 (so early in the Internet's history that there was no perceived need for further discrimination of its target audience), was followed by hundreds of additional mailing lists throughout the nineties (the Institute for Advanced Technology in the Humanities alone maintained dozens on its jefferson.village server, as did Michigan State University through the H-Net umbrella, the archives of which are now the subject of an organized digital preservation effort).[8] Instant chat, from Internet Relay Chat through commercial services like AIM and Google, has also been widely used by digital humanities. But the next major communications outlet was undoubtedly blogs, which began appearing in the humanities computing (or digital humanities) community predictably early in their general cultural onset (certainly by 2003 one could construct a robust digital humanities blogroll, and the comments fields on blog posts served as important venues for discussion). None of these new technologies, I would hasten to add, supplanted or replaced prior channels of public communication; rather, they coexisted with them, thickening the collective network ecology with each new addition. So, despite Twitter and the bevy of other social networking services at our disposal, Humanist still publishes its listserv digests every two or three days, and many digital humanists remain active bloggers. Indeed, the increasingly porous boundaries between blogs and Twitter (in particular) are one of the salient features of the contemporary network environment, with platforms like WordPress capable of harvesting tweets referring to a given entry and accreting them alongside of comments posted to the blog site. This dynamic allows for strikingly robust real-time conversations to unfold, as has been demonstrated (for example) in the wake of both the 2009 and the 2011 Modern Language Association (MLA) conventions, when the heavy Twitter presence from the digital humanities entourage in turn provoked longer, more substantive blog postings engaging the issues emerging from the ballrooms of the Hiltons and Marriotts.

Just as Googling digital humanities to yield the Wikipedia definition is one surefire way of defining the field—not only for the particulars of the definition but also because its continuous shaping and policing by the community lends it a kind of tactical authenticity—so, too, does Twitter allow one to quickly limn the contours of an up-to-the-minute moving image of the digital humanities. I know of no better example of this than *Digital Humanities Now*, "a real-time, crowdsourced publication" that "takes the pulse of the digital humanities community and tries to discern what articles, blogs, projects, tools, collections, and announcements are worthy of greater attention."[9] "It is created," the site goes on to explain, "by ingesting the Twitter feeds of hundreds of scholars . . . processing these feeds through Twittertim.es to generate a more narrow feed of common interest and debate, and reformatting that feed on this site, in part to allow for further (non-Twitter) discussions." The tweets the service scans are those of several hundred self-identified DHers on a Twitter list maintained by the site's originator Dan Cohen, itself generally considered the most comprehensive listing of its kind. (It's important to emphasize that Dan will add anyone who asks if they are not on his radar screen already.) Collectively, these individuals are referred to as the site's "editorial board." *Digital Humanities Now*, or *dhnow*, thus combines the conceit of a scholarly journal with the real-time automated aggregation enabled by Twitter's open Application Programming Interface.

In practice, the site works only middling well, with many overtly non-DH topics getting promoted to the status of a "refereed" entry on the *dhnow* feed simply by virtue of their popularity among the demographic who happens to identify with DH. But while Cohen and the others behind the service clearly understand that it is an often arbitrary snapshot of the conversations and currents within the digital humanities community at any given moment, it nonetheless masquerades, through both its title and its publication strategy, as an impartial reflector *of* digital humanities in a larger professional sense. This *is* what's happening now, it purports to say, and *dhnow* thus reinforces the conceit of digital humanities as a stable, self-consistent signifier; as Cohen writes, "I often say to non-digital humanists that every Friday at five I know all of the most important books, articles, projects, and news of the week—without the benefit of a journal, a newsletter, or indeed any kind of formal publication by a scholarly society. I pick up this knowledge by osmosis from the people I follow online."[10] Digital humanities thus emerges as "tactical" in the sense that it is also *procedural* in such an instance, operationalized through the automated functions of a site that harvests a self-selecting group of users who voluntarily affiliate and align themselves within the scope of coverage.

While an aggregated publication like *Digital Humanities Now* is ferociously democratic—"one retweet one vote," we might say—it would be disingenuous to pretend that digital humanities online doesn't also participate in certain celebrity economies and reputation metrics.[11] For example, Twitter's "Who to Follow" feature functions as a sort of phonebook for the service, allowing users to search for user accounts based on topic relevance. The first dozen or so hits on a search for "digital humanities," undertaken in early May 2011, revealed the following users:

- @dancohen (Dan Cohen): Director, Roy Rosenzweig Center for History & New Media, resources & platforms (Zotero, Omeka) for history & beyond, Mason prof of history & digital humanities
- @digitalhumanist (Dave Lester): Assistant Director at MITH (@umd_mith), digital humanities, open source, #DHapi, #thatcamp
- @dhnow (DigitalHumanitiesNow): What people in the digital humanities are reading and discussing, by @dancohen and the poeple @dhnow follows.
- @brettbobley (Brett Bobley): I like music, cooking, lasers, helicopters, computers, and I director the Office of Digital Humanities at the NEH.
- @nowviskie (Bethany Nowviskie): Director, Digital Research and Scholarship; UVA Library, Assoc. Director, Scholarly Communication Institute; VP, Assoc Computers & Humanities
- @JenServenti (Jennifer Serventi): Civil servant and friend of the digital humanities, food trucks, chocolate, ice cream, and cheese.
- @melissaterras (melissa terras): Reader, Dept of Information Studies, University College London. Digital Humanities, Digital Culture: Computing Science vs. cultural heritage
- @mkirschenbaum (Matthew Kirschenbaum): Assoc. Prof. English, Assoc. Director, MITH and Director, Digital Cultures and Creativity Living/Learning Program
- @amandafrench (Amanda French): PhD in English lit, singer-songwriter, tech fan
- @foundhistory (Tom Scheinfeldt): Managing Director of the Center for History and New Media at George Mason Univ (http://chnm.gmu.edu); chief Omekan (http://omeka.org); public historian

My concern here is not the accuracy or integrity of the "Who to Follow" algorithm—the users listed here would all be excellent people to follow as thought leaders in the digital humanities, and the list accords with my own off-the-cuff choices (though we might note the somehow recursive presence of *dhnow*)—but rather that a user may not realize that this particular mapping of digital humanities is itself tactical, a product of an inexorable calculus of influence and reputation that continually sorts, ranks, and situates, plucking patterns and trends from the data stream, orienting them around accounts and avatars to generate a set of cohesive user identities, and collectively packaging the lot as a fast, honest answer to the simple question, who should I follow? which is really another way of asking, who's important? who matters? And not only who should I *follow*, but whose eyeballs do *I* want on *me*? Indeed, the very fact that everyone on Twitter is subjectified as a "who"—even institutions and services take on that singular pronoun—speaks to the odd flattening of agency that characterizes this multivalent social topology. While there is no public documentation available on how the "Who to Follow" feature actually works, it seems safe to assume that the algorithm harvests profile data, the content of tweets, hashtags, and most of all who follows who and who their followers follow in order to arrive at its influence mappings around any given topic. Of course, the end result is obvious: the mappings are self-perpetuating, so that those who are currently identified as influential users in a given topic space will accumulate even more followers as a result of their visibility through the "Who to Follow" feature, which will in turn contribute to reinforcing their ranking by the algorithm.

Some observers will, of course, suggest that such stuff has been a feature of scholarly life since at least the days of the Royal Academy (or maybe Plato's academy). But a better and more specific frame of reference might be the "star system" in literary studies. (The contentious suggestion of a "star system" in digital humanities was memorably lofted in a blog piece by William Pannapacker covering DH sessions at the 2011 MLA conference in Los Angeles, which is reprinted here.[12]) The scholar most closely identified with a diagnosis and critical analysis of the workings of the academic star system is David R. Shumway, who in 1997 wrote a much-talked-about piece in *PMLA* on the phenomenon. Shumway, of course, is himself adopting the phrase from Hollywood, recounting the genealogy of "stardom" as a new and distinct form of celebrity manufactured by the studios. Shumway makes several trenchant points, yoking the emergence of stars in literary studies not only to the rise of high theory but also to the rise of the international academic conference, the airlines that transport us to them, the ongoing institutionalization of academic literary studies as a research discipline (and the attendant search for legitimization), and the proliferation of images of the professoriate amid the ferment of the culture wars. Ultimately, he concludes that the star system in literary studies is a distinct historical phenomenon that originates in the late 1970s; he also concludes that the disproportionate resources required to maintain it likely contribute to the unhealthy rise of contingent labor and the general deterioration of academic working conditions. Moreover, he sees it as serving to undermine the public's confidence in the academy by diluting the authority of the rank-and-file professoriate.

Several of Shumway's characterizations of the star system map all too easily onto digital humanities. The management of public image, for example: we do this both trivially in the form of avatars as well as more substantively through our daily online "presences" on blogs, Twitter, listservs, and more. Likewise, it's worth noting that, like "high theory," the digital humanities is routinely positioned as a kind of metadiscourse (or methodology) that cuts across individual subdisciplines and fields. This is an enormously powerful and seductive base of operations. Most tellingly, for Shumway star quality is not simply a function of public image or the number of frequent flier miles the academic logs but rather of a specific kind of relationship between consumers, or "fans," and the celebrity: "It is the feeling of personal connection that transforms the merely famous scholar into a star" (92). In the digital humanities, I would argue, this special relationship is less a function of the performativity of a lecture (most of us are simply not that interesting to watch) than the ruthless metrics of online community, the *frisson* that comes from an @reply from someone more famous than you or *you'll never believe who just started following me!* For those of us who spend time online in Twitter and (to a lesser degree) other social networks, including Facebook and the looser tissues of the blogosphere, this star system is reified (and sometimes even quantified or visualized) in the ongoing accumulation of network relations that describe—often all too precisely—influence and impact, pitilessly allowing one to locate oneself in the ecosystem at any given instant. This seems to me to go some way toward explaining why there is so much anxiety around the Twitter/DH nexus (as reflected in other essays in this volume, for example)—its constant mappings and metrics have come to inhabit that intangible performative dimension that Shumway earlier ascribed to the public (and in-person) appearances of the high-theory stars.

Online relationships are eminently portable across the analog/digital membrane, so those who are in positions of visibility and impact online reap rewards that have more tangible consequences in meatspace. As Phil Agre reminded us a long time ago, the network is a terrific place to, well, network.[13] At its best, this can be a great multiplier, or democratizer: the individual with a 4/4 load at an isolated teaching institution can wield influence in ways that would have been unthinkable in the theory-driven era Shumway describes. That kind of load balancing—no longer Yale deconstruction or Duke English but centers of influence at big public land-grant institutions or small "teaching colleges"—is dramatically different from the star system characterized by daring publicity stills of Derrida or De Man (of the sort Shumway reproduced in his essay), or the faux-fanzine *Judy*. But it is not any less divorced from the real world balance of academic power, which still manifests in the form of jobs, grants, publications, invitations, and all the rest of the apparatus that Shumway's high-theory stars defined by transcending. As cycles of influence flicker ever more rapidly back and forth between the analog and digital worlds, as tenure committees in the humanities begin to import impact metrics (citation indices and the like) from the sciences, and as the success stories of the disempowered few who rise above their rank through social networking become more commonplace, digital humanities must do better than simply brush off any suggestion of ins and outs on the networks that connect it day to day. It must acknowledge, openly and frankly, that while Twitter (and other online social networks) and DH are not coextensive, the interactions among and between them are real and consequential.

And yes, tactical. Networks, as Dianne Rocheleau and Robin Roth remind us, are "relational webs shot through with power," and "an individual's position within the network is not neutral or arbitrary, but has implications for how the individual views the network and how s/he/it may act within it (or against it)" (434). It's not just that our avatars are now the real stars—it's that stardom (or else simply surviving) is also now a function of one's ability to arbitrage influence across all manner of networks, "real" and virtual alike.

And Not an End

My own contribution of this essay to this volume at this time is itself ineluctably tactical, a positioning and an intervention. But it is not a provocation, or at least it is not intended to be. I have brought together some bits of obscure institutional history dredged from a decade ago and observations about the dynamics of reputation and community online at the present moment in order to make a simple point: not only is digital humanities constantly in flux, but also the term is one whose mojo may be harnessed, either rhetorically or algorithmically or both, to make a statement, make a change, and otherwise get stuff done. Lately other commentators have also wanted to insist that digital humanities is a tactical construct, but for them such insistence seems to serve more of a means of disarming the term from a stance of perceived disenfranchisement. If DH is merely tactical, this line of attack goes, it can be outflanked in favor of some alternative nomenclature that is more inclusive, more pluralistic, more democratic, and so forth. This in my view is precisely wrong since it is oblivious to the import of the institutional, material, and social contexts in which the term digital humanities has already been taken up and operationally embedded.[14]

While not particularly revelatory in and of itself, my "tactical" view of what digital humanities *really* is offers a necessary counterbalance, I believe, to some current tensions and debates within the wider community represented in this volume and beyond. Much energy is now being expended on defining what digital humanities is, on whether a paper or proposal was accepted or rejected because it was or was not "real" digital humanities, and so forth—as though appeals to higher authorities can transcend the reality that review panels and committees and boards are nearly always staffed by overworked and undercompensated individuals (who are by no means exclusively tenured or tenure-track faculty) doing what they can do to do the best with what they have. But digital humanities has also been claimed, some might even say radicalized, as precisely that space where traditional academic and institutional practices are vulnerable to intervention, with individual scholars or self-organizing affinity groups utilizing the tools and channels of online communication to effect real institutional change. This often (arguably only) happens one policy statement, one proposal approval, one new ad-hoc committee, one new budget line item, one promotion, or one new job at a time. Successes can only sometimes be leveraged across institutions or, indeed, across departments and units within the same institution. The oppositional and activist connotations of my reliance on the word tactical here are thus not incidental and refer to the outsider status some in digital humanities increasingly wish to claim, as well as to related phenomena such as tactical media and hacktivism. Digital humanities is not only about such things, of course, but a lot of angst and anxiety at this moment could perhaps more productively be channeled elsewhere if we simply remind ourselves that DH is a means and not an end.[15]

NOTES

1. http://www.iath.virginia.edu/hcs/.
2. http://www.virginia.edu/topnews/releases/humanities-sept-16-1999.html.
3. http://www.iath.virginia.edu/hcs/dhcs/.
4. http://www3.isrl.illinois.edu/~unsworth/laval.html.
5. http://www.iath.virginia.edu/hcs/conclusions.html.
6. http://www.iath.virginia.edu/hcs/9–24.html.
7. In a note on a draft of this essay, Johanna Drucker comments as follows: "[I]t might be interesting to describe the curriculum we came up with because it was so dedicated to crossing the doing/describing divide that seems to be a persistent plague in DH discussions. Our 'spine' in that curriculum went from digitization, data types, database design, computer languages/programming, interface design, information visualization, text analysis/markup, intellectual property, communities of practice, diversity of communities, etc. through a series of units EACH of which had a set of theoretical readings AND a set of exercises created for it. Geoff Rockwell was in that seminar, along with a few other interesting visitors at UVA that year, and then the UVA folks—McGann, Pitti, Laue, Nowviskie, Ramsay, Unsworth, Martin, and others I'm forgetting and don't mean to slight. But the principle of making sure that theory and practice talked to each other was crucial. The adoption of the 'digital media' rubric was, as you note correctly, a tactical one within UVA's environment, meant to aim at a compromise in which critical/theoretical issues from media studies might feel legitimate as part of the practice."
8. http://www.h-net.org/archive/.
9. http://digitalhumanitiesnow.org/.

10. http://www.dancohen.org/2009/11/18/introducing-digital-humanities-now/. Reprinted in this volume.

11. Portions of the paragraphs that follow were originally published as a blog post, "The (DH) Stars Come Out in LA" (http://mkirschenbaum.wordpress.com/2011/01/13/the-dh-stars-come-out-in-la-2/).

12. http://chronicle.com/blogs/brainstorm/pannapacker-at-mla-digital-humanities-triumphant/30915.

13. http://vlsicad.ucsd.edu/Research/Advice/network.html.

14. See, for example, this exchange between Alex Reid and myself: http://www.alex-reid.net/2011/06/digital-humanities-tactics.html.

15. For comments that helped me clarify my thinking I am grateful to Luke Waltzer, Neil Fraistat, Johanna Drucker, Jentery Sayers, Liz Losh, and Matt Gold.

BIBLIOGRAPHY

"The Digital Humanities Manifesto 2.0." http://manifesto.humanities.ucla.edu/2009/05/29/the-digital-humanities-manifesto-20/.

Kirschenbaum, Matthew G. "What Is Digital Humanities and What's It Doing in English Departments?" *ADE Bulletin* 150 (2010): 55–61. Reprinted in this volume.

Rochelau, Dianne, and Robin Roth. "Rooted Networks, Relational Webs, and Powers of Connection: Rethinking Human and Political Ecologies." *Geoforum* 38 (2007): 433–37.

Schreibman, Susan, Ray Siemens, and John Unsworth. "The Digital Humanities and Humanities Computing: An Introduction." In *A Companion to Digital Humanities*, xxiii–xxvii. Oxford: Blackwell, 2004.

Shumway, David R. "The Star System in Literary Studies." *PMLA* 112, no. 1 (1997): 85–100.

Svensson, Patrik. "Humanities Computing as Digital Humanities." *Digital Humanities Quarterly* 3, no. 3 (2009). http://digitalhumanities.org/dhq/vol/3/3/000065/000065.html.

The Digital Humanities or a Digital Humanism

DAVE PARRY

We should all probably start by admitting that none of us really knows what digital humanities is or, more precisely, that none of us is fully in control of what digital humanities (DH) is. As with so many disciplinary practices, the answer to the "what is" question is likely to be legion. And as Matthew Kirschenbaum has noted in a recent ADE Bulletin article, defining DH has become something of a genre essay. But contrary to any suggestion that the definition is settled or has been fully explored, the rising number of conference presentations along with the surplus of writings on the topic would suggest that many see the question as somehow crucial. Indeed, the significant rise in discourse around the question "What is DH?" reveals, I would suggest, not only a certain angst about the constitution of the field, a not-so-unconscious uneasiness on the part of the practitioners, but a recognition that DH has become a significant force discursively and economically within the institution.

Establishing a definition by asking after the essence of something seems a futile project. What is the essence of the digital humanities? is an impossible question to answer, as if there is an ideal form of digital humanities out there to which one can point, a central Platonic ideal from which all other digital humanities can be judged in relation. (I am not really into Platonic ideals.) It is, however, possible to engage the question from another angle, performing a discursive analysis. Rather than asking, what is the digital humanities? we can ask, what do we talk about when we talk about digital humanities?

For the past three years, scholars identifying as digital humanists have participated in a project called "A Day in the Life of the Digital Humanities," or "Day of DH," for short. In an effort to create a picture of what it is that DH scholars actually do, practitioners write about what scholarly (and sometimes not so scholarly) activities they engage in throughout the day. Typically, this takes the form of writing blog posts documenting one's work day, attempting to render transparent one's individual work, while simultaneously representing the diversity of work that is collected under the name DH. This year, over two hundred scholars (up from roughly one hundred two years ago and one hundred and fifty last year) registered and posted to the official Day of DH site, with numerous others engaging through other venues such as Twitter. As such, the textual corpus produced on this day, while not a definite answer to the question of what is DH, serves as an important representative sampling of how it is that a group of scholars who self-identify as DH practitioners talk about their work. The text produced on this day represents an inclusive example, not a restrictive one, of how it is people talk—or more precisely, write—about what it means to "do DH."

Unfortunately, though, with such a large sampling, it would be difficult to closely read all of the essays listed on the Day of DH website, which is to say nothing of the material and conversations produced via other means not archived on the official Day of DH website. Reading all of this material would indeed be a Sisyphean task, whereby any close engagement would necessarily yield numerous other texts that would have to be read, a black hole to be sure. Luckily, however, digital humanists have provided us with computational tools that enable a more efficient reading practice, textual analysis tools that look for frequency of word use across a large textual corpus, saving us the task of actually having to read the entire body of work. So rather than engaging in a close reading of what practitioners actually wrote, it is possible and certainly more convenient to use a computer to aid in the reading process.

The data that such an analysis yields is, as with many such projects, largely predictable, indeed largely knowable without the use of a computer. The most frequent words by far are digital, humanities, day, and work. Again, not surprising, given that these are the terms that frame the discussion: what a day looks like for those who work in the digital humanities. But the next level of words with high frequency are revealing, if mostly predictable: research, design, project, data, text (and its variants such as textual), and tool(s), which is to suggest that people who identify as DH practitioners see themselves as designing and building tools and projects that deal with text and data, producing text and data about said text and data. Perhaps, tellingly, all of these words have a higher occurrence than "reading" and "writing."

None of this is particularly surprising, though; it merely reinforces a sense that many scholars have already articulated: digital humanities is largely, or primarily, about using computing technologies as tools to do traditional humanities-based research. One could, I suspect, perform this type of textual analysis on a range of sources producing similar results. The Digital Humanities Conference programs, Blackwell's *A Companion to Digital Humanities*, or even the recipients of National Endowment for the Humanities (NEH) funding would all present a similar distribution of words and conversations. This is not to make an evaluative claim (at least not yet) but simply to make an observational one: those who identify their work as digital humanities primarily talk about using computers to do humanities research.

Indeed, there is a strong connection between digital humanities and humanities computing. The first sentence in Kirschenbaum's essay suggests as much, quickly conflating the two terms: "What is (or are) the 'digital humanities,' aka 'humanities computing?'" (1). As his essay goes on to argue, the term "digital humanities" itself is a (re)branding of the term "humanities computing," specifically chosen by Blackwell's book project and later, perhaps crucially, as Kirschenbaum suggests, with respect to the formation of the NEH Office of the Digital Humanities. What Kirschenbaum illustrates is how the term "digital humanities" was a strategic choice made by several key players. It is these events that serve as one of the focal points for Kirschenbaum's essay, as he argues that they will "earn a place in histories of the profession alongside major critical movements like the Birmingham School or Yale deconstruction" (4). And this, ultimately, is what is at stake in the "what is DH?" debate. Digital humanities has become "something of a movement," indeed perhaps the next big movement in humanities-based scholarship (4). As scholars look to define what it is that constitutes the movement, and by extension what it is that is not part of the movement, "digital humanities" comes to serve as a rather deft switch from the phrase "humanities computing," stressing that humanities remains the focus, the next moment in a continuum of scholarship rather than a rupture with the past.

Consider the fact that we do not have "pencil humanists" or "typewriter humanists." This might seem like an odd observation, but we should ask what the adjective "digital" is doing in "digital humanities." As the earlier introductory word-frequency analysis suggests, what digital humanists mean by "digital humanities" is not that they use computers to write or read humanities-based texts; rather, a digital humanities scholar uses digital devices to perform critical and theoretical observations that are not possible with traditional pencil or typewriter aided analysis. That is, computers and by extension the digital enable a new critical lens for understanding traditional humanistic subjects of inquiry, a lens not available prior to the invention of computing technologies. At this point we do not even have to distinguish between the people who make tools for this type of analysis and those who use these tools for analysis. The defining feature is the relation of a digital tool to the scholarship being performed.

In the same way that the Birmingham School or Yale deconstruction opened up new ways of critiquing texts not possible prior to their inception, computers inaugurate a school of critique, a new series of tools through which we can analyze texts. This is to say nothing of the relative significance of any of these movements but rather to point out that all of them see themselves as movements, as ways of critiquing and analyzing texts that illustrate or reveal textual meaning in a way previously unavailable prior to the invention of their particular methodologies. Simply using a computer does not make one a digital humanities scholar—typing your manuscript on a word processor does not let you in the club; your work needs to share an affinity with a certain method of approach to humanities scholarship. In this regard, the computer is a necessary, but not sufficient, factor in the digital humanities. One could certainly imagine the digital being incorporated in other ways, but certainly it is a primary enabling factor for the rise of digital humanities.

Perhaps the best way to explain this view of digital humanities is, as Alex Reid suggests, through a Venn diagram in which the humanities is one circle, the digital another, and their overlap constitutes the field of digital humanities. In many respects, this works to describe any one of a number of methodological approaches to the humanities. A Venn diagram with the feminism school as one circle, humanities another, and their overlap constitutes a humanities scholar who practices feminist humanism—or similarly Marxism as one circle, humanities as another, constitutes Marxist humanities scholarship. This is often how scholars describe their endeavors: "I work at the intersection of computing, feminism, and eighteenth-century writing."

On the whole, this version of the digital humanities treats the digital as an adjective, a word that modifies the unchanged notion of the humanities, leaving the core of what happens unaltered, instead updating the means by which it is done. It makes humanities relevant in the age of computing and demonstrates that humanists, too, can use computers to do better, more elaborate projects; deal with large data sets; count word occurrences; and produce interesting textual visualizations. In this sense, the rhetorical shift from humanities computing—humanities as the adjective that modifies computing, humanities as a way of computing—to digital humanities, the digital as a way of doing humanities, seems rather predictable. It is both more descriptive of actual practice and less threatening to traditional humanistic scholars. Using computers to engage in more efficient textual analysis does little to disrupt the framing values and ideals of the field; rather, it merely allows them to be accomplished on a larger scale and at a faster pace.

In this respect, digital humanists talk about the digital as something added to the humanities, a supplement to the existing scholarly paradigm. The question in this type of scholarship is how the digital can be used to enhance, reframe, or illuminate scholarship that is already done or, in some cases, how the digital can do it more efficiently. While texts become data and word frequency counts substitute for sentence-level analysis, the goal remains markedly the same: a hermeneutics of the text meant to discern what it is a text (or a large corpora of texts) means.

This all suggests that there is a nondigital humanities—a humanities unaffected by the digital. This comes to be a rather problematic claim when we realize that the digital has so altered the academic culture that there are relatively few scholarly activities that are not already significantly altered by the digital. Almost all scholars at this point use computers rather than typewriters and use e-mail to converse with colleagues dispersed around the globe. Library card catalogs have been replaced by computer searches, and journal articles are often available only by electronic means. The practice of the humanities, of the academy as a whole (certainly within the American and European contexts), is thoroughly integrated with the digital and is, at this point, impossible to separate from it.

But for the most part, epistemological claims of large data sets notwithstanding, the digital has done little to alter the *structure* of the humanities. Digital humanities now means that one can build tools to read texts and produce data—for instance, to design a tool as part of a project to study eighteenth-century manuscripts—but the work of the humanities scholar remains largely unchanged by the existence of the computational device. The digital is a means to do what has always been done, a means to do it more efficiently and better, but still to do what has always been done. To be sure, the incorporation of the digital has led to the emergence of more varied scholarly writing practices, such as the ability to have multimodal scholarly writing that incorporates images and sound within a work. However, I still see this work along a continuum of academic writing, rather than work that marks any sort of significant rupture: using the new to do more of the same. I think the speed at which the digital humanities have been so easily incorporated into humanities programs—Kirschenbaum notes that the transition from term of convenience to whole scale movement was less than five years—should give us pause. It certainly suggests that the digital humanities are not all that transformative and certainly not a threat to the business of humanities departments or the university as a whole.

This is not to suggest that there are not some significant and interesting projects being done under the banner of DH both within and outside of academia but rather that a great deal of what is being done, what is seen as central and representative of digital humanities scholarship, does little to question the founding principles of academic knowledge, again, especially within the humanities. A digital humanism that replaces an ivory tower of bricks and mortar with one of supercomputers and server farms crunching large amounts of textual data and producing more and more textual analysis simply replaces one form of isolationism with another, reinscribing and reenforcing a very conservative form of humanities-based scholarship.

Now, we could juxtapose this digital humanism to another, the one not represented in the textual analysis of the Day of DH that began this essay. Tellingly, there are a group of words that appear less frequently in scholars' posts about the digital humanities, ones often associated with the digital and the humanities that are, nonetheless, significantly less represented, in some place all together absent. Social media, video games, or even contemporary web services and objects are significantly underrepresented. Even popular services such as Facebook or Twitter have a relatively low occurrence and, when mentioned, often are used in the context referring to using the service rather than studying the tool. The most popular word used with either of these two services is "checked," indicating that they are referenced as a medium of communication and not a medium of study.

And so, there are at least two digital humanisms: one that sees the digital as a set of tools to be applied to humanistic inquiry (design, project, tools, data) and another that sees the digital as an object of study (social media, digital games, mobile computing). As Kathleen Fitzpatrick observes, digital humanities can be defined as "a nexus of fields within which scholars use computing technologies to investigate the kinds of questions that are traditional to the humanities or, as is more true of my own work, who ask traditional kinds of humanities-oriented questions about computing technologies."

This definition would be more inclusive than the one derived from the word-frequency approach used at the beginning of this essay. Indeed, it is in the group that asks humanities-oriented questions about computing technologies, where Kathleen places her own work, that I would also include mine. And so here we have two versions (under one definition), sometimes in conflict, over what constitutes the digital humanities. The first is the sense that the digital is a direct, almost practical use of computational means for research in the humanities: computer-enabled reading. The second invokes scholars who study media or, more popularly, "new media" (a somewhat problematic term as "new media" is neither new nor media).

Given what the data reveals about how people who identify as digital humanists talk about their work, given what is included in journals and conferences under the rubric of "digital humanities," the first definition appears to be carrying the day—that is, that the digital humanities I have been discussing for the majority of this essay, the one that sees the computational as a tool for doing humanities-based research, is becoming the privileged term, with the media studies version of the digital humanities serving a marginal role. As much as the "big tent" definition and narrative is iterated, the practice of what actually occurs points to a different reality.

Now, I could argue that this type of polarity or conflict, between a digital humanism of computational technologies as adjectival modification of humanities research trumping a digital humanities of humanities-based research into the digital, is an unfortunate academic development. Indeed, it seems to me that the dominant type of digital humanism privileges the old at the expense of the new, even while it brings computational technologies into humanities buildings. And, personally, I find the first form of digital humanism, well, frankly, rather boring. I am not really interested in scholarship that counts word occurrence in Jane Austen texts, or even word occurrence across all the texts written in the same year as Austen's. While Ngram viewers might illuminate certain interesting, up until now unnoticed statistical trends regarding word usage and ultimately, perhaps, cultural meaning, if they become the paradigmatic example of what it means to perform a humanities reading, I fear not only for the future relevance of the humanities but also for our ability to resist being easily replaced by Watson-style computers. (There is nothing particularly new here. Italo Calvino imagined just such a computational reading practice in *If on a Winter's Night a Traveler* far before the instance of any humanities-based computing.) If using computational technologies to perform text analysis becomes just the latest way to make humanities exciting and relevant, to argue for funding, to beg not to be eliminated from the university, then DH will soon also go the way of any number of other textual reading schools: historically important, yes, culturally transformative, no. My hope is that DH can be something more than text analysis done more quickly.

But, actually, I am not going to make a claim as to why we should reverse this privileging, arguing for my flavor of DH over another. Really, that is just an etymological battle that might only reflect a preference for studying Facebook over *Pride and Prejudice* and which a particular scholar thinks is more socially relevant. What we choose to call these practices seems less significant than actually doing them, and if within the academy we end up dividing humanities computing from emerging media studies, with each getting its own name, I am not sure this would be an entirely unproductive division. Instead, though, I want to suggest we think about a different way to conceive of this problem, via Walter Benjamin.

I have become convinced over the last few years that Benjamin's "The Work of Art in the Age of Mechanical Reproduction" is one of the most important essays in media studies, not because of Benjamin's careful reading of the photograph, film, mechanization, and art or the effects these things have on culture but rather for the discursive approach that he uses during his investigation. That is, it is less the precise contours of the argument in relation to art or fascism but rather his methodology that I find crucial. What Benjamin says is that rather than ask, is photography art? we need to ask the more important questions: What does having the photograph do to our concept of art? How does the mere existence of the photograph change our ability to conceive of art as such? What change does the existence of the photograph bring about from which there is no going back?

By extension, asking, what is the digital humanities? or, should this particular approach to humanities be included under a tent of digital humanism? is to perform a less than productive inquiry. Rather, we should be asking what the digital does to our concept of the humanities and, by extension, even our concept of the human.

It is clear to me now, and I think it should be clear to any scholar, that the digital does not merely transform all means by which we do scholarship—word processors instead of pencils, computers instead of card catalogs, text encoding instead of notes scribbled in margins and notecards. The existence of the digital transforms the very meaning of the word "scholarship." Simply put, the existence of the digital transforms all areas of culture, not just scholarship. Indeed, scholarly transformations are just one small piece of the puzzle. We live in a world that is so thoroughly digital it is impossible, at this point, to talk about the nondigital. To treat the digital as simply an adjective that can be added onto the humanities is to attempt to contain it, to discipline the digital, to regulate it to one among a range of approaches to scholarship, rather than to recognize that the *only* way to do scholarship now is digital. Even if one never turns on a computer, answers an e-mail, or sends a text message, our cultural support structures are digital to the core: the world is digital now, not analog. If what adding "digital" to the humanities does is just take old disciplines, old ways of talking about texts and other objects of study, and make them digital, leaving the disciplinarity and the silo structure of the university intact, it will have failed or, more precisely, perhaps, simply reduced itself to an adjective. This critique holds equally well for studying Facebook or *Pride and Prejudice*: what is at stake here is not the object of study or even epistemology but rather ontology. The digital changes what it means to be human and by extension what it means to study the humanities. (Still, I would argue that you cannot begin to understand the complexities of these questions without engaging the present. No amount of Shakespeare and claiming his centrality to expressing a universal human condition will help you understand the role of WikiLeaks in the Tunisia uprising.)

In discussing the Venn diagram of the digital humanities, Alex Reid posits a second option. Rather than think of "the digital" and "the humanities" as two separate spheres of influence, which overlap and intersect in a field known as "digital humanities," we should think rather of one giant circle labeled "digital humanities." That is, there is no studying of the humanities separate from the digital. To study the humanities (or any kind of socially relevant, engaged-in-the-present object of inquiry) necessitates a realization that the world is now digital. There is no humanism separate from the digital. This is not about the means of study (computers to process text), nor is it about the object of the study (digital media)—although both are implicated. Rather, it is about how the idea of studying itself is altered by the existence of the digital.

It is in this respect, I think, that the digital humanities has something to offer the academy and that there is perhaps a third definition, one we could oppose to either the first or the second: the digital humanities as an understanding of new modes of scholarship, as a change not only in tools and objects but in scholarship itself. What is important about the Day of DH was not what was talked about, using text analyzers to rank word counts. Rather, the importance of the Day of DH lies in the fact that a community of scholars was differently constituted: publicly performing scholarship, blogging, tweeting, facebooking about what it means to be an academic. That such a discussion took place around a specific, ultimately narrowly defined academic discipline seems less important to me than the fact that such a demonstration and public conversation took place. Doing digital work means working differently, whether that work is humanities or sociology or physics.

Indeed, it is the indirect benefits of the scholarship that goes by the name humanities computing that tends to be of the most importance. Humanistic inquiry that involves conversation between computer scientists and classically trained humanists cannot but help to produce a different kind of crossdisciplinary understanding, even if said scholarship is limited by a focus on traditional objects of study. A program that reads all of the texts published in England in 1784 to measure occurrences of the word "God" ultimately seems of less importance to me than a project that necessitates (by its digital nature) a collaboration and merging of disciplinary silos.

Of course, collaborative and collective scholarship has a long history both inside and outside of the academy, especially when we look at the work performed in other disciplines, especially the sciences, where collaborative scholarship is the standard, not the exception. But within the humanities, and especially over the recent history of our discipline, scholarship is seen as an individual, indeed often solitary, performance. Digital humanities did not invent collaborative scholarship, but it does make such work more acceptable and transparent.

In the end, debates will occur about digital humanities, with various practitioners carving out ground and staking claim to their particular fields and methods of inquiry. If I were to guess, I suspect that the primary definition of digital humanities as humanities computing, using computers as tools to do humanities research, will win the day, a concession I am more than willing to make. I have very little to no desire to label myself a digital humanist. The real transformation will come, or not come, based on the way the academy, and even humanists, transform the nature of scholarship based on the digital and, more importantly, come to terms with the way the digital transforms what it means to have a humanism.

BIBLIOGRAPHY

Fitzpatrick, Kathleen. "Reporting from the Digital Humanities 2010 Conference." *Chronicle of Higher Education*, July 13, 2010. http://chronicle.com/blogs/profhacker/reporting-from-the-digital-humanities-2010-conference/25473.

Kirschenbaum, Matthew. "What Is Digital Humanities and What's It Doing in English Departments?" *ADE Bulletin* 150 (2010): 1–7. http://mkirschenbaum.files.wordpress.com/2011/01/kirschenbaum_ade150.pdf. Reprinted in this volume.

Reid, Alex. "Digital Humanities: Two Venn Diagrams." *Alex-Reid.net*. March 10, 2011. http://www.alex-reid.net/2011/03/digital-humanities-two-venn-diagrams.html.

The Resistance to Digital Humanities

DAVID GREETHAM

This essay is a perhaps foreseeable follow-up to an earlier piece on "The Resistance to Philology" (Greetham),[1] published in the collection *The Margins of the Text*. That volume dealt not just with those parts of a text that typically were relegated to the bibliographical margins (titles, annotations, marginalia, etc.) but also with those features of textual discourse (race, gender, sexual orientation, class, among others) that had been *marginalized* in discussions of textual scholarship. The collection had been prompted by the discovery that in some otherwise highly regarded academic institutions, a scholarly edition, bibliography, or textual study counted as only one *half* of a "real" book in promotion and tenure decisions. The critical hardback monograph was the gold standard by which scholarly and intellectual achievement was to be measured.

Now, a decade and more later, it is unclear whether that institutional prejudice against bibliographical and editorial work has been overcome or whether it has been compounded by a newer dismissive attitude, this time toward digital and electronic "publications." Since the great majority of new scholarly editions established in the last twenty years and more have some prominent digital component (electronic text, hyperlinks and hypermedia, and so on), if the institutional marginalization of *text* has been joined by a similar prejudice (or, at best, an equivocal attitude) toward *medium*, then those of us working with *electronic text* are confronted with a double whammy in an increasingly competitive academic atmosphere. Put in a related form: is the very concept of digital humanities (DH) seen in some quarters as an oxymoron, the passing off of *technē* as if it were *critique*; and, *a fortiori*, if this oxymoronic DH is concerned with the production of textual or bibliographical resources, are those scholars engaging in such pursuits under a two-fold suspicion by the general community of "humanists"?

In a short essay describing the potential problem, it is unlikely that we will find a smoking gun or that the usual cloak of confidentiality regarding tenure and promotion will be sufficiently lifted to provide a clear view of academic predispositions. Nonetheless, there is little sign of the old prejudices against textual study having been lifted. In part, this continued disdain may be related to the positivist and antihermeneutical postures of the more technical (and less critical) claims of some textuists (e.g., that textual scholarship is a "science," with demonstrable proofs), a self-characterization that only feeds the suspicions of some humanities scholars that bibliographical and textual research belongs in current humanities departments only as a "service" activity, not fully integrated in or related to the loftier philosophical aspirations of postformalist humanities. In the original "Resistance" essay, I argued that textuists should embrace hermeneutics rather than science to become "dangerous" again; and Hans Walter Gabler (2010) has recently promoted a recognition of textual *criticism* as the *sine qua non* of editorial and bibliographical activity.

It is probably true that, because digital work has at least acquired a veneer of the "sexy" and the "new," while there may be some chartable unease about the quantification and the technical coding (SGML, HTML, XML) aspects of electronic work, the proliferation of recent *print* publications (and even movies) on the Internet, information (see Gleick), online social networks, and so on has given a public prominence to digital humanities, whatever that is. The ongoing series of *New York Times* articles on "Humanities 2.0"; the citing of blogs as evidence in the popular press; the use of Twitter and digital phones in recent political movements (Iran, Egypt, Tunisia, Yemen); and the continued, perhaps exacerbated, concerns of government with the control of copyright in digital environments—all of these features of what Bourdieu calls "fields" of "cultural production"—show that the electronic environment is a persistent and well-traversed area of our common discourse. Whether that discourse will admit digital bibliographical scholarship, digital editing, and digital textuality as academic credentials is another matter.

As in the case of the earlier "Resistance" essay, this problem can be seen as one of rhetoric (though recognizing that this usage is not meant to undervalue the very real and practical concerns of scholars, particularly younger scholars, facing the career-determining decisions of review committees). Thus, in the first issue of *Digital Humanities Quarterly* (*DHQ*, whose very title shows an indebtedness to, or desire to connect with, an established "print" mode of production), Joseph Raben's *apologia* ("Tenure, Promotion and Digital Publication") makes much of the fact that *DHQ* is a "a totally online scholarly publication," while at the same time noting that "the absence of parallel publications in other sectors of humanities research is a measure of the distance still to be traveled before computer publishing is regarded as fully equal to the book and the print journal." Raben puts the issue very starkly when he recognizes that some potential contributors to *DHQ* may be all too aware that "appearance in electronic media is not as highly regarded by the gatekeepers of tenure and promotion as the traditional hard-bound book and the article offprint, at least in the humanities." The enthusiastic embrace of electronic work by such senior scholars as Jerome J. McGann (whose hypermedia archive of Dante Gabriel Rossetti and such foundational critical writings as the "Rationale of HyperText" have provided a paradigm for DH) has to be measured against the reluctance of other textual critics to grant DH, and specifically electronic editing, the status of supersessionist medium. So G. Thomas Tanselle, who is generally regarded as the exemplary contemporary figure in the continuity of the print-based Greg-Bowers school of "copytext" editing, was (unexpectedly) brought in (co-opted) by the Modern Language Association (MLA) to write a preface to the volume on *Electronic Textual Editing*, in which he discounted the "hyperbolic writing and speaking about the computer age, as if the computer age were basically discontinuous with what went before" and warned that "when the excitement leads to the idea that the computer alters the ontology of texts and makes possible new kinds of reading and analysis, it has gone too far" (Tanselle). I share Tanselle's view that much of what Paul Duguid has pointedly referred to as early "liberation technology" by computer proselytes placed the rhetoric of DH in a dangerously vertiginous position. And I also agree that, if DH is to be accorded a recognizable and stable position in academic writing, it must not cut itself loose from the textual and critical history that precedes it. As I have remarked elsewhere, I would maintain that the rhetorical stance of Matthew G. Kirschenbaum's *Mechanisms: New Media and the Forensic Imagination* (in which digital forensics is linked to the bibliographical principles of W. W. Greg, Fredson Bowers, and G. Thomas Tanselle) is not just an appropriate ideological tactic but may also serve to head off the potential ghettoization of DH and electronic editing with it.

But how far has the ghettoization already gone; and, in the absence of the smoking gun, how do we measure the "resistance" of my title? In his brief introduction to the scholarly mandate of *DHQ*, Raben cites some disturbing statistics from a 2006–7 MLA *Report of the MLA Task Force on Evaluating Scholarship for Tenure and Promotion.* Raben concentrates on the findings that "40.8% of departments in doctorate-granting institutions report no experience in evaluating refereed articles in electronic format, and 65.7% report no experience in evaluating monographs in electronic format," although 88.9 percent of doctorate-granting institutions rate the publication of a monograph as "very important" or "important" for tenure. These statistics are telling enough, but the report itself contains much more that should be of continuing concern to DH practitioners. It is hardly promising that across the board, only 28.1 percent of departments considered monographs in electronic format "important" to the evaluation of scholarship, and overall "[r]efereed articles in digital media count for tenure and promotion in less than half as many departments as refereed articles in print," and "[m]onographs in electronic formats have a place in the evaluation of scholarship for tenure and promotion in only about one-third as many departments as print monographs" (MLA *Report of the Task Force*, 43–44). There is clearly a suspicion that somehow the "open access" principles of a good deal of electronic scholarship produce a less than rigorous evaluation procedure than in traditional print contexts. This suspicion was one of the reasons that Hoyt Duggan founded SEENET (Society for Early English and Norse Texts)—to create a forum for peer review that would match that usually associated with print publication, which was also a founding principle of NINES (Networked Infrastructure for Nineteenth-Century Electronic Scholarship). The MLA report finds that such rigorous scholarly procedures are now evident in electronic journals, which are "increasingly run by editorial boards committed to peer review" (44). The institutional paradox is that while "digital forms of scholarship increasingly pervade academic life, work in this area has not yet received proper recognition when candidates are evaluated for promotion and tenure" (44). It is impossible to estimate how many younger scholars may hesitate to begin work on digital projects, knowing (or sensing) that their labors will count for less during the important career-making moments, a challenge that I think may be compounded when the electronic scholarship is editorial or bibliographical. So although I can testify from thirty years involvement with the interdisciplinary Society for Textual Scholarship that the proportion of younger (and, I believe, of female) participants in recent conferences has greatly increased in the last decade or so, we must wonder how many of these younger people will make it into even the midranks of the profession.

What is this scholarly environment as it promotes (or fails to promote) digital and digital *textual* work? The MLA report was published only five years ago; and while at several points its authors look toward a more collegial institutional atmosphere in the near future, we should not expect that moment to have yet arrived. Nonetheless, in part as a response to the grim findings of the report, the MLA has been in the forefront of an attempt to make literature and language scholars and administrators more familiar with digital work and its demands.

In a very helpful e-mail correspondence, Stephen Olsen (associate director of research and manager of digital services at the MLA) points to a number of such "outreach" programs by and within the MLA, including a series of electronic roundtables at the annual conventions, together with presentations of digital projects at individual computer stations. Workshops on evaluating digital scholarship are also organized at the MLA, as they are at Association of Departments of English (ADE) and Association of Departments of Foreign Languages (ADFL; especially notable being the summer seminars for administrators). The MLA *Guidelines for Evaluating Work with Digital Media in the Modern Languages* together with several important publications by the ADE (see Fitzpatrick, "Planned Obsolescence"; Hayles, "How We Read"; and Kirschenbaum, "What Is Digital Humanities?") have emerged from the summer seminars and are now available on the ADE website. Such forceful programs from the leading U.S. professional organizations may indeed lead to an administrative adjustment of perspective, but reports from other quarters suggest that there is a good deal of proselytizing still to be done. The real test will be to see whether there is substantial change in the statistics when the MLA next conducts a follow-up report to the earlier one.

In the series of e-mail, personal, and phone interviews (which must clearly remain impressionistic rather than statistical) I conducted for this article, those scholars who primarily occupied a position in a research or archival wing of an institution tended to be more hopeful about the recognition of electronic work. Thus Bethany Nowviskie, who serves as director of dgital research and scholarship at the University of Virginia Library and sits on the MLA Committee on Information Technology, has drafted an article on the "preconditions" to the evaluation of collaborative digital scholarship, to be published in a cluster in *Profession*, edited by Laura Mandell and Susan Schreibman. This will build upon the 2006–7 report and provide what may become a template for future evaluations. Similarly, Michael Bérubé, director of the Institute for Arts and Humanities and Paterno family professor in literature at Pennsylvania State University and coauthor of the MLA report, finds that "forms of scholarship other than the monograph are absurdly devalued in some quarters" but that the work of Kirschenbaum and others is "beginning to change things . . . however gradually." A less hopeful diagnosis (and prognosis) is offered by Stephen Ramsay, associate professor in English at the University of Nebraska–Lincoln and a fellow in the Center for Digital Research in the Humanities, in an e-mail and phone conversation about recent case histories. Ramsay noted that such cases "provide a sad commentary on the state of DH acceptance. Just when I think we've arrived, [these cases] remind me that in some quarters things are precisely as they were when I started (fifteen years or so ago)." Ramsay also feels that there may be an institutional "fear" of some of the more technical (and less "humanistic") aspects of DH, especially quantification and data mining, but that, for institutions like his own University of Nebraska, DH offers an opportunity to create an academic and intellectual "presence" that would not have been available in predigital days.

The problem may be, as both Ramsay and Bérubé suggest, that during a period of transition it may be particularly difficult to determine where we are in the unfolding of that transition (and even more difficult to predict when and if DH will have been fully accepted as a "respectable" element in humanities research). As Morris Eaves (also a coauthor of the MLA report) observes, in characteristically pointed language,

> When it comes to DH/resistance: resistance certainly remains, but it's hard to gauge its character—maybe chiefly because things happen so slowly, or should I say gradually, or even carefully, in the humanities. One (I) would hope that DH would simply be digested like a rat in a python—slowly but inexorably. But there are some signs, as you say, of uphill battles with faculties and administrations fighting what I regard as rearguard battles—against whatever "digital" means, against statistics, etc. It seems to me that there's a lot of "mere" prejudice involved—kneejerk "humanism," complete with eyerolling, inattention to detail, refusal to listen, and so on. And of course the (perfectly natural, comfortable, maybe inevitable) combination of DH with textual criticism is in some respects lethal—compounding the opportunities to restage familiar old battles on new turf.

> However, there are plenty of hopeful signs for us optimists . . . A certain level of resignation that, well, this digital stuff *is* happening, and we can resist only so much. A vast amount of sheer interest among Ph.D. students and recent Ph.Ds, cluster hires, the spread of digital humanities centers/institutes with a variety of missions, more and more Ph.D. candidates with serious investments in *some* flavor of DH.

Eaves's recognition that a resistance to DH may be another form of the resistance I charted earlier to "philology" is particularly telling, for it means that textual scholars working in electronic environments (i.e., pretty much everyone) have to parry a two-pronged hostility: that textual study is not *critical*; and that, if presented digitally, is a mere *technē*. So the "hopeful signs" that Eaves looks for may depend on what "flavor" of DH is being offered.

There can be no doubt that the sheer range of DH projects, institutes, and scholarly investment has increased enormously in the last decade or so. The survey of DH activities in Matthew G. Kirschenbaum's "What Is Digital Humanities and What Is It Doing in English Departments?" (2010) sees a "robust professional apparatus that is probably more rooted in English than any other departmental home" (1) but then cites examples that are challenging if not perplexing or professionally disturbing (the book series Topics in the Digital Humanities from the University of Illinois Press, like this current volume, in codex format, and the well-circulated story of Brain Croxall, a recent Emory PhD whose 2009 MLA paper "The Absent Present: Today's Faculty" was read in absentia because he could not get travel funds to attend the convention in Philadelphia). That Kirschenbaum chooses a particularly dystopian citation from Cynthia Selfe as his epigraph ("People who say that the last battles of the computer revolution in English departments have been fought and won don't know what they're talking about") enfolds the account of apparent progress within a rhetoric of immobility, even regression.

And in conversation at the Society for Textual Scholarship conference at Penn State in March 2011, Kirschenbaum (who is both author of the highly regarded *Mechanisms* and the forthcoming *Track Changes* and associate professor in the Department of English at the University of Maryland as well as associate director of the Maryland Institute for Technology in the Humanities and thus of the "double appointment" model of a number of successful DHers) agreed that the print monograph still overwhelmingly influences tenure and promotion decisions and this at a time when print publication is becoming more difficult to sustain economically. It may be that promotion and tenure committees will be reasonably tolerant of a candidate's involvement with DH but that this tolerance will not necessarily extend to a faculty member whose primary work has been digital and who has yet to produce the traditional print monograph. This problem is in part addressed by the MLA wiki "Short Guide to Evaluation of Digital Work," which poses a series of questions that institutions should consider in trying to evaluate nonprint work. These questions include the following: Is it accessible to the community of study? Have there been expert consultations? Has this been shown to others for expert opinion? Has the work been reviewed? Can it be submitted for peer review? Has the work been presented at conferences? (a question that in a qualification, "It should, however, be recognized that many candidates don't have the funding to travel to international conferences," recognizes the practical issues raised by the Croxall case). The wiki takes the funding issue as indicative of the phenomenological divide between print and digital production: "Digital work is hard to review once it is done and published online as our peer review mechanisms are typically connected to publication decisions. For this reason competitive funding decisions like the allocation of a grant should be considered as an alternative form of review. While what is reviewed is not the finished work so much as the project and track record of the principal investigators, a history of getting grants is a good indication that the candidate is submitting her research potential for review where there is real competition."

A broader view of the status of DH was undertaken during the workshop session of Project Bamboo, held in Princeton in 2008. Among the concerns raised were those similar to the MLA report, for example, that while "new faculty are brave and will try new stuff," in terms of "career incentives," they are "worried about what they're judged on" because "[h]umanities are rewarded by publishing a book" (Project Bamboo, "Exercise 6A Scribe Notes"). The same (unidentified) speaker went on to describe such a bias as confirming current emphasis on "the glory of the book" although conceding that "[w]e are at the cusp of a reward system changing for humanities," which might reflect a shift whereby the "distinction between technologists and people who use technology [is] disappearing . . . and that "people think through technology" (Project Bamboo, "Exercise 6A Scribe Notes").

The anxieties surrounding DH that emerged at the conference were wide ranging and included a greater concern about getting published early in graduate school than in previous generations; observations that digital work had actually failed to produce academic advancement; a worry that campuses don't know how to credit online work; a nostalgia—among certain Bamboo participants—for older, more "reliable" analog technologies; and a fear of information overload, particularly as it affects younger students learning to organize their research and citations for the first time. Despite all of these reservations, the conference also made a tentative distinction between "standing faculty [who] are more about just writing books" and incoming hires who will "incorporate technology in the classroom. They use blackboard, can digitize clips, work with library, Instructional Technology. I look to my new colleagues for inspiration on how to use technology" (Project Bamboo, "Exercise 6A Scribe Notes"). Nowhere else was the paradox between the anxieties over DH and the expectation that professional academics are utilizing and advancing digital scholarship more apparent.

Indeed, these anxieties might be increasing, with not only an institutional expectation of two published books in humanities combined with the widespread failure of digital publication to produce advancement. One solution suggested "targeting select senior faculty who are not dinosaurs and developing their projects. . . . These are the people who can influence tenure decisions" (26), a view reinforced later that "rather than a parallel peer review system, what we should do is look for senior established colleagues who can take risks and would do something different—persuade them to publish something in a digital form. By taking that step it makes it more respectable for junior people to do" (33). But a step like this would have to address entrenched institution-wide predispositions that would not be easily overcome and that this could have a cumulative effect: "if they don't get tenure at our place, it will be hard for them elsewhere" (26).

Unlike the almost contemporary and statistically based MLA report, these comments from the initial Bamboo conference are clearly largely impressionistic, albeit informed by many specific examples of the problems faced by DH. And these examples must be recognized as issuing from a self-selected group of international institutions that were all, to one extent or another, supportive of and involved in the new digital media, unlike the MLA respondents who were not so selected but instead represented language and literature programs throughout North America. If the Bamboo conferees could register fairly widespread unease about the status of DH, how widespread must the problem be in the academy at large? Of course, it may be that those at Bamboo, precisely because they are self-selected, are more aware of the problems and barriers facing digital scholarship than are the more comprehensive MLA respondents.

It is clearly appropriate to consider some hard cases. Both examples to follow come from my own experience, and both recognize the "resistance" that is my subject and (the first more than the second) some signs of overcoming this problem. I cite first the testimony of Dr. Stephen Brier, senior academic technology officer at my institution, the CUNY Graduate Center.

> There has been growing interest over the past few years among our doctoral students (and, to a lesser degree among our faculty) in the digital humanities, both with respect to research methodologies that they hope to employ in conceptualizing and producing their dissertations and in DH's pedagogical implications and possibilities for transforming classroom teaching. Since many hundreds of our doctoral students teach undergraduate courses at CUNY's various senior and community colleges, they have manifested a particular interest in using digital technology to enhance the quality of their teaching and the possibilities for student learning at CUNY. As coordinator of the Graduate Çenter's Interactive Technology and Pedagogy certificate program and co-director of the New Media Lab, I have seen this heightened interest in DH among students from across the social sciences and humanities. Moreover, several GC faculty and doctoral students have launched a Digital Humanities Initiative, sponsored by the Digital Studies Group and under the aegis of the GC's Center for the Humanities.

> The DHI has organized a series of well-attended seminars over the past year on DH issues and questions, which have focused equally on new digital research methodologies and digital pedagogy. This heightened interest in DH has led us to propose the development of a new interdisciplinary M.A. track in Digital Humanities under the umbrella of GC's M.A. in Liberal Studies program, which is currently being developed with encouragement from the Provost's office. I am excited by the multiple venues in which DH is manifested at GC. At the same time, I am not sanguine that DH will easily or rapidly transform the more conventional academic arenas in which doctoral education takes place at our institution. My money is on the next generation of scholars we are producing at the Graduate Center, who I believe will carry the DH banner into the next phase of their academic careers.

The two most striking elements of this testimony from an administrator (rather than the faculty and students recorded in the Bamboo conversations) are (1) the recognition that the impetus for institutional and scholarly advances in DH comes primarily from graduate students and only secondarily from doctoral faculty, and (2) there will be no easy or quick transformation toward DH within the "conventional academic arenas." This latter prognosis reflects the uncertainties expressed by Ramsay and others about our current position in the progress of DH. The fact that the support of DH within the Graduate Center comes from two levels—the top administration and the present and future students—does reinforce that frequent complaint within Bamboo that the problems lie with entrenched senior faculty and with the departments they represent, and this condition is doubtless widespread in the current academy. There is, however, one further part of Brier's institutional description that may make movement within CUNY easier than at other graduate and doctoral programs. Unlike the norm elsewhere, CUNY Graduate Center students typically teach (as independent instructors rather than as TAs) their own courses throughout the undergraduate (and sometimes graduate) levels. They thus get an opportunity to test and improve DH techniques in pedagogical as well as research circumstances and of course to react with (and learn from) the next generation of potential scholars in electronic environments. Even so, Brier is not "sanguine" (any more than MLA or Bamboo) that we should expect major reappraisals of the scholarly validity of DH research throughout the profession.

And that caveat leads to my second example—of a former graduate student of mine who had done a dissertation on the relations between electronic and print media and who then got a tenure-track position in a branch of a state university, continued to work on digital issues, and was then denied tenure and promotion, in a complex case that exemplifies several of the issues in this survey. For example, like the MLA's reporting that all too few institutions had experience in evaluating DH scholarship, a senior administrator admitted that "I would be more confident of recommending promotion if I knew better how to assess [the candidate's] achievement in digital scholarship" but lay the responsibility for providing this information on the specific department: "[i]t would help considerably if the Department [which had denied tenure] would clarify what it expects in the way of scholarship that justifies promotion," a demonstration of (at best) an ambivalence to DH at midlevel and (at worst) an outright hostility. This same administrator wrote that "when I compare [the candidate's] scholarly and professional activities to some elsewhere in the college who have achieved promotion to Associate Professor, I cannot see that [the candidate] has been less successful than them in showing a persistent, dedicated engagement with getting articles published and with involvement in a variety of professional activities." It is, of course, very unlikely that a department denying tenure and promotion will be overtly dismissive of all forms of digital scholarship; but, when such a denial invokes the hoary distinction of "form" (i.e., medium) over "substance," it seems fairly clear that this is indeed another "resistance" to the new medium: the negative evaluation from the department includes the comment that "[t]he evidence presented for the pedagogical value of [the candidate's] work in digital humanities appears to pride form over substance." There are those who have apparently still not been able to accept the dicta of Marshall McLuhan and for whom "medium" continues to be a nonsubject. When that medium is digital, substance is no longer visible to those who will not see. When this sort of prejudice occurs in promotion and tenure decisions, it raises the wider issue of whether such decisions should be based on form, substance, or both and what should be the relationship between the two.

And what one sees is obviously dependent on what one is looking for and the valuation one places on these data. A particularly apt demonstration of this question of fact and significance occurred in one of the "Humanities 2.0" series of articles in the *New York Times*. If we examine the content, methodology, results of, and response to "In 500 Billion Words, New Window on Culture" (Cohen), we can chart a range of opinions on the utility and critical value of the data. In brief, the report on the digitization of the five hundred billion words makes clear that the research should illuminate such fields as "lexicography, the evolution of grammar, collective memory, the adoption of technology, the pursuit of fame, censorship, and historical epidemiology" and that this new "culturomics . . . extends the boundaries of rigorous quantitative inquiry to a wide array of new phenomena spanning the social sciences and the humanities" (Michel).

Despite the evidence of the report itself (e.g., that the Nazi repression of references to Marc Chagall is very clearly documentable by the word frequency statistics, with only a single mention in German from 1933 through 1944), in the *Times* coverage of the research the well-known critic Louis Menand found the value of the statistics limited and claims for its relevance to humanities overblown. While acknowledging that the Google Books NGram Viewer could be particularly useful for linguists, he suggested that "obviously some of the claims [about cultural history] are a little exaggerated" (Menand). He was also troubled that, among the paper's thirteen named authors, there was not a single humanist involved. "There's not even a historian of the book connected to the project," Menand noted. I share Menand's unease that there appear to have been no humanists on board (unless one counts linguists in this group) and certainly nobody representing history of the book. In subsequent e-mail correspondence, Menand elaborated on his concerns: "What I had in mind was the various things the authors of the paper claimed to have proved by counting changes in the number of words or phrases. I thought it was a completely superficial way to do cultural history. It's not that the data might not be relevant, but you'd have to do a lot more work before you could make some of the claims they were making—hence my noting that they did not have a humanist on their team. They seemed to think this could be a purely empirical exercise."

Menand's demurrals are well taken, and doubtless the involvement of a representative group of humanists would have affected the interpretative positions that the report covers. But I am less certain that quantitative analyses are a "superficial" way to provide information for "cultural history." If that were so, then the research of the *annaliste* school of French history (challenging the previously dominant "great-figure" focus) would be vitiated in relegating its data and, yes, its quantification to a form of nonhumanistic "counting." It does indeed require a humanistic intervention to try to characterize the raw evidence of the so-called Ngrams that the Google-powered research recorded and analyzed (and admittedly there has been some complaint that the Ngrams may be based on "dirty" data). But when the authors of the report on the perhaps unfortunately named "culturomics" note that the research should illuminate various "humanistic" fields and that this new "culturomics . . . extends the boundaries of rigorous quantitative inquiry to a wide array of new phenomena" spanning the social sciences and the humanities, I am not sure that these claims are necessarily "exaggerated" (Michel). In the Chagall example, the quantifiable "disappearance" in German-language publications during the Nazi years has to be set against the continued presence of the artist in languages other than German throughout the Nazi hegemony; and, even in German, the references pick up again after 1945. This quantification is "superficial" only in the sense that it provides a numerical series of raw facts; but the moment that we place these mere facts against the template of mid-twentieth-century political history, an interpretive strategy is forced upon us, a strategy that can then be checked and if necessary modified by running other Ngrams involving other (Jewish and non-Jewish) painters, other art forms, other places and types of publication, and other historical periods. Menand is right that the Ngram in and of itself does not *prove* anything beyond the limited values encoded in the statistics; but I suspect that much of the "resistance" that the traditional culture critic finds in culturomics is derived from the combination of the quantification itself and its being presented in a digital (i.e., machine-produced and machine-readable) format.

In other words, the addition of digitization to quantification makes the data seem even less humanistic and critical. The resistance is simply a more recent form of that distrust of "detail" that Julia Flanders finds in stylometrics and related "pedantic" studies. She cites a 1989 review of John Burrows, *Computation into Criticism*: "From his pages of tables, graphs, and figures he proves that each of the characters under consideration [from Jane Austen's novels] has his or her own idiolect . . . While there seems to be no reason—or at least none that a non-statistician can see—to doubt the validity of his findings, the thought does occur as to whether five years of work . . . by Professor Burrows to tell his readers this was really necessary" (La Faye, 429). Flanders notes that La Faye has misunderstood Burrows's argument; but, in addition, the relevance of the review is its resistance to (and devaluation of) the pedantry required to produce a quantifiable result—much the same position of the antiphilological critics I cited in the predecessor to this article (e.g., that "the prestige of fiddling with minute variants and bibliographical details should be low" [Sisson, 616]).

In the various forms of "resistance" encountered in this essay, I think we can see that the critical dismissal of Ngrams and culturomics, the devaluing of digital-based research, the institutional unwillingness to regard work conducted in an electronic medium as on a par with print, and the related continuation of the "gold standard" of the monograph in tenure and promotion decisions are all symptoms of the fact that, to cite again Morris Eave's colorful figure, the rat has not yet been digested by the python.

NOTES

This report inevitably depends on leads and information provided by a number of practitioners of DH, some of them contributors to this volume. I would specifically like to acknowledge the valuable help and guidance from Michael Bérubé, Stephen Brier, Morris Eaves, Charlotte Edwards, Matthew K. Gold, Katherine D. Harris, Sarah Ruth Jacobs, Matthew G. Kirschenbaum, David Laurence, Louis Menand, Bethany Nowviskie, Stephen Olsen, Stephen Ramsay, Bowen Slate-Greene, Lisa Spiro, and Domna Stanton.

1. The title of that earlier essay was a deliberate conflation, derived from two pieces by Paul De Man, "The Resistance to Theory" and "The Return to Philology" (1986), and initially appeared in the volume *The Margins of the Text*" (Greetham).

BIBLIOGRAPHY

Association of Departments of English. *ADE Bulletin* 150 (2010). http://www.ade.org/.

Bérubé, Michael. "Advice on Status of DH." E-mail. March 14, 2011.

Bourdieu, Pierre. *The Field of Cultural Production.* Edited by Randall Johnson. Cambridge, Mass.: Polity Press, 1993.

Brier, Steven. E-mail to author. April 1, 2011.

Cohen, Patricia. "In 500 Billion Words, New Window on Culture." *New York Times,* December 16, 2010. http://www.nytimes.com/2010/12/17/books/17words.html?ref =humanities20.

De Man, Paul. "The Resistance to Theory." In *The Resistance to Theory*. Minneapolis: University of Minnesota Press, 1986.

———. "The Return to Philology." In *The Resistance to Theory*. Minneapolis: University of Minnesota Press, 1986.

Digital Humanities Quarterly. http://www.digitalhumanities.org/dhq/.

Duguid, Paul. "Material Matters: The Past and Futurology of the Book." In *The Future of the Book*, edited by Geoffrey Nunberg. Berkeley and Los Angeles: University of California Press, 1996.

Eaves, Morris. "After STS." E-mail. March 25, 2011.

Fitzpatrick, Kathleen. "Planned Obsolescence: Publishing, Technology, and the Future of the Academy." *ADE Bulletin* 150 (2010): 41–54. http://www.ade.org/cgi-shl/docstudio/docs.pl?adefl_bulletin_c_ade_150_41.

Flanders, Julia. "Detailism, Digital Texts, and the Problem of Pedantry." *TEXT Technology* 14, no. 2 (2005). http://texttechnology.mcmaster.ca/pdf/vol14_2/flanders14-2.pdf.

Gabler, Hans Walter. "Theorizing the Scholarly Edition." Special Issue, "Scholarly Editing in the Twenty-First Century," *Literature Compass* 7, no. 2 (2010): 43–56.

Gleick, James. *The Information: A History, A Theory, A Flood.* New York: Pantheon, 2011.

Greetham, David. "The Resistance to Philology." In *The Margins of the Text.* Ann Arbor: University of Michigan Press, 1997. Repr. *The Pleasures of Contamination.* Bloomington: Indiana University Press, 2010.

Harley, Diane, et al. *Assessing the Future Landscape of Scholarly Communication: An Exploration of Faculty Values and Needs in Seven Disciplines.* Center for Studies in Higher Education, University of California Berkeley, 2010. http://escholarship.org/uc/cshe_fsc.

Hayles, N. Katherine. "How We Read: Close, Hyper, Machine." *ADE Bulletin* 150 (2010): 62–79. http://www.mla.org/adefl_bulletin_c_ade_150_62.

Kirschenbaum, Matthew G. *Mechanisms: New Media and the Forensic Imagination.* Cambridge, Mass. and London: MIT Press, 2008.

———. "What Is Digital Humanities and What's It Doing in English Departments?" *ADE Bulletin* 150 (2010): 55–61. http://www.ade.org/cgi-shl/docstudio/docs.pl?adefl_bulletin_c_ade_150_55. Reprinted in this volume.

La Faye, Dierdre. Rev. of *Computation into Criticism: A study of Jane Austen's novels and an Experiment in Method. Review of English Studies* 40, no. 159 (1989): 429–30 (qtd. in Flanders).

McGann, Jerome J., ed. "The Complete Writings and Pictures of Dante Gabriel Rossetti: A Hypermedia Archive." http://www.rossettiarchive.org/.

———. "The Rationale of HyperText." *Text* 9 (1996). Repr. *Electronic Text: Investigations in Method and Theory.* Edited by Kathryn Sutherland. Oxford: Clarendon, 1997. Repr. *Radiant Textuality: Literature After the World Wide Web.* New York: Palgrave, 2001.

Menand, Louis. "Debates in Digital Humanities." E-mail. February 20, 2011.

Michel, Jean-Baptiste, et al. *Quantitative Analysis of Culture Using Millions of Digitized Books. Science* 331, no. 6014 (January 2011): 176–82.

Modern Language Association. *The Evaluation of Digital Work.* http://wiki.mla.org/index.php/Evaluation_Wiki.

———. *Guidelines for Evaluating Work with Digital Media in the Modern Languages.* http://www.mla.org/resources/documents/rep_it/guidelines_evaluation_digital.

———. *Report of the Task Force on Evaluating Scholarship for Tenure and Promotion.* December, 2006; *Profession* 2007. http://www.mla.org/tenure_promotion.

NINES (Ninetenth-Century Scholarship Online). http://www.nines.org/about/what_is.html.

Nowviskie, Bethany. Interview with author. March 18, 2011.

———. "'Inventing the Map' in the Digital Humanities: A Young Lady's Primer." *Poetes Archive Journal* 2, no. 1 (2010). http://paj.muohio.edu/paj/index.php/paj/article/viewArticle/11.

Olsen, Stephen. "Digital Humanities." E-mail. April 8, 2011.

Parry, Dave. "Be Online or Be Irrelevant." AcademHack. http://academhack.outsidethetext.com/home/2010/be-online-or-be-irrelevant/.

Project Bamboo. "Exercise 6A Scribe Notes." Princeton, N.J. 2007. https://wiki.projectbamboo.org/display/BPUB/Exercise+6a+Scribe+Notes.

Raben, Joseph. "Tenure, Promotion and Digital Publication." *Digital Humanities Quarterly* 1, no. 1 (Spring 2007). http://www.digitalhumanities.org/dhq/vol/1/1/000006/000006.html.

Ramsay, Stephen. E-mail to author. March 24, 2011.

———. Telephone interview. March 28, 2011.

SEENET (Society for Early English and Norse Electronic Texts). http://www3.iath.virginia.edu/seenet/piers/archivegoals.htm.

Sisson, C. H. "Pound Among the Pedants." *Times Literary Supplement,* May 20, 1979, 616.

Tanselle, G. Thomas. "Preface." In *Electronic Textual Editing,* edited by Lou Barnard, Katherine O'Brien O'Keefe, and John Unsworth. New York: MLA, 2006.

Beyond Metrics: Community Authorization and Open Peer Review

KATHLEEN FITZPATRICK

I originally began writing about peer review—its history, its present status, and its digital future—a couple of years ago, as it became increasingly clear that addressing the question of digital scholarship required a prior reckoning with the issue. I hadn't ever really intended to give it that much of my attention; but, as my colleagues and I worked on the development of the digital scholarly network MediaCommons, it kept crowding in, as it has for many digital humanities projects: at every meeting, conference presentation, panel discussion, or other venue where we discussed the kinds of work we were interested in publishing, one of the first questions we were asked was what we intended to do about peer review.

Coming to the development of MediaCommons at one and the same time from the position of being a scholar and that of being a blogger, I was of two distinct minds in responding to that question. The blogger in me wanted to wave the question off; enormous amounts of influential intellectual work are being done on the Internet today without the benefit of prepublication peer review. The scholar in me got it, however: influential as that intellectual work online may be, what is it worth within the academy's systems of accounting? What kind of value can it have, unless behind it stands some form of peer review, the gold standard of scholarly merit?

In thinking through that disjuncture in my responses, I came to understand there to exist a profound mismatch between conventional peer review as it has been practiced since the mid-twentieth century and the structures of intellectual engagement on the Internet.[1] This should not be terribly surprising; all our assumptions about scholarly communication since the eighteenth century have been predicated on the print technologies alongside and in conjunction with which they arose. These technologies operate under the conditions of certain kinds of material scarcity that, far from being hindrances, in fact give them their authority. That same relationship between scarcity and authority was operative in manuscript culture; a text's authenticity derived from the trustworthiness of its source, the hand that produced it. In print, that sense of authority transferred from the hand to the publisher's imprimatur, which similarly served as a warranty of sorts, authorizing the book's content as being complete, correct, and stable.[2] Within the scholarly universe, however, the value of a publisher's imprimatur is not simply about that authorizing gesture but is instead directly tied to selectivity, to using the scarce resources of print in the wisest possible way. The value of a journal's name or a press's imprint varies directly with the perception that the texts it publishes are the "best"; perhaps perversely, that sense of bestness derives in significant part from the number of texts that the journal or press rejects.

The disjuncture between this model and Internet-based publishing is immediately obvious: while access to a publisher's imprimatur is intentionally limited in print, anyone with the right hardware, software, and network connection could simply publish anything online. This promiscuity is precisely what makes the open web suspect for many academics, and the usual response of those who seek to defend digital publication is to point to those online venues that employ traditional peer review and are thus equally selective as many print publishers. The problem, however, with this kind of online reproduction of the systems that govern print publishing is that the Internet operates within a completely different set of technological affordances, which have in turn helped to foster a very different understanding of the creation of authority. In contrast with print, the scarcities involved in Internet-based publishing are not material; they are, rather, shortages of time and attention—shortages, in other words, that are experienced by those who are looking for information rather than by those who provide it.

As a result, over the course of the last twenty years, the publisher-derived imprimatur declaring selectivity has gradually become less important online than the imprimatur that is conferred by community. Within the current structures of Internet-based communication, in other words, it is far less important to a given reader that some authorizing producer has declared a text to be of value—and even less important that this entity has done so by selecting this text from numerous other rejected possibilities—than it is that someone whom the reader knows, even if only by reputation, has read and recommended the text. This community imprimatur manifests itself most substantively as links that direct one's own circle of readers to valuable information elsewhere, but the relatively recent rise of the "like" button indicates the desire for and pervasiveness of lightweight community-based recommendations on the web. Liking and linking both enact a new kind of selectivity in creating a mode of community-based authorization, a selectivity that is imposed at the point of consumption rather than production.

This shift in the locus of selectivity, between the publisher's role in creating a text's authority in print and the role of communities in creating that authority online, poses key challenges for scholarship as it begins to move into networked spaces. These challenges are most pressing for the forms of scholarship that must make use of these networked environments as well as those that are attempting to understand those environments. Fields such as the digital humanities, digital media studies, and Internet research must take the lead in reconsidering their reliance on conventionally determined and awarded imprimatur and instead consider the ways that field-based community models of authorization might more accurately reflect the innovations taking place in the field. After all, the principle of exclusion on which conventional peer review relies for its authority is part of a cluster of well-established disciplinary practices, practices that (in a most Foucauldian manner) not only create a set of accepted procedures and methods through which scholars in a field do their work but also draw the borders of acceptability—of field, of method, of knowledge—as an exercise of power. The self-policing nature of peer review, coupled with its reliance on the opinions of a very small number of usually well-established scholars, runs the risk of producing an ingrained conservatism, a risk-averse attitude toward innovation, and a resistance to new or controversial approaches.[3]

Crowdsourcing presents the potential to correct for the kind of conservatism that exclusivity can foster. Just as many eyes make all bugs shallow, as the saying has it, so many readers might make the value of a piece of scholarship more apparent. Twenty readers, with twenty different perspectives, might be able to see what two to three well-established readers cannot. Even more importantly, those twenty readers, if required not simply to respond to the work under review but to engage with one another in the process, will push one another to deeper understandings not just of the objects of their discussion but of the broader field with which their scholarship engages. In other words, crowdsourced review can improve on traditional review practices not just by adding more readers but by placing those readers into conversation with one another and with the author, deepening the relationship between the text and its audience.

It is important, on the one hand, to distinguish between the popular conception of crowdsourcing, with its sense that participation is open to "just anybody," and the kinds of crowdsourcing that can be accomplished within a preexisting community of practice, which Katherine Rowe has referred to as "our-crowd sourcing."[4] Getting the members of a scholarly field into open dialogue with one another around the evaluation of scholarship offers the possibility, as Rowe and I have explored elsewhere, of airing methodological or theoretical assumptions and biases rather than allowing them to remain covert points of contention within fields.[5] On the other hand, new forms of networked communication have raised questions about the relationship between expertise and credentials, suggesting that in many cases readers from outside our narrowly defined fields, and even outside the academy, may bring much-needed perspectives to our work. It's easy to see how open reviewing can benefit interdisciplinary work by provoking discussion among scholars from multiple disciplinary perspectives in the evaluation of a project. Beyond such obvious conversations across scholarly communities, however, many of us would benefit from discussions with readers located outside the academy. Most of our fields, and the work we produce within them, would benefit from the kinds of aeration that exposure to other perspectives can provide; having our work discussed by readers with different forms of expertise than our own can only help us produce more robust projects.

New work being done in and on the digital not only *can* but *should* transgress the existing borders of knowledge, as these fields wrestle with new methods, new formats, and new affordances for scholarly work. The guiding principle for these fields, like that of the network technologies that facilitate them, should be openness. The Internet operates as an end-to-end network, in which any packet of data is treated exactly like any other, leaving it to the endpoints of the network to differentiate among data types, figuring out how each should be produced and used.[6] Digital fields should explore what such an end-to-end model might hold for them; if the communication network of the digital humanities were patterned after such an open principle and all scholarship were openly transmitted through it, might we find a way to allow selectivity to be exercised at the network's endpoint, with the consumers of scholarship?

This is of course the "publish, then filter" model that Clay Shirky has argued is most conducive to communication in a peer-based network, a mode of open communication that not only relocates the point of selectivity from the publisher to the reader but that also suggests, as Chris Anderson has pointed out, that network-based communication presents scholars with a radical new understanding of the notion of the "peer."[7] This understanding shifted once at the birth of scholarly communication, when the delegation of the royal imprimatur from the crown to early scholarly associations like the Royal Society of London began to press the dominant conception of the "peer" from "peer of the realm" to "scholarly peer," a colleague whose status derived less from social privilege than from earned credentials.[8] Today, that notion is shifting again, as the meritocratic notion of the peer gives way in the age of the Internet to an understanding of a peer as any node connected to a network. While I hope to avoid being overly utopian in assessing the democratizing potential of this shift, I do want us to consider how this new notion of the peer might affect scholarly communication. What would happen if we were to recognize that all members of a scholarly community—all of the nodes on our particular disciplinary or interdisciplinary network—have potentially valuable contributions to make to the development and evaluation of our work? What if we opened that network even further, to all interested readers inside and outside our fields, inside and outside the academy? What kinds of community-based filtering would such recognition make possible?

More importantly, perhaps, we also need to ask how we can get such communal processes of evaluation to *count as* evaluation in the academic sense. As academic processes of credentialing have become increasingly tied to the imprimatur granted by publisher selectivity, it has become, in turn, increasingly difficult to imagine suitable alternatives. And while it suits my inner blogger to dismiss this kind of concern—throw open the floodgates, I'd like to say; let a thousand flowers bloom;

force the traditionalists to sort the problem out for themselves—I know full well the risks that such an attitude presents for the future of the field. Scholars working in digital fields are already subject to personnel-based processes (hiring, tenure, promotion) overseen and conducted by faculty and administrators who often do not see the value of the new forms of scholarship that they are producing. The imprimatur granted by traditional peer review has often been an important recourse for those scholars whose work is controversial or defies traditional form. And yet, if that mode of peer review doesn't provide digital scholarship with the most suitable form of evaluation, the digital humanities must take control in developing a system of evaluation that does suit our needs.

Moreover, I would argue that we must develop means of articulating, clearly and compellingly, the value of open peer review—both the importance of these processes for the free and open exchange among peers and the kinds of data that such processes can provide as a means of evaluating the reception of the scholarship under consideration. As I have recently suggested elsewhere, tenure and promotion committees must find ways to understand the forms of assessment that take place around and in digital scholarship, but those of us engaging in that digital scholarship must help make our modes of assessment comprehensible to those committees, to articulate to them how the forms of review that take place at the network's endpoints function and how their results might be interpreted.[9]

In imagining ways that scholars in the digital humanities might support the robust evaluation of their work in open formats, we will need to consider a number of somewhat different cases: there are differences between the requirements for review of traditional textual scholarship published in digital environments, such as that in open access journals and online monograph series, as opposed to the review of work that does not take the form of textual argumentation, such as archival projects or multimodal work, or the review, post hoc, of DIY-published online material such as scholarly blogs. The latter two cases obviously cry out for new modes of open review, as they concern work that is nearly always published, in the sense of having been made public, without being subjected to prepublication peer review and very often without the benefit of a publisher's imprimatur. But in all three of these cases, institutional acceptance of the publications for credentialing purposes will require making visible what John Guillory has referred to as the immanent scene of judgment—laying bare for future evaluators the mechanisms by which this material has been judged by experts within the field—and finding ways to translate that immanent judgment into information that can be comprehended at the sites of review that move further and further outside the field (the department, the college, the university).

Open review online provides a number of mechanisms through which this immanent scene of review can be examined; we already have the capacity to gather a lot of data about how digital publications are received and responded to, including things like the number of page views, of visitors, and of inbound links. We have not yet, however, found robust ways to put this kind of data to work in assessing the impact or importance of an online publication or to connect these use-metrics to peer review in a nonreductive fashion. Take something as seemingly simple as web traffic. There are many fine-grained ways of slicing this data (including entrances, exits, average time on page, and bounce rate, not to mention a metric as basic and yet amorphous as the "unique visit"), but perhaps unsurprisingly most of the readily available analytical tools are focused on the ultimate goal of "conversion": the transformation of a visit into a sale. Digital scholarly publishing will require rethinking the ways that such traffic is measured and assessed, moving from a focus on conversion to a focus on engagement—and engagement can be quite difficult to measure. A visitor to a substantive scholarly blog post, for instance, who simply snagged the post in Instapaper and moved on but then later sat and read the article at leisure would not appear to have had a significant engagement with the text when in fact that engagement could well have been far more in depth than the average. We need far better markers for that kind of engagement in order for basic traffic to become legible.

This kind of data must of course be employed in review processes with great care; many of our colleagues in the natural sciences would no doubt warn us about the dangers posed by a failure to recognize or properly contextualize the somewhat arbitrary nature of metrics such as journal impact factor. Certainly the value of scholarship in the humanities cannot be reduced to a numerical representation. We will also need to develop safeguards against certain kinds of gaming the system, such that the metrics we obtain are as nonmanipulable as possible. Nonetheless, there is a wealth of data that we're not currently putting to good use in these review processes, relying instead on the even more reductive metric of publisher imprimatur that results from traditional review.

Moreover, in addition to the quantitative data that online publications generate, there is also rich qualitative data about how they're received. The discussions on texts published in open review processes are available for examination; in networks such as MediaCommons that encourage or require commenters to sign their names to their responses, the authority that the commenters bring to the discussion can be assessed (avoiding the sneaking sense that participants in open review processes online could be "just anybody"). Similarly, inbound links, rather than simply providing numerical evidence of citation, often result from substantive discussion of the project in question. Of course, examining those discussions requires actual reading, a prospect that, as I have noted elsewhere, may be an uphill climb.[10] However, at least at the stage in which reviews for tenure and promotion move outside the subfield to the department as a whole, reviewers *should* be reading this material and, if not directly assessing the work, certainly assessing the assessment, seeing how readers directly engaged with the work have responded to it. Just as external reviewers' letters bring expert opinion to bear in the tenure process, so the results of open peer review processes can demonstrate expert judgment as it is brought to bear on the work under consideration.

There are undoubtedly other forms of data that we should be gathering about work published online; Michael Jensen, in "Authority 3.0," presents a lengthy list of the kinds of data that might in the future be compiled in computational assessments of scholarly reputation.[11] And there are richer things that should be done with that data—the kinds of analysis for which scholars in digital humanities, digital media studies, and Internet research are ideally trained. We could, for instance, use the skill set we bring to our research to perform sophisticated network analysis on the communities that surround our digitally published texts, or semantic analysis of the discussions that they inspire. And we could, most importantly, find ways to communicate the results of that analysis in forms that would be comprehensible to members of review committees and administrators from outside the field. This solution is part computational, as Jensen argues, but also crucially qualitative and interpretive, not simply a boiling down of authority to metrics but a means of explicating what it is we value in scholarship and how we know when it has succeeded.

Scholars in the digital humanities, digital media studies, and Internet research are poised to make a profound contribution to the development of a better model of peer review, one that works with, rather than against, the Internet's open architecture and social modes of producing authority—but only if we are willing to resist the modes of discipline that we have inherited from other fields, to insist that our methods of review must more appropriately resemble and make use of our scholarly methods, and to develop the tools and modes of analysis necessary to communicate the authority generated by such review to those outside the field.

NOTES

1. For a more fully elaborated version of this argument, see chapter 1, "Peer Review," in Kathleen Fitzpatrick, *Planned Obsolescence*.
2. See Simone, especially 241.
3. See, for instance, Thurner and Hanel, whose study finds that a small number of poor referees in a conventional peer review system results in a significant reduction of the quality of work selected for publication and a tilt toward the "average." See also Dacey.
4. See Cohen.
5. See Fitzpatrick and Rowe, 139.
6. See Lessig, 44.
7. See Shirky, 98; Anderson.
8. See Biagioli, 18.
9. See Fitzpatrick, "Peer Review, Judgment, and Reading."
10. See Fitzpatrick, "Peer Review, Judgment, and Reading."
11. See Jensen, 304–5.

BIBLIOGRAPHY

Anderson, Chris. "Wisdom of the Crowds." *Nature* 2006. http://www.nature.com/nature/peerreview/debate/nature04992.html.

Biagioli, Mario. "From Book Censorship to Academic Peer Review." *Emergences* 12, no. 1 (2002): 11–45.

Cohen, Patricia. "Scholars Test Web Alternative to Peer Review." *New York Times,* August 24, 2010. http://www.nytimes.com/2010/08/24/arts/24peer.html.

Dacey, James. "Peer Review Highly Sensitive to Poor Refereeing, Claim Researchers." *PhysicsWorld.com.* September 9, 2010. http://physicsworld.com/cws/article/news/43691.

Fitzpatrick, Kathleen. "Peer Review, Judgment, and Reading." *Profession* 2011. Forthcoming.

———. *Planned Obsolescence: Publishing, Technology, and the Future of the Academy.* MediaCommons, 2009. http://mediacommons.futureofthebook.org/mcpress/plannedobsolescence/.

Fitzpatrick, Kathleen, and Katherine Rowe. "Keywords for Open Review." *LOGOS: The Journal of the World Book Community* 21, no. 3–4 (2010): 133–41.

Guillory, John. "Evaluating Scholarship in the Humanities: Principles and Procedures." *ADE Bulletin* 137 (Spring 2005): 18–33.

Jensen, Michael. "Authority 3.0: Friend or Foe to Scholars?" *Journal of Scholarly Publishing* 39, no. 1 (2007): 297–307.

Lessig, Lawrence. *Code: Version 2.0.* New York: Basic Books, 2006.

Shirky, Clay. *Here Comes Everybody: The Power of Organizing Without Organizations.* New York: Penguin, 2008.

Simone, Raffaelle. "The Body of the Text." In *The Future of the Book,* edited by Geoffrey Nunberg, 239–51. Berkeley: University of California Press, 1996.

Thurner, Stefan, and Rudolf Hanel. "Peer-review in a World with Rational Scientists: Toward Selection of the Average." *arXiv* 1008.4324 (2010). http://arxiv.org/abs/1008.4324.

Trending: The Promises and the Challenges of Big Social Data

LEV MANOVICH

Today, the term "big data" is often used in popular media, business, computer science, and the computer industry. For instance, in June 2008, *Wired* magazine opened its special section on "The Petabyte Age" by stating, "Our ability to capture, warehouse, and understand massive amounts of data is changing science, medicine, business, and technology. As our collection of facts and figures grows, so will the opportunity to find answers to fundamental questions." In February 2010, *The Economist* started its special report "Data, Data Everywhere" with the phrase "the industrial revolution of data" (coined by computer scientist Joe Hellerstein) and then went to note that "the effect is being felt everywhere, from business to science, from government to the arts."

Discussions in popular media usually do not define big data in qualitative terms. However, in the computer industry, the term has a more precise meaning: "Big Data is a term applied to data sets whose size is beyond the ability of commonly used software tools to capture, manage, and process the data within a tolerable elapsed time. Big data sizes are a constantly moving target currently ranging from a few dozen terabytes to many petabytes of data in a single data set" ("Big Data").

Since its formation in 2008, the Office of Digital Humanities at the National Endowment for Humanities (NEH) has been systematically creating grant opportunities to help humanists work with large data sets. The following statement from a 2011 grant competition organized by the NEH together with a number of other research agencies in the United States, Canada, the UK, and the Netherlands provides an excellent description of what is at stake: "The idea behind the Digging into Data Challenge is to address how 'big data' changes the research landscape for the humanities and social sciences. Now that we have massive databases of materials used by scholars in the humanities and social sciences—ranging from digitized books, newspapers, and music to transactional data like web searches, sensor data or cell phone records—what new, computationally-based research methods might we apply? As the world becomes increasingly digital, new techniques will be needed to search, analyze, and understand these everyday materials" ("Digging into Data

Challenge"). The projects funded by the 2009 Digging into Data Challenge and the earlier NEH 2008 Humanities High Performance Computing Grant Program have begun to map the landscape of data-intensive humanities. They include analysis of the correspondence of European thinkers between 1500 and 1800; maps, texts, and images associated with nineteenth-century railroads in the United States; criminal trial accounts (data size: 127 million words); ancient texts; detailed 3-D maps of ancient Rome; and the research by my lab to develop tools for the analysis and visualization of large image and video data sets.

At the moment of this writing, the largest data sets being used in digital humanities projects are much smaller than big data used by scientists; in fact, if we use industry's definition, almost none of them qualify as big data (i.e., the work can be done on desktop computers using standard software, as opposed to supercomputers). But this gap will eventually disappear when humanists start working with born-digital user-generated content (such as billions of photos on Flickr), online user communication (comments about photos), user created metadata (tags), and transaction data (when and from where the photos were uploaded). This web content and data is infinitely larger than all already digitized cultural heritage; and, in contrast to the fixed number of historical artifacts, it grows constantly. (I expect that the number of photos uploaded to Facebook daily is larger than all artifacts stored in all the world's museums.)

In this chapter, I want to address some of the theoretical and practical issues raised by the possibility of using massive amounts of such social and cultural data in the humanities and social sciences. My observations are based on my own experience working since 2007 with large cultural data sets at the Software Studies Initiative (softwarestudies.com) at the University of California, San Diego (UCSD). The issues that I will discuss include the differences between "deep data" about a few people and "surface data" about many people, getting access to transactional data, and the new "data analysis divide" between data experts and researchers without training in computer science.

The emergence of social media in the middle of the 2000s created opportunities to study social and cultural processes and dynamics in new ways. For the first time, we can follow imaginations, opinions, ideas, and feelings of hundreds of millions of people. We can see the images and the videos they create and comment on, monitor the conversations they are engaged in, read their blog posts and tweets, navigate their maps, listen to their track lists, and follow their trajectories in physical space. And we don't need to ask their permission to do this, since they themselves encourage us to do so by making all of this data public.

In the twentieth century, the study of the social and the cultural relied on two types of data: "surface data" about lots of people and "deep data" about the few individuals or small groups.[1] The first approach was used in all disciplines that adapted quantitative methods (i.e., statistical, mathematical, or computational techniques for analyzing data). The relevant fields include quantitative schools of sociology, economics, political science, communication studies, and marketing research.

The second approach was used in humanities fields such as literary studies, art history, film studies, and history. It was also used in qualitative schools in psychology (for instance, psychoanalysis and Gestalt psychology), sociology (Wilhelm Dilthey, Max Weber, Georg Simmel), anthropology, and ethnography. The examples of relevant methods are hermeneutics, participant observation, thick description, semiotics, and close reading.

For example, a quantitative sociologist worked with census data that covered most of the country's citizens. However, this data was collected only every ten years, and it represented each individual only on a macro level, living out her or his opinions, feelings, tastes, moods, and motivations ("U.S. Census Bureau"). In contrast, a psychologist would be engaged with a single patient for years, tracking and interpreting exactly the kind of data that the census did not capture.

In between these two methodologies of surface data and deep data were statistics and the concept of sampling. By carefully choosing her sample, a researcher could expand certain types of data about the few into the knowledge about the many. For example, starting in the 1950s, the Nielsen Company collected television viewing data in a sample of American homes (via diaries and special devices connected to television sets in twenty-five thousand homes) and then used this sample data to predict television ratings for the whole country (i.e., percentages of the population which watched particular shows). But the use of samples to learn about larger populations had many limitations.

For instance, in the example of Nielson's television ratings, the small sample did not tell us anything about the actual hour-by-hour, day-to-day patterns of television viewing of every individual or every family outside of this sample. Maybe certain people watched only news the whole day; others only tuned in to concerts; others had the television on but never paid attention to it; still others happened to prefer the shows that got very low ratings by the sample group, and so on. The sample stats could not tell us anything about this. It was also possible that a particular television program would get zero shares because nobody in the sample audience happened to watch it—and in fact, this occurred more than once ("Nielsen Ratings").

Imagine that we want to scale up a low-resolution image using a digital image editor like Photoshop. For example, we start with a ten-by-ten pixel image (one hundred pixels in total) and resize it to one thousand by one thousand (one million pixels in total). We do not get any new details—only larger pixels. This is exactly what happens when you use a small sample to predict the behavior of a much larger population. A "pixel" that originally represented one person comes to represent one thousand people who are all assumed to behave in exactly the same way.

The rise of social media, along with new computational tools that can process massive amounts of data, makes possible a fundamentally new approach to the study of human beings and society. We no longer have to choose between data size and data depth. We can study exact trajectories formed by billions of cultural expressions, experiences, texts, and links. The detailed knowledge and insights that before could only be reached about a few people can now be reached about many more people. In 2007, Bruno Latour summarized these developments as follows: "The precise forces that mould our subjectivities and the precise characters that furnish our imaginations are all open to inquiries by the social sciences. It is as if the inner workings of private worlds have been pried open because their inputs and outputs have become thoroughly traceable." (Latour).

Two years earlier, in 2005, PhD student Nathan Eagle at the MIT Media Lab was already thinking along the similar lines. He and his advisor Alex Pentland put up a website called Reality Mining ("MIT Media Lab: Reality Mining") and described how the new possibilities of capturing details of peoples' daily behavior and communication via mobile phones could create sociology in the twenty-first century ("Sociology in the 21st Century"). To put this idea into practice, they distributed Nokia phones with special software to one hundred MIT students who then used these phones for nine months, which generated approximately sixty years of "continuous data on daily human behavior." Eagle and Pentland published a number of articles based on the analysis of data they collected. Today, many more computer scientists are working with large social data sets; they call their new field "social computing." According to the definition provided by the website of the Third IEEE International Conference on Social Computing (2011), social computing refers to "computational facilitation of social studies and human social dynamics as well as design and use of information and communication technologies that consider social context" ("Social Computing").

Now let us consider Google search. Google's algorithms analyze billions of web pages, plus PDF, Word documents, Excel spreadsheets, Flash files, plain text files, and since 2009 Facebook and Twitter content.[2] Currently, Google does not offer any service that would allow a user to analyze patterns directly in all of this data the way Google Insights for Search does with search queries and Google's Ngram Viewer does with digitized books, but it is certainly technologically conceivable. Imagine being able to study the collective intellectual space of the whole planet, seeing how ideas emerge, diffuse, burst, and die and how they get linked together and so on—across the data set estimated to contain at least 14.55 billion pages (de Kunder).

To quote *Wired*'s "The Petabyte Age" issue again, "In the era of big data, more isn't just more. More is different."

Does all this sound exciting? It certainly does. So what might be wrong with these arguments? Are we indeed witnessing the collapse of the deep-data/surface-data divide? If so, could this collapse open a new era for social and cultural research?

I am going to discuss four objections to the optimistic vision I have just presented. These objections do not imply that we should not use new data sources about human culture and human social life or not analyze them with computational tools.

I strongly believe that we should do this. But we need to carefully understand what is possible in practice as opposed to in principle. We also need to be clear about what skills digital humanists need to take advantage of the new scale of human data.

1. Only social media companies have access to really large social data sets, especially transactional data. An anthropologist working for Facebook or a sociologist working for Google will have access to data that the rest of the scholarly community will not.

A researcher can obtain some of this data through APIs provided by most social media services and the largest media online retailers (YouTube, Flickr, Amazon, etc.). An API (Application Programming Interface) is a set of commands that can be used by a user program to retrieve the data stored in a company's databases. For example, the Flickr API can be used to download all photos in a particular group and also to retrieve information about the size of each photo, available comments, geolocation, the list of people who favored this photo, and so on ("Flickr API Methods").

The public APIs provided by social media and social network companies do not give all data that these companies themselves are capturing about the users. Still, you can certainly do very interesting new cultural and social research by collecting data via APIs and then analyzing it—if you are good at programming, statistics, and other data analysis methods. (In my lab, we have recently used Flickr API to download one hundred and sixty-seven thousand images from the "Art Now" Flickr group, and we are currently working to analyze these images to create a "map" of "user-generated art.")

Although APIs themselves are not complicated, all truly large-scale research projects that use the data with these APIs so far have been undertaken by researchers in computer science. A good way to follow the work in this area is to look at papers presented at yearly World Wide Web conferences (WWW2009 and WWW2010). Recent papers have investigated how information spreads on Twitter (data: 100 million tweets, Kwak, Lee, Park, and Moon), what qualities are shared by the most favored photos on Flickr (data: 2.2 million photos), how geotagged Flickr photos are distributed spatially (data: 35 million photos, Crandall, Backstrom, Huttenlocher, and Kleinberg), and how user-generated videos on YouTube compare with similar videos on Daum, the most popular UGC (user-generated content) service in Korea (data: 2.1 million videos, Cha, Kwak, Rodriguez, Ahn, and Moon).

It is worth pointing out that even researchers working inside the largest social media companies can't simply access all the data collected by different services in a company. Some time ago, I went to a talk by a researcher from Sprint, one of the largest U.S. phone companies, who was analyzing the relations between geographic addresses of phone users and how frequently they called other people. He did have access to this data for all Sprint customers (around fifty million). However, when he was asked why he did not use other data collected by Sprint, such as instant messages and apps usage, he explained that these services are operated by a different part of the company and that the laws prohibit employees to have access to all of this data together. He pointed out that like any other company, Sprint does not want to get into lawsuits for breach of privacy and pay huge fines and damage their brand image; therefore they are being very careful in terms of who gets to look at what data. You don't have to believe this, but I do. For example, do you think Google enjoys all the lawsuits about Street View? If you were running a business, would you risk losing hundreds of millions of dollars and badly damaging your company image?

2. We need to be careful of reading communications over social networks and digital footprints as "authentic." Peoples' posts, tweets, uploaded photographs, comments, and other types of online participation are not transparent windows into their selves; instead, they are usually carefully curated and systematically managed (Ellison, Heino, and Gibbs).

Imagine that you wanted to study the cultural imagination of people in Russia in the second part of 1930s and you only looked at newspapers, books, films, and other cultural texts, which of course all went through government censors before being approved for publication. You would conclude that indeed everybody in Russia loved Lenin and Stalin, was very happy, and was ready to sacrifice his or her life to build communism. You may say that this is an unfair comparison and that it would be more appropriate to look instead at people's diaries. Yes, indeed it would be better; however, if you were living in Russia in that period and you knew that any night a black car might stop in front of your house and you would be taken away and probably shot soon thereafter, would you really commit all your true thoughts about Stalin and government to paper? In 1993, the famous Russian poet Osip Mandelstam wrote a short poem that criticized Stalin only indirectly without even naming him, and he paid for this with his life ("Stalin Epigram").

Today, if you live in a pretty large part of the world, you know that the government is likely to scan your electronic communications systematically ("Internet Censorship by country"). In some countries, citizens may be arrested simply for visiting a wrong website. In these countries, you will be careful about what you are saying online. Some of us live in other countries where a statement against the government does not automatically put you in prison, and therefore people feel they can be more open. In other words, it does not matter if the government is tracking us or not; what is important is what it can do with this information. (I grew up in the Soviet Union in the 1970s and then moved to the United States; based on my experience living in both societies, in this respect the difference between them is very big. In the USSR, we never made any political jokes on the phone and only discussed politics with close friends at home.)

Now let us assume that we are living in a country where we are highly unlikely to be prosecuted for occasional antigovernment remarks. But still, how authentic are all the rest of our online expressions? As Ervin Goffman and other sociologists pointed out a long time ago, people always construct their public presence, carefully shaping how they present themselves to others, and social media is certainly not an exception to this ("Ervin Goffman"), though the degree of this public self-construction varies. For instance, most of us tend to do less self-censorship and editing on Facebook than in the profiles on dating sites or in a job interview. Others carefully curate their profile pictures to construct an image they want to project. (If you scan your friends' Facebook profile pictures, you are likely to find a big range). But just as we do in all other areas of our everyday lives, we exercise some control all the time when we are online—what we say, what we upload, what we show as our interests, and so on.

Again, this does not mean that we can't do interesting research by analyzing larger numbers of tweets, Facebook photos, YouTube videos, or any other social media site—we just have to keep in mind that all these data are not a transparent window into peoples' imaginations, intentions, motifs, opinions, and ideas. It's more appropriate to think of it as an interface people present to the world—that is, a particular view that shows only some parts of their actual lives and imaginations and may also include other fictional data designed to project a particular image (Ellison, Heino, and Gibbs).

3. Is it really true that "we no longer have to choose between data size and data depth," as I stated? Yes and no. Imagine this hypothetical scenario. On the one side, we have ethnographers who are spending years inside a particular community. On another side, we have computer scientists who never meet people in this community but have access to their social media and digital footprints—daily spatial trajectories captured with GPS and all video recorded by surveillance cameras, online and offline conversations, uploaded media, comments, likes, and so on. According to my earlier argument, both parties have "deep data," but the advantage of a computer science team is that they can capture this data about hundreds of millions of people as opposed to only small community.

How plausible is this argument? For thousands of years, we would learn about other people exclusively through personal interactions. Later, letter writing became an important new mechanism for building personal (especially romantic) relationships. In the twenty-first century, we can have access to a whole new set of machine-captured traces and records of individuals' activities. Given that this situation is very new, it is to be expected that some people will find it hard to accept the concept that such machine records can be as meaningful in helping us to understand communities and individuals as face-to-face interaction. They will argue that whatever the quality of the data sources, data analysis ideas, and algorithms used by computer scientists, they will never arrive at the same insights and understanding of people and dynamics in the community as ethnographers. They will say that even the most comprehensive social data about people which can be automatically captured via cameras, sensors, computer devices (phones, game consoles), and web servers can't be used to arrive at the same "deep" knowledge.

It is possible to defend both positions, but what if both are incorrect? I believe that in our hypothetical scenario, ethnographers and computer scientists have access to *different* kinds of data. Therefore they are likely to ask different questions, notice different patterns, and arrive at different insights.

This does not mean that the new computer-captured "deep surface" of data is less "deep" than the data obtained through long-term personal contact. In terms of the sheer number of "data points," it is likely to be much deeper. However, many of these data points are quite different than the data points available to ethnographers.

For instance, if you are physically present in some situation, you may notice some things that you would not notice if you were watching a high-res video of the same situation. But at the same time, if you do computer analysis of this video you may find patterns you would not notice if you were on the scene only physically. Of course, people keep coming up with new techniques that combine on-the-scene physical presence and computer and network-assisted techniques. For a good example of such innovation, see the Valley of the Khans project at UCSD. In this project, photos captured by small unmanned aerial vehicles sent out by an archeological team moving around a large area in Mongolia are immediately uploaded to a special *National Geographic* site, exploration.nationalgeographic.com. Thousands of people immediately start tagging these photos for interesting details, which tells archeologists what to look for on the ground ("Help Find Genghis Khan's Tomb").

The questions of what can be discovered and understood with computer analysis of social and cultural data versus traditional qualitative methods are particularly important for the digital humanities. My hypothetical example used data about social behavior, but the "data" can also be eighteenth-century letters of European thinkers, nineteenth-century maps and texts about railroads, hundreds of thousands of images uploaded by users to a Flickr group, or any other set of cultural artifacts. When we start reading these artifacts with computers, humanists become very nervous.

I often experience this reaction when I lecture about digital humanities research done in my lab Software Studies Initiative at UCSD (softwarestudies.com). The lab focuses on the development of methods and tools for exploration and the research of massive cultural visual data, both digitized visual artifacts and contemporary visual and interactive media ("Software Studies: Cultural Analytics"). We use digital image analysis and new visualization techniques to explore cultural patterns in large sets of images and video: user-generated video, visual art, magazine covers and pages, graphic design, photographs, feature films, cartoons, and motion graphics. Examples of the visual data sets we have analyzed include 20,000 pages of *Science* and *Popular Science* magazines issues published between 1872 and 1922, 780 paintings by Van Gogh, 4,535 covers of *Time* magazine (1923–2009), and 1,074,790 pages ("One Million Manga Pages").

In our experience, almost every time we analyze and then visualize a new image or video collection, or even a single time-based media artifact (a music video, a feature film, a video recording of a game play), we find some surprising new patterns. This applies equally to collections of visual artifacts about which we had few a priori assumptions (for instance, one hundred and sixty-seven thousand images uploaded by users to "Art Now" Flickr) and artifacts that already were studied in detail by multiple authors.

As an example of the latter, I will discuss a visualization of the film *The Eleventh Year* by a famous twentieth-century Russian director Dziga Vertov (Manovich, "Visualizing Large Image Collections for Humanities Research"). The visualization itself can be downloaded from our Flickr account (Manovich, "Motion Studies: Vertov's The Eleventh Year").

My sources were the digitized copy of the film provided by Austrian Film Museum and the information about all shot boundaries created manually by a museum researcher. (With other moving image sources, we use the open source software Shotdetect, which automatically detects most shot boundaries in a typical film.) The visualization uses only the first and last frame of every shot in the film, disregarding all other frames. Each shot is represented as a column: the first frame is on the top, and the last frame is right below.

"Vertov" is a neologism invented by the director who adapted it as his last name early in his career. It comes from the Russian verb *vertet*, which means "to rotate something." "Vertov" may refer to the basic motion involved in filming in the 1920s—rotating the handle of a camera—and also the dynamism of film language developed by Vertov who, along with a number of other Russian and European artists and designers and photographers working in that decade, wanted to defamiliarize reality by using dynamic diagonal compositions and shooting from unusual points of view. However, my visualization suggests a very different picture of Vertov. Almost every shot of *The Eleventh Year* starts and ends with practically the same composition and subject. In other words, the shots are largely static. Going back to the actual film and studying these shots further, we find that some of them are indeed completely static—such as the close-ups of people's faces looking in various directions without moving. Other shots employ a static camera that frames some movement—such as working machines, or workers at work—but the movement is localized completely inside the frame (in other words, the objects and human figures do not cross the view framed by the camera.) Of course, we may recall that a number of shots in Vertov's most famous film, *Man with a Movie Camera* (1929), were designed specifically as opposites: shooting from a moving car meant that the subjects were constantly crossing the camera view. But even in this most experimental of Vertov's films, such shots constitute a very small part of a film.

One of the typical responses to my lectures is that computers can't lead to the same nuanced interpretation as traditional humanities methods and that they can't help understand deep meanings of artworks. My response is that we don't want to replace human experts with computers. As I will describe in the hypothetical scenario of working with one million YouTube documentary-style videos, we can use computers to quickly explore massive visual data sets and then select the objects for closer manual analysis. While computer-assisted examination of massive cultural data sets typically reveals new patterns in this data that even the best manual "close reading" would miss—and of course, even an army of humanists will not be able to carefully close read massive data sets in the first place—a human is still needed to make sense of these patterns.

Ultimately, completely automatic analysis of social and cultural data will not produce meaningful results today because computers still have a limited ability to understand the context of texts, images, video, and other media. (Recall the mistakes made by the IBM Watson artificial intelligence computer when it competed on the television quiz show *Jeopardy!* in early 2011 ["Watson (computer)"].)

Ideally, we want to combine the human ability to understand and interpret—which computers can't completely match yet—and the computer's ability to analyze massive data sets using algorithms we create. Let us imagine the following research scenario. You want to study documentary-type YouTube videos created by users in country X during the period Y, and you were able to determine that the relevant data set contains one million videos. So what do you do next? Computational analysis would be perfect as the next step to map the overall "data landscape": identify the most typical and most unique videos; automatically cluster all videos into a number of categories; find all videos that follow the same strategies, and so on. At the end of this analytical stage, you may be able to reduce the set of one million videos to one hundred videos, which represent it in a more comprehensive way than if you simply used a standard sampling procedure. For instance, your reduced set may contain both the most typical and the most unique videos in various categories. Now that you have a manageable number of videos, you can actually start watching them. If you find some video to be particularly interesting, you can then ask the computer to fetch more videos that have similar characteristics, so you can look at all of them. At any point in the analysis, you can go back and forth between particular videos, groups of videos, and the whole collection of one million videos, experimenting with new categories and groupings. And just as Google Analytics allows you to select any subset of data about your website and look at its patterns over time (number of viewed pages) and space (where do visitors come from), you will be able to select any subset of the videos and see various patterns across this subsets.

This is my vision of how we can study large cultural data sets, whether these are billions of videos on YouTube or billions of photos on Flickr, or smaller samples of semiprofessional or professional creative productions such as one hundred million images on deviantart.com or two hundred and fifty thousand design portfolios on coroflot.com. Since 2007, our lab has been gradually working on visualization techniques that would enable such research exploration.

4. Imagine that you have software that combines large-scale automatic data analysis and interactive visualization. (We are gradually working to integrate various tools that we designed in our lab to create such a system. See "Cultural Analytics Research Environment.") If you also have skills to examine individual artifacts and the openness to ask new questions, the software will help you to take

research in many new exiting directions. However, there are also many kinds of interesting questions that require expertise in computer science, statistics, and data mining—something that social and humanities researchers typically don't have. This is another serious objection to the optimistic view of big data-driven humanities and social research I presented earlier.

The explosion of data and the emergence of computational data analysis as the key scientific and economic approach in contemporary societies create new kinds of divisions. Specifically, people and organizations are divided into three categories: those who create data (both consciously and by leaving digital footprints), those who have the means to collect it, and those who have the expertise to analyze it. The first group includes pretty much everybody in the world who is using the web or mobile phones; the second group is smaller; and the third group is much smaller still. We can refer to these three groups as the new "data classes" of our "big-data society" (my neologisms).

At Google, computer scientists are working on the algorithms that scan a web page a user is on currently and select which ads to display. At YouTube, computer scientists work on algorithms that automatically show a list of other videos deemed to be relevant to one you are currently watching. At BlogPulse, computer scientists work on algorithms that allow companies to use sentiment analysis to study the feelings that millions of people express about their products in blog posts. At certain Hollywood movie studios, computer scientists work on algorithms that predict the popularity of forthcoming movies by analyzing tweets about them (it works). In each case, the data and the algorithms can also reveal really interesting things about human cultural behavior in general, but this is not what the companies who are employing these computer scientists are interested in. Instead, the analytics are used for specific business ends. For more examples, see "What People Want (and How to Predict it)."

So what about the rest of us? Today we are given a variety of sophisticated and free software tools to select the content of interest to us from this massive and constantly expanding universe of professional media offerings and user-generated media. These tools include search engines, RSS feeds, and recommendation systems. But while they can help you find what to read, view, listen to, play, remix, share, comment on, and contribute to, in general they are not designed for carrying systematic social and cultural research along the lines of the "cultural analytics" scenario I described earlier.

While a number of free data analysis and visualization tools have become available on the web during last few years (Many Eyes, Tableau, Google docs, etc.), they are not useful unless you have access to large social data sets. Some commercial web tools allow anybody to analyze certain kinds of trends in certain data sets they are coupled with in some limited ways (or, at least, they whet our appetites by showing what is possible). I am thinking of already mentioned Google Books Ngram Viewer, Trends, Insights for Search, Blogpulse, and also YouTube Trends Dashboard,

Social Radar, and Klout. (Searching for "social media analytics" or "Twitter analytics" brings up lists of dozens of other tools.)

For example, the Google Ngram Viewer plots relative frequencies of words or phrases you input across a few million English language books published over the last four hundred years and digitized by Google. (Data sets in other languages are also available.) You can use it to reveal all kinds of interesting cultural patterns. Here are some of my favorite combinations of words and phrases to use as input: "data, knowledge"; "engineer, designer"; "industrial design, graphic design." In another example, YouTube Trends Dashboard allows you to compare most-viewed videos across different geographic locations and age groups.

Still, what you can do with these tools today is quite limited. One of the reasons for this is that companies make money by analyzing patterns in the data they collect about our online and physical behavior and target their offerings, ads, sales events, and promotions accordingly; in other cases, they sell this data to other companies. Therefore they don't want to give consumers direct access to all of their data. (According to an estimate by ComScore, in the end of 2007, five large web companies were recording "at least 336 billion transmission events in a month" ["To Aim Ads, Web Is Keeping Closer Eye on You"].)

If a consumer wants to analyze patterns in the data that constitutes or reflects her or his economic relations with a company, the situation is different. The companies often provide the consumers with professional-level analysis of this data—financial activities (e.g., my bank website shows a detailed breakdown of my spending categories), websites and blogs (Google Analytics), or online ad campaigns (Google AdWords).

Another relevant trend is to let a user compare her or his data against the statistical summaries of data about others. For instance, Google Analytics shows the performance of my website against all websites of similar type, while many fitness devices and sites allow you to compare your performance against the summarized performance of other users. However, in each case, the companies do not open the actual data but only provide the summaries.

Outside of the commercial sphere, we do see a gradual opening up of the data collected by government agencies. For U.S. examples, check Data.gov, HealthData.gov, and Radar.Oreilly.com. As Alex Howard notes in "Making Open Government Data Visualizations That Matter," "every month, more open government data is available online. Local governments are becoming data suppliers." Note, however, that these data are typically statistical summaries as opposed to transactional data (the traces of online behavior) or their media collected by social media companies.

The limited access to massive amounts of transactional social data that is being collected by companies is one of the reasons why today large contemporary data-driven social science and large contemporary data-driven humanities are not easy to do in practice. (For examples of digitized cultural archives available at the moment, see the list of repositories ["List of Data Repositories"] that agreed to make their data available to Digging into Data competitors.) Another key reason is the large gap between what can be done with the right software tools, right data, and no knowledge of computer science and advanced statistics and what can only be done if you do have this knowledge.

For example, imagine that you were given full access to the digitized books used in Ngram Viewer (or maybe you created your own large data set by assembling texts from Project Guttenberg or another source) and you want software to construct graphs that show changing frequencies of topics over time, as opposed to individual words. If you want to do this, you better have knowledge of computational linguistics or text mining. (A search for "topic analysis" on Google Scholar returned 239,000 articles for the first field and 39,000 articles for the second newer field.)

Or imagine that you were interested in how social media facilitates information diffusion, and you want to use Twitter data for your study. In this case, you can obtain the data using Twitter APIs or third-party services that collect this data and make it available for free or for a fee. But again, you must have the right background to make use of this data. The software itself is free and readily available—R, Weka, Gate, Mallet, and so on—but you need the right training (at least some classes in computer science and statistics) and prior practical experience to get meaningful results.

Here is an example of what can be done by people with the right background. In 2010, four researchers from the Computer Science Department at KAIST (South Korea's leading university for technology) published a paper titled "What Is Twitter, a social network or a news media?" Using Twitter APIs, they were able to study the entire Twittersphere as of 2009: 41.7 million user profiles, 1.47 billion social relations, 106 million tweets. Among their discoveries, over 85 percent of trending topics are "headline news or persistent news in nature." (Note that the lead author on the paper was a PhD student. It is also relevant to note that the authors make their complete collected data sets freely available for download, so that they can be used by other researchers. For more examples of the analysis of "social flows," see papers presented at IEEE International Conference on Social Computing 2010.)

In this chapter, I have sketched an optimistic vision of a new paradigm opened to humanities and social sciences. I have then discussed four objections to this optimistic vision. There are other equally important objections that I did not discuss because they are already debated in popular media and in academia by many people. For example, a very big issue is privacy; would you trust academic researchers to have all your communication and behavior data automatically captured?

So what conclusions should we draw from this analysis? Is it true that "surface is the new depth," in a sense that the quantities of "deep" data that in the past were obtainable about a few can now be automatically obtained about many? Theoretically, the answer is yes, as long as we keep in mind that the two kinds of deep data have different content.

Practically, there are a number of obstacles before this can become a reality. I have tried to describe a few of these obstacles, but there are also others I did not analyze. However, with what we already can use today (social media companies, APIs, Infochimps.com data marketplace and data commons, free archives such as Project Guttenberg, Internet Archive, etc.), the possibilities are endless—if you know some programming and data analytics and also are open to asking new types of questions about human beings, their social lives, their cultural expressions, and their experiences.

I have no doubt that eventually we will see many more humanities and social science researchers who will be equally as good at implementing the latest data analysis algorithms themselves, without relying on computer scientists, as they are at formulating abstract theoretical arguments. However, this requires a big change in how students in humanities are being educated.

The model of big-data humanities research that exists now is that of collaboration between humanists and computer scientists. It is the right way to start "digging into data." However, if each data-intensive project done in the humanities would have to be supported by a research grant, which would allow such collaboration, our progress will be very slow. We want humanists to be able to use data analysis and visualization software in their daily work, so they can combine quantitative and qualitative approaches in all their work. How to make this happen is one of the key questions for the digital humanities.

NOTES

1. I am grateful to UCSD faculty member James Fowler for an inspiring conversation a few years ago about the collapse of depth/surface distinction. See his work at jhfowler .ucsd.edu.

2. More details at http://en.wikipedia.org/wiki/Google_Search.

BIBLIOGRAPHY

"Big data." Wikipedia.org. September 14, 2011. http://en.wikipedia.org/wiki/Big_data.

Cha, Meeyoung, Haewoon Kwak, Pablo Rodriguez, Yong-Yeol Ahn, and Sue Moon. I Tube, You Tube, Everybody Tubes: Analyzing the World's Largest User Generated Content Video System. Internet Measurement Conference 2007. http://conferences.sigcomm .org/imc/2007/.

Crandall, David J., Lars Backstrom, Daniel Huttenlocher, and Jon Kleinberg. Mapping the world's photos. 18th International World Wide Web Conference, 2009. http://www .cs.cornell.edu/~dph/papers/photomap-www09.pdf.

"Cultural Analytics Research Environment." Softwarestudies.com. Software Studies Intitative. May 2008. http://lab.softwarestudies.com/2008/05/visualizing-cultural-patterns .html.

"Data.gov." Data.gov. http://www.data.gov/.

"Data, Data Everywhere." *The Economist*. February 10, 2010. March 29, 2011, http://www.economist.com/node/15557443/print?story_id=15557443.

de Kunder, Maurice. "The Size of the World Wide Web." WorldWideWebSize.com. http://www.worldwidewebsize.com/.

"Digital footprint." Wikipedia.org. March 31, 2011. http://en.wikipedia.org/wiki/Digital_footprint.

"Digging into Data Challenge." DiggingIntoData. http://diggingintodata.org/.

Ellison, Nicole, Rebecca Heino, and Jennifer Gibbs. Managing Impressions Online: Self-presentation Processes in the Online Dating Environment. *Journal of Computer-Mediated Communication* 11, no. 2 (2006). http://jcmc.indiana.edu/vol11/issue2/ellison.html.

"Ervin Goffman." Wikipedia.org. March 27, 2011. http://en.wikipedia.org/wiki/Erving_Goffman.

"Flickr API Methods." Flickr.com. http://www.flickr.com/services/api/.

"GOV 2.0 Coverage and Insight." O'Reilly Media. http://radar.oreilly.com/gov2/.

"Health.Data.gov." Data.gov. http://www.data.gov/health.

"Help Find Genghis Khan's Tomb from the Comfort of Your Home." Wired.com. http://www.wired.com/geekdad/2010/07/mongolia-valley-of-the-khans/.

Howard, Alex. "Making Open Government Data Visualizations That Matter." Gov20.govfresh.com. March 13, 2011. http://gov20.govfresh.com/making-open-government-data-visualizations-that-matter/.

"Internet Censorship by country." Wikipedia.org. April 30, 2011. http://en.wikipedia.org/wiki/Internet_censorship_by_country.

Latour, Bruno. "Beware, Your Imagination Leaves Digital Traces." *Times Higher Education Literary Supplement*, April 6, 2007. http://www.bruno-latour.fr/poparticles/index.html,

"List of Data Repositories." DiggingIntoData. April 14, 2011. http://diggingintodata.org/Home/Repositories/tabid/167/Default.aspx.

Kwak, Haewoon, Changhyun Lee, Hosung Park, and Sue Moon. "What Is Twitter, a Social Network or a News Media?" 19th International World Wide Web Conference. July 17, 2011. an.kaist.ac.kr/~haewoon/papers/2010-http-twitter.pdf.

Manovich, Lev. "Motion Studies: Vertov's The Eleventh Year." http://www.flickr.com/photos/culturevis/5952098107/in/set-72157623326872241.

———. "Visualizing Large Image Collections for Humanities Research." In *Media Studies Futures*, edited by Kelly Gates. Blackwell, forthcoming 2012. http://manovich.net/DOCS/media_visualization.2011.pdf.

"MIT Media Lab: Reality Mining." Reality.media.mit.edu. MIT. http://reality.media.mit.edu/.

"Nielsen Company." Wikipedia.org. April 5, 2011. http://en.wikipedia.org/wiki/Nielsen_Company.

"Nielsen ratings." Wikipedia.org. July 17, 2011. http://en.wikipedia.org/wiki/Nielsen_ratings.

"One Million Manga Pages." Softwarestudies.com. Software Studies Intitative. http://lab.softwarestudies.com/2010/11/one-million-manga-pages.html.

"The Petabyte Age: Because More Isn't Just More—More Is Different." *Wired,* June 7, 2008. http://www.wired.com/science/discoveries/magazine/16-07/pb_intro.

"Social Computing: Introduction." Third IEEE International Conference on Social Computing. http://www.iisocialcom.org/conference/socialcom2011/.

"Sociology in the 21st Century." Reality.media.mit.edu. MIT. http://reality.media.mit.edu/soc.php.

"Software Studies: Cultural Analytics." Softwarestudies.com. Software Studies Initiative. http://lab.softwarestudies.com/2008/09/cultural-analytics.html.

"Stalin Epigram." Wikipedia.org. July 17, 2011. http://en.wikipedia.org/wiki/Stalin_Epigram.

Story, Louise. "To Aim Ads, Web Is Keeping Closer Eye on You." NYTimes.com. Louise Story. March 10, 2008. http://www.nytimes.com/2008/03/10/technology/10privacy.html.

"U.S. Census Bureau." Census.gov. U.S. CensusBureau. http://www.census.gov/.

"Watson (computer)." Wikipedia.org. May 2, 2011. http://en.wikipedia.org/wiki/Watson_%28artificial_intelligence_software%29.

Davenport, Thomas H., and Jeanne G. Harris. "What People Want (and How to Predict It)." MIT Sloan Management Review. MIT. http://sloanreview.mit.edu/the-magazine/2009-winter/50207/what-people-want-and-how-to-predict-it/.

"WWW2009." www2009.org. http://www2009.org/.

"WWW2010." www2010.org. http://www2010.org/www/.

Humanities 2.0: Promise, Perils, Predictions

CATHY N. DAVIDSON

There has never been a great age of science and technology without a corresponding flourishing of the arts and humanities. In any time or place of rapid technological advance, those creatures we would now call humanists—literary commentators; historians; philosophers; logicians; theologians; linguists; scholars of the arts; and all manner of writers, musicians, and artists—have also had a field day. Perhaps that generalization is actually a tautology. Great ages of science are great ages of the humanities because an age isn't a historical period but a construct, and constructs are the work of humanists. Throughout history, there have been many momentous scientific discoveries that simply drift into the culture and are adapted without any particular new social or philosophical arrangements. It is the humanistic articulation of the significance of scientific change that announces a new episteme, a world-altering, even metaphysical, transformation. While scientists and engineers are responsible for the discoveries and inventions, humanists consolidate those experimental findings, explain them, and aggregate their impact in such a way that we suddenly have not just the new but an epoch-defining paradigm shift. ($E = mc^2$ is an equation; the concept of relativity is a defining intellectual model.) The humanistic turn of mind provides the historical perspective, interpretive skill, critical analysis, and narrative form required to articulate the significance of the scientific discoveries of an era, show how they change our sense of what it means to be human, and demarcate their continuity with or difference from existing ideologies.

Although we live in an unusually vibrant moment that, in historical terms, can be defined by its flourishing of technology and humanism, the contemporary rhetoric of academic humanists is one of exclusion, as if we had not been invited to sit at the table. It is outside the province of this essay to demonstrate that this is an age of populist humanism, and so I simply point to the phenomenon of artistic, architectural, historical, and crosscultural tourism and the concomitant building of concert halls and museums on a scale unequaled since the late nineteenth century, a comparable era of technological transformation. It is difficult to understand why so many humanists feel irrelevant to a culture that names the "creative class" as one of its defining features. As scholars such as Toby Miller and George Yudice have noted, humanists should be addressing the role of humanistic culture and cultural policy in the neoliberal economy instead of wringing their hands over the lack of their role in that economy.

Since the advent of the desktop computer interface (commonly figured as 1983) and the Internet (1991), virtually every mode of expression has been altered, and the very valuing of self-expression is rampant. "What oft was thought, but ne'er so well express'd" has so many new venues that a term such as "new media" needs an addendum almost daily. We live in the information age, not the age of computation, not the age of genomics. I would insist that this is our age and that it is time we claimed it and engaged with it in serious, sustained, and systemic ways.

One impetus of this essay, then, is to counter the academic humanist's pervasive stance of isolation with an intellectual call to attention and action. Are the material conditions for the production of humanistic scholarship as good as they should be? Of course not. Dozens of educators, including me, have noted that humanists occupy an increasingly fraught space in the academy (Perloff; Weisbuch). However, I am not convinced that science and technology are the problem any more now than they have been for the last seventy or eighty years. The so-called crisis in the humanities is nothing new. Even in *The Two Cultures and the Scientific Revolution* (1959), C. P. Snow was already lamenting that "thirty years ago the cultures had long ceased to speak to each other" and blamed the bifurcation in part on the devaluing of humanists: "young scientists now feel that they are part of a culture on the rise," while humanists feel their worth "in retreat" (18, 19). If humanists have been feeling put down for that long, clearly our sky-is-falling rhetoric isn't helping matters.

Perhaps we need a paradigm shift. Perhaps we need to see technology and the humanities not as a binary but as two sides of a necessarily interdependent, conjoined, and mutually constitutive set of intellectual, educational, social, political, and economic practices. More to the point, we need to acknowledge how much the massive computational abilities that have transformed the sciences have also changed our field in ways large and small and hold possibilities for far greater transformation in the three areas—research, writing, and teaching—that matter most.[1] We are not exempt from the technological changes of our era, and we need to take greater responsibility for them. We should be thinking about them critically, considering what they mean for us, and working to shape them to the future that we desire.

Humanities 1.0: A Brief Sketch

For the title of this essay, I draw from the popular (if contested) terminology coined by the media prognosticator Tim O'Reilly—Web 1.0 and Web 2.0. The distinctions between these phases of the Internet are becoming murky, and the terms have been appropriated for a range of commercial and even propagandistic uses that humanists need to be more cognizant of. Still, the terms are useful for this essay in that they help delineate the developmental stages of the Internet, which in turn help us envision an ever-expanding role for the humanities vis-à-vis technology.

Historically, Web 1.0 demarcates the first generation of the World Wide Web, basically from 1991 to the dot-com bust of fall 2001. Functionally, Web 1.0 is best characterized under the general rubric of data: primarily websites and tools that allowed for massive amounts of archiving, data collection, data manipulation, and searching, sites and tools mostly created by experts or commercial interests for the benefit of users worldwide. Web 1.0 has been described as an approach from the few to the many.

Web 2.0 characterizes the second generation of the Internet, after the collapse of 2001. O'Reilly was not oblivious to the financial implications of the dot-com bust and coined the term Web 2.0 partly to reassure and rally investors, to suggest that the new version of the information age could be profitable. Web 2.0 describes not only the new set of tools but also the new relationships between producers and consumers of those tools. In its most idealistic manifestation, Web 2.0 is best defined by interactivity and user participation (rather than data aggregation). According to O'Reilly, networking is the new Internet's single most important attribute, while others point to the significance of customization and collaboration. Web 2.0 includes all forms of corporate or social networking (from Google to MySpace); collaborative knowledge building (sites such as Wikipedia); user-generated content (including photo-sharing sites like Flickr or video-posting sites like YouTube); and blogs, wikis, virtual environments, and other sites that use a many-to-many model of participation and customization.

O'Reilly's terminology is an oversimplification, but it is useful for historicizing first-generation humanities computing (Humanities 1.0) and for suggesting the possibilities and perils of a networked, interactive, collaborative Humanities 2.0.[2] Humanities computing includes the careful digitizing of textual and, increasingly, multimedia archives engaged in by scholars and librarians the world over for something like the last two decades. These online resources have transformed how we do research and who can do it. Except for a few holdouts, we all now do much of our research online. Anyone reading this essay online or who has spent the morning perusing articles at Project Muse or JSTOR should be grateful that the humanities were not left behind in the most massive project of synthesizing, aggregating, and archiving data that the world has ever known.

Whether our particular scholarly interests draw us to the Perseus Digital Library (http://www.perseus.tufts.edu), containing classical texts, or to Ars Electronica (http://www.aec.at/en/), a platform for digital media and culture, we have at our disposal an array of rich, diverse, and compelling digital resources.[3] Nor are these merely tools. Great archives such as the International Dunhuang Project (http://idp.bl.uk) have recreated vibrant transnational cultural centers that were obliterated in the eighteenth and nineteenth centuries as part of colonialism's quest for loot. The Dunhuang Project challenges accepted definitions in the humanities, such as what constitutes and is constituted by the West.

My area of research was transformed by Humanities 1.0. In the 1980s, when I was working on *Revolution and the Word: The Rise of the Novel in America,* I spent hours in archives, poring over microfilms in the dizzying light of a discarded microfilm reader that I carted up to my office.[4] I called it the Green Monster, without affection, and I cannot summon up even an ounce of nostalgia for that creature, which captured so many hours of my early career. I can't say whether or not my overall arguments would have changed had they been written with the support of the new digital archives, but if I were to start this research today, what I cited, what I claimed, and where I made hypotheses or even speculations would be given far greater materiality. Whereas early American fiction was barely a category in card catalogs when I was researching *Revolution and the Word,* there are now searchable databases of early American imprints, eighteenth-century European imprints, South American and (growing) African archives, and archives in Asia as well. A contemporary scholar could, in far less time than it took me, not only search U.S. databases but also make comparisons across and among popular political movements worldwide (from democracy to feminism to abolitionism) and possibly make arguments about the spread of the popular novel and about its ideologies of self-governance along with the worldwide transportation of commodities and human beings (through travel, migration, indenture, enslavement, and escape).

Suffice it to say that Humanities 1.0—computational humanities—has changed the way we do research; the kinds of questions we can ask; and the depth, breadth, and detail of the answers we can provide to those questions. My colleague Peter H. Wood, a historian whose seminal 1974 *Black Majority: Negroes in Colonial South Carolina from 1670 through the Stono Rebellion* was reissued in 1996, suggested whimsically that books written before the advent of digital archives and search engines should come with a special sticker affixed to the front cover: "Extra Credit."

Toward Humanities 2.0: Collaborative Archives, Interpretation, Theory

The computational tools, the multilingual and transnational archives at the disposal of humanists, and the numbers of scholars and students globally who have access to any given digital textual database have, I believe, been factors in transforming the paradigms of humanistic scholarship and moving us toward Humanities 2.0. Hybridity, exchange, flow, and cultural transaction are all explored more responsibly and adventurously when the resources of many nations, in many languages, have been digitized, made interoperable, and offered for research by scholars around the world, each of whom brings a local store of knowledge and experience to the theoretical, interpretive enterprise. Data transform theory, theory stated or assumed, transforms data into interpretation. As any student of Foucault would insist, data collection is really data *selection*. Which archives should we preserve? Choices based on a complex ideational architecture of canonical, institutional, and personal preferences are constantly being made.

As more and more archives are opening themselves not just to unrestricted access by users, not just to questions and challenges posed by users, but to actual input and contribution by users (including the input of multiple interpretations and theories), we are moving to a new generation of digital humanities. Long-standing projects such as NINES (Networked Infrastructure for Nineteenth-Century Electronic Scholarship), led by the romanticist and textual theorist Jerome McGann, are augmenting professional, refereed, peer-reviewed archives with features that allow individual users to customize the archive (http://www.nines.org). Users can reissue NINES objects in their own exhibits, syllabi, essays, and timelines. They can tag objects and post their personal classification systems ("folksonomies") on the NINES site where other users can view them.

I suspect that soon this kind of Humanities 2.0 customization and collaboration will be pushed to another level, as Wikipedia-like functions augment professionally archived sources. At sites with such functions, users might contribute information about the projects in which they are using the archive (from syllabi to ethnographic reports), or engage in theoretical debates in an open forum, or even contribute digitized content to the archive itself. A memoir site, for example, might have a hosting function where any user can upload an ancestor's diary accompanied by photographs or portrait paintings. Other users might comment on, augment, and correct content or offer different interpretations of what the content means for a new theory of affect and intersubjectivity or for new understandings of the interactions among governmental policy, migration, race, gender, and religion. Courses might be based on students' participating in such a knowledge-sharing enterprise. A professor might teach a course on global information flows in which students engage their worldwide social networks in cocreating an archive that traces deployments of specific technologies, networking sites, and corporate or national policies. The possibilities for topics and uses are as limitless as our imaginations.

The questions that open repositories pose are also limitless. Once we champion openness, we enter a new world of social, intellectual, and curatorial rules.[5] An open repository challenges the borders between disciplines as well as between professionals and amateurs, between scholars and knowledge enthusiasts. It raises questions of privilege and authority as well as ethical issues of credibility and responsibility, privacy and security, neutrality and freedom of expression.

Decentering Knowledge and Authority

Much of our lives as academics depends on peer review. For a profession to relinquish the authority of the referee is a major step. As John Seely Brown has noted, it took professional astronomers several years before they came to appreciate that their field would be richer if they were more open to the energetic observations and theories of amateur astronomers. While most amateur astronomers are good observers who report useful, even incalculably valuable, celestial findings, some among the army of amateur sky watchers are motivated by a desire to protect Earth from martians and other invading space aliens. At some point, professional astronomers had to make a judgment call. They realized there were more advantages than disadvantages to openness and evolved checks for the credibility of observations offered by amateur astronomers.[6]

These profound issues are at the heart of our profession and at the heart of the various debates on the use, importance, and credibility of Wikipedia (the largest encyclopedia the world has ever known, one created partly by volunteer and amateur collaborative labor and the standard bearer for both the controversy and the intellectual potential of Web 2.0).[7] How does one put value on a source when the refereeing is performed by someone who has not been authorized and credentialed to judge?[8] Who are one's peers when the validity of the sources is determined by community standards enforced by various users, not by professionals who have been certified as the authorities of the community?[9] The distinction is important, because for many of us in the humanities it is foundational to our belief system, our reward system, and the implicit (and rarely spoken) assumptions about who constitutes a peer in peer review, a process on which our profession is based.

As so often happens when we analyze the new, the discussion of peer review for collaborative knowledge-building sites such as Wikipedia throws into relief practices so widely accepted that we rarely question them anymore.[10] The very concept of peer review needs to be defined and interrogated. We use the term as if it were self-explanatory and unitary, and yet who does and does not count as a peer is complex and part of a subtle and often self-constituting (and circular) system of accrediting and credentialing (i.e., "good schools" decide what constitutes a "good school"). We peer review in different modes in different circumstances. (I've known some kind teachers to be savage conference respondents and vice versa.) Humanities 2.0 peer review extends and makes public the various ways in which we act as professionals who judge one another and contribute to one another's work, whether subtly or substantively.

Peer review is not the only practice whose assumptions are at stake in this next phase of digital humanities. Humanities 2.0 is distinguished from monumental, first-generation, data-based projects not just by its interactivity but also by an openness about participation grounded in a different set of theoretical premises, which decenter knowledge and authority. Additional concepts decentered by Web 2.0 epistemologies include authorship, publication, refereeing, collaboration, participation, customizing, interdisciplinarity, credentialing, expertise, norms, training, mastery, hierarchy, taxonomy, professionalism, rigor, excellence, standards, and status.

Collaborative Writing: "The Future of Learning Institutions in a Digital Age"

I turn my focus on two projects (in one of which I am a participant) that underscore the paradigm-shifting potentialities of next-generation digital humanism. The first, "The Future of Learning Institutions in a Digital Age," deals primarily with collaborative thinking and writing; the second, the Law in Slavery and Freedom Project, is organized primarily around collaborative research and teaching.

The first draft of "The Future of Learning Institutions in a Digital Age" is conventional enough. It is a concept paper cowritten by me and my frequent collaborator on digital humanities projects, the philosopher and race theorist David Theo Goldberg. The process of proceeding from that draft to a final one, however, is quite unusual. It is a collaborative effort, incorporating contributions made by literally dozens of scholars, students, teachers, and concerned individuals who are contributing to discussions happening both online and in a series of public forums.

The concept paper considers the physical and intellectual arrangements of education, especially higher education. It is both a theoretical discussion and an activist proposal for educational reform.[11] Among other things, we directly challenge the national educational policy euphemistically called No Child Left Behind, a policy that in fact leaves behind over 30 percent of those entering high school. That 30 percent dropout rate makes the United States seventeenth in educational attainment levels among industrialized nations. We also critique the current academy, examining the obstacles to intellectual life posed by disciplinary and institutional structures and envisioning ways that digitality can help make intellectual linkages against odds. We are also concerned that education (on all levels) is becoming less relevant to the lives of youth today, and we propose institutional reforms directed at the multimedia, multitasking skills and interests of contemporary students. Finally, we advocate engaged, informed, creative, and critical thinking about the information age, which this generation of students has inherited and will shape.

Beginning in January 2006, "The Future of Learning Institutions in a Digital Age" was hosted on a collaborative, online writing tool developed by the Institute for the Future of the Book, a small nonprofit organization dedicated to "investigating the evolution of intellectual discourse as it shifts from printed pages to networked screens" (Davidson and Goldberg, *The Institute for the Future of the Book*). This site allowed dozens of readers to post public commentary on our draft and make bibliographic additions to it. It was rather like a "track changes" document, except that, instead of being shared with one or two readers, the draft was open to anyone on the World Wide Web. The point was not only to write about collaborative modes of thinking but also to engage in them.[12]

In addition to using the collaborative online tool, we held three public forums with humanists and social scientists concerned with creative learning. Possibly because of the high value an English professor places on the written word, the online feedback sometimes felt more intimidating than the critique offered in face-to-face exchanges. Texts have status in our profession. Our system of reward and recognition depends on publication. What does it mean to expose one's writing before it is final? Psychologically (I speak only for myself here), I have to restrain myself when there is a new comment posted for all the world to see on the institute's site. I have to stifle the voice that wants to shout, "Hey! It's just a first draft," or, "We already thought of that but just haven't put it in the paper yet." Those defensive responses are not what collaborative thinking is supposed to be about.

Is this new process worth the trouble? Immeasurably. The project has exposed us to bibliographies from many different fields, to the specific uses of terminologies (and their histories) within fields. It has been one of the most fluidly interdisciplinary exchanges that I have yet experienced. It has also taught me how one's words can signal meanings one didn't intend. Reader response is humbling; it is also illuminating. So much of what passes in our profession for response is actually restatement of one's original premises. In an interactive collaborative exchange, one often gains a better sense of assumptions unfolding, a process that helps make one's unstated premises visible (especially to oneself).

So what happens to authorship in such a collaborative environment? Goldberg and I address this issue, both a theoretical and an institutional (i.e., professional) one, in "The Future of Learning Institutions in a Digital Age." I am not sure we know the answer yet (it is one area where we seek the input of others), but we are mindful of what the digital media activist Nicholas Carr has referred to as the "sharecropper" downside of Web 2.0: that is, the many volunteer their time and insights, but too often someone else walks off with the profit or the credit. Needless to say, there will be no monetary profits from "The Future of Learning Institutions in a Digital Age," and we are evolving a model of authorship that both takes responsibility and gives credit. Because the online tool keeps a record of interactions, we will be able to footnote contributors who offered ideas that changed our thinking. We will be able to address contributors with whom we disagree, acknowledging that debate has influenced our final ideas. We will also include, as collaborators, a list of all who participated in the forums and the website discussion, whether or not we used their ideas explicitly in our project, whether or not we agree or disagree with their input. In one way or another, all have helped shape our final project, just as teaching does, if only through forcing us to articulate ideas that seemed self-evident but turned out to embed assumptions we had not consciously addressed. We know that whatever form we devise to acknowledge attribution will be imperfect. But that's the point of Humanities 2.0. It's a process, not a product. There is a latest version but never a final one.

Collaborative Research and Teaching: Law in Slavery and Freedom Project

A second project that fits under the rubric of Humanities 2.0 is also a hybrid of authority and participation, peer review and community contribution. It combines collaborative pedagogy with collaborative research. I refer to the Law in Slavery and Freedom Project, under the leadership of the history professors Martha S. Jones (University of Michigan), Rebecca J. Scott (University of Michigan), and Jean M. Hébrard (École des Hautes Études en Sciences Sociales). This team of scholars, their collaborators, and their students work in the United States, France, Germany, Brazil, Canada, Cuba, the Caribbean, and West Africa. The remarkable project has developed through the close analysis of manuscript documentation from archives in various countries that once were slaveholding societies. Courses are taught simultaneously in different locations, and collaborators work transnationally on projects about the movement and displacement of persons. The participants have, for example, traced the life histories of a Senegambian woman enslaved in Saint-Domingue and her descendants through to the twentieth century, and they have a parallel project on a slaveholding Saint-Domingue emigre and her Atlantic itinerary. They are using digitized images to compare a small set of freedom papers from Senegal with others from Cuba and Saint-Domingue. Pedagogy and research, archive and theory line up to produce an expansive humanism with intellectual breadth, rigor, and inclusiveness. As the Law in Slavery and Freedom Project matures and more of its documents go online, participation will extend beyond the students in the class to a much wider community. If the project ever becomes completely open, it is even possible that anyone could become a collaborator, adding interpretive content, offering critique, or positing new information. This multinational, multilingual, collaborative, interpretive framing of a major intellectual project, where research and teaching are practiced and demonstrated simultaneously and in a public forum, strikes me as the essence of what higher education strives to accomplish. The research and pedagogical possibilities of an open-knowledge commons are breathtaking for scholars and students of the humanities and for a more general public who might be invited into projects that encourage humanistic thinking. Scientists talk about Big Science. I am proposing a Big Humanities. I would venture to say that digitizing (with interoperability and universal access) the entire record of human expression and accomplishment would be as significant and as technologically challenging an accomplishment of the information age as sequencing the human genome or labeling every visible celestial object.[13]

Humanities 2.1: Perils and Predictions

Since May 2007, when I was invited to write this essay, I have revised it twice, motivated by corporate or governmental changes that fuel my concerns about the future of the Internet. In my daily blogging on the HASTAC site (http://www.hastac.org), I find myself alternating between enthusiasm for expansive collaborative projects and jeremiads against such things as Facebook's incursions against privacy, hackers' near-successful attempts to destroy security systems, and corporate and regulatory inroads into so-called net neutrality. With copyright and patent rulings, changes in national security policy, and unseemly corporate mergers, it seems that every day the scholar interested in technology has to be on the alert. Any paean to the potential of Humanities 2.0 thus needs a software update, Humanities 2.1, a reminder that there are always glitches and bugs and viruses in transitional eras. We're still in the beta version of the information age, and there is an urgent need for sustained, humanistic participation to ensure a better version.

Among the frightening issues that need to be addressed are those associated with what Siva Vaidhyanathan calls "the Googlization of everything." His online book in progress is subtitled "How One Company Is Disrupting Culture, Commerce, and Community and Why We Should Worry." What does it mean that Google is, according to Nicholas Carr, an "oligopoly" ("Do You Trust Google?") that already functions as despotically as a utility company? What does it mean that our universities, presses, and libraries are turning over their content to Google and not necessarily with a business plan that will profit any of the participants except Google? Whether we like it or not, Google now has access to much of our personal information. Managing payroll, medical, and customer accounts of corporations and municipalities is one of the fastest-growing web applications of the moment. What will it mean as those applications are increasingly centralized and ripe for next-generation data mining and management? "Search engine" hardly defines what Google makes, controls, censors, does, or has the potential to do. "Information" does not adequately alert us to its potential control over all the material, intellectual, cultural, and social arrangements of our life. Google Earth, indeed.

At the time of this writing, the U.S. corporate giant Cisco is supplying routers to China that allow government censors to restrict what citizens can find on the Internet and how they can communicate with one another. Google is cooperating with that venture in censorship, creating granular settings that allow the government to select what search engines deliver. And Yahoo has admitted turning over information about a dissident Chinese journalist's e-mail accounts to the Chinese government. Of course, similar processes are at work in the United States. One need not be either a Luddite or an alarmist to assert that technology (and its enabling economic and political preconditions) is contributing to state monopoly capitalism on a scale unprecedented in human history.

Conclusion

I began by asserting that, like any great age of science and technology, the twenty-first century is a great age also of humanism. However, we live in an oddly contradictory time, when many humanists feel they do not count. Discoveries in the computational, natural, and biological sciences evoke the deepest issues about what it means to be human, but in the academy the humanities no longer occupy the central place where those issues might be productively explored. Public policy has increasingly become an alternative to humanistic inquiry rather than a subset or extension of it. This situation must change—not just for the sake of the humanities but for the full realization of the goals of the social and natural sciences as well.

Humanities 2.0 is a humanities of engagement that addresses our collective histories and concern for history. To be valued by one's time requires making oneself responsible and responsive to one's time. For academics, this engagement entails a willingness to reconsider the most cherished assumptions and structures of their discipline. It is not clear that humanists welcome the disciplinary self-scrutiny, self-evaluation, and reshaping that colleagues in the natural sciences (and, to a lesser extent, some of the social sciences) have gone through in the past two decades. Indeed, a real conversation, rather than a contest, across the humanities and sciences about the benefits and costs of disciplinary change could turn out to be enlightening for all of us and on many levels practical, professional, and intellectual. In a time of paradigm shifts, moral and political treachery, historical amnesia, and psychic and spiritual turmoil, humanistic issues are central—if only funding agencies, media interests, and we humanists ourselves will recognize the momentousness of this era for our discipline and take seriously the need for our intellectual centrality.

NOTES

1. To demonstrate the application of those abilities, participants in the 2006–2007 John Hope Franklin Humanities Institute Seminar Interface (Duke's contribution to the national HASTAC InFormation Year Project) developed visualization tools for complex humanistic data sets. A subset of the group, led by Rachael Brady, Harry Halpin, and Timothy Lenoir, designed a three-dimensional virtual reality data display that allows one to put up hundreds of patents and physically separate out strands to see, for example, social, intellectual, corporate, governmental, and scientific connections too complex to imagine without a visualization tool or in a two-dimensional graphical representation.

2. Others and I began using the term "Humanities 2.0" at a 2005 HASTAC gathering held shortly after O'Reilly coined the term "Web 2.0." Cofounded by David Theo Goldberg and me, HASTAC ("haystack," an acronym for the Humanities, Arts, Science and Technology Advanced Collaboratory) is a network of educators and digital visionaries who have worked together since 2003 both to codevelop creative new collaborative learning technologies and to think critically about the role of technology in life, learning, and society (www.hastac.org).

3. For a survey of humanities computing, see McCarty. A list of digital humanities centers and projects can be found at CenterNet (digitalhumanities.org/centernet), an international network of digital humanities centers developed in response to the American

Council of Learned Societies report "Cyberinfrastructure for the Humanities and Social Sciences" (2006).

4. Recently, when Oxford University Press asked me to prepare an expanded edition of *Revolution and the Word* (2004), I briefly toyed with and then rejected the idea of updating content. Instead, I decided to write a monographic overview of the field, including a discussion of the impact of new technologies on the history of the book (41–45).

5. The *Mozilla Manifesto* is a fascinating collaborative document (combining elements of Hobbes, Locke, Hume, Smith, and Marx) that addresses individual and collective relationships in an open-source network.

6. What O'Reilly has called "harnessing collective intelligence" entails rules for credibility and sociability. Kathy Sierra, cofounder of the Head First book series for O'Reilly, reminds us that the "crowds" and "mobs" that Surowieki and Rheingold champion come with caveats and constraints.

7. For discussions of *Wikipedia*, see Davidson, "We Can't Ignore"; and Jenkins. For an especially thoughtful discussion of the pros and cons of *Wikipedia* (with a fine bibliography on the con side), see "Wikipedia: Policies and Guidelines."

8. For a witty discussion of the cognitive prejudices against openness, see Boyle. James Boyle, with Lawrence Lessig and others, is one of the founders of Creative Commons and Science Commons. Although issues of intellectual property and fair use are outside the scope of this essay, it is not an exaggeration to say that all forms of humanistic scholarship are threatened by current copyright legislation.

9. In August 2006, the Internet activist and designer Virgil Griffith unveiled a tool called WikiScanner that revealed how the CIA, the FBI, Disney, Fox News, and other corporate and political interests were editing *Wikipedia* entries for purposes of propaganda and, in some cases, defamation of character. *Wikipedia* invited the use of WikiScanner and revised its own editing practices and community rules to curb the practices of those who would use the many-to-many tool to injure, obscure, or prevaricate. If only we had such community rules and the equivalent of WikiScanner for mainstream media.

10. Credibility and authority were also at issue in the nineteenth century when the Philological Society of London assembled volunteer readers to locate unregistered words and usages of words for the *Oxford English Dictionary (OED)*. Deception was as much a problem then as it is now: one of the most trusted contributors to the *OED* turned out to be not a don but an inmate of a mental institution (Winchester).

11. This project is funded as part of the John D. and Catherine T. MacArthur Foundation's new initiative Digital Media and Learning (www.digitallearning.macfound.org).

12. At the time of this writing (April 2008), a research assistant, Zoe Marie Jones, continues to solicit contributions to "Models and Resources," an extensive bibliography of exemplary learning institutions (www.hastac.org/ node/1106). What forms the final monographic publication takes will depend on the future technologies that best promote interactivity, access, and collaboration.

13. For the purposes of this *PMLA* essay, I have concentrated on archives. Elsewhere I wrote about other technologies of relevance to the humanities, including a virtual reality

data-correlating installation conceived at Duke as well as virtual environment role-playing games and global positioning systems ("Data Mining"). Imagine, for example, if the slavery and freedom collaboratory I proposed came with GPS mapping and tracking devices.

BIBLIOGRAPHY

Boyle, James. "A Closed Mind about an Open World." *Financial Times,* August 7, 2006. http://www.It.com/home/us. Path: Search; Boyle Closed Mind.

Brown, John Seely. "The Social Life of Learning in the Net Age." Electronic Techtonics: Thinking at the Interface: 1st International HASTAC Conference. Nasher Museum, Duke University. April 19, 2007.

Carr, Nicholas. "Do You Trust Google?" *Wired* 16, no. 1 (2008): 42.

———. "Sharecropping the Long TaiL" *Rough Type*. December 19, 2006. http://www.roughtype.com/archives/2006/12/sharecropping_t.php.

Davidson, Cathy N. "Data Mining. Collaboration and Institutional Infrastructure for Transforming Research and Teaching in the Human Sciences and Beyond." *CTWatch Quarterly* 3, no. 2 (2007): 3–6. http://www.ctwatch.org. Path: Back Issues; May 2007.

———. *Revolution and the Word: The Rise of the Novel in America*. 1986. Rev. ed., New York: Oxford University Press. 2004.

———. "We Can't Ignore the Influence of Digital Technologies." *Chronicle of Higher Education Review,* March 23, 2007, B20.

Davidson, Cathy N., and David Theo Goldberg. *The Future of Learning Institutions in a Digital Age*. John D. and Catherine T. MacArthur Foundation Occasional Paper Series on Digital Media and Learning. MIT Press, forthcoming.

———. *The Institute for the Future of the Book*. March 7, 2008, http://www.futureofthebook.org/.

Jenkins, Henry. *Convergence Culture: Where Old and New Media Collide*. New York: New York University Press, 2006.

"The Law in Slavery and Freedom Project: Overview." *The Law in Slavery and Freedom*. University of Michigan. 2006. http://sitemaker.umich.edu/law.slavery.freedom/overview.

McCarty, Willard. *Humanities Computing*. Houndmills, England: Palgrave-Macmillan, 2005.

Miller, Toby, and George Yudice. *Cultural Policy*. London: Sage, 2002.

The Mozilla Manifesto, vO.9. Mozilla.org. Mozilla Foundation. April 17, 2007. http://www-archive.mozilla.org/about/mozilla-manifesto.html.

O'Reilly, Tim. "What Is Web 2.0: Design Patterns and Business Models for the Next Generation of Software." *O'Reilly*. September 30, 2005. http://oreilly.com/web2/archive/what-is-web-20.html.

Perloff, Marjorie. *Crisis in the Humanities.* 7 Mar. 2008 http://epc.buffalo.edu/authors/perloff/articles/crisis.html.

Rheingold, Howard. *Smart Mobs: The Next Social Revolution*. New York: Basic, 2003.

Sierra, Kathy. "The Dumbness of Crowds." *Creating Passionate Users*. January 2, 2007. http://headrush.typepad.com/creating_passionate_users/2007/01/the_dumbness_of.html.

Snow, C. P. *The Two Cultures and the Scientific Revolution*. 1959. Edited and introduction by Stefan Collini. Cambridge, Mass.: Cambridge University Press, 1993.

Surowiecki, James. *The Wisdom of Crowds: Why the Many Are Smarter than the Few and How Collective Wisdom Shapes Business, Economies, Societies, and Nations*. New York: Anchor, 2005.

Vaidhyanathan, Siva. *The Googlization of Everything*. March 8, 2008. http://www.googlizationofeverything.com/.

Weisbuch, Robert. "Six Proposals to Revive the Humanities." *Chronicle of Higher Education*, March 26, 1999, B4–5.

"Wikipedia: Policies and Guidelines." *Wikipedia*. June 15, 2007. http://en.wikipedia.org/wiki/Category:Wikipedia_policies_and_guidelines.

Winchester, Simon. *The Meaning of Everything: The Story of the Oxford English Dictionary*. Oxford: Oxford University Press, 2003.

Wood, Peter H. *Black Majority: Negroes in Colonial South Carolina from 1670 through the Stono Rebellion*. 1974. New York: Norton, 1996.

Where Is Cultural Criticism in the Digital Humanities?

ALAN LIU

As the cue for a thesis I wish to offer about the future of the digital humanities, I start by confessing to a lie I inserted in the last paragraph of the mission statement of 4Humanities. 4Humanities is an initiative I helped cofound with other digital humanists in November 2010 to advocate for the humanities at a time when economic retrenchment has accelerated a long-term decline in the perceived value of the humanities.[1] It serves as a platform for advocacy statements and campaigns, international news on the state of the humanities, showcase examples of humanities work, "student voices" for the humanities, and other ways of speaking up publicly for the humanities. But unlike other humanities advocacy campaigns—for example, those of the National Humanities Alliance in the United States or the Defend the Arts and Humanities and Humanities and Social Sciences Matter initiatives in the United Kingdom—it has a special premise. As emblematized in the motto on its website, 4Humanities is "powered by the digital humanities community." The idea is that in today's world of networked communications the digital humanities have a special role to play in helping the humanities reach out. The last paragraph of the 4Humanities mission statement (which I wrote) thus asserts,

> 4Humanities began because the digital humanities community—which specializes in making creative use of digital technology to advance humanities research and teaching as well as to think about the basic nature of the new media and technologies—woke up to its special potential and responsibility to assist humanities advocacy. The digital humanities are increasingly integrated in the humanities at large. They catch the eye of administrators and funding agencies who otherwise dismiss the humanities as yesterday's news. They connect across disciplines with science and engineering fields. They have the potential to use new technologies to help the humanities communicate with, and adapt to, contemporary society.

But, in reality, the past tense in the wake-up call here ("the digital humanities community . . . woke up to its special potential and responsibility to assist humanities advocacy") is counterfactual or, at best, proleptic. It's a tactical lie in the service of a hope.

In outline form, my thesis about the digital humanities is as follows. While my opening stance is critical, my final goal is hopeful: to recommend how the deficit in the digital humanities I identify may convert antithetically into an opportunity.

The digital humanities have been oblivious to cultural criticism

After the era of May 1968, one of the leading features of the humanities has been cultural criticism, including both interpretive cultural studies and edgier cultural critique.[2] In parallel, we recall, the computer industry developed the personal computer and networking in the 1970s and 1980s in a Zeitgeist marked by its own kind of cultural criticism: cyberlibertarianism in conjunction with social-justice activism (e.g., in the vintage manner of the Computer Professionals for Social Responsibility or the Electronic Frontier Foundation).[3] Yet in all that time, as it were, the digital humanities (initially known even more soberly as "humanities computing") never once inhaled. Especially by contrast with "new media studies," whose provocateur artists, net critics, tactical media theorists, hacktivists, and so on, blend post-1960s media theory, poststructuralist theory, and political critique into "net critique" and other kinds of digital cultural criticism, the digital humanities are noticeably missing in action on the cultural-critical scene.[4] While digital humanists develop tools, data, and metadata critically, therefore (e.g., debating the "ordered hierarchy of content objects" principle; disputing whether computation is best used for truth finding or, as Lisa Samuels and Jerome McGann put it, "deformance"; and so on) rarely do they extend their critique to the full register of society, economics, politics, or culture.[5] How the digital humanities advances, channels, or resists today's great postindustrial, neoliberal, corporate, and global flows of information-cum-capital is thus a question rarely heard in the digital humanities associations, conferences, journals, and projects with which I am familiar. Not even the clichéd forms of such issues—for example, "the digital divide," "surveillance," "privacy," "copyright," and so on—get much play.

It is as if, when the order comes down from the funding agencies, university administrations, and other bodies mediating today's dominant socioeconomic and political beliefs, digital humanists just concentrate on pushing the "execute" button on projects that amass the most data for the greatest number, process that data most efficiently and flexibly (flexible efficiency being the hallmark of postindustrialism), and manage the whole through ever "smarter" standards, protocols, schema, templates, and databases uplifting Frederick Winslow Taylor's original scientific industrialism into ultraflexible postindustrial content management systems camouflaged as digital editions, libraries, and archives—all without pausing to reflect on the relation of the whole digital juggernaut to the new world order.

As I have argued in my *Laws of Cool*, producers and consumers in other social sectors who are uneasy about the new world order of "knowledge work" at least express their paradoxical conformance and resistance to that order though the subtle ethos of "cool." Digital humanists are not even cool.

The lack of cultural criticism blocks the digital humanities from becoming a full partner of the humanities

Of course, cultural criticism is not without its problems (about which more later). But for the sake of the digital humanities, I call special attention to the lack of cultural criticism because I fear that it will block the field's further growth just as it is at a threshold point.

Consider that digital humanists are finally coming close to their long deferred dream of being recognized as full partners of the humanities. Extrinsic indicators include stories in the press about the digital humanities being "the next big thing"; the proliferation of digital humanities jobs, programs, panels, grants, and publications; and in general (as I have summed up elsewhere in taking stock of the field) more mind share.[6] Perhaps most telling, however, is an intrinsic methodological indicator: the proximity of the digital humanities to the current "close reading" versus "distant reading" debate (as it is called in literary studies, with analogies in other humanities and social science fields).[7] In this regard, Katherine Hayles's "How We Read: Close, Hyper, Machine"—one of the recent wave of essays, talks, and panels contributing to the debate—is quite shrewd in observing that the whole issue is supercharged because, after literary scholars turned to cultural texts beyond traditional literature, close reading (originally theorized and practiced by the New Criticism) assumed a compensatory role as what remained quintessentially *literary*, thus assuming "a preeminent role as the essence of the disciplinary identity" of literary studies (63).

While this is not the place for a detailed examination of the close versus distant reading debate (to which I have myself contributed [Liu, "Close"]), it is apropos to recognize that the debate serves as a proxy for the present state of the running battle between New Critical method and post–May 1968 cultural criticism. Indeed, we recall that close reading came into dominance only after the New Critics fought polemical battles against a *prior* age of cultural criticism whose methods were in their own way distant reading. I refer to nineteenth-century historicist, philosophical, religious, moral, and philological reading, which culled archives of documents to synthesize a "spirit" (*Geist*) of the times, nations, languages, and peoples capable of redeeming the other, darker people's identity haunting the century: the French revolutionary mob. The New Critics displaced such *Historismus* (as the Germans called such historism), but only to urge an equivalent project of modern reclamation. Rejecting alongside *Historismus* (and the related intellectual tradition of *Geistesgeschicte)* also the "paraphrase" of contemporary scientific discourse and mass media information, they defended their notion of an individual human sensibility rooted in organic culture (originally, the yeoman small-farm culture idealized in their southern agrarian phase) against the other, "northern" people's identity of the time: modern mass industrial society.[8]

May 1968 marked the return of the repressed: a surge in postmodern, rather than modern, theories of discourse and culture that identified the human as ipso facto collective and systemic. Even if a distinctively new decentralized and bottom-up ideology inspired Gilles Deleuze and Félix Guattari, for instance, to celebrate wolf packs, Mongol hordes, and schizos quite different from the nineteenth-century *Geist*, it seemed clear that humanity was congenitally structural, epistemic, class based, identity-group based (gendered, racial, ethnic), and so on. Currently, distant reading is a catch-all for that. Indeed, the method is a catch-all for cultural-critical methods extending back even earlier than May 1968 to some of the main influences on the work of Franco Moretti (the leading practitioner and theorist of distant reading): Braudelian (Annales) historiography and Marxist literary sociology, which—mixed into New Criticism and genre theory (the latter descending, for example, from Western Marxist criticism in Georg Lukács's mode)—generate Moretti's powerful thesis of the social "force" of "forms."[9]

Now enter the digital humanities, which have been invited to the main table of debate. As symbolized by Moretti's collaboration at Stanford with the digital humanist Matthew Jockers (the two have started the Stanford Literary Lab and worked together on quantitative stylistics research), the digital humanities are now what may be called the *practicing partner* of distant reading. I choose this phrase not to imply that everyone else since May 1968 has been disengaged from practice but to spotlight the fact that digital humanities practice assumes a special significance qua practice because it is positioned at a destabilizing location in the post–May 1968 balance of methods. In reality, we recall, the running battle between the New Criticism and critical methods après 1968 fairly quickly settled into a cold war. Generation '68, including cultural critics, occupied the high ground of "theory." The New Criticism, meanwhile, dug into the ordinary, pedagogical, and even existential levels of reading practice—to the extent that even high theorists took pride in grounding their method in close reading. Just as deconstruction was ultraclose reading, for instance, so the New Historicism read the microhistory of "anecdotes."[10] An unspoken demilitarized zone thus intervened between close and cultural-critical reading.

The digital humanities break this détente. Sophisticated digital humanities methods that require explicit programmatic instructions and metadata schema now take the ground of elemental practice previously occupied by equally sophisticated but tacit close reading methods. Moretti and his collaborators, therefore, explore "the great unread" of vast quantities of literature (rather than only exceptional literature) through text analysis, topic modeling, data mining, pattern recognition, and visualization methods that have to be practiced at the *beginning* and not just interpretive or theoretical end of literary study.[11] Adding to the casus belli is the fact that the contrast between the practices of close reading and the digital humanities is so stark that it is changing the very nature of the ground being fought over: the text. The relevant text is no longer the New Critical "poem [text] itself" but instead the digital humanities archive, corpus, or network—a situation aggravated even further because block quotations serving as a middle ground for fluid movement between close and distant reading are disappearing from view. We imagine, after all, that even as bold a distant reader as Moretti still at times—or even most times—wants to pause to close read en bloc literary passages as he encounters them. But block quotations have a different status in the digital humanities. Either they drop out of perception entirely because text analysis focuses on microlevel linguistic features (e.g., word frequencies) that map directly over macrolevel phenomena (e.g., different genres or nationalities of novels) without need for the middle level of quoted passages; or they exist as what hypertext theorists, originally inspired by Roland Barthes, call "lexia"—that is, modular chunks in a larger network where the real interest inheres in the global pattern of the network.[12] In either case, one noticeable effect of distant reading in Moretti and Jockers's mode is that data visualizations of large patterns increasingly replace block quotations as the objects of sustained focus. One now close reads graphs and diagrams that have roughly the same cognitive weight (and even visual size on the page) as block quotations of old, even if the mode of "meaningfulness" to be read off such visualizations is of a different order (linking the act of analysis more to breadth of field than to a sense of depth or emplacement).

The upshot is that digital humanists will never get a better invite to the table, as I put it, where the mainstream humanities are renegotiating the relation between qualitative methods premised on a high quotient of tacit understanding and quantitative methods requiring a different rigor of programmatic understanding. All those lonely decades of work on text encoding, text analysis, digital archives or editions, online reading tools or environments, and other incunabula of digital scholarship are now not so lonely. Mainstream humanists have come to recognize that, at minimum, they need a search function to do research; and the nature of digital media is such that the transition from the minimum to the maximum is almost instantaneous. No sooner does one come to depend on online searching then it becomes intuitive that one also needs advanced digital humanities tools and resources to practice scholarship in the age of Google Books. Indeed, Google itself has encouraged the creation of new digital humanities methods for using Google Books through its Digital Humanities Research Awards (Orwant).

But will digital humanists be able to claim their place at the table? Or, as in the past, will they once more be merely servants at the table whose practice is perceived to be purely instrumental to the main work of the humanities?[13] This is the blockage in the growth of the field that I fear. Consider the nature of some of the scholarly works that have recently had the greatest impact in turning the attention of the humanities to large literary systems—for example, Moretti's *Graphs, Maps, Trees* and Pascale Casanova's *The World Republic of Letters*. Both of these remarkable books, which participate in what James F. English calls the "new sociology of literature," frame their corporate- or system-scale analyses of literature in cultural criticism—specifically, a combination of Braudelian historiography, Marxist sociology (in Casanova's case, an Immanuel Wallerstein–like "core versus periphery" analysis of world literature), and global-scale literary comparatism. The lesson to digital humanists should be clear. While digital humanists have the practical tools and data, they will never be in the same league as Moretti, Casanova, and others unless they can move seamlessly between text analysis and cultural analysis. After all, it can be said that digital materials on the scale of corpora, databases, distributed repositories, and so on—specialties of the digital humanities—are ipso facto cultural phenomena. The people behind Google Books Ngram Viewer say it. In their groundbreaking *Science* article (paralleled by Google's release of its Ngram Viewer), Jean-Baptiste Michel and Erez Lieberman Aiden (with their collaborators) call their quantitative analyses of Google Books a contribution to "culturomics." So, too, the Software Studies Initiative at the University of California, San Diego, is well advanced in developing what it calls "cultural analytics."[14] Where are the digital humanists in the picture? To be an equal partner—rather than, again, just a servant—at the table, digital humanists will need to show that thinking critically about metadata, for instance, scales into thinking critically about the power, finance, and other governance protocols of the world.

The digital humanities can transcend their "servant" role in the humanities through leadership in advocating for the humanities

Engagement with cultural criticism, I am saying, is necessary for the digital humanities to be a full partner of the mainstream humanities today. But it is not enough for digital humanists to add cultural criticism to their brief in a "me too" way. Partners are not just followers. They become partners only by being able to rotate into the leadership role when their special competencies are needed. Truly to partner with the mainstream humanities, digital humanists now need to incorporate cultural criticism in a way that shows leadership in the humanities.

I believe that the service function of the digital humanities—as literal as running the actual servers, if need be—can convert into leadership if such service can be extended beyond facilitating research in the academy (the usual digital humanities remit) to assisting in advocacy *outside* the academy in the humanities' present hour of social, economic, and political need. I refer to the economic recession beginning in 2007 that gave warrant to nations, regional governments, and universities to cut funding for the humanities and arts in favor of fields perceived to apply more directly to society's well-being, especially the STEM fields (science, technology, engineering, mathematics).[15] Of course, this is an old story that goes back as far as the "two cultures" problem named by C. P. Snow. What is new is that the scale of the Great Recession of 2007—bringing a climax to decades of neoliberal and postindustrial trends that shift the work and value of knowledge away from the academy—is leading to a changed paradigm. Especially in public university systems, which are exposed most directly to changing social, economic, and political attitudes, the new normal threatens to solve the two cultures problem by effectively subtracting one of the cultures. The humanities, arts, and other disciplines that rely disproportionately on funds not supplied by industry or national agencies for science, medicine, and defense are in peril of systematic defunding.

Simultaneous with such defunding, another peril threatens the humanities: the continuing breakdown in their ability to communicate with the public. This, too, is an old story that extends back, for instance, to the decline of the fabled "public intellectual" in the twentieth century. What is new today is that the Internet and, most recently, Web 2.0 have altered the very idea of effective public communication by changing the relation between "experts," traditionally those with something valuable to communicate, and the public, who traditionally listened to expertise (or at least media reports about expertise) and responded with votes, tuition dollars, fees, and so on to support the various expert institutions and professions. As perhaps best exemplified by Wikipedia, the new networked public is now developing its own faculty of expertise through bottom-up processes of credentialing (e.g., Wikipedia's "administrators"), refereeing, governance, and so on. It will take at least a generation for the academy (and mediating agencies such as journalism) to create or adapt the institutional protocols, practices, and technologies that can negotiate a new compact of knowledge between expertise and networked public knowledge—for example, between the standards of peer review and crowdsourcing. In the meantime, the humanities are caught in a particularly vicious form of the communicational impasse of expertise. While the networked public still tolerates specialized knowledge from scientists, engineers, doctors, and others, it seems to have ever less patience for specialized humanities knowledge, since in the domain of "human" experience everyman with his blog is an autodidact. And this is not even to mention the ridiculous mismatch between the forms of humanities knowledge and the new networked public knowledge—for example, between the scale, structure, and cadence of a humanities monograph and those of a blog post or tweet.[16]

In short, just when the humanities need more than ever to communicate their vision of humanity (and so their own value) to the public, they find themselves increasingly cut off from the modes of communication that produce some of today's most robust discourses of public knowledge. While able like anyone else to reach out through the new media, humanities scholars by and large must do so as *individuals* unsupported by any of the institutional and professional structures that afford them their particular identity qua humanists or scholars.

Hence the unique leadership opportunity for the digital humanities. As digital humanists simultaneously evolve institutional identities for themselves tied to the mainstream humanities and explore new technologies, they become ideally positioned to create, adapt, and disseminate new methods for communicating between the humanities and the public. At a minimum, digital humanists—perhaps in alliance with social scientists who study Internet social activism—might facilitate innovative uses of new media for such traditional forms of advocacy as essays, editorials, petitions, letter-writing campaigns, and so on. But really, digital humanists should create technologies that fundamentally reimagine humanities advocacy. The goal, I suggest, is to build advocacy into the ordinary work of the humanities, so that research and teaching organically generate advocacy in the form of publicly meaningful representations of the humanities. As a starting point, for example, consider how something like the Open Journal Systems (OJS) publication platform might be extended for this purpose. Created by the Public Knowledge Project, OJS facilitates the publication and management of online journals while also providing "reading tools" that assist users in pursuing additional research (e.g., looking beyond an individual text through search and aggregation tools that give a glimpse of the relevant context). Imagine that OJS could be mashed up with text analysis and extraction tools as well as output platforms like OMEKA or the Simile Exhibit and Timeline widgets designed to break scholarship free of the "document" format, with the result that the publication process automatically generates from every article a "capture" of humanities scholarship that is not just an abstract but something more akin to a brochure, poster, video, or other high-impact brief—that is, something that could expose the gist of scholarship for public view and use.

The idea is to create ways to allow humanities scholars deliberately, spontaneously, or collaboratively to generate a bow wave of public awareness about their research and teaching that propagates outward as part of the natural process of research and teaching. After all, millions tune in each week to watch crab fishermen on the Discovery Channel (*Deadliest Catch*). Humanists may not be salt-of-the-earth crabbers, and archives may not be as stormy as the high seas. But surely, humanists ought on occasion to try to share the excitement of the chase by which breakthrough intellectual discoveries and movements occur. A beautifully designed, visually rich report published by the United Kingdom's JISC (Joint Information Systems Committee) in 2010 titled "Inspiring Research, Inspiring Scholarship: The Value and Benefits of Digitised Resources for Learning, Teaching, Research and Enjoyment" gives the flavor of what I mean (Tanner). The text of the brochure begins in an everyman-as-researcher mode as follows: "Imagine walking into one of Britain's great cathedrals. As you take in the architectural, cultural and religious ambience, your personal mobile device automatically engages with content on your behalf." Similarly, one of my initiatives while participating during 2009 through 2010 in a working group of the University of California (UC) Commission on the Future (convened by the regents of the UC system to explore new paradigms for the university in a bleak future of permanently reduced state funding) was to canvass humanities, arts, and social science scholars throughout UC for showcase research examples that might be presented to the public in an advocacy effort. The results, which I mocked up as a document full of blurbs and pictures for each example, are not ready for publication, but I can attest that the examples are definitively there. Sample headlines include "Treasure of Previously Unknown Letters by Benjamin Franklin," "World History For Us All," "Students Learn from California Holocaust Survivors," "The Prehistory of Multitasking," "UC and Human Rights Around the World," and "What is the Community Reading?" (Liu, "UC Research Contributions to the Public"). While humanities scholarship can sometimes seem abstruse, minute, or nonsensical to the public (true of all fields), there are also a stunning number of projects that intuitively, profoundly, and movingly demonstrate the public value of the humanities—many of them, not incidentally, designed around or otherwise centrally facilitated by digital technologies.

Beyond acting in an instrumental role, the digital humanities can most profoundly advocate for the humanities by helping to broaden the very idea of instrumentalism, technological, and otherwise. This could be its unique contribution to cultural criticism

Earlier, I deprecated the idea of "service." The digital humanities, I said, need to transcend their role as "just a servant" of the humanities to take a leadership role. Yet in apparent contradiction, my imagination of such leadership has so far been instrumental in a manner that does not exceed a narrow, if cutting-edge, service concept. The digital humanities, I argued, can create, adapt, and disseminate new tools and methods for reestablishing communication between the humanities and the public. This contradiction brings to view a complex matrix of issues that is both a problem and an opportunity for the digital humanities, since ultimately it shows digital humanists to occupy a strategic niche in the humanities and even society as a whole, where the same issues are in play.

Within the digital humanities, to start with, we observe that service and instrumentalism are part of a tangle of related concepts—including functionalism, tools, and (as I earlier deployed the term) practice—about which the field is deeply insecure. On the one hand, digital humanists worry that their field is too instrumental. Witness the vigorous thread on the *Humanist* list in 2010 on "Industrialisation of the Digital Humanities?" (McCarty, "Industrialisation"). Willard McCarty, the list's moderator, touched off the discussion by reflecting, "I fear that the digital humanities is becoming dominated by purely technical concerns of implementation. . . . One sign of this industrialization is the spread of technological orthodoxy under the banner of technical standards." Just as rambunctious was the *Humanist* thread that McCarty triggered the next year with his post titled "In Denial?" where—to use Internet parlance—he trolled (i.e., baited) the list with the statement, "I'd be interested to know if you have recently heard anyone assert that the computer is 'just a tool' and what you think [they] may have been meant by that phrase." The sustained discussion that followed shows that McCarty hit a sensitive nerve.

Yet on the other hand, digital humanists also worry that their field is not instrumental *enough* by comparison with engineering fields where instrumentality has the prestige of "innovation" and "building." Thus the "I am more builder than thou" controversy that arose around Stephen Ramsay's paper at the 2011 Modern Language Association Convention, which threw down the gauntlet to those in the digital humanities who mainly just study, interpret, or supervise by saying, "Do you have to know how to code? . . . I say 'yes.' . . . Personally, I think Digital Humanities is about building things. I'm willing to entertain highly expansive definitions of what it means to build something. . . . If you are not making anything, you are not . . . a digital humanist" ("Who's In and Who's Out"; see also his follow-up post "On Building").

But now I will widen the context. The insecurity of the digital humanities about instrumentalism, we should realize, simply shifts to a new register a worry experienced by the humanities at large. On the one hand, the humanities also struggle against the perception that they are primarily instrumental because their assigned role is to provide students with a skill set needed for future life and work. For example, the rhetoric of university course catalogs (which speak of the humanities as providers of "skills" in critical analysis, language, and so on) combines with the insidious logic of higher teaching loads for humanists to imply that the main function of the humanities is service: they teach the analytical, communicational, and other abilities needed as means to other ends. In truth, it may be that no matter how much the humanities try to position themselves as research or ethical pursuits in their own right, they will find it hard to break out of the instrumentalist syndrome simply because, by comparison with the STEM (and, to a lesser extent, social science) fields, they are identified almost entirely with the academy itself as a means of student preparation. There are relatively few extra-academic research labs, think tanks, clinics, and so on able to give a home to the humanities in autonomous or advanced, rather than preparatory, social roles.

On the other hand, clearly, the humanities suffer even more from seeming to be noninstrumental to the point of uselessness. In hard economic times (a real-life incident from my own experience), parents actually come up to chairs of English departments at graduation to complain that their daughter's humanities degree is only good for working at Starbucks.[17] The catch-22 is that the harder the humanities work to become research enterprises equipping students with specialized competencies and vocabularies, the more cut off they seem from practical use. This is particularly galling for post–May 1968 cultural critics, who addressed their advanced research methods to praxis but, if anything, reinforced the impression that humanist critique is only interpretive, reflective, politically marginal, skeptical, or nihilist—that is, unrealpolitik.[18] Much of my own early work in cultural criticism (and also as an internal critic of the method) was devoted to exploring this and related problems—for example, in the essays on subversion collected in my *Local Transcendence: Essays on Postmodern Historicism and the Database*. As I put it, "what kind of movement is subversion anyway—the single action still allowed in a New Historicist universe become like a gigantic, too-quiet house within which, somewhere, in one of the walls, perhaps, insects chew?" (47).

Now let me widen the context to the furthest extent. To be fair to the humanities, they are just the canary in the mine for the problem that modern society has with instrumentalism generally. A thumbnail history (or fable) of the issue might be as follows. In the premodern version, the players were God, nature, man, and free will. God determined what happened; nature was the instrumentality of that happening; humanity received the instruction set; and then humanity messed up by listening to the serpent, hacking the tree of knowledge, and staking human identity on free will and all its woe. At the moment of the fall, which was also the Promethean ascent into knowledge for its own sake, instrumentality became radically overdetermined. Nature (the tree) became more than an instrument. It became a mark of human identity. Instrumentality, specifically in regard to knowledge, exceeded the status of a means/medium to become an end that was at once necessary for the full experience of humanity and (because it meant exile from paradise) dehumanizing.

In the modern (and postmodern) version of the tale, the players are determination, technology, humanity, and—again—free will. It is hard to underestimate the problem that modernity has had with determination of all sorts after the age of God. Accusations of "media determinism" and "technological determinism" leveled at media theorists, for instance, are merely symptomatic of the uncertainty that modernity feels about secular determinism in toto. Touch just one of the levers of media or technological determinism, and it soon becomes clear that they connect to the total machine of historical, material, and social determinism that is both the condition and dilemma of modernity. Once the Enlightenment desacralized God, modernity came to believe that things happen because they are caused by material-cum-historical determination. Nature and history were now the compound instrumentality that became overdetermined. Nature and history, as invoked in the French Revolution and its aftermath, marked human identity as freedom (since causality became an affair of humans endowed by nature with the possibility of self-determination). Yet of course, nature and history also rapidly became a new dehumanizing slavery to nineteenth- and twentieth-century modes of empire, evolution, economics, and industry.

To put it mildly, in sum, contemporary society is existentially uncomfortable about determination and its instrumental agencies. It may very well be that the concept of "culture" originally rose into prominence to make the problem of determination if not solvable then what Claude Lévi-Strauss, in a memorable phrase, called "good to think" (89). *Historismus* and *Geistesgeschichte* in the nineteenth century, for example, converged in a *Kulturgeschichte* (cultural history or history of civilization) whose metanarratives created the fiction of an equivocal middle ground between determination and free will. Humanity was constrained by natural, psychological, historical, and social forces; yet a will to be human, or *Geist,* nevertheless came to light through the cultural workings of those forces. A compelling recent example is the idea of corporate culture in the United States, which emerged after the 1970s in conjunction with the expansion of the so-called service industries, especially in the areas of "knowledge work." In the new service industries, men and women were imprisoned by global socioeconomic forces in little cubicles staring at even smaller cells in a spreadsheet. Corporate culture was an expression of that, since the idea was that strong corporations have totalizing cultures that determine (and are constantly reinforced by) everything from information technology practices to company slogans and social events. Yet paradoxically, corporate culture was also supposed to incubate in workers the spirit of "disruptive" innovation and entrepreneurship that is the mark of neoliberal freedom.[19] It's as if we all live in the universe of Iain M. Banks's richly imagined science fiction novels set in the universe of "the Culture," a sprawling galactic civilization that dominates in a totally distributed, decentralized, Western-liberal style at once wholly determinative and utterly laissez-faire in its encouragement of individual freedom.[20]

My conclusion—or, perhaps, just a hopeful guess—is that the appropriate, unique contribution that the digital humanities can make to cultural criticism at the present time is to use the tools, paradigms, and concepts of digital technologies to help rethink the idea of instrumentality. The goal, as I put it earlier, is to think "critically about metadata" (and everything else related to digital technologies) in a way that "scales into thinking critically about the power, finance, and other governance protocols of the world." Phrased even more expansively, the goal is to rethink instrumentality so that it includes both humanistic and STEM fields in a culturally broad, and not just narrowly purposive, ideal of service.

In particular, my recommendation for the digital humanities is two-fold: First, while continuing to concentrate on research and development in its core areas (e.g., text encoding, text analysis, pattern discovery, the creation of digital archives and resources), digital humanists should enter into fuller dialogue with the adjacent fields of new media studies and media archaeology so as to extend reflection on core instrumental technologies in cultural and historical directions. The time is long overdue for staging major conferences or programs designed specifically to put digital humanists in the same room, for example, with new media artists, hackers, and media theorists. In that room, standard issues in the digital humanities (such as "standards" themselves) could be enlarged with sociocultural meaning. Individuals working in the digital humanities, or who straddle fields, already increasingly engage in such dialogue. What is needed now is the elevation of the dialogue to the front and center of the discipline of the digital humanities.

Second, digital humanists should also enter into dialogue with science-technology studies. On reflection, it is remarkable how little the field draws on contemporary science-technology studies to enrich its discussion of tools, building, and instrumentality through new understandings of the way researchers, technicians, processes, communication media, and literal instruments come together in what

Andrew Pickering calls the "mangle of practice" that is inextricably linked to society and culture. Science-technology studies by Lorraine Daston, Peter Galison, and Bruno Latour, for example, are canonical in this respect—for example, Daston and Galison's work on the history of changing ideals of "objectivity" (variously mediated by instruments and interpreters) and Latour's well-known melding of the concepts of human agency and machine instrumentality in "actor-network theory." Engaging with science-technology studies would help the digital humanities develop an understanding of instrumentalism—including that of its own methods—*as* a culture embedded in wider culture.[21]

Steps like these would give digital humanists a more solid foundation or, better, a heretofore missing technological and intellectual *infrastructure* (by analogy with modern programming, which evolved infrastructural software layers to mediate between low-level resources and high-level applications) through which to grapple with cultural issues.[22] Only by creating a methodological infrastructure in which culturally aware technology complements technologically aware cultural criticism can the digital humanities more effectively serve humanists by augmenting their ability to engage today's global-scale cultural issues.

Ultimately, the greatest service that the digital humanities can contribute to the humanities is to practice instrumentalism in a way that demonstrates the necessity of breaking down the artificial divide of the "two cultures" to show that the humanities are needed alongside the sciences to solve the intricately interwoven natural, technological, economic, social, political, *and* cultural problems of the global age. For example, there is not a single "grand challenge" announced by the Obama Administration, the Grand Challenges in Global Health initiative, the U.S. National Academy of Engineering, and other agencies or foundations in the areas of energy, environment, biomedicine, food, water, education, and so on that does not require humanistic involvement.[23] All these issues have a necessary cultural dimension, whether as cause or effect; and all, therefore, need the public service of humanist and, increasingly, digital humanist participants.

NOTES

This chapter is a substantially extended version of a brief paper by the same title that I originally presented in truncated form at the Modern Language Association convention in 2011 and subsequently posted online (Liu, "Where Is Cultural Criticism in the Digital Humanities?"). I have benefited from posts and criticisms that appeared in response to the online version and from discussions with the audience after later, fuller versions of the paper at Cambridge University and University of Nottingham.

1. Geoffrey Rockwell, Melissa Terras, and I cofounded 4Humanities in November 2010 with a collective of digital humanists located initially in Canada, the United Kingdom, and the United States (with other nations added later). The creation of the initiative was prompted by two discussion threads on the *Humanist* listserv in October 2010—one

worrying that the digital humanities were too narrowly "industrialised" or technologically instrumental, the other discussing the severe budget cuts in the United Kingdom imposed by the then newly formed conservative-liberal democrat coalition government. (For the posts that started these threads, see, respectively, McCarty, "Industrialisation," and Prescott.)

2. Here and throughout, I use "May 1968" for convenience as the symbolic name for an epoch rather than as an exact historical date (since some of the intellectual movements I refer to began somewhat earlier or later).

3. The Computer Professionals for Social Responsibility (CPSR) started in the Silicon Valley area in 1981 to express concern over the military use of computer systems and later broadened its scope to other social justice concerns related to computing. The Electronic Frontier Foundation (EFF) began in 1990 to champion "the public interest in every critical battle affecting digital rights" (Electronic Frontier Foundation, "About EFF").

4. This is a simplification, of course. A more extended discussion would note that much of the latent cultural-critical interest of the digital humanities lay under the surface in textual-editing theory, hypertext theory, and other registers of method specialized around the idea of textuality. In this regard, Jerome McGann's *A Critique of Modern Textual Criticism* and "The Rationale of Hypertext" (e.g., the coda on "the decentered text") are of a piece with cultural criticism in the post–May 1968 era, as is Matthew Kirschenbaum's invocation of D. F. McKenzie's *Bibliography and the Sociology of Texts* to discuss the "complex network of individuals, communities, ideologies, markets, technologies, and motivations" that inform the task of preserving digital media with "a pronounced social dimension that is at least as important as purely technical considerations" (Kirschenbaum, 240–41). "Net Critique" is the title of the blog of the network theorist and critic Geert Lovink. The phrase is also aptly generic for cultural criticism of the digital age.

5. Susan Schreibman discusses the debate over the "ordered hierarchy of content objects" (OHCO) thesis engaged in most famously by Allan Renear and Jerome McGann (e.g., in the latter's "Rethinking Textuality"). On the deformance thesis, see Samuels and McGann.

6. On the digital humanities as the "next big thing," see for example Pannapacker. The piece I refer to as an attempt to take stock of the field is my forthcoming "The State of the Digital Humanities: A Report and a Critique."

7. I concentrate here on the distant reading versus close reading issue in literary studies. However, I am aware that this has a somewhat distorting effect because the underlying issue of quantitative versus qualitative methods is older in other humanities fields and social science disciplines, with the result that recent digital technologies enter into play in those fields in a different methodological context. In historiography, for instance, the Annales movement brought distant reading and quantitative methods to the fore in the mid-twentieth century. One difference in the contemporary history field, therefore, is that the front line of recent digital history concerns such methods as geographic information systems (GIS) or social-network analysis that evolve quantitative methods further or differently (rather than redebate the first principles of the quantitative approach). The social sciences, of course, have long been familiar with the quantitative versus qualitative

problem. (My thanks to Zephyr Frank for conversation on this topic in relation to history at the Digital Humanities 2011 conference at Stanford University. In regard to the social sciences, my thanks to Astrid Mager for excellent commentary on this issue from her perspective as a digital social scientist during the question and answer period after my talk at HUMlab on "Close, Distant, and Unexpected Reading.")

8. I discuss the origin of the New Criticism in Liu, "Close, Distant, and Unexpected Reading."

9. See, for example, Moretti's reflections on "form" as a "diagram of forces" (*Graphs, Maps, Trees*, 56–57, 64).

10. Hayles, 63–64, gives other examples of high theorists and critics claiming allegiance to close reading. On the New Historicist "anecdote," see my discussions in *Local Transcendence* (e.g., 23-24, 29–30, 258–61).

11. See Allison et al. (including Jockers and Moretti) on "the Great Unread—the vast, unexplored archive that lies underneath the narrow canon of literary history" (10).

12. For "lexia" in hypertext theory, see Landow's influential adaptation of Barthes's term (4).

13. Julia Flanders nicely captures the stigma of servitude that has marked the digital humanities when she writes, "Representational technologies like XML, or databases, or digital visualization tools appear to stand apart from the humanities research activities they support. . . . Humanities scholarship has historically understood this separateness as indicating an ancillary role—that of the handmaiden, the good servant/poor master—in which humanities insight masters and subsumes what these technologies can offer" (para. 11).

14. One of the main emphases in the article on culturomics by Michel and Lieberman Aiden et al. is that the study of language enabled by their ngram analysis of Google Books facilitates the study of culture generally. Some of their specific examples (such as censorship of names of intellectuals in Nazi Germany) are closely analogous to humanities cultural criticism (181). Similarly, specific projects in "cultural analytics" at the University of California San Diego Software Studies Initiative include not just those that define culture in terms of aesthetic or media artifacts but also those that use the initiative's methods to study culture in a recognizably cultural-critical sense—e.g., projects on "2008 U.S. presidential campaign ads"; "visualizing art, industry, territory, and global economy in Brazil"; or "mapping 28 years of TV news" (Software Studies Initiative, "Projects").

15. To be fair, society's ever narrower focus on applied research threatens the STEM fields themselves, causing scientists to worry ever more about how to argue for the need for basic research. During 2009–2010, I led a subgroup (on research mission and principles) for the research strategies working group of the University of California Commission on the Future (UCOF, a body convened by the regents of the university to rethink the paradigm of the University of California in the face of systemic, long-term cuts in state funding). One of my takeaway lessons from that subgroup, which included scientists such as John Birely, University of California's associate vice president for laboratory management (who led our subgroup's work on a recommendation about basic research), is the extent

to which the STEM fields are acutely sensitive to the need to defend the very idea of basic research. While only a part of the recommendations of the various working groups made it into the UCOF's *Final Report*, that report does contain the following defensive language about basic research: "It is also critical that federal support for research be sustained or even increased given that the federal government underwrites so much of the basic research conducted at U.S. research universities, laboratories and research organizations. Although the President's budget calls for a steady increase in the financing of research, due to pressure to reduce federal budgets, Congress may look for short-term monetary gains and neglect basic research and its long-term impact on economic health" (24).

16. The academic use of social networking, blogs, and a variety of experimental platforms such as CommentPress (a blog-like platform capable of presenting monographs in modular paragraph units each of which can be commented on by users) attests that the adoption of the new protocols, practices, technologies, and forms in the academy is underway. But, as I mention later, there is a difference between scholars using such methods on an individual or ad hoc basis and using them in an *institutional* framework, which so far does not exist to integrate or, in many cases, even support the new communication media. (For a description of CommentPress, see Knight; and Hovey and Hudson.)

17. Personal communication from a parent to me at the English Department commencement ceremony, University of California, Santa Barbara, June 12, 2011.

18. See Alex Reid's response to my short paper on which this essay is originally based. Among other excellent commentary, Reid reflects, "I don't think it is unreasonable to argue that cultural critique as it has developed over the past 30–40 years has been a contributing factor to the general cultural decline of the humanities. At the very least, with historical hindsight, it was not the change that we needed if our intention was to remain culturally relevant. . . . Cultural critique has led us to be overspecialized, largely irrelevant, and barely intelligible, even to one another, let alone to the broader society. Yes, digital humanities can help us address that by providing new means to reach new audiences, but that won't help unless we are prepared to shift our discourse."

19. For my extended analysis of the idea of corporate culture, see my *Laws of Cool*, chap. 4.

20. The first of Banks's Culture novels (currently numbering nine) was *Consider Phlebas*, 1987.

21. In a manner analogous to science-technology studies, David M. Berry asks digital humanists to reflect on their own field as a culture. He writes that "to understand the contemporary born-digital culture and the everyday practices that populate it . . . we need a corresponding focus on the computer code that is entangled with all aspects of our lives, including reflexivity about how much code is infiltrating the academy itself" (4). This means problematizing "the unspoken assumptions and ontological foundations which support the 'normal' research that humanities scholars undertake on an everyday basis" (4) and recognizing that "there is an undeniable cultural dimension to computation and the media affordances of software" (5). Ultimately, he reflects, the culture of the digital humanities may well scale up to the future evolution of academic culture generally: "we

are beginning to see . . . the cultural importance of the digital as the unifying idea of the university" (7).

22. I am influenced here by Jean-Françoise Blanchette's excellent talk at the Digital Humanities 2011 conference, which gave an overview of the development of modern software focused on the nature of the "infrastructure" created to negotiate modularly between applications and underlying network, storage, and processor resources. (See also his more detailed article on this topic, "A Material History of Bits.") By analogy, I am suggesting that digital humanists currently lack an adequate infrastructural layer—both (or modularly) technological and methodological—through which to address their practices to cultural issues.

23. See the Obama White House's "A Strategy for American Innovation"; the U.S. National Academy of Engineering's "Grand Challenges"; and the Grand Challenges in Global Health initiative.

BIBLIOGRAPHY

Allison, Sarah, et al. *Quantitative Formalism: An Experiment*. Stanford Literary Lab Pamphlet Series 1, January 2011, http://litlab.stanford.edu/LiteraryLabPamphlet1.pdf.

Banks, Iain M. *Consider Phlebas*. New York: Bantam, 1987.

Berry, David M. "The Computational Turn: Thinking About the Digital Humanities." *Culture Machine* 12 (2011): 1–22, http://www.culturemachine.net/index.php/cm/article/viewArticle/440.

Blanchette, Jean-Françoise. "Infrastructural Thinking as Core Computing Skill." Lecture. New Models of Digital Materialities Panel. Digital Humanities 2011 conference. Stanford University, June 21, 2011.

———. "A Material History of Bits." *Journal of the American Society for Information Science and Technology* 62, no. 6 (2011): 1042–57. Wiley Online Library. April 20, 2011. http://onlinelibrary.wiley.com/doi/10.1002/asi.21542/abstract.

Casanova, Pascale. *The World Republic of Letters*. Translated by M. B. DeBevoise. Cambridge, Mass.: Harvard University Press, 2004.

Computer Professionals for Social Responsibility. Home page. Last modified December 1, 2008. http://cpsr.org/.

Cultural Analytics. Home page. Software Studies Initiative. University of California, San Diego. http://lab.softwarestudies.com/2008/09/cultural-analytics.html.

Daston, Lorraine, and Peter Galison. *Objectivity*. Cambridge, Mass.: Zone Books, 2007.

Deadliest Catch. Discovery Channel. 2005 to present. Television.

Defend the Arts and Humanities. Home page. http://defendartsandhums.blogspot.com/.

Deleuze, Gilles, and Félix Guattari. *A Thousand Plateaus: Capitalism and Schizophrenia*. Translated by Brian Massumi. Minneapolis: University of Minnesota Press, 1987.

Electronic Frontier Foundation. "About EFF." https://www.eff.org/about.

English, James F. "Everywhere and Nowhere: The Sociology of Literature After 'the Sociology of Literature.'" *New Literary History* 41, no. 1 (2010): v–xxiii.

Flanders, Julia. "The Productive Unease of 21st-century Digital Scholarship." *Digital Humanities Quarterly* 3, no. 3 (2009). http://digitalhumanities.org/dhq/vol/3/3/000055/000055.html.

4Humanities: Advocating for the Humanities. 4Humanities Collective. Initiated November 2010. http://humanistica.ualberta.ca/.

Google Books Ngram Viewer. Google Labs, Google Inc. 2010. http://ngrams.googlelabs.com/.

Grand Challenges in Global Health. Home page. http://www.grandchallenges.org/Pages/Default.aspx.

Hayles, N. Katherine, "How We Read: Close, Hyper, Machine" *ADE Bulletin* 150 (2010): 62–79.

Hovey, Pehr, and Renee Hudson. "CommentPress Research Paper." Transliteracies Project. University of California. April 22, 2009. http://transliteracies.english.ucsb.edu/post/research-project/research-clearinghouse-individual/research-papers/commentpress-research-paper.

Humanities and Social Sciences Matter: The Campaign for the Arts, Humanities and Social Sciences. Chair of Steering Committee, Nicola Miller. http://humanitiesmatter.com/?p=32.

Kirschenbaum, Matthew G. *Mechanisms: New Media and the Forensic Imagination.* Cambridge, Mass.: MIT Press, 2008.

Knight, Kim. "CommentPress." Transliteracies Project. University of California. May 7, 2008. http://transliteracies.english.ucsb.edu/post/research-project/research-clearinghouse-individual/research-reports/commentpress-2.

Landow, George P. *Hypertext: The Convergence of Contemporary Critical Theory and Technology*. Baltimore: Johns Hopkins University Press, 1992.

Latour, Bruno. *Reassembling the Social: An Introduction to Actor-Network-Theory*. Oxford: Oxford University Press, 2005.

Lévi-Strauss, Claude. *Totemism*. Translated by R. Needham. Boston: Beacon, 1963.

Liu, Alan. "Close, Distant, and Unexpected Reading: New Forms of Literary Reading in the Digital Age." Lecture. HUMlab, Umeå University, Sweden. May 10, 2011. http://blog.humlab.umu.se/?p=3366.

———. *The Laws of Cool: Knowledge Work and the Culture of Information*. Chicago: University of Chicago Press, 2004.

———. *Local Transcendence: Essays on Postmodern Historicism and the Database*. Chicago: University of Chicago Press, 2008.

———. "The State of the Digital Humanities: A Report and a Critique." *Arts and Humanities in Higher Education* 11, no. 1 (2012): 1–34 (forthcoming).

———, ed. "UC Research Contributions to the Public." Unpublished internal working paper for Research Strategies working group of University of California Commission on the Future. June 6, 2010.

———. "Where Is Cultural Criticism in the Digital Humanities?" Lecture presented in truncated form. The History and Future of the Digital Humanities panel. MLA

Annual Convention. Los Angeles, January 7, 2011. Full version subsequently posted on Alan Liu personal blog. http://liu.english.ucsb.edu/where-is-cultural-criticism-in-the-digital-humanities.

Lovink, Geert. *Net Critique*. Personal blog. Institute of Network Cultures. http://networkcultures.org/wpmu/geert/.

Lukács, Georg. *The Theory of the Novel: A Historico-Philosophical Essay on the Forms of Great Epic Literature*. Translated by Anna Bostock. Cambridge, Mass.: MIT Press, 1971.

McCarty, Willard. "In Denial?" *Humanist* listserv 24.905. April 25, 2011. http://lists.digitalhumanities.org/pipermail/humanist/2011-April/002122.html.

———. "Industrialisation of the Digital Humanities?" *Humanist* listserv 24.422. October 21, 2010. http://lists.digitalhumanities.org/pipermail/humanist/2010-October/001644.html.

McGann, Jerome J. *A Critique of Modern Textual Criticism*. Chicago: University of Chicago Press, 1983.

———. "The Rationale of Hypertext." In *Radiant Textuality: Literature after the World Wide Web*, 53–74. New York: Palgrave, 2001.

———. "Rethinking Textuality." In *Radiant Textuality: Literature after the World Wide Web* 137–60. New York: Palgrave, 2001.

McKenzie, D. F. *Bibliography and the Sociology of Texts*. Cambridge, Mass.: Cambridge University Press, 1999.

Michel, Jean-Baptiste, Erez Lieberman Aiden et al. "Quantitative Analysis of Culture Using Millions of Digitized Books." *Science* 331, no. 6014 (January 14, 2011): 176–82, http://www.sciencemag.org/content/331/6014/176.

Moretti, Franco. *Graphs, Maps, Trees: Abstract Models for a Literary History*. London; New York: Verso, 2005.

National Academy of Engineering. "Grand Challenges for Engineering." http://www.engineeringchallenges.org/.

National Humanities Alliance. Home page. June 16, 2011. http://www.nhalliance.org/index.shtml.

OMEKA. Home page. Roy Rosenzweig Center for History and New Media, George Mason University. http://omeka.org/.

Open Journal Systems. Home page. Public Knowledge Project. http://pkp.sfu.ca/?q=ojs.

Orwant, Jon. "Our Commitment to the Digital Humanities." Official Google Blog. July 14, 2010. http://googleblog.blogspot.com/2010/07/our-commitment-to-digital-humanities.html.

Pannapacker, William. "The MLA and the Digital Humanities." Brainstorm blog, *Chronicle of Higher Education*, December 28, 2009. http://chronicle.com/blogPost/The-MLAthe-Digital/19468/.

Pickering, Andrew. *The Mangle of Practice: Time, Agency, and Science*. Chicago: University of Chicago Press, 1995.

Prescott, Andrew. "Digital Humanities and the Cuts." *Humanist* listserv 24.427. October 24, 2010. http://lists.digitalhumanities.org/pipermail/humanist/2010-October/001649.html.

Ramsay, Stephen. "On Building." Stephen Ramsay personal website. January 11, 2011. http://lenz.unl.edu/papers/2011/01/11/on-building.html.

———. "Who's In and Who's Out." Lecture. The History and Future of the Digital Humanities panel. MLA Annual Convention. Los Angeles, January 7, 2011. Stephen Ramsay personal website, January 8, 2011. http://lenz.unl.edu/papers/2011/01/08/whos-in-and-whos-out.html.

Reid, Alex. "Alan Liu, Cultural Criticism, the Digital Humanities, and Problem Solving?" *Digital Digs* (personal blog). January 17, 2011. http://www.alex-reid.net/2011/01/alan-liu-cultural-criticism-and-the-digital-humanities.html.

Renear, Allen, et al. "Refining Our Notion of What Text Really Is: The Problem of Overlapping Hierarchies." January 6, 1993. Scholarly Technology Group, Brown University Library. http://www.stg.brown.edu/resources/stg/monographs/ohco.html.

Samuels, Lisa, and Jerome McGann. "Deformance and Interpretation." *New Literary History* 30, no. 1 (1999): 25–56.

Schreibman, Susan. "Computer-mediated Texts and Textuality: Theory and Practice." *Computers and the Humanities* 36, no. 3 (2002): 283–93. http://www.jstor.org/pss/30200528.

SIMILE Widgets. Home page. Massachusetts Institute of Technology and Contributors. http://www.simile-widgets.org/.

Snow, C. P. *The Two Cultures and the Scientific Revolution*. New York: Cambridge University Press, 1959.

Software Studies Initiative, University of San Diego. Home page. http://lab.softwarestudies.com/.

Stanford Literary Lab. Home page. Stanford University. http://litlab.stanford.edu/.

Tanner, Simon. "Inspiring Research, Inspiring Scholarship: The Value and Benefits of Digitised Resources for Learning, Teaching, Research and Enjoyment." November 2010. JISC (Joint Information Systems Committee). http://www.jisc.ac.uk/media/documents/programmes/digitisation/12pagefinaldocumentbenefitssynthesis.pdf.

University of California Commission on the Future. *Final Report*. November 2010. Office of the President, University of California. http://ucfuture.universityofcalifornia.edu/presentations/cotf_final_report.pdf.

White House (President Obama). "A Strategy for American Innovation: Driving Towards Sustainable Growth and Quality Jobs." September 2009. http://www.whitehouse.gov/administration/eop/nec/StrategyforAmericanInnovation/.

Acknowledgments

Every book is a product of many hands, a commonplace that is especially true for an edited collection of the size and scope of *Debates in the Digital Humanities*. And thus, first and foremost, I would like to thank the authors who contributed their work to this book. They persevered through a series of extremely tight deadlines, took part in a demanding peer-to-peer review process, and turned around revision after revision with dispatch. I am honored and humbled to count them as colleagues, peers, and friends, and I am proud of the work we have assembled together.

I am deeply thankful to the entire team at the University of Minnesota Press for taking on this project and seeing it through to completion. In particular, I would like to thank Douglas Armato, director of the press, whose astute advice and clear vision sustained the book as it moved from initial conception through final publication. I am also grateful to editorial assistant Danielle Kasprzak, who carefully shepherded the project through its editorial stages. I appreciate the insightful and erudite reports from the press's anonymous reviewers, which strengthened key sections of the text. Collaborating with Doug, Dani, and the rest of the Minnesota team has been one of the signal pleasures of this project.

For their support of work that informed my editing of this volume, I am grateful to the NEH Office of Digital Humanities (special thanks to Brett Bobley, Jen Serventi, and Jason Rhody), the U.S. Department of Education, New York City College of Technology, the CUNY Graduate Center, and the City University of New York Office of Academic Affairs. At CUNY, I would like to thank George Otte, Steve Brier, Joan Richardson, Bill Kelly, Bonne August, Russell Hotzler, Chase Robinson, Alexandra Logue, Louise Lennihan, Roberta Matthews, David S. Reynolds, Nina Bannett, Pamela Brown, Joe Ugoretz, Mikhail Gershovich, Boone Gorges, Luke Waltzer, Jeff Allred, Jody Rosen, Maura Smale, Barbara Burke, Richard Hanley, Shelley Smith, and Charlie Edwards for their advice, collegiality, support, and friendship. I am grateful, too, to the mentors whose intellectual generosity shaped me in earlier years, including Scott Mosenthal, Robert D. Richardson Jr., Annie Dillard, and Luke Menand.

Personal thanks go to Jeanne and Danny Gold, Heather Peterson, and my extended family for their steadfast love and encouragement. I thank my wife Liza for the unwavering support and wise counsel she provides on a daily basis. Finally, I thank my son Felix, whose ability to take unrestrained delight in the world around him is happily beyond debate.

Contributors

Bryan Alexander is senior fellow at the National Institute for Technology in Liberal Education (NITLE). He is author of *The New Digital Storytelling: Creating Narratives with New Media.*

Rafael C. Alvarado is associate director of the Sciences, Humanities, and Arts Network of Technological Initiatives (SHANTI) and lecturer in anthropology at the University of Virginia.

Jamie "Skye" Bianco is assistant professor of English and director of Digital Media at Pitt (DM@P) at the University of Pittsburgh.

Ian Bogost is professor of digital media at the Georgia Institute of Technology. He is author of *Unit Operations, Persuasive Games, How to Do Things with Videogames* (Minnesota, 2011), and *Alien Phenomenology* (Minnesota, 2012) and coauthor of *Racing the Beam* and *Newsgames.*

Stephen Brier is professor of urban education and the founder of the Interactive Technology and Pedagogy Doctoral Certificate Program at the CUNY Graduate Center. He served as author, executive producer, and editor of the American Social History Project's *Who Built America* multimedia curriculum.

Daniel J. Cohen is associate professor of history and the director of the Roy Rosenzweig Center for History and New Media at George Mason University. He is the author of *Equations from God: Pure Mathematics and Victorian Faith* and coauthor of *Digital History: A Guide to Gathering, Preserving, and Presenting the Past on the Web.*

Cathy N. Davidson is Ruth F. DeVarney Professor of English and John Hope Franklin Humanities Institute Professor of Interdisciplinary Studies at Duke University. She has published more than twenty books, including *Revolution and the Word: The Rise of the Novel in America; Reading in America: Literature and Social History; Closing: The Life and Death of An American Factory* (with photographer Bill Bamberger); *The Future of Thinking: Learning Institutions in a Digital Age* (with David Theo Goldberg); and *Now You See It: How the Brain Science of Attention Will Transform the Way We Live, Work, and Learn.*

Rebecca Frost Davis is the program officer for the humanities at the National Institute for Technology in Liberal Education (NITLE).

Johanna Drucker is Breslauer Professor of Information Studies at the University of California, Los Angeles. She is the author of many books, including *SpecLab: Digital Aesthetics and Projects in Speculative Computing; Sweet Dreams: Contemporary Art and Complicity*; *The Visible Word: Experimental Typography and Modern Art;* and *The Alphabetic Labyrinth: The Letters in History and Imagination,* among others.

AMY E. EARHART is assistant professor of English at Texas A&M University. She is coeditor of *The American Literature Scholar in the Digital Age.*

CHARLIE EDWARDS is a graduate student in the English PhD and Interactive Technology and Pedagogy Certificate Programs at CUNY Graduate Center.

KATHLEEN FITZPATRICK is director of scholarly communication of the Modern Language Association and professor of media studies at Pomona College. She is author of *The Anxiety of Obsolescence: The American Novel in the Age of Television* and of *Planned Obsolescence: Publishing, Technology, and the Future of the Academy.*

JULIA FLANDERS is director of the Women Writers Project in the Center for Digital Scholarship in the Brown University Library. She is the coeditor of the forthcoming *Cambridge Companion to Textual Scholarship*.

NEIL FRAISTAT is professor of English and director of the Maryland Institute for Technology in the Humanities (MITH) at the University of Maryland. He is author or editor of ten books, including the forthcoming *Cambridge Companion to Textual Scholarship* and Volume III of the *Complete Poetry of Percy Bysshe Shelley.*

PAUL FYFE is assistant professor of English and History of Text Technologies at Florida State University.

MICHAEL GAVIN is an A. W. Mellon Postdoctoral Fellow with the Humanities Research Center at Rice University.

MATTHEW K. GOLD is assistant professor of English at New York City College of Technology and a faculty member in the Interactive Technology and Pedagogy Doctoral Certificate Program at the CUNY Graduate Center. He is advisor to the provost for master's programs and digital initiatives at the CUNY Graduate Center, director of the CUNY Academic Commons, and codirector of the CUNY Digital Humanities Initiative.

DAVID GREETHAM is distinguished professor of English, medieval studies, and interactive technology and pedagogy at the CUNY Graduate Center. He is the author of *Textual Scholarship: An Introduction; Textual Transgressions: Essays toward the Construction of a Biobibliography; Theories of the Text; The Pleasures of Contamination: Evidence, Text, and Voice in Textual Studies;* editor of *The Margins of the Text, Scholarly Editing: A Guide to Research*, and of Book XV of *John Trevisa, On The Properties of Things.*

JIM GROOM is an instructional technology specialist at the University of Mary Washington.

GARY HALL is professor of media and performing arts in the School of Art and Design at Coventry University, UK. He is the author of *Culture in Bits* and *Digitize This Book! The Politics of New Media, or Why We Need Open Access Now* (Minnesota, 2008), and coeditor of *New Cultural Studies: Adventures in Theory* and *Experimenting: Essays with Samuel Weber.*

MILLS KELLY is associate professor of history at George Mason University and associate director of the Roy Rosenzweig Center for History and New Media.

MATTHEW KIRSCHENBAUM is associate professor of English at the University of Maryland and associate director of the Maryland Institute for Technology in the Humanities (MITH). He is the author of *Mechanisms: New Media and the Forensic Imagination.*

ALAN LIU is professor and chair of English at the University of California, Santa Barbara. He is the author of *Wordsworth: The Sense of History; The Laws of Cool: Knowledge Work and the Culture of Information;* and *Local Transcendence: Essays on Postmodern Historicism and the Database.*

ELIZABETH LOSH is director of the Culture, Art, and Technology Program at the University of California, San Diego. She is the author of *Virtualpolitik: An Electronic History of Government Media-Making in a Time of War, Scandal, Disaster, Miscommunication, and Mistakes* and coauthor of the forthcoming *Understanding Rhetoric.*

LEV MANOVICH is professor of visual art at the University of California, San Diego. He is the author of *Software Takes Command; Black Box–White Cube; Soft Cinema: Navigating the Database; The Language of New Media; Metamediji;* and *Tekstura: Russian Essays on Visual Culture.*

WILLARD MCCARTY is professor of humanities computing at King's College London and professor at University of Western Sydney. He is author of *Humanities Computing,* coauthor of the *Humanities Computing Yearbook,* and editor of *Text and Genre in Reconstruction: Effects of Digitalization on Ideas, Behaviours, Products, and Institutions.*

TARA MCPHERSON is associate professor of critical studies at University of Southern California's School of Cinematic Arts. She is author of *Reconstructing Dixie: Race, Gender and Nostalgia in the Imagined South,* coeditor of *Hop on Pop: The Politics and Pleasures of Popular Culture,* and editor of *Digital Youth, Innovation, and the Unexpected.*

BETHANY NOWVISKIE is director of digital research and scholarship at the University of Virginia Library Scholars' Lab and associate director of the Scholarly Communication Institute. She is the editor of *#Alt-Academy: Alternative Careers for Humanities Scholars.*

TREVOR OWENS is a digital archivist with the National Digital Information Infrastructure and Preservation Program at the Library of Congress.

WILLIAM PANNAPACKER is associate professor of English and director of the Andrew W. Mellon Scholars Program in the Arts and Humanities at Hope College. He is the author of *Revised Lives: Walt Whitman and Nineteenth-Century Authorship.*

DAVE PARRY is assistant professor of emerging media and communications at the University of Texas at Dallas.

STEPHEN RAMSAY is associate professor of English and a fellow at the Center for Digital Research in the Humanities at the University of Nebraska, Lincoln. He is the author of *Reading Machines: Toward an Algorithmic Criticism.*

ALEXANDER REID is associate professor of English and director of composition and teaching fellows at the State University of New York at Buffalo. He is the author of *The Two Virtuals: New Media and Composition* and coeditor of *Design Discourse: Composing and Revising Programs in Professional and Technical Writing.*

GEOFFREY ROCKWELL is professor of philosophy and director of the Canadian Institute for Research Computing in the Arts (CIRCA) at the University of Alberta. He is the author of *Defining Dialogue: From Socrates to the Internet.*

MARK L. SAMPLE is assistant professor of English at George Mason University.

TOM SCHEINFELDT is managing director of the Roy Rosenzweig Center for History and New Media at George Mason University. He is coeditor with Dan Cohen of *Hacking the Academy*.

KATHLEEN MARIE SMITH is a PhD candidate in the Department of Germanic Languages and Literatures at the University of Illinois at Urbana-Champaign.

LISA SPIRO is director of National Institute for Technology in Liberal Education (NITLE) Labs.

PATRIK SVENSSON is associate professor of digital humanities and director of HUMlab at Umeå University.

LUKE WALTZER is assistant director for educational technology at the Bernard L. Schwartz Communications Institute, Baruch College.

MATTHEW WILKENS is assistant professor of English at the University of Notre Dame.

GEORGE H. WILLIAMS is assistant professor of English at the University of South Carolina Upstate.

MICHAEL WITMORE is director of the Folger Shakespeare Library. He is the author of *Culture of Accidents: Unexpected Knowledges in Early Modern England*; *Pretty Creatures: Fiction and the English Renaissance*; *Shakespearean Metaphysics*; and, with Rosamond Purcell, *Landscapes of the Passing Strange: Reflections from Shakespeare*.